Footprint **Northeast India**

David Stott and Vanessa Betts
1st edition

D0995486

"I was stunned by the richness of the land, by its lush beauty and exotic architecture, by its ability to overload the senses with the pure, concentrated intensity of its colors, smells, tastes, and sounds. It was as if all my life I had been seeing the world in black and white and, when brought face-to-face with India, experienced everything re-rendered in brilliant technicolor."

Keith Bellows (Vice-President, National Geographic Society)

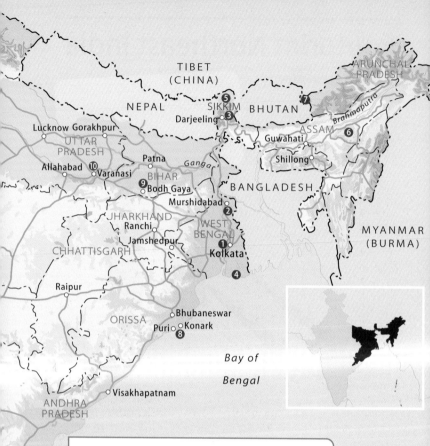

Northeast India Highlights

See colour maps at back of book

① Kolkata
Intellectual, cultural and sporting capital of India, page 57.

② Murshidabad
Historic Bengali ruins on the banks of the Ganga, page 90.

③ Darjeeling
Tea estates and trekking in the shadow of the Himalaya, page 95.

④ Sunderbans
Tiger-spotting among the mangrove archipelago, page 111.

⑤ Sikkim
Khangchendzonga, monasteries, orchids and more, page 113.

⑥ Kaziranga National Park
Spot one-horned rhinos before taking Assam tea on the veranda, page 138.

⑦ Tawang Monastery
Search for Buddhist isolation in secretive Arunachal Pradesh, page 155.

⑧ Puri and Konark
Exquisite temples, hectic festivals and sandy beaches, pages 185 and 187.

⑨ Bodh Gaya
Meditate in the "birthplace" of the Buddha, page 224.

⑩ Varanasi
India in the raw, page 236.

⑪ Andamans
Scuba, snorkel and scooter in a pristine paradise, page 253.

0 km   100
0 miles   100

The Government of India state that "the external boundaries of India are neither correct nor authenticated"

Contents

City of temples

Varanasi draws pilgrims from all over the globe to meditate, worship and bathe in the waters of the river Ganga.

A foot in the door

Veteran broadcaster Mark Tully perfectly summed up India's northeast when he described the country as "a land where there are no full stops". Here, the India of old – steam trains lumbering through misty tea gardens, Bengal tigers stalking the mangrove forests, golden monasteries perched on mountain peaks – collides with the tensions that underlie the modernization of the New India.

As societies long-starved of opportunity now race to grab their share of the consumer dream, and governments embrace a vision of progress involving forcible land grabs, the marginalized millions counter forcefully, striking back for any number of issues – Maoism, separatism, or national independence – that in themselves seem to keep the nation in its miraculous equilibrium.

A journey through the northeast can take you from a coffee house political debate in intellectual Kolkata to ash-smeared Varanasi, gazing across the Ganga through plumes of smoke – another soul's blissful release into moksha; from Bodh Gaya, where pilgrims seek peace beneath the Buddha's Bodhi tree, to Puri, home to one of Hinduism's most riotous festivals; from tiny Sikkim, so ethnically Himalayan and so clean that you can forget you're in India altogether, to the Christianized hills on the frontier with Myanmar, where elders in hornbill-feather headgear oversee traditions that predate the 'universal' religions by millennia.

The romantic rhythms, the chaos and madness are all here. This is a land of unrelenting change and colour – the India of your imagination.

6

1 Saffron-clad gurus enjoy some shade during a parade at one of the regions chaotic and extraordinary festivals. ›› See page 40.

2 Markets decorate the streets of every Kolkatan neighbourhood; haggling for fruit and veg is a daily activity. ›› See page 79.

3 Kaziranga National Park is one of the last havens of the one-horned rhino, best viewed on an elephant safari. ›› See page 138.

4 Protected from over-development by their remoteness, the Andaman Islands offer pure white beaches and colourful marine life. ›› See page 253.

5 Terracotta temples adorned with reliefs from the Hindu epics offer a sacred meeting place for the community to congregate and revitalize their energies. ›› See page 297.

6 The toy train puffs its way through bustling towns, loops among the tea plantations and performs figures-of-eight on it's route to the hill stations. ›› See page 96.

7 Northeast India is home to more than 300 distinct tribes, many of whom still maintain traditional forms of dress and culture. ›› See page 317.

8 Buddhist culture thrives in tiny Sikkim, where brightly decorated monasteries such as this one at Enchey dot the hilltops. ›› See page 113.

9 Royal Bengal tigers are a magical sight; and a leisurely boat trip in the Sunderbans offers the chance to glimpse this elusive creature in its natural habitat. ›› See page 111.

10 Thirsty work: blocks of ice are transported by cycle-rickshaw to the West Bengali town of Digha. ›› See page 112.

11 Picking the freshest tips on the tea estates near Darjeeling has traditionally offered employment to the local Nepali population. ›› See page 95.

12 The trek to Mt Khangchendzonga is one of several excellent routes in the little-visited eastern Himalaya. ›› See page129.

Head for heights
A rope bridge in Aranachal Pradesh crosses the turbulent reaches of the Brahmaputra River, known locally as the Siang.

Essentials

❣ Footprint features

Planning your trip

Where to go

Northeast India encompasses a vast land of diverse peoples, languages, adventures and geography. Although many of the key destinations are connected by an overnight train ride, and cheaper domestic flights are making the distances involved less daunting, if you have limited time it is best to stick to your main goals and not get over-ambitious. If, however, you have more than a couple of weeks at your disposal, the Northeast offers the chance to experience beach life, the Himalaya and tribal cultures, as well as some of the country's holiest places, all in one trip. Travel agencies, which can make the necessary arrangements for a relatively small fee are listed throughout the text, but remember that air tickets can be difficult to get at short notice for some trips (such as to the Andamans during Indian holiday periods, and to Varanasi at any time). Regardless of budget, travel in India is invariably tiring so build in an opportunity for a rest: Puri on the east coast, the hill stations, or Bodh Gaya, are all relaxing places to spend a few days. Kolkata, where you are likely to start your trip, is both a good and a bad introduction to India. On one hand, expect poverty, over-crowding and choking pollution, yet because it is not as heavily touristed as other points of entry (such as Delhi or Mumbai) there is less risk of being scammed and locals are genuinely friendly. There are plenty of top- and mid-range hotels in Kolkata and Varanasi and it is advisable to book your first night in advance if you're a first-time visitor.

Two weeks

Starting in Kolkata, give yourself a couple of days to acclimatize and view the wealth of colonial architecture and cultural offerings. If you are feeling overwhelmed by the city, leave this for the end of the trip when you are better adjusted. Fly or take an overnight train to Siliguri, then a jeep to Kalimpong or Darjeeling for a few days to soak up the Kangchendzonga views, before heading to Varanasi by train. Steep yourself in the holiest Hindu city, then strike east to catch the Buddhist vibe at Bodh Gaya, from where you might also squeeze in a day trip to Nalanda. From here return to Kolkata and spend time in the city, or kick back on a launch among the islands of the Sunderbans.

An excellent trekking experience is manageable in Sikkim or the north of West Bengal in a fortnight. Head straight up to Darjeeling or Gangtok, where the majority of treks last three to eight days, and breath the Himalayan air. After your trek, retreat and relax for a couple of nights in a quiet settlement such as Mirik (near Darjeeling) or Khecheopalri Lake (Sikkim) to just admire the snowy peaks. Back down in the plains, head east and get up close to the wildlife in Jaldapara Park before hopping slowly south to Kolkata via Malda's historic ruins and sleepy Murshidabad's charms.

For two weeks in paradise, take a flight to the Andamans and make for Havelock or (depending on boat schedules) one of the more pristine, isolated islands such as Little Andaman or Neil Island. For more accessible beach action, head south to Puri, where you might coincide with a Yatra festival if it's April or July. Take in the majestic Sun Temple at Konark, then perhaps head south down the coast, diverting inland to visit the tribal belt of southern Orissa. Do this trip in reverse if you prefer to unwind at the end of a holiday.

Three weeks

Visit the Northeastern Hill States, flying from Kolkata to Guwahati and on to Tezpur, where you can branch off into Arunachal Pradesh for the four-day journey to the magical Tawang Monastery. Back in Tezpur, it's a short road trip to Kaziranga to spot one-horned rhinos. Next, if it's December, the Hornbill Festival in jungly Nagaland is

⁝ Packing for India

You can buy most essentials in larger cities and shops in five-star hotels. Items you might find useful include a loose-fitting, light cotton clothes including a sarong (women should dress modestly at all times; brief shorts and tight vest tops are best avoided, though on the beach modest swimwear is fine). It can be cold in the north from December to February and everywhere over 1500 m, where warmer clothing is essential. Comfortable shoes, sandals or trainers are essential. Take high-factor sun screen and a sun hat. It's almost impossible to buy film outside the 100 to 400 ASA range. Indian pharmacies can be very cheap but aren't always reliable, so take a supply of medicines from home, including inhalers and anti-malarial drugs (Proguanil is not available). For protection against mosquitoes, take repellent. See also Health, page 44.

Photocopies of documents, passport ID and visa pages, and spare photos are useful when applying for permits or in case of loss or theft.

For budget travellers: moquito nets aren't always provided in cheap hotels so take one with you. Earplugs are handy. Take a good padlock to secure your budget room too, though these are cheaply bought in India. A cotton or silk sheet sleeping bag are useful when you can't be sure of clean linen.

worth a detour and while there absorb Kohima and its memories of World War II. Otherwise, carry straight on by road to Meghalaya to see the archery stakes and colourful bazars in Shillong, from where day-trips allow you to visit Jaintia tribal villages or the wettest place on earth, Mawsynram. Cross over again to Guwahati to fly back to Kolkata or, if you have time to spare, fly to Bagdogra and travel by land to Sikkim, Darjeeling or Murshidabad.

Four weeks

In a month and at a brisk pace, it is possible to see all the main sights of Northeast India (excluding the Hill States) and really get an impression of the distinct regional cultures. Flying wherever possible, you could take on Kolkata, the Himalaya, Jaldapara, Varanasi, Bhubaneswar, and either Puri/Digha/Havelock. Alternatively, selecting two or three states, and seeing them at a more leisurely pace, meandering through less touristy towns (such as Kurseong, Bishnupur or Sasaram) could be more enriching and less stressful.

When to go

As in most of India, the best time to be in the Northeast is from the end of the monsoon in October to the end of March, after which the temperatures and humidity level in the lowlands begin to build up. Some of the country's great festivals, such as Dasara and Diwali across India and Durga Puja in West Bengal, are celebrated in the autumn and winter. From April to June the Himalayan hill stations bring much-needed respite from the heat, while the monsoon months of June to September can bring serious disruption in the shape of flooding and landslides. On the other hand, the spectacular Rath Yatra festival in Puri is one compelling reason to visit during July, and devotees of wet weather might pick this time of year to visit Meghalaya – officially home of the wettest town on earth – if only to see nature at one of its extremes.

Trekking in the eastern Himalaya is best in October, with clear blue skies and relatively mild temperatures; the spring months are also good, though visibility may by hazy. Winter in the mountains can be extremely cold, and many guesthouses close.

Activities and tours

There are now many opportunities in adventure sports. Such thrills can be combined with more conventional sightseeing. Apart from the activities listed here, you can also try ballooning, heli-skiing, hang gliding, mountain or rock climbing and even motor rallying. ▸▸ *For tour operators, see page 53.*

Biking

For those keen on moving faster along the road, by travelling on the 2 wheels of a motorbike (preferably a 'Bullet'), see page 34.

Birdwatching

The country's diverse and rich natural habitats harbour over 1200 species of birds of which around 150 are endemic. Visitors can enjoy spotting Oriental species whether it is in towns, in the countryside or more abundantly in the national parks and sanctuaries. On the plains, the cooler months (Nov-Mar) are the most comfortable for a chance to see migratory birds from the hills, but the highlands themselves are ideal in May-Jun and again after the monsoons when visibility improves in Oct-Nov. Bodies of water of all sizes draw visiting water fowl from other continents during the winter.

It is quite easy to get to some parks from the important tourist centres. *A Birdwatcher's Guide to India* by Krys Kazmierczak and Raj Singh (Prion Ltd, Sandy, Bedfordshire, UK, 1998), is well researched and comprehensive with helpful practical information and maps. See also Background, page 326.

★ **Head for ...**
Chilika Lake, Orissa, page 204, **Sikkim**, page 113; the **foothills of Arunachal Pradesh**, page 153.

Contact
www.delhibird.net, www.kolkatabirds.com, www.orientalbirdclub.org, www.sacon.org, **Bird Link**, biks@giasdl01.vsnl.net.in, is concerned with conservation of birds and their habitat.

Cricket

Sport has become one of India's greatest and most popular entertainments. Cricket has an almost fanatical following across India. Reinforced by satellite TV and radio and a national side that enjoys high world rankings and much outstanding individual talent, cricket has become a national obsession. Stars have cult status, and you can see children trying to model themselves on their game on any and every open space.

Contact
India's cricket board (BCCI), www.bcci. cricket.deepthi.com, www.abcofcricket.com, www.focricinfo.com, a good section to keep up to date with all the latest in Indian cricket, and for information and tickets.

Cycling

Cycling offers a peaceful and healthy alternative to cars, buses or trains. Touring on locally hired bicycles is possible along country roads – ideal if you want to see village life in India and the lesser known wildlife parks. Consult a good Indian agent for advice. Expert guides, cycles and support vehicle, accommodation in simple rest houses or tents, are included, see page 33.

Football

Football is played from professional level to kickabout in any open space. The season is Oct-Mar and details of matches are published in the local papers. Top class game tickets are Rs 25, but they are sold for much more on the black market. The crowds generate tremendous fervour for big matches, and standards are improving. African players are now featuring more frequently with Indian teams and monthly salaries have risen to over Rs 40,000 per month, an excellent wage by Indian standards.

Contact
www.indianfootball.com, for the latest news.

★ 5 of the best yoga retreats

Bamboo Resort, Sikkim, www.bambooresort.com.
Basunti, Himachal Pradesh, www.basunti.com.
Bihar School of Yoga, Bihar, www.yogavision.net.
Glenburn Tea Estate, West Bengal, www.glenburnteaestate.com.
Yoga Adventure with Jane Craggs, West Bengal, www.janecraggs.co.uk.

Watersports

Snorkelling, parasailing, windsurfing and water skiing are among the attractions along the long stretches of unspoilt coastal India. There are scuba diving centres in the Andamans. Courses are well run and cost US$85 for an introductory dive, US$400 for 4 days, or US$600 for a 2-week Dive Master course.

★ Head for …
Puri (Orissa) page 185; **Andaman Islands**, page 253.

Contact
PADI Europe, Oberwilerstrasse 3, CH-8442, Hettlingen, Switzerland, T52-304 1414, admin@padi.ch.
PADI International Head Office, Unit 6, Unicorn Park, Whitby Rd, Bristol, BS4 4EX, T0117-971 1717, www.padi.co.uk.

Whitewater rafting

The snow-fed rivers that flow through regions like Sikkim offer excellent white-water rafting. The popular waters range from grades II-III for amateurs to the greater challenges of grades IV-VI for the experienced (eg Rangit and Teesta in Sikkim; Brahmaputra, known as the Siang in Arunachal Pradesh). Trips range from a half day to several days and allow a chance to see scenery, places and people off the beaten track. The trips are organized and managed by professional teams who have trained abroad. The rivers can sometimes be dangerous in Aug-Sep.

★ Head for …
Sikkim, page 113, **Assam**, page 134, **Arunachal Pradesh**, page 153.

Yoga and meditation

There has been a growing Western interest in the ancient life disciplines in search of physical and spiritual wellbeing, as practised in ancient India. Yoga is supposed to regulate the nervous system and aims to attain the union of body, mind and spirit through the practice of *asanas* (body postures), breath control, discipline, cleansing, contemplation and awareness. It seeks to achieve moral purification through abstinence and restraint (dietary and sexual). Meditation which complements yoga to relieve stress, increase awareness and bring inner peace prescribes the practice of *dhyana* (purposeful concentration) by withdrawing oneself from external distractions and focusing ones attention to consciousness itself. This leads ultimately to *samadhi* (release from worldly bonds). Hatha yoga has captured the Western imagination as it promises good health through postural exercises, while the search for inner peace leads others to learn meditation techniques.

Centres across the country offer courses for beginners and practitioners. Some are at special resort hotels which offer all inclusive packages in idyllic locations, some advocate simple communal living in an ashram while others may require rigorous discipline in austere monastic surroundings. Whether you wish to embark on a serious study of yoga or sample an hour's introductory meditation session, India offers opportunities for all, though you may need to apply in advance for some popular courses. Popular centres in places frequented by travellers are listed throughout the book. The **International Yoga Festival** is held in Varanasi annually in Feb.

Essentials Planning your trip Activities & tours

Trekking

The Himalaya offers unlimited opportunities to view the natural beauty of mountains, unique flora and fauna and the diverse groups of people who live in the ranges and valleys, many of whom have retained unique cultural identities because of their isolation. The treks described in this book are only for guidance. They try to give you a flavour of an area or a destination. Some trails fall within the 'Inner Line' for which special permits are required (see page 16). For books on Trekking, see page 330.

Types of trekking

Independent trekking There are some outstandingly beautiful treks, though they are often not through the wilderness sometimes conjured up. However, trekking alone is not recommended as you will be in unfamiliar territory where you may not be able to communicate with the local people and if injured you may not have help at hand. Independent trekkers should get a specialist publication with detailed route descriptions and a good map. Remember, mountain topography is subject to constant change, and tracks and crossings can be affected very rapidly. Speak to those who know the area well and have been trekking to the places you intend visiting.

Backpacking camping Hundreds of people arrive each year with a pack and some personal equipment, buy some food and set off trekking, carrying their own gear and choosing their own campsites or places to stay. Serious trekkers will need a framed backpack. Supplies of fuel wood are scarce and flat ground suitable for camping rare. It is not always easy to find isolated and 'private' campsites.

Trekking without a tent Although common in Nepal, only a few trails in India offer the ease and comfort of this option. Exceptions are the Singalila Ridge trail in the Darjeeling area and the Sikkim Khangchendzonga trek. On these, it is often possible to stay in trekking huts or in simple village homes. You carry clothes and bedding, as with youth hostelling, and for a few rupees a night you get a space on the floor, a wooden pallet or a camp bed, or in the more luxurious inns, a room and shower. The food is simple, usually vegetable curry, rice and dhal *which, although repetitive, is healthy and can be tasty. This approach brings you into more contact with the local population, the limiting factor being the routes where accommodation is available.*

Locally organized treks Porters can usually be hired through an agent in the town or village at the start of a trek. Porters hired in the bazar may be cheaper than agency porters but may be unreliable. Make sure they are experienced in carrying loads over distances at high altitude. They will help carry your baggage, sometimes cook for you, and communicate with the local people. A good porter will know the area and some can tell you about local customs and point out interesting details en route. Away from roads, the footpath is the principal line of communication between villages. Tracks tend to be very good, well graded and in good condition. In remoter areas away from all habitation, tracks may be indistinct and a local guide is recommended. Although some porters speak a little English, you may have communication problems. Remember, you may be expected to provide your porter's warm clothing and protective wear including shoes, gloves and goggles on high altitude treks.

Hiring a *sardar* and crew is more expensive but well worthwhile since he will speak some English, act as a guide, take care of engaging porters and cooks, arrange for provisions and sort out all logistical problems. A *sardar* will cost more and although he may be prepared to carry a load, his principal function will be as a guide and overseer for the porters. Make sure your *sardar* is experienced in the area you will be travelling in and can show good references which are his own and not borrowed.

⁞ Himalayan environment trust code of practice

Deforestation Make no open fires and discourage others making one for you. Limit use of firewood and heated water and use only permitted dead wood. Choose accommodation where kerosene or fuel-efficient wood burning stoves are used.

Litter Remove it. Burn or bury paper and carry away non-degradable litter. If you find other people's litter, remove theirs too. Pack food in biodegradable containers.

Water Keep local water clean. Do not use detergents and pollutants in streams and springs. Where there are no toilets be sure you are at least 30 m away from water source and bury or cover. Do not allow cooks or porters to throw rubbish in nearby streams and rivers.

Plants Do not take cuttings, seeds and roots – it is illegal in all parts of the Himalaya.

Begging Giving to children can encourage begging. Donations to a project, health centre or school may be more constructive.

Be aware of **local traditions and cultures**; respect their privacy, and ask permission before taking photographs; respect their holy places, never touching or removing religious objects, and removing shoes before entering temples; be aware of local etiquette, dressing modestly particularly when visiting temples and shrines and while walking through villages avoiding shorts, skimpy tops and tight-fitting outfits. Do not hold hands and kiss in public.

Using a trekking agent Trekking agents based in Delhi or Kolkata or at hill stations (eg Leh, Darjeeling, Gangtok) will organize treks for a fee and provide a *sardar*, porters, cooks, food and equipment, but it requires effort and careful thought on your part. This method can be excellent and is recommended for a group, preferably with some experience, that wants to follow a specific itinerary. You have to follow a pre-arranged itinerary in some areas, as required by the government, and also as porters expect to arrive at certain points on schedule. You can make arrangements from abroad in advance; often a protracted business with faxes and emails. Alternatively, wait until you get to India but allow at least a week to make arrangements.

Fully organized and escorted trek A company or individual with local knowledge and expertise organizes a trip and sells it. Some or all camp equipment, food, cooking, planning the stages, decision-making based on progress and weather conditions, liaison with porters, shopkeepers, etc are all taken care of. When operating abroad, the agency may take care of all travel arrangements, ticketing, visas and permits. Make sure that both you and the trekking company understand exactly who is to provide what equipment. This has the advantage of being a good, safe introduction to the country. You will be able to travel with limited knowledge of the region and its culture and get to places more easily which as an individual you might not reach, without the expense of completely kitting yourself out. You should read and follow any advice in the preparatory material you are sent, as your enjoyment greatly depends on it.

An escorted trek involves going with a group; you will camp together but not necessarily all walk together. If you are willing to trade some of your independence for careful, efficient organization and make the effort to ensure the group works well together, the experience can be very rewarding. Ideally there should be no more than 20 trekkers (preferably around 12). Companies have reputations to maintain and try to comply with western concepts of hygiene. Before booking, check the itinerary – is it too demanding, or not adventurous enough? Also find out whether the leader is qualified and is familiar with the route and what equipment is provided.

Local agents

Tourist offices and government approved trekking agents in **Delhi** and the hill stations will organize fairly inexpensive treks (on some routes, it is compulsory to trek in this way). Tour operators and travel agents are listed in each town. The following are recommended:

Adventure Quests, www.adventure quests.net. Run by ex-servicemen, with a range of adventurous trekking and rafting trips in Arunachal Pradesh.

Himalayan Mountaineering Institutes, in hill stations in Darjeeling.

Ibex Expeditions, see page 54.

Mountain Adventures, A-51, SFS Mount Kailash, New Delhi, T011-2622 2202, www.mountainindia.com.

NEI (Nature Expedition India), B-966 Ansals Palam Vihar, Gurgaon, New Delhi Suburb, T0124-236 8601, www.himalaya-india.com.

Wanderlust, G-18,2nd floor, Masjid Moth, Greater Kailash Part-II, New Delhi-110048 T011-3292 0231, www.wanderlustindia.com.

Foreign operators

Australia and New Zealand

Adventure World, see page 54.

Himalayan Travellers, Wellington, T04-863325.

Peregrine Adventures, see page 54.

UK

Exodus, see page 53.

Explore Worldwide, T0870-333 4001, www.explore.co.uk.

High Places, T0845-257 7500, www.highplaces.co.uk.

Himalayan Kingdoms, T0845-330 8579, www.himalayankingdoms.com.

KE Adventure, T01768-773966, www.ke adventure.com.

Snow Lion Expeditions, T0800-525 8735, www.snowlion.com.

USA

Air Treks, T1877-247 8735, www.airtreks.com.

Mercury, T0800-2231474.

Mountain Travel Sobek, T1510-594 6000, www.mtsobek.com.

Trekking seasons

These vary with the area you plan to visit and the elevation. Autumn is best in most parts of the Himalaya though March to May can be pleasant. The monsoons (mid-June to end-September) can obviously be very wet and localized thunderstorms can occur at any time, particularly in the spring and summer. Start your trek early in the morning as the monsoon approaches. It often continues to rain heavily up to mid-October in the eastern Himalaya. Be prepared for extremes in temperatures in all seasons so come prepared with light clothing as well as enough waterproof protection. Winters can be exceptionally cold; high passes can be closed and you need more equipment. Winter treks on all but a few low-altitude ones (up to 3200 m) are only recommended for the experienced trekker accompanied by a knowledgeable local guide. In the **Darjeeling** area (pages 99-101), April to May has occasional showers but the rhododendrons and magnolias are in full bloom; October and November are usually dry with excellent visibility. Early December is possible but very cold. Trekking is possible in **Sikkim** (page 128) from mid-February to late May and again from October to early December; April, May, October and November are best.

Trekking permits

Trekking is permitted in all areas other than those described as Restricted or Protected and within the **'Inner Line'**, so that you may not go close to the international boundary in many places. Often, destinations falling within these 'sensitive' zones which have recently been opened for trekking, require treks to be organized by a recognized Indian travel agent for groups of at least four, travelling on a specified route, accompanied by a representative/liaison officer. Sometimes there are restrictions on the maximum number of days, season and type of transport used. The 'Inner Line' runs parallel and 40 km inside the international boundary. Other areas now open to tourists include Tsangu Lake, Lachung and Yumthang (Sikkim) and Kameng Valley (Arunachal Pradesh). On arrival in India, government-approved

❊ Water purification

There are various ways of purifying water in order to make it safe to drink. Dirty water should be strained through a filter bag, and then boiled or treated.

Bringing water to a rolling **boil** at sea level will make water safe for drinking, but at higher altitudes you have to boil the water for longer to ensure that all the microbes are killed.

Various sterilizing methods can be used, with preparations containing **chlorine** (eg 'Puritabs') or **iodine** (eg 'Pota Aqua') compounds. Chlorine compounds generally do not kill protozoa (eg giardia). Prolonged usage of iodine compounds may lead to thyroid problems, although this is rare if used for less than a year.

There are a number of **water filters** now on the market, available both in personal and expedition size. There are two types of water filter, mechanical and chemical. Mechanical filters are usually a combination of carbon, ceramic and paper, although they can be difficult to use. Although cheaper, the disadvantage of mechanical filters is that they do not always remove viruses or protozoa. Chemical filters use a combination of an iodine resin filter and a mechanical filter. The advantage is that according to the manufacturers' claims, everything in the water will be killed. The disadvantage is that the filters need replacing, adding a third to the price.

Essentials Planning your trip Trekking

trekking agencies can obtain permits relatively easily, usually within three or four days. It can be much slower applying for trekking permits from abroad and may also slow down your visa application. Some restricted areas are still totally closed to foreigners. For other restricted areas, permits are issued at the Foreigners' Regional Registration Offices in Delhi, Mumbai, Kolkata and Chennai (and sometimes at a local FRRO), from immigration officers at some points of entry, and sometimes at the district magistrate's. There are also entrance fees for the various national parks and conservation areas which can be as much as Rs 350 for foreigners.

❊ *Always carry your passport. Without one you can be turned back or, if in a restricted area, be deported at one of the regular trekking permit inspection points.*

Mountaineering courses

Courses in mountaineering, skiing, high altitude trekking and mountain rescue: **Himalayan Mountaineering Institute**, Nehru Hill, Darjeeling.

Indian Mountaineering Federation, T011-2411 1211, www.indmount.org. Information on mountaineering.

Equipment and clothing

If you have good equipment, it is worth taking it, especially your own boots. Mountaineering and trekking equipment can sometimes be hired from various hill stations. Ask the Institutes of Mountaineering and tourist offices there. Guard against cold, wet, sudden changes of temperature, strong sun and wind! Waterproof jacket with hood and over-trousers (windproof, waterproof and 'breather' type); warm sweater; fleece jacket; tracksuit; hiking trousers or shorts (knee length but not cycling); cotton T-shirts; cotton underwear; thermal underwear (vests, long johns); gloves; balaclava or ski toque; sun hat; swimwear. Try to carry lightweight, quick-drying fabrics that can be easily washed in cold water streams. (After the trek, you might consider offering clothes you can part with to your porter.) Good lightweight walking boots with ankle support should be comfortable and well worn in, as blisters can ruin a trek; spare laces, good trainers (for resting the feet; also suitable for many low-level treks except in snow and off-the-trails); polypropylene undersocks, heavy walking socks. Sunglasses (with

UV filter), snow glasses if you are planning to go above the snow line, high-factor sun block (SPF 15+), lip cream, a good sleeping bag (cheap ones from a local market are unsuitable above 4000 m) plus cotton liner, a Thermarest pad or a double thickness foam sleeping mat, 2-m-sq plastic sheet (sold locally), torch (flashlight) with replacement batteries or a Petzl headtorch, a compass, binoculars, insulated bag water-bottle (to also take to bed!), a day pack, a tent (in certain areas). Those expecting to climb high, cross glaciers etc may need to hire crampons, ice axes, snow gaiters, ropes etc as well as a silver survival blanket and a reinforced plastic 'bivouac bag'. A kerosene stove and strong fuel container suitable for high altitudes (kerosene is widely available); water filter and containers; nesting cooking pots (at least two); enamel mug and spoon and bags for provisions. Be sure to eat a balanced diet. Local foods will be available along the trail, and in fact the porters' meal of chapati or rice, vegetables, dhal and sweet milky tea is quite nutritious. Some shops stock limited amounts of dry goods for trekkers (noodles, chocolate bars, canned foods, fruit, nuts, porridge oats etc). You might prefer to take some freeze-dried packs of favourites from home. Remember to thoroughly boil the fresh (unpasteurized) local milk.

Maps

Survey of India has started producing trekking maps, Scale 1:250,000; but at present these cover only the Himachal and Uttarakhand areas; none are available for the Northeast. For information on Sikkim trekking maps, see page 129.

Taking a tour

You may choose to try an inclusive package holiday or let a specialist operator quote for a tailor-made tour. Out of season these can be worth exploring. The lowest prices quoted from the UK vary from about US$550 for a week (flights, hotel and breakfast) in the low season to over US$3000 for three weeks during the peak season. Most will chalk out individual itineraries and cover the major sights with small groups. A list of specialist tour operators, who arrange anything from general tours to wildlife safaris to ashram retreats, can be found on page 53.

Local customs and laws

Customs

Most travellers experience great warmth and hospitality. With it comes an open curiosity about personal matters. You should not be surprised if total strangers ask for details of your job, income and family circumstances or discuss politics and religion.

Conduct

Respect for the foreign visitor should be reciprocated by a sensitivity towards local customs and culture. How you dress is how people will judge you; cleanliness, modest clothes and a smile go a long way. Scanty, tight clothing draws unwanted attention. Public displays of intimacy are inappropriate in public. You may at times be frustrated by delays, bureaucracy and inefficiency, but displays of anger and rudeness will not achieve anything positive, and often make things worse. People's concept of time and punctuality is also often rather vague so be prepared to be kept waiting.

Courtesy

It takes little effort to learn common gestures of courtesy and they are greatly appreciated. The greeting when meeting or parting, used universally among the Hindus across India, is the palms joined together as in prayer, sometimes accompanied with

⦙ First impressions

On arrival at any of India's major cities the first impressions can take you aback. The exciting images of an ancient and richly diverse culture which draw many visitors to India can be overwhelmed by the immediate sensations which first greet you. These can be daunting and make adjustment to India early on in your trip difficult. Even on a short visit give yourself time and space to adjust.

Pollution All cities seriously suffer.

Noise Many find India incredibly noisy, as radios, videos and loudspeakers blare at all times.

Smells India has a baffling mix of smells, from the richly pungent and unpleasant to the delicately subtle.

Pressure On stepping out of your hotel everybody seems to clamour to sell you their services. Taxi and rickshaw drivers are always there when you don't want them. There often seems to be no sense of personal space or privacy. Young women are often stared at.

Public hygiene (or lack of it) It is common to see people urinating in public places and defecating in the open countryside.

the word *namaste* (North and West) or *namoshkar* (East). Muslims use the greeting *assalām aleikum*, with the response *waleikum assalām*, meaning 'peace be with you'; 'please' is *mehrbani-se*; 'thank you' is often expressed by a smile, or with the somewhat formal *dhannyabad* or *shukriya* (Urdu). For useful Hindi phrases, see box page 21.

Hands and eating

Traditionally, Indians use the right hand for giving, receiving, shaking hands and eating, as the left is considered to be unclean since it is associated with washing after using the toilet. In much of rural India cutlery is alien at the table except for serving spoons, and at most humble restaurants you will be offered only small spoons to eat with. If you visit an ashram or are lucky enough to be invited to a temple feast day, you will almost certainly be expected to eat with your hands. Watch and copy others until the technique becomes familiar.

Women → *See also page 55.*

Indian women in urban and rural areas differ in their social interactions with men. To the Westerner, Indian women may seem to remain in the background and appear shy when approached. Yet you will see them working in public, often in jobs traditionally associated with men in the West, in the fields or on construction sites. It is not considered polite for men to photograph women without their consent, so ask before you start snapping.

Women do not usually shake hands with men as physical contact between the sexes is not acceptable. A westernized city woman, however, may feel free to shake hands with a foreign visitor. In certain, very traditional rural circles, it is still the custom for men to be offered food first, separately, so don't be surprised if you, as foreign guest (man or woman), are awarded this special status when invited to an Indian home.

Visiting religious sites

Visitors to all religious places should be dressed in clean, modest clothes; shorts and vests are inappropriate. Always remove shoes before entering (and all leather items in Jain temples). Take thick socks for protection when walking on sun-baked stone floors. Menstruating women are considered 'unclean' and should not enter places of worship. It is discourteous to sit with one's back to a temple or shrine. You will be expected to sit cross-legged on the floor – avoid pointing your feet at others when attending prayers at a temple. Walk clockwise around a shrine (keeping it to your right).

⁞ Leave a small footprint

As well as respecting local cultural sensitivities, travellers can take a number of simple steps to reduce, or even improve, their impact on the local environment. Environmental concern is relatively new in India, but don't be afraid to pressurize businesses by asking about their policies.

Litter Many travellers think that there is little point in disposing of rubbish properly when the tossing of water bottles, plastic cups and other non-biodegradable items out of train windows is already so widespread. You can immediately reduce your impact by refusing plastic bags and other excess packaging when shopping – use a small backpack or cloth bag instead – and if you do collect a few, keep them with you to store other rubbish until you get to a litter bin.

Filtered water versus bottled water Plastic mineral water bottles, an inevitable corollary to poor water hygiene standards, are a major contributor to India's litter mountain. However, many hotels, including nearly all of the upmarket ones, most restaurants and bus and train stations, provide drinking water purified using a combination of ceramic and carbon filters, chlorine and sometimes UV irradiation. Ask for 'filter paani'; if the water tastes at all like a swimming pool it is probably quite safe to drink,

though it's worth introducing your body gradually to the new water. See box, page 17, on water purification.

Bucket baths versus showers The biggest issue relating to responsible and sustainable tourism is water. Much of northwest India is afflicted by severe water restrictions, with certain cities in Rajasthan and Gujarat having water supply for as little as 20 minutes a day. The traditional Indian 'bucket bath', in which you wet, soap then rinse off using a small hand-held plastic jug dipped into a large bucket, uses on average around 15 litres of water, as compared to 30-45 for a shower. These are commonly offered except in four- and five-star hotels.

Support responsible tourism Spending your money carefully can have a positive impact. Sleeping, eating and shopping at small, locally owned businesses directly supports communities, while specific community tourism concerns provide an economic motivation for people to stay in remote communities, protect natural areas and revive traditional cultures, rather than exploit the environment or move to the cities for work.

Transport Choose walking, cycling or public transport over fuel-guzzling cars and motorbikes.

Non-Hindus are sometimes excluded from the inner sanctum of **Hindu** temples and occasionally even from the temple itself. Look for signs or ask. In certain temples and on special occasions you may enter only if you wear unstitched clothing such as a *dhoti*.

In **Buddhist** shrines, turn prayer wheels in a clockwise direction. In **Sikh** *gurud-waras*, everyone should cover their head, even if it is with a handkerchief. Tobacco and cigarettes should not be taken in. In **Muslim** mosques, visitors should only have their face, hands and feet exposed; women should also cover their heads. Mosques may be closed to non-Muslims shortly before formal prayers.

Some temples have a register or a receipt book for **donations** which works like an obligatory entry fee. The money is normally used for the upkeep and services of the temple or monastery. In some pilgrimage centres, priests can become unpleasantly persistent. If you wish to leave a donation, put money in the donation box; priests and Buddhist monks often do not handle money. It is also not customary to shake hands with a priest or monk. *Sanyasis* (holy men) and some pilgrims depend on donations.

⦂ Basic Hindi words and phrases

Pronunciation: a as in ah; i as in bee; o as in oh; u as oo in book
Hello namaste/nomoshkar
Thank you/no thank you dhanyavad or shukriya/nahin shukriya
Yes/no ji han/ji nahin
What is your name? apka nam kya hai?
My name is... mera nam... hai
How are you? kya hal hai?
I am well, thanks, and you? main thik hun, aur ap?
How much? Kitna?
That is very expensive! bahut mahanga hai!

Guide fees

Guides vary considerably in their knowledge and ability. Government licensed guides are covered by specified fees. Local temple and site guides should charge less. Charges for four people for half a day are about Rs 280, for a full day Rs 400; for five to 15 people for half a day Rs 400, for a full day Rs 530. Rs 125 for a language other than English

Begging

Beggars are found in busy street corners in large Indian cities, as well as at bus and train stations where they often target foreigners. Visitors can find this distressing, especially the sight of severely undernourished children or those displaying physical deformity. You may be particularly affected when some persist in making physical contact. In the larger cities, beggars are often exploited by syndicates which cream off most of their takings. Yet those seeking alms near religious sites are another matter, and you may see Indian worshippers giving freely to those less fortunate than themselves, since this is tied up with gaining 'merit'. How you deal with begging is a personal choice but it is perhaps better to give to a recognized charity than to make largely ineffectual handouts to individuals. Young children sometimes offer to do 'jobs' such as call a taxi, carry shopping or pose for a photo. You may want to give a coin in exchange. While travelling, some visitors prefer to hand out fruit to the many open-palmed children they encounter.

Charitable giving

A pledge to donate a part of one's holiday budget to a local charity could be an effective formula for 'giving'. Some visitors like to support self-help cooperatives, orphanages, refugee centres, disabled or disadvantaged groups, or international charities like Oxfam, Save the Children or Christian Aid which work with local partners, by either making a donation or by buying their products. Also see information about charities and organizations that welcome volunteers on pages 56 and 80.

Concern India Foundation, 6K Dubash Marg, Mumbai, T022-2202 9708, www.concernindia.org. An umbrella organization working with local charities.
Oxfam, Sushil Bhawan, 210 Shahpur Jat, New Delhi 110049, T011-2649 1774; 274 Banbury Rd, Oxford OX2 7D2, UK, www.oxfam.org (400 grassroots projects).
SOS Children's Villages, A-7 Nizamuddin West, New Delhi 110013, T011-2435 9450, www.soscvindia.org. Over 30 children's projects in India, eg opposite Pital Factory, Jhotwara Rd, Jaipur 302016, T0141-228 0787.
Save the Children India, 4C Swapnalok, 47 LJ Mard, Mumbai 400036, www.savethechildrenindia.org.
Trek-Aid, 2 Somerset Cottages, Stoke Villages, Plymouth, Devon, PL3 4AZ, www.a38.com/trekaid. Health, education, etc, through self-help schemes for displaced Tibetan refugees.

Photography

Many monuments and national parks charge a camera fee ranging from Rs 20-100 for still cameras, and as much as Rs 500 for video cameras (more for professionals). Special permits are needed from the Archaeological Survey of India, New Delhi, for using tripods and artificial lights. When photographing people, it is polite to first ask – they will usually respond warmly with smiles. Visitors often promise to send copies of the photos – don't unless you really mean to do so. Photography of airports, military installations, bridges and in tribal and 'sensitive border areas', is not permitted.

Drugs

Certain areas, such as Puri (Orissa), have become associated with foreigners who take drugs. These are likely to attract local and foreign drug dealers but be aware that the government takes the misuse of drugs very seriously. Anyone charged with the illegal possession of drugs risks facing a fine of Rs 100,000 and a minimum 10 years' imprisonment. Several foreigners have been imprisoned for drugs-related offences in the last decade.

Getting there

India is accessible by air from virtually every continent. Most international flights arrive in Delhi or Mumbai, both of which have good internal connections to Kolkata and other airports in the Northeast India. Some carriers permit 'open-jaw' travel, arriving in and departing from different cities.

Buying a ticket

Discounts The cheapest fares from Europe tend to be with Central European, Central Asian or Middle Eastern airlines. With these airlines it pays to confirm your return flight as early as possible. You can also get good discounts from Australasia, Southeast Asia and Japan. If you plan to visit two or more South Asian countries within three weeks, you may qualify for a 30% discount on your international tickets. Ask your national tourist office. International air tickets can be bought in India though payment must be made in foreign exchange.

Ticket agents Companies dealing in volume and taking reduced commissions for ticket sales can offer better deals than the airlines themselves. The national press carry their advertisements. **Trailfinders,** T0845-058 5858, www.trailfinders.co.uk, has worldwide agencies; **STA,** T0870-160 0599, www.statravel.co.uk, with over 100 offices worldwide, offers special deals for under-26s; **Travelbag,** T0800-082 5000, www.travel bag.co.uk, quotes competitive fares and is part of ebookers. General Sales Agents (GSAs) for specific airlines can sometimes offer attractive deals: try **Jet Air,** 188 Hammersmith Road, London W6 7DJ, T020-8970 1555, for Gulf Air, Kuwait Airways; **Welcome Travels,** 58 Wells Street, London W1P 3RA, T020-7436 3011, for Air India.

Stopovers and Round-the-World (RTW) tickets You can arrange several stopovers in India on RTW and long-distance tickets. RTW tickets allow you to fly in to one and out from another international airport. You may be able to arrange some internal flights using international carriers eg **Air India** sometimes allows stopovers within India for a small extra charge. **Emirates/Sri Lankan** offers some attractive return fares to Australia that allow stops in Dubai, India, Sri Lanka and either Thailand or Singapore. If you plan to visit two or more South Asian countries within three weeks, you may qualify for a 30% discount on your international tickets. Ask your travel agent. International air tickets can be bought in India, often at excellent prices, though payment must be made in foreign currency.

From Europe

The best deals are from the UK (try www.cheapflights.com, which also has lots of useful information). In 2007 the cheapest return flights direct to Kolkata from London cost around £450, but rose above £700 approaching the high season of Christmas, New Year and Easter. Alternatively, an off-season return flight to Delhi can cost as little as £300, and airlines such as **Jet Airways** offer good deals on internal flights when booked in conjunction with an international leg.

Direct services from London to Kolkata are offered by a limited number of airlines, including **Air India** and **British Airways**, with flights taking as little as 10 hours. **Lufthansa, Emirates** and **Gulf Air** offer good discounts but fly via their hub cities, adding to the journey time. Flight consolidators in the UK offering competitive fares include: **Flight bookers**, T0800-082 3000, www.ebookers.com; and **North South Travel**, T01245-608291, www.northsouthtravel.co.uk, (profits to charity). Air India has relaunched the **companion-free** scheme for routes between USA/Canada and UK/Europe. It's valid until 31 March 2008.

From Australasia

Qantas, Singapore Airlines, Thai Airways, Malaysian Airlines, Cathay Pacific and **Air India** are the principal airlines connecting the continents, although **Qantas** is the only one that flies direct. Coming from Asia, **Singapore Airlines** and **Thai Airways** have direct services to Kolkata. **STA** and **Flight Centre** offer discounted tickets from their branches in major cities in Australia and New Zealand. **Abercrombie & Kent, Adventure World, Peregrine** and **Travel Corporation of India**, organize tours; see Ticket agents and airlines, page 24.

From North America

From the east coast, it is best to fly direct to India from New York via London by **Air India** (18 hours). Discounted tickets on **British Airways, KLM, Lufthansa, Gulf Air** and **Kuwait Airways** are sold through agents although they will invariably fly via their country's capital cities. From the west coast, it is best to fly via Hong Kong, Singapore or Bangkok to Delhi or Kolkata using one of those countries' national carriers. **Air Canada** operates between Vancouver and Delhi. **Air Brokers International,** www.airbrokers.com, is competitive and reputable. **STA**, www.statravel.co.uk, has offices in many US cities, Toronto and Ontario. Student fares are also available from **Travel Cuts,** T0800-6672887, www.travelcuts.com, in Canada.

Departure tax

Rs 500 is payable for all international departures other than those to neighbouring SAARC countries, when the tax is Rs 250 (not reciprocated by Sri Lanka). This is normally included in your international ticket; check when buying. (To save time 'Security Check' your baggage before checking in at departure.)

Road

Crossings between India and its neighbours are affected by the political relations between them. Get your Indian visa in advance, before arriving at the border. Several road border crossings are open periodically, but permission to cross cannot be guaranteed. Those listed below are the main crossings which are usually open all year to tourists. New direct 'friendship' buses have been introduced between Dhaka and Kolkata.

From Bangladesh To Kolkata from Dhaka and Jessore. The Bangaon-Benapol crossing is the most reliable. On the Bangladesh side rickshaws are available from Benapol, while buses and minibuses go to Bangaon railway station from the border. **To Tripura** from Dhaka is only four hours by road from the border crossing, just 2 km from the centre of Agartala, with flights to Kolkata. The border post is efficient when open but arrive there before 1500, as formalities often take time. Regulations are subject to change so find out in advance. In London, Bangladesh High Commission, T020-7584 0081.

From Bhutan To Bagdogra, the nearest airport is three to four hours' drive from Jaigaon, the rather untidy and unkempt Indian border town. The Indian Immigration checkpost is on the main street, about 1 km from the 'Bhutan Gate' at the border town of Phuntsholing where it is possible to spend a night. Accommodation ranges from the simple **Central Hotel** to the moderate government run **Druk Hotel**. To enter Bhutan you need an entry permit and a visa.

From Burma/Myanmar The recently reopened Moreh/Tamu border crossing links Myanmar with the state of Manipur. However, foreigners have reported great difficulty in securing permission to either leave or enter Myanmar by land. Anyone intending to try will need a permit to visit Manipur from the Indian government (see page 55 for permit information).

From Nepal Four crossings are in common use: To **Delhi via Banbassa** is the shortest direct route between Kathmandu and Delhi, via the Nepali town of Mahendranagar and Banbassa. **To Varanasi via Gorakhpur** you must go to the **Sonauli-Bhairawa** crossing, the shortest and fastest route to Varanasi; many continue to Delhi from there. From Kathmandu or Pokhara you can get to Bhairawa, 6 km inside the Nepal border, Sonauli on the border itself, and Nautanwa on the Indian side. From there, buses take 3½ hours to Gorakhpur, with train connections for Delhi, or 5½ hours by bus to Varanasi, see page 252. **To Patna via Raxaul-Birganj** several buses run daily from Raxaul to Patna (five to seven hours) but timings are unreliable and the buses are crowded and uncomfortable. Night buses from Patna reach the border in the early morning; morning buses from Patna connect with the night bus to Kathmandu. Either way you have to have at least one night bus journey unless you stay overnight at Birganj or Raxaul, which is not recommended. The bus journey between Kathmandu or Pokhara and the border takes about 11-12 hours. Even Express buses are slow and packed. Tourist minibuses are the only moderately comfortable option. For details see Patna, page 219. **Kakarbhitta** (Kakarvita) is on the Nepalese side of a wide river which forms the border here between India and Nepal. A kilometre-long road bridge links it to the Indian town of Raniganj on the east bank. Cycle rickshaws run between the two. A small notice and an Indian flag are all that mark the Indian Immigration checkpost which is in a shady grove of trees by the road. The larger Indian town of Bagdogra is 15 km away. For details see under Siliguri, page 103.

Ticket agents and airlines

Agents
Abercrombie & Kent, www.abercrombie kent.com, www.abercrombiekent.com.au.
Adventure Company, T0870-794 1009, www.adventurecompany.co.uk. Quotes competitive fares.
Adventure World, www.adventureworld.com.au.
Bridge the world, T020-7911 0900, www.b-t-w.co.uk.

Council Travel, www.counciltravel.com.
Ebookers, T020-7757 3000, www.ebookers.com.
Flight Centres, www.flightcentre.com.
Hari World Travels, www.hariworld.com.
Jet Airways, 188 Hammersmith Rd, London W6 7DJ, T020-8970 1500. For Gulf Air, Kuwait Airways, etc.
North South Travel, T01245-492882, www.northsouthtravel.co.uk. Profits go to charity.
Orient International Ltd, 91 Charlotte St, London W1P 1LB, T020-7637 1330.
Peregrine, www.peregrine.net.au.

STA, London, T0871-230 0040, www.sta
travel.co.uk. Over 100 offices worldwide.
Trailfinders, London, T0845-058 5858,
www.trailfinders.com. Worldwide agencies.
Travel Corporation of India, www.tcindia.com.
Travel Cuts, www.travelcuts.com. US and
Canadian agent.
Welcome Travels, 58 Wells St, London
W1P 3RA, T020-7436 3011, www.welcome
travels.com. For Air India.
www.bargainholidays.com,
www.expedia.co.uk,
www.lastminute.com
www.travelocity.com.

Airlines
Air India, www.airindia.com.
British Airways, www.ba.com.

Cathay Pacific, www.cathaypacific.com.
Emirates, www.emirates.com.
Gulf Air, www.gulfairco.com.
Indian Airlines, www.indian-airlines.nic.in.
Jet, www.jetairways.com.
Kingfisher, www.flykingfisher.com.
KLM, www.klm.com.
Kuwait Airways, www.kuwait-airways.com.
Lufthansa, www.lufthansa.com.
Malaysian Airlines, www.malaysiaairlines.com.
Qantas, www.qantas.com.au.
Royal Jordanian, www.rja.com.jo.
Sahara, www.airsahara.net.
Singapore Airlines, www.singaporeair.com.
Thai Airways, www.thaiair.com.
Virgin Atlantic, www.virgin-atlantic.com

Getting around

Air

India has a comprehensive network linking the major cities of the different states. Deregulation of the airline industry has had a transformative effect on travel within India, with a host of low-budget private carriers offering sometimes unbelievably cheap fares on an ever expanding network of routes in a bid to woo the train-travelling middle class. Promotional one-way fares as low as Rs 9 (US$0.20) are not unknown, and on any given day, booking a week or two in advance, you can hope to fly between Delhi and Kolkata for around US$50-80.

Kolkata is the hub of northeast air travel, with direct flights to the capitals of most states in the region, as well as to Delhi, Mumbai, Varanasi and other major cities. Guwahati in Assam, and Bagdogra, the air hub for the Himalayan hill stations, also have good connections to Delhi. Some approximate one-way fares include: Delhi-Guwahati US$75-200; Delhi-Bagdogra US$85-160; Kolkata-Varanasi US$160-200; Kolkata-Guwahati US$35-70; and Kolkata-Imphal US$35-65.

Competition from the efficiently run private sector has, in general, improved the quality of services provided by the nationalized airlines. It also seems to herald the end of the two-tier pricing structure, meaning that ticket prices are now usually the same for foreign and Indian travellers. The airport authorities too have made efforts to improve handling on the ground.

For covering vast distances or awkward links on a route, internal flights are worth considering, though delays and re-routing can be irritating, and there are environmental issues to consider. For short distances it makes more sense to travel by train.

The best way to get an idea of the current routes, carriers and fares is to use a third-party booking website such as **www.flightraja.com**, **www.cleartrip.com** or **www.yatra.com**; the latter also deals with international flights. Booking with these is a different matter: some refuse foreign credit cards outright, while others have to be persuaded to give your card special clearance. Tickets booked on these sites are typically issued as an email ticket or an SMS text message – the simplest option if you have an Indian mobile phone, though it must be converted to a paper ticket at the relevant carrier's airport offices before you will be allowed into the terminal.

The following airlines were well established at the time of writing, though the pace of change is rapid:

Air Deccan, T011-3900 8888, www.air deccan.net. The best connected out of all the budget airlines, with flights to more obscure destinations and ambitious expansion plans.

Indian Airlines, www.indian-airlines.com. The nationalized carrier, with the widest network of routes. Subsidiary **Alliance Air** flies some of the oldest aircraft in Indian skies and has a poor safety record.

Indigo, T099-1038 3838, www.goindigo.in. Comparable to SpiceJet.

Jet Airways, T1800-225522, T011-3989 3333, www.jetairways.com. The longest-established of the private airlines, offering full-service domestic flights.

Kingfisher, T0124-284 4700, www.flyking fisher.com. Similar service and prices to Jet.

SpiceJet, T1800-180 3333, www.spicejet.com. No-frills service between major cities.

Airport information The formalities on arrival in India have been increasingly streamlined during the last few years and the facilities at the major international airports greatly improved. However, arrival can still be a slow process. Disembarkation cards, with an attached customs declaration, are handed out to passengers during the inward flight. The immigration form should be handed in at the immigration counter on arrival. The customs slip will be returned, for handing over to the customs on leaving the baggage collection hall. You may well find that there are delays of over an hour at immigration in processing passengers passing through immigration who need help with filling in forms.

Pre-paid taxis to the city are available at all major airports. Insist on being taken to your chosen destination even if the driver claims the city is unsafe or the hotel has closed down. ►► *For details on getting from Kolkata airport into the city centre, see page 60.*

Air tickets All the major airlines are connected to the local travel agents who will book your tickets for a fee if you don't want to spend precious time searching online or waiting in a queue. Remember that tickets are in great demand in the peak season so it is essential to get them weeks or months ahead. If you are able to pre-plan your trip, it is even possible to book internal flights at home when you buy your international air ticket. This can done through an agent or direct with the airline (eg **Indian Airlines** or **Jet Airways**). Both Jet and Indian offer a variety of flight passes, valid on certain sections of their networks; these can be useful if you plan to travel extensively and quickly in areas beyond the reach of the budget airlines. You can also book internal flights on the internet, www.welcometravel.com, and collect and pay for them on your arrival in India. **Indian Airlines** and **Jet Airways** offer special 7, 15 and 21-day unlimited travel deals (some are limited to one area of the country) from around US$300 to US$800. A 25% discount is given on US dollar fares for travellers aged 12-30 years and 25% discount fares exist on some late-night flights (between 2000 and 0800) between major cities.

Delays Be prepared for delays, especially during the winter. Nearly all northern routes originate in Delhi where from early December to February smog has become a common morning hazard, sometimes delaying departures by several hours.

Air travel tips **Security:** You may need to identify your bags after they have been checked in and just before they are loaded onto the plane. All baggage destined for the hold must be X-rayed by security before checking in, so do this first on arrival at the airport.

Telephone: There is a free telephone service at major airports (occasionally through the tourist office counter) to contact any hotel of your choice.

Waiting lists: If you don't have a confirmed booking and are 'wait-listed' it pays to arrive early at the airport and be persistent in enquiring about your position.

⁞ Riding the rails

High class, comfortable, and by Indian standards, quick new Express trains have brought many journeys within daytime reach. But while they offer an increasingly functional means of covering long distances in comfort, it is the overnight trips which still retain something of the early feel of Indian train travel. The bedding carefully prepared – and now available on air conditioned second class trains – the early morning light illuminating another stretch of hazy Indian landscape, spontaneous conversations with fellow travellers – these are still on offer, giving a value far beyond the still modest prices. Furthermore, India still has a complete guide to its rail timetables.

Rail

Trains can still be the cheapest and most comfortable means of travelling long distances saving you hotel expenses on overnight journeys. It gives access to booking station Retiring Rooms, which can be useful from time to time (see page 36). Above all, you have an ideal opportunity to meet local travellers and catch a glimpse of life on the ground. Remember the dark glass fitted on air-conditioned coaches does restrict vision. See also www.indianrail.gov.in.

High-speed trains There are several air-conditioned 'high-speed' **Shatabdi** (or 'Century') Express for day travel, and **Rajdhani Express** ('Capital City') for overnight journeys. These cover large sections of the network but due to high demand you need to book them well in advance (up to 90 days). Meals and drinks are usually included.

Steam For rail enthusiasts, the steam-hauled narrow-gauge train between Kurseong and Darjeeling in North Bengal (a World Heritage Site) is an attraction. See the IRCTC and Indian Railways website, www.irctc.co.in. **Williams Travel** ① *18/20 Howard St, Belfast BT1 6FQ, Northern Ireland, T01232-329477*, and **SD Enterprises** (see page 28) are recommended for tailor-made trips.

Classes A/c First Class, available only on main routes, is very comfortable (bedding provided). It will also be possible for tourists to reserve special coaches (some air conditioning) which are normally allocated to senior railway officials only. **A/c Sleeper**, two and three-tier configurations (known as 2AC and 3AC), are clean and comfortable and good value. **A/c Executive Class**, with wide reclining seats, are available on many *Shatabdi* trains at double the price of the ordinary **a/c Chair Car** which are equally comfortable. **1st Class (non-a/c)** is gradually being phased out (now rather run down but still pleasant if you like open windows). **Sleeper Class** provides basic upholstered seats and is a 'Reserved' class though tickets are sometimes 'subject to available accommodation'. **2nd Class** (non-a/c) two and three-tier (commonly called Sleeper), provides exceptionally cheap and atmospheric travel but can be crowded and uncomfortable, and toilet facilities can be unpleasant; it is nearly always better to use the Indian-style squat loos rather than the Western-style ones as they are better maintained. At the bottom rung is **Unreserved Second Class**, with hard wooden benches. You can travel long distances for a trivial amount of money, but unreserved carriages are often ridiculously crowded, and getting off at your station may involve a battle of will and strength against the hordes trying to shove their way on.

Indrail passes These allow travel across the network without having to pay extra reservation fees and sleeper charges but you have to spend a high proportion of

Train touts

Many railway stations – and some bus stations and major tourist sites – are heavily populated with touts. Self-styled 'agents' will board trains before they enter the station and seek out tourists, often picking up their luggage and setting off with words such as "Madam!/Sir! Come with me madam/sir! You need top class hotel ...". They will even select porters to take your luggage without giving you any say.

If you have succeeded in getting off the train or even in obtaining a trolley you will find hands eager to push it for you.

For a first time visitor such touts can be more than a nuisance. You need to keep calm and firm. Decide in advance where you want to stay. If you need a porter on trains, select one yourself and agree a price **before** the porter sets off with your baggage. If travelling with a companion one can stay guarding the luggage while the other gets hold of a taxi and negotiates the price to the hotel. It sounds complicated and sometimes it feels it. The most important thing is to behave as if you know what you are doing!

your time on the train to make it worthwhile. However, the advantages of pre-arranged reservations and automatic access to 'Tourist Quotas' can tip the balance in favour of the pass for some travellers. Tourists (foreigners and Indians resident abroad) may buy these passes from the tourist sections of principal railway booking offices and pay in foreign currency, major credit cards, travellers' cheques or rupees with encashment certificates. Fares range from US$57 to US$1060 for adults or around half that for children. Rail-cum-air tickets are also to be made available. Indrail passes can also conveniently be bought abroad from special agents. For people contemplating a single long journey soon after arriving in India, the half- or one-day Pass with a confirmed reservation is worth the peace of mind; two- or four-day passes are also sold. The UK agent is **SD Enterprises Ltd,** 103 Wembley Park Drive, Wembley, Middlesex, HA9 8HG, UK, T020-8200 9549, www.indiarail.co.uk. They make all necessary reservations and offer excellent advice. They can also book Indian Airlines and Jet Airways internal flights.

Cost A/c first class costs about double the rate for two-tier shown below, and non a/c second class about half. Children (five-12) travel at half the adult fare. The young (12-30 years) and senior citizens (65 years and over) are allowed a 30% discount on journeys over 500 km (just show your passport).

Duration	US$ a/c 2-tier	Duration	US$ a/c 2-tier
½ day	34.50	21 days	229
1 day	53	30 days	280
7 days	156	60 days	462
15 days	215	90 days	614

Fares for individual journeys are based on distance covered and reflect both the class and the type of train. Higher rates apply on the Mail and Express trains and the air-conditioned *Shatabdi* and *Rajdhani Expresses*.

Rail travel tips Bedding: It can get cold in air-conditioned coaches when travelling at night. Bedding is provide on second class air-conditioned sleepers. On others it can be hired for Rs 30 from the Station Baggage Office for second class.

Berths: It is worth asking for upper berths, especially in second class three-tier sleepers, as they can also be used during the day when the lower berths are used as seats. Once the middle berth is lowered for sleeping the lower berth becomes too cramped to sit on.

Credit cards: Some main stations now have separate credit card booking queues – even shorter than women's queues!

Delays: Always allow plenty of time for booking and for making connections. Delays are common on all types of transport. The special **Shatabdi** and **Rajdhani Express** are generally quite reliable. Ordinary Express and Mail trains have priority over local services and occasionally surprise by being punctual, but generally the longer the journey time, the greater the delay. Delays on the rail network are cumulative, so arrivals and departures from mid-stations are often several hours behind schedule. Allow at least two hours for connections, more if the first part of the journey is long distance.

Food and drink: It is best to carry some though tea, bottled water and snacks are sold on the platforms (through the windows). Carry plenty of small notes and coins on long journeys. Rs 50 and Rs 100 notes can be difficult to change when purchasing small food items. On long-distance trains, the restaurant car is often near the upper class carriages (bogies).

Getting a seat: It is usually impossible to make seat reservations at small 'intermediate' stations as they don't have an allocation. You can sometimes use a porter to get you a seat in a 2nd class carriage. For about Rs 20 he will take the luggage and ensure that you get a seat!

Internet services: Much information is now available online via the websites www.railtourismindia.com, www.indianrail.gov.in and www.trainenquiry.com, where you can check timetables (which change frequently), numbers, seat availability and even the running status of your train. The third party site, www.indiagroove.com, can also help plan complex itineraries with various changes of train. Internet tickets can theoretically be bought on www.irctc.co.in, though a credit card is required; foreign cards may not be accepted. An alternative is to seek out a local agent who can sell e-tickets, which can cost as little as Rs 5-10 (plus Rs 20 reservation fee), and can save hours of hassle; simply present the printout to the ticket collector.

Left luggage: Bags can be left for up to 30 days in station cloakrooms. These are especially useful when there is time to go sightseeing before an evening train. The bags must be lockable and you are advised not to leave any food in them.

Ladies' compartments: A woman travelling alone, overnight, on an unreserved second class train can ask if there is one of these. Lone female travellers may feel more comfortable in air-conditioned sleeper coaches, which require reservations and are used extensively by Indian families.

Ladies' and seniors' queues: Separate (much shorter) ticket queues may be available for women and senior citizens. Travellers over 60 can ask for a 30% discount on the ticket price.

Overbooking: Passengers with valid tickets but no berth reservations are sometimes permitted to travel overnight, causing great discomfort to travellers occupying lower berths. Wait-listed passengers should confirm the status of their ticket in advance by calling enquiries at the nearest computerised reservation office. At the station, check the reservation charts (usually on the relevant platform) and contact the Station Manager or Ticket Collector.

Porters: These can carry prodigious amounts of luggage. Rates vary from station to station (sometimes listed on a board on the platform) but are usually around Rs 10-25 per item of luggage.

Pre-paid taxis: Many main stations have a pre-paid taxi (or auto-rickshaw) service which offers a reliable service at a fair price.

Quotas: A large number of seats are technically reserved as quotas for various groups of travellers (civil servants, military personnel, foreign tourists, etc). Tourist quota is available at main stations. As a tourist you are not obliged to use it, but it can get you on an otherwise 'full' train; you will need your passport, and either pay in US dollars or pounds sterling or in rupees with a currency encashment certificate/ATM receipt. In addition, many stations have their own quota for particular trains so that a train may be 'fully booked' when there are still some tickets available from the special quota of other stations. These are only sold on the day of departure so wait-listed passengers are often able to travel at the last minute. Ask the superintendent on duty to try the 'Special' or 'VIP Quota'. The 'Tatkal' system releases a small percentage of seats at 0800 on the day before a train departs; you pay an extra Rs 75-200 (depending on class and season) to get on an otherwise heavily booked train.

Security: Keep valuables close to you, securely locked, and away from windows. For security, carry a good lock and chain to attach your luggage.

Tickets and reservations: Unreserved second class tickets are available at any station by queueing at the window – a skill in itself – and represent the quickest way to get on a train that is about to depart. On most trains (not Rajdhani or Shatabdi Express) you can attempt to upgrade an unreserved ticket by seeking out the Station Manager's office, or the black-suited TTE (Travelling Ticket Examiner) if the train is at the platform, and asking if a seat is available; an upgrade fee is payable. This can save time waiting in the slower line for reservations.

It is now possible to reserve tickets for virtually any train on the network from one of the 520 computerised reservation centres across India. It is always best to book as far in advance as possible (usually up to 60 days). To reserve a seat on a particular train, note down the train's name, number and departure time, and fill in a reservation form while you line up at the ticket window; you can use one form for up to four passengers. At busy stations the wait can take an hour or more; you can save a lot of time and effort by asking a travel agent to get yours for a small fee, usually of around Rs 50-100. If the class you want is full, ask at the ticket window if special 'quotas' are available (see above). If not, consider buying a 'wait list' ticket, as seats often become available close to the train's departure time; phone the station on the day of departure to check your ticket's status. If you don't have a reservation for a particular train but carry an Indrail Pass, you may get one by arriving about three hours early. Be wary of touts at the station offering tickets, hotels or money changing.

Timetables: Regional timetables are available cheaply from station bookstalls; the monthly 'Indian Bradshaw' is sold in principal stations. The handy 'Trains at a Glance' (Rs 30) lists popular trains likely to be used by most foreign travellers and is available in the UK from SD Enterprises Ltd (see under Indrail passes, page 28).

Road

Road travel is often the only choice for reaching many of the places of outstanding interest in which India is so rich. For the uninitiated, travel by road can also be a worrying experience because of the apparent absence of conventional traffic regulations and also in the mountains, especially during the rainy season when landslides are possible. Vehicles drive on the left – in theory. Routes around the major cities are usually crowded with lorry traffic, especially at night, and the main roads are often poor and slow. There are a few motorway-style expressways, but most main roads are single track. Some district roads are quiet, and although they are not fast they can be a good way of seeing the country and village life if you have the time.

Bus Buses now reach virtually every part of India, offering a cheap, if often uncomfortable, means of visiting places off the rail network. Very few villages are now more than 2-3 km from a bus stop. Services are run by the State Corporation from the State Bus Stand (and private companies which often have offices nearby). The latter allow advance reservation and though tickets prices are a little higher, they have fewer stops and are a bit more comfortable.

⁞ The hazards of road travel

On most routes it is impossible to average more than 50-60 kph in a car. Journeys are often very long, and can seem an endless succession of horn blowing, unexpected dangers, and unforeseen delays. Villages are often congested – beware of the concealed spine-breaking speed bumps – and cattle, sheep and goats may wander at will across the road. Directions can also be difficult to find. Drivers frequently don't know the way, maps are often hopelessly inaccurate and map reading is an almost entirely unknown skill. Training in driving is negligible and the test often a farce. You will note a characteristic side-saddle posture, one hand constantly on the horn, but there can be real dangers from poor judgement, irresponsible overtaking and a general philosophy of 'might is right'.

Bus categories: Though comfortable for sightseeing trips, apart from the very best 'sleeper coaches' even **air conditioned luxury coaches** can be very uncomfortable for really long journeys. Often the air conditioning is very cold so wrap up. Journeys over 10 hours can be extremely tiring so it is better to go by train if there is a choice. **Express buses** run over long distances (frequently overnight), these are often called 'video coaches' and can be an appalling experience unless you appreciate loud film music blasting through the night. Ear plugs and eye masks may ease the pain. They rarely average more than 45 km per hour. **Local buses** are often very crowded, quite bumpy, slow and usually poorly maintained. However, over short distances, they can be a very cheap, friendly and easy way of getting about. Even where signboards are not in English someone will usually give you directions. Many larger towns have **minibus** services which charge a little more than the buses and pick up and drop passengers on request. Again very crowded, and with restricted headroom, they are the fastest way of getting about many of the larger towns.

Bus travel tips: Some towns have different bus stations for different destinations. Booking on major long-distance routes is now computerized. Book in advance where possible and avoid the back of the bus where it can be very bumpy. If your destination is only served by a local bus you may do better to take the Express bus and 'persuade' the driver, with a tip in advance, to stop where you want to get off. You will have to pay the full fare to the first stop beyond your destination but you will get there faster and more comfortably. When an unreserved bus pulls into a bus station, there is usually an unholy scramble for seats, whilst those arriving have to struggle to get off! In many areas there is an unwritten 'rule of reservation' using handkerchiefs or bags thrust through the windows to reserve seats. Some visitors may feel a more justified right to a seat having fought their way through the crowd, but it is generally best to do as local people do and be prepared with a handkerchief or 'sarong'. As soon as it touches the seat, it is yours! Leave it on your seat when getting off to use the toilet at bus stations.

Car A car provides a chance to travel off the beaten track, and gives unrivalled opportunities for seeing something of India's great variety of villages and small towns. Until recently, the most widely used hire car was the Hindustan Ambassador. However, except for the newest model, they are often very unreliable, and although they still have their devotees, many find them uncomfortable for long journeys. For a similar price, Maruti cars and vans (Omni) are much more reliable and are now the preferred choice in many areas. Gypsy 4WDs and Jeeps are also available, especially in the hills, where larger Sumos have made an appearance. Maruti Esteems and Toyota Qualis are comfortable and have optional reliable air conditioning. A specialist operator can be very helpful in arranging itineraries and car hire in advance.

Car hire: With a driver, car hire is cheaper than in the West. A car shared by three or four can be very good value. Be sure to check carefully the mileage at the beginning and end of the trip. Two- or three-day trips from main towns can also give excellent opportunities for sightseeing off the beaten track in reasonable comfort. Local drivers often know their way much better than drivers from other states, so where possible it is a good idea to get a local driver who speaks the state language, in addition to being able to communicate with you. In the mountains, it is better to use a driver who knows the roads. Drivers may sleep in the car overnight though hotels sometimes provide a bed for them. They are responsible for their expenses, including meals. Car (and auto) drivers increase their earnings by taking you to hotels and shops where they get a handsome commission (which you will pay for). If you feel inclined, a tip at the end of the tour of Rs 100 per day in addition to their daily allowance is perfectly acceptable. Check beforehand if fuel and inter-state taxes are included in the hire charge.

Cars can be hired through private companies. International companies such as **Hertz, Europcar** and **Budget** operate in some major cities and offer reliable cars; their rates are generally higher than those of local firms (eg **Sai Service, Wheels**). The price of an imported car can be three times that of the Ambassador.

Car with driver	Economy Maruti 800 Ambassador	Regular A/C Maruti 800 Contessa	Premium A/C Maruti 1000 Opel etc	Luxury A/C Esteem Qualis
8 hrs/80 km	Rs 800	Rs 1000	Rs 1400	Rs 1800+
Extra km	Rs 4-7	Rs 9	Rs 13	Rs 18
Extra hour	Rs 40	Rs 50	Rs 70	Rs 100
Out of town				
Per km	Rs 7	Rs 9	Rs 13	Rs 18
Night halt	Rs 100	Rs 200	Rs 250	Rs 250

Car travel tips: When booking emphasize the importance of good tyres and general roadworthiness. On main roads across India **petrol stations** are reasonably frequent, but some areas are poorly served. Some service stations only have diesel pumps though they may have small reserves of petrol. Always carry a spare can. Diesel is widely available and normally much cheaper than petrol. Petrol is rarely above 92 octane. Drivers must have third party **insurance**. This may have to be with an Indian insurer, or with a foreign insurer who has a national guarantor. You must also be in possession of an International Driving Permit, issued by a recognised driving authority in your home country (eg the AA in the UK, apply at least six weeks before leaving). **Asking the way** can be very frustrating as you are likely to get widely conflicting advice each time you stop to ask. On the main roads, 'mile' posts periodically appear in English and can help. Elsewhere, it is best to ask directions often and follow the average direction! **Accidents** often produce large and angry crowds very quickly. It is best to leave the scene of the accident and report it to the police as quickly as possible thereafter. Ensure that you have adequate provisions, plenty of food and drink and a basic tool set in the car.

The **AA** offers a range of services to members; contact **Automobile Association of Eastern India** ① *13 Promothesh Barman Sarani, Kolkata, T033-2247 5131.*

Taxi: Yellow-top taxis in cities and large towns are metered, although tariffs change frequently. These changes are shown on a fare chart which should be read in conjunction with the meter reading. Increased night time rates apply in some cities, and there is a small charge for luggage. Insist on the taxi meter being flagged in your presence. If the driver refuses, the official advice is to contact the police. This may not work, but it is worth trying. When a taxi doesn't have a meter, you will need to fix the fare before starting the journey. Ask at your hotel desk for a guide price.

At stations and airports it is often possible to share taxis to a central point. It is worth looking for fellow passengers who may be travelling in your direction and get a pre-paid taxi. At night, always have a clear idea of where you want to go and insist on being taken there. Taxi drivers may try to convince you that the hotel you have chosen 'closed three years ago' or is 'completely full'. Say that you have a reservation.

Rickshaw: Auto-rickshaws (autos) are almost universally available in towns across India and are the cheapest and most convenient way of getting about. It is best to walk a short distance away from a hotel gate before picking up an auto to avoid paying an inflated rate. In addition to using them for short journeys it is often possible to hire them by the hour, or for a half or full day's sightseeing. In some areas younger drivers who speak some English and know their local area well may want to show you around. However, rickshaw drivers are often paid a commission by hotels, restaurants and gift shops so advice is not always impartial. Drivers generally refuse to use a meter, often quote a ridiculous price or may sometimes stop short of your destination. If you have real problems it can help to note down the vehicle license number and threaten to go to the police. Beware of some rickshaw drivers who show the fare chart for taxis.

Cycle-rickshaws and **horse-drawn tongas** are more common in the more rustic setting of a small town or the outskirts of a large one. You will need to fix a price by bargaining. The animal attached to a tonga usually looks too undernourished to have the strength to pull the driver, let alone passengers.

Kolkata holds the dubious honour of being the only city in the world where **hand-pulled rickshaws** remain an essential means of transport; in the monsoon, they are often the only vehicles that can get through the flooded streets. The government periodically tries to ban them, but until another form of employment can be found for 18,000 men, they are likely to remain. Always agree a price before getting on board and expect a very bumpy ride.

Cycling Cycling is an excellent way of seeing the quiet byways of India. It is easy to hire bikes in most small towns for about Rs 20-30 per day. Indian bikes are heavy and without gears, but on the flat they offer a good way of exploring comparatively short distances outside towns. In the more prosperous tourist resorts, mountain bikes are now becoming available, but at a higher charge. It is also quite possible to tour more extensively and you may then want to buy a cycle.

There are shops in every town and the local Hero brand is considered the best, with Atlas and BSA good alternatives; expect to pay around Rs 1200-1500 for a second-hand Indian bike but remember to bargain. At the end of your trip you could sell it easily at half price. Imported bikes have lighter weight and gears, but are more difficult to get repaired and carry the much greater risk of being stolen or damaged. If you wish to take your own, it is quite easy if you dismantle it and pack it in its original shipping carton; be sure to take all essential spares including a pump. It is possible to get Indian spares for 26" wheel cycles. All cyclists should take bungy cords (to strap down a backpack) and good lights from home, although cycling at night is not recommended; take care not to leave your bike parked anywhere with your belongings. Bike repair shops are universal and charges are nominal.

You are usually not far from a 'puncture wallah' who can make minor repairs cheaply.

It is possible to cover 50-80 km a day quite comfortably. One cyclist reported that the national highways are manic but country roads, especially along the coast, can be idyllic, if rather dusty and bumpy. You can even put your bike on a boat for a backwater trip or on top of a bus. If you want to take your bike on the train, allow plenty of time for booking it in on the brake van at the Parcels office and for filling in forms.

It is best to start a journey early in the morning, stopping at midday and then resuming your journey in the late afternoon. Night riding, though cooler, can be hazardous because of lack of lighting and poor road surfaces. Try to avoid major highways as far as possible. Fortunately foreign cyclists are usually greeted with cheers, waves and smiles and truck drivers are sometimes happy to give lifts to cyclists (and their bikes). This is a good way of taking some of the hardship out of cycling round India. For expert advice contact the **Cyclists' Touring Club** ① *T0870-873 0060, www.ctc.org.uk.*

Motorcycling This is a particularly attractive way of getting around. It is easy to buy new Indian-made motorcycles including the 350cc Enfield Bullet and several 100cc Japanese models, including Suzukis and Hondas made in collaboration with Indian firms; Indian Rajdoots are less expensive but have a poor reputation for reliability. Buying new at a fixed price ensures greater ease and reliability. Buying second hand in rupees takes more time but is quite possible (expect to get a 30-40% discount) and repairs are usually easy to arrange and quite cheap. You can get a broker to help with the paperwork involved (certificate of ownership, insurance etc) for a fee (see also Insurance, page 47). They charge about Rs 5000 for a No Objection Certificate (NOC), essential for reselling; it's easier to have the bike in your name. Bring your own helmet and an International Driving Permit. Vespa, Kinetic Honda and other makes of scooters in India are slower than motorbikes but comfortable for short hauls of less than 100 km and have the advantage of a 'dicky' (small, lockable box) for spares, and a spare tyre.

Hitchhiking Hitchhiking is uncommon, partly because public transport is so cheap. If you try, you are likely to spend a very long time on the roadside. However, getting a lift on scooters and on trucks in areas with little public transport can be worthwhile, whilst those riding motorbikes or scooters in tourist areas can be expected to pick up the occasional hitchhiking policeman! It is not recommended for women on their own.

Maps
For anyone interested in the geography of India, or even simply getting around, trying to buy good maps is a depressing experience. For security reasons it is illegal to sell large-scale maps of areas within 80 km of the coast or national borders, and it is illegal to export any large scale maps.

The **Bartholomew** 1:4 m map sheet of India is the most authoritative, detailed and easy to use map available. It can be bought worldwide. **GeoCenter World Map** 1:2 m, covers India in three regional sections and are clearly printed. **Nelles'** regional maps of India at the scale of 1:1.5 m offer generally clear route maps, though neither the road classifications nor alignments are wholly reliable. The same criticism applies to the attractively produced and easy-to-read **Lonely Planet Travel Atlas of India and Bangladesh** (2001).

State and town plans are published by the **TTK Company**. These are often the best available though they are not wholly reliable. For the larger cities they provide the most compact yet clear map sheets (generally 50 mm by 75 mm format).

The Survey of India publishes large scale 1:10,000 town plans of approximately 70 cities. These detailed plans are the only surveyed town maps in India, and some are over 20 years old. The Survey also has topographic maps at the scale of 1:25,000 and 1:50,000 in addition to its 1:250,000 scale coverage, some of which are as recent as the late 1980s. However, maps are regarded as highly sensitive and it is only possible to buy these from main agents of the Survey of India.

Stanfords, 12-14 Long Acre, London, WC2, T020 78361321, www.stanfords.co.uk, offers a mail order service.

Sleeping

India has an enormously wide range of accommodation. You can stay safely and very cheaply by Western standards right across the country. In all the major cities there are also high-quality hotels, offering a full range of facilities. In small centres even the best hotels are far more variable. The heritage hotels so widespread in Rajasthan are virtually unheard of in the Northeast. Hotels in hill stations, because of their location and special appeal, often deviate from the description of our different categories. In the peak season (October to April for most of India) bookings can be extremely heavy in popular destinations. It is sometimes possible to book in advance by phone, fax or email, but double check your reservation, and always try to arrive as early as possible in the day.

Hotels → *See box, page 37, for Sleeping price codes.*

Price categories The category codes used in this book are based on prices of double rooms excluding taxes. They are **not** star ratings and individual facilities vary considerably. The most expensive hotels charge in US dollars only. Modest hotels may not have their own restaurant but will often offer 'room service', bringing in food from outside. Many hotels operate a 24-hour checkout system. Make sure that this means that you can stay 24 hours from the time of check-in. Expect to pay more in Delhi and, to a lesser extent, Kolkata, for all categories. Prices away from large cities tend to be lower.

Off-season rates Large reductions are made by hotels in all categories out-of-season in many resorts. Always ask if any is available. You may also request the 10-15% agent's commission to be deducted from your bill if you book direct. Clarify whether the agreed figure includes all taxes.

Taxes In general most hotel rooms rated at Rs 1200 or above are subject to a tax of 10%. Many states levy an additional luxury tax of between 10 and 25%, and some hotels add a service charge of 10% on top of this. Taxes are not necessarily payable on meals, so it is worth settling your meals bill separately. Most hotels in the C category and above accept payment by credit card. Check your final bill carefully. Visitors have complained of incorrect bills, even in the most expensive hotels. The problem particularly afflicts groups, when last-minute extras appear mysteriously on some guests' bills. Check the evening before departure, and keep all receipts.

Hotel facilities You have to be prepared for difficulties which are uncommon in the West. It is best to inspect the room and check that all equipment (air conditioning, TV, water heater, flush) works before checking in at a modest hotel.

In some states **power cuts** are common, or hot water may be restricted to certain times of day. The largest hotels have their own generators but it is best to carry a good torch. Usually, only category C and above have **central air conditioning**. Elsewhere air conditioned rooms are cooled by individual units and occasionally by large 'air-coolers' which can be noisy and unreliable. When they fail to operate tell the management as it is often possible to get a rapid repair done, or to transfer to a room where the unit is working. During power cuts generators may not be able to cope with providing air conditioning. Fans are provided in all but the cheapest of hotels.

Apart from those in the A category and above, 'attached bath' does not necessarily refer to a bathroom with a bathtub. Most will provide a **bathroom** with a toilet, basin and a shower. In the lower priced hotels and outside large towns, a bucket and tap may replace the shower, and an Indian squat toilet instead of a Western WC (squat toilets are very often cleaner). Even mid-price hotels, which are clean and pleasant, don't always provide towels, soap and toilet paper.

In some regions **water supply** is rationed periodically. Keep a bucket filled to use for flushing the toilet during water cuts. Occasionally, tap water may be discoloured due to rusty tanks. During the cold weather and in hill stations, hot water will be available at certain times of the day, sometimes in buckets, but is usually very restricted in quantity. Electric water heaters may provide enough for a shower but not enough to fill a bath tub! For details on drinking water, see page 38.

At some times of the year and in some places **mosquitoes** can be a real problem, and not all hotels have mosquito-proof rooms or mosquito nets. If you have any doubts check before confirming your room booking. In cheap hotels you need to be prepared for the presence of flies, cockroaches, spiders, ants and geckos (harmless house lizards). Poisonous insects and scorpions are extremely rare in towns. Hotel managements are nearly always prepared with insecticide sprays. Few small hotels in mosquito-prone areas supply nets so it is best for budget travellers to take one from home. An impregnated, wedge-shaped one (for single-point fixing) is preferable, available in all good camping/outdoor shops. Remember to shut windows and doors at dusk. Electrical mats and pellets are now widely available, as are mosquito coils that burn slowly. One traveller recommends Dettol soap to discourage mosquitoes. Dusk and early evening are the worst times for mosquitoes so trousers and long-sleeved shirts are advisable, especially outdoors. At night, fans can be very effective in keeping mosquitoes off; remember to tuck the net under the mattress all round. As well as insects, expect to find spiders larger and hairier than those you see at home; they are mostly harmless and more frightened of you than you are of them!

Hotels close to temples can be very **noisy**, especially during festivals. Music blares from loudspeakers late at night and from very early in the morning, often making sleep impossible. Mosques call the faithful to prayers at dawn. Some find ear plugs helpful.

Hotels in hill stations often supply **wood fires** in rooms. Usually there is plenty of ventilation, but ensure that there is always good air circulation, especially when charcoal fires are provided in a basket.

Where staff training is lacking, the person who brings up your cases may proceed to show you light switches, room facilities, TV tuning, and hang around waiting for a **tip**. Room boys may enter your room without knocking or without waiting for a response to a knock. Both for security and privacy, it is a good idea to lock your door when you are in the room. At the higher end, you should expect to tip bellboys a little for every favour. Don't be surprised that staff don't always wait for a response to knocking before entering: lock your door when you are in your room if this is a problem.

Tourist 'bungalows'

The different state tourism development corporations run their own hotels and hostels which are often in places of special interest. These are very reasonably priced, though they may be rather dated, restaurant menus may be limited and service is often slow.

Railway and airport retiring rooms

Railway stations often have 'Retiring Rooms' or 'Rest Rooms' which may be hired for periods of between one and 24 hours by anyone holding an onward train ticket. They are cheap and simple though often heavily booked. Some major airports (eg Mumbai) have similar facilities.

Government rest houses

Rest houses may be available for overnight stays, especially in remote areas. They are usually very basic, with a caretaker who can sometimes provide a simple meal, with notice. Check the room rate in advance as foreigners can be overcharged. Government officials always take precedence, even over guests who have booked.

Sleeping and eating price codes

Sleeping

LL Over US$200	**B** US$46-65	**E** US$12-20
L US$151-200	**C** US$31-45	**F** US$7-11
AL US$101-150	**D** US$21-30	**G** US$6 and under
A US$66-100		

Price of a double room in high season, excluding taxes.

Eating

ŦŦŦ Over US$12	ŦŦ US$7-12	Ŧ Under US$6

For a two-course meal for one person, excluding drinks and taxes.

Indian-style hotels

These, catering for Indian businessmen, are springing up fast in or on the outskirts of many small- and medium-sized towns. Most have some air-conditioned rooms and attached showers. They are variable in quality but it is increasingly possible to find excellent value accommodation even in remote areas.

Hostels

The Department of Tourism runs 16 youth hostels, each with about 50 beds, usually organized into dormitory accommodation. The YHA also have a few sites all over India. Travellers may also stay in religious hostels (*dharamshalas*) for up to three days. These are primarily intended for pilgrims and are sometimes free, though voluntary offerings are welcome. Usually only vegetarian food is permitted; smoking and alcohol are not.

Camping

Mid-price hotels with large grounds are sometimes willing to allow camping. Regional tourist offices have details of new developments. For information on YMCA camping facilities contact: **YMCA**, The National General Secretary, National Council of YMCAs of India, PB No 14, Massey Hall, Jai Singh Rd, New Delhi 1.

Eating and drinking

Food

You find just as much variety in dishes and presentation crossing India as you would on an equivalent journey across Europe. Combinations of spices give each region its distinctive flavour.

The larger hotels, open to non-residents, often offer **buffet** lunches with Indian, Western and sometimes Chinese dishes. These can be good value (Rs 250-300; but Rs 450 in the top grades) and can provide a welcome, comfortable break in the cool. The health risks, however, of food kept warm for long periods in metal containers are considerable, especially if turnover at the buffet is slow. We have received several complaints of stomach trouble following a buffet meal, even in five-star hotels.

It is essential to be very careful since food hygiene may be poor, flies abound and refrigeration in the hot weather may be inadequate and intermittent because of power cuts. It is best to eat only freshly prepared food by ordering from the menu (especially meat and fish dishes). Avoid salads and cut fruit.

If you are unused to spicy food, go slow! Stick to Western or mild Chinese meals in good restaurants and try the odd Indian dish to test your reaction. Popular local restaurants are obvious from the number of people eating in them. Try a traditional thali, which is a complete meal served on a large stainless steel plate (or very occasionally on a banana leaf). Several preparations, placed in small bowls, surround the central serving of wholewheat chapati and rice. A vegetarian *thali* would include *dhal* (lentils), two or three curries (which can be quite hot) and crisp poppadums, although there are regional variations. A var iety of pickles are offered – mango and lime are two of the most popular. These can be exceptionally hot, and are designed to be taken in minute quantities alongside the main dishes. Plain *dahi* (yoghurt) in the south, or *raita* in the north, usually acts as a bland 'cooler'. Simple *dhabas* (rustic roadside eateries) are an alternative experience for sampling authentic local dishes.

❖ See page 332 for a food glossary. Regional cuisine is covered in the introduction to each state.

Many city restaurants offer a choice of so-called **European options** such as toasted sandwiches, pancakes, apple pies, fruit crumbles and cheesecakes. Italian favourites (pizzas, pastas) can be very different from what you are used to. Western confectionery, in general, is disappointing. **Ice creams**, on the other hand, can be exceptionally good; there are excellent Indian ones as well as some international brands.

India has many delicious tropical **fruits**. Some are seasonal (eg mangoes, pineapples and lychees), while others (eg bananas, grapes and oranges) are available throughout the year. It is safe to eat the ones you can wash and peel.

Drink

Drinking water used to be regarded as one of India's biggest hazards. It is still true that water from the tap or a well should never be considered safe to drink since public water supplies are often polluted. Bottled water is now widely available although not all bottled water is mineral water; most is simply purified water from an urban supply. Buy from a shop or stall, check the seal carefully (some companies now add a second clear plastic seal around the bottle top) and avoid street hawkers; when disposing bottles puncture the neck which prevents misuse but allows recycling for storage. There is growing concern over the mountains of plastic bottles that are collecting and the waste of resources needed to produce them, so travellers are encouraged to use alternative methods of getting safe drinking water. Many hotels will have a water filter from which to fill your bottle, and in the more advanced towns and cities, even simple restaurants provide glasses of filltered water, which is generally quite safe to drink (see box, page 20). You may wish to purify water yourself, see box, page 17. A portable water filter is a good idea, carrying the drinking water in a plastic bottle in an insulated carrier. Always carry enough drinking water with you when travelling. It is important to use pure water for cleaning teeth.

Tea and **coffee** are safe and widely available. Both are normally served sweet, and with milk. If you wish, say 'no sugar' (*chini nahin*), 'no milk' (*dudh nahin*) when ordering. Alternatively, ask for a pot of tea and milk and sugar to be brought separately. Freshly brewed coffee is a common drink in South India, but in the North, ordinary city restaurants will usually serve the instant variety. Even in aspiring smart cafés, espresso or cappuccino may not turn out quite as you'd expect in the West.

Bottled **soft drinks** such as Coke, Pepsi, Limca and Thums Up are universally available but always check the seal when you buy from a street stall. There are also several brands of fruit juice sold in cartons, including mango, pineapple and apple. Don't add ice cubes as the water source may be contaminated. Take care with fresh fruit juices or *lassis* as ice is often added.

Indians rarely drink **alcohol** with a meal, water being on hand. In the past wines and spirits were generally either imported and extremely expensive, or local and of poor quality. Now, the best Indian whisky, rum and brandy (IMFL or 'Indian Made

⁞ A cup of chai

Not long ago, when you stopped at a roadside tea stall nearly anywhere in India and asked for a cup of chai, the steaming hot sweet tea would be poured out into your very own, finely handthrown, beautifully shaped clay cup. Similarly, whenever a train drew into a railway station, almost any time of day or night, and you heard the familiar loud call of "chai garam, garam chai!" go past your window, you could have the tea served to you in your own porous clay cup.

True, it made the tea taste rather earthy but it added to the romance of travelling. Best of all, when you had done with it, you threw it away and it would shatter to bits on the roadside (or down on the railway track) – returning 'earth to earth'. It was the eco-friendly disposable cup of old – no question of an unwashed cup which someone else had drunk out of, hence unpolluted and 'clean'.

And, of course, it was good business for the potter.

But time has moved on, bringing with it tea stalls that prefer thick glass tumblers (which leave you anxious when you glance down at the murky rinsing water), and for the transient customer, hot chai in an understandably convenient, light, hygienic, easy-to-stack, thin plastic cup, which sadly lacks the bio-degradability of the earthenware pot. Hence, travellers must balance the desire for a hit of hot milky sweetness against the fact that they will be adding to India's unsightly and ever growing mountain of plastic waste.

The fast-disappearing terracotta cup can still be found at a few stations. Yet despite vague threats by the railways minister to banish plastic, we are still in danger of losing another little piece of the magic of travelling in India.

Foreign Liquor') are widely accepted, as are good Champagnoise and other wines from Maharashtra. If you hanker after a bottle of imported wine, you will only find it in the top restaurants and have to pay at least Rs 800-1000.

For the urban elite, refreshing Indian beers are popular when eating out and so are widely available. 'Pubs' have sprung up in the major cities. Elsewhere, seedy, all-male drinking dens in the larger cities are best avoided for women travellers, but can make quite an experience otherwise – you will sometimes be locked into cubicles for clandestine drinking. If that sounds unsavoury then head for the better hotel bars instead; prices aren't that steep. In rural India, local rice, palm, cashew or date juice *toddy* and *arak* is deceptively potent. However, the Sikkimese *chhang* makes a pleasant change drunk out of a wooden tankard through a bamboo straw!

Most states have alcohol-free dry days or enforce degrees of Prohibition. Some upmarket restaurants may serve beer even if it's not listed, so it's worth asking. For dry states and Liquor Permits, see page 42.

Entertainment

Despite the rapid growth of a young business class, Northeast India's 'nightlife' remains meagre and is mainly focused on discos in the largest hotels. Kolkata has a few such clubs to choose from, although new and more ambient bars/lounges are beginning to appear. For more basic drinking, there are options ranging from English-style pubs within hotels to men-only, cabaret-feel bars. More traditional, popular entertainment is widespread across the villages in the form of folk drama, dance and music, each region having its own styles, with open-air village performances. The hugely popular local film industry comes largely out of this tradition, and *Bhojpuri* films are now flourishing as a reaction against recent slick Bollywood and Tollywood offerings. It's always easy to find a cinema, even in small towns, but prepare for a long sitting with standard storylines and characters plus lots of action, singing and dancing. In big cities, multiplexes are becoming commonplace and usually show English-language movies as well as the latest Indian hits, while the Nandan complex in Kolkata has art-house and foreign film screenings. As the intellectual and cultural hub of India, Kolkata offers a wealth of opportunities and venues to see theatre, concerts and exhibitions in both Bengali and English. See also page 12 for cricket and football, which are both popular popular forms of entertainment.

Festivals and events

Northeast India has an extraordinary wealth of festivals, many specific to a particular state or community or even a particular temple. The biggest festival of all, and the largest gathering of humanity on the planet, is the **Kumbh Mela**, which draws millions of pilgrims to four holy sites in India in a rotation system. One of these sites is Allahabad, 125 km to the west of Varanasi, although the next Maha (great) Kumbh Mela won't be held there until 2013. Festivals tend to fall on different dates each year depending on the Hindu lunar calendar, so check with the tourist office. Some major festivals are given below; details of these and others appear under the particular state or town.

A few count as national holidays: **Republic Day** (26 January); **Independence Day** (15 August); **Mahatma Gandhi's Birthday** (2 October); and **Christmas Day** (25 December). 1 January (when following the Gregorian calendar) is accepted officially as **New Year's Day**, but there are regional variations that fall on different dates, often coinciding with spring/harvest time, such as **Naba Barsha** in Bengal (14 April) and **Rongali Bihu** in Assam (mid-April). **Makar Sankranti** always falls on 14 January and is highly auspicious in Bengal, when the huge Gangasagar mela sees the gathering of pilgrims at the mouth of the Ganga to mark the end of winter. During the spring festival of **Vasant Panchami** (January/February) people wear bright yellow clothes to herald the advent of the season with singing, dancing and feasting. In Bengal this festival is commonly called **Saraswati Puja**, as the goddess of learning is worshipped, and it is a state holiday. **Maha Sivaratri** (February/March) marks the night when Siva danced his celestial dance of destruction; it is celebrated with feasting and fairs at Siva temples, but preceded by a night of devotional readings and hymn singing. Varanasi sees Siva devotees collect en masse, when the ghats become a camping ground for sadhus, naga babas and their followers.

Holi, the festival of colours, occurs at the end of February or the start of March and is particularly vibrant in North India. On the first night, bonfires are lit symbolizing the end of winter (and conquering of evil). People have fun throwing coloured powder and water at each other and in the evening some gamble with friends. If you don't mind getting covered in colours, you can risk going out but celebrations can sometimes get very rowdy (and unpleasant, especially for lone women) in urban areas, even though alcohol is not for sale during festival. There is also a **Bengali Holi** (Dol Jatra) the day before, which means celebrations stretch over three days in many places in this region.

Buddha Jayanti, the first full moon night in April/May marks the birth of the Buddha and Bodh Gaya collects pilgrims from all over the world to celebrate in its temples. Puri in Orissa witnesses the spectacle of **Rath Yatra** in June/July, when crowds gather to help tow Lord Jagannath and his brother and sister through the streets in extraordinary decorated chariots. **Raksha Bandhan** (or Rakhi Purnima) in July/August symbolizes the love between brother and sister. A sister says special prayers for her brother and ties artful coloured threads around his wrist to remind him of the special bond. He in turn gives a gift and promises to protect and care for her. August/September sees **Janmashtami**, when the birth of Krishna is celebrated at midnight at Krishna (ISKCON) temples. The September/October festival of **Dasara** has many local variations. In North India, celebrations for the nine nights (navaratri) are marked with **Ramlila**, various episodes of the Ramayana story (see page 302) being enacted with particular reference to the battle between the forces of good and evil. In Bengal, the focus is on Durga's victory over the demon Mahishasura and

⁞ Purnima (Full Moon)

Many religious festivals depend on the phases of the moon. Full moon days are particularly significant and can mean extra crowding and merrymaking in temple towns throughout India, and are sometimes public holidays.

Durga puja is celebrated in a massive way, with huge pandals erected in public spaces, often themed to reflect current events or mimic world monuments, containing images of the Goddess, her consorts and her enemies.

In Bengal, **Lakshmi puja** follows soon after Durga puja, and offers worship to the Goddess of Wealth. However, the rest of India worships Lakshmi with **Diwali/Deepavali**, the festival of lights, which falls on the dark chaturdasi (14th) night (the one preceding the new moon) in October/November, when rows of lamps or candles are lit in remembrance and rangolis are painted on the floor as a sign of welcome. Fireworks have become an integral part of the celebrations, often set off days before Diwali. In Bengal, **Kali Puja** is celebrated the day before Diwali but is a distinct festival. **Sonepur Cattle Fair** takes place in Bihar in October/November. Nagaland unites its many tribes for dancing, song and sport during the **Hornbill Festival** in the first week of December. The **Konark Dance Festival** (early December), held in Orissa, runs for five days and showcases classical Indian dance against a backdrop of the Sun Temple. **Christmas Day** sees Indian Christians celebrate the birth of Christ in much the same way as in the West, many churches hold midnight masses and decorations go up.

Muslim holy days

These are fixed according to the lunar calendar, see box above. According to the Gregorian calendar, they tend to fall 11 days earlier each year, depending on the sighting of the new moon. **Ramadan** is the start of the month of fasting when all Muslims (except young children, the very elderly, the sick, pregnant women and travellers) must abstain from food and drink, from sunrise to sunset. **Id ul Fitr**, with much gift-giving, is the three-day festival that marks the end of Ramadan. **Id-ul-Zuha/ Bakr-Id** is when Muslims commemorate Ibrahim's sacrifice of his son according to God's commandment; this is the main time of pilgrimage to Mecca (the Hajj). It is marked by the sacrifice of a goat, feasting and alms giving. **Muharram** is when the killing of the Prophet's grandson, Hussain, is commemorated by Shi'a Muslims. Decorated *tazias* (replicas of the martyr's tomb) are carried in procession by devout wailing followers who beat their chests to express their grief. **Murshidabad** in West Bengal celebrates Murharram with much festivity, and the Muslim areas of Kolkata are highly atmospheric at this time.

Shopping

India excels in producing fine crafts at affordable prices through the passing down of ancestral skills. You can get handicrafts from the different states at the government emporia in the major cities, which guarantee quality at fixed prices, although many goods are poorly displayed. Upmarket shops and top hotel arcades offer better quality, choice and service but at a price. Vibrant and colourful local bazars are often a great experience but you must be prepared to bargain.

Bargaining can be fun and quite satisfying but it is important to get an idea of prices by asking at several different stalls before taking the plunge. Some shopkeepers will happily quote twice the actual price (or more) to a foreigner showing interest, so you might well start by halving the asking price. On the other hand, it would be inappropriate to do the same in an established shop with price tags, though a plea for the 'best price' or a 'special discount' might reap results even here. Remain good humoured throughout. Walking away slowly can test whether your custom is sought, if you are then called back. Taxi/rickshaw drivers and guides get a commission when they deliver tourists to certain shops, but prices are invariably inflated. Small shops can't always be trusted to pack and post your purchases: unless you have a specific recommendation from a person you know, only make such arrangements in government emporia or a large store. Never enter into any arrangement to help 'export' marble items, jewellery, etc, no matter how lucrative your 'cut' of the profits may sound. Make sure, too, that credit cards are run off just once when making a purchase. Export of certain items is controlled or banned (see page 43).

The superb hand-knotted **carpets** of Kashmir, using old Persian designs woven in wool or silk or both, are hard to beat for their beauty and quality, and Kashmiri traders can be found wherever there are foreign tourists. Tibetan refugees in Darjeeling and Gangtok also produce excellent carpets, which are less expensive. They will make carpets to order and parcel post them safely. You'll find **jewellery** catching your eye at wayside stalls and from sparkling shops, whether it's chunky tribal necklaces from the Himalaya, fine Orissan filigree, or glass bangles from Varanasi. It's best to buy from reputable shops as street stalls often pass off fake silver, gems and stones as real; and beware of being hustled in Kolkata's New Market. **Silver** and **gold** are sold by weight – check the price in newspapers. The choice of metal work is vast, from brass, copper and white-metal ware with ornate patterns, tribal lost-wax dhokra toys from Orissa, Bihar and Bengal, to Tibetan 'singing' bowls which are available from refugee communities. Stone temple carvings are produced for sale in Orissa (Puri, Konark) whilst terracotta images and items are still made in Bihar and Jharkhand. Santiniketan is renowned for colourful embossed **leatherwork**. Exquisite **textiles** are plentiful: handlooms produce skilful ikat from Orissa, brocades from Varanasi, golden muga from Assam and printed silks and batiks from Bengal. Sober handspun *khadi*, tribal weaving from remote Himalayan villages and hand block-printed saris from Serampur are easier on the pocket. The pashmina shawl from Kashmir is available in dozens of colours, widths and qualities (often mixed with silk) in every city. All trade in *tush* (toosh) wool is banned. Cane and bamboo work is a speciality of the Northeastern Hill States, offering a variety of furniture or intricately **woven baskets** in unusual shapes and designs.

Essentials A to Z

Accident and emergency

Contact the relevant emergency service (police T100, fire T101, ambulance T102) and your embassy (see Directory in Kolkata, page 82). Make sure you obtain police/medical reports required for insurance claims.

Alcohol

Periodically some Indian states have tried to enforce prohibition. When applying for your visa you can ask for an **All India Liquor Permit**. Foreigners can also get the permit from any Government of India Tourist Office in Delhi or the state capitals. Instant 'spot' permits are issued by some hotels.

Children

Children of all ages are widely welcomed. However, care should be taken when travelling to remote areas where health services are primitive. It's best to visit in the cooler months since you need to protect children from the sun, heat, dehydration and mosquito bites. Cool showers or baths help; avoid being out during the hottest part of the day. Diarrhoea and vomiting are the most common problems, so take the usual precautions. Breastfeeding is best and most convenient for babies. In the big cities you can get safe baby foods and formula milk. It doesn't harm a baby to eat an unvaried and limited diet of familiar food carried in packets for a few weeks if local dishes are not acceptable, but it may be an idea to give vitamin and mineral supplements. Wet wipes and disposable nappies are difficult to find. The biggest hotels provide babysitting. See also Health, page 44.

Customs and duty free

Duty free

Tourists are allowed to bring in all personal effects 'which may reasonably be required', without charge. The official allowance includes 200 cigarettes, 0.95 litres of alcohol, a camera with 5 rolls of film and a pair of binoculars. Valuable personal effects and professional equipment including jewellery, camera equipment and laptop computers must be declared on a Tourist Baggage Re-Export Form (TBRE) in order for them to be taken back out of the country. These forms require the equipment's serial numbers. Find out the numbers in advance and be ready to show them on the equipment. Details of imported equipment may be entered into your passport. Save time by completing the formalities while waiting for your baggage. Keep these forms to show to the customs when leaving India, otherwise considerable delays are very likely.

Currency regulations

There are no restrictions on the amount of foreign currency or TCs a tourist may bring into India. If you are carrying more than US$5000 in cash or US$10,000 or its equivalent in cash and TCs you need to fill in a currency declaration form. This could change with a relaxation in the currency regulations.

Prohibited items

The import of dangerous drugs, live plants, gold coins, gold and silver bullion and silver coins not in current use is subject to strict regulation. It is illegal to import firearms into India without special permission. Enquire at consular offices abroad for details.

Export restrictions

Export of gold jewellery purchased in India is allowed up to a value of Rs 2000 and other jewellery (including precious stones) up to a value of Rs 10,000. Export of antiquities and art objects over 100 years old is restricted. Ivory, musk, skins of all animals, *toosh* and *pashmina* wool, snake-skin and articles made from them are banned, unless you get permission for export. For further information, contact the Indian High Commission or consulate, or access the Central Board of Excise and Customs website, www.cbec.gov.in/travellers.htm.

Disabled travellers

India is not specially geared up for making provisions for the physically handicapped or wheelchair-bound traveller. Access to buildings, toilets (sometimes squat type), pavements, kerbs and public transport can prove frustrating, but it is easy to find people to give a hand to help with lifting and carrying. Provided there is an able-bodied companion to help and you are prepared to pay for at least mid-price accommodation, car hire and taxis, India should be rewarding, even if in a somewhat limited way.

Some travel companies specialize in exciting holidays, tailor-made for individuals depending on their level of disability. **Global Access**, Disabled Travel Network, www.globalaccessnews.com, provides travel information for 'disabled adventurers' and includes a number of reviews and tips. *Nothing Ventured*, edited by Alison Walsh (HarperCollins), gives personal accounts of worldwide journeys by disabled travellers, plus advice and listings. **Accessible Journeys Inc**, 35 West Sellers Av, Ridley Park, PA 19078, T610-521 0339, www.disability travel.com, runs some packages to India. **Responsible Travel.com**, 3rd floor, Pavillion House, 6 Old Steine, Brighton, BN1 1EJ, UK, T01273-600030, www.responsible travel.com, specializes in eco-holidays and has some tailored to the needs of disabled travellers.

Essentials A to Z

Electricity

India supply is 220-240 volts AC. There may be pronounced variations in the voltage, and power cuts are common. Power back-up by generator or inverter is becoming more widespread, though it may not cover a/c. Socket sizes vary so take a universal adaptor; low quality versions are available locally. Many hotels, even in the higher categories, don't have electric razor sockets.

Embassies and consulates

For information on visas and immigration, see page 55. For a complete list of embassies and consulates, see http://meaindia.nic.in/onmouse/mission.htm.

Indian embassies abroad

Australia 3-5 Moonah Pl, Yarralumla, Canberra, T02-6273 3999, www.hcindia-au.org; Level 2, 210 Pitt St, Sydney, T02-9223 9500; 15 Munro St, Coburg, Melbourne, T03-9384 0141.
Canada 10 Springfield Rd, Ottawa, K1M 1C9, T613-744 3751, www.hciottawa.ca. Toronto, T416-960 0751, Vancouver, T604-662 8811.
France 15 Rue Alfred Dehodencq, Paris, T01-4050 7070, www.amb-inde.fr.
Germany Tiergartenstrasse 17, 10785 Berlin, T030-257950. Consulates: Bonn T0228-540132; Frankfurt T069-153 0050, Hamburg T040-338036, Munich T089-210 2390, Stuttgart T0711-153 0050.
Ireland 6 Leeson Park, Dublin 6, T01-497 0843, www.indianembassy.ie.
Nepal 336 Kapurdhara Marg, Kathmandu, T+9771-441 0900, www.south-asia.com/embassy-india.
Netherlands Buitenrustweg-2, 2517 KD, The Hague, T070-346 9771, www.indianembassy.nl.
New Zealand 180 Molesworth St, Wellington, T+64-4473 6390, www.hicomind.org.nz.
Singapore India House, 31 Grange Rd, T6737 6777, www.embassyofindia.com.
South Africa 852 Schoeman St, Arcadia, Pretoria 0083, T012-342 5392, www.india.org.za.
Sri Lanka 36-38 Galle Rd, PO Box 882, Colombo 3, T+94-1-2327587, www.indiahcsl.org.
Switzerland 9 Rue de Valais, CH-1202, Geneva, T022-906 8686.
UK India House, Aldwych, London, WC2B 4NA, T020-7836 8484 (visas 0800-1200), www.hcilondon.net. Consulates: 20 Augusta St, Jewellery Quarter, Hockley, Birmingham, B18 6JL, T0121-212 2782, www.cgibirmingham.org; 17 Rutland Sq, Edinburgh, EH1 2BB, T0131-229 2144, www.cgiedinburgh.org.
USA 2107 Massachusetts Av, Washington DC 20008, T202-939 7000. Consulates: New York, T212-774 8600, San Francisco, T415-668 0662, Chicago, T312-595 0405.

Gay and lesbian travellers

Indian law forbids homosexual acts for men (but not women) and carries a maximum sentence of life imprisonment. Although it is common to see young males holding hands in public, this very rarely indicates a gay relationship and is usually an expression of friendship. Overt displays of affection between homosexuals (and heterosexuals) give offence and should be avoided. Nevertheless, in 2007 Kolkata held its inaugural **Gay and Lesbian Film Festival**, a sign that in the cities at least, attitudes may be starting to shift.

Health

Local populations in India are exposed to a range of health risks not encountered in the Western world. Many of the diseases are major problems for the local poor and destitute and, although the risk to travellers is more remote, they cannot be ignored. Obviously 5-star travel is going to carry less risk than backpacking on a budget.

There are many excellent private and government clinics/hospitals. As with all medical care, first impressions count. It's worth contacting your embassy on arrival and asking where the recommended (ie those used by diplomats) clinics are.

Before you go

Visit your GP or travel clinic at least 6 weeks before your departure for general advice on travel risks, malaria and vaccinations; see also page 54. Make sure you have travel insurance, get a dental check, know your own blood group and if you suffer a long-term condition such as diabetes or epilepsy make sure someone knows or that you have a Medic Alert bracelet/necklace. Remember that it is risky to buy medicinal tablets abroad because the doses may differ and India has a huge trade in false drugs.

A-Z of health risks

Altitude sickness can creep up on you as just a mild headache with nausea or lethargy. The more serious disease is caused by fluid collecting in the brain and can lead to coma and death. There is also a lung disease version with breathlessness and fluid infiltration of the lungs. The best cure is to descend as soon as possible. Preventative measures include getting acclimatized and ascending gradually. Try to avoid flying directly into the cities of high altitude. Climbers like to take treatment drugs as protective measures but this can lead to macho idiocy and death. The peaks are still there and so are the trails, whether it takes you a bit longer than someone else does not matter as long as you come back down alive.

If you are unlucky (or careless) enough to receive a venomous **bite or sting** by a snake, spider, scorpion or sea creature, try to identify the creature, without putting yourself in further danger (do not try to catch a live snake). Snake bites are very frightening but rarely poisonous – even venomous snakes bite without injecting venom. Victims should be taken to a hospital or a doctor without delay so treatment can be given. To prevent bites, do not walk in snake territory in bare feet or sandals – wear proper shoes or boots. For scorpions and spiders, keep beds away from the walls and check your shoes and under the toilet seat. Certain tropical sea fish when trodden upon inject venom into bathers' feet. This can be very painful. Wear plastic shoes if such creatures are reported. The pain can be relieved by immersing the foot in hot water (as hot as you can bear). Citric acid juices in fruits such as lemon are reported as being useful.

Dengue fever is a mosquito-borne disease and unfortunately there is no vaccine. The mosquitoes that carry it bite during the day. You will be ill for 2-3 days, then get better for a few days and then feel ill again. It should all be over in 7-10 days. Heed all the anti-mosquito measures that you can.

The standard advice for **diarrhoea** prevention is to be careful with drinking water and ice. If you have any doubts about the water then boil it or filter and treat it (see also page 17). Food can also transmit disease. Be wary of salads (what were they washed in, who handled them), re-heated foods or food that has been left out in the sun. There is a simple adage that says wash it, peel it, boil it or forget it. Also be wary of unpasteurized dairy products, these can transmit a range of diseases from brucellosis (fevers and constipation), to listeria (meningitis) and tuberculosis of the gut (constipation, fevers and weight loss).

The key treatment with all diarrhoea is rehydration. Try to keep hydrated by taking the right mixture of salt and water. This is available as Oral Rehydration Salts (ORS) in ready-made sachets or can be made up by adding a teaspoon of sugar and a half teaspoon of salt to a litre of clean water. Drink at least 1 large cup of this drink for each loose stool. You can also use flat carbonated drinks as an alternative. Immodium (or Pepto-Bismol) is good if you have a long coach/train journey or on a trek, although is not a cure. Antibiotics like Ciproxin (Ciprofloaxcin) – obtained by private prescription in the UK – can be a useful antibiotic for some forms of travellers' diarrhoea. If it persists beyond 2 weeks, with blood or pain, seek medical attention.

If you go **diving** make sure that you are fit to do so. The **British Sub-Aqua Club** **(BSAC)**, Telford's Quay, South Pier Rd, Ellesmere Port, Cheshire CH65 4FL, UK, T01513-506200, www.bsac.com, can recommend doctors who do medical examinations. Protect your feet from cuts, beach dog parasites (larva migrans) and sea urchins. The latter are almost impossible to remove but can be dissolved with lime or vinegar. Keep an eye out for secondary infection. Check that the dive company know what they are doing, have appropriate certification from **BSAC** or **PADI**, Unit 7, St Philips Central, Albert Rd, St Philips, Bristol BS2 0TD, T0117-300 7234, www.padi.com, and that the equipment is well maintained.

Hepatitis means inflammation of the liver. The most obvious symptom is a yellowing of your skin or the whites of your eyes. Prior to this all that you may notice is itching and tiredness. Early on, depending on the type of hepatitis, a vaccine or immunoglobulin may reduce the duration of the illness. There are vaccines for hepatitis A and B; the latter spread through blood and unprotected sexual intercourse, both of these can be avoided. Unfortunately there is no vaccine for hepatitis C or other hepatitis viruses.

If infected with **leishmaniasis**, you may notice a raised lump, which leads to a purplish discolouration on white skin and a possible ulcer. The parasite is transmitted by the bite of a sandfly. Sandflies do not fly very far and the greatest risk is at ground levels, so if you can avoid sleeping on the jungle floor do so, under a permethrin treated net and use insect repellent. Seek advice for any persistent skin lesion or nasal symptom.

Various forms of **leptospirosis** occur throughout the world, transmitted by a bacterium which is excreted in rodent urine. Fresh water and moist soil harbour the organisms, which enter the body through cuts and scratches. If you suffer from any form of prolonged fever consult a doctor.

Malaria has some seasonality but it is too unpredictable to not take prophylaxis. In the UK we still believe that Chloroquine and Paludrine are sufficient for Northeast India, except in Assam where Mefloquine, Doxycycline or Progranil (Malarone) are recommended. Doctors in the US recommend the latter 3 drugs throughout India.

For **mosquito repellents**, DEET (Di-ethyltoluamide) is the gold standard but is an environmental contaminant. Apply the repellent 4-6 hrs but more often if you are sweating heavily. If a non-DEET product is used check who tested it. Validated products (tested at the London School of Hygiene and Tropical Medicine) include Mosiguard, Non-DEET Jungle formula and non-DEET Autan. If you want to use citronella remember that it must be applied very frequently (hourly) to be effective. If you are a target for insect bites or develop lumps quite soon after being bitten, carry an Aspivenin kit.

Prickly heat is a common intensely itchy rash, avoided by frequent washing and by wearing loose clothing. It is cured by allowing skin to dry off through use of powder – and spending a few nights in an a/c hotel.

Rabies is endemic in certain parts of India, so avoid dogs that are behaving strangely and cover your toes at night from the vampire bats. If you are bitten by a domestic or wild animal, scrub the wound with soap and water and/or disinfectant and seek medical assistance at once. The treatment depends on whether you have already been satisfactorily vaccinated against rabies. If you have, then some further doses of vaccine are all that is required. If you are not already vaccinated then anti-rabies serum (immunoglobulin) may also be required. It is important to finish the course of treatment.

The range of visible and invisible **sexually transmitted diseases** is awesome. Unprotected sex can spread HIV, hepatitis B and C, gonorrhea (green discharge), chlamydia (may cause painful urination and later female infertility), painful recurrent herpes, syphilis and warts, just to name a few. You can cut down the risk by using condoms, a femidom or avoiding sex altogether.

Make sure you protect yourself from the **sun** with high-factor sun screen and don't forget to wear a hat.

Ticks usually attach themselves to the lower parts of the body often after walking in areas where cattle have grazed. They swell up as they start to suck blood. The important thing is to remove them gently, so that they do not leave their head parts in your skin, because this can cause a nasty allergic reaction later. Do not use petrol, Vaseline, lighted cigarettes, etc to remove the tick, but, with a pair of tweezers remove the beast gently by gripping it at the attached (head) end and rock it out in very much the same way that a tooth is extracted.

Certain **tropical flies** which lay their eggs under the skin of sheep and cattle also occasionally do the same thing to humans with the unpleasant result that a maggot grows under the skin and pops up as a boil or pimple. The best way to remove these is to cover the boil with oil, Vaseline or nail varnish to stop the maggot breathing, then to squeeze it out gently the next day.

Further information
Blood Care Foundation (UK), www.bloodcare.org.uk Charity 'dedicated to the provision of screened blood and resuscitation fluids in countries where these are not readily available'. They will dispatch certified non-infected blood of the right type to your hospital/clinic in India.
British Travel Health Association (UK), www.btha.org The official website of an organization of travel health professionals.
Department of Health Travel Advice (UK), www.doh.gov.uk/traveladvice Excellent site, also available as a free booklet, T6, from post offices. Lists vaccine requirements.

Fit for Travel, www.fitfortravel.scot.nhs.uk
Provides an A-Z of vaccine and travel health
advice for each country.
**Foreign and Commonwealth Office (FCO)
(UK), www.fco.gov.uk** A key travel advice
site, with information on the country, people,
climate and lists the UK embassies/consulates.
It promotes the concept of 'know before you
go' and offers advice on travel health.
**The Health Protection Agency
www.hpa.org.uk** Up-to-date malaria advice
guidelines and specific advice about which
drugs to take. Also has useful information for
those who are pregnant, suffering from
epilepsy or planning to travel with children.
Medic Alert (UK), www.medicalalert.co.uk
Produces bracelets and necklaces for those
with existing medical problems.
**Travel Screening Services (UK),
www.travelscreening.co.uk** A private clinic
for travel health. Gives vaccines, travel health
advice, email and SMS text vaccine reminders
and screens returned travellers for diseases.
World Health Organisation, www.who.int
The Blue Book on travel advice lists the
diseases around the world and offers advice
on vaccination.

Books

International Travel and Health, World Health
Organisation Geneva, ISBN 92 4 158026 7.
Lankester, T, *The Travellers Good Health
Guide*, ISBN 0-85969-827-0.
Warrell, D and Anderson, A (eds),
*Expedition Medicine (The Royal Geographic
Society)*, ISBN 1 86197 040-4.
Young Pelton, R, Aral, C and Dulles, W,
The World's Most Dangerous Places,
ISBN 1-566952-140-9.

Insurance

Buying insurance with your air ticket is the
most costly way of doing things: better go
to an independent. Some banks now offer
travel insurance for account holders. See
also www.dh.gov.uk/policyandguidance/
healthadvicefortravellers.

If you are carrying specialist equipment –
expensive cameras, VCRs, laptops – you will
probably need to get separate cover for
these items (claims for individual items are
often limited to £250) unless they are
covered by existing home contents

insurance. Dig out the receipts for these
expensive personal effects. Take photos of
the items and note down all serial numbers.

Check exactly what your medical cover
includes, eg ambulance, helicopter rescue or
emergency flights back home, and check for
exclusions: you may find that activities such
as mountain biking are not covered. Note
that drinking alcohol is likely to invalidate a
claim in the event of an accident. Also check
the payment protocol. You may have to pay
first – known as an excess charge – before
the insurance company reimburses you.

Always carry with you the telephone
number of your insurer's 24-hr emergency
helpline and your insurance policy number.

Most annual policies have a trip limit of
around a month. If you plan to be abroad
for longer insurers including **Columbus**,
Direct Travel Insurance, **Flexicover** and
Insure and Go offer suitable cover. If
travelling abroad several times in a year,
an annual, worldwide insurance policy
will save you money.

Senior travellers should note that some
companies will not cover people over 65
years old, or may charge higher premiums.

Insurance companies
In North America
Young travellers from North America can try
the **International Student Insurance Service**
(ISIS), available through **STA Travel**, T1-
800-777 0112, www.sta-travel.com. Other
recommended travel insurance companies
include: **Access America**, T1-800-284
8300; **Council Travel**, T1-888-COUNCIL,
www.counciltravel.com; **Travel Assistance
International**, T1-800-8212828; **Travel Guard**,
T1-800-8261300, www.noelgroup.com;
Travel Insurance Services, T1-800-937 1387.

In the UK
STA Travel offers good-value policies for
students. Several companies specialize in gap
year travel insurance, including **Columbus
Direct**, www.columbusdirect.com, **Down
Under Travel Insurance**, www.duinsure.com,
and **Endsleigh**, www.endsleigh.co.uk. Other
companies include: **American Express**, T0800-
028 7573, www.americanexpress.co.uk/travel;
Biba, T0870-950 1790, www.biba.org.uk;
Churchill, T0800-026 4050, www.churc
hill.com; **Direct Line**, T0845-246 8704,

www.directline.com; **Esure**, T0845-600 3950, www.esure.com; **Flexicover**, www.flexi cover.com; **Moneysupermarket.com**, www.moneysupermarket.com; **MRL**, T0870-876 7677, www.mrlinsurance.co.uk, **MIA Online**, www.miaonline.co.uk; **Preferential**, T0870-600 7766, www.preferential.co.uk; **World Nomads**, www.worldnomads.com.

The best policies for senior travellers in the UK are offered by **Age Concern**, T01883-346964 and **Saga**, T0800-056 5464, www.saga.co.uk.

Internet

India is the 4th highest user behind the USA, China and Japan, and the number of people online is estimated to be between 25 and 60 million. You're never far from an internet café or PCO (public call office). The Indian communications ministry declared 2007 the year of broadband, which will include a major focus on providing Wi-Fi.

In small towns there is less internet access and power is sporadic; it is best to write lengthy emails in Word, saving frequently, then paste them into your web-based email. Costs vary dramatically from Rs 20-100, with most somewhere in between. As a general rule, avoid emailing from upmarket hotels as their prices can be exorbitant unless you are a guest, in which case it's often free. If you intend to stay in India for a while, sign up for membership with the internet chain **I-way**.

Language

The most widely spoken Indo-Aryan languages in Northeast India are Bengali (spoken by 8.3% of the Indian population) and Oriya (3.7%), spoken alongside Hindi in Orissa. Nepali and Sikkimese are the dominant languages in Sikkim, while in the Northeastern hill states, hundreds of distinct Sino-Tibetan tribal languages and dialects are still spoken, despite the dominance in the region of Bengali, Assamese and the Manipuri-Meiteiolon language. For food and drink and a glossary of terms, see page 332.

Laundry

Laundry services are generally speedy and can be arranged very cheaply (eg a shirt washed and pressed for Rs 15-20 in **C-D** category; but Rs 50 or more in **LL-AL** hotels) and quickly (in 12-24 hours). It is best not to risk delicate fibres, though luxury hotels can usually handle these.

Media

International **newspapers** (mainly English language) are sold in the bookshops of top hotels in major cities and occasionally by booksellers elsewhere. India has a large and lively English language press. They all have extensive analysis of contemporary Indian and some international issues. The major papers now have websites, excellent for keeping daily track on events, news and weather.

The best known are the traditionalist *The Hindu*, www.hinduonline.com/today. *The Hindustan Times*, www.hindustantimes.com, the slightly more tabloid-establishment *Times of India*, www.timesofindia.com/ and *The Statesman*, www.thestatesman.org. *The Economic Times* is good for world coverage. *The Telegraph*, www.telegraphindia.com, has good foreign coverage. *The Indian Express*, www.expressindia.com, stands out as being consistently critical of the Congress Party and the government. *The Asian Age* is now published in the UK and India simultaneously and gives good coverage of Indian and international affairs. Of the news weeklies, some of the most widely read are current affairs *India Today*, *Frontline* and *The Week*, which are journals in the *Time* or *Newsweek* mould. *Business Today* is of course economy-based, while *Outlook* has a broader remit and has good general interest features. There is also *Outlook Traveller*, probably the best of the domestic travel titles.

India's national **radio** and **television** network, *Doordarshan*, broadcasts in national and regional languages but things have moved on. The advent of satellite TV has hit even remote rural areas and there are over 500 local broadcast television stations – each state has its own local-language current affairs broadcaster plus normally at least one other channel for entertainment. The 'Dish' can help travellers keep in touch through Star TV from Hong Kong, accessing BBC World, CNN etc, VTV (music) and Sport, is now available even in modest hotels in the smallest of towns.

: Money matters

It can be difficult to use torn or very worn currency notes. Check notes when you are given them and refuse any that are damaged.

Request some Rs 100 and 50 notes. Rs 500 (can be mistaken for Rs 100) notes reduce 'wallet bulge' but can be difficult to change.

A good supply of small denomination notes always comes in handy for bus tickets, cheap meals and tipping. Remember that if offered a large note, the recipient will never have any change!

It can be worth carrying a few clean, new sterling or dollar notes for use where travellers' cheques and credit cards are not accepted. It is likely to be quite a while before euro notes are widely accepted.

Money

Indian currency is the Indian Rupee (Re/Rs). It is **not** possible to purchase these before you arrive. If you want cash on arrival it is best to get it at the airport bank. Rupee notes are printed in denominations of Rs 1000, 500, 100, 50, 20, 10. The rupee is divided into 100 paise. Coins are minted in denominations of Rs 5, Rs 2, Rs 1 and 50 paise. **Note** Carry money, mostly as TCs, in a money belt worn under clothing. Have a small amount in an accessible place.

Exchange rates (August 2007)
US$1 = Rs 40; UK £1 = Rs 83; AUS$1 = Rs 36; NZ$1 = Rs 32; €1 = Rs 56

Travellers' cheques (TCs)
TCs issued by reputable companies (eg **Thomas Cook, American Express**) are widely accepted and can be easily exchanged at local travel agents and tourist internet cafés. Try to avoid changing at banks, where the process can be time consuming; opt for hotels and agents instead. Most banks will accept US dollars, pounds sterling and euro TCs. Replacement of lost Amex TCs may take weeks. If travelling to remote areas it can be worth buying Indian rupee TCs from a major bank, as these are more widely accepted than foreign currency ones.

Credit cards
Major credit cards are accepted in the main centres, but rarely in smaller cities and towns. Payment by credit card can sometimes be more expensive than payment by cash and some credit card companies charge a premium on cash withdrawals. **Visa** and **Mastercard** have a growing number of ATMs in major cities and several banks offer withdrawal facilities for **Cirrus** and **Maestro**. It is easy to obtain a cash advance against a credit card. Some railway reservation centres are now taking payment for train tickets by Visa, which can be very quick as the queue is short, but they cannot be used for Tourist Quota tickets.

ATMs
By far the most convenient method of accessing money, ATMs are appearing all over India, usually attended by security guards. Banks with ATMs for Cirrus, Maestro, Visa and Mastercard include: **Bank of Baroda, Citibank, HDFC, HSBC, ICICI, IDBI, Punjab National Bank, State Bank of India** (SBI), **Standard Chartered** and **UTI**. A withdrawal fee is usually charged by the issuing bank on top of the various conversion charges applied by your own bank. Fraud prevention measures may result in travellers having their cards blocked by the bank when unexpected overseas transactions occur; advise your bank of your travel plans before leaving.

Changing money
The **State Bank of India** and several others in major towns are authorized to deal in foreign exchange. Some give cash against Visa/Mastercard (eg **ANZ, Bank of Baroda** who print a list of their participating branches, **Andhra Bank**). The larger cities have licensed money changers with offices usually in the commercial sector. Changing money through unauthorized dealers is illegal. Premiums on the currency black market are very small and highly risky.

Large hotels change money 24 hrs a day for guests, but banks often give a much better rate of exchange. It is best to exchange money on arrival at the airport bank or the Thomas Cook counter. You should be given a foreign currency encashment certificate when you change money through a bank or authorized dealer; ask for one if it is not automatically given. It allows you to change Indian rupees back to your own currency on departure. It also enables you to use rupees to pay hotel bills or buy air tickets for which payment in foreign exchange may be required. The certificates are only valid for 3 months.

Transferring money to India

HSBC, Barclays and ANZGrindlays and others can make 'instant' transfers to their offices in India but charge a high fee (about US$30). Standard Chartered Bank issues US$ TCs. Sending a bank draft (up to US$1000) by post (4-7 days by Speedpost) is the cheapest option.

Cost of living

The cost of living in India remains well below that in the West. The average wage per capita is about Rs 34,000 per year (US$800). Manual, unskilled labourers (women are often paid less than men), farmers and others in rural areas earn considerably less. However, thanks to booming global demand for workers who can provide cheaper IT and technology support functions, salaries in certain sectors have sky rocketed. An IT specialist can earn an average Rs 500,000 per year (US$12,000) and upwards – a rate that is rising by around 15% a year.

Cost of travelling

Most food, accommodation and public transport are exceptionally cheap. Budget travellers sharing a room, using public transport and eating nothing but rice and dhal can get away with a budget of Rs 350-400 (about US$8 or £4) a day. This sum leaps up if you drink booze (about US$2, £1 or Rs 80 for a pint), smoke fags or want to have your own wheels. Those planning to stay in fairly comfortable hotels and use taxis sightseeing should budget at US$30 (£15) a day. Then again, you could always check into the Park Hotel in Kolkata and notch up a $300 credit card bill on your room alone.

Opening hours

Banks open Mon-Fri 1030-1430, Sat 1030-1230. Top hotels sometimes have a 24-hr money changing service. Post offices open Mon-Fri 1000-1700 and Sat mornings. Government offices open Mon-Fri 0930-1700, Sat 0930-1300 (some on alternate Sat only). Shops open Mon-Sat 0930-1800. Bazars keep longer hours.

Post

The post is frequently unreliable, and delays are common. Send mail from a post office where possible, or a top hotel post box. Valuable items should only be sent by registered mail. Government emporia or shops in the larger hotels will send purchases home if the items are difficult to carry.

Airmail services to Europe and Australia take at least a week and a little longer for the Americas. Speed post (about 4 days to the UK) is available from major towns. **Speed post** to the UK costs around Rs 675 for the first 250g sent and an extra Rs 75 for each 250g thereafter. Courier services (eg DHL) are available in the larger towns. At some main post offices you can send small packages under 2 kg as **letter post** (rather than parcel post), which is much cheaper at Rs 220. **Book post** (for printed paper only, sent by sea mail) is cheaper still at around Rs 170 for 5 kg; delivery takes at least 3 months. **Sea mail** costs Rs 800 for 10 kg. Maximum dimensions: height 1 m, width 0.8 m, circumference 1.8 m. Specialist shippers deal with larger items, normally around US$150 per cubic metre.

Poste restante facilities are widely available in even quite small towns at the GPO where mail is held for 1 month. Ask for mail to be addressed to you with your surname in capitals and underlined. When asking for mail at poste restante check under surname as well as first name.

Safety

Personal security

In general the threats to personal security for travellers in India are low. However, incidents of petty theft and violence directed at tourists have been on the increase so care is necessary in some places, and common sense needs to be used. Follow the same precautions you would when at home. There have been incidents of sexual assault in and around the main tourist beach centres. Avoid wandering alone outdoors late at night. During daylight hours be careful in remote places, especially when alone. If you are under threat, scream loudly. Never accept food or drink from casual acquaintances, it may be drugged.

Some parts of India are subject to political violence. Separatist movements in the Northeastern states, particularly Assam and Nagaland, have been responsible for a number of bombings and kidnappings in recent years, and the situation in these areas remains tense. The Left-wing Maoist extremist Naxalites are active in east central India, particularly in rural Bihar. They have a long history of conflict with state and national authorities, including attacks on police and government officials. The Naxalites have not specifically targeted Westerners, but have attacked symbolic targets including Western companies.

As a general rule, travellers are advised to be vigilant in the lead up to and on days of national significance, such as Republic Day (26 January) and Independence Day (15 August) as militants have in the past used such occasions to mount attacks.

Following a major explosion on the Delhi to Lahore (Pakistan) train in February 2007, increased security has been implemented on many trains and stations. Similar measures at airports may cause delays for passengers so factor this into your timing. Also check your airline's website for up-to-date information on luggage restrictions.

In the great majority of places visited by tourists, violent crime and personal attacks are extremely rare.

Travel advice

Seek advice from your consulate before you travel. Also contact: **British Foreign & Commonwealth Office Travel Advice Unit**, T0845-850 2829, www.fco.gov.uk. **US State Department's Bureau of Consular Affairs**, Overseas Citizens Services, Room 4800, Department of State, Washington, DC 20520-4818, USA, T202-647 1488, http://travel. state.gov. **Australian Department of Foreign Affairs Canberra**, Australia, T02-62613305, www.smartraveller.gov.au. Canadian official advice is on www.voyage.gc.ca.

Theft

Theft is not uncommon. Keep TCs, passports and valuables with you at all times. Don't regard hotel rooms as being automatically safe; even hotel safes don't guarantee secure storage. Avoid leaving valuables near open windows even when you are in the room. Use your own padlock in a budget hotel when you go out. Pickpockets and other thieves operate in the big cities. Crowded areas are particularly high risk. Take special care of your belongings when getting on or off public transport.

If you have items stolen, they should be reported to the police as soon as possible. Keep a separate record of vital documents, including passport details and numbers of TCs. Larger hotels will be able to assist in contacting and dealing with the police. Dealings with the police can be very difficult and in the worst regions such as Bihar even dangerous. The paperwork involved in reporting losses can be time consuming and irritating and your own documentation (eg passport and visas) may be demanded. In some states the police themselves sometimes demand bribes, though you should not assume that if procedures move slowly you are being expected to offer a bribe.

Confidence tricksters are particularly common around railway stations or places where budget tourists gather. A common plea is some sudden and desperate calamity; sometimes a letter will be produced in English to back up the claim. The demands are likely to increase sharply if sympathy is shown. See also Shopping, page 41.

Travel safety

The traffic police are tightening up very hard on traffic offences in some places. They have the right to make on-the-spot fines for speeding and illegal parking. If you face a demand for a fine, insist on a receipt. If you have to go to a police station, try to take someone with you.

If you face really serious problems, for example in connection with a driving accident, you should contact your consular office as quickly as possible. Always ensure you always have your international driving licence and vehicle documentation with you.

Motorcycles don't come fitted with helmets and accidents are commonplace so exercise caution, the horn and the brake. Horns carry their own code: pip to make pedestrians, stray dogs and other bikers aware you're about to overtake, or hold a screaming continuous note to communicate urgent alarm to anything fast bearing down on you – be prepared to dive from the tarmac.

Thefts on **trains**, particularly between Kolkata, Varanasi and Delhi, are on the rise. First-class compartments are self-contained and normally completely secure, although nothing of value should be left close to open train windows. Most thefts occur in non a/c sleeper class carriages. Luggage should be chained to a seat for security overnight. Locks and chains are available at main stations and bazars. Strong locks for travelling cases are invaluable. Use a leather strap around a case for extra security. If you put your bags on the upper berth during the day, beware of fellow passengers climbing up for a 'sleep'. Be guarded with new friends on trains who show particular interest in the contents of your bag and be extra wary of accepting food or drink from casual acquaintances; travellers have reported being drugged and then robbed. Pickpockets and other thieves operate in crowded areas.

Senior travellers

Travellers over the age of 60 can take advantage of several discounts on travel, including 30% on train fares and up to 50% on some air tickets. Ask when booking, as these will not be offered automatically.

Smoking

Several state governments have passed a law banning smoking in all public buildings and transport but exempting open spaces. To avoid fines, check for notices.

Student travellers

Full-time students qualify for an **ISIC** (**International Student Identity Card**) which is issued by student travel and specialist agencies (eg Usit, Campus, STA) at home. The card allows certain travel benefits such as reduced prices and concessions into certain sites. For details see www.isic.org or contact **STIC** in Imperial Hotel, Janpath, New Delhi, T011-2334 3302. Those intending to study in India may get a year's student visa (see page 55). For insurance, see page 47.

Telephone

The international code for India is +91. The IDD prefix for dialling out of India is 00. International Direct Dialling is now widely available in privately run call booths, usually labelled on yellow boards with the letters 'PCO-STD-ISD'. You dial the call yourself, and the time and cost are displayed on a screen. Cheap rate is 2100-0600, but expect queues. Calls from hotels are usually much more expensive, though some will allow local calls free of charge. Internet phone booths are the cheapest way of calling overseas.

A double ring repeated means it is ringing. Equal tones with equal pauses means engaged, similar to in the UK.

Due to the tremendous pace of the telecommunications revolution, millions of telephone numbers go out of date every year. Current telephone directories are often out of date and some of the numbers given in this book will have been changed even as we go to press. The best advice is to **put an additional 2 on the front of existing numbers**. Directory enquiries, T197, can be helpful but works only for the local area code.

Mobile phones are for sale everywhere, as are local SIM cards that allow you to make calls within India and overseas at much lower rates than using a 'roaming' service – sometimes for as little as Rs 0.5 per min. Private companies such as **Airtel**, **Hutch**, **Reliance** and **Tata Indicom** allow foreigners to sign, but the deals change frequently. To connect you'll need to complete a form, have a local address or know a friendly hotel owner who'll vouch for you, and present photocopies of your passport and visa plus 2 passport photos. Most phone dealers will be able to help, and can also sell top-up vouchers. India is divided into a number of 'calling circles' or regions, and if you travel outside the region where your connection is based (eg from West Bengal into Orissa), you will pay higher charges for calls.

Fax services are available from many PCOs and larger hotels, who charge either by the minute or per page.

Time

India doesn't change its clocks, so from the last Sun in Oct to the last Sun in Mar the time is GMT +5½ hrs, and the rest of the year it's +4½ hrs (USA, EST +10½ and +9½ hrs; Australia, EST -5½ and -4½ hrs).

Tipping

A tip of Rs 10 to a luggage porter in a modest hotel (Rs 20 in a higher category) would be appropriate. In upmarket restaurants, a 10% tip is acceptable when service is not already included; in cheaper places round off the bill with small change. Indians don't normally tip taxi drivers but a small extra amount over the fare is welcomed. Porters at airports and railway stations often have a fixed rate displayed but will usually press for more. Ask fellow passengers what a fair rate is.

Tourist information

There are Government of India tourist offices in the state capitals, as well as state tourist offices (sometimes Tourism Development Corporations) in the major cities and a few important sites. They produce their own tourist literature and some also have lists of city hotels and guest houses. The quality of material is improving though maps are often poor. Many offer tours of the city and sights, and overnight and regional packages. Some run modest hotels and midway motels with restaurants and may also arrange car hire and guides. The staff in the regional and local offices are usually helpful.

Tourist offices overseas

Australia Level 5, Glasshouse,135 King St, Sydney, NSW 2000, T02-9221 9555, info@indiatourism.com.au.
Canada 60 Bloor St West, Suite No 1003, Toronto, Ontario, T416-962 3787, indiatourism@bellnet.ca.
France 11-13 Bis Boulevard Hausmann, 75009, Paris T01-4523 3045.
Germany Baserler St 48, 60329, Frankfurt AM-Main 1, T069-242 9490, www.india-tourism.de.
Italy Via Albricci 9, Milan 20122, T02-805 3506, info@indiatourismmilan.com.
Japan B9F Chiyoda Building, 6-5-12 Ginza, Chuo-Ku, Tokyo 104-0061, T03-3571 5062, indiatourt@smile.ocn.ne.jp.
The Netherlands Rokin 9-15, 1012 KK Amsterdam, T020-620 8991, info@indiatourismamsterdam.com.
South Africa PO Box 412452, Craig Hall 2024, 2000 Johannesburg, T011-325 0880, goito@global.co.za.
UK 7 Cork St, London WIS 3LH, T020-7437 3677, info@indiatouristoffice.org.
USA 3550 Wilshire Boulevard, Room 204, Los Angeles, California 90010, T213-380 8855, goitola@aol.com; Suite 1808, 1270 Av of Americas, New York, NY 10020-1700, T212-5864901, ny@itony.com.

Tour operators

In the UK

Ace, T01223-835055, www.study-tours.org. Expert-led cultural study tours.
Adventures Abroad, T0114-247 3400, www.adventures-abroad.com. Outward bound and more.
The Adventure Company, Cross and Pillory House, Cross and Pillory Lane, Alton, GU34 1HL, T0845-450 5316, www.adventure company.co.uk. Adventure tours, small groups.
Colours Of India, Marlborough House, 298 Regents Park Rd, London, N3 2TJ, T020-8343 3446, www.colours-of-india.co.uk. Tailor-made cultural, adventure, spa and cooking tours.
Coromandel (Andrew Brock Travel Ltd), 29a Main St, Lyddington, Oakham, Rutland LE15 9LR, T01572-821330, www.coromandel abt.com. Tailor-made tours (by car and river cruise) in East India.
Cox & Kings (Taj Group), T020-7873 5006, www.coxandkings.co.uk.
Discovery Initiatives, The Travel House, 51 Castle St, Cirencester, GL7 1QD, T01285-643333, www.discoveryinitiatives.com. Wildlife safaris, tiger study tours and cultural tours with strong conservation ethic.
Dragoman, T01728-861133, www.dragoman.com. Overland, adventure, camping.
Exodus, T0870-950 0039, www.exodus.co.uk. Small group overland and trekking tours.
Gateway to India, T0870-442 3204, www.gateway-to-india.com. Tailor-made, off the beaten track, local reps.
Greaves Tours, 53 Welbeck St, London, T020-7487 9111, www.greavesindia.com.

Luxury, tailor-made tours using scheduled flights. Traditional travel such as road and rail preferred to flights between major cities.

Guerba Expeditions, T01373-826611, www.guerba.co.uk. Adventure, treks.

High & Wild, Compass House, Gate Lane, Wells, T01749-671777, www.highandwild .co.uk. Range of individual and group tours.

Indian Explorations, Afex House, Holwell, Burford, Oxfordshire, OX18 4JS, T01993-822443, www.indianexplorations.com. Bespoke holidays to the Andaman Islands.

On the go, 68 North End Rd, London W14 9EP, T020-7371 1113, www.onthegotours.com. Legendary tours and tailor-made itineraries at amazing prices.

Palanquin Travels, T020-7580 6700, www.palanquin.co.uk. Culture, wildlife.

Pettitts, T01892-515966, www.pettitts.co.uk. Unusual locations.

STA Travel, T0870-160 6070, www.sta travel.co.uk. Student and youth travel agent.

Select Connections, T01892-725555, www.selectconnections.co.uk. Excellent tailor-made breaks throughout India.

Steppes Travel, 51 Castle St, Cirencester, Gloucestershire, GL7 1QD, T01285-651010, www.steppestravel.co.uk.

Trans Indus, Northumberland House, 11 The Pavement, Popes Lane, London W5 4NG, T020-8566 2729, www.transindus.com. Upmarket tailor-made or group trips. Unusual locations.

In India

The Blue Yonder, Bengaluru (Bangalore), T080-3290 6620. Highly regarded sustainable and community tourism operators, mainly active in Kerala and Sikkim but soon to start work in Sikkim, Bhutan and Nepal.

Ibex Expeditions, G 66 East of Kailash, New Delhi 110065, T011-2691 2641, www.ibexpeditions.com. Award-winning tour operator for tours, safaris and treks.

Paradise Holidays, 312-Ansal Cassique Tower, Rajouri Garden, New Delhi 110027, T981-105 2376, www.paradiseholidays.com. Wide range of tailor-made tours, from cultural to wildlife.

Royal Expeditions, 26 Community Center (II Floor), East of Kailash, New Delhi, T011-2623 8545 (UK T020-8150 6158), www.royal expeditions.com. Tailor-made tours in culture, photography and wildlife. Specializes in easy options for senior travellers.

In North America

Absolute Asia, 180 Varick St, 16th Floor, New York, T212-627 1950, www.absoluteasia.com. Luxury custom-designed tours, including an Eastern Himalaya tour combining Sikkim, Bhutan and Nepal.

Adventures Abroad, T800-665 3998, www.adventures-abroad.com.

Greaves Tours, 304 Randolph St, Chicago, T1-800-318 7801. See under UK entry above.

High Asia, 33 Thornton St, Hamden, Connecticut, T609-269-5332. Adventurous and exploratory tours in Assam and Arunachal Pradesh, including elephant trekking, tribal culture tours and trips linking India to China via the Burma Road.

Myths and Mountains, USA T800-670 6984, www.mythsandmountains.com. Culture, crafts, religion.

Sita World Travel, 350 Fifth Av, Suite 1421, New York, T212-279 6865, www.sitatours .com. Top-end packages.

Spirit of India, USA T888-3676147, www.spirit-of-india.com. General and spirituality-focused tours, local experts.

In Australia and New Zealand

Abercrombie & Kent, 19-29 Martin Pl, Sydney, T02-92382356, www.abercrombiekent.com.au.

Adventure World, 73 Walkers St, Sydney, T02-89130755, www.adventureworld.com.au. Independent tour operator. Also at 101 Great South Rd, Remuera, Auckland, T64-9524 5118, www.adventureworld.co.nz.

Classic Oriental Tours, 35 Grafton St, Woollahara, T02-96572020, www.classic oriental.com.au. Travel arrangements in groups and for independent travellers, at all standards from budget to de luxe.

Intrepid Travel, 11-13 Spring St, Fitzroy, Victoria 3065, T1300-360 887, www.intrepid travel.com. Cookery courses and village stays.

Peregrine Adventures, Australia, T03-9662 2700, www.peregrineadventures.com. Small group overland and trekking tours.

Vaccinations

If you need vaccinations, see your doctor well in advance of your travel. Most courses must be completed in a minimum of 4 weeks. Travel clinics may provide rapid courses of vaccination, but are likely to be more expensive. Typhoid, polio, tetanus, infectious hepatitis and diptheria are recommended. The following vaccinations may also be considered: rabies, possibly BCG (since tuberculosis is still common in the region) and in some cases meningitis and diphtheria (if you're staying in the country for a long time). Yellow fever is not required in India but you may be asked to show a certificate if you have travelled from Africa or South America. Japanese encephalitis may be required for rural travel during rainy seasons. A new and effective oral cholera vaccine (Dukoral) is now available as 2 doses (1 week apart) providing 3 months' protection. For details of malaria prevention, see the health section on page 44.

Visas and immigration

For embassies and consulates, see page 44. More foreign nationals, including children, require a visa to enter India. Nationals of Bhutan and Nepal only require a suitable means of identification. Visa regulations change frequently so it is essential to check details and costs with the relevant embassy or consulate. These remain closed on Indian national holidays (see page 40). In London, applications are processed in a couple of hours (0800-1200) if you apply in person. At other offices, it can be much easier to apply in advance by post, to avoid queues and low visa quotas. Postal applications can take up to 15 working days.

Applications should be accompanied by 2 passport photographs and your passport which should be valid 6 months beyond the period of your visit. Note that visas are valid from the date granted, not from the date of entry. For the most up-to-date information on visa requirements visit www.india-visa.com.

All foreign visitors who stay in India for more than 180 days need to get an income tax clearance exemption certificate from the Foreign Section of the Income Tax Department in Delhi or Kolkata.

Currently the following visa rules apply:
Transit For passengers en route to another country (no more than 72 hours in India).
Tourist 3-6 month visa from the date of issue with multiple entry.
Business 3-6 months or up to 2 years with multiple entry. A letter from the company giving the nature of business is required.

5 year For those of Indian origin only, who have held Indian passports.
Student Valid up to 1 year from the date of issue. Attach a letter of acceptance from Indian institution and an AIDS test certificate. Allow up to 3 months for approval.
Visa extensions Applications should be made to the Foreigners' Regional Registration Offices at New Delhi or Kolkata, or an office of the Superintendent of Police in the District Headquarters. After 6 months, you must leave India and apply for a new visa – the Nepal office is known to be difficult. Anyone staying in India for a period of more than 180 days (6 months) must register at a convenient Foreigners' Registration Office, see Registration below.

Permits and restricted areas
Some areas are politically sensitive and special permits may be needed to visit them though the government is relaxing its regulations. The border regions, tribal areas and Himalayan zones are subject to restrictions and special permits may be needed to visit them, although the government is relaxing its regulations.

Currently the following require special permits: Arunachal Pradesh, Manipur (for 5 days), Mizoram and Nagaland. Apply to the Under Secretary, Ministry of Home Affairs, Foreigners Division, Lok Nayak Bhavan, Khan Market, New Delhi 110003, at least 4 weeks in advance. Special permission is no longer needed to visit **Assam**, **Meghalaya** and **Tripura**. For more information, see box page 134. For the **Andaman Islands**, permits are issued for 30 days to visit some of the islands on arrival at Port Blair, see page 258. For **Sikkim**, permits for 15 days are issued by several government offices; see box, page 117.

Weights and measures

Metric system has come into universal use in the cities. In remote areas local measures are sometimes used. One lakh is 100,000 and 1 crore is 10 million.

Women travellers

Independent travel is still largely unheard of for Indian women. Although it is relatively safe for women to travel around India, most people find it an advantage to travel with a companion. Even then, privacy is rarely respected and there can be a lot of hassle, pressure and intrusion on your personal space. Backpackers often meet like-minded travelling companions at budget hotels. Cautious solo women travellers recommend dying blonde hair black and wearing wedding rings, but the most important measure is to dress appropriately, in loose-fitting, non-see-through clothes, covering shoulders, arms and legs. Take advantage of the gender segregation on public transport, both to avoid hassle and talk with local women. In mosques women should be covered from head to ankle. **Independent Traveller**, T0870-760 5001, www.independenttraveller.com, runs women-only tours to India.

'Eve teasing', the euphemism for physical harassment, is an unfortunate result of the sexual repression latent in Indian culture, combined with a young male population whose only access to sex education is via the back corners of dingy cyber cafés. Unaccompanied women are most vulnerable in major cities, crowded bazars, beach resorts and tourist centres where men may follow them and touch them; festival nights are particularly bad for this. Women have reported that they have been molested while being measured for clothing in tailors' shops. If you are harassed, it can be effective to make a scene. Be firm and clear if you don't wish to speak to someone. The best response to staring, whether lascivious or curious, is to avert your eyes down and away. This is not the submissive gesture it might seem, but an effective tool to communicate that you have no interest in any further interaction. Aggressively staring back or verbally confronting the starer can be construed as a come-on. It is best to be accompanied at night, especially when travelling by rickshaw or taxi in towns. Be prepared to raise an alarm if anything unpleasant threatens.

Most railway booking offices have separate women's ticket queues or ask women to go to the head of the general queue. Some buses have seats reserved for women. See also page 19.

Working in India

It is best to arrange voluntary work well in advance with organizations in India (see Kolkata, page 80); alternatively, contact an organization abroad. Students may spend part of their year off helping in a school or teaching English. Foreigners should apply to the Indian representative in their own country for the latest information about **work permits**.

Voluntary work
In the UK
1 to 1, Woodside House, 261 Low Lane, Leeds, LS18 5NY, T0800-011 1156, www.i-to-i.com.
International Voluntary Service (IVS), Old Hall, East Bergholt, Colchester, CO7 6TQ, T01206-298215; Oxford Place Centre, Oxford Place, Leeds, LS1 3AX, T0113-246 9900; St John's Centre, Edinburgh EH2 4BJ, www.ivs-gb.org.uk.
VSO, 317 Putney Bridge Rd, London, SW15 2PN, www.vso.org.uk.
Volunteer Work Information Service, PO Box 2759, Lewes, BN7 1WU, UK, T01273-470015, www.workingabroad.com.

In the USA
Council for International Programs, 1700 East 13th St, Suite 4ME, Cleveland, Ohio, T216-566-108, www.cipusa.org.

In Australia
The website www.ampersand.org.au has links to a variety of volunteer organizations.
Australian Volunteers International, 71 Argyle St, Fitzroy, VIC 3065, T03-9279 1788, www.australianvolunteers.com.

Kolkata (Calcutta)

⸭ Footprint features

Introduction

Kolkata is considered by many to be the countrys cultural and intellectual hub. The vibrant daily theatre and concert performances, sprawling annual book fair and art-house film festivals are rooted in the legacy of the great Tagore and evoke the iconic films of Satajit Ray. From being at the centre of the Indian independence movement, Kolkata is today ruled by the longest-running democratically elected communist government in the world. Politics and reform continue to be discussed amidst the fan-swirled smoke in the Indian Coffee House, and by the businessmen gathered for *adda* (chatting) in one of the historic clubhouses.

Many visitors have a preconceived idea of this oft-maligned city, and for a long time the "black hole" tag and the work of Mother Teresa conjured up images of a disintegrating, filthy conurbation engulfed in desperate poverty. But a little time spent here is enough for those ideas to be rapidly dispelled, and to gain a fascinating glimpse of how 14 million people live together. From rich to poor and educated to illiterate, Kolkatans melt together in a way that isn't seen in other cities. Although the *bustees* (slums) continue to swell and street living is more visible here than anywhere, the warmth and humanity of the population is palpable. The city's many volunteers find that this is the memory that stays with them, as intensely as the smell of kati-rolls cooking, the jingle of rickshaw bells and the ever-vocal horns of the city's yellow Ambassadors.

Since 2000, Kolkata has been rejuvenating itself economically and, more recently, visually: the impressive relics of colonialism are being given a facelift and Hoara Bridge is lit up at night. Kolkatans are immensely proud of their heritage and they love their city – and visitors to this fascinating and surprising metropolis generally discover that they do too.

★ Don't miss ...

1 **Sporting fever** Kolkatans are sport fanatics, so join the wild throngs of cricket supporters at Eden Gardens, the locals on the Maidan for fielding practice, or enjoy a flutter at the glorious colonial racecourse, page 63.

2 **Park Street Cemetery** Soak up the atmosphere and history while wandering between soaring obelisks and curious epitaphs in this quiet havens, page 65.

3 **Victorial Memorial** Relive the rise and fall of the Raj inside Lord Curzon's white marble edifice, the city's most visited landmark, page 66.

4 **Riverside** Take a ferry to Haora and view the colonial cityscape from the water, walk back over the bridge among 100,000 commuters and basket-wallahs, then immerse yourself in the neon-bright flower market beneath, page 67.

5 **Street food** You can taste all of India along 100 m of one street, whether it's *chola batura* on Chowringhee, *sambar vada* on the Strand or *dal* fry by Dalhousie – but leave room for some famed Bengali *mishti doi*, page 74.

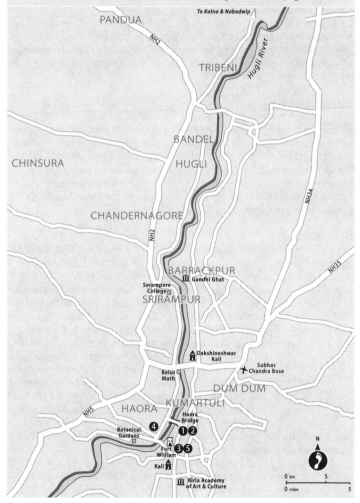

Kolkata (Calcutta)

Kolkata (Calcutta)

➔ *Phone code: 033. Colour map 2, grid C2. Population: 13.22 million.*

To Bengalis Kolkata is the proud intellectual capital of India, with an outstanding contribution to the arts, services, medicine and social reform in its past, and a rich contemporary cultural life. As the former imperial capital, Kolkata retains some of the country's most striking colonial buildings, yet at the same time it is truly an Indian city. Unique in India in retaining trams, and the only place in the world to still have hand-pulled rickshaws, you take your life in your hands each time you cross Kolkata's streets. Hugely crowded, Kolkata's maidan, the parkland, give lungs to a city packed with some of the most densely populated slums, or bustees, anywhere in the world.

➤➤ *For Sleeping, Eating and other listings, see pages 70-82.*

Ins and outs

Getting there Subhas Chandra Bose airport at Dum Dum serves international and domestic flights. Taxis to the city centre take 30-60 minutes. Haora (Howrah) station, on the west bank of the Hugli, can be daunting and the taxi rank outside is often chaotic; the prepaid taxi booth is to the right as you exit. Trains to the north use the slightly less chaotic Sealdah terminal east of the centre, which also has prepaid taxis. Long-distance buses arrive at Esplanade, 15-20 minutes' walk from most budget hotels.

➤➤ *See Transport, page 80, for further details.*

Getting around You can cover much of Central Kolkata on foot. For the rest you need transport. You may not fancy using hand-pulled rickshaws, but they become indispensable when the streets are flooded. Buses and minibuses are often jam packed, but routes comprehensively cover the city and conductors will help find the correct bus. The electric trams can be slightly better outside peak periods. The Metro, though on a limited route, is one of the easiest ways of getting around the city. Taxis are relatively cheap but allow plenty of time to get through very congested traffic. Despite the footpath, it is not permitted to walk across the Vidyasagar Bridge. Taxi drivers expect passengers to pay the Rs 10 toll.

Background

Calcutta, as it came to be named, was founded by the remarkable English merchant trader **Job Charnock** in 1690. He was in charge of the East India Company factory (ie warehouse) in Hugli, then the centre of British trade from eastern India. Attacks from the local Muslim ruler forced him to flee – first down river to Sutanuti and then 1500 km south to Chennai. However, in 1690 he selected three villages – Kalikata, Sutanuti and Govindpur – where Armenian and Portuguese traders had already settled, leased them from Emperor Aurangzeb and returned to what became the capital of British India.

The first fort here, named after King William III (completed 1707), was on the site of the present BBD Bagh. A deep defensive moat was dug in 1742 to strengthen the fort – the Maratha ditch. The Maratha threat never materialized but the city was captured easily by the 20-year-old **Siraj-ud-Daula**, the new Nawab of Bengal, in 1756. The 146 British residents who failed to escape by the fort's river gate were imprisoned for a night in a small guard room about 6 m by 5 m with only one window – the infamous '**Black Hole of Calcutta**'. Some records suggest 64 were imprisoned and only 23 survived.

✦ *Kolkata can be very hot and humid outside from mid-March to October. Asthma sufferers find the traffic pollution very trying.*

The following year **Robert Clive** re-took the city. The new Fort William was built and in 1772 Calcutta became the capital of British administration in India with Warren

❗ Kolkata's place in the cosmic dance

Kolkata's site was particularly holy to Hindus. According to one myth, **King Daksa** was enraged when his daughter **Sati** married **Siva**. He organized a **Yajna** (grand sacrifice) to which he invited everyone in the kingdom – except his son-in-law. Distraught, **Kali** (Sati) threw herself on the sacrificial flames. Siva in turn arrived on the scene to find his wife's body already burnt. Tearing it from the flames, he started his dance of cosmic destruction. All the other gods, witnessing the devastation that Siva was causing in his anguish, pleaded with Vishnu to step in and end the chaos. **Vishnu** intercepted him with his chakra (discus-like weapon) and, in order to dislodge Kali's body from Siva's shoulder, chopped it into 51 pieces, which were flung far and wide. The place where each one fell became a place of pilgrimage – a pithasthana. Kali's little toe fell at Kali Ghat. The place, Kalikshetra or Kalikata, gave the city its name.

Hastings as the first Governor of Bengal, see page 282. Some of Calcutta's most impressive colonial buildings were built in the years that followed, when it became the first city of British India. It was also a time of Hindu and Muslim resurgence.

Colonial Calcutta grew as new traders, soldiers and administrators arrived, establishing their exclusive social and sports clubs. Trade in cloth, silk, lac, indigo, rice, areca nut and tobacco had originally attracted the Portuguese and British to Bengal. Later Calcutta's hinterland producing jute, iron ore, tea and coal led to large British firms setting up headquarters in the city. Calcutta prospered as the commercial and political capital of British India up to 1911, when the capital was transferred to Delhi.

Kolkata had to absorb huge numbers of migrants immediately after Partition in 1947. When Pakistan ceased trading with India in 1949, Kolkata's economy suffered a massive blow as it lost its supplies of raw jute and its failure to attract new investment created critical economic problems. In the late 1960s the election of the Communist Party of India Marxist, the **CPI(M)**, led to a period of stability. The CPI(M) has become committed to a mixed economy and has sought foreign private investment.

Central Kolkata

BBD Bagh (Dalhousie Square) and around

Many historic Raj buildings surround the square which is quietest before 0900. Renamed Benoy Badal Dinesh (BBD) Bagh after three Bengali martyrs, the square has an artificial lake fed by natural springs. On Strand Road North is the dilapidated **Silver Mint** (1824-1831). The **Writers' Building** (1780), designed by Thomas Lyon as the trading HQ of the East India Company, was refaced in 1880. It is now the state Government Secretariat. The classical block with 57 sets of identical windows was built like barracks inside. **Mission Row** (now RN Mukharji Road) is Kolkata's oldest street, and contains the **Old Mission Church** (consecrated 1770), built by the Swedish missionary Johann Kiernander.

South of BBD Bagh is the imposing **Raj Bhavan** (1799-1802), the residence of the Governor of West Bengal, formerly Government House. It was modelled on Kedleston Hall in Derbyshire, England (later Lord Curzon's home), and designed by **Charles Wyatt**, one of many Bengal engineers who based their designs on famous British buildings. The **Town Hall** (1813) has been converted into a **museum** ① *1100-1800, foreigners Rs 10,*

Kolkata

Related maps
A Central Kolkata,
page 64.
B Around Sudder Street,
page 71.
C Park Street, page 72.

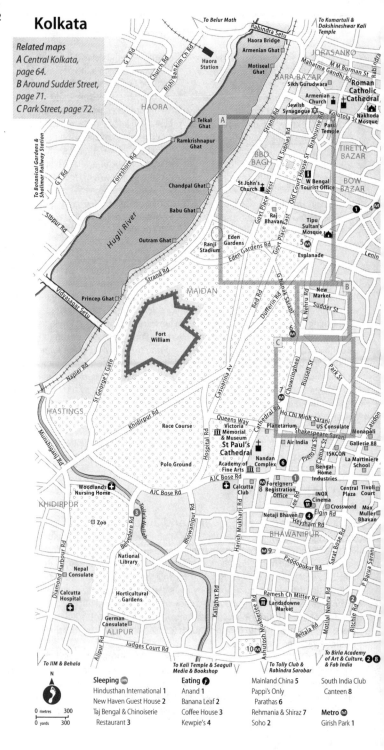

Sleeping 🛏
Hindusthan International 1
New Haven Guest House 2
Taj Bengal & Chinoiserie
Restaurant 3

Eating 🍴
Anand 1
Banana Leaf 2
Coffee House 3
Kewpie's 4

Mainland China 5
Pappi's Only
Parathas 6
Rehmania & Shiraz 7
Soho 2

South India Club
Canteen 8

Metro Ⓜ
Girish Park 1

0 metres 300
0 yards 300

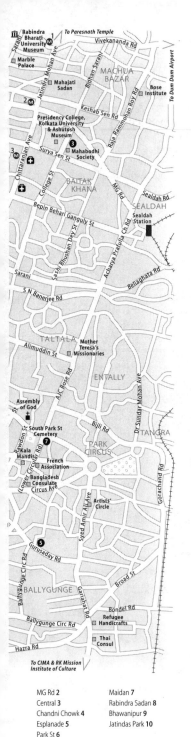

MG Rd **2**

Central **3**

Chandni Chowk **4**

Esplanade **5**

Park St **6**

Maidan **7**

Rabindra Sadan **8**

Bhawanipur **9**

Jatindas Park **10**

no bags allowed, which tells the story of the independence movement in Bengal through a panoramic, cinematic display, starring an animatronic Rabindranath Tagore. The **High Court** (1872) was apparently modelled on the medieval cloth merchants' hall at Ypres in Flanders.

Ochterlony Monument (1828), renamed as Shahid Minar (the Martyrs' Memorial) in 1969, was built as a memorial to **Sir David Ochterlony**, who led East India Company troops against the Nepalese in 1814-1816. The 46-m tall Greek Doric column has an Egyptian base and is topped by a Turkish cupola.

St John's Church (1787) ① *0900-1200, 1700-1800*, like the later St Andrew's Kirk (1818), was modelled partially on the church of St Martin-in-the-Fields, London. The soft subsoil did not allow it to have a tall spire and architecturally it was thought to be "full of blunders". Verandas were added to the north and south in 1811 to reduce the glare of the sun. Inside the vestry can be found Warren Hastings's desk and chair, plus paintings, prints and assorted dusty memorabilia of the Raj. *The Last Supper* by **Johann Zoffany** in the south aisle shows the city's residents dressed as the Apostles. Job Charnock is buried in the old cemetery. His octagonal mausoleum, the oldest piece of masonry in the city, is of Pallavaram granite (from Madras Presidency), which is named charnockite after him. The monument to the **Black Hole of Calcutta** was brought here from Dalhousie Square (BBD Bagh) in 1940.

Eden Gardens ① *usually open for matches only, a small tip at Gate 14 gains entry on other days*. These gardens, which are situated in the northwest corner of the Maidan, were named after Lord Auckland's sisters Emily and Fanny Eden. There are pleasant walks, a lake and a small Burmese pagoda (typical of this type of Pyatthat). Laid out in 1834, part forms the Ranji Stadium where the first cricket match was played in 1864. Today, Test matches (played November to February), international tennis championships and various other sports fixtures attract crowds of 100,000.

Conveniently close to Chowringhee and the vast shopping arcade, New Market, Sudder Street is the focus for Kolkata's backpackers and attracts touts and drug pushers. Beggars on Chowringhee and Park Street often belong to organized syndicates who have to pay a large percentage of their 'earnings' for the privilege of working that area.

Around the corner from Sudder Street is the **Indian Museum** ① *27 JL Nehru Rd, T033-2286 1679, Tue-Sun Mar-Nov 1000-1700, Dec-Feb 1000-1630, foreigners Rs 150, Indians Rs 10, cameras Rs 50/100 with tripod*, possibly Asia's largest. The Jadu Ghar (House of Magic) was founded in 1814 and has a worthwhile collection. The colonnaded Italianate building facing the Maidan has 36 galleries (though large sections are often closed off). Parts are poorly lit and gathering dust so it is best to be selective. Highlights include the geological collection with Siwalik fossils, natural

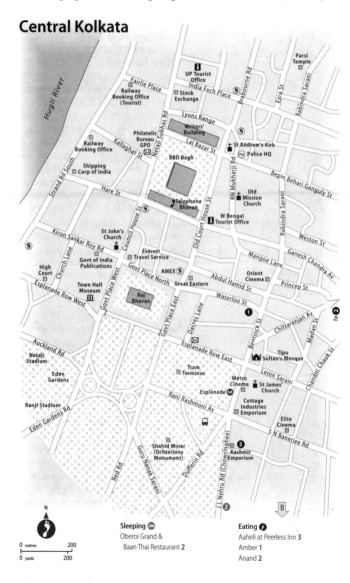

Central Kolkata

Sleeping 🛏
Oberoi Grand &
  Baan Thai Restaurant 2

Eating 🍴
Aaheli at Peerless Inn 3
Amber 1
Anand 2

history and anthropology, outstanding exhibits from the Harappa and Moenjodaro periods, a prized collection of Buddhist art, miniature paintings, 'Art and Textile' with ivory, glass and silverware, Theme Gallery with rare paintings and 200-year-old hand-drawn maps, and many more. You need permission to see the exceptional collection of over 50,000 coins. Allow a couple of hours.

Park Street → *See map, page 72.*

South Park St Cemetery ① *daily 0800-1630, free, booklet Rs 100, security guard opens gate for foreigners and will expect you to sign the visitors' book,* was opened in 1767 to accommodate the large number of British who died serving their country. The cemetery is a quiet space on the south side of one of Kolkata's busiest streets. The heavily inscribed decaying headstones, obelisks, pyramids and urns have been somewhat restored, and gardeners are actively trying to beautify the grounds. Several of the inscriptions make interesting reading. Death, often untimely, came from tropical diseases or other hazards such as battles, childbirth and even melancholia. More uncommonly, it was an excess of alcohol, or as for Sir Thomas D'Oyly, through "an inordinate use of the hokkah". Rose Aylmer died after eating too many pineapples! Tombs include those of **Col Kyd**, founder of the Botanical Gardens, and the great oriental scholar **Sir William Jones**.

Asiatic Society ① *1 Park St, Mon-Fri 1000-1800, free,* the oldest institution of Oriental studies in the world, was founded in 1784 by the great Orientalist, Sir William Jones. It is a treasure house of 150,000 books and 60,000 ancient manuscripts in most Asian languages, although permission is required to see specific pieces. The museum includes an Ashokan edict, rare coins and paintings.

The Maidan

This area, 200 years ago, was covered in dense jungle. Often called the lungs of the city, it is a unique green, covering over 400 ha along Chowringhee (JL Nehru Road). Larger than New York's Central Park, it is perhaps the largest urban park in the world. In it stands Fort William and several clubhouses providing tennis, football, rugby, cricket and even crown green bowls. Thousands each day pursue a hundred different interests – from early morning yogis, model plane enthusiasts, weekend cricketers and performers earning their living, to vast political gatherings.

The massive **Fort William** was built by the British after their defeat in 1756, see page 86, on the site of the village of Govindapur. Designed to be impregnable, it was roughly octagonal and large enough to house all the Europeans in the city in case of an attack. Water from the Hugli was channelled to fill the wide moat and the surrounding jungle was cleared to give a clear field of fire; this later became the Maidan. The barracks, stables, arsenal, prison and St Peter's Church are still there, but the fort now forms the Eastern Region's Military Headquarters and entry is forbidden.

Chowringhee and around

You can still see some of the old imposing structures with pillared verandas (designed by Italian architects as residences of prominent Englishmen) though modern high rise buildings have transformed the skyline of this ancient pilgrim route to Kalighat.

St Paul's Cathedral ① *0900-1200, 1500-1800, 5 services on Sun,* is the original metropolitan church of British India. Completed in 1847, its Gothic tower (dedicated in 1938) was designed to replace the earlier steeples which were destroyed by earthquakes. The cathedral has a fine altar piece, three 'Gothic' stained glass windows, two Florentine frescoes and the great West window by **Burne-Jones**. The original stained glass East window, intended for St George's Windsor, was destroyed by a cyclone in 1964 and was replaced by the present one four years later.

Academy of Fine Arts① *Cathedral Rd, Tue-Sun 1500-1800*, was founded in 1933. The collection includes miniature paintings, textiles, works of Jamini Roy, Tagore and Desmond Doig and modern Indian sculpture in the gardens. Galleries exhibit works of local artists. Guide service and occasional films.

Victoria Memorial ① *Tue-Sun 1000-1630; museum 1000-1530 (very crowded on Sun), foreigners Rs 150, Indians Rs 10, cameras not permitted inside. Sound & Light show, summer 1945, winter 1915, 45 mins, Rs 20 front seats, Rs 10 elsewhere*, (1906-1921) was designed by Lord Curzon. The white marble monument to Queen Victoria and the Raj designed in Italian Renaissance-Mughal style stands in large, well-kept grounds with ornamental pools. A seated bronze Queen Victoria dominates the approach, while a marble statue stands in the main hall where visitors sometimes leave flowers at her feet. The building is illuminated in the evening; the musical fountain is a special draw. The statues over the entrance porches (including Motherhood, Prudence and Learning), and around the central dome (of Art, Architecture, Justice, Charity) came from Italy. The impressive weather vane, a 5 m tall bronze winged figure of Victory weighing three tonnes, looks tiny from below. The principal gallery, covering the history of the city, includes a wealth of Raj memorabilia. There are fine miniatures, a rare collection of Persian manuscripts, and paintings by **Zoffany**, the two **Daniells**, and Samuel **Davis**.

North Kolkata

Belur Math and the Dakshineshwar Kali temple

Some 16 km north of the city is **Belur Math**① *0600-1200, 1600-1900*, the international headquarters of the **Ramakrishna Mission**, founded in 1899 by **Swami Vivekananda**, a disciple of the 19th-century Hindu saint **Ramakrishna**. He preached the unity of all religions and to symbolize this the *Math* ('monastery') synthesizes Hindu, Christian and Islamic architectural styles in a peaceful and meditative atmosphere.

On the opposite side of the river from Belur Math is the **Dakshineshwar Kali temple** ① *0600-1200, 1530-2100*. This temple was built in 1847 by Rani Rashmoni. The 12 smaller temples in the courtyard are dedicated to Siva, Radha and Krishna. Because of the Rani's low caste, no priest would serve there until Ramakrishna's elder brother agreed and was succeeded by Ramakrishna himself. Here, Ramakrishna achieved his spiritual vision of the unity of all religions. The temple is crowded with colourfully clad devotees, and is open to all faiths. A boat (Rs 7) takes 20 minutes to cross to Belur Math.

Kumartuli

South of the Dakshineshwar temple is Kumartuli. Off Chitpur Road, the *kumars* or potters work all year, preparing clay images around cores of bamboo and straw. For generations they have been making life-size idols for the *pujas* or festivals, particularly of Goddess Durga on a lion, slaying the demon. The images are usually unbaked since they are immersed in the holy river at the end of the festival. As the time of the *pujas* approaches, you will see thousands of images, often very brightly painted and gaudily dressed, awaiting the final finishing touch by the master painter. There are also *shola* artists who make decorations for festivals and weddings.

Just north of the Belgachia Metro station is the ornate Digambar Jain **Paresnath Temple**① *0600-1130, 1500-1900, no leather*, which is dedicated to the 10th Tirthankara. Consecrated around 1867, it is richly decorated with mirrors and Venetian glass mosaics.

College Street

This is the heart of intellectual Kolkata with the **university** and several academic institutions, including the old **Sanskrit College** and the elite **Presidency College**.

Europeans and Indian benefactors established the Hindu College (1817) to provide a liberal education. In 1855, this became the Presidency College. A centre for 19th-century Bengali writers, artists and reformers, it spawned the early 20th-century Swadeshi Movement. The famous **Coffee House** (opened in 1944), the smoke-filled, cavernous haunt of the city's intelligentsia, still sells a good cup of coffee. Along the pavements are interesting second-hand book stalls. **Asutosh Museum** ① *University Centenary Building, Mon-Fri 1030-1630, Sat 1030-1500, closed university holidays*, of eastern Indian art and antiquity, includes textiles, terracotta figures and Bengali folk art, but is poorly maintained with large sections frequently closed off.

Rabindra Bharati University Museum
① *6/4 Dwarakanath Tagore Lane (red walls visible down lane opposite 263 Rabindra Sarani), Mon-Fri 1000-1700, Sat 1000-1330, Sun and holidays 1100-1400.*
This museum, in a peaceful enclave away from the teeming chaos of Rabindra Sarani, occupies the family home of Rabindranath Tagore, who won the Nobel prize for Literature in 1913. It showcases Tagore's life and works, as well as the 19th-century Renaissance movement in Bengal.

Marble Palace
① *46 Muktaram Babu St, closed Mon and Thu, 1000-1600, free pass from WB Tourist Bureau, 3/2 BBD Bagh, 24 hrs ahead, shoes must be removed, restricted photography.*
Located in Chor Bagan (Thieves' Garden), the one-man collection of Raja Rajendra Mullick is in his ornate home (1835) with an Italianate courtyard, classical columns, a large tank and Egyptian sphinxes. Six sleeping marble lions and statuary grace the lawns. The long galleries are crammed with statues, pottery, mirrors, chandeliers and English, Dutch and Italian paintings, disorganized and gathering dust. Allow 45 minutes. The rambling museum on two floors has curiosity appeal.

Haora Bridge area
North of the Marble Palace on Baghbazar Street is the **Girish Mancha**, the government theatre complex. The gorgeously well-kept **Armenian Church** of Holy Nazareth (1724) reminds us of the important trading role the small Armenian community who mostly came from Iran, played from the 17th century. Though the church is locked on weekdays you may ask to look around as the vestry is open during office hours. The 200 or so Armenians in the city still hold a service in Armenian in one of their two churches here every Sunday. Their college in Mirza Ghalib Street only has about half-a-dozen pupils since it admits only those of Armenian descent. On its east side is the **Roman Catholic Cathedral** (1797) built by the Portuguese. The **Jewish** community, mostly Sephardic, of Baghdadi origin, was also once very prominent in commerce. Their two cavernous synagogues, the grander in Canning Street, are well maintained and still used for services on alternate Saturdays. There are only around 50 Jews left in the city who continue to congregate at Nahoum's bakery in the New Market; the Jewish Girls School in Park Street has no pupils from the community.

Haora Bridge (pronounced How-ra), or Rabindra Setu, was opened in 1943. This single-span cantilever bridge, a prominent landmark, replaced the old pontoon bridge that joined the city with Haora and the railway station. To avoid affecting river currents and silting, the two 80-m high piers rise from road level; the 450 m span expands by a metre on a hot day. It is the busiest bridge in the world in terms of foot passengers; go during rush hour to join with the 100,000 commuters and men with improbable loads on their heads. Wrestlers can be seen underneath and there is a daily flower market beneath the eastern end, with piles of marigolds glowing amongst the mud. The pedestrian-free **Vidyasagar Setu**, further south, has eased the traffic burden.

South Kolkata

Kali Temple

ⓘ *Off Ashok Mukherjee Rd, 0500-1500, 1700-2200.* This is the temple to Kali (1809), the patron goddess of Kolkata, usually seen in her bloodthirsty form garlanded with skulls. There was an older temple here, where the goddess's little toe is said to have fallen when **Siva** carried her charred corpse in a frenzied dance of mourning, and she was cut into pieces by Vishnu's *chakra*, see page 61. Non-Hindus have limited access to this important Hindu pilgrimage centre. Where once human sacrifices were made, the lives of goats are offered daily on two wooden blocks to the south of the temple. When visiting the temple, priests will attempt to snare foreigners for the obligatory *puja*. A barrage may start as far away as 500 m from the temple. Don't be fooled in to handing over your shoes and succumbing to any priests until you are clearly inside the temple, despite being shown 'priest ID' cards. Once settled with a priest the experience can be well worth the initial hassle. An acceptable minimum donation is Rs 50-60. Books showing previous donations of Rs 1000 are probably faked. Having done the *puja*, you'll probably be left alone to soak up the atmosphere.

Mother Teresa's Homes

Mother Teresa, an Albanian by birth, came to India to teach as a Loreto nun in 1931. She started her Order of the Missionaries of Charity in Kalighat to serve the destitute and dying 19 years later. *Nirmal Hriday* (Pure Heart), near the Kali Temple, the first home for the dying, was opened in 1952. Mother Teresa died on 5 September 1997 but her work continues. You may see nuns in their white cotton saris with blue borders busy working in the many homes, clinics and orphanages in the city.

Botanical Gardens and Birla Academy of Art and Culture

Kolkata's **Botanical Gardens** ⓘ *0700-1700, Rs 50, avoid Sun and public holidays when it is very crowded*, on the west bank of the Hugli 20 km south from BBD Bagh, were founded in 1787 by the East India Company. The flourishing 250-year-old **banyan tree**, with a circumference of over 300 m, is perhaps the largest in the world. The original trunk was destroyed by lightning in 1919 but over 1500 offshoots form an impressive sight. The gardens are peaceful and deserted during the week and make a welcome change from the city. To reach the Botanical Gardens catch a bus from Esplanade; minibuses and CTC buses (No C-12) ply the route.

The Birla Academy of Art and Culture ⓘ *108/109 Southern Av, T033-2466 2843, Tue-Sun 1600-2000*, housed in a modern high rise, concentrates on medieval and contemporary paintings and sculpture. It is worth visiting.

Around Kolkata

There are several interesting places for a day's outing north of Kolkata. It's best to take a train (buses are slow); avoid peak hours, and keep an eye on your possessions

Barrackpur and Hugli District → *25 km north of Kolkata.*

The riverside Gandhi Ghat has a museum and there is a pleasant garden in memory of Jawaharlal Nehru. The bronze Raj statues removed from their pedestals in Central Kolkata after Independence have found their way to the gardens of the bungalow of the former governor (now a hospital) in Barrackpur. The tower was part of the river signalling system.

Many European nations had outposts along the River Hugli. Hugli District has a rich history. When the Mughals lost power, several of the ancient seats of earlier rulers of Bengal became centres of foreign trade. The Portuguese and British settled at Hugli, the

Srirampur (Serampore) → *24 km north of Kolkata.*

Founded by the Danes in 1616 as Fredricnagore, Serampore, a garden city, became a Danish colony in 1755. From the early 19th century it was the centre of missionary activity, until sold to the East India Company in 1845. The Government House, two churches and a Danish cemetery remain. **College of Textile Technology** ① *12 Carey Rd, 1000-1630 (Sat 1000-1300).* The Baptist missionaries **Carey**, **Marshman** and **Ward** came to Serampore since they were not welcomed by the English administrators in Calcutta. They set up the Baptist Mission Press, which by 1805 was printing in seven Indian languages. **Serampore College** (1818) ① *Mon-Fri 1000-1600, Sat 1000-1300, with permission from the principal,* India's first Christian Theological college, was allowed to award degrees by the Danish king in 1829. The library has rare Sanskrit, Pali and Tibetan manuscripts and the Bible in over 40 Asian languages.

Chandernagore

The former French colony, which dates back to 1673, was one of the tiny pockets of non-British India that did not gain Independence in 1947, but was handed over to India after a referendum in 1950. The churches, convents and cemeteries of the French are still there, although the old French street names have been replaced by Bengali. The former Quai de Dupleix, with its riverfront benches, still has a somewhat Gallic air. The Bhubanesvari and Nandadulal **temples** are worth visiting, especially during *Jagaddhatri Puja*. **Institute Chandernagar** ① *Mon-Sat except Thu 1600-1830, Sun 1100-11700,* at the **Residency** has interesting documents and relics of the French in India. The orange-painted Italian missionary **church** (1726) also stands witness to Chandernagore's European past.

Chinsura and Hugli

The Dutch acquired Chinsura from the Nawab of Murshidabad in 1628 and built the **Fort Gustavus**, but it was exchanged with Sumatra (Indonesia) and became British in 1825. The octagonal **Dutch church** (1678) with its cemetery nearby, a 17th-century Armenian church and three East India Company barracks remain. The Dutch are still remembered at the **Shandesvar Siva temple** on special occasions, when the lingam is bizarrely decked in Western clothes and a Dutch sword!

The Portuguese set up a factory in Hugli in 1537 but Emperor Shah Jahan took the important trading post in 1632. The East India Company built their factory in 1651, destroyed in skirmishes marking the following six years, but Clive regained Hugli for the Company in 1757.

The Shi'a **Imambara** of Hazi Mohammed Mohasin (1836-1876) has fine marble inlay decoration, a silver pulpit and elaborate lanterns. In **Chota Pandua** nearby, interesting Muslim buildings include the ruins of the 14th-century Bari Masjid with elements of Buddhist sculpture. In Rajbalhat, the **Amulya Pratnasala Museum** ① *closed 2nd and 4th Tue, Wed 1400-2100,* shows sculpture, coins, terracottas and manuscripts.

Bandel

Bandel (Portuguese *bandar* or wharf) is now a railway junction town. The Portuguese built **Bandel Church** to Our Lady of the Rosary around 1660, on the site of an older Augustinian monastery. The keystone of the original church (1599), perhaps the earliest in Bengal, is on the riverside gate. Destroyed in 1640 by Shah Jahan, the church was reinstated 20 years later. The seafaring Portuguese believed that the statue of Our Lady of Happy Voyages in the bell tower could work miracles. Lost in the river, while being carried to save it from Shah Jahan's soldiers, it miraculously reappeared two centuries later. The 18th-century stone and terracotta **Hanseswari Temple** is 4 km away.

Tribeni and Pandua

Originally *Saptagram* (seven villages), **Tribeni** (three rivers) is particularly holy, being at the confluence of the Ganga, Saraswati and Kunti. It has many Hindu temples and 11th- to 12th-century Vaishnavite and Buddhist structures. The remains of the **Mazar of Zafarkhan Ghazi** (1313), the earliest mausoleum in eastern India, shows how black basalt sculpture and columns of earlier Hindu temples and palaces were incorporated into Muslim buildings. **Pandua** (Hugli District) has several remains of the Pala and Sena periods. Shah Sufi-ud-din is thought to have built the 39 m **Victory Tower** after defeating the local Hindu ruler in 1340. Its circular base had a court house. Outside, a staircase spirals up the fluted surface, while inside there is enamelled decoration. Hoards of Kushana and Gupta Dynasty gold coins have been found in nearby **Mahanad**.

Kalna

The town north of Pandua, centred on the Maharaja of Burdwan's palace, has several fine 18th-century terracotta temples. Look for the Ramayana scenes on the large Lalji (1739), Krishna panels on the Krishnachandra (1752), assorted friezes on the Ananta Vasudeva (1754) and the later Pratapesvara (1849). Across the way is the unusual circular Siva temple (1809) with 108 small double-vaulted shrines. Kalna has trains from Kolkata and rickshaws at the station, 3 km from the temples.

Nabadwip

The birthplace of Sri Chaitanya, see page 92, is a pilgrimage centre for his followers and the river ghats are lined with temples where devotees worship by singing *keertans* and *bhajans*. **ISKCON** (International Society for Krishna Consciousness) has its Chandrodaya Mandir at **Mayapur** ① *until 1300*, across the river. Nabadwip has trains from Sealdah and Haora, and ferries across to Mayapur.

⬤ Sleeping

Watch out for 10% luxury tax, 10% service charge and 20% expenditure tax. Medium price and budget hotels attracting foreigners are concentrated in the Sudder St area. Mid-priced hotels often have a few a/c rooms but may not have a generator and so have power cuts, especially in summer. For telephone number changes T1952 (dial old number to get new). 'Ask Me', T033-2474 6363, advises on local affairs/numbers/addresses etc.

Central Kolkata *p61, maps p62, p64, p71 and p72*
LL Oberoi Grand, 15 JL Nehru, T033-2249 2323, www.oberoihotels.com. Atmospheric Victorian building opposite the Maidan, exquisitely restored, suites have giant 4 posters, tea lounge, excellent restaurants including Thai, lovely pool for guests.
LL Park, 17 Park St, T033-2249 9000, www.theparkhotels.com. Trendy designer hotel, good restaurants, health club, nightclubs, 24-hr café, service can be disappointing, entrance themed on underground car park.
LL Taj Bengal, 34B Belvedere Rd, Alipore, T033-2223 3939, www.tajhotels.com. Opulent and modern, restaurants are plush, imaginative, intimate, with good food (ground floor Indian cheaper than 5th floor), leisurely service (unusual Bengali breakfast), *Khazana* shop for excellent textiles, *Baluchari* saris, *kantha* embroidery etc.
L New Kenilworth, 1-2 Little Russell St, T033-2282 3939, www.kenilworth hotels.com. 105 well appointed rooms with good buffet breakfast and coffee shop (excellent lunch buffet), English-style pub, quiet. Recommended.
AL Golden Park, 13 Ho Chi Minh Sarani, T033-2288 3939. Boutique hotel, 78 rooms with all facilities including pool and health club, restaurants.

⬤ *For an explanation of the sleeping and eating price codes used in this guide, see the inside*
⬤ *front cover. Other relevant information is found on pages 35-39.*

AL Lytton, 14 Sudder St, T033-2249 1872, www.lyttonhotelindia.com. Comfortable, tastefully furnished rooms, better in new block, good restaurants, bar, efficient, good value.

AL-A Housez 43, 43 Mirza Ghalib St, T033-2227 6021, rmehrotra@connectworld.co.in. New "value boutique" hotel making slightly wide-of-the-mark attempt at trendy, nice public areas with beanbags, well-presented rooms, pleasant staff.

A Lindsay, 8-A Lindsay St, T033-2252 2237, hotellindsay@vsnl.net. Recently refurbished hotel towering over New Market, **Blue & Beyond** restaurant with panoramic city views.

Around Sudder Street

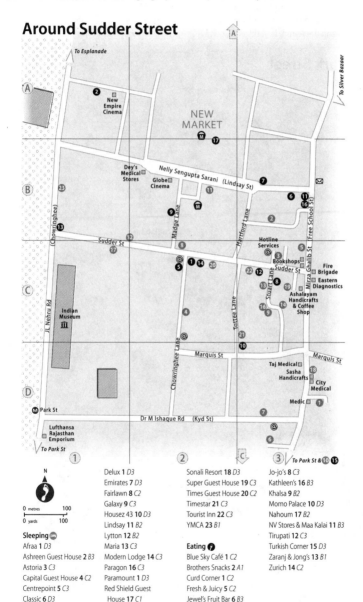

B Astor, 15 Shakespeare Sarani, T033-2282 9950. Comfortable a/c rooms with bath tubs (inferior annexe), open-air restaurant. Gives off-season discounts.

B Fairlawn, 13A Sudder St, T033-2252 1510, www.fairlawnhotel.com. 20 a/c old-fashioned rooms (US$50 full board), semi-formal meals at set times. The hotel and management provide a throwback to the Raj, bric-a-brac everywhere, quite a place and the terrace is good for a beer.

B Middleton Inn, 10 Middleton St, T033-2216 0449, mchamber@vsnl.net. Pleasantly furnished a/c rooms with hot bath (fridge, TV), not particularly spacious though spotlessly clean, original art, quiet and convenient, breakfast included. Recommended.

B-C Kenilworth, 7 Little Russell St, T033-2282 5325. The "original" Kenilworth provides old-world comforts in enormous colonial rooms with antique furnishings. Bit faded but atmospheric, away from tourist scene.

Park Street

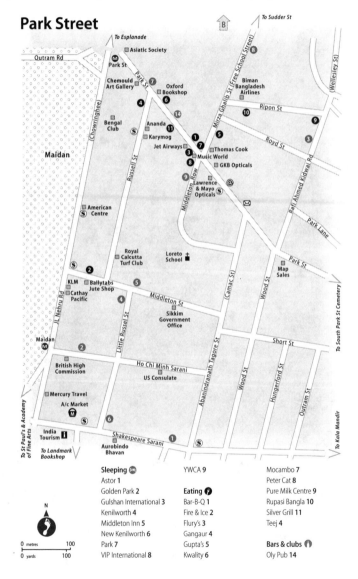

Sleeping
Astor 1
Golden Park 2
Gulshan International 3
Kenilworth 4
Middleton Inn 5
New Kenilworth 6
Park 7
VIP International 8

YWCA 9

Eating
Bar-B-Q 1
Fire & Ice 2
Flury's 3
Gangaur 4
Gupta's 5
Kwality 6

Mocambo 7
Peter Cat 8
Pure Milk Centre 9
Rupasi Bangla 10
Silver Grill 11
Teej 4

Bars & clubs
Oly Pub 14

B-C VIP International, 51 Mirza Ghalib St, T033-2229 6495, www.hotelvipgroups.com. A/c rooms, clean and comfortable, hot bath, friendly efficient staff make up for a drab hotel.

C Astoria Hotel, 6 Sudder St, near fire station, T033-2252 2241. Offers 41 rooms of various standards.

C Gulshan International, 21B Royd St, T033-2229 0566. Efficient staff, 16 clean, comfortable rooms, complimentary breakfast.

D YMCA, 25 Jl Nehru Rd, T033-2249 2192, www.calcuttaymca.org. 17 rooms, including 2 a/c, with bath, in large, rambling colonial building, run down but clean linen, check room first, some better than others. Helpful staff, rates include breakfast.

D-E Super Guest House, 30A Mirza Ghalib St, T033-2252 0995, super_guesthouse@ hotmail.com. This super guest house has the only truly spotless rooms in the area, a/c with hot bath, friendly management.

E Crystal, 11/1 Kyd St, T033-2226 6400, hcrystal@vsnl.net. Good, clean rooms (mostly a/c), phone and TV, those on top floor are light and airy (and cheaper).

E Delux, B/33/H/4 Mirza Ghalib St, 3rd floor, T033-2229 2703. Tucked away, friendly staff, 8 small but clean rooms with bath.

E Shilton, 5A Sudder St, T033-2252 1512, shiltoncal@hotmail.com. 27 decent-sized rooms with bath, some triples, clean.

E YWCA, 1 Middleton Row, T033-2229 2494. Nice old airy colonial building with good atmosphere, but students only. Some rooms with bath, dorm, very friendly staff. Rates include breakfast, alcohol forbidden, a pleasant oasis in the city. A recommended alternative to Sudder St.

E-F Emirates, 11/1 Kyd St, T033-2217 8487. Fresh, bright rooms in a building with character, a/c and non-a/c rooms, good standard, pleasant terrace.

E-G Afraa, B/33/H/3 Mirza Ghalib St, 3rd floor, T033-2217 7222. Clean, small rooms, TV, ask for one with a window, friendly place.

F Ashreen Guest House, 2 Cowie Lane, T033-2252 0889, ashreen_guesthouse@yahoo .com. Modern rooms of excellent standard, ideal place to break yourself into Kolkata gently, super-friendly staff, book ahead.

F Capital Guest House, 11B Chowringhee Lane, T033-2252 0598. Not a bad place, tucked away from the road, relatively quiet.

F Galaxy, 3 Stuart Lane, T033-2252 4565. 4 good rooms with attached bath and TV, decent choice but often full. Try at around 1030 just after checkout.

F Sonali Resort, 21A Mirza Ghalib St, T033-2252 3223. Good choice, with 13 good, clean rooms with bath and TV.

F-G Centrepoint, 20 Mirza Ghalib St, T033-2252 8184, ian_rashid@yahoo.com. Decent enough small rooms, some a/c, clean sheets and bath, grubby carpet, dorm (Rs 75), best for long stays.

F-G Maria, 5/1 Sudder St, T033-2252 0860. 24 clean, basic rooms (hard beds), some with bath, dorm (Rs 70), internet, shared TV, pleasant staff. Popular budget place.

G Classic, 6/1A Kyd St, T033-2227 6386. 18 clean rooms (some a/c), some with bath, singles with shared bath.

G Modern Lodge, 1 Stuart Lane, T033-2252 4960. Very popular, almost always full with long-term volunteers, 14 rooms, attached or shared bath, breezy rooftop, lounge, quirky staff, no reservations so try at 1000.

G Paragon, 2 Stuart Lane, T033-2252 2445. 45 rooms and dorms (Rs 80/100 with shared/private bath), some tiny but clean. Water heater to fill buckets. Open communal spaces, friendly but indifferent management, popular with backpackers.

G Paramount, 33/4 Mirza Ghalib St, T033-2229 0066. Clean rooms with bath and TV, helpful staff, brighter than many others.

G Red Shield Guest House, 2 Sudder St, T033-2286 1659. Characterful building and a good place to stay (popular with Mother Teresa volunteers). 7 modest rooms, some with bath, varying rates, cramped bumper to bumper 6- and 10-bedded dorms (Rs 70/ Rs 75), TV/sitting room, lights out at 2200.

G Times Guest House, 3 Sudder St, T033-2252 1796. Get a room at the front with balcony to view the action on the street below. Atmospheric, jolly staff.

G Timestar, 2 Tottee Lane, T033-225 2 8028. Reasonable airy rooms, some with proper windows attached bath. Singles to 4-bedded, TV optional.

G Tourist Inn, 4/1 Sudder St, T033-2252 9818. Has 9 small, clean rooms with common bath, rooftop catches the precious breeze.

LL Hindusthan International, 235/1 AJC Bose Rd, T033-2283 0505 www.hindu sthan.com. 212 rooms on 8 floors, railway 10 km, good buffet lunches and almost cool bar, popular Underground nightclub, pool (non-residents Rs 300).
D New Haven Guest House, 19B Ritchie Rd, T033-2475 4097. Simply furnished, cleanish rooms with bath, small front garden, only breakfast, residential area with good *dhaba* and Chinese restaurants within around 10 mins' walk.

Around Kolkata *p68*

The following are in Nabadwip.
E-G ISKCON Guesthouse, some with bath, a/c, inexpensive 4-6 bed dorm, cheap meals.
F Indrajit, rooms with bath and restaurant.
F Trimurti, rooms with bath and restaurant.
G Akintak Kutir is basic.
G Baishakhi, some rooms with bath.

Eating

Thursdays are traditionally 'meatless' days and in smaller places only chicken and fish are available. Licensed restaurants serve alcohol (some are no longer pleasant places to eat in since the emphasis is on drink). Be prepared for a large surcharge for live (or even recorded) music. This, plus taxes, can double the price on the menu. Many restaurants outside hotels do not accept credit cards. Special Bengali sweets are made fresh every afternoon at thousands of sweet shops (1600-1730): try *shingaras, kochuris* and *nimkis*.

BBD Bagh and around *p61, map p64*

Baan Thai, Oberoi Grand, T033-2249 2323. Excellent selection, imaginative decor, some Thai-style seating on floor.
Aaheli at Peerless Inn, T033-2228 0301. Excellent, unusual menu of Bengali specialities, comfortable a/c, fairly pricey.
Amber, 11 Waterloo St, T033-2248 3477. North Indian and continental. 3 floors of gourmet delights (try tandoori), generous helpings, fast service, **Essence** on 2nd floor fancies itself as a cocktail bar. Recommended.
Anand, 19 Chittaranjan Av, closed Wed. Great South Indian. Mammoth dosas, all-vegetarian. Possible queues at busy times.

Around Sudder Street *p64, map p71*

Zaranj and **Jong's**, 26 JL Nehru Rd. Adjacent restaurants, both tasteful, stylish, subdued decor, excellent food. Try *pudina paratha, murgh makhani*, tandoori fish in Zaranj, or delectable Burmese fare in Jong's.
Gupta's, 53C Mirza Ghalib St, T033-2229 6541. Good Indian and Chinese. Small, intimate, softly lit, low ceilings (beware of fans!), try paneer and *bekti tikka*.
Jimmy's, 14D Lindsay St. Chinese. Small, a/c, good *momos*, Szechuan dishes, ice cream. Alcohol served.
Blue Sky Café, 3 Sudder St. Chiefly Western. Very popular budget travellers' meeting place, a/c, always full and cramped, good food.
Curd Corner, Sudder St. Very small but popular, excellent breakfast.
Fresh and Juicy, Chowringhee Lane. Snug space for a sociable breakfast with some of the best coffee around, reasonably authentic Indian meals, attracts a loyal following.
Jewels Fruit Bar, 12B Lindsay St. Good for South Indian snacks and dosas, good summer retreat with blasting a/c in upstairs section.
Jo-jo's, Stuart Lane. Average Indian snacks and meals but superb juices, first floor a/c, good escape during summer.
Khalsa, 4C Madge Lane. Excellent lassi, Western breakfasts, Indian mains, all super-cheap, beyond excellent service from utterly charming Sikh owners. No smoking.
Momo Palace, 1B Tottee Lane. The tiniest palace imaginable, but fabulous soups, hakka noodles and momos.
NV Stores and Maa Kali, 12/2 Lindsay St. Stand-up street stalls making surprisingly good sandwiches from any possible combination of ingredients; great lassis too.
Rupasi Bangla, 1/1C Ripon St. Excellent vegetarian and non-vegetarian Bengali dishes; try begun nohey bari and palong monohari. Delivery to hotel room available.
Tirupati, street stall next to Hotel Maria. A Sudder Street institution; find a perch on the busy benches and enjoy enormous helpings of food from every continent.
Turkish Corner, 43 Mirza Ghalib St. Range of superb kebabs, the best of which is the felafel sandwich. Standing room only, but they'll deliver on orders over Rs 200.
Zurich, 3 Sudder St. Attempts a café atmosphere, reliable snacks and breakfasts, often full, portions can be a bit niggardly.

Park Street *p65, map p72*

Visitors craving Western fast food will find plenty of familiar names in this area.

♔♔ Bar-B-Q, 43 Park St, T033-2229 9169. Always popular, always delicious; bar.

♔♔ Fire and Ice, Kanak Building, Middleton St, T033-2288 4073. Pizzas here are the real deal, service is excellent, and the ambience is relaxing. Definitely worth it.

♔♔ Flury's, 18 Park St. Classic Kolkata venue with hit-and-miss Western menu, but pastries and afternoon tea are winners and the bakery has brown bread.

♔♔ Gangaur, 2 Russell St. A wide menu of Indian delights, if you can resist the superb Rs 100 *thali* (1130-1530). Afterwards you can head next door for Bengali sweets.

♔♔ Kwality, 21 Park St and 2 Gariahat Rd. Famous for ice creams at Park Street, but also for excellent Indian and continental, usually crowded, pleasant old-time feel.

♔♔ Mocambo, 25B Park St. International. A/c, pleasant lighting, highly descriptive menu. Longstanding reliable favourite.

♔♔ Peter Cat, T033-2229 8841, 18A Park St (entrance on Middleton Row). International. Good kebabs and sizzlers, hilarious menu of cheap cocktails, pleasant ambience but can rush you out on busy weekend nights.

♔♔ Silver Grill, 18E Park St, T033-2229 4549. Chinese. Extensive menu, specialities *Limkai* chicken, Thai prawns, slightly shabby setting with red leather seats.

♔♔ Teej, 2 Russell St, T033-2217 0730. Pure vegetarian Rajasthani delights washed down with cold beer, colourful *haveli*-esque setting.

South Kolkata *p68, map p62*

♔♔♔ Chinoiserie, Taj Bengal, T033-2223 3939. Good for a splurge on excellent Chinese.

♔♔♔ Mainland China, 3A Gurusaday Rd, T033-2283 7964. Sublime Chinese. Unusual offerings, especially fish and seafood, tastefully decorated with burnished ceiling and wall mural, pleasant ambience, courteous. Book ahead.

♔♔♔ Soho, Ideal Plaza, 11/1 Sarat Bose Rd, T033-2289 6059. Slick new outfit serving mainly Mediterranean cuisine, good wine list, Sunday brunch buffet (Rs 350) with North Indian and mezze choices, Soho bar and club next door.

♔♔ Kewpie's, 2 Elgin Lane (between Elgin and Heysham rds), T033-2475 9880. Tue-Sun 1200-1500, 1730-2245. Authentic Bengali, home cooking at its best, add on special

dishes to basic *thali* (Rs 200), unusual fish and vegetarian. Few tables in rooms in a residence, a/c, sells recipe book. Highly recommended, reserve in advance.

♔♔ Pappi's Only Parathas, 1 AJC Bose Rd. This pure vegetarian enterprise offers every possible combination of vegetable and paratha. The menu has over 100 delicious choices.

♔ Banana Leaf, 73-75 Rash Behari Av. Vegetarian South Indian, top-notch dosas and thalis plus superb mini-iddli and even decent coffee.

♔ South India Club canteen, 70B Hindustan Park (off Rash Behari Av). An authentic taste of the South serving full meals for Rs 35, and a good place to experiment with less commonly seen dishes such as pongal or upma. Strange hours (Mon-Sat 0700-1100, 1400-2130, Sun 0700-1200, 1500-2130), but recommended.

Other areas

Connoisseurs of Chinese cuisine go to South Tangra Rd off EM bypass, east of the city centre. Eateries are basic – formica-top tables, etc – and the approach is none too picturesque, past tanneries and open drains, but they serve excellent food.

♔♔ Ka Fu Lok and **Sin Fa**, do excellent soups, jumbo prawns and honey chicken, best to go early (1200 for lunch, 2000 for dinner).

♔♔ Lily's Kitchen, try garlic chicken, sweet and sour fish, chop suey, steamed fish (40 mins), very generous so order half plates.

Coffee shops

Ashalayam, 44 Mirza Ghalib St. Peaceful oasis run by NGO, sells handicrafts made by street children.

Indian Coffee House, College St (see page 67).

Confectionery

Kathleen's, several branches, including 12 Mirza Ghalib St, corner of Lord Sinha Rd.

Kookie Jar, Rawdon St. One of the best, though pricey.

Nahoum, F20, New Market. Good pastries, cakes, savouries.

Nepal Sweets, 16B Sarat Bose Rd. Very good for *chandrakala*, almond *pista barfi*, mango *roshogolla*, *kheer mohan* (also savouries).

Pure Milk Centre, near Rafi Ahmed Kidwai St/ Ripon St corner. Good sweet 'curd' (*mishti doi*). Excellent hot *roshogollas*. Get there early.

Kati-rolls

Kati-rolls (tender kebabs wrapped in *parathas*) are hard to beat. Try mutton/chicken egg roll (if you don't want raw onions and green chillis, order "no piaaz e mirchi").

Brothers Snacks, 1 Humayun Place, New Market. Safe, tasty bet with outdoor seats. **Rehmania** and **Shiraz**, both on Park St/AJC Bose Rd corner. Muslim joints famed for their mutton rolls and kebabs.

Bars and clubs

Kolkata *p61, maps p62, p64, p71 and p72*
Bars
The larger hotels have pleasant bars and upmarket restaurants serve alcohol. The top hotels are well stocked, luxurious but pricey. In Sudder St, **Fairlawn's** pleasant garden terrace is popular at dusk attracting anyone seeking a chilled beer, while **Lyttons** is also open to thirsty travellers from neighbouring hotels. **Super Pub Bar**, Sudder St, is always busy and sociable, but expect gruff service and check your change. The 9th floor bar at the **Lindsay Hotel** has good views over New Market and Kolkata. Independent bars, open usually until 2230, lack atmosphere; some are positively men only. The bar at the **New Empire Cinema**, between New Market and Chowringhee, is more pleasant than most. **Oly Pub**, 21 Park St, is an institution: very smoky, very noisy, serves steak and eggs, no women allowed downstairs.

Clubs
Some are affiliated to a number of Indian and foreign clubs including Royal Overseas League, Travellers, St-James's, National Liberal, Oxford and Cambridge Universities. To use the facilities you need to be a member of these clubs, or the guest of a local member.
Bengal Club, 1/1 Russell St, T033-2249 9443, the former house of Lord Macaulay, has an excellent dining room.
Tollygunge Club, 120 DP Sasmal Rd, T033-2473 2316. Built on an old indigo plantation, 18-hole golf course, riding, tennis, pool, away from centre, atmosphere and location make up for average rooms and restaurant.

Entertainment

Kolkata *p61, maps p62, p64, p71 and p72*
Calcutta: This Fortnight is distributed free by **West Bengal Tourist Office**. The English language dailies (Telegraph, *Times of India* etc) carry a comprehensive list. *CalCalling* is a monthly listings booklet available from **Oxford Book Shop**, Park St. Rs 20.

Cinema
A/c and comfortable cinemas showing English language films are a good escape from the heat, and many are still very cheap. Check the newspapers for timings, programmes change every Fri. **Elite**, SN Banerjee Rd, **Globe**, Lindsay St, and **New Empire Cinema**, New Market St, are all conveniently close to Sudder St. **Nandan Complex**, AJC Bose Rd, T033-2223 1210, shows classics and art house movies; entrants in Kolkata International Film Festival (Nov) are screened here. Swish **Inox** multiplexes (www.inoxmovies.com) are scattered around town; tickets for these are Rs 100-150 and can be booked by credit card over the phone.

Dance, music, theatre and art
Regular performances at **Rabindra Sadan**, Cathedral Rd. **Kala Mandir**, 48 Shakespeare Sarani. **Gorky Sadan**, Gorky Terrace, near Minto Park. **Sisir Mancha**, 1/1 AJC Bose Rd. Some of these also hold art exhibition as at **Academy of Fine Arts**, Cathedral Rd, and **Ramakrishna Mission**, Golpark. **Seagull Arts and Media Centre**, 36C SP Mukherjee Rd, T033-2455 6492, www.seagullindia.com, holds regular photography exhibitions. You can see Bengali theatre of a high standard at **Biswaroopa**, 2A Raja Raj Kissen St and **Star Theatre**, 79/34 Bidhan Sarani.

Discos and nightclubs
Sheesha, 22 Camac St. Dark and stylish with expensive hookahs adding to the chilled atmosphere.
Soho, Ideal Plaza, 11/1 Sarat Bose Rd. Becoming the place to be seen, with a curved bar, funky lighting, a good mix of Western and Hindi tunes and flatscreen TVs showing big sporting events. Open until 0200 Fri and Sat.

⦂ Worship of the clay goddess

Durga Puja, the 17th-century festival in honour of the clay goddess, precedes the full moon in late September/early October, when all offices and institutions close down and the Metro only operates from the late afternoon.

Images of the 10-armed, three-eyed goddess, a form of Shakti or Kali (see page 303) astride her 'vehicle' the lion, portray Durga slaying Mahisasura, the evil buffalo demon. Durga, shown with her four children Lakshmi, Sarasvati, Ganesh and Kartik, is worshipped in hundreds of brightly illuminated and beautifully decorated *pandals* (marquees) made of bamboo and coloured cloth. The priests perform prayers at appointed times in the morning and evening. On the fourth and last day of festivities, huge and often emotionally charged processions follow devotees who carry the clay figures to be immersed in the river at many points along the banks. The potters return to collect clay from the river bank once again for the following year.

You can see the imagemakers in Kumartuli (see page 66) a few days earlier and visit the pandals early in the evening, before they become crowded. Local communities are immensely proud of their pandals and no effort is spared to put on the most impressive display. The images are decorated with intricate silver, golden or shola (white pith) ornaments, there are moving electric light displays and huge structures are built (sometimes resembling a temple) in order to win competitions. The WB Tourist Bureau offers an all-night bus tour (Rs 50) as well as a two-hour launch trip on the Hugli to watch the immersion ceremony on the last night.

At hotels (see Sleeping, above) **Incognito** (Taj Bengal). Understated, relaxed ambience, 30-plus crowd, good food, taped music, fussy dress codes (closed Mon). **Someplace Else** (Park). Pub, live bands favoured by the young. **Tantra** (Park). Taped music, large floor, young crowd, no shorts or flip-flops, cover charge. Next door **Roxy** is less popular, but has free entry and is more relaxed. **Underground** (Hindustan International). Good live band, young crowd, good sizzlers, pool tables.

Performing arts

English language productions staged by **British Council** and theatre clubs. **Sangeet Research Academy**, near Tollygunge Metro station, a national centre for training in Indian Classical music, stages free concert on Wed evenings. **Rabindra Bharati University**, 6/4 Dwarakanath Tagore Lane, holds performances, particularly during the winter, including singing, dancing and *jatras*. *Jatra* is community theatre, highly colourful and exaggerated both in delivery and make-up, drawing for its subject romantic favourites from mythology or more up to date social, political and religious themes.

⊛ Festivals and events

Kolkata p61, maps p62, p64, p71 and p72
See also Essentials, page 40.
Jan Ganga Sagar Mela, Sagar, 105 km south of Kolkata, where the Hugli joins the sea, draws thousands of Hindu pilgrims. See page 111.
Mar/Apr Holi (Dol Purnima), spring festival.
Jun-Jul The Ratha Yatra at Mahesh, nearby.
Sep-Oct Durga Puja, Bengal's celebration of the goddess during Dasara. See box, above.
Oct-Nov Diwali (*Kali Puja* in Bengal) is the festival of lights.
Dec Christmas. Numerous churches hold special services, including Midnight Mass, and the New Market takes on a new look in Dec as **Barra Din** (Big Day) approaches with temporary stalls selling trees and baubles. Other religious festivals are observed as elsewhere in India.

O Shopping

Kolkata *p61, maps p62, p64, p71 and p72*
Most shops open 1000-1730 or later
(some break for lunch) weekdays,
1000-1300 on Sat.

Art

Artists' Circle, 46 Circus Av, T033-2283 3176.
Interesting exhibitions by emerging artists.
Centre Art Gallery, 87C Park St. Mainly
works by Bengali artists.
Centre for International Modern Art
(**CIMA**), Sunny Towers, 43 Ashutosh
Chowdhury Av, www.cimaartindia.com.
Diverse exhibitions and excellent shop.
Chemould Art Gallery, 12F Park St. One
of the big names in contemporary art,
and worth keeping an eye on.
Galerie 88, 28B Shakespeare Sarani, www.
galerie88.in. Contemporary art (1200-2000).

Books

College St, a wealth of second-hand
pavement bookstalls along this street mainly
for students but may reveal an interesting
first edition for a keen collector (see page 66).
Crossword, Elgin Rd. Deservedly popular
chain store, with 2 floors of books, CDs
and films and a busy coffee shop.
Kolkata Book Fair, check venue with tourist
office. End of Jan for a fortnight, stalls sell
paperback fiction to antiquarian books.
Landmark, top floor, Emami Centre, Lord
Sinha Rd. A great selection of fiction.
Mirza Ghalib St has a string of small shops
selling new, used and photocopied versions
of current favourites. Bargaining required.
Oxford Book Shop, Park St. Huge selection
of new English titles, some films, tiny café.
Seagull, 31A SP Mukherjee Rd. Amazing
stock of art-related coffee table books.

Clothes and accessories

Ananda, 13 Russell St. Fancy saris.
Ballytubs Jute Shop, 5 Middleton St.
Unique, delightfully decorated bags in jute.
Fabindia, 16 Hindustan Park (also branches
at Woodburn Park, and City Centre Mall in
Salt Lake). 1000-2000. Clothes, textiles and
home furnishings from fair trade company.
Hotline Services, 7 Sudder St. Traveller
wear, plus a range of scarves and throws.
Monapali, 15 Louden St. Designer *salwar*.

Ogaan, P545 Lake Rd Extn. High quality
clothes including swimwear and lingerie.
Ritu's Boutique, 46A Rafi Ahmed Kidwai
Rd. A good place to find *kurtas* and saris.
Taj Bengal arcade. For pricey leather goods.

Government emporia

Government emporia are mainly in the town
centre and are fixed price shops. Several at
Dakshinapan, near Dhakuria Bridge, Mon-
Fri 1030-1930, Sat 1030-1400, convenient,
excellent selection of handloom and
handicrafts. **Central Cottage Industries**,
7 JL Nehru Rd. **Kashmir Art**, 12 JL Nehru Rd.
Phulkari, Punjab Emporium, 26B Camac St.
Rajasthali, 30E JL Nehru Rd. **Tripura**, 58 JL
Nehru Rd. **UP**, 12B Lindsay St.

Handicrafts and handloom

There are many handicraft shops around
New Market, selling batik prints, handloom,
blockprints and embroidery, but starting
prices are usually excessive so bargain hard.
Shops listed below are all either fair trade-
based or associated with self-help groups.
Ashalayam Handicrafts, 1st floor, 44 Mirza
Ghalib St. Products made by street children
who have been trained and given shelter by
the Don Bosco Ashalayam Project. Proceeds
are split between the artisans and the trust.
Bengal Home Industries Association,
11 Camac St. Good selection of printed
cotton (bedspreads, saris) and assorted
knick-knacks. Relaxed, fixed price.
Calcutta Rescue Handicrafts, at Modern
Lodge (Wed) and Fairlawn Hotel (Thu (1830-
1930). Medical NGO sells great selection of
cards, bags and trinkets made by patients.
Karma Kutir, 32 Ballygunge Place.
Excellent embroidered clothes.
Karmyog, 12B Russell St. Gorgeous
handcrafted paper products.
Sasha, 27 Mirza Ghalib St, www.sasha
world.com. Attractive, good-quality, fair trade
textiles, furnishings in contemporary a/c space.

Jewellery

Bepin Behari Ganguly St (Bow Bazar)
is lined with mirrored jewellers' shops;
PC Chandra, **BB Dutt**, **B Sirkar** are well
known. Also many on Rash Behari Av.
Silver market (Rupa Bajar) is off Mirza Ghalib
St opposite New Market. Gold and silver
prices are listed daily in the newspapers.

Markets

New Market, Lindsay St, behind the original Hogg Market (largely rebuilt since a fire in 1985 and recently revamped), has over 2500 shops. It used to be said that you could buy anything from a needle to an elephant (on order) in one of its stalls. Today it's still worth a visit; come early morning to watch it come alive. You will find mundane everyday necessities to exotic luxuries, from fragrant florists to gory meat stalls. Be prepared to deal with pestering basket-wallahs.

For conventional shopping try a/c **Market**, Shakespeare Sarani; **The Forum**, Elgin Rd; **City Centre**, Salt Lake; and **Planet M** on Camac St.

Kolkata has a number of **bazars**, each with a character of its own. In **Bentinck St** are Muslim tailors, Chinese shoemakers interspersed with Indian sweetmeat shops and tea stalls. **Gariahat** market early in the morning attracts a diverse clientele (businessmen, academics, cooks) who come to select choice fresh fish. In **Shyambazar** the coconut market starts business at 0500 and ends by 0700. Burra Bazar is a hectic wholesale fruit market held daily. The colourful flower market is on **Jagannath Ghat** on the river bank. The old **China Bazar** no longer exists although Tiretta Bazar area still retains its ethnic flavour; try an exceptional Chinese breakfast from a street stall.

Music

Music World, 18G Park St, T033-2217 0751. Sells a wide range of all genres.

Tailors

Garments can be skilfully copied around New Market and on Madge Lane. Tailors will try to overcharge foreigners as a matter of course.

▲ Activities and tours

Kolkata *p61, maps p62, p64, p71 and p72*
Body and soul
Aurobindo Bhavan, 8 Shakespeare Sarani, T033-2282 3057. Informal drop-in classes for men and women (separate classes), 3 times a week. Phone for times.
Satyananda Yoga Kendra, 20 South End Park, Golpark, T033-2463 8191. Offers 2- and 3-week courses (3 morning and 5 evening sessions a week) plus chanting on Sat afternoons, in a pleasant peaceful environment, but somewhat inconvenient for city centre.

Look out for adverts around Sudder St for informal yoga classes held on hotel rooftops.

Cricket
Occasional Test matches and One Day Internationals at Eden Gardens, see page 63, 100,000 capacity; get tickets in advance.

Football
The season starts in May and continues through the monsoons. The club grounds are on the Maidan (try **East Bengal Football Club**, T033-2248 4642).

Golf
Several courses including:
Royal Calcutta Golf Club, 18 Golf Club Rd, T033-2473 1352. Founded in 1829, the oldest golf club in the world outside the UK. It moved to its present course in 1910 having taken the radical step of admitting women in 1886.
The Tollygunge Club, 120 Despran Sasmal Rd, T033-2473 5954. The course is on land that was once an indigo plantation.

Horse racing
Royal Calcutta Turf Club, T033-2229 1104. Racing takes place in the cool season (Nov to early Apr) and monsoon (Jun-Oct); tote, bookmakers available. The Derby is in the first week of Jan.

Sightseeing tours
WBTDC Tours, departure point is Tourism Centre, 3/2 BBD Bagh E, 1st floor, T033-2248 8271. Daily tours, 0830-1730, Rs 150 in non a/c bus, Rs 200 in a car for 4-5 passengers. Tour stops at: Eden Gardens, High Court, Writers' Building, Belur Math, Dakshineswar Kali Temple, Jain Temple, Netaji Bhavan, Kolkata Panorama and Esplanade, Victoria Memorial, St Paul's Cathedral and Kali Ghat. Entry fees not included. Private tour operators also offer city tours. Approved guides from Govt of India Tourist Office, T033-2582 5813.

Swimming
Hindustan International hotel pool is open to non-residents (Rs 300).

Best deals in air tickets to/from the East (through Bangkok) are offered by agents in the Sudder St area (about US$120).
Help Tourism, Sadananda Kothi (1st floor), 67A Kali Temple Rd, Kalighat, T033-2455 0917, www.helptourism.com. Wide variety of wildlife and adventure tours. Recommended.
American Express, 21 Old Court House St, T033-2248 6181. **Mercury**, 46 JL Nehru Rd, T033-2288 3554. **Thomas Cook**, 198 Chitrakut (2nd floor), Shakespeare Sarani, T033-2283 0473. **Travel Planners**, 7 Red Cross Pl, T033-2443 5138. Recommended.

Volunteer work

Many people come to Kolkata to work as volunteers for an NGO. The following organizations happily accept volunteers, though it's wise to contact them in advance.
Calcutta Stations Mission, www.calcutta stationsmission.com. A new NGO providing food relief and medical care to disadvantaged communities in various parts of the city.
Don Bosco Ashalayam Project, T033-2643 5037, www.ashalayam.org. Rehabilitates young homeless people by teaching skills.
Missionaries of Charity (Mother Teresa), The Mother House, 54A AJC Bose Rd, T033-2249 7115. The majority of volunteers work at one of the Mother Teresa homes. Induction/registration sessions are at 1500 on Mon, Wed and Fri in various languages.

⊙ Transport

Kolkata *p61, maps p62, p64, p71 and p72*
Kolkata is at the eastern end of the Grand Trunk Rd (NH2). Many city centre roads become one way or change direction from 1400 to 2100 so expect tortuous detours.

Air

Enquiries T033-2511 8787. The spacious terminals are well organized and spotless. There is adequate seating in the departure lounge as well as a bookshop, drink dispenser and clean toilets. A reservation counter for rail (same day travel only) and one for hotels are in the arrivals hall. There are money changers at the exit of the **International terminal**.

For transport to town the pre-paid taxi service (closes at 2200) to the city centre is about Rs 210 (but de luxe cars, Rs 400-650).

Return from the city centre costs the same if you bargain. The public bus is a nightmare; strongly not recommended. The nearest Metro station is at Dum Dum (Rs 6 to city centre); auto-rickshaws to there cost about Rs 60; total 40 mins. Transit passengers with onward flights may use the Airport Rest Rooms (some a/c, doubles, dorm, all good value).

Airlines offering domestic services include **Indian Airlines** (IA) and **Jet Airways** (JA), T033-3989 3333, www.jetairways.com, which have flights to **Agartala** (IA, JA), **Ahmadabad** (IA), **Aizwal** (IA), **Bagdogra** (IA, JA), **Bengaluru (Bangalore)** (IA, JA), **Bhubaneswar** (IA), **Chennai** (IA, JA), **Delhi** (IA, JA), **Dibrugarh**, **Dimapur**, **Guwahati** (IA, JA), **Hyderabad** (JA), **Imphal** (IA, JA), **Jaipur**, **Jorhat** (IA, JA), **Mumbai** (IA, JA), **Patna**, **Port Blair** (IA, JA), **Pune** (JA), **Silchar**, **Tezpur**.
Air Deccan, T983-677008, www.airdeccan .net; **Indigo**, T033-4003 6208, www.go indigo.com; **Kingfisher**, T1800-180 0101, www.flykingfisher.com; and **Spicejet**, T1800-180 3333, www.spicejet.com operate to major destinations. For schedules and prices it's best to visit a third-party booking site such as www.yatra.com or www.flightraja.com. For international flights, see page 22.

Airline offices

International Bangladesh Biman, 55B Mirza Ghalib St, T033-2227 6001, airport T033-2511 8787. **British Airways**, Apeejay House, 15 Park St, reservations T098313-77470, airport T033-2511 8262. **Cathay Pacific**, 1 Middleton St, T033-2288 4312. **Druk Air**, 51 Tivoli Court, 1A Ballygunge Circular Rd T033-2290 2429. **Gulf Air**, 230A AJC Bose Rd, T033-2233 7996. **KLM**, 1 Middleton St, T033-2283 0151. **Kuwait Airways**, 230A AJC Bose Rd, T033-2280 1335. **Lufthansa**, 30A/B JL Nehru Rd, T033-2229 9367. **SAS**, 228A AJC Bose Rd T033-2240 5182. **Singapore Airlines**, 1 Lee Rd, 2nd floor T033-2280 9898. **Sri Lankan**, 230A AJC Bose Rd, T033-2247 7783. **Thai Airways**, 229 AJC Bose Rd, 8th floor, T033-2283 8865.

National airlines Air India, 50 Chowringhee Rd, T033-2282 2356, Airport T033-2511 9031. **Indian Airlines**, 39 Chittaranjan Av, T033-2211 0810, reservations T1407/033-2211 6869 and Hotel Hindusthan International, T033-2247 6606, airport T033-2511 9721. **Jet Airways**, 18D Park St, T033-3989 3333, airport T033-2511 9894.

Bicycle

Bike hire is not easy; ask at your hotel if a staff bike is free. Spares are sold along Bentinck St, north of Chowringhee.

Bus

Local State Transport services run throughout the city and suburbs from 0500-2030; usually overcrowded after 0830, but very cheap (minimum Rs 4). Faster, private minibuses (little more expensive) cover major routes. South Bengal minibuses are bigger and will often stop on request.

Long distance An extensive hub and spoke bus operation from Kolkata allows cheap travel within West Bengal and beyond, but long bus journeys in this region are gruelling, and are a last resort when trains are full. The Tourist Office, 3/2 BBD Bagh, has timetables. Advance bookings at computerized office of Kolkata State Transport Corp (STC), Esplanade, T033-2248 1916. Kolkata STC: to **Balurghat**; **Digha**; **Farakka**; **Mayapur**; **Jalpaiguri**; **Cooch Behar**; **Malda**; **Siliguri**; 12 hrs; **Bankura**; **Bishnupur**; and **Purulia**. More comfortable a/c buses to Siliguri depart from Esplanade, Rs 550-700. **Orissa & Bihar STC**, Babu Ghat: to **Bokaro**; **Dhaka**, **Gaya**, **Puri**, 11 hrs. Bhutan Govt, **Phuntsholing** via Siliguri, 1900, Rs 300, 16 hrs. Private buses to **Dhaka** can be booked from agencies on Marquis St, from where they also depart.

Ferry

Local To cross the Hugli, between Haora station and Babu Ghat, Rs 4, except Sun. During festivals a ferry goes from Babu Ghat to Belur Math, 1 hr.

Long distance Shipping Corp of India, 1st floor, 13 Strand Rd (enter from Hare St), T033-2248 4921 (recorded information T033-2248 5420), 1000-1300 (for tickets), 1400-1745 (information only), operates a steamer to **Port Blair** in the Andamans. Some 3 or 4 sailings a month (3-4 days), Rs 1500 to Rs 5861 one way. For tickets go 4 days in advance, and be there by 0830; huge queue for 'bunk class'. See page 264.

Metro

The Metro is usually clean, efficient and punctual. The 16½-km route from Dum Dum to Tollygunge runs 0700-2145, Sun 1400-2145,

every 7-15 mins; fare Rs 4-9. Note that trains are sometimes longer than the platforms.

Rickshaw

Hand-pulled rickshaws are used by the local people especially along the narrow congested lanes. Auto-rickshaws operate outside the city centre, especially as shuttle service to/from Metro stations along set routes. Auto-rickshaws from Sealdah station to Sudder St, Rs 60.

Taxi

Car hire with driver: **Everett**, 4 Government Pl North, T033-2248 7038; **Gainwell**, 8 Ho Chi Minh Sarani, T033-2454 5010; **Mercury**, 46 JL Nehru Rd, T033-2288 3554. Tourist taxis from India and WB Tourist Offices. Local taxis are yellow. Ambassadors: insist on the meter, then use conversion chart to calculate correct fare.

Train

Kolkata is served by 2 railway stations, **Haora** (Howrah is still used on timetables) and **Sealdah**. Haora station has a separate complex for platforms 18-21. Enquiries, Haora, T033-2660 7395, 'New' Complex, T033-2660 2217, Sealdah, T033-2350 3535. Central Enquiries, T033-2220 3545. Reservation, T138 (computerized). Railway Reservations, 6 Fairlie Place, BBD Bagh; 0800-1300, 1330-2000, Sun 0800-1400 (best to go early). At Fairlie Place, tourists are automatically told to go to the Foreign Tourist Counter next door to get Foreign Tourist Quota. If the trains you want are listed as full, try the Tourist Counter, upstairs. It usually takes at least 30 mins. You will need to show your passport and an encashment or ATM receipt as well as the completed form. You can pay in US$, sterling or euros, but expect a poor exchange rate.

Trains listed depart from Haora (Howrah), unless marked '**S**' for Sealdah (timings change every Apr and Oct). To **Allahabad**: see New Delhi. **Agra Fort**: *Jodhpur Exp 2307*, 2330, 20½ hrs. **Bhubaneswar**: *Dhauli Exp 2821*, 0600, 7½ hrs; *Falaknuma Exp 2703*, 1720, 7½ hrs; *Howrah Puri Exp 2837*, 2335, 7½ hrs. **Chennai**: *Coromandel Exp 2841*, 1450, 28½ hrs; *Howrah Chennai Mail 2603*, 2330, 33½ hrs. **Mumbai (CST)**: *Gitanjali Exp 2860*, 1330, 32½ hrs (via **Nagpur**, 18½ hrs); *Howrah Mumbai Mail 2810*, 2015, 35½ hrs (via

Nagpur, 19½ hrs); *Howrah Mumbai Mail 2321*, 2200, 38 hrs, via **Gaya**. **Mumbai (Lokmanya Tilak)**: *Jnaneswari SD Exp 2102*, 2255 (Mon, Wed, Thu, Sun), 32½ hrs (via **Nagpur**, 19 hrs). **Nagpur**: See Mumbai trains plus *Howrah Ahmedabad Exp 2834*, 2015, 22½ hrs. **New Delhi** via **Patna** and **Allahabad**: *Rajdhani Exp 2301*, 1655 (except Sun), 16½ hrs; *Rajdhani Exp 2305*, 1355 (Sun), 20 hrs, via **Gaya**; (**S**) *Rajdhani Exp 2313*, 1655 (daily), 17½ hrs. **New Jalpaiguri (NJP)**: (**S**) *Kanchenjunga Exp 5657*, 0645, 11½ hrs; (**S**) *Darjeeling Mail 2343*, 2205, 13 hrs; *Kamrup Exp 5959*, 1735, 14 hrs. **Puri**: *Jagannath Exp 8409*, 1900, 11 hrs; *Howrah Puri Exp 2837*, 2235, 11 hrs. **Ranchi**: *Howrah Hatia Exp 8615*, 2155, 8 hrs; *Howrah Shatabdi Exp 2019*,0605, 7 hrs.

Tram

Kolkata is the only Indian city to run a network. 0430-2300. Second-class carriage Rs 3.50-4, front 'first class' Rs 4-4.50, but no discernable difference. Trams originate at Esplanade depot and are a great way to see the city – ride route 1 to Belgachia through the heart of North Kolkata's heritage.

❶ Directory

Kolkata *p61, maps p62, p64, p71 and p72*

Banks

There are 24-hr ATMs all over the city centre. Money changers proliferate on Sudder St. **Thomas Cook**, 4/A ground floor, Park Mansions, Park St.

Chemists

Many around Lindsay St and New Market. **Angel**, 151 Park St (24-hr). **Dey's**, 6/2B Lindsay St. **Lawrence & Mayo**, 20E Park St (opticians). **Moonlight**, 180 SP Mukherjee Rd (24-hr).

Consulates and high commissions

Bangladesh, 9 Bangabandhu, Sheikh Mujib Sarani T033-2247 5208. **Denmark**, 3 Netaji Subhas Rd, T033-2248 7476. **France**, 4th floor, 2 Clive Ghat St, T033-2230 4571. **Germany**, 1 Hastings Park Rd, T033-2479 1141. **Nepal**, 1 National Library Av, T033-2456 1224. **Netherlands**, 502 Mangalam Av, 24 Hemant Basu Sarani, T033-2242 4979. **Norway**, 5B, Roudon St, T033-2287 8804. **Spain**, 1 Taratolla Rd, T033-2469 5954. **Sri Lanka**, 2 Sarani Shakespeare St, T033-2281 5354. **Sweden**, 9 Elgin Rd, T033-2280 7136. **Switzerland** 113 Park St, T033-229 5557. **Thailand**, 18B Mandeville Gardens, T033-2440 7836. **UK**, 1A Ho-Chi-Minh Sarani, T033-2288 5172. **USA**, 5/1 Ho-Chi-Minh Sarani, T033-2282 3611.

Cultural centres and libraries

British Council Information Centre, L&T Chambers, 16 Camac St, T033-2282 5370. Good for UK newspapers, reference books. Mon-Sat 1100-1900. **French Association**, 217 AJC Bose Rd, T033-2281 5198. **Goethe Institut**, Max Mueller Bhavan, 8 Pramathesh Barua Sarani, T033-2486 6398, www.goethe .de/kolkata. Mon-Fri 0930-1730, Sat 1500-1700.

Hospitals

Apollo Gleneagles, 5B Canel Circular Rd, T033-2358 5211. **Wockhardt Medical Centre**, 2/7 Sarat Bose Rd, T033-2475 4096, reliable diagnostic centre. **Woodlands**, 8B Alipore Rd, T033-2456 7075.

Internet

Many across the city; several in Sudder St area. Some charge as little as Rs 15 per hr.

Post

Poste restante at GPO, 0800-2000. Closed Sun and holidays. **DHL**, 6 Marquis St, T033-2217 1675. **Speed Post** At major post offices including airport, Esplanade and Park St.

Tourist offices

India Tourism, 4 Shakespeare Sarani, T033-2282 5813, Mon-Fri 0900-1800, Sat 0900-1300. **WBTDC**, 3/2 BBD Bagh (E), T033-2248 8217. Mon-Fri 1030-1600, Sat 1030-1300. **State Governments: Andaman & Nicobar Islands**, 2nd floor, 3a Auckland Place, T033-2247 5084. **Arunachal Pradesh**, Block CE, 109 Sector 1, Salt Lake, T033-2321 3627. **Assam**, 8 Russell St, T033-2229 5094. **Manipur**, 26 Rowland Rd, T033-2475 8163. **Meghalaya**, 120 Shantipally, EM Bypass T033-2441 1932. **Mizoram**, 24 Old Ballygunge Rd, T033-2475 7887. **Nagaland**, 11 Shakespeare Sarani, T033-2282 5247. **Orissa**, 41 Lenin Sarani, T033-2216 4556. **Rajasthan**, 2 Ganesh Chandra Av, T033-2215 9740. **Sikkim**, 4/1 Middleton St, T033-2281 5328. **Tripura**, 1 Pretoria St, T033-2242 5703. **Uttar Pradesh**, 12A NSC Bose Rd, T033-2248 5917.

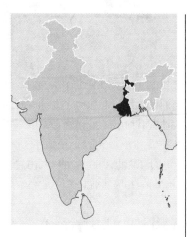

⁑ Footprint features

Introduction

This cultured corner of the sub-continent has added immeasurably to India's overall identity. The heritage of the great Hindu saint Ramakrishna, a rich literary tradition presided over by the ghost of Rabindranath Tagore and a wealth of unique festivals, not to mention the region's ingrained leftist leanings, all unite to make the most densely-populated Indian state deliciously vibrant.

Travelling north takes you through a land that has been left wonderfully fertile by the ever-shifting River Gangas and run-off from the Himalayas. Intensely populated and cultivated, the area contains such treasures as the terracotta temples at Bishnupur, and Santiniketan, the placid rural oasis in which Tagore established his artistic university. Historic palaces and spectacular mosques crumble against a backdrop of village life in Murshidabad, the delightful former capital of the Nawabs of Bengal. Luminescent expanses of green paddies and clusters of banana trees trace the river north towards the Himalayan foothills, via the Sultanate monuments at Gaur and Pandua and east to the one-horned rhinos in Jaldapara Park.

Synonymous with tea the world over, Darjeeling has always been a holiday destination, particularly during the summer months when the cool mountain air provides relief from the heat of the plains. With large Tibetan and Nepali populations, the hill stations have a very different feel: monasteries, prayer flags and steamed dumplings give a taste of the land and peoples that lie deeper in the Himalayas.

South of Kolkata, the sultry Sunderbans, a World Heritage Site, comprise 54 mangroved islands interwoven by streams, home to a large Bengal tiger population. Also in the south is Digha, which offers a surprisingly relaxing beach break on the Bay of Bengal, just a few hours away from the capital.

★ Don't miss ...

1 **Murshidabad** After the noise and bustle of Kolkata, spend a peaceful weekend at this historic town with its quiet rural charm, see page 90.

2 **Festivals** Bengalis throw a great party. Experience a snake worship in Bishnupur or a *baul* gathering in Santiniketan, page 94.

3 **Darjeeling** Visit a tea estate and trek through the flowering magnolias and rhododendron bushes in the spring, page 95.

4 **Kalimpong** There is a great Wednesday and Sunday market here with a range of bizarre goods on offer, plus amazing *momos* and *thukpas* are available every day, page 102.

5 **Sunderbans** If it's too cold in the hills, head south to this mysterious archipelago and see if you can spot a tiger swimming in the mangrove swamps, page 111.

West Bengal

Background → *Population: 80.2 mn. Area: 88,752 sq km.*

The land

Geography Graphically described as being made up of 'new mud, old mud and marsh', most of West Bengal lies on the western delta of the Ganga. Its limited higher ground, the basalt **Rajmahal Hills** just west of Murshidabad, are an extension of the ancient rocks of the peninsula. All that remains of the dense forests that once covered the state are the mangrove swamps of the **Sunderbans** in the far south and a narrow wooded belt along the southern slopes of the Himalaya. The apparently unchanging face of the Bengali countryside is highly misleading. Rivers have constantly changed their courses and over the last 300 years the Ganga has shifted progressively east, leaving the Hugli as a relatively minor channel. Minor variations in height make enormous differences to the quality of land for farming. The chief variety in the landscape of the plains of Bengal, however, comes from the contrasting greens of the different varieties of rice, often producing startlingly attractive countryside. The dominating mountains to the north and the plateau and hills of the southwest provide far greater scenic contrasts though. The gently rising slopes which lead from the delta to the peninsular rocks of Bihar and Orissa, are the home of some of India's most isolated tribal peoples, though their forest habitat has been severely degraded.

Climate Hot and oppressively humid summers are followed by much cooler and clearer winters. Heavy storms occur in late March and April. These electric storms are marked by massive cloud formations, strong winds and heavy rain. Occasionally tropical cyclones also strike coastal areas at this time of year, though they are far more common between October and December. The monsoon hits between June and September, when large parts of Kolkata are knee-deep in water for hours at a time.

History

In **prehistoric times** Bengal was home to Dravidian hunter-gatherers. In the first millennium BC, the Aryans from Central Asia, who had learned the agricultural techniques and the art of weaving and pottery, arrived in Bengal, bringing with them the Sanskrit language. From about the fifth century BC trade in cotton, silk and coral from Ganga Nagar flourished. In the third century BC Bengal was part of the Mauryan Empire, but it remained densely forested and comparatively sparsely populated.

The **Guptas** conquered Bengal in the fourth century AD and trade with the Mediterranean expanded for the next 200 years, particularly with Rome. The fall of the Roman Empire in the fifth century led to a decline in Bengal's fortunes. Only with the founding of the **Pala Dynasty** in AD 750 was the region united once again. Bengal became a centre of Buddhism and art and learning flourished. The **Senas** followed. They were great patrons of the arts and ruled for 50 years until deposed by the invading Turks, who began a century of Muslim rule under the Khaljis of the Delhi Sultanate. The most notable of the Pathan kings who followed the Khaljis was **Sher Shah**, who extended his territory from Bihar into Bengal, which was taken back by the Mughal emperor Akbar, anxious to obtain the rich resources of rice, silk and saltpetre in 1574-1576.

The increasing power of the Muslims spurred the **Portuguese** towards the subcontinent and they began trading with Bengal in the mid-16th century. Before long they faced competition from the Dutch and the British and in 1632 an attack on their port near Kolkata by Emperor Shah Jahan reduced their merchant power.

In 1690 the purchase of the three villages which grew into Calcutta enabled the British to build a fort and consolidate their power. In 1700, Bengal became an independent presidency and Calcutta prospered. The *firmans* (permits) granted were for trading from the ports but the British took the opportunity of gaining a monopoly over internal trade as well. After the death of the Emperor Aurangzeb, the authority of Delhi slowly crumbled. In 1756, Siraj-ud-Daula, the then Nawab of Bengal, began to take note of Kolkata's growing wealth. Finding the British strengthening the fortifications he attacked Fort William, finding little difficulty in capturing the city. Within a year, however, Clive took the city back and then defeated the Nawab at Plassey; a turning point for the British in India. Through the 19th century West Bengal became the economic and political centre of **British India**.

Calcutta developed as the principal centre of cultural and political activity in modern India. Bengali literature, drama, art and music flourished. Religious reform movements such as the **Brahmo Samaj**, under the leadership of **Raja Ram Mohan Roy** in the 1830s, developed from the juxtaposition of traditional Hinduism with Christian missionary activity at the beginning of the 19th century. Later, one of India's greatest poets, Nobel Prize winner **Rabindranath Tagore** (1861-1941), dominated India's cultural world, breathing moral and spiritual life into the political movement for independence.

Until 1905 Bengal had included much of modern Bihar and Orissa, as well as the whole of Bengal. Lord Curzon's short-lived Partition of Bengal in 1905 roused fierce opposition, and also encouraged the split between Muslims and Hindus which finally resulted in Bengali Muslim support for the creation of Pakistan in 1947. The division into the two new states was accompanied by the migration of over five million people and appalling massacres as Hindus and Muslims fled. West Bengal was again directly affected by the struggle to create Bangladesh, when about 10 million refugees arrived from East Pakistan after 25 March 1971. Most returned after Bangladesh gained its Independence in December 1971.

Culture

The majority of the people are Bengalis. Tribal groups include Santals, Oraons and Mundas in the plains and the borders of Chota Nagpur and Lepchas and Bhotias in the Himalaya. Over 85% of the population speak Bengali. Hindi, Urdu and tribal languages account for most of the remainder.

Bengalis are said to be obsessed about what they eat. The men often take a keen interest in buying the most important elements of the day's meal, namely fresh fish. Typically, it is river fish, the most popular being *hilsa* and *bekti* or the widely available shellfish, especially king prawns. *Bekti* is grilled or fried and is tastier than the fried fish of the west as it has often been marinated in mild spices first. The prized smoked *hilsa*, although delicious, has thousands of fine bones. *Maachh* (fish) comes in many forms as *jhol* (in a thin gravy), *jhal* (spicy and hot), *malai curry* (in coconut milk, mildly spiced), chop (in a covering of mashed potato and crumbs) or *chingri maachher* cutlet (flattened king prawn 'fillets', crumbed and fried). Bengali cooking uses mustard oil and mustard which grows in abundance, and a subtle mixture of spices. *Mishti* (sweetmeats) are another distinctive feature. Many are milk based and the famous *sandesh, roshogolla, roshomalai, pantua* and *ledikeni* (named after Lady Canning, the wife of the first Viceroy of India) are prepared with a kind of cottage cheese, in dozens of different textures, shapes, colours and tastes. Pale pinkish brown, *mishti doi*, is an excellent sweet yoghurt eaten as a dessert, typically sold in hand-thrown clay pots.

Crafts

Silk has been woven in India for more than 3500 years and continues today with the weaving of the natural-coloured wild silk called *tassar*. Bengal silk, found as block-printed saris, has had a revival in the exquisite brocade weaving of *baluchari*, produced in the past under royal patronage, and is now carried out in Bankura. The saris are woven in traditional style with untwisted silk and have beautiful borders and *pallu* (the end section), which depict peacocks, flowers and human figures. **Fine cotton** is woven also.

The Bankura horse has become a symbol of **pottery** in West Bengal which still flourishes in the districts of Bankura, Midnapore and Birbhum. Soft **soap stone** is used for carving copies of temple images, while **shell** bangles are considered auspicious. **Ivory** carvers once produced superb decorative items, a skill developed in the Mughal period. Today, bone and plastic have largely replaced ivory in inlay work. **Metal** workers produce brass and bell-metal ware while the tribal *dhokra* casters still follow the ancient *cire perdue* method, see page 175. Kalighat *pat* paintings are in a primitive style using bold colours.

Modern West Bengal

Since the mid-1960s political life has been dominated by the confrontation between the Communist Party of India (Marxist) (the CPI(M)) and the Congress Party. The CPI(M) has held power in the State Assembly since June 1977, making it the world's longest-running democratically elected Communist government. The Congress, the second largest party, has performed better in the Lok Sabha parliamentary elections. Although the CPI(M) has lost some of its share of the urban vote, especially in Kolkata, Assembly elections have continued to be won convincingly by the CPI(M)-led Left Front under Chief Minister Buddhadeb Bhattacharjee. This pattern continued in the 2006 State Assembly elections, when the CPM won 233 of the 293 Assembly seats. Recent years have seen economic liberalisation attempts and communal agitation against the policy of annexing land from poor villages to give multinational companies access to Special Enterprise Zones (SEZs), erupting in the village of Nandigram on 14 March 2007. At least 12 protesters were killed in police firing during a move against compulsory land purchase by a Indonesian multinational project.

North of Kolkata

The plains north of Kolkata are home to the peaceful University town of Santiniketan, home of Tagore, and the 300-year-old terracotta temples of Bishnupur. The legacy of the Muslim nawabs lives on in the impressive ruins of Gaur and Pandua, while atmospheric Murshidabad provides an accessible blend of Bengali history and relaxation. ▸▸ *For Sleeping, Eating and other listings, see pages 93-95.*

Bishnupur ●❀○◘◖ ▸▸ *pp93-95. Colour map 2, grid C1.*

➔ *Phone code: 03244. Population: 61,900.*

The warrior Malla Kings of Bengal ruled this area from Bishnupur for nearly two centuries. The British subsequently sold it to the Maharajah of Burdwan. The Mallas were great patrons of the arts and built uniquely ornamental terracotta temples. It is also where the Dhrupad style of classical Indian singing originated. Local handicrafts include silk, tassar, conch-shell and bell-metal ware and the famous terracotta Bankura horse, Dokhra, and also slate statues and artefacts. Bengali sweetmeats and flavoured tobacco are local specialities.

Sights

There are more than two dozen temples in Bishnupur, mostly dedicated to Krishna and Radha. They are usually built of brick but sometimes of laterite and on a square plan with a gently curved roof imitating the Bengali thatched (*chala*) hut. The terracotta tiles depict episodes from the *Ramayana* and *Mahabharata*, and also scenes from daily life. Inside, there is a sanctuary (*thakurbari*) and a platform (*vedi*) for the image, on one side. The upper storey has a gallery topped by one, five or even nine towers.

Most of the temples are concentrated within the fort, which was built later by Muslim rulers. Distances given are from the **Tourist Lodge**. The **Rasmancha** (3 km) is a unique Vishnu shrine. The well-preserved cannons, in particular the 4-m long **Dalmadal** to the south of the Rasmancha, date back to the Mallas. The **Jor Mandir** (5 km), a pair of

hut-shaped temples with a single *sikhara*, built in 1655 by Raghunath Singh, has
attractively ornamented panels. He also built the **Shyam Rai Temple** (7 km), perhaps
the earliest example of the *pancharatna* (five towers) and a fine *sikhara*. Each façade
is triple arched and the terracotta panels show scenes from the *Ramayana* and
Krishna's life. The large **Madan Mohan Temple** (5 km), with a
white façade, was built of brick with terracotta panels in 1694
by King Durjan, while the 17th-century **Lalji** and **Madan Gopal**
are built of laterite. The **Mrinmoyee Mandir** (3 km) has a clay
idol of Durga dating from AD 997, and in the courtyard a
curiosity of nine trees growing together. Little remains of the
Malla Kings' **Fort** (3½ km). You can see the gate of laterite, with
firing holes drilled in different directions and a 13th-century stone chariot. The water
reservoirs are still there though the moat, once served by seven lakes, is partly dry.

> ⁝ The temples can be very
> difficult to find on foot in
> the maze of narrow streets.
> It is best to arrange a cycle-
> rickshaw for a tour, Rs 50
> for 2½ hours.

Santiniketan ⬤🚲❂⬤🚌❶ ⤳ *pp93-95. Colour map 2, grid C1.*

→ *Phone code: 03463. Population: 65,700.*
Santiniketan, the 'Abode of Peace', is a welcome change from the hectic traffic, noise
and dirt of Kolkata. Even a brief visit to the shady university campus, with its artistic
heritage and its quiet, rural charm, makes a profound impression on most visitors,
and is a must for aficionados of Bengal's greatest poet.

Ins and outs

Getting there The nearest railway station is Bolpur, which has trains from Kolkata's
Haora and Sealdah stations. Cycle-rickshaws charge Rs 15-20 to Santiniketan, 3 km
away. Local buses use a stand near the station. The road journey from Kolkata on the
congested NH2 (213 km) can be very slow.

Getting around The Visva Bharati campus and Santiniketan's residential area are
ideal for exploring on foot. To get further afield you will need a cycle-rickshaw.

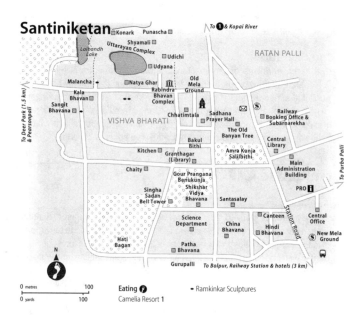

Vishva Bharati University① *closed Wed and Tue afternoon, sightseeing is permitted only after university hours: summer 1430-1700, winter 1415-1630 and during holidays 0700-1200, Rs 5, no photography, all compounds are subdivided by wire fences*, has an interesting history. The Maharishi Debendranath Tagore, father of Rabindranath Tagore, the Nobel Laureate, started an *ashram*, later named Santiniketan. In 1901 Rabindranath started an experimental place of learning with a classroom under the trees, and a group of five pupils. It went on to become the Vishva Bharati University in 1921. It now attracts students from all over the world and aspires to be a spiritual meeting ground in a serene, culturally rich and artistic environment. Open-air classes are still a feature of this unique university. Among the many *Bhavans* are those concentrating on fine art (Kala Bhavan) and music and dance (Sangit Bhavan). The **Uttarayan Complex** where the poet lived consists of several buildings in distinctive architectural styles. **Sadhana** Prayer Hall, where Brahmo prayers are held on Wednesday, was founded in 1863. The unusual hall enclosed by stained glass panels has a polished marble floor which is usually decorated with fresh *alpana* designs. **Chhatimtala**, where Maharishi Debendranath sat and meditated, is the site of special prayers at Convocation time. In keeping with its simplicity, graduates are presented with a twig with five leaves from the locally widespread *Saptaparni* trees.

Rabindra Bhavan ① *Thu-Mon 1030-1330 and 1400-1630, Tue 1030-1330, no photography, bags may not be permitted, shoes must be removed before entering each building*, is a museum and research centre in the Uttarayan complex, containing photographs, manuscripts and Tagore's personal belongings; the peripheral buildings contain photos too. Well documented and very informative so allow at least an hour to read the small print. The garden is delightful, particularly when the roses are blooming. **Kala Bhavan** ① *Thu-Mon 1500-1700*, has a rich collection of 20th-century Indian art, particularly sculptures, murals and paintings by famous Bengali artists. **Nandan Museum**① *Thu-Mon 1000-1330 and 1400-1700, Tue 1000-1330,* has a collection of terracotta, paintings and original tracings of Ajanta murals.

Surul (4 km), with its evocative village atmosphere and small terracotta temples with interesting panels on their façades, makes a pleasant trip. The *zamindari* 'Rajbari' with its durga shrine gives an impression of times past.

Ballavpur Deer Park (3 km)① *Thu-Tue 1000-1600*, is a reclaimed wooded area of rapidly eroding laterite *khowai* with spotted deer and winter migratory birds.

Around Bishnupur

Bakresvar, 58 km northwest of Santiniketan, is known for its medicinal sulphurous hot springs (separate bathing areas for men and women, though you may not fancy the tepid pools full of people doing laundry). There are seven major *kunds* (springs) from 36°C to 67°C, the hottest being Agnikunda (fire spring). Temples to Siva, Sakti, Kali and Vishnu make it a Hindu pilgrimage centre. The temples are modern and white tiled though the Kali temple is old and painted red. Allow five hours for the trip.

Murshidabad ▣◐◉ ➠ *pp93-95. Colour map 2, grid B1.*

➔ *Phone code 03482. Population: 36,900.*

Named after Nawab Murshid Kuli Khan, a Diwan under Emperor Aurangzeb, Murshidabad became the capital of Bengal in 1705 and remained so up to the time of the battle of Plassey. The town lies on the east bank of the Bhagirathi, a picturesque tributary of the Ganga, with imposing ruins scattered around and an enchanting time warp feel. A vibrant vegetable bazar takes place each morning beneath decaying columns left over from the days of the *nawabs*, and the town comes to life for the famed Muslim festival of Muhurram at the end of January. Come during the week to avoid crowds of Indian tourists.

doors) **Palace** ⓘ *Sat-Thu 1000-1500, Rs 100, no photography*, built in 1837. It is now a splendid museum with a portrait gallery, library and circular durbar hall and contains a rare collection of old arms, curios, china and paintings. The large newer **Imambara** (1847) opposite, also Italianate in style, is being extensively renovated. The domed, square pavilion (**Madina**) with a veranda that stands nearby may be what remains of the original Imambara. There are numerous 18th-century monuments in the city which are best visited by cycle-rickshaw (Rs 75 for three hours). Mir Jafar and his son Miran lived at **Jafaragunj Deorhi**, known as the traitor's gate. **Kat-gola**, the garden house of a rich Jain merchant, has a collection of curios and a hugely atmospheric old Jain temple. The **Palace of Jagat Sett**, one of the richest financiers of the 18th century, is 2 km from the Jafargung Cemetery to the north of the palace. The **Katra Mosque** (1724), modelled on the great mosque at Mecca and an important centre of learning, is outside the city to the east. It was built by Murshid Kuli Khan who lies buried under the staircase. **Moti Jheel** (pearl lake) and the ruins of **Begum Ghaseti's palace** are 3 km south of the city. Only a mosque and a room remain. **Khosbagh** (Garden of Delight) across the river has three walled enclosures.

Malde 🏠🚌 ⇢ *pp93-95. Colour map 2, grid B1.*

→ *Phone code: 03512.*

Malda is a convenient and comfortable base from which to visit the atmospheric ruins of Gaur and Pandua, with plenty of banks and other amenities in the town centre. Now famous mainly for its large juicy Fajli mangoes, Malda was established around 1680 by the English, who bought an entire village from a local landlord and built it into a market town. **Malda Museum** (1937) has a collection of stone images, coins and inscriptions from Gaur and Pandua. The **market** behind the **Tourist Lodge** is fascinating. Old Malda, which lies at a confluence of rivers 4 km away, has the **Jami Masjid**, built in 1596 out of decorated brick and stone with some good carving on the entrance pillars. The 17-m **Nimasarai tower** across the river dates from the same period, and has strange stones embedded on the outer surface, which may once have been used to display beheaded criminals.

Gaur and Pandua

→ *Colour map 2, grid B1.*

Gaur's situation on the banks of the River Ganga, yet within easy reach of the Rajmahal Hills with their fine black basalt, made it possible for gifted stonemasons to construct beautiful religious and secular buildings. Muslim monuments of the Sultanate period are strewn around the quiet, deserted city. Pandua alternated with Gaur as a capital of Bengal between 1338 and 1500, when it was abandoned. Some of the ruins here show clearly how the Muslims made free use of material from Hindu temples near Malda.

Gaur

On the ancient site of Lakshanavati, Gaur was the capital of King Sasanka in the seventh century, followed by the Buddhist Pala kings. The city became famous as a centre of education and culture during the reign of the Hindu Sena kings in the 12th century. In the early 13th century it was invaded by Bhaktiar Khalji and then captured by the Afghan Fakhr-ud-din Dynasty in the 14th century. They plundered the temples to construct their own mosques and tombs. Gaur was sacked by Sher Shah Suri in 1537 and the city's population was wiped out by plague in 1575.

The remains of the embankments of the fort are to the south on the bank of the Bhagirati. The great golden mosque, **Bari Sona Masjid** or Baroduari (12-door), was built in 1526 and is an enormous rectangular stone-faced brick structure with a large open square in front. Fine marble carving is still visible on the remains of the minarets. Note the small Kali temple at the entrance.

Bangladesh can be seen from the **Dakhil Darwaza** (early 15th century), the main fort gateway with its five-storeyed towers. It was built of small red bricks embossed with terracotta decorations. The turrets and circular bastions produce a striking contrast of light and shade with decorative motifs of suns, rosettes, lamps and fretted borders. During the 15th century, a number of mosques and mausoleums were built in the new architectural style.

The **Firuz Minar** (Victory Tower), built by Sultan Firuz Shah in 1486, has a spiral staircase. The lower storeys are 12 sided while the upper are circular, with striking blue and white glazed tiles, used in addition to the terracotta and brick. The builders of the **Chika Mosque** (Bat Mosque, early 15th century), near the Kadam Rasul, made free use of Hindu idols in its construction. The **Chamkati Mosque** (circa 1475) shows the vaulted ceiling of the veranda. Inside the southeast corner of the Fort is the massive **Baisgazi Wall** (height being '22 yard') which enclosed the Old Palace with its *darbar,* harem etc. **Kadam Rasul** (1513) is a domed building with a Bengali *chala* roof, which housed the relic of the Prophet, a footprint in stone. The two-storeyed **Lukochuri Darwaza** (Hide-and-Seek Gate, circa 1655) is in the later Mughal style.

The **Tantipara Mosque** (circa 1475; *tanti*, weaver) has superbly decorated red brick with octagonal turrets and five entrance arches. The elegant **Lattan** (Painted) **Mosque** (1475), attributed to Yusuf Shah, was decorated with bands of blue, green, yellow and white glazed tiles. Some 2 km south, close to the Bangladeshi border, is the ruined **Chhoti Sona Masjid**, has a carved gate.

Ramkeli, not far from the Bari Sona Masjid, has the Madan Mohan Jiu Mandir and is of religious significance for followers of **Sri Chaitanya**, the 14th-century Bengali religious reformer. **Tamaltola** marks where he meditated under a tree and pilgrims come to see a footprint in stone.

To get here, from near the Tourist Lodge in Malda get a bus for Mohodipur and ask to be dropped at Pyasbari (tea and snacks available). Stay on the narrow tarmac road and you won't get lost. Turn right from the NH34 for the site, which you can wander around free. To return to Malda, stop a bus or share a taxi. Or arrange a half-day taxi hire through the tourist office in Malda (Rs 600).

Pandua

The old brick-paved road, nearly 4 m wide and about 10 km long, passes through the town and most of the monuments stand close to it. The **Adina Masjid** (1364-1374) ① *free*, exemplifies Muslim architecture in medieval Bengal. Built by Sultan Sikander Shah and once comparable to the great eighth-century mosque at Damascus, it is sadly in a poor state of repair. The vast space

Gaur

To Malda
After Cunningham & Tim Makin
PYASBARI
NH34
Little Bhagirathi
Bari Sona Masjid
Dakhil Darwaza
Firuz Minar
Kumbhir Pir Dighi
Chika Mosque
Kadam Rasul
Palace
Lukochuri Darwaza
Belbari Madrassa
Chamkati Mosque
Chhota Sagar Dighi
Gunmant Mosque
Tantipara Mosque
Lattan Mosque
Kotwali Darwaza
N
0 metres 800
0 yards 800
Balua Dighi
To Chhoti Sona Masjid

enclosed by pillared aisles has an 88-arch screen around a quadrangle with the mosque. Influence of 12th-century Sena architecture is evident in the tall, ornate, tiered *sikhara* and trefoil arches and the remarkable absence of a large entrance gateway. Most of the substructure, and some pillars, was of basalt plundered from existing Hindu temples and palaces. A small doorway in the western back wall of the mosque, clearly taken from an earlier Vishnu temple, exhibits the stonemasons' skill and the exceptional metalwork of the time. The **Eklakhi Mausoleum**, built of brick (circa 1412), has a Hindu idol carved on its front lintel. The **Qutb Shahi Mosque** (also *Sona* or Golden Mosque) was built in 1582. Further along are the ruins of the 17th-century **Chhoti** and **Bari Dargahs**.

To get to the site, from the **Tourist Lodge** in Malda get a Siliguri or Raiganj bus and ask to be dropped at Pandua Bus Stand. The narrow tarmac road to the site, off the NH34, is easy to follow and gives a fascinating behind-the-scenes view of Bengali village life. Buses from Adina return to Malda.

⊜ Sleeping

Bishnupur *p88*
D-E Tourist Lodge, T03244-252013, 10 rooms, 5 a/c, 4-bed dorm (Rs 80), restaurant, also serves beer.
F Retiring Rooms. Guest 'n Rest, near Tagore's statue, serves Bengali food only.

Santiniketan *p89, map p89*
There are a couple of cheap guest houses within the campus; to arrange a stay (maximum 3 days) contact the Public Relations Officer (PRO), T03463-252751.
C Camellia Resort, Prantik (3 km from campus), T03463-262043, www.camellia group.org. Clean but dull rooms (some a/c) on 3 floors around a central courtyard, good restaurant, beautiful large garden, pool, well located in open countryside but you need transport, rickshaws or car hire available, free transport to/from Bolpur station.
C-E Chhuti Holiday Resort, 241 Charupalli, Jamboni, T03463-252692, www.chhuti resort.com. Comfortable thatched rooms with bath, some a/c, good restaurant, innovative.
D-E Rangamati, Prabhat Sarani, Bhubandanga, Bolpur, T03463-252305. 22 decent rooms, some with balcony, dorm (Rs 150), restaurant (Indian and Chinese).
D-F Royal Bengal, Bhubandanga, Bolpur, T03463-257148. Clean and modern, all rooms with balcony and attached bath, dorm (Rs 200), soulless restaurant.
D-F Santiniketan Tourist Lodge (WBTDC), off main road, Bolpur, T03463-252699. Slightly faded rooms, varying sized a/c rooms, small non-a/c (**E**), 13-bed dorm (Rs 80), pleasant garden, poor food.

D-F Sathi, Bhubandanga Rd, Bolpur, T03463-254630. Some a/c, 3, 4 and 5-bedded rooms, best on first-floor terrace (front and back).
F-G Manasi Lodge, Santiniketan Rd, Bolpur, T03463-254200. Clean rooms, attached bath, lovely staff, popular courtyard restaurant.
G Nisa, opposite Mela Polo Ground, Bolpur, T03463-253101. Basic but clean rooms with fan, those at rear have balconies.
G Railway Retiring Rooms, Bolpur. 1 a/c, restaurant.

Murshidabad *p90*
E Whitehouse, 30 KN Rd, near local bus stand, T03482-255443.
F Ashoke Mahal, past the market, T03482-320855. Clean and pleasant, rear room has a balcony by the river.
F Manjusha, by Hazarduari Palace, T03482-270321. The best location in town, with serene riverside garden, charming manager can help with bike and boat hire, food by arrangement.
F Youth Hostels at Lalbagh and Murshidabad, reserve through Youth Services, 32/1 BBD Bagh S, Kolkata, T03482-280626.
F-G Indrajit, near railway station, T03482-271858. Wide choice of rooms of all standards, friendly staff, excellent multi-cuisine restaurant, alcohol available.
G Youth Hostel, reserve through Youth Services Office, Kolkata, T033-2248 0626. Amazingly cheap.

Malda *p91*
D-G Continental Lodge, 22 KJ Sanyal Rd, by State Bus Stand, T03512-252388. Reasonable

rooms, restaurant, friendly, views over town from public balcony.

E-G Tourist Lodge, NH34, T03512-266123. Reservations (Kolkata) T033-2248 8271. 13 rooms around courtyard (4 a/c) some with bath, a/c bar, restaurant, dorm (Rs 80).

F Chanakya, NH34, town centre, T03512-266620. Some a/c in the 22 rooms, restaurant, bar, clean, modern.

G Railway Retiring Rooms. A/c rooms and dorm, modernized, helpful staff. (South Indian platform snacks recommended).

🍴 Eating

Santiniketan *p89, map p89*
Camelia Resort, Prantik. Good food, wide choice, well priced.

Chhuti, see Sleeping, has restaurants but may require advance notice.

Kalor Dokan, an institution, open all hours.

Maduram, this sweet shop in Bolpur on Santiniketan Rd is highly recommended.

Railway canteen, cheap and reliable.

✹ Festivals and events

Bishnupur *p88*
Aug Jhapan, in honour of the serpent goddess *Manasa*, dates from the 17th century. This regional harvest festival is linked with the fertility cult and is unique. Venomous snakes (cobras, pythons, vipers, kraits, flying snakes) are brought in baskets by snake-charmers who display amazing tricks.

Santiniketan *p89, map p89*
23-25 Dec Poush Mela, an important fair, coinciding with the village's Foundation Day. Folk performances include *Santals* dances and *baul* songs. Bauls are Bengal's wandering minstrels, who are worshippers of Vishnu. They travel from village to village singing their songs, accompanied by a single string instrument, *ektara*, and a tiny drum. Tribal silver and Dhokra metal crafts make attractive buys.

End Jan/early Feb Magh Mela, a rural crafts and agricultural fair at Sriniketan, marks the anniversary of the founding of *Brahmo Samaj*. Vasanta Utsav coincides with *Holi*. Dance, music and singing are held throughout the year, particularly good during festivals.

🛍 Shopping

Bishnupur *p88*
Cottage industries flourish in the different *paras* (quarters) each devoted to a specialized craft: pottery in Kamarpara, *sankha* (conch-shell) cutting in Sankharipara, and weaving, particularly Baluchari silk saris, in Tantipara. **Silk Khadi Seva Mandal**, Boltala, and **Terracotta Crafts**, 500 m from the Tourist Lodge, are recommended.

Santiniketan *p89, map p89*
The local embossed leather work is distinctive. **Suprabhat Women Handicrafts**, Prabhat Sarani, Bhuban Nagar, opposite **Tourist Lodge**, Bolpur, 0930-1300, 1700-1900. Excellent, creative embroidery (including *kantha*), ready made or to order, crafted by local village women. **Smaranika Handicraft Centre**, opposite Bolpur Station. Interesting embroidery, jewellery and saris at fixed prices.

Subarnarekha, next to railway booking office in Santiniketan, sells rare books.

Murshidabad *p90*
Woven and handblock-printed silk saris and bell-metal ware are the main local industries.

⊖ Transport

Bishnupur *p88*
For the area around car hire from **Tourist Lodge**; **Kiron Homeo Hall**, Matukgunge. Cycle rickshaws are widely available.

WBSTC buses from Esplanade, Kolkata, 5½ hrs on local roads. **STC Super Express** buses from Durgapur (1 hr). Train from Kolkata (H) to **Bankura**: *Howrah-Purulia Exp 8017*, 1645, 4 hrs.

Santiniketan *p89, map p89*
There are mainly cycle-rickshaws and taxis available.

Train from **Kolkata** (**H**): *Ganadevata Exp 3017*, 0605, 2¾ hrs; *Shantiniketan Exp 3015*, 1010, 2½ hrs. From **Bolpur** to **Kolkata** (**H**): *Shantiniketan Exp 3016*, 1310, 2½ hrs; *Kanchenjunga Exp 5658*, (**S**), 1611, 4 hrs, booking recommended (avoid station counter as the better University booking office, 0800-1400, has a daily quota of 50 reserved seats). Also trains to New Jalpaiguri (for Darjeeling) via Malda.

Murshidabad *p90*

Jeeps from Baharampur local bus stand to Lalbagh, 40 mins, Rs 8; or shared auto-rickshaw, 30 mins, Rs 6. Then cycle-rickshaw to Hazarduari gate, Rs 8. The train *Lalgola Passenger* from **Kolkata** (**S**) leaves 2300, 5½ hrs. Buses from Baharampur to Kolkata are painful.

Malda *p91*

Buses are cheap and rickshaws common. For **Gaur and Pandua**, buses, taxis (Rs 600 for half-day tour) and tongas. Bus to **Murshidabad**, 3-4 hrs, Rs 60. **Siliguri**, WBSTC Rocket buses 1700-2400, 6½ hrs. Bus to Kolkata not recommended. **Trains:** to **New Jalpaiguri**: *Kanchenjunga Exp 5658*, 1330, 6 hrs. **Kolkata (S)**: *Kanchenjunga Exp 5659* (AC/II), 1242, 8 hrs.

❶ Directory

Bishnupur *p88*

Banks State Bank of India changes foreign cash. **Hospital** Sub-Division Hospital, near the Court. Vishnu Pharmacy in Maruee Bazar.

Santiniketan *p89, map p89*

Banks State Bank of India, Bolpur and Santiniketan. **Hospital** Pearson Memorial Hospital, Santiniketan. **Tourist information** PRO, Vishva Bharati Office, T03463-252751, Thu-Tue 1000-1700.

West Bengal Hills

The Himalayan foothills of northern West Bengal contain a wealth of trekking opportunities and hill stations in stunning locations including the region's prime tourist destination, Darjeeling. The old colonial summer retreat is surrounded by spectacular views and still draws plenty of visitors to enjoy cooler climes and a good cuppa. The area also holds one of the Indian one-horned rhino's last safe havens in the Jaldapara Wildlife Sanctuary. ▸▸ *For Sleeping, Eating and other listings see pages 104-110.*

Darjeeling ⊜⦿⊛⊙▲⊖❶ ▸▸ *pp104-110. Colour map 2, grid A1.*

➜ *Phone code: 0354. Population: 107,500. Altitude: 2134 m.*

For tens of thousands of visitors from Kolkata and the steamy plains Darjeeling has been the place to get away from the summer heat. Built on a crescent-shaped ridge Darjeeling is surrounded by hills which are thickly covered with coniferous forests and terraced tea gardens. The idyllic setting, the exhilarating air outside town, and stunning views of the Kangchendzonga range – when you can see through the clouds – attract plenty of trekkers too. Nevertheless, Darjeeling's modern reality is a crowed, noisy and in places shockingly dirty and polluted town. From June to September the monsoons bring heavy downpours, sometimes causing landslides, but the air clears after mid-September. Winter evenings are cold enough to demand log fires and lots of warm clothing.

Ins and outs

Getting there Bagdogra, near Siliguri, is Darjeeling's nearest airport, where jeeps and share-taxis tout for business since buses only run from Siliguri. Trains connect New Jalpaiguri/Siliguri with Kolkata and other major cities. The diesel 'toy train' runs from Siliguri/NJP in season but is very slow. Most people reach Darjeeling by bus or share-taxi and arrive at the Bazar Bus stand in the lower town, though some taxis go to Clubside on the Mall, which is more convenient for most accommodation. Buses from Gangtok arrive near the GPO. ▸▸ *See Transport, page 108, for further details.*

> ♦ *Roads can get washed away during the monsoons and may remain in poor condition even in October.*

⦂ Darjeeling Himalayan Railway – a mini miracle

For many people, the somewhat erratic narrow gauge Toy Train between New Jalpaiguri and Darjeeling, with its 0.6 m gauge track which used to be hauled by sparkling tank engines, is a rewarding experience. The brainchild of East Bengal railway agent Franklyn Prestage, the train promised to improve access to the hills from the sweltering humidity of the Kolkata plains in the summer. Following the line of an earlier steam tramway, the name was changed to the Darjeeling Himalayan Railway Company in 1881.

It is a stunning achievement, winding its way up the hillside, often with brilliant views over the plains covering the 82 km with gradients of up to one in 19. At Ghoom it reaches 2438 m and then descends 305 m to Darjeeling. The DHR has been upgraded to a World Heritage Site and has newly refurbished carriages with cushioned seats and window curtains for the tourist trains. It is a must for steam buffs – despite derailments which are "swiftly dealt with and you are lifted back on the tracks within 20 minutes".

Getting around Darjeeling's roads slope quite gently so it is easy to walk around the town. The railway station is in the lower part of town on Hill Cart Road, with the taxi and bus stands. The lower and upper roads are linked by a series of connecting roads and steep steps. For sights away from the centre you need to hire a taxi. Be prepared for seasonal water shortages and frequent power cuts. After dark a torch is essential.

History

Darjeeling means region of the *dorje* (thunderbolt) and its official but rarely used spelling is Darjiling. The surrounding area once belonged to Sikkim, although parts were annexed from time to time by the Bhutanese and Nepalese. The East India Company returned the territory's sovereignty to the Rajas of Sikkim, which led to the British obtaining permission to gain the site of the hill station called Darjeeling in 1835, in return for an annual payment. It was practically uninhabited and thickly forested but soon grew into a popular health resort after a road and several houses were built and tea growing was introduced. The Bengal Government escaped from the Kolkata heat to take up its official summer residence here. The upper reaches were originally occupied by the Europeans, who built houses with commanding views. Down the hillside on terraces sprawled the humbler huts and bazars of the Indian town.

Sights

Observatory Hill, sacred to Siva, is pleasant for walks though the views of the mountains are obscured by tall trees. Further north is **Himalayan Mountaineering Institute and Everest Museum** ① *To354-225 4087, daily 0830-1300 and 1400-1600 except Thu in winter, Rs 100 (includes zoo), still camera Rs 10, video Rs 20, entrance is through the zoo on Jawahar Rd West*, recommended. Previously headed by the late Tenzing Norgay who shared the first climb of Everest in 1953, it traces the history of attempted climbs from 1857 and displays old mountaineering equipment including that used on that historic Tenzing-Hillary climb. The **zoo** ① *1000-1600, Rs 100 (includes Institute)*, is next to the Mountaineering Institute. High-altitude wildlife includes Himalayan black bears, Siberian tigers, red pandas, yaks and llama. There are large enclosures over a section of the hillside but at feeding time and during wet weather they retreat into their small cement enclosures giving the impression that they are restricted to their cells. There is a reasonably successful snow leopard breeding programme.

⦂ *Visit the Shrubbery behind Raj Bhawan on Birch Hill for spectacular views of Kangchendzonga.*

Back into the centre of the town, the pedestrianized **Mall** to the east of Observatory Hill offers good views near the Chowrasta. Beware of the monkeys as they bite. The decaying **Natural History Museum** ① *Bishop Eric Benjamin Rd, 1000-1600, Rs 5*, has a large collection of fauna of the region. The **Tibetan Refugee Self-help Centre** ① *T0354-225 3122, Mon-Sat, walk to viewpoint 500 m beyond Windamere hotel and then walk down for about 30 mins (ask around)*, with its temple, school and hospital is north of town. After the Chinese invasion, thousands of Tibetan refugees settled in Darjeeling (many having accompanied the Dalai Lama) and the rehabilitation centre was set up in 1959 to enable them to continue to practise their skills and provide a sales

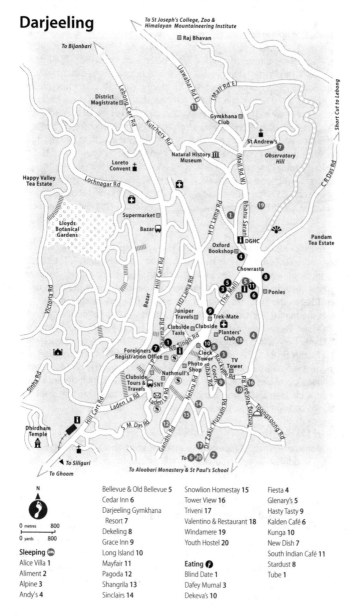

Darjeeling

To St Joseph's College, Zoo &
Himalayan Mountaineering Institute

To Bijanbari

Raj Bhavan

To Siliguri

To Ghoom

To Aloobari Monastery & St Paul's School

N

0 metres 800
0 yards 800

Quali-tea brew

An ancient Chinese legend suggests that 'tay', or tea, originated in India, although tea was known to have been grown in China around 2700 BC.

It is a species of Camellia, Camellia thea. After 1833, when its monopoly on importing tea from China was abolished, the East India Company made attempts to grow tea in Assam using wild chai plants found growing there and later introduced it in Darjeeling and in the Nilgiri hills in the South. Today India is the largest producer of tea in the world. Assam grows over half and Darjeeling about a quarter of the nation's output. Once drunk only by the tribal people, it has now become India's national drink.

The old orthodox method of tea processing produces the aromatic lighter coloured liquor of the Golden Flowery Orange Pekoe in its most superior grade. The fresh leaves are dried by fans on withering troughs to reduce the moisture content and then rolled and pressed to express the juices which coat the leaves. These are left to ferment in a controlled environment to produce the desired aroma. Finally the leaves are dried by passing them through a heated drying chamber and then graded – the unbroken being the best quality, down to the fannings and dust. The more common crushing, tearing, curling (CTC) method produces tea which gives a much darker liquor.

Most of Darjeeling's tea is sold through auction houses, the largest centre being in Kolkata. Tea tasting and blending are skills have developed over a long period of time and are highly prized. The industry provides vital employment in the hill areas and is an assured foreign exchange earner.

outlet. You can watch them at work (carpet weaving, spinning, dyeing, woodwork, etc) during the season, when it is well worth a visit (closes for lunch). The shop sells carpets (orders taken and posted), textiles, curios or jewellery, though not cheap to buy. South of town, the **Aloobari Monastery**, on Tenzing Norgay Road, is open to visitors. Tibetan and Sikkimese handicrafts made by the monks are for sale.

Near the market are **Lloyds Botanical Gardens** ① *Mon-Sat 0600-1700, closed bank holidays*. These were laid out in 1878 on land given by Mr W Lloyd, owner of the Lloyd's Bank. They have a modest collection of Himalayan and Alpine flora including banks of azaleas and rhododendrons, magnolias, a good orchid house and a herbarium. It is a pleasant and quiet spot. **Victoria Falls**, which is only impressive in the monsoons, provides added interest to a three-hour nature trail. There are several tea gardens close to Darjeeling, but not all welcome visitors. One that does is the **Pattabong Estate** on the road towards Sikkim.

Around Darjeeling

Ghoom Monastery, at an altitude of 2550 m, is the important Yiga-Choling Gompa, a Yellow-hat Buddhist Monastery. Built in 1875, it houses famous Buddhist scriptures. You can visit Ghoom (8 km away) on the steam Tourist Train from April to June and October to November. There is an interesting Darjeeling Himalayan Railway museum at the station. A few spruced up carriages do a tourist-only ride in summer with a photo stop at Batasia, departing at 1000, returning at 1230 (but check times), Rs 240. It's limited to 40 passengers so go early to join the queue; tickets go on sale at 0800. See also Toy Train on page 110. Alternatively, go on the diesel train at 0900, Rs 25 (first class); Rs 4 (second class) and return on foot or by bus. Both pass through **Batasia Loop**, 5 km from Darjeeling on the way to Ghoom, which allows the narrow gauge rail to do a figure-of-eight loop. There's a war memorial here in a pleasant park with mountain views (Rs 3).

The disused **Lebong Race Course**, 8 km away, was once the smallest and highest in the world and is still pleasant for a walk. It was started as a parade ground in 1885.

It is worth rising as early as 0400 to make the hour's journey for a breathtaking view (weather permitting) of the sunrise on Kangchendzonga at **Tiger Hill** ① *jeeps from Darjeeling, Rs 600, you may wish to walk back from Tiger Hill (about 2 hrs, 11 km) or visit Ghoom on the way back.* Mount Everest (8846 m), 225 km away, is visible on a clear day. The crowds at sunrise disappear by mid-morning.

Trekking around Darjeeling ⌂ ⇢ *p105.*

The trekking routes around Darjeeling are well established, having been popular for nearly 100 years. Walks lead in gentle stages along safe roads and through wooded hills up to altitudes of 3660 m. Trails pass through untouched nature filled with rhododendrons, magnolias, orchids and wild flowers, together with forests, meadows and small villages. All this to a backdrop of mountains stretching from Mount Everest to the Bhutan hills, including the third highest mountain in the world, Khangchendzonga. The best trekking seasons are April to May, when the magnolias and rhododendrons are in full bloom, and October to November. In spring there may be the occasional shower. In autumn the air is dry and the visibility excellent. In winter the lower altitude trails that link Rimbick with Jhepi (18 km) can be very attractive for birdwatchers. There is an extensive network of varied trails that link the hillside towns and villages. Agents in Darjeeling can organize four- to seven-day treks, providing guide, equipment and accommodation (see page 108). Trekking gear can also be hired from the youth hostel where there is a useful book of suggestions from other trekkers.

In a bid to provide employment for local youth, the West Bengal Forest and Wildlife Department have stipulated that visitors must have a guide (porters are optional) in order to enter the Singalila National Park. Checks to this effect are made at the

Darjeeling treks

Not to scale

Manebhanjang checkpoint at the entrance to the park. If you haven't arranged a trek through an agent in Darjeeling, local guides can be hired in Manebhanjang for around Rs 300 per day. Entry fees for the park are also paid at the checkpoint (foreigners Rs 100, Indians Rs 20, still camera Rs 50, video camera Rs 100). If you prefer to go alone, it is possible (though a bit risky) to pay for a guide but not actually take one, just showing the payment receipt at the checkpoint to gain entry to the ridge.

Singalila trek

The 160-km Singalila trek starts from the small border town of **Manebhanjang**, 26 km from Darjeeling. The journey to and from Darjeeling can be done by shared or private jeep in 1½ hours. Walking from Manebhanjang north to Sandakphu (rather than starting in Sandakphu and heading south) means you are always walking towards the most stunning views. If you have not arranged for transport to meet you at a particular point then it is entirely possible to travel back to Darjeeling from any roadhead by public bus, with services at least once daily, often three to four times daily.

There are plenty of trekkers huts of varying standards and prices (if on an organised trek these will have been booked for you) at Tonglu, Sandakphu, Phalut, Gorkhey, Molley, Rammam, Rimbick, Siri Khola and other villages. Although room is usually available, it's wise to book in advance during May/June and October when trails can be very busy. Any trekking agent in Darjeeling can arrange these bookings for a small fee. Private lodges, such as Sherpa Lodge in Rimbick and Rammam, and other trailside lodges in Meghma, Jaubari and Kalpokhri, are generally friendly, flexible and provide reasonable basic accommodation. Some places can prepare yak curry on request, and be sure to sample hot chhang, the local millet brew, served in a wooden keg and sipped through a bamboo straw.

The area is a birdwatcher's paradise with over 600 species including orioles, fly-catchers, minivets, finches, sunbirds, thrushes, piculets, falconets and Hoodson's Imperial pigeons. The rhododendron, oak and conifer forests are particularly well preserved.

Day 1 To Tonglu (or Tumling) 1 km beyond Manebhanjang town you reach a rough stone paved track leading sharply up to the left. Tonglu (3,030 m) is 11 km from this point if you follow the jeep track, slightly less if you take the frequent but very steep short cuts. Alternatively, head for Tumling, just the other side of the peak of the hill from Tonglu (you take the alternative road from Meghma and rejoin the main route 1 km after Tumling). There is a trekkers' hut at **Tonglu** with 24 beds and a fine view of the Khangchendzonga range. From here you can also see the plains of North Bengal and some valleys of Nepal in the distance. Closer to hand are the snow fed rivers, the Teesta in the east and Koshi in the west. You can also sleep in **Tumling** where Shikhar Lodge has simple basic and clean rooms, run by a local teacher's friendly family, "fabulous supper and breakfast" plus a lovely garden. There are tea shops at **Chitre** and at **Meghma**, which has an interesting monastery noted for its large collection of Buddhist statues; 108, according to locals. Ask at the tea house opposite to get in.

Day 2 To Jaubari and Gairibans A level walk along the ridge takes you past the long 'mani' wall to the Nepalese village of Jaubari; no visa is needed and good accommodation is available should you wish to spend a night in Nepal. After Jaubari the trail turns sharply to the right back into Indian territory and down through bamboo and rhododendron forests to the village of Gairibans in a forest clearing. You could carry on all the way to Sandakphu, a long hard day's hiking.

Day 3 To Sandakphu It is 14 km uphill to Sandakphu, with a lunch break in Kalpokhri with its attractive 'black' lake surrounded by fir trees, about midway. Even in winter the lake never freezes. The last 3 km from Bhikebhanjang (tea shop) to Sandakphu are particularly steep; this section takes more than an hour but the views from the

Singalila Ridge make it all worthwhile. **Sandakphu**, a small settlement located at 3636 m, is considered the finest viewpoint on the trek, and is the prime destination for most visitors. Located 57 km from Darjeeling, it is accessible by jeep (the same narrow bumpy track used by trekkers), which is how many Indian tourists make the journey during the season. A viewpoint 100 m above Sandakphu offers fantastic views, including the northern face of Everest (8846 m), 140 km away as the crow flies, Khangchendzonga (8598 m), Chomolhari, the highest peak in Bhutan, and numerous peaks such as Pandim that lie in Sikkim.

There are several trekkers' huts and lodges, each with a dining area, toilets and cookhouse. These vary widely in standards and price, some costing up to Rs 500 per person; it's worth seeing a few. The drive back to Manebhanjang by pre-arranged four-wheel drive can take four hours along the very rough track, if finishing the trek here.

Day 4 Sandakphu to Phalut Phalut, 22 km from Sandakphu along an undulating jeepable track, is at the junction of Nepal, Sikkim and West Bengal. It offers even closer views of Khangchendzonga. It is best to avoid trekking here in May and June and mid-September to 25 October when large numbers of college trekking teams from West Bengal descend on the area. From Phalut it's possible to get a jeep back the way you came, via Sandakphu. Alternatively you can walk south for 4 km back towards **Bhikebhanjang** and then take a 16 km long trail through fine forests of the Singalila National Park down to **Rimbick**.

Day 5 Phalut to Rimbick From Phalut, there is **Gorkhey**, with accommodation, and it's a further 3 km to the village of **Samanden**, hidden in a hanging valley. From Samanden, it is a 6 km walk to **Rammam** where there is a clean, comfortable Sherpa Lodge in a pleasant garden, recommended for friendly service and good food. Alternatively, the Trekkers' Hut is about 1 km before Rammam village. From Rammam it is a two-hour walk down to a couple of attractive trekkers' huts at **Siri Khola** and a further two hours to Rimbick. Again, this area has a wealth of birdlife. From Rimbick there are three jeeps a day to take you back to Darjeeling.

Although Gorkhey, Phalut, Rammam and Rimbick lie just south of the border with Sikkim, entering Sikkim is not permitted on this route, though agents say this may change in future; ask in Darjeeling about the current situation.

Sabarkum via Ramman to Molley or Bijanbari

An alternative quieter trail links Sabarkum (7 km before Phalut on the main Sandakphu-Phalut trail) with Rammam, with a possible overnight halting place at the **Molley** Trekkers' Hut. Those with five days to spare can return by the **Rammam-Rimbick-Jhepi-Bijanbari** route (153 km). From Rammam you can cross by a suspension bridge over the Siri Khola River and follow the path up the valley, which leads to Dentam in Sikkim (entry into Sikkim not permitted). This less-trodden valley has rich birdlife, particularly kingfishers, and excellent views of undisturbed forest. From **Bijanbari** (762 m) it is possible to return to Darjeeling, 36 km away by jeep, or climb a further 2 km to Pulbazar and then return to Darjeeling 16 km away. Those wishing only to go to Rimbick can get a jeep from there, or may return to Manebhanjang via Palmajua and Batasi (180 km), which takes one day.

Mirik and Kurseong ⬛🏍⬛ ⟫ *pp105-109.*

Mirik, 49 km from Darjeeling, at an altitude of 1730 m, has forests of japonica, orange orchards, tea gardens and cardamom plantations. Its restful ambience, dramatic views and homely accommodation make it an appealing stop for a few days of relaxation. **Sumendu Lake**, with its 3½ km cobbled promenade, offers boating, while **Krishannagar**, south of the lake, has a carpet weaving centre and the impressive **Bokar**

Gompa, a 15-minute stroll from the main road. You can trek to **Kurseong** and **Sandakphu**, or less ambitiously, take a bus a few miles up the Darjeeling road and walk back through rolling tea estates, flower-laden cottages and villages.

Kurseong or Place of the White Orchid east of Mirik, is surrounded by tea gardens and orange orchards and has some popular boarding schools. Travellers suggest stopping here overnight on the Toy Train between Siliguri and Darjeeling. You can visit the **Makaibari Tea Estate** 4 km away ① *Tue-Sun*, and the **Forest Museum** on Dow Hill.

At **Tung** nearby, the St Alphonsus Social and Agricultural Centre, run by a Canadian Jesuit, is working with the local community through education, housing, agricultural, forestry and marketing projects. They welcome volunteers; contact **SASAC** ① *Tung, Darjeeling, West Bengal, T0354-234 2059, sasac@satyam.net.in.*

Kalimpong 🚌🚻🚹🏕🚍🚹 » *pp105-110. Colour map 2, grid A2.*

→ *Phone code: 03552. Population: 43,000. Altitude: 1250 m.*

Set in beautiful wooded mountain scenery with an unhurried air about it, Kalimpong was a meeting point of the once 'Three Closed Lands' on the trade route to Tibet, Bhutan and Nepal. Away from the crowded and scruffy centre near the motor stand, the

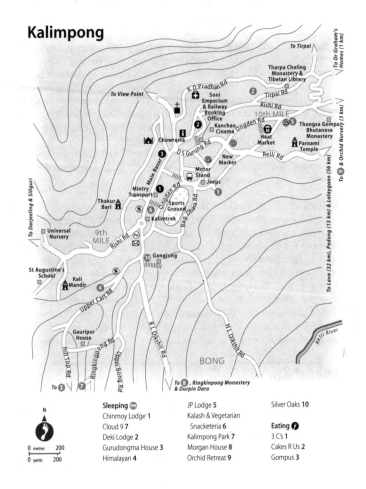

Kalimpong

Sleeping 🛏	JP Lodge 5	Silver Oaks 10
Chinmoy Lodge 1	Kalash & Vegetarian	
Cloud 9 7	Snacketeria 6	**Eating** 🍴
Deki Lodge 2	Kalimpong Park 7	3 C's 1
Gurudongma House 3	Morgan House 8	Cakes R Us 2
Himalayan 4	Orchid Retreat 9	Gompus 3

N

0 metres 200
0 yards 200

town becomes more spaced out as mountain roads wind up the hillsides leading to monasteries, mission schools and orchid nurseries. Some say that the name is derived from *pong* (stronghold) of *kalon* (king's minister), or from *kalibong*, a plant fibre.

Ins and outs

Getting there and around Bagdogra is the nearest airport and New Jalpaiguri the nearest railhead. Buses and shared jeeps from there arrive at the Bazar Motor Stand in two to three hours. From Darjeeling, the 51-km journey (2½ hours) is through beautiful scenery. The road winds down through tea estates and then descends to 250 m at Tista where it crosses the river on a 'new' concrete bridge. 'Lovers' Meet' and 'View Point' give superb views of the Rangit and Tista rivers. The centre of Kalimpong is compact enough to be seen comfortably on foot. ►► *See Transport, page 109, for further details.*

Sights

The traditional market at the 10th Mile has great atmosphere. The *haat* here every Wednesday and Saturday draws colourful villagers who come to sell fruit, unfamiliar vegetables, traditional medicines, woollen cloth, yarn and much more. It is remarkably clean and laid back, a delight to explore and find unusual merchandise: curly young fern tops, bamboo shoots, dried mushrooms, fragrant spices, musk, *chaang* paraphernalia, large chunks of brown soap, and tiny chickens in baskets alongside gaudy posters. The oldest, the **Thongsa Gompa Bhutanese monastery**, 10th Mile (1692) has been renovated. Further north, the Tibetan monastery (Yellow Hat) at Tirpai, the **Tharpa Choling** (1922) has a library of Tibetan manuscripts and *thangkas*. The **Pedong Bhutanese monastery** (1837) near the old Bhutanese Damsang Fort at Algara (15 km) holds ceremonial dances every February. At Durpin Dara, the highest point in Kalimpong with superb views, stands the **Ringkinpong monastery** of Zang Dog Palri Phodrang. Unique outside Tibet, it has a school of Tibetan Medicine and is particularly interesting when prayers are being chanted. **Doctor Graham's Homes**, 3 km, was started by the missionary Doctor John Anderson Graham in 1900 when he admitted six needy children. Now there are 1300 pupils. Volunteers able to spend at least six months should write in advance. There are pleasant **hikes** through Tista Road and rice fields to **Chitray Falls**, 9 km, a three-hour walk to **Bhalu Khop** and a 1½ hours' downhill walk from the motor stand to the Relli River. Scenic two-three hour **treks** leave from **Lava** (32 km; monastery and weekly market on Tuesday), and **Lolaygaon** (56 km), which has spectacular views of Kangchendzonga; both villages have a good choice of accommodation. You can picnic on the river beaches at Tista Bazar and Kalijhora.

Kalimpong excels in producing orchids, amaryllis, roses, cacti, dahlias and gladioli. Nurseries include Ganesh Mani Pradhan on 12th Mile, Universal on 8th Mile, Shanti Kunj on BL Dikshit Road and Himalayan on East Main Road.

Siliguri and Jaldapara 🖫⊜🔾 ►► *pp106-110. Colour map 2, grid A1/A2.*

Surrounded by tea plantations, **Siliguri** is a largely unattractive transport junction with a vast truck park to the north and a busy main road lined with shops. The narrow-gauge steam Toy Train to Darjeeling starts from here during the tourist season. It is also used as a base for travel into the hills and to the Jaldapara National Park.

The River Torsa flows through **Jaldapara National Park.** The riverine forests of sal, khair and sheeshu harbour the one-horned rhino, elephants, wild boar, bison, deer, leopards, gaur and the occasional tiger. It covers an area of 116 sq km and is situated close to Phuntsholing in Bhutan. Trained elephants and vehicle safaris are available to take visitors around. It is 160 km from Bagdogra airport, 224 km from Darjeeling. The best time to visit is from November to April when forest cover is thinner.

● Sleeping

Darjeeling *p95, map p97*

Most hotels are within 1 km of the station. Several include all meals in season (Mar-Jun, Sep-Nov) and offer discounts off season. Some charge extra for Christmas and New Year. Prices listed are for high season.

L Windamere, Observatory Hill, T0354-225 4041, www.windamerehotel.com. Enviable location, good views when clear, 27 spacious rooms (no phone or TV), dated bathrooms (limited hot water), terraces, charming, characterful, Raj experience with memorabilia, coal fires (can be smoky), hotties in bed, pre-war piano favourites accompany tea.

L-AL Mayfair, The Mall, opposite Raj Bhavan gate, T0354-225 6376, www.mayfairhotels.com. Superb location, among terrace gardens, 31 lavish rooms (5 attractive wooden attics), plus cottages on hillside below Mall, good Tiffany's restaurant.

AL Cedar Inn, Dr Zakir Hussain Rd, T0354-225 4446, www.cedarinndarjeeling.com. Slightly out of town, but with great views. Free taxi service around town. Family friendly, sauna/gym, nice garden. Wood panelled rooms.

A Sinclairs, 18/1 Gandhi Rd, T0354-225 6431, www.sinclairshotels.com. 54 rooms, central heating, restaurant, bar, central location.

A-B Darjeeling Gymkhana Resort, The Mall, T0354-225 7320, www.sunflower-hotels.com. Modern rooms, Indian vegetarian restaurant, club on doorstep for sports/activities, wooded location. Good spot.

C Alice Villa, 41 HD Lama Rd below DGHC Tourist Office, Chowrasta, T0354-225 4181. 21 large clean rooms (fireplace in some, bucket of coal Rs 75), cosy bungalow, food by arrangement, good value.

C-D Shangrila, 5 Nehru Rd, near Chowrasta, T0354-225 4149. Some of the 10 rooms have good views, decent restaurant.

C-E Bellevue, Chowrasta, T0354-225 4075, www.darjeeling-bellevuehotel.com. Central, 43 rooms with bath and hot water, some large, bright and airy (eg rooms 35, 49), all have loads of character with old wooden fittings, good K'dzonga view from roof at sunrise, limited food. Ask the owner, Lawang, for tourist information. Friendly management.

D Main Old Bellevue Hotel, Chowrasta, T0354-225 4178. Rooms with character in the Heritage building in a pleasant garden.

D Valentino, 6 Rockville Rd, T0354-225 2228. 17 clean rooms with mountain views, central heating, good Chinese restaurant, bar.

D-E Dekeling, 51 Gandhi Rd (the Mall), on Club side, T0354-225 4159, www.dekeling.com. 11 rooms with bath on upper floors, 4 attic front rooms with views (noisy when jeeps depart at 0400 for Tiger Hill with lots of hooting), good restaurant, charming family, 'brilliant hosts', reserve ahead.

D-E Grace Inn, 8/B Cooch Bihar Rd, T0354-225 8106. Large, well-furnished rooms with chalet feel, subtly lit restaurant with ambitious menu, cheerful staff. Big off-season discounts.

E Alpine Hotel, 104 Rockvile Rd, T0354-225 6355, alpinedarj@yahoo.com. Just down from TV tower, clean and bright rooms.

E Snowlion Homestay, 27/A Gandhi Rd, T0354-225 5521. Sparkling new rooms with a jolly Tibetan family, smart bathrooms, some rooms have electric heater.

F-G Andy's, 102 Zakir Hussain Rd, 5 mins from Chowrasta past pony sheds towards TV tower, T0354-225 3125, www.andysguesthouse.biz. Very clean, airy rooms, some with Indian WC, upper floors with small hot shower, bird's-eye views from rooftop, kitchenette, storage for trekkers, friendly family atmosphere. Recommended.

G Aliment, 40 Zakir Hussain Rd, 100 m below youth hostel, T0354-225 5068, alimentweb@sify.com. Small, clean, bright rooms, hot shower, cheap food, internet Rs 30 per hr, packed with travellers, good atmosphere, excellent library, friendly owner.

G Long Island, Rochville Dham, down the back of TV tower, near Tower View, T0354-225 2043, pritaya19@yahoo.com. Attractively painted, quaint exterior, clean basic rooms with communal hot shower, restaurant, quiet location, great views from rooftop and upper rooms. Run by very friendly Nepali family. Highly recommended.

G Pagoda, 1 Upper Beechwood Rd. Very friendly, clean but basic rooms, some with bath (limited bucket hot water), central yet quite peaceful, good value.

G Tower View, Rockville Dham, down the back of TV Tower, T0354-225 4452. Pleasant, clean rooms with toilet, shared hot shower, wood stove and dusty book collection in appealing restaurant.

G Triveni, 85 Dr Zakir Hussain Rd, T0354-225 3878. Well-kept basic rooms, home-cooked meals, popular.

G Youth Hostel (WB), Dr Zakir Hussain Rd, T0354-225 2290. Mainly dorm (Rs 25), being renovated, superb position, no restaurant, trekking information, slightly out of town but popular.

Trekking around Darjeeling *p99*

C Karmi Farm, Bijanbari, contact **Samsara Travel** in Darjeeling, T0354-225 6370, samsara@dte.vsnl.net.in. A haven of rural peace at Kolbong, which you may choose to use as a base, north of Bijanbari (access via Kaijali, 4WDs stop 20 mins' walk away, or it's 2-3 hrs by pony from Pulbazar). 7 doubles with bath, simple but spotless, superb food, US$20 includes food, porters etc.

F Teacher's Lodge, Jaubari, excellent value. There is a large **Trekkers' Hut** at Gairibans with about 20 beds.

Mirik and Kurseong *p101*

A-C Orange County Retreat, Mirik, T0354-244 3612. Catering more to Indian tourists, 12 stone cottages, plus a honeymoon suite. Plenty of views and nature. Arranges treks in the Singalila range.

B-E Jagjeet, Mirik, T0354-224 3231, www.jag jeethotel.com. Large, well-furnished rooms, although cheaper ones are a bit musty. Good restaurant and bar.

D-F Ratnagiri, Mirik, T0354-224 3243. Bright spotless rooms with great views, and a cute garden restaurant. Excellent choice.

E Tourist Lodge, Hill Cart Rd, Kurseong, T0354-234 4409. Good views, 16 rooms, fast food restaurant, bar.

E Tourist Lodge, Mirik, T0354-224 3371. Huge wood-panelled rooms with balconies, ignore the faded exterior.

F-G Lodge Ashirvad, Mirik, T0354-224 3272. The best budget option, with 24-hr hot water in some rooms, rooftop with monastery views and a helpful owner.

Kalimpong *p102, map p102*

Hotels offer discounts during winter and monsoon; not all accept credit cards.

A Silver Oaks, Main Rd, T03552-255296, www .elginhotels.com. Beautiful rooms, some with fabulous views, good restaurant (own fruit and vegetables), pleasant terraced garden.

B Gurudongma House, Hill Top Rd, T03552-255204, www.gurudongma.com. Rooms in charming family house and cottage with meals, Alpine tents, gardens, personal service (collect from motor stand), book ahead. Also restored farmhouse at Samthar where you can enjoy country pleasures and wonderful food; contact **Gurudongma Tours and Treks**, gurutt@satyam.net.in.

B Himalayan, Upper Cart Rd, 10-min walk town centre, T03552-255248, www.himalayan hotel.co.in. 20 rooms, 8 spacious suites in newer imaginatively designed 'cottages', rest in stone-built characterful family home of the MacDonalds, rooms better upstairs, lovely veranda, mountain views, attractive gardens, set menu meals, helpful management.

B Orchid Retreat, Ganesh Villa, longish walk from town, T03552-255389, thakro@cal2. vsnl.net.in. In interesting orchid nursery, 6 rooms in traditional thatched cottages (built with local materials), hot water (no TV or phone), home-cooked meals (Rs 100-150), lovely terrace garden with special palm collection, personal attention, peaceful.

B-C Kalimpong Park, Ringkingpong Rd, T03552-255304, www.indiamart.com/ kalimpongparkhotel. Raj atmosphere aplenty in good-sized, airy rooms, **B** suites (some in older 2-storeyed house), good restaurant and bar, garden, pleasant peaceful location, knowledgeable owner.

B-C Morgan House, Singamari, Durpin Dara Hill, T03552-255384, 3 km from centre. Beautiful location, 7 rooms with bath (good views from upstairs), restaurant, bar, gardens.

D Crown Lodge, off Bag Dhara Rd, near Motor Stand, T03552-255846, slg_ramklg@ sancharnet.in. 21 clean well-maintained rooms with bath, hot water, generator, very friendly and helpful, pleasant.

D-E Kalash, on main road above Vegetarian Snacketeria, T03552-259564. Spotless rooms over a great restaurant, but traffic noise can be a problem.

D-F JP Lodge, RC Mintry Rd, T03552-257457, www.jplodge.com. Clean comfortable rooms with charming staff, designated meditation space in a wood-panelled garret.

E Cloud 9, Ringkingpong Rd, T03552-259554. Clean attractive rooms, good multi-cuisine restaurant.

E-F Chinmoy Lodge, below motor stand, T03552-2256364. Set amongst quaint old buildings, with sweeping views from roof and cheery, freshly painted rooms.

E-G Deki Lodge, Tirpai Rd, uphill from Motor Stand, T03552-255095, www.geocities.com/dekilodge. Pristine rooms aimed at various budgets, cosy terrace restaurant with great views, kind and knowledgeable staff, a place with character.

Siliguri and Jaldapara *p103*
Siliguri

Hill Cart Rd is officially Tenzing Norgay Rd.
A Cindrella, Sevoke Rd, '3rd mile' (out of town), T0353-2547136, www.cindrella hotels.com. Comfortable a/c rooms, vegetarian restaurant, pool, internet, car hire, airport pick-up, efficient.
B Sinclairs, Pradhan Nagar, T0353-251 2440, www.sinclairhotels.com. 46 comfortable rooms, good restaurant and service, pool.
B-D Conclave, Hill Cart Rd, (opposite SNT bus stand), T0353-2516144, www.hotelconclave .com. A brand new hotel in town centre. Good quality rooms, a/c, satellite TV, licensed bar, restaurant serving quality Indian/European food, intermittent internet, parking.
B-D Mainak (WBTDC), Hill Cart Rd (near railway station; auto from NJP Rs 120), T0353-251 3989, maitd@dte.vsnl.net.in. 38 comfortable rooms, 14 a/c (rooms vary), well-kept gardens, restaurant and bar, helpful staff.
C-F Heritage, Hill Cart Rd, T0353-251 9621, hotel_heritage@sancharnet.in. Prices proportional to the shabbiness of the rooms, but the location is good.
C-F Rajdarbar, Hill Cart Rd next to **Hotel Conclave**, T0353-251 4316, tapas_gh@hot mail.com. A friendly place, well situated with restaurant, hot water in all rooms.
C-F Vinayak, Hill Cart Rd, T0353-243 1130. Clean rooms with bath, some a/c, good restaurant.
E Mount View, Hill Cart Rd, opposite main bus station, T0353-251 5919. Basic rooms, **Khana Khazana** restaurant next door has a busy terrace and generous portions.
E-G Yatri Hotel, Hill Cart Rd opposite main bus stand, T0353-251 4707, yatrihotel98@ yahoo.com. Basic, cheap rooms with bath, restaurant and cosy bar next door.
G Hillview, Hill Cart Rd, T0353-251 9951. Shabby old place, but the only hotel in town with any character.

G Railway Retiring Rooms, Siliguri Junction and New Jalpaiguri. 4 rooms and 6 dorm beds in each, good vegetarian snacks.
G Siliguri Lodge, Hill Cart Rd (near SNS bus stand), T0353-251 5290. Grotty exterior but clean sheets and relatively quiet.
G Youth Hostel, Kangchendzonga Stadium, 130 beds.

Jaldapara
C Hollong Forest Tourist Lodge, Hollong, 6 km from Madarihat, T03563-262228, book well in advance either directly, or via the Tourist Bureau, Siliguri, T0353-251 1974. Built of timber on stilts deep inside the park. 6 rooms (all meals), the lodge is very popular and is en route to Phuntsholing in Bhutan.
F Nilpara Forest Bungalow, Hasimara. 2 rooms, very basic, caretaker will prepare a simple meal if requested but take all provisions.
F Youth Hostel and Lodge, 4 km from Hasimara railway station, 18 km from Madarihat, at Baradabri. 3 rooms, 14 beds in 4 dorms, poor catering, reserve through DFO, Tourism Centre, Jalpaiguri, T03563-262239 or Kolkata, T033-2248 8271.

● Eating

Darjeeling *p95, map p97*
Hotels with restaurants will usually serve non-residents. Several have bars.
♥♥♥ New Elgin. Charming dining room with character, good meals, very pleasant service.
♥♥ Glenary's, Nehru Rd (the Mall), T0354-225 7554, glens_getaways@sancharnet.in. Modern tea room with excellent confectionery, friendly, first class breakfast, Kalimpong cheese and wholemeal bread sold, licensed restaurant upstairs pricier, bar downstairs with a local band on Sat 1900-2200. Internet café (Rs 30 per hr).
♥♥ Hasty Tasty, Nehru Rd. Very good pure vegetarian Indian fast food, not the cheapest but worth it.
♥♥ Kalden Café, Chowrasta. Squash yourself onto the benches crowded with locals and foreigners for Tibetan delights and curious-sounding Western dishes. Super friendly and super cheap.
♥♥ New Dish JP Sharma Rd. Chinese. Adventurous menu, excellent chicken entrées, friendly staff.

The Tube, in alley left of Fancy Market, NB Singh Rd. Something for everyone (thali recommended) in a semi-groovy setting with great views.

Valentino, Chinese and Continental.

Blind Date, top floor, Fancy Market, NB Singh Rd. Warm and friendly place, cheap Tibetan and Chinese mains, divine soups and clean kitchen in open view. A must.

Dafey Mumal, Laden La Rd. Buzzing bar and good Chinese and Tibetan meals.

Dekeva's, 52 Gandhi Rd, near club side. Nice little Tibetan place, cosy, local meals, also fast food.

Fiesta, Chowrasta. Café-style restaurant serving a mainly Western menu. A bit faded, but a good spot to watch the world go by.

Kunga, Gandhi Rd. Cheerful unpretentious Tibetan joint, with great *momos* and backpacker-friendly breakfasts.

South Indian Café, Chowrasta. Indian food. Very good vegetarian meals.

Stardust, Chowrasta. Basic range of North and South Indian dishes, pure vegetarian, great views from the terrace.

Mirik and Kurseong *p101*
Cheap *dhabas near the bus stand offer passable noodle dishes.*

Samden, main road, Krishnanagar. Great Tibetan food.

Kalimpong *p102, map p102*
Most restaurants shut at 2000. Local canteens behind the jeep stand dish out delicious *momos* and noodle soups at rock-bottom prices.

Gompus, Chowrasta (in hotel). Largely meat-based menu, good for Tibetan and Chinese, very popular, alcohol served.

3C's (formerly **Glenary's**), Main Rd. Hangout for local youth, with Western food, good breakfasts, cakes and decent coffee.

Cakes R Us, past DGTC on DB Giri Rd. Café-style offerings.

Vegetarian Snacketeria, Main Rd, opposite Main Bazar. Tasty South and North Indian plus a wide choice of drinks.

❂ Festivals and events

Darjeeling *p95, map p97*
Apr-May Buddha Jayanti celebrates the birth of the Buddha in the monasteries.

O Shopping

Darjeeling *p95, map p97*
Books
Greenland, Laden La Rd, up some steps near entrance to **Prestige Hotel**. Book swap.
Oxford Bookshop, Chowrasta, good stock especially local interest, amiable staff.

Handicrafts
Local handicrafts sold widely include Buddhist *tankhas* (hand-painted scrolls surrounded by Chinese brocade), good wood carving, carpets, hand-woven cloth, jewellery, copper, brass and white metal religious curios such as prayer wheels, bowls and statues. Chowrasta shops are closed on Sun, Chowk Bazar and Middle Bazar on Thu.

Dorjee, Laden La Rd. **Eastern Arts**, Chowrasta. **H Mullick**, curios from Chowrasta, a cut above the rest. **Nepal Curios**, Laden La Rd. **Tibetan Refugee Self-Help Centre**, Gandhi Rd. See page 97.

Photography
Das Studios, Nehru Rd. Stationery, postcards, interesting black-and-white prints from Raj days; order from album (1-2 days).

Tea
Nathmull's, Laden La Rd (above GPO) and at Rink Mall, nathmulls@goldentipstea.com. An institution, vast selection (Rs 140-10,000 per kg), avoid fancy packs, knowledgeable owner.

Kalimpong *p102, map p102*
Handicrafts
Tibetan and Nepalese handicrafts and woven fabrics are particularly good. There is an abundance of shops on RC Mintry Rd.
Gangjong, Primtam Rd (ask at Silver Oaks Hotel for directions). Interesting hand-made paper factory.
Soni Emporium, near Motor Stand, Mani Link Rd, specializes in Himalayan handicrafts.

▲ Activities and tours

Darjeeling *p95, map p97*
Clubs
The old **Gymkhana Club** has 3 good snooker tables, badminton, squash, tennis and roller skating. Temporary membership Rs 30 per day, up to Rs 55 for activities, excellent staff.

Darjeeling Club, Nehru Rd, T0354-225 4348, the old Planters' Club, a relic of the Raj, membership (Rs 50 per day), allows use of pleasant colonial restaurant (Rs 200 buffet), bar, billiards, a bit run down, but log fires, warm and friendly.

Mountaineering
Himalayan Mountaineering Institute, T0354-225 4087. Runs basic to advanced courses Mar-Dec. 28-day courses cost $650.

Riding
Pony rides are popular on the Mall starting at Chowrasta; also possible to do a scenic half-day ride to Ghoom – agree price in writing!

River rafting
On the Tista, a range of trips from 1½ hrs to 2-day camps with fishing (Rs 2500 for 6 or more, transport extra), contact DGHC Tourism.

Tour operators
Clubside Tours & Travels, JP Sharma Rd, T0354-225 5123. Hotel booking, tours, treks, good jeep hire, air tickets for all domestic carriers.
Darjeeling Transport Corp, 30 Laden La Rd. Maruti vans, jeeps, Land Rovers and a few Sumos are available. Prices vary according to the season so negotiate rates.
DGHC, from Tourist Office. A variety of tours, including to Mirik, Tiger Hill, and Darjeeling town and surrounding areas. Price lists are available at the DGTC office.
Juniper Tours, behind police island, New Car Park, Laden La Rd, T0354-225 2095, also Indian Airlines and Jet Airways agent.
Meghma Tours & Travels, 51 Gandhi Rd, T0354 2289073, meghmatourstravels@yahoo.co.in. A variety of day tours as well as trips into Sikkim.

Trekking agents
Clubside Tours & Travels, see Tour operators above.
Himalayan Adventures, Das Studios, Nehru Rd, T0354-225 4090, dastrek@aussiemail.com.au.
Himalayan Travels, at Sinclairs, Gandhi Rd, T0354-225 5405. Long established.
Trek-Mate, Singalila Arcade, Nehru Rd, T0354-225 6611, chagpori@satyam.net.in. Well-equipped, English-speaking guides, excellent service, recommended.

Kalimpong p102, map p102
DGAHC Tourist Information Centre, DB Giri Rd, can advise on walking routes and rafting.
Gurudongma Tours & Travels, T03552-225204, www.gurudongma.com. High-quality, personalized treks, priced accordingly.
Mintry Transport, Main Rd. Jet Airways and Indian Airlines agent.

◉ Transport

Darjeeling p95, map p97
Air Nearest airport is Bagdogra (90 km), see below. Transfer by car takes 3 hrs. Pre-paid taxi counter to left of exit, around Rs 1200 (sharing possible). **Indian Airlines**, Belle Vue Hotel, Chowrasta, T0354-225 2355.

Bus NH31 connects Darjeeling with other parts of India. Buses go from the main transport stand to nearby hill stations but run infrequently, are slower than jeeps, and not much cheaper. Services run from 0630-1530. A comprehensive timetable is posted at the ticket counter beside the main stand. Private buses have connections to **Kolkata** via **Siliguri**, through ticket Rs 575.

Jeep Shared jeep is the quickest and most convenient way of getting around the mountains. Jeeps leave regularly to most local destinations, and if you find one that is almost full, you won't be waiting long. The price per person in a share jeep are: Rs 70 to **Siliguri** (2½ hrs via short cut); to **Gangtok** Rs 125, to **Kalimpong** 3 hrs, Rs 50-70; **Mirik** ½ hrs, Rs 55. The journey to Kalimpong is stunning, along narrow ridges planted with tea bushes and past wooden villages teetering on precipices.

Ropeway Cable Car Currently closed after an accident, with no fixed date for reopening.

Taxi Easily available in the lower part of town.

Train Darjeeling station has some old steam engines. Computerized reservation allows nationwide booking, 0800-1400. Diesel service to **Siliguri** at 0915, 7½ hrs (narrow gauge, see page 110), 80 km away; services to **New Jalpaiguri** resume in the near future. The narrow gauge steam tourist train to **Ghoom** departs 1000, stops at Batasia Loop, Rs 240 (see Ghoom Monastery, page 98).

Mirik and Kurseong p101
Mirik

Access from Bagdogra airport, Siliguri (52 km) and Darjeeling (55 km). Buses and jeeps to and from other hill stations 0630-1800.

Kurseong

51 km from Siliguri, off the main Darjeeling road, or via Pankhabari. Buses and jeeps from **Siliguri**, 3 hrs, **Darjeeling**, 2 hrs.

The Toy Train stops here; passenger service from 0645 to Darjeeling most of the year, Rs 10, 3½ hrs. The refurbished steam train runs a school service between Darjeeling and Kurseong on weekdays in term time.

Kalimpong p102, map p102

Air Nearest airport is at Bagdogra, 80 km, 3-3½ hrs by car, Rs 1200 (see Siliguri); seat in shared taxi or bus, Rs 75. **Indian Airlines** and Jet Airways bookings with Mintry Transport.

Bus State and private buses use the Motor Stand. Several to **Siliguri**, 3 hrs; **Darjeeling**, 3½ hrs; **Gangtok**: 3½ hrs (very scenic). **Kolkata**: fast 'Rocket' buses.

Jeep Shared jeeps depart 0630-1500, depending on demand; much quicker than buses. To **Darjeeling**, Rs 70 (Rs 50, on cramped back seat); **Siliguri** Rs 70/Rs 50; **Gangtok** Rs 120.

Train The nearest railhead is New Jalpaiguri/ Siliguri station, 67 km. Tickets from **Rly Out Agency**, next to Soni Emporium, motor stand. Computerized bookings and a small tourist quota for trains departing to New Jalpaiguri.

Siliguri and Jaldapara p103
Siliguri

Try to arrive in Siliguri or New Jalpaiguri (NJP) in daylight (before 1900). Rickshaw drivers can be quite aggressive at NJP).

Air Nearest airport, **Bagdogra**, 14 km away, with tourist information counter and little else; security checks can be rigorous. Flights to **Kolkata**, Delhi and Guwahati. **Indian Airlines**, Mainak Tourist Lodge, T0353-251 1495, airport T0353-255 1192; **Jet Airways**, Vinayak Building, Hill Cart Rd, T0353-243 5876, airport T0353-255 1675, daily. **Air Deccan**, T3900-8888, to **Delhi** daily and **Guwahati**, 3 times a

week. **Helicopter** daily in fine weather to Sikkim (see page 122), depending on demand. Transfer: STC buses to **Darjeeling** and **Gangtok**. Taxis (for sharing) to Darjeeling (Rs 1200), Gangtok (Rs 1600), Kalimpong (Rs 1200) and Siliguri (Rs 300).

Bus Siliguri is on NH31, well connected with Darjeeling (80 km), Gangtok (114 km) and Kalimpong (54 km) and served by state buses from WB, Bihar, Sikkim and Bhutan. **Tenzing Norgay Central Bus Terminus** (CBT) is next to the Junction Railway Station; **SNT Bus Station**, is across Hill Cart Rd. Buses to N Bengal go from the **Dooars Bus Stand** at the junction of Sevoke and Bidhan roads. The North Bengal STC's overnight Rocket bus to **Kolkata** depart hourly from 1700-2000 from Hill Cart Rd, 12 hrs, Rs 215, but it's a torturous journey on terrible roads. There are also many private operators just outside the bus stand offering similar services. **Kalimpong** 0700, 2-3 hrs, Rs 55, from N Bengal STC, Sevoke Rd. **Madarihat** (for Jaldapara) leave from bus station on Hill Cart Rd. Malda, many buses from 0430-2000, 6 hrs, Rs 112. Mirik, 0730, 2-3 hrs, Rs 50. **Gangtok**, SNT buses leave regularly thoughout the morning, Rs 70-90, 5 hrs; reserve near Mahananda Bridge, Hill Cart Rd. De luxe private buses from CBT, Junction Station (separate ticket window), Rs 100. **Bhutan**: Bhutan Government buses, tickets from Counter 14 at CBT, 0600-0730, 1000-1400. To **Phuntsholing**: buses at 0720, 1200, 1400, 1500, Rs 70, 3-4 hrs. N Bengal STC buses run at 0700, Rs 70.

To Nepal: to **Kathmandu** buses (or more conveniently taxi or Land Rover) to Panitanki on the border (35 km, 1 hr); transfer to Kakarbhitta by cycle-rickshaw. **Kakarbhitta**, the Nepalese border town, has only basic accommodation. **Visas** cost US$30 to be paid in exact cash and you'll need 2 passport photos. Buses depart 0300-2400, arriving the same evening at Kathmandu (595 km, 15-16 hrs); the journey can be very tiring. Tickets from Tourist Services Agency, Pradhan Nagar, Siliguri, T0353-253 1959, bytours@ cal2.vsnl.net.in; Siliguri to Kakarbhitta (Rs 120); Kakarbhitta to Kathmandu/Pokhara (Nep Rs 520); also through tickets. From Kakarbhitta it is also possible to **fly** (seasonal) from Bhadrapur (34 km, with free transfer to airstrip) to Kathmandu (1 hr) by RNAC,

Everest Air or Buddha Air (Nep Rs 1400); agent Sharma Travels. Alternatively, get a taxi to Biratnagar in Nepal (150 km) and fly from there to Kathmandu (US$99).

Jeep Shared jeeps are the best way to get to and around the hills, as they leave more frequently and are faster than buses, and only a little more expensive. **Kalimpong**, from Sevoke Rd stand, 2½ hrs Rs 50; **Gangtok**, Sevoke Rd or outside CBT on Hill Cart Rd, 3½-4 hrs Rs 120; Darjeeling, from Hill Cart Rd, 3-3½ hrs, Rs 85.

Train Siliguri Junction (narrow gauge, T0353-242 3333) and **New Jalpaiguri** (NJP broad gauge, T0353-256 1555), 5 km away, both for **Toy Train**, with tourist information. There are buses, cycle-rickshaws (Rs 25), trains and taxis (Rs 80) between the two. NJP has good connections to other major destinations in India. For long distance rail journeys from NJP, first buy tickets at Siliguri (Computerized Reservations, Bidhan Rd near Stadium), 1000-1300, 1330-1700 (to avoid the queue go to Chief Reservations Officer at side of building), then go to NJP station for train. Porters demand Rs 50 for 2 cases. **Darjeeling**: the Toy Train normally leaves from NJP, calling at Siliguri Junction on its way to Darjeeling, but due to construction works it has recently been starting from Siliguri. Services from NJP are expected to resume; check when buying your ticket. The daily service leaves at 1030, 7½ hrs (Rs 35 in 2nd class). Services are often disrupted by landslides during the rains, though the upper section from Kurseong (accessible by bus/jeep) continues to run; check beforehand. Take special care of luggage; thefts reported. From NJP to **Kolkata (S)**: *Darjeeling Mail 2344* (AC/CC&AC/II), 2000, 12½ hrs. **Kolkata (H)**: *Kamrup Exp 5960* (AC/II), 1645, 13½ hrs; *Kanchenjunga Exp 5658* (AC/II), 0800, 12 hrs. **New Delhi**: *NE Exp 5621*, 1720, 27 hrs; *Rajdhani Exp* (Mon, Wed, Thu, Fri), 2423, 1240, 21 hrs. From **Kolkata (S)**: *Darjeeling Mail 2343*, 2205, 13 hrs, connects with the Toy Train from NJP.

Jaldapara
Air Indian Airlines has daily flights from Kolkata to Bagdogra (50 mins) and from Delhi and Guwahati. From airport, bus to Siliguri; then 4 hrs' scenic drive to Jaldapara (155 km). There is an airfield at Hasimara.

Bus Express buses from Kolkata to Madarihat or Siliguri to Park (128 km). Forest Department transport to Hollong inside the sanctuary.

Train Hasimara/Madarihat Station (18 km from park) has trains from Siliguri Junction.

Directory

Darjeeling *p95, map p97*
Banks Many ATMs and exchange houses all over town. **Hospitals** Planters' Hospital, Nehru Rd, T0354-225 4327. Sadar Hospital, T0354-225 4218. **Post** GPO, Laden La Rd. **Tourist offices** W Bengal, Belle Vue, 1st floor, 1 Nehru Rd, T0354-225 4102. 1000-1700, off-season 1030-1600. Also at railway station, and at New Car Park, Laden La Rd. Darjeeling, **Gorkha Hill Council (DGHC)**, Silver Fir (below Windamere), The Mall, T/F0354-225 5351. Sikkim, T0354-222 5277, issues permits free of charge. **Useful addresses** Foreigners' Registration Office: Laden La Rd, T0354-225 4204; for Sikkim permits: go to District Magistrate, Lebong Cart Rd (north of centre), then get form stamped at FRO, and return to DM; 2 hrs.

Kalimpong *p102, map p102*
Banks Banks don't change money; Emporium, Mani Link Rd, accepts Visa and Mastercard. **Useful addresses** There is a hospital and a post office near the police station.

Siliguri *p103*
Banks Several ATMs on Hill Cart and Sevoke roads; there's a convenient one opposite the CBT by Hotel Heritage. **Hospital** T0353-252 1920; North Bengal Clinic, T0353-242 0441. Recommended. **Chemist** On College Rd. **Internet** Moulik, behind Vinayak, Hill Cart Rd, T0353-243 2312. Net-N-Net, Hill Cart Rd opposite bus stand. **Tourist offices** Bhutan, near railway station. Sikkim, Hill Cart Rd; W Bengal, 1st floor, M4 Hill Cart Rd, T0353-251 1974, sig_omntdc@sancharnet.in, also at Mainak, NJP Station and airport. **Travel agent** Help Tourism (Association of Conservation & Tourism), 143 Hill Cart Rd (1st floor), T0353-253 5893, helptour@shiva net.com. Recommended for eastern Himalaya. **Useful addresses** Railway booking office, Bidhan Rd, T0353-423333, railway enquiry at NJP, T0353-256 1555.

South of Kolkata

To the south of Kolkata are the tidal estuary of the Hugli and the mangrove forests of the Sundarbans. Famous for their population of Bengal tigers, the Sundarbans reach into Bangladesh, but it's possible to take a day trip down to the mouth of the Hugli or boat trips into the Sundarbans themselves. ▸▸ *For Sleeping, Eating and other listings, see page 112.*

Sagardwip

Ganga Sagar Mela is held in mid-January, attracting over 500,000 pilgrims each year who come to bathe and then visit the **Kapil Muni Temple**. The island has been devastated many times by cyclones. To reach the island catch a bus from Esplanade or take a taxi to Kakdwip and then take a ferry across to Kochuberia Ghat (Sagardwip). From there it is a 30-minute bus ride across island to where the Ganga meets the sea.

Sunderbans Tiger Reserve → *Colour map 2, grid C2.*

① *You need a permit – valid for a maximum of 5 days – from the WB Tourist Office, 3/2 BBD Bagh, Kolkata, T033-2248 8271, where you can also book a package tour (take your passport). Alternativley, contact the Secretary, Department of Forests, G Block (top floor), Writers Building (top floor), T033-2221 5999.*

Sunderbans (pronounced Soonder-buns) or 'beautiful forests', is named after the Sunderi trees. The mangrove swamps are said to be the largest estuarine forests in the world. Improved management is battling to halt the loss of mangrove cover as it is exploited for fuel. Most villagers depend on fishing and forestry, while local honey gatherers who are active in April and May are said to wear masks on the backs of their heads to frighten away tigers, which they believe only attack from the rear! You will notice large areas of *bheries* for aquaculture. Prawn fisheries are the most lucrative and co-operative efforts are being encouraged by the government.

The biosphere reserve, a World Heritage Site, still preserves the natural habitat of about 300 **Bengal tigers** (*Panthera tigris*). They are bigger and richer in colour than elsewhere in South Asia and are thought to survive on salt water; rainwater is the only source of fresh water in the park. Tigers here have become strong swimmers and are known to attack fishermen. Methods of improved management include providing permanent sources of fresh water for tigers by digging deep, monsoon-fed ponds, installing solar-powered lighting to scare them away from villages and electrifying dummy woodcutters. Spotted deer, wild boar, monkeys, snakes, fishing cats, water monitors, Olive Ridley sea turtles and a few large estuarine crocodiles are the other wildlife here, particularly on Lothian Island and Chamta block. You may see deer, boar, macaque and birds but are unlikely to see a tiger. However, it is wonderfully peaceful.

The best season is from September to March. Heavy rains and occasional severe cyclones in April to May and November to December can make an independent visit impossible. Carry bottled water, torch, mosquito repellent and be prepared for cool nights in winter. You must always be accompanied by armed forest rangers. Motor launches can be hired from Canning and Sonakhali (Basanti), but it is better to go down the narrow creeks in human-powered country boats. Occasionally you can go ashore on bamboo-and-palm jetties to walk in the fenced-in areas of the forest which have watchtowers, open dawn to dusk only.

Sajnekhali has a **sanctuary** for water birds and a Mangrove Interpretation Centre with a turtle hatchery, a crocodile tank and a mangrove nursery.

West Bengal South of Kolkata

Digha → *185 km from Kolkata.*
Digha was described by Warren Hastings visiting over 200 years ago as the 'Brighton of the East', though there is not a pebble for at least 2000 km. The casuarina-lined, firm wide beach is popular with Bengalis. The small **Chandaneswar Temple**, 10 km away, actually in Orissa, is an important Siva temple which can be reached by bus.

● Sleeping

Sagardwip *p111*
WBTDC organizes 2-day boat trips with accommodation on board (**L-C**) during Ganga Sagar Mela. You can also arrange to stay at the Dharamshala and leave a donation.
F Youth Hostel. Book via the Youth Services Office in Kolkata, T033-2248 0626, ext 27.

Sunderbans Tiger Reserve *p111*
A few basic lodges are in Gosaba. One is in Pakhirala, the last village before Sajnekhali.
E Tourist Lodge, Sajnekhali, contact through WBTDC, T033-2248 8271. Raised on pillars and fenced from wildlife, solar power, small basic rooms with mosquito nets (ask for linen), 14 with Western toilets, hot water in buckets, 20-bed dorm (Rs 220), simple meals (poor choice but if you buy local fish, restaurant will cook it), no alcohol. Reserve in advance and carry your permit.

Digha *p112*
There is plenty of accommodation.
C Sea Coast, T03220-266305. With some a/c rooms, this is the best 3-star option.
E-F Sea Hawk, T03220-266235. Comfortable rooms, on 3 floors, some a/c.
E-F Tourist Lodge, T03220-266255. Rooms on 3 floors, 4 a/c, 5-bed dorm (Rs 80), meals, bar.

▲ Activities and tours

Sunderbans Tiger Reserve *p111*
Sunderban Tiger Camp, office at 9 Mitter House (2nd floor), 71 Ganesh Chandra Av, T033-2237 5012, www.sunderbantigercamp.com. Situated near Gosaba. Year-round tours with great food, evening entertainment and accommodation in either tents (Rs 2,150 for 2 days/1 night) or cottages (Rs 2800-3400).
WBTDC Tours: 2-day and 3-day trips (infrequent during monsoon, Jul-Sep), by coach from Kolkata then 'luxury' launch with onboard accommodation. Prices vary

with standard of lodging: a 2-day tour costs Rs 1175 for a bedroll to Rs 2550 for a 2-person coupé; 4% tax is added. The launch is the only way to visit the Sunderbans during monsoon.

● Transport

Sunderbans Tiger Reserve *p111*
Road and boat From Kolkata: CSTC bus from Babu Ghat, Strand Rd, to **Sonakhali** (first depart 0630 then hourly, Rs 36, 3½ hrs), then hire a boat to Sajnekhali (Rs 400-500, 3 hrs). Alternatively, from Basanti, take public ferry to **Gosaba**, (1½ hrs, Rs 8), then travel across the island by flat-bed van rickshaw (5 km, 45 mins), which enables you to see interesting village life, and finally take a boat to **Sajnekhali**; recommended for at least one way. Lodge staff will arrange boat hire with park guide (About Rs 600 for 4 hrs, Rs 1000 for 8 hrs; boats can take 6-8 people). Since these are tidal waterways, boats are not always able to moor near the ghats, and during monsoons or bad weather they will not sail.

Train and boat Kolkata (Sealdah) to **Canning** (105 km) and then boat to **Docghat** where you can get a shared auto or bus to Sonakhali, where you get another boat. From Canning you can get a private boat direct to **Sajnekhali** Lodge (Rs 800 per day), but the journey is long and dependent on the tide.

Digha *p112*
Bus A/c luxury buses leave from Esplanade, taking 4 hrs (Rs 170). Public buses leave from Esplanade and Howrah, 4½-5 hrs (Rs 75).

Train Direct train from Howrah on Sun, 2867A, 0755, 3½ hrs. From Mon-Sat trains depart Salimar (on west bank of Hugli south of Howrah) at 0800.

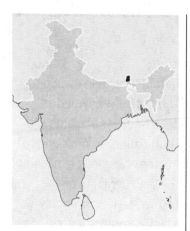

Sikkim

113

⁝ Footprint features

Introduction

Khangchendzonga, the third highest mountain in the world, dominates the skyline of Sikkim. The state is renowned as much for its wonderful wildlife and rich variety of plants and flowers as for its ethnically varied population. Sikkim's original inhabitants, the Lepchas, call the region Nye-mae-el, meaning paradise. To the later Bhutias it is Beymul Denjong, or The Hidden Valley of Rice. The name Sikkim itself is commonly attributed to the Tsong word Su-khim, meaning New or Happy House.

With 660 species of orchids, some found at altitudes as high as 3000 m, Sikkim is an orchid-lovers' paradise, while the monasteries of Rumtek and Pemayangtse are just two among a wealth of fascinating centres of Buddhism in the state. Organic farming and ecotourism are officially enshrined in government policy, and although trekking is less developed than in other parts of the Himalaya, the state is beginning to attract ramblers and trekkers in serious numbers.

You can stay a few days in Gangtok, making day trips to Rumtek and Phodong, then move on to Pelling or Yuksom, visiting Pemayangtse Monastery and Khecheopalri Lake, before continuing to Kalimpong or Darjeeling in West Bengal. Road journeys within Sikkim are very scenic, but numerous hairpin bends and unsealed sections can also make them extremely slow, so expect to cover anything from 10 to 40 km per hour. Conditions deteriorate considerably during the monsoon, which can sometimes make travel impossible.

★ Don't miss ...

1 **Tashi Viewpoint** Get up early and watch the sunrise over the Kangchendzonga range, page 120.
2 **Rumtek Monastery** This faithful reproduction of Chhofuk in Tibet is very impressive, page 123.
3 **Saramsa Gardens** If orchids are your thing, head here where there are over 500 species, page 123.
4 **Pemayangtse Monastery** Stay overnight at this awe-inspiring place and take an early morning walk to see a breathtaking sunrise in perfect peace, page 125.
5 **Khecheopalri Lake** Trek to the lake and watch leaflamps float on the clear water during evening prayers, page 126.

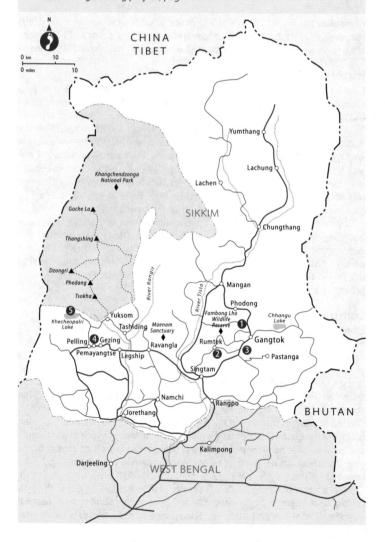

Background → *Population: 540,500. Area: 7298 sq km.*

The land

Geography Sikkim nestles between the peaks of the eastern Himalaya, stretching only 112 km from south to north and 64 km from east to west. Within this area is contained a vast range of landscapes and habitats, from subtropical river valleys to snow-covered peaks, and despite comprising just 0.2% of India's land mass Sikkim accounts for an astounding 26% of its biodiversity. The state encompasses the upper valley of the Tista River, a tributary of the Brahmaputra, the watershed of which forms the borders with Tibet and Nepal. In the east lies the Chumbi valley, a tongue of Tibetan land separating Sikkim from Bhutan that gives the state its strategic and political sensitivity. The Sikkimese believe Khangchendzonga (8586 m, *Kanchenjunga*), the 'Five Treasures of the Great Snows', to be the repository of minerals, grains, salt, weapons and holy scriptures. On its west is the massive 31 km-long Zemu glacier.

Climate In the lower valleys Sikkim's climate is subtropical. Above 1000 m, it is temperate, while the higher mountain tops are permanently under snow. Sikkim is one of the Himalaya's wettest regions, most rain falling between mid-May and September.

History

From the 13th century Tibetans, like the Namgyal clan, immigrated to Sikkim. In 1642 Phuntsog Namgyal (1604-1670) became the Chogyal (king). With a social system based on Tibetan Lamaistic Buddhism, the land was split into 12 *Dzongs* (fortified districts).

In the 18th century Sikkim lost land to Nepal, Bhutan and the British. When the Gurkhas of Nepal launched a campaign into Tibet and were defeated by the Chinese in 1791-1792, Sikkim won back its northern territories. The narrow Chumbi Valley that separates Sikkim from Bhutan remained with Tibet. When the British defeated Nepal in 1815, the southern part of the country was given back to Sikkim. However, in the next conflict with Nepal, Darjeeling was handed over to the British in return for their assistance. In 1848 the Terai region at the foot of the mountains was annexed by the British.

Nepalis migrated into Sikkim from the beginning of the 19th century, eventually becoming more numerous than the local inhabitants. This led to internal conflict also involving the British and the Tibetans. The British won the ensuing battles and declared Sikkim a Protectorate in 1890. The state was controlled by a British Political Officer who effectively stripped the *Gyalpos*, of executive power. It was many years before the Sikkimese regained control.

Culture

Ethnic groups The Naong, Chang and Mon are believed to have inhabited Sikkim in prehistoric times. Each ethnic group has an impressive repertoire of folk songs and dances. The **Lepchas**, who call themselves Rongpas and claim to be the original inhabitants of Sikkim, may have come from Tibet well before the eighth century and brought Lamaistic Buddhism, which is still practised. They are now regarded as the indigenous peoples. They are deeply religious, peace loving and shy but cheerful. The government has reserved the **Dzongu** area in North and Central Sikkim for Lepchas, now making up less than 10% of the population. For a long time, the Lepchas' main contact with the outside world was the market-place at Mangan, where they bartered oranges and cardamom. Their alphabet was only devised in the 18th century by the king. The **Magar**, a minority group, are renowned as warriors and were involved in the coronation of Phuntsog Namgyal, the first Chogyal of Sikkim in 1642.

The **Bhotias** (meaning 'of Bhot/Tibet') or Bhutias entered Sikkim in the 13th century from Kham in Tibet. Many adapted to sedentary farming from pastoral nomadism and displaced the Lepchas. Some, however, retained their older lifestyle,

⁝ Permits

Free Inner Line Permits (ILPs) are issued to foreigners to enter Sikkim for up to 15 days (renewable twice). These allow visits to Gangtok, Rumtek, Phodong, Mangan, Rabangla, Namchi, Gezing, Pemayangtse, Pelling, Yuksam, Pakyong and Soreng. Contact an Indian mission abroad when applying for an Indian visa (enclosing two extra photos), or at any FRO (Foreigners' Registration Office) or the Sikkim Tourism Office in New Delhi, Kolkata or Siliguri (check www.sikkim.gov.in for office details). Rangpo can issue a 15-day permit extendable in Gangtok or by the Superintendent of Police in Namchi, Geyzing and Mangan. Certain areas in north and west Sikkim (Chungthang, Yumthang, Lachen, Chhangu, Dzongri) have been opened to groups of two to 20 trekkers, on condition that travel is with a registered agency. Protected Areas Permits (PAP) can be arranged by most local travel agents; apply with photocopies of passport (Indian visa and personal details pages), ILP and two photos.

To get your permit extended at the Foreigners' Registration Office at Gangtok, first visit the Magistrate's Office at the Secretariat on the ridge overlooking town to get a 'No Objection' endorsement.

Sikkim Background

and combined animal husbandry with trading over the Trans-Himalayan passes: Nathula (4392 m), Jelepla (4388 m), Donkiala (5520 m) and Kongrala (4809 m). Over the years the Bhotia have come into increased contact with the Lepcha and intermarried with them. Nearly every Bhotia family has one member who becomes a monk. Monasteries remain the repositories of Bhotia culture and festivals here are the principal social events. However, those who have visited Ladakh or Zanskar may find them architecturally and artistically a little disappointing. The Bhotias are famous for their weaving and are also skilled wood carvers.

The **Newars** entered Sikkim in large numbers from Nepal in the 19th century. Skilled in metal and woodwork, they were granted the right by the Chogyal to mine copper and mint the Sikkimese coinage. Other Nepali groups followed. With high-altitude farming skills, they settled new lands and built houses directly on the ground unlike the Lepcha custom of building on stilts. The Newars were followed by the Chettris and other Nepali clans who introduced Hinduism, which became more popular as their numbers swelled.

Religion In Sikkim, as in Nepal, Hinduism and Buddhism have interacted and amalgamated so Himalayan Hinduism includes a pantheon of Buddhist *bodhisattvas* as well as Hindu deities. The animist tradition also retains a belief in evil spirits.

Buddhist **prayer flags** flutter in the breeze everywhere. The different types, such as wind, luck and victory, are printed with texts and symbols on coloured pieces of cloth and are tied to bamboo poles or trees. **Prayer wheels** carrying inscriptions (which should be turned clockwise) vary in size from small hand-held ones to vast drums which are installed by a monastery or stupa. Whitewashed masonry **chortens** (stupas) usually commemorate the Buddha or Bodhisattva, the structure symbolizing the elements (earth, water, fire, air, ether). The eight **lucky signs** appear as parasol, pot or vase, conch shell, banner, two fishes, lotus, knot of eternity and the wheel of law (Dharma Chakra). Bowls of water (Thing Duen Tsar) are offered in prayer from left to right during Buddhist worship. The gift of water from one who is free from greed and meanness is offered to quench thirsty spirits and to wash the feet, and represents flower (or welcome), incense, lamp, perfume and food.

Festivals Since the 22 major festivals are dictated by the agricultural cycle and the Hindu-Buddhist calendar, it is best to check dates with the tourist office.

In **February, Losar** takes place, Tibetan New Year – preceded by Lama dances in Rumtek. **Bumche** at Tashiding. In **June** is **Saga Dawn**, a Buddhist festival with huge religious processions round Gangtok. **Rumtek Chaams Dance festival** is held in commemoration of the eight manifestations of Guru Padmasambhava, who established Buddhism in Tibet. In **August/September, Pang Lhabsol** commemorates the consecration of Khangchendzonga as Sikkim's guardian deity; the Lepchas believe that the mountain is their birthplace. The masked warrior dance is especially spectacular; warriors wear traditional armour of helmets, swords and shields. Celebrations are held in Pemayangtse. In **September/October, Dasain** is one of the most important Nepali festivals. It coincides with **Dasara** in North India, see page 41. On the first day barley seeds are planted in prayer rooms, invocations are made to Durga, and on the eighth day buffalo and goats are ritually sacrificed. **Diwali** (the Festival of Lights) follows **Dasain**. In **December, Kagyat Dances** performed by monks (especially at Enchey), with religious music and chanting, enact themes from Buddhist mythology and end with the burning of effigies made of flour, wood and paper. This symbolizes the exorcism of evil spirits and the ushering in of prosperity for the coming year. **Losoog** (**Namsoong** for Lepchas at Gangtok) is the Sikkimese New Year, also called **Sonam Losar**. Farmers celebrate their harvest and beginning of their new cropping calendar.

Modern Sikkim

In 1950, Sikkim became a Protectorate of India. In 1973 there were growing demands for accession to India by the local population, consisting mainly of Nepalis, and Sikkim was formally made an associate state. The Gyalpos lost their power as a result of the new democratic constitution and Sikkim became the 22nd state in the Union in 1975. Although there is no separatist movement, India's takeover and the abolition of the monarchy, supported by many of Nepali origin, is still resented by many Sikkimese who don't regard themselves as Indians. The state enjoys special tax and other privileges, partly because of its highly sensitive geopolitical location on the disputed border with China. In the 2004 State Assembnly the Sikkim Democratic Front, a party confined to Sikkim, won 31 of the 32 seats under the Chief Minister Pawan Kumar Chamling.

Gangtok

→ *Phone code: 03592. Colour map 2, grid A2. Population: 55,200. Altitude: 1547 m.*

Gangtok or High Hill, the capital, sits on a ridge overlooking the Ranipul River. The setting is spectacular with fine views of the Khangchendzonga range, but the town has lost some of its quaint charm with the mushrooming of concrete buildings along the national highway and the main road. The crowded Mahatma Gandhi Marg and the colourful bazars below it are where all the town's commercial activity is concentrated. Away from here, there are many serene areas and quiet back alleys which remain virtually untouched. ▸▸ *For Sleeping, Eating and other listings, see pages 120-122.*

Ins and outs

Getting there There is an airport near Gangtok linked to Bagdogra airport (see page 108), 124 km away, by a regular helicopter service. Most visitors arrive from North Bengal by the attractive road following the Tista (NH31A), which is acessible all year except in very wet weather (mid-June to September) when there may be landslips. Permits and passports are checked at Rangpo where 15-day permits (extendable in Gangtok or district headquarters for up to 45 days) are available (passport and two photos required). SNT buses terminate at the Paljor Stadium Road stand, while private buses and jeeps from Siliguri/Bagdogra stop on NH31A just below the tourist office, which has some hotels within easy reach. Jeeps for West Sikkim use the Nam Nang jeep stand, a 15-minute walk south along MG Marg.

▸ *See Transport, page 122, for further details.*

Getting around The busy hub around MG Marg, pedestrianized in the evening, is a 20-minute walk from end to end. Away from the bazars, the town is pleasant for walking around (see Rajesh Verma's *Sikkim: A Guide and Handbook*, Rs 140). For further afield you'll need to hire a jeep or taxi; rates are fixed and displayed on the back window.

Sights

At the north end of town the **Government Institute of Cottage Industries** ① *Mon-Sat 0900-1230 and 1330-1530, closed 2nd Sat of month*, produces a wide range of local handicrafts, including wool carpets, dolls, jackets, handmade paper, carved and painted wooden tables. Good quality and prices but no parcel service.

Enchey Monastery is 3 km northeast of the main bazar, a pleasant walk that takes you past the small flower garden at Whitehall (orchids on show March-April). Built by the eighth Chogyal in the 1840s, the present building dates from 1909. Religious dances are held in August and December; see Festivals, page 118.

The **Palace of the Chogyal** is only open once a year in the last week of December for the **Pang Lhabsol Festival**. Below this is the **Tsuklakhang** or Royal Chapel, standing on a high ridge where royal marriages and coronations took place. This is the major place of worship and has a large and impressive collection of scriptures. The interior houses Buddha images and is lavishly decorated with woodcarving and murals. Visitors are welcome during Tibetan New Year but may not be permitted at other times; photography is prohibited.

Moving south along the road you pass the **Secretariat** complex on your left. Beyond this is the **Deer Park**, loosely modelled on the famous one at Sarnath, see page 243, with a statue of the Buddha. From here a recently built **Ropeway** ① *0930-1700, Rs 50 one way*, descends the hill to Deorali Bazar, near which is the unique **Research Institute of Tibetology** ① *Mon-Sat 1000-1600*, established in 1958 to promote research into Tibet and Mahayana Buddhism. The library maintains a large and important Buddhist collection with many fine *thangkas*, icons and art treasures on

Gangtok

*Related map
A Gangtok centre,
page 120*

To Tashi View Point (9 km), Phodong & Yumthang
Gate (No Entry)
Raj Bhawan
Saibaba Mandir
TV Tower
Himalayan Nursery
Government Institute of Cottage Industries
Zero Point
Council House
Enchey Monastery
Helipad
Tashi Namgyal Academy
N Sikkim Highway
SNT & Booking Office
Hanuman Mandir
Paljor Stadium Rd
Catholic Centre
Paljor Stadium
Flower Show
To Nathula & Chhangu Lake
Whitehall
CNI Church
The Ridge
Bhanu Path
Kazi Rd
Tibet Rd
Gate
Private Bus Taxis ii
Palace of the Chogyal
Foreigners' Reg Office
Tsuklakhang (Royal Chapel)
Supermarket
Taxis i
Kanchenjunga Bazar
MG Marg
Kazi Rd
Secretariat
Deer Park
NH31A
Government Press
Ropeway
Nam Nang Taxis iii
Research Institute of Tibetology
Do-drul Chorten
To Orchidarium, Rangpo, Rumtek & Kalimpong

N

0 metres 100
0 yards 100

Sleeping 🛌
Denzong Inn **1**
Hidden Forest **2**
Norkhill **3**
Siniolchu Lodge **4**
Tashi Delek & Blue Poppy Restaurant **5**

Eating 🍴
China Pilot **1**
Oberoi's Barbique **2**
Ocean **3**
Taste of Tibet **4**

display. To the south, surrounded by 108 prayer wheels, the gold-topped **Do-drul Chorten** contains relics and a complete set of holy texts. Nearby is a monastery for young lamas with large statues of the Buddha and Guru Padmasambhava.

There are some lovely walks around the capital. **Tashi Viewpoint** via Enchey Monastery is 9 km away. Go early to watch the sun rise over the Khangchendzonga range. **Hanuman Tok**, a hill with a small temple, 8 km away, is another viewpoint.

● Sleeping

Gangtok *p118, maps p119 and below*
Heating is essential in winter (some budget hotels charge extra). Dogs bark at night so take ear plugs. Discounts Jul-Aug, Dec-Jan.
AL-A Norkhill, T03592-205637, www.elgin hotels.com. 26 clean rooms in old palace, meals included, spacious public rooms, good views and gardens, exchange, curio shop, once excellent but standards are slipping.
AL-B Tashi Delek, MG Marg, T03592-202991, www.hoteltashidelek.com. 46 rooms and some suites (better on top floors), excellent restaurant, bar, exchange, airlines counter, terrace garden with enthralling views, friendly service. Pricey but recommended.
A Netuk House, Tibet Rd, T03592-202374, netuk@sikkim.org. 8 comfortable, clean rooms with modern shower in a traditional family home, excellent Sikkimese meals, bar, quiet, mountain views, friendly, excellent service.
B-C Chumbi Residency, Tibet Rd, T03592-226618, www.sikkiminfo.net/chumbi. Tall modern hotel, 25 good rooms, suites too, clean and quiet, dynamic manager.
B-C Tibet (Dalai Lama Trust), PS Rd, T03592-202523, www.sikkiminfo.net/hoteltibet. 34 rooms, good views from those at rear, restaurant, bar, exchange, Tibetan books and crafts for sale, very pleasant, peaceful and charming (but some critical reports).
C Hidden Forest, 2km from centre in Middle Sichey, T03592-205197, www.hiddenforest retreat.com. 8 spacious, timber-floored rooms in the home of a forest officer and his family, set in a 3-acre nursery full of orchids and medicinal plants, with paths leading into the surrounding forest, homegrown organic food served in cozy dining room, a unique choice. Recommended.
C-E Denzong Inn, near Kanchenjunga Bazar, T03592-202692. Set in an interesting complex with faint Chinese-mafia feel, 24 rooms and good if slightly threadbare suites. Some rooms on the terrace come with proper green baize card tables.

C-E Sonam Delek, Tibet Rd, T03592-202566, www.sikkiminfo.net/sonamdelek. 15 rooms with bath, best choice for views though **E** rooms losing theirs to new extension, pleasant restaurant, terrace garden.
D Mintokling Guest House, Bhanu Path, T03592-204226, mintokling@hotmail.com. Prettily decorated, timber-floored rooms with bath among flower gardens and lawns, good restaurant, charming owner. Recommended.
E Mount Jopuno (Sikkim Tourism), PS Rd, T03592-203502. Out of 12 rooms, 4 de luxe (**C**), good restaurant and service, eager young staff (at Institute of Hotel Management).
E-F Siniolchu Lodge, near Enchey Monastery, T03592-202074. Good views, 24 rooms on 3 floors up a hillside, some with bath and heating, restaurant, bar, tours.

Gangtok centre

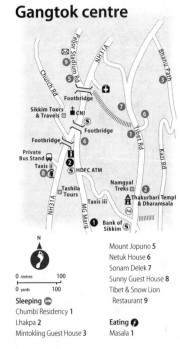

Mount Jopuno 5
Netuk House 6
Sonam Delek 7
Sunny Guest House 8
Tibet & Snow Lion
Restaurant 9

Sleeping ●
Chumbi Residency 1
Lhakpa 2
Mintokling Guest House 3

Eating ●
Masala 1

E-F Sunny Guest House, by Siliguri jeep stand on NH31A, T03592-202179. Pleasantly old-school rooms with bath, super K'dzonga views from top floor, forgettable room service.
F-G Modern Central Lodge, MG Marg, T03592-204670, www.modernhospitality.com. Simple, clean and colourful rooms with bath, best on upper floors, a bit noisy, great lounge with lots of books, basic but good restaurant, good-value jeep tours, very friendly and helpful.
G Lhakpa, Tibet Rd, T03592-223002. Good value, 3 clean rooms in traditional house, some with bath, cheaper dorm, restaurant/bar (excellent Chinese), roof terrace, views.

● Eating

Gangtok *p118, maps p119 and p120*
Lightly spiced Sikkimese meat and vegetable dishes are usually eaten with noodles or rice. Churpi is a local yak milk curd cheese.
♔♔ Blue Poppy, Tashi Delek. International. Good meals at Rs 350 (Sikkimese recommended, order in advance).
♔♔ Masala, MG Marg under Karma Hotel. Quirkily decorated and fastidiously clean, serving pure vegetarian Indian and Chinese.
♔♔ Snow Lion, in Hotel Tibet. Good Tibetan and Sikkimese in elaborately decorated room, but service can be glacial and vegetarian meals may come with flecks of meat.
♔♔ Taste of Tibet, MG Marg. Swish and modern, serving excellent Tibetan soups and noodles to an accompaniment of whatever internet radio channel happens to be tuned in.
♔ China Pilot, Star Cinema Building, MG Rd. Excellent value Chinese.
♔ Oberoi's Barbique, MG Marg. Reasonable versions of Tibetan cuisine; the window tables make a pleasant place to hang out.
♔ Ocean, MG Marg near steps to Kanchenjunga Bazar. Laid back dining-and-drinking venue run by young locals; good *momos* and vegetarian Sikkimese set meal, variable music.
♔ Rasoi/Blue Sheep, Tourist Office Building. Tasty Pan-Indian and continental food, clean and smart and extremely popular at night.

● Bars and clubs

Gangtok *p118, maps p119 and p120*
Bars in most restaurants serve local spirits distilled at Rangpo: brandy, rum, whiskey and liqueurs. *Chhang* is the unofficial national drink. A bamboo mug (*thungba*) is filled with fermented millet through which boiled water is allowed to percolate; the drink is sipped through a bamboo straw. You can enjoy this mildly intoxicating pleasant drink for over an hour simply by adding hot water.

● Shopping

Gangtok *p118, maps p119 and p120*
Books
Good Books, down steps off MG Marg near Gandhi statue. Many local interest titles.

Handicrafts
Traditional crafts include carpets, *thangkas*, traditional jewellery, shirts, boots and fur caps and wood carving.
Charitrust Handicrafts, Tibet Hotel. Modest collection, good quality, books on Tibet.
Handcrafts Centre, Zero Point. Mon-Sat 0930-1230, 1300-1530. Here you can watch artisans at work.

Markets
The markets are interesting; **Kanchenjunga Bazar** (Haat on Sun, closed Thu), in a new concrete building, sells some unusual local fruit and vegetables and yak's milk cheese fresh and dried (skewered on string).

▲ Activities and tours

Gangtok *p118, maps p119 and p120*
Mountaineering
Himalayan Mountaineering Institute based in Yuksom offers climbing courses in stunning surroundings.

River rafting
On rivers Tista (from Dikchu or Singtam, 1 hr drive from Gangtok) and Rangit (from Melli Bazar, 4 km from Tista Bridge, which has a **Wayside Inn** for refreshments, or **Rishi**) arranged by Tourism Department and private travel agents, eg Tashila, 1 day US$45, 2-day US$70, some Grade 2-3 rapids. A 2-hr ride is ideal for the beginner; wonderful scenery.

Tour operators
Some offer tours before the season opens, eg to North Sikkim in Jan/Feb when roads and trekking routes may be closed. To support ecologically responsible tourism, contact

ECOSS (Ecotourism Society of Sikkim), T03592-228211, www.ecossikkim.org, for a list of approved tour operators. Most agents help to arrange Protected Area Permits for trekkers.

Namgyal Treks and Tours, 75 Tibet Rd, T03592-223701, www.namgyaltreks.net. Experienced, well organized.

Singalila, NH31A, opposite petrol pump, T03592-221556, singalila@hotmail.com. Arranges coach tours and river rafting.

Yuksom Tours and Treks, above Telephone Exchange, T03592-226822, www.yuksom-tours.com. Professional, well-equipped treks, good food, all inclusive US$55 per day.

Tours

Gangtok From Tourist Information Centre, T03592-221634. **Morning tour**: Government Institute of Cottage Industries, Deer Park, Chorten, Research Institute of Tibetology, Orchid Sanctuary and Enchey Monastery. In season daily (0930, Rs 45). **Afternoon tour**: Orchidarium and Rumtek Monastery (1400). **Phodong** Rs 70 (more expensive by car). **West Sikkim** Requires a minimum 16. Fri at 1030 returning Sun 1600 (2 nights), Rs 600.

⊖ Transport

Gangtok *p118, maps p119 and p120*
Air
Nearest airport is Bagdogra (124 km), see page 109. **Indian Airlines**, above Green Hotel, MG Marg, T03592-223354, www.indian-airlines.nic.in, 1000-1300, 1400-1600; **Jet Airways**, RNC, MG Marg, T03592-223556, www.jetairways.com. To Gangtok: taxi Rs 1500, 4-5 hrs; or get bus/ shared taxi to Siliguri from where buses/taxis to Gangtok are available. A daily government 5-seater helicopter (Gangtok T03592-281372, Bagdogra T0353-2531959) runs between Bagdogra and Gangtok; unreliable since heavy cloud or rain prevents flights, but is an excellent option (Rs 2000 each way, 45 mins, 10 kg luggage) with mesmerizing views.

Bus
SNT (Sikkim Nationalized Transport) Bus Stand, NH31A, 0900-1300, 1400-1600. Private buses from **West Point Taxi Stand**, NH31A, T03592 202858. Some only operate in the high season. Buy tickets 24 hrs in advance; hotels can help. Long-distance journeys about

Rs 60. To **Rumtek**, 1600 (1500 holidays) 1 hr; **Namchi**, 0800, 1500 (4½ hrs); **Namok, Phodong, Chungthang, Mangan**, 0800, 1300 (return 1500); **Gezing**, 0700, 1300 (5 hrs); **Jorethang (then Pelling)**, 0800. For North Bengal: **Bagdogra** (about 5 hrs); **Darjeeling**, 94 km, between 0700-1330 (6-7 hrs); from Darjeeling 0730-1400; to **Kalimpong**, 75 km, 0830-1930 (4-4½ hrs), from Kalimpong 0700-1315; to **NJP/ Siliguri** (5 hrs), 0700-1415 (4½-5 hrs); from Siliguri 0630-1300. To **Kolkata** 1300; from Kolkata 1700; a/c bus Rs 380.

Taxi/jeep
Shared taxis (Rs 10) run along NH31A, stopping at marked taxi stops. Charter taxis charge fixed, relatively high rates around town. Rates for sightseeing negotiable; around Rs 1500 per day for travel outside Sikkim, Rs 1200 within Sikkim; plus night halt Rs 200. Tourist office has a list of official rates.

For sharing: Stands (i) Lal Bazar (East Sikkim) (ii), Private Bus Stand (for North Bengal) and (iii) Nam Nang (West Sikkim). **Rumtek**, from Kanchenjunga Bazar, Rs 25; **Mangan**, Rs 80; **Ravangla**, around Rs 80; **Pelling**, Rs 150. Share jeeps leave on a fixed schedule, most departing early morning; much quicker and more frequent than buses to most destinations.

Train
Nearest railway stations are at **Siliguri/New Jalpaiguri (NJP)**, Computerized Bookings, SNT Compound, 0800-1400. NJP Enquiries, T0353-269 1555.

⊖ Directory

Gangtok *p118, maps p119 and p120*
Banks 1000-1400, Sat 1000-1200 (difficult to get exchange). **State Bank of India**, MG Marg. **State Bank of Sikkim**, Tibet Rd, Several ATMs on MG Marg, including UTI, HDFC. **Hospitals** On Stadium Rd: STNM Hospital, opposite Hotel Mayur, T03592-222944. **Internet** Several on MG Marg; around Rs 30/hr. **Post** GPO, Stadium Rd and PO in Gangtok Bazar. **Tourist offices** Sikkim, MG Marg, Gangtok Bazar, T03592-221634. In season Mon-Sat 0900-1900, off season 1000-1600. Apply for permits here. Dept of Tourism, T03592-223425. **Useful contacts** Ambulance: T03592-231137. **Fire**: T03592-222001. **Police**: T03592-202033.

Around Gangtok

Rumtek Monastery

→ *Phone code: 03592. Colour map 2, grid A2. 24 km southwest of Gangtok. Altitude: 1550 m. www.rumtek.org.*

Standing in one of the attractive lower valleys with fluttering prayer flags, the monastery is the headquarters of the Kagyu ('Black Hat') order of Tibetan Lamaistic Buddhism. The monks fled Tibet after the Chinese invasion, bringing with them whatever statues, *thangkas* and scriptures they could carry. At the invitation of the Chogyal they settled in Rumtek. The new monastery was built in the 1960s in the traditional style as a faithful copy of the Kagyu headquarters in Chhofuk, Tibet, with typical monastic paintings and intricate woodwork. The **Dharma Chakra Centre** with the unique **golden reliquary** of the 16th Gyalwa Karmapa, who died in 1981, is here.

Visitors are dropped at the gate at the bottom of a gentle uphill path; passports may be checked. A 20-minute walk past local houses and curio shops leads to the monastery. Outside, you may see pairs of monks chanting prayers in their quarters or catch some younger ones playing football in the field. The main hall is impressive but lacks Pemayangtse's atmosphere. Visitors are welcome but are asked not to disturb the monks during prayers (0400, 1800). In the adjacent building you can watch the wood-block printing of texts on handmade paper. The peace is broken when hordes of tourists arrive.

Fambong Lho Wildlife Reserve

A little beyond Rumtek, 25 km from Gangtok across the Ranipool Valley, this reserve ① *Rs 5*, has serene jungle walks in the hills, with waterfalls, mountain views, orchids and wildlife (marten, fox, red panda, boar; even wolf and sloth bear). You are free to go on your own (though this is not advisable on some stretches) and can climb or walk for one to six days. There are log huts at Golitar and Tumin, Rs 50.

Saramsa Gardens → *14 km south of Gangtok.*

The gardens contain over 500 indigenous species in what is more like a botanical garden with large orchidariums. The best season is March to early May; you may be disappointed at other times. The road to Saramsa forks east off the NH31a a few kilometres south of **Tadong** which has a couple of places with rooms and refreshments including the fairly modern **Tashi Tadong** and the **Daragaon**.

Kyongnosla Alpine Sanctuary → *Altitude: 3200 m-4100 m.*

Located 31 km from Gangtok on the Nathula highway, which until 1962 was the main route for mule trains trading between Gangtok and Lhasa in Tibet, the sanctuary extends from the '15th Mile' check post to the ridges bordering Rongchu and Chhangu Lake. Among the junipers and silver firs the sanctuary harbours some rare ground orchids and rhododendrons and numerous medicinal plants including the *Panax pseudo-ginseng*. The best season is April-August or October-November. The Himalayan marmot has been reintroduced here. Other mammals include goral, serow, red panda, Himalayan black bear, Tibetan fox and yellow-throated martens, and very colourful pheasants.

Two easy treks lead to the Shiv Gufa (1 km from the road), where you can crawl into a tiny cave on your hands and knees to see a small Siva image and several tridents embedded in the soft floor, and to Kheding (4 km), while longer and more difficult ones to Simulakha, Namnang Lakha and Nakcho are very scenic. Trekkers with permits for Chhangu may return from Nakcho via the lake.

Chhangu (Tsomgo) Lake → *36 km from Gangtok. Altitude: 3774 m.*

The holy Chhangu lake lies 5km further along the precipitous Nathula road. Completely frozen in mid-winter, it's best to visit March-May and September to mid-December.

There are excellent views of Khangchendzonga from the nearby ridge and superb sunsets, but the lake area is overcrowded and spoilt by snack kiosks and loud Hindi music. You can walk around the 1-km long lake in an hour. There are organized tours and permits are needed (apply with photo and passport a day ahead). If you go independently, allow six hours for the return trip; a jeep/minivan costs about Rs 800.

● Sleeping

Rumtek Monastery *p123*
A Martam Village Resort, Gangkha, Upper Martam, 5 km from the monastery, T03592-203314. Overlooking the valley, 11 pleasant, traditional-style thatched cottages with large picture windows, good meals. Recommended.
B Shamhbala Mountain Resort, T03592-252241, parekh.house@gems.net.in. In a large estate, 500 m before monastery. 31 cottages in traditional tribal styles, or comfortable rooms in main building, most with good views from balconies, vegetarian restaurant, bar, exchange, pick-up from Siliguri arranged.
D-E Jharna, T03592-202714. Some rooms with hot water, restaurant, bar.
F Sungay, near monastery gate. Basic rooms in old guest house, cleanish shared toilet, friendly.

Kyongnosla Alpine Sanctuary *p123*
F Log Huts, 2 rooms in each at Kyongnosla and Lamnang Lakha. You must apply for a permit (Rs 5) to Chief Wildlife Warden, Sikkim Forest Dept, Deorali, Sikkim, to enter sanctuary.

● Festivals and events

Rumtek Monastery *p123*
Feb Special colourful **Losar** dances are held 2 days before the Tibetan New Year (check date). Arrive 3 days earlier to see rehearsals without masks, *pujas* and ceremonies are held during this period.
Jun The important Rumtek *chaam* is performed on the 10th day of the 5th month of the Tibetan calendar; masked dancers present 8 manifestations of the Guru Rimpoche. Tours in Jul-Aug from Gangtok.

● Transport

Rumtek Monastery *p123*
To get the monastery there is a bus from **Gangtok** about 1600 (1 hr) along a steep narrow road, return depart about 0800. A shared jeep: Rs 25 each; last return to Gangtok 1300. **Rumtek** to **Pemayangtse**, 4 hrs. Taxi from Gangtok, Rs 300 (return Rs 500, 1½ hr wait).

South and West Sikkim

Ravangla and Maenam Sanctuary → *Altitude: 2155-3260 m.*

Ravangla (Rabongla), 65 km southwest of Gangtok, is a small village whose timber-fronted main street retains a strong frontier flavour, and is the gateway to one of Sikkim's best day hikes. The 12-km trek through the sanctuary to **Maenam Peak** (3260 m), which dominates the town, takes about three hours. The sanctuary harbours red panda, civet, blood pheasant and black eagle and is most beautiful when the magnolia and rhododendron are in bloom in April-May. **Bhaledunga**, another 30-minute hike along the ridge, on the steep cliff edge above the Tista, juts out in the shape of a cock's head.

Some 30 km south of Ravangla and 76 km southwest of Gangtok is the town of Namchi. Towering above it on the 'wish-fulfilling hill' of Samdruptse is a 45-m statue of Guru Padmasambhava, the patron saint of Sikkim who spread Buddhism to Tibet in the ninth century. Resplendent in copper and a coat of bronze paint, the **statue** ① *0700-1700, free,* can be seen from Darjeeling, around 40 km away. A ropeway from Namchi is planned; otherwise take a taxi, Rs 250 return. Not to be outdone, a 33-m statue of Siva is rising on another hill outside Namchi.

The administrative headquarters of West Sikkim, **Gezing** (Gayzing, Gyalshing), 105 km west of Gangtok, is at the crossroads of bus routes and has a busy market with food stalls, shops, a few hotels (none recommended) but little else to detain visitors.

Forty kilometres north of Gezing is the gold-topped **Tashiding monastery**, built in 1716, which stands on a conical hill between the Rathong and Rangit rivers on a spot consecrated by Guru Rimpoche. The gompa has been refurbished and all the frescos repainted. The most sacred *chorten* in Sikkim is here so even the sight of Tashiding is thought to bring blessing. You will see numerous stones with high-class carvings of *mantras* around the monastery. Pilgrims attend the **Bumchu festival** in February/ March to drink water from the sacred pot which has never run dry for over 300 years. Below the monastery is the small Tshchu Phur cave where Guru Rinpoche meditated; follow the trail on the left of the entrance to Tashiding until you see a small house opposite and the painting on the rocks. Carry a torch if you plan to crawl into the cave.

Pemayangtse → *112 km west of Gangtok. 72 km from Darjeeling. Altitude: 2085 m.*

A full day trip by car from Gangtok, along a very scenic road, Pemayangste (Perfect Sublime Lotus) was built during the reign of the third Chogyal Chador Namgyal in 1705. It is about 7 km from Gezing, above the main road to Pelling.

The awe-inspiring **monastery** ① *0700-1600, Rs 10, good guided tours, 0700-1000 and 1400-1600 (if closed, ask for key), no photography inside,* Sikkim's second oldest, is for many visitors the highlight of their visit; it has a certain aura about it. Take an early morning walk to the rear of the monastery to see a breathtaking sunrise in perfect peace. The walls and ceiling of the large *Dukhang* (prayer hall) have numerous *thangkas* and wall paintings, and there is an exceptional collection of religious artworks including an exquisite wooden sculpture on the top floor depicting the heavenly palace of Guru Rimpoche, the *Santhokpalri,* which was believed to have been revealed in a dream. The old stone and wood buildings to the side are the monks' quarters. According to tradition the monks have been recruited from Sikkim's leading families as this is the headquarters of the Nyingmapa sect. Annual *chaam* dances are held in late February and in September.

Denjong Padma Choeling Academy (DPCA), set up to educate needy children, runs several projects, such as crafts and dairy, and welcomes volunteers, who can also learn about Buddhism and local culture. The Meditation Centre offers courses and can accommodate visitors for a small charge and volunteers for free at the new hostel (see below); a rewarding experience. Volunteers spend up to six weeks, March-December. Contact Jules Stewart, London, T0207-229 4774, jjulesstewart@aol.com.

Rabdanste, the ruined palace of the 17th- to 18th-century capital of Sikkim, is along the Gezing-bound track from the monastery, 3 km from Pelling. From the main road, turn left just before the white sign "Gezing 6 km", cross the archery field and turn right behind the hill (road branches off just below Pemanyangtse). Follow the narrow rocky track for 500 m to reach the palace.

Pelling → *2 km from the monastery and 9 km by road from Gezing.*

Pelling sits on a ridge with good views of the mountains. The rather bleak little town has three areas linked by a winding road, Upper and Middle with views and hotels, and Lower Pelling with banks and other services. Upper Pelling is expanding rapidly with new hotels springing up to accommodate honeymooners from Kolkata, and makes the most convenient base for visits to Pemayangtse. You can also visit the **Sanga Choelling Monastery** (circa 1697), possibly the oldest in Sikkim, which has some colourful mural paintings. The hilltop monastery is about 3 km along a fairly steep track through thick woods (about 30 minutes). The area is excellent for walking.

A road west of the Pelling-Yuksom road leads to this tranquil lake where the clear waters reflect the surrounding densely wooded slopes of the hills with a monastery above; Lepchas believe that birds remove any leaf that floats down. Prayer flags flutter around the lake and it is particularly moving when leaflamps are floated with special prayers at dusk. The sanctity of the lake may be attributed to its shape in the form of a foot (symbolizing the Buddha's footprint), which can be seen from the surrounding hills. You can trek from Pelling to Yuksom via the lake without a permit.

Yuksom (Yuksam), 42 km north from Pelling by jeepable road, is where the first Chogyal was crowned in 1641, thus establishing the kingdom of Sikkim. The wooden altar and stone throne above the Kathok lake stand beside Norbu Ghang chorten, which has an enormous prayer wheel, in a beautifully peaceful pine forest. The simple Hermit's retreat at **Dhubdi** (circa 1700) is up on a hill, 45 minutes' walk away. Yuksom makes a quiet and relaxing base for a few days' stay, with several day walks and longer treks leading out from the village centre.

◉ Sleeping

Ravangla and around *p124*
A Kewzing homestays, Kewzing village, 8 km towards Legship, T03595-260141, T094348-65154, ktdc@sikkimfoundation.org. A community-driven programme allows guests to stay in family homes in a quiet Bhutia village. Rooms vary widely, some better value than others, and there is a maximum 2-night stay in any house to ensure even distribution of income. A rare and fascinating insight into traditional rural life. Rates include all meals and guide; cultural programme extra Rs 1000.
D-F Maenamla, Kewzing Rd, T03595-263861, maenamla@hotmail.com. Smartest choice in town, with carpeted rooms, clean baths, hot water from geyser, friendly and welcoming.
F Melody, Ralang Rd, T03595-260817. Basic but charming, wooden floors, clean, friendly.

Tashiding
G Blue Bird, T03595-243248. Very basic rooms, Sikkimese food.
G Siniolchu,T03595-243211. Friendly, 5 clean rooms (3 big and beautiful ones on upper floor). Dorm, shared bath, hot water, meals.

Pemayangtse *p125*
A Mount Pandim (15-min walk below monastery), T03593-250756, www.elgin hotels.com. Sparkling bright rooms with bath, some with beautiful mountain views, in freshly renovated and upmarket lodge.

Pelling *p125*
Power and water cuts can last 4 hrs or more and dogs often bark all night. Several **G** in Upper Pelling, with excellent views if you can overlook the often dubious cleanliness. Best is **Kabur**, T03595-258504, with a terrace restaurant and internet. With over 30 places to choose from, and hotel building going on unchecked, the following are recommended.
D-E Sikkim Tourist Centre, Upper Pelling, near Jeep Stand, T03595-258556. Simple rooms, some with views, cheaper on roadside, rooftop restaurant (cooking excellent but service limited; only snacks after 1400), tours.
E Norbu Ghang, Main Rd, T03595-250566. Rooms with bath, better views from those away from road, views from the terrace are superb. Restaurant.
E-F Haven, Khecheopalri Rd, Middle Pelling, T03595-258238. Clean doubles with running hot water.
G Garuda, Upper Pelling, near bus stop, T03595-250614. Rooms in basic lodge with bath, hot water (heaters Rs 100-150), dorm, restaurant (breakfast on rooftop, mountain views), internet, backpackers favourite.
G Sisters Family Guest House, near Garuda, T03595-250569. Friendly, 8 simple clean rooms, shared bath (bucket hot water), great food.

Khecheopalri Lake *p126*
Families also offer to take in guests (further 25 mins' walk up the hill).
G Pilgrims' Lodge, on edge of lake. Enterprising Mr Tenang provides Sikkimese porridge and millet bread (and much more), and leads short circular hikes around the lodge.

Yuksom *p126*

For **E** home stays in the village contact Khang-chendzonga Conservation Committee, T03595-241211, kcc_sikkim@hotmail.com. Highly recommended, meals and activities included. **D Tashigang**, Main Road, T03595 241202, tashigang2@yahoo.com. 21 good, clean rooms with lovely views, own vegetable garden, tennis, quiet, very welcoming. **G Dragon**, Main Road, T03595-241290. Friendly and sociable guest house with clean rooms (shared bath), good for swapping trekking stories with other travellers.

● Eating

Pelling *p125*
Don't miss local *chhang* brewed in the area. **Alpine**, Khecheopalri Rd (below Garuda). Chinese, Kashmiri especially good. Yellow, wooden cottage run by friendly Ladakhi lady. **Mock-Too**, Upper Pelling opposite Sikkim Tourist Centre. Excellent fresh snacks including *momos*, paratha and samosas.

Yuksom *p126*
G Yak, on main street. Good food includes delicious fresh Tibetan bread with yak's cheese.

▲ Activities and tours

Pelling *p125*
Help Tourism, Sikkim Tourist Centre, T03595-250855, good information and tours.

Yuksom *p126*
Khangchendzonga Conservation Committee (KCC) helps arrange trekking guides and porters. Agents arrange permits with 2 days' notice, saving a trip to Gangtok.

● Transport

Buses can be crowded, especially during *Pujas* and *Diwali*. SNT buses and quicker, more convenient jeeps run to/from Gangtok and between all main towns in the west, often leaving early morning; check locally for current times. If no jeep is going directly to your destination, it may be best to go to Gezing, Jorethang or Namchi, which have

frequent services in all directions. Direct jeeps leave from all three towns for Siliguri, 4-5 hrs, and Darjeeling, 2-3 hrs.

Ravangla and around *p125*
Tashiding
Several jeeps from Gezing via Legship, and from Yuksom (early morning). From Pemayangtse: a day's trek.

Pemayangtse *p125*
From Gezing: bus or shared jeep to monastery, 1000-1430, Rs 15-20. From Pelling, taxi Rs 50 one way, easy walk back.

Pelling *p125*
To **Gezing** reasonably frequent jeeps (Rs 20) or walk along steep downhill track, 1-2hrs. To **Khecheopalri Lake**: last bus dep 1400, or you can walk 5 hrs (part very steep; last 3 hrs follows road, with short cuts). Buses and share-jeeps to **Yuksom** (until 1500, 3 hrs), Damthang, Gangtok (4 hrs); **Darjeeling** via Jorethang, tickets from stand opposite **Hotel Garuda**, Rs 180. **Siliguri**: SNT bus 0700; tickets sold at provision store next to **Hotel Pelling** where bus starts, and stops uphill at jeep stand near **Garuda**.

Khecheopalri Lake *p126*
From **Pelling**: jeep share, 1½ hrs; **Tashiding** (3 options): **1** 0700 bus to Gezing, then jeep. **2** Bus to Yuksom 1500 (irregular) from 'junction', 10 km from lake, overnight in Yuksom, then bus at 0700 (or jeep) to Tashiding, 1 hr. **3** Hitching a lift on the Pelling to Tashiding jeep, which passes the 'junction' at about 1400 (try sitting on top of jeep to enjoy the beautiful scenery).

Yuksom *p126*
Bus To **Gezing and Tashiding**, 0700. Shared jeep: to **Pelling**, 0600, 0700, 3 hrs, Rs 40 each, from market place; buy ticket a day ahead in season. **Gangtok**, Rs 150 each.

● Directory

Pelling *p125*
Tourist office Sikkim, Upper Pelling, near Garuda, T03595-250855. Helpful staff.

● *For an explanation of the sleeping and eating price codes used in this guide, see the inside front cover. Other relevant information is found on pages 35-39.*

North Sikkim

Phodong → *Colour map 2, grid A2.*

The renovated early 18th-century monastery is 1 km above the north Sikkim Highway, about 2 km before Phodong village. It is a pleasant walk up to the little-visited gompa where friendly monks show you around; the track is jeepable. A further hike of 2 km takes you to **Labrang** monastery of the Nyingmapa sect. Below the track nearby is the ruined palace of **Tumlong**, the capital of Sikkim for most of the 19th century.

Lachung, Shingba Rhododendron Sanctuary and Yumthang

→ *Colour map 2, grid A2. 135 km north of Gangtok.*

Recently opened to tourists, Lachung sits among spectacular mountain scenery at 2400 m and acts as a gateway to the increasingly popular Yumthang valley. Still run on the traditional democratic Dzomsa system, the village is a stronghold of Lepcha culture, though the daily influx of tourists from Gangtok and the rapid construction of lodges to accommodate them has begun to take its toll.

The road north to Yumthang passes through the Rhododendron Sanctuary, which has 24 of the 40 rhododendron species found in Sikkim, along with attractive aconites, gentians, poppies, saxifrages, potentillas and primulas.

The attractive high valley of **Yumthang** is surrounded by mountains. The alpine meadow near the tree line is a seasonal grazing ground for yaks. A few minutes' walk from the main road beyond a log bridge over the river Lachung are sulphur hot springs. There is also a **Log House** (no electricity); contact the Forest Department (permit needed). Hire a jeep from Gangtok or go on an organized tour.

⊜ Sleeping

Phodong *p128*
F Yak and Yeti, T03595-260884. Quiet and clean. Some rooms with toilet, hot water in buckets, but meals are pricey. Recommended.

Lachung *p128*
B-C Sonam Palgey, T03592-2810777. 10 basic comfortable rooms in great location by waterfall overlooking valley, tasty meals.

Northway serves excellent Indian food, and is friendly, relaxed, efficient and good value.

⊙ Transport

Phodong *p128*
From Gangtok bus to start of jeep track, 0800 (2 hrs), Rs 35; return bus, 1500. Jeeps travel up to **Labrang**.

Trekking in Sikkim

Trekking is in its infancy and many of the routes are through areas that seldom see foreigners. Consequently, facilities are poorly developed though the paths are usually clear. You do not need previous experience since most treks go no higher than 2000-3800 m. An added attraction is that dzos (cross between a cow and a yak) will carry your gear instead of porters, though they are slower. The trekking routes also pass through villages that give an insight into the tribal people's lifestyle. With this area coming under threat from pollution by rubbish left by trekkers, be sure to choose a trekking agency that enforces good environmental practices; ECOSS in Gangtok and the KCC in Yuksom (see pages 122 and 127) can point you in the right direction.

Ins and outs

Foreigners must be in a group of two at least before applying for a **permit** to trek. Approved **trekking agents** can assist with permits. Areas open to foreigners include the Khangchendzonga Biosphere Reserve near Yuksom, the Lachung and Yumthang valleys in North Sikkim and Chhangu in East Sikkim (one day). Yuksom can arrange guides (Rs 300-400 a day), cook (Rs 250), porter (Rs 100(and yak/pony (Rs 150), and book trekkers' huts (Rs 50 per head). **Leeches** can be a problem in the wet season below 2000 m. *Sikkim: A Guide and Handbook* by **Rajesh Verma**, updated annually, introduces the state and has descriptions of treks, with trekking profiles. The U 502 sheets for Sikkim are NG 45-3 and NG 45-4. PP Karan

> ‡ *The best time to visit is March to late May and October to early December. April is best for flowers.*

published a map at the scale of 1:150,000 in 1969. Price US$3, available from the Program Director of Geography, George Mason University, Fairfax, VA 22030, US. *Sikkim Himalaya* (Swiss Alpine Club) – Huber 1:50,000. Very detailed, £16.

Khangchendzonga National Park

① *Rs 180 (5 days), Rs 50 for each extra day, camera Rs 10, porter Rs 5, pack animal Rs 5, camping Rs 25 per tent, trekkers' hut Rs 50 per person, Tsokha Hut Rs 75 per bed.*
The park offers trekking routes through picturesque terraced fields of barley, past fruit orchards to lush green forests of pines, oak, chestnut, rhododendrons, giant magnolias, then to high passes crossing fast mountain streams and rugged terrain. Animals in the park include Himalayan brown bear, black bear, the endangered musk deer, flying squirrel, Tibetan antelope, wild ass and Himalayan wild goat. The red panda lives mostly on treetops at 3000-4000 m. There are about 600 species of birds.

The Khangchendzonga trek now falls wholly within the newly designated national park, from which all forms of industry and agriculture have been officially

Sikkim treks

banished. The park office in **Yuksom**, housed in a shiny new building about 100 m below the trekkers' huts, has interesting exhibits and helpful staff.

The classic trekking route goes from **Yuksom to Gocha La** (variously spelt Goecha La and Gochela). This eight to nine day trek includes some magnificent scenery around Khangchendzonga, and there are excellent views as you travel up the Ratong Chu River to the amphitheatre of peaks at the head of the valley. These include Kokthang (6150 m), Ratong (6683 m), Kabru Dome (6604 m), Forked Peak (6116 m) and the pyramid of Pandim (6720 m) past which the trail runs.

Trekkers' Huts (F), in picturesque places at Yuksom, Tsokha and Dzongri, are fairly clean with basic toilets. Bring sleeping bags; meals are cooked by a caretaker.

Day 1 Yuksom to Tsokha An eight-hour climb to the growing village of Tsokha, settled by Tibetan refugees. The first half of the climb passes through dense semi-tropical forests and across the Prek Chu on a suspension bridge. A steep climb of two hours leads first to **Bakhim** (2,740 m) which has a tea stall, a Forest Bungalow and good views back. The track goes through silver fir and magnolia to Tsokha (2950 m), the last village on the trek. Trekkers' hut, campsite and good Mountain Hut private lodge at Tsokha.

Day 2 Tsokha to Dzongri Mixed temperate forests give way to rhododendron. **Phedang** is less than three hours up the track. Pandim, Narsingh and Joponu peaks are clearly visible, and a further hour's climb takes the track above the rhododendrons to a ridge. A gentle descent leads to Dzongri (4030 m, 8 km from Bakhim). There is a trekkers' hut and campsite. Dzongri attracts pilgrims to its *chortens* holding Buddhist relics. From exposed and windswept hillsides nearby are good panoramic views of the surrounding mountains and of spectacular sunrises or sunsets on Khangchendzonga.

Day 3 Dzongri to Thangshing A trail through dwarf rhododendron and juniper climbs the ridge for 5 km. Pandim is immediately ahead. A steep drop descends to the Prek Chu again, crossed by a bridge, followed by a gentle climb to Thangshing (3900 m). The southern ridge of Khangchendzonga is ahead. There is a trekkers' hut and campsite.

Day 4 Thangshing to Samity Lake The track leads through juniper scrub to a steeper section up a lateral moraine, followed by the drop down to the glacial and holy Samity Lake. The surrounding moraines give superb views of Khangchendzonga and other major peaks. You can't camp at the lake; a new campsite is 1 km away at Lammuney.

Day 5 To Zemathang and Gocha La and return The climb up to Zemathang (4800 m) and Gocha La (4900 m) gives views up to the sheer face of the eastern wall of Khangchendzonga. It is a vigorous walk to reach the pass, but equally impressive views can be gained from nearby slopes. Much of the walk is on rough moraine.

Day 6 Samity Lake to Thangshing Return to Thangshing. This is only a two-hour walk, so it is possible to take it gently and make a diversion to the former yak grazing grounds of Lam Pokhari Lake (3900 m) above Thangshing. The area is rich in medicinal plants, and you may see some rare high altitude birds and blue sheep.

Days 7 and 8 Thangshing to Tsokha The return route can be made by a lower track, avoiding Dzongri. Dense rhododendrons flank the right bank of the Prek Chu, rich in birdlife. Day 7 ends in Tsokha village. The next morning you retrace your steps to Yuksom.

Other treks in Sikkim

It's possible to trek from town to town, if you're prepared to do a lot of road walking and ask villagers to show you short cuts. One of the best circuits, for up to seven days but also enjoyable in smaller sections, begins from Pelling or Pemayangtse, descending through terraced fields to the Rimbi Khola river, then climbing up to Khecheopalri Lake. From here you can easily reach Yuksom in a day, then continue on to Tashiding, and either return to Pemayangtse or climb eastwards towards Kewzing and Ravangla.

● Footprint features

Northeastern Hill States

Introduction

The Northeast is a true frontier region. It has over 2000 km of border with Bhutan, China, Myanmar (Burma) and Bangladesh and is connected to the rest of India by a narrow 20 km wide corridor of land. One of the most ethnically and linguistically diverse regions in Asia, each of the seven Northeastern Hill states has its distinct culture and tradition.

Deep forests cover the sparsely populated Himalayan foothills of Arunachal Pradesh, only recently opened to visitors. To its south, Assam, which occupies the lush lowlands of the Brahmaputra Valley, is the most densely populated and largest of the states. Meghalaya's beautiful hills have the dubious distinction of being the wettest region in the world. The little-visited four southeastern states of the region, Nagaland, Manipur, Mizoram and Tripura, make up a fascinating area, hilly, remote, and a zone where the tribal cultures of South and Southeast Asia intertwine.

The Northeast has been a politically sensitive region since Independence. Insurgency in places continues to surface making travel in some areas unsafe. Arunachal Pradesh, most of Assam, Meghalaya and Mizoram are largely free of problems. Nevertheless, advice on travel to these and the other states should be taken locally. Permits are required for Arunachal Pradesh, Mizoram, Nagaland and Manipur.

Don't miss ...

1 **Kaziranga National Park** The place to see the Indian greater one-horned rhino (from the back of an elephant), page 138.
2 **Nameri National Park** Stay at the eco camp and go rafting and fishing, page 139.
3 **Archery Stakes** Place a bet at this daily occurrence in Shillong, page 150.
4 **Mawsynram** Visit the wettest place in the world, which had over 20 m one year. Nearby Cherrapunji has an annual rainfall of over 11 m, page 150.
5 **Tawang Monastery** Embark on the spectacular four-day journey to this remote place, page 155.
6 **Kohima** Pay your respects at the cemetery where the British prevented the Japanese invasion of India in April 1944, page 158.

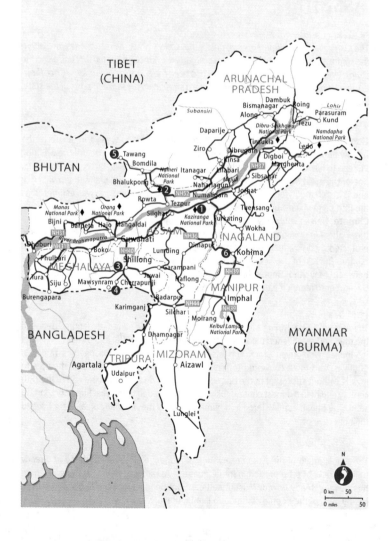

Northeastern Hill States

🔢 Visiting the Hill States

Visitors to Assam, Meghalaya and Tripura do not need permits but may need to register on arrival and departure. Foreigners visiting Arunachal Pradesh, Nagaland, Manipur and Mizoram can apply for Restricted Area Permits from the Ministry of Home Affairs, Foreigners Division, Lok Nayak Bhavan, Khan Market, New Delhi 110003. Send two photos and allow up to six weeks; success is by no means guaranteed. Groups of four and married couples stand a better chance. The State Tourist Offices and local travel agents can usually help, and save bureaucratic hassle. Indians require Inner Line Permits from the Ministry of Home Affairs.

Assam

➔ *Population: 26.6 mn. Area: 78,438 sq km.*

The lush valley of the Brahmaputra, one of the world's great rivers, provides the setting for Assam's culturally rich and diverse communities. Although it is tea that has given the state a world name, the fertile river valley has been the home to generations of rice farmers, and tribal populations continue to have a significant presence in parts of the state.

▸▸ *For Sleeing, Eating and other listings, see pages 142-147.*

The land

Geography Assam stretches nearly 800 km from east to west, the length of the narrow floor of the Brahmaputra Valley. The Himalaya to the north and the Shillong Plateau to the south can be clearly seen. The state is dominated by the Brahmaputra, one of the great rivers of the world, which has a fertile alluvial plain for growing rice and is also famous for tea. Earthquakes are common; one in 1950 was estimated as the fifth biggest earthquake ever recorded.

Climate Unless you really want to see rain, avoid the monsoon! Assam is in one of the wettest monsoon belts in the world. Even the central Brahmaputra Valley, protected by the rain shadow of the Shillong Plateau, has over 1600 mm of annual rainfall. The rest of the Assam Valley has up to 3200 mm a year, mostly concentrated between May and September. Although summer temperatures are high, from December to March it can be cold, especially at night.

History

The Ahoms, a Shan ruling tribe, arrived in the area in the early 13th century, deposed the ruler and established the kingdom of Assam with its capital in Sibsagar. They later intermixed with Aryan stock and also with existing indigenous peoples (Morans, Chutiyas) and most converted to Hinduism. The Mughals made several attempts to invade without success, but the Burmese finally invaded Assam at the end of the 18th century and held it almost continuously until it was ceded to the East India Company in 1826. The British administered it in name until 1947 though many areas were beyond their effective control.

People

The ethnic origin of the Assamese varies from Mongoloid tribes to those of directly Indian stock, but the predominant language is Assamese, similar to Bengali. There has been a steady flow of Muslim settlers from Bengal since the late 19th century. Nearly 90% of the people continue to live in rural areas.

Modern Assam

The Assam Valley is in a strategically sensitive corridor for India, lying close to the Chinese frontier. Its sensitivity has been increased by the tension between local Assamese and immigrant groups. The failure of the AGP (Assam Gana Parishad) to hold its alliance together and to control the violence that has become endemic through Assam contributed to its downfall. Congress returned to power in the 2006 elections under Chief Minister Tarun Gogoi, a lawyer and long serving member of the Lok Sabha. The state has suffered a long-running low-intensity conflict and in late 2006 and early 2007 a number of bombings occurred in the capital Guwahati. Seek advice from your consulate before travelling.

Guwahati ●●●●▲●● ⇢ pp142-147. Colour map 2, grid B4.

→ *Phone code: 0361. Population: 808,000.*

Despite its commanding position on the south bank of the mighty Brahmaputra, it is easy to forget that Guwahati is a riverside town, the waterside having little impact on people's lives. The main entrance point for visitors to the Northeastern states, the city retains a relaxed and friendly atmosphere. Paltan Bazar, where most visitors arrive, is very busy and crowded. The area north of the railway is quieter with an almost rural feel.

Ins and outs

Getting there Borjhar airport (23 km) has flights to Kolkata, Delhi, Bagdogra and airports throughout the Northeast. It has occasional coaches, shared taxis and auto-rickshaws for transfer to town. Some 1150 km from Kolkata, Guwahati is at the junction of NH31, 37 and 40, and is well connected by road to all major centres of the northeast region. The railway station is in the central Paltan Bazar, while most state and private buses arrive immediately to its south. ⇢ *See Transport, page 145, for further details.*

Getting around It is easy to walk around the two main commercial areas of Paltan and Pan (pronounced *Paan*) Bazars, which have most of the hotels and restaurants. Red minibuses or canters are cheap and very efficient around the city (conductors call out the stops), whereas auto-rickshaws need hard bargaining. Political incidents in the city are rare so military presence usually remains discreet and low key. Carry a torch when walking at night; large holes in the pavement lie in wait to plunge unwary travellers straight down into the sewers!

History

Guwahati, on the site of the ancient capital of a succession of local chieftains, was once known as *Pragjyotishpur* ('the City of Astrology'). The **Navagrah** (nine planets) **Temple** on a hill here was the ancient centre of astronomy and astrology. It was also a centre of learning and a place of Hindu pilgrimage. In the seventh century, Hiuen Tsang described its beautiful mountains, forests and wildlife. Today it is the business capital while **Dispur**, the 'Capital Area', is just to the south.

Sights

The 10th-century **Janardhan Temple**, in the heart of the city, was rebuilt in the 17th century. The Buddha image here uniquely blends Hindu and Buddhist features. The **Umananda** (Siva) **Temple**, on Peacock Island in the Brahmaputra, can be reached by ferry. An Ahom king built the temple in 1594, believing Uma, Siva's consort, had stayed there. Ask the priests about the few rare golden langurs here. **Assam State Museum** ① *Tue-Sun 1000-1615 (Nov-Mar), 1000-1700 (Apr-Oct) and 2nd, 4th Sat, Rs 2, photography with permission*, covers epigraphy, sculpture and natural history, among others; sections on village life, crafts and ethnography are particularly interesting. This small, well-lit museum is thoughtfully displayed with some information in English and is informative on the neighbouring cultures. **Srimata Sankaradeva Kalakshetra** ⓘ *Panjabari, on road to Narangi, Tue-Sun 0800-2200, Rs 10, bus No 8*, is a cultural complex set up to serve as a centre for Assamese dance, drama, music, fine arts and literature ("a theme park of Assamese life"). It features a museum, theatre, artists' village and heritage park.

Excursions from Guwahati

Kamakhya Temple ⓘ *Mon-Sat 0830-1300, 1500-1600, Sun 0830-1200*, 8 km southwest, is believed to be an old Khasi sacrificial site on Nilachal Hill. It has been a centre for Tantric Hinduism and Sakti worship. Rebuilt in 1665 after the 10th-century temple was destroyed by a Brahmin convert to Islam, it typifies Assamese temple architecture with its distinctive beehive-shape *sikhara* (spire), the nymph motifs and the long turtleback hall. The dark sanctum contains the creative part of the goddess which is said to have fallen here, see page 68, and pilgrims enter to touch the wet *yoni* of Kamakhya (Sakti). Western visitors may be allowed into the sanctum but should be prepared for the charged atmosphere and to walk barefoot on a floor sprinkled with the sacrificial blood of a goat. Ask for Hemen Sarma, a knowledgeable resident Brahmin, on entering the complex. Further up the hill is a smaller temple and

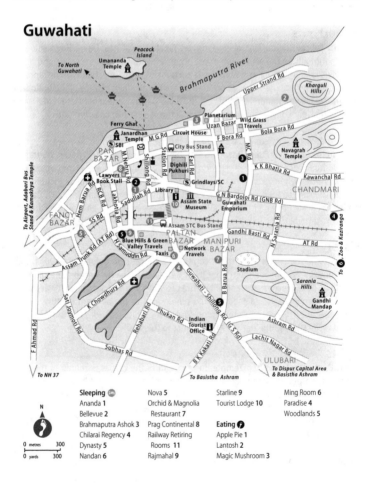

Guwahati

Sleeping
Ananda 1
Bellevue 2
Brahmaputra Ashok 3
Chilarai Regency 4
Dynasty 5
Nandan 6

Nova 5
Orchid & Magnolia
  Restaurant 7
Prag Continental 8
Railway Retiring
  Rooms 11
Rajmahal 9

Starline 9
Tourist Lodge 10

Eating
Apple Pie 1
Lantosh 2
Magic Mushroom 3

Ming Room 6
Paradise 4
Woodlands 5

a viewpoint with panoramic views of the Brahmaputra. See Festivals, page 144. It can be visited by bus from MG Rd (towards Adabari Bus Stand) which can drop you near Kamakhya. From here take a canter (red minibus) from AT Road to the temple or walk up the steep and slippery rocky path at the back of the hill.

Basistha Ashram, 12 km away, is believed to be sage Basistha's (Vasistha) hermitage. It is a scenic spot with three mountain streams nearby. **North Guwahati** is a sleepy town across Saraighat Bridge, which can also be reached by any ferry from the ghat. The **Digheswari Temple** is worth a visit. Take a rickshaw from the other bank, an auto-rickshaw or a shared four-wheeler.

Around Guwahati

Hajo, a friendly and peaceful town, 34 km across the river, produces bell-metal work and is sacred to three religions. **Hayagriba Madhab** Hindu temple is said to contain a Buddhist relic. Some believe this is where the Buddha attained Nirvana. Its hilltop location is more spectacular than the temple itself. The main street behind the tank stocked with fish leads to an old Ganesh temple after 2 km; a friendly priest might allow you in. Hajo is also sacred to Muslims since the **Pao Mecca Mosque** built by Pir Ghiasuddin Aulia is supposed to have a quarter (*pao*) of the sanctity of Mecca. Take a bus from Adabari Bus Stand ① *1 hr, last return departs around 1600 but very crowded; you may have to travel on the roof.*

The small village of **Sualkuchi**, situated on the north bank of the Brahmaputra, is famous for silk production from non mulberry leaf-fed worms, hence its unique natural colour. Every household is involved with weaving of *muga*, *endi* or *pat* silk; prices are 30% cheaper than in Guwahati. Take the ferry from Guwahati or a bus from Hajo taking 20 minutes.

Pabitora is a small wildlife sanctuary a two-hour drive from Guwahati (60 km), on the border of Nagaon and Kamrup districts; rhinos can be found here. **Madan Kamdev**, 45 km north of Guwahati, has been called Assam's Khajuraho. The temples which may date from the 11th to 12th centuries, possibly reconstructed in the 18th, are believed to be associated with tantric practices. The principle shrine to Uma-Mahesvara or Siva-Parvati is still in use. Buses from Guwahati go to Baihata on NH31, 5 km from the site; rickshaws take over.

Manas National Park ⊟⊟ » *pp142-146. Colour map 2, grid A3.*

→ *Phone code: 03666.*

A World Heritage Site, and one of India's most beautiful sanctuaries, Manas lies in the Himalayan foothills, southeast of the river Manas, on the Assam-Bhutan border. Over half the area is covered with tall grass and scattered patches of woodland. This changes to dense semi-evergreen forest in the upper reaches and even to conifer on hills towards Bhutan.

Ins and outs

It is essential to enter via Barpeta Road by car or taxi. Permits are issued by the Field Director, Manas Project Tiger, Barpeta Road, after he obtains confirmation of a police escort to accompany you. Pick up provisions beforehand. Use the Bansbari gate with a Forest Range Office to get to Mathanguri inside the park (20 km, 30 minutes). Book a car or taxi for the return trip. If you travel during dawn (0500) and before sunset (1600) you may see some wildlife. Travel is not allowed after sunset. The maximum temperature is summer is 35°C, minimum 18°C; the winter maximum is 24°C, minimum 7°C. Annual rainfall is 4100 mm. Season: November-March. Take something warm, a hat and shoes for wading through slippery streams.

‖ *The town has medical facilities, a tourist information office, banks and a post office.*

Manas, with a buffer zone of 2800 sq km (including two other far-flung sanctuaries) and a core area of 391 sq km, was demarcated in 1977-1978 when the preservation programme Project Tiger was launched. At the last count there were over 80 tigers. UNESCO has released funds to help the national park recover from damage caused by Bodo rebels. Political troubles can lead to sudden closure of the park so get local advice before visiting; contact Wild Grass Tours, see page 145.

Sights

The forests are home to most of the larger animals found in Kaziranga, most common being wild buffalo, swamp deer, hog deer, sambar and elephant. Some 22 of the animal and bird species are on the endangered list of the IUCN including the rare capped and golden langur which can be seen among the flowering trees, mostly on the Bhutan side. There are also pigmy hog, hispid hare, slow loris, clouded leopard, rhino and tiger. The sanctuary is rich in birdlife (over 400 species), and attracts migratory flocks of redstarts, forktails, mergansers and ruddy shelduck. Otters are frequently seen in the Manas River.

Occasionally boats, for two to eight, are for hire from the Forest Beat Officer, Mathanguri. To see the animals at close range, an elephant ride is best. These start from Mathanguri ① *0900-1200, 1400-1700, 1 hr, Rs 525 for foreigners.* Charges for entry and camera are similar to Kaziranga, see below.

Kaziranga National Park ⬤▲⬛⬤ ↠ *pp142-147.*

Colour map 2, grid B4.

→ *Phone code: 03776.*

Kaziranga Reserve Forest was declared a game sanctuary in 1916 to save the Indian greater one-horned rhino and became a national park in 1974. It is now a World Heritage Site. In a beautiful setting on the banks of the Brahmaputra, and with the Karbi Anglong Hills to the south, the 430 sq km park combines elephant grass mixed with thorny rattan cane, areas of semi-evergreen forest and shallow swamps.

Ins and outs

Guwahati is 215 km from Kohora, the entry point to Kaziranga on the NH37. Park roads open 0800-1100, 1400-1630. Foreigners, Rs 250. Camera fees change regularly: still, Rs 50, video, Rs 500, though may alter depending on length of lens. There's a 25% discount on fees after three consecutive days. Summer maximum 35°C, minimum 18°C; Winter maximum 24°C, minimum 7°C. Annual rainfall 2300 mm, heavy in

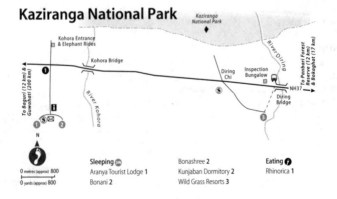

Kaziranga National Park

Sleeping ⬤	Bonashree **2**	Eating ⬤
Aranya Tourist Lodge **1**	Kunjaban Dormitory **2**	Rhinorica **1**
Bonani **2**	Wild Grass Resorts **3**	

0 metres (approx) 800
0 yards (approx) 800

the best for birds); closed mid April to mid October during monsoons. Wear cotton clothing but take a jacket. ▸ *See Transport, page 146, for details.*

Sights

The **rhino** population is about 1800 here and they can be easily seen in the marshes and grasslands. Despite Kaziranga's status as a World Heritage National Park, poachers still manage to kill the animal for its horn, which is used in Chinese and Tibetan medicine. The park also has over 1000 wild buffalo, sambar, swamp deer (over 500), hog deer, wild pig, hoolock gibbon, elephant (about 1000) python and tiger (around 85 at last count in 2000), the only predator of the docile rhino. There is a rich variety of shallow-water fowl including egrets, pond herons, river terns, black-necked stork, fishing eagles and adjutant storks, pelicans and the rare Bengal florican. There are otters and dolphins in the river.

There are three road routes for visiting the park: **The Kaziranga Range** – Kohora, Daflang, Foliomari which is full of big mammals; the **Western Range** – Baguri, Monabeel, Bimoli, Kanchanjuri with tall elephant grass so visibility not great; and the **Eastern Range** – Agortoli, Sohola, Rangamatia, where you may see a lot of wildlife but at a distance. Keep receipts as fees are valid for several trips during one day.

Entry into the park is by your own vehicle, hired jeep or trained elephants. Although elephants cover less ground than motor vehicles, they can get a lot closer to the wildlife, particularly rhinos and buffalo. However, the elephant rides get mixed reports; the general consensus seems to be that they are less enjoyable when demand is heavy. They carry four and a seat may be booked through the Forest Range Officer, the night before the visit ① *0530-0630 or 0630-0730, Rs 1000 foreigners (Indians Rs 120), plus jeep transfer from town to the elephant pick-up, Rs 120.* The viewing posts just inside the park may offer quieter viewing.

The Department of Tourism, Kaziranga and private agents hire out **jeeps** for five to six people. Government ones cost Rs 700 (or Rs 120 per person shared) for three hours; private ones Rs 900-1000 for 50 km or 2½ hours. A car or jeep must be accompanied by a Forest Department guard (Rs 50), who can give directions as well as spot wildlife. Cars and jeeps pay a road toll, Rs 150. Total price per jeep is Rs 920-1220.

Panbari Forest Reserve, 12 km from Kaziranga, has hoolock gibbons and a good variety of birdlife. Contact the Forest Office, Guwahati, for permission to visit.

Tezpur and around ▣▲◉ ▸ *pp142-146. Colour map 2, grid A4.*

→ *Phone code: 03712.*

Tezpur, on the north bank of the Brahmaputra, 180 km northeast of Guwahati, is the site of Assam's first tea plantations. Its ancient origins can be seen at Da Parbatia, west of town, which has the entrance gate of an early Gupta style temple.

An interesting excursion is to take a Guwahati-bound bus, get off at the bridge over the Brahmaputra, then negotiate with a boatman to take you to the river's confluence with the Bhoreli for some river dolphin watching. Some hotels, **Luit** for example, offer such trips. It involves a 30-minute rickshaw ride, Rs 150, followed by boat hire, around Rs 1000.

Nameri National Park, a 210 sq km park on the Arunachal border, is on the river Jia Bhoreli, about 40 km north of Tezpur. There are tigers (26 in 2006), elephants, Indian bison, barking and hog deer. It is home to about 20 endangered white-winged wood ducks among 300 bird species, with evergreens, bamboo and some open grassland. The best time to visit is from October to April. Viewing is on elephant back as there are no roads; you can trek within the park with a forest guide. Entry and camera fees are similar to Kaziranga.

Plantation labour

Today Assam produces most of India's tea. Old colonial tea planters' bungalows surrounded by neat rows of emerald green tea bushes dominate the landscape, particularly in Upper Assam. After an early experiment using imported Chinese labourers ended in near mutiny, the British began the mass recruitment of Adivasis from the Choto Nagpur plateau, Andhra Pradesh and Orissa. They have now been assimilated into Assamese society. One of the largest groups of organized labour in India today, they enjoy benefits undreamed of by other workers including free health care, education and subsidized food. The lifestyle of the plantation, hardly changed since the Raj, has been tarnished lately by the rise of insurgency, with tea companies being targeted for extortion and kidnapping.

Bhalukpong, 20 km west of Nameri, just beyond the Arunachal Pradesh border, en route to Tawang, has a hot spring, an orchid garden and good fishing. You can camp (own tent) on the picturesque bank of the River Jia Bhoreli. A taxi to Tezpur, taking one hour, costs around Rs 250. Or catch a bus from Balipura, change for Bhalukpong.

Orang National Park is often called a miniature Kaziranga. The 76 sq km park, 66 km northwest of Tezpur, has similar flora and fauna, though viewing is not as rewarding. This is compensated by its peaceful and intimate atmosphere, especially if staying inside the park. Arriving by car is best from Tezpur. From Orang, it is a 15-km bumpy, dust track to the park.

Northeast Assam ⬤🏍🏨🎵 ›› *pp142-147.*

Jorhat → *Colour map 2, grid A5.*
Jorhat is one of Assam's major tea centres and is convenient for visiting Majuli Island to the north. The **Tea Festival** is held in November.

Majuli Island → *Colour map 2, grid A5.*
Majuli Island is one of the largest river islands in the world, though constantly changing, and now reduced to around 700 sq km. The flooding of the Brahmaputra River means that at times Majuli is reduced to a cluster of islands, some as small as a hut top. Roads keep shifting but villagers adapt to re-routing by building cost-effective bamboo bridges. Cut off from the mainland to the south about 400 years ago, it is served by ferries from Jorhat and North Lakhimpur, but it can still be accessed from the north by road during summer. Majuli is also a birdwatchers' paradise. Foreigners must register on arrival and departure at the nearest police station.

At the forefront of Assamese Vaishnava culture, the island is an important centre for arts, crafts and science. Work is in progress to declare it a World Heritage Site. The *satras* (monasteries) here, inspired by the 15th-century saint Sankardeva and his disciple Madhavdeva, are worth visiting. They are essentially small, self-sufficient villages where Vishnu is worshipped through regular performances of dance dramas at the temples.

Some *satras* can be visited on foot in and around **Kamalabari** and **Garmur** but for others a rickshaw is handy. **Auniati**, a few kilometres west of Kamalabari, has an Angami tribal museum with old manuscripts, utensils, jewellery and handicrafts. **Bengenatti**, east of Uttar Kamalabari, is a centre for performing arts and tribal dance forms. Others worth visiting are at Nauten Kamalabari and Dekhinpat.

Hollong Park Gibbon Sanctuary

The sanctuary at **Bhalowguri**, 16 km from Majuli Island, was designated in 1998, but is scarcely visited by tourists. Indeed, the low-key nature of the operation is a big part of the appeal, and few leave disappointed. Viewing the wild elephants requires an overnight stay in the specially constructed hut on stilts. The current fee is a meagre Rs 20 per person (four hours' viewing), which includes an armed escort/guide, though the dense forest growth makes the gibbons hard to spot. Contact District Forest Officer in Jorhat, then Forest Range Officer at Mariani. To reach the park catch a bus from the top of MG Road in Jorhat and go via Mariani, 18 km southeast.

Sibsagar and around

District headquarters of the largest tea and oil producing area in the Northeast, **Sibsagar** was the Ahom capital for two centuries. There are several royal tanks. Daupadi (the Ahom King's wife) built the huge tank here in 1734. On the east bank there is a birdwatching tower and a library. The tower of the Siva Dol on its bank is one of the tallest Siva temples in India. **Sivaratri** is celebrated in March.

The **Joysagar** at **Rangpur**, 5 km away, and the three temples on its bank date from 1697. **Talatal Ghar**, 6 km away, is a seven-storeyed palace with three underground floors, built between 1696-1714. Take a bus from BG Rd Bali Ghat in Sibsagar (Rs 5, 20 minutes); then cycle-rickshaw (Rs 15).

Dibrugarh, Tinsukia and Borajan Reserve Forest

Much of the old town of Dibrugarh was destroyed during the 1950 earthquake. The new town on the Brahmaputra is surrounded by tea estates. Tinsukia, a major transport junction in the Northeast, is convenient for visiting the nearby Dibru-Saikhowa National Park and the small Borajan Reserve Forest.

Borajan Reserve Forest, 5 km from Tinsukia, is a small (500 sq m) patch of forest which is home to five species of primate (Hoolock gibbon, capped langur, slow loris, stump tailed macaque and common macaque), though not all are easy to spot.

Dibru-Saikhowa National Park

A national park since March 1999, on the southern flood plain of the Brahmaputra near Tinsukia, this is largely a semi-wet evergreen forest. The 340 sq km core area within a large biosphere reserve is a refuge for some endangered species: tiger, leopard, leopard cat, clouded leopard and elephant. The rich birdlife includes the very rare white-winged wood duck. The best time to visit is November to March. Temperature ranges from 6 to 36°C. Average annual rainfall ranges from 2300 to 3600 mm.

Entry points are at **Guijan** on the southern edge and **Dhola** (near Saikhowa Ghat) in the north, both accessible by bus from Tinsukia. From Guijan, a boat across the river takes you to the Range Office at the park entrance. If you cross from Dhola, the Range Office is 5 km into the park at Narbarmora; it is better to notify your arrival beforehand. See Kaziranga above for usual park fees. The Forest Department has one double room at Guijan; carry provisions. Contact DFO, Rangagora Road, Tinsukia, T0374-233 1472.

Margherita → Colour map 2, grid A6.

Margherita, the constituency of the present Chief Minister, is on Dihing river at the foot of the Patkoi Range and was named by Italian railway engineers in the 19th century after the Queen of Italy. The town is surrounded by tea estates and is the Northeast head-quarters of Coal India Ltd. The last of the steam railway engines in Assam is still operating.

Ledo → Colour map 2, grid A6.

The small coal mining town of Ledo, 6 km northwest of Margherita, was the headquarters of Northern Combat Area Command during the Second World War and is the start of the 470-km Stilwell Road. Named after General Joseph Stilwell, the road was

⁝ The burning bush

As well as rhinos and tea, Assam is the home of the world's hottest chilli. The Naga Jalokia chilli, which grows naturally in the northeast, has been tested to have a firepower of 855,000 Scoville Heat Units, meaning that one drop of its juice would need diluting that many times in order to be rendered neutral. This makes it more than twice as hot as the previous titleholder, the Mexican red savina Habanero, though whether your mouth and stomach would notice the difference is debatable: anything above 5000 SHUs is considered super-hot.

the most ambitious and costly engineering project of the war, US$137 million at the time. Once a two lane, all-weather bitumen highway linking Ledo with Myitkyina in North Burma through the Pangso Pass and with Kunming in China (1656 km) it is now closed beyond Nampong in Arunachal Pradesh. A sign, 6 km west of Ledo, commemorates the Road to Mandalay but little else remains of the massive Allied presence here.

⬤ Sleeping

Guwahati *p135, map p136*
Hotel staff often speak little English. There are some budget hotels at Sadullah and M Nehru Rd crossing; those in Paltan Bazar are often full by the afternoon. Most medium priced hotels have some a/c rooms and tend to serve Indian meals only. You may need to complete 4 copies of the hotel registration slip and then register with the police (fairly quickly). Most hotels outside Guwahati require photocopies of passport ID and the visa page.
A Brahmaputra Ashok, MG Rd, T0361-254 1064, www.theashokgroup.com. 49 rooms (the riverside ones are best), central a/c, TV, bamboo and cane furniture, good restaurant, credit cards, good travel agency.
A Dynasty, SS Rd, T0361-251 6021, www.hoteldynastyindia.com. 68 comfortable rooms, good restaurants.
B Nandan, GS Rd, opposite Indian Airlines, T0361-254 0855, www.hotelnandan.com. 55 rooms, some a/c, expensive suites, restaurants, **Upavan** for snacks, bar.
B Rajmahal, Paltan Bazar (near bus stand), T0361-254 9141, www.rajmahalhotel.com. 80 rooms, good value, excellent restaurant, pool open in summer (non-residents Rs 75 for 45 mins).
B-C Prag Continental, M Nehru Rd, Pan Bazar, T0361-254 0850. 62 rooms, some a/c, terrace restaurants, **Continental Café**.
C-D Bellevue, MG Rd, on river front opposite Raj Bhawan, T0361-254 0847. Not the

plushest in town, but quiet and with great elevated views over the river. 45 rooms, restaurant (continental recommended).
C-D Chilarai Regency, HP Brahmachari Rd, Paltan Bazar, T0361-263 9748. Some of the 44 large rooms have a/c. Bar, exchange.
C-D Nova, SS Rd, T0361-252 3464. Clean rooms (some **C** a/c), decent restaurant (Indian, Chinese) but slow service (room service quicker), pleasant, friendly and helpful.
D-E Starline, Md Shah Rd, Paltan Bazar, T0361-251 8541. Of the 74 clean rooms, 12 have a/c with hot water 24 hrs. Chinese/ Indian restaurant, polite and helpful staff.
F-G Ananda, M Nehru Rd, T0361-254 4832. Small dark rooms but pleasant, vegetarian dining hall.
F-G Orchid, B Barua Rd, opposite stadium, T0361-254 4471. Set back from road in own compound, 23 clean rooms, 5 a/c, hot water in buckets, excellent **Magnolia** restaurant.
G Railway Retiring Rooms, rooms (some a/c), small dorm, book at Enquiry Counter.
G Tourist Lodge (Assam Tourism), opposite railway station, T0361-254 4475. 21 fairly clean simple rooms with nets, toilets and balcony, canteen, staff speak little English but are friendly, tourist information, good value.

Manas National Park *p137*
E Doli, 200 m from station, 18 rooms with fan, net, bath, abundant food, helpful.

G Mathanguri Forest Lodge, built on hill overlooking Manas River. Despite being in a poor state, it's situated within the park.

Forest Deparment's **Forest Lodge**, and **Bhutan Tourist Lodge**, Mathanguri, are very simple but clean and well maintained, cook available but bring provisions (from Barpeta Rd), camping possible, book well in advance. Prefabricated **Rest House** provides linen but no electricity, open Nov-Apr. Contact Field Director, Manas Tiger Reserve, PO Barpeta Rd, T03666-233413. If you arrive late at Barpeta Rd you will need to spend the night there.

Kaziranga National Park *p138, map p138*
B-C Wild Grass Resorts, lovely location, 1½ km from NH37, 5½ km from Kohora, ask for Kaziranga IB Bus Stop, 400 m north of resort, T03776-262085, www.nivalink.com/wildgrass. 19 rooms, wooden floors, cane furniture, de luxe camping (4 tents, common bath), can get very cold in winter, excellent buffet lunch (Rs 50/65), huge pool, great service, spotless, relaxing, beautiful walks through forests and tea plantations, tours, pick-up from Guwahati for groups, occasional cultural shows.
D Aranya Tourist Lodge, 1 km south of Kohora, T03776-262429. Friendly, 24 rooms with bath and balcony, some a/c, simple garden, restaurant, bar (slow service).
D-E Bonani, near **Aranya Tourist Lodge**, T03776-262423. 5 a/c rooms, limited menu.
G Bonashree, still cheaper, 9 rooms, a large veranda, pleasant garden, but often full.
Kunjaban Dormitory, linen optional, 5- or 12-bed (Rs 30-50). Book via Deputy Director, Tourism, Bonani, Kaziranga, T03776-266 2423.

Tezpur and around *p139*
C-D Eco Camp, Nameri National Park, T03714-244246, or contact **Wild Grass Tours**, see page 144. Swiss cottage tents with thatched cover, some with bath, 6-bed dorm (Rs 125), wash block, meals.
C-D Luit, Ranu Singh Rd, 100 m bus stand, Tezpur, T03712-221220. 38 clean rooms, some a/c, best in new wing, restaurant, bar.
E Basanth, Main Rd, Tezpur, T03712-230831. Good, clean, well-maintained rooms (Rs 250).
E Durba, KK Rd, Tezpur, T03712-224276. Clean rooms with TV, **Appayam** restaurant.
G Bungalows, Orang National Park. 2 at the entrance, 2 located 1½ km inside the park, overlooking river. Bring your own provisions;

the cook/guide will prepare your food. Reservations, Divisional Forest Officer, Mangal Doi, T03713-222065.
G Forest Lodge, Nameri National Park, contact Range Officer.
G Tourist Lodge, opposite Chitralekha Udyan, Tezpur, T03712-221016. 6 large rooms with bath and dorm, very quiet and peaceful, tourist information.

Johhat *p140*
D Dilip, near **Paradise Hotel**, Jorhat, T0376-2332 1610. Clean, friendly, one of few places to accept foreigners.
D Paradise, Solicitor's Rd (off AT Rd), Jorhat, T0376-332 1521, F332 3512. Restaurant, bar, 31 rooms, 9 a/c, hot water, exchange.

Majuli Island *p140*
G Circuit House, Kamalabari, Majuli Island, Garmur (Rs 100), contact SDO, Majuli, T03775-274424, ahead but often booked.
G Guest House, at Nauten Kamalabari (8 km from Garmur), Majuli Island. Spartan and no hot water but incredibly cheap.
G Uttar Kamalabari Satra, Kamalabari, Majuli Island. Very basic, bring own bedding and leave a donation, usually booked through **Wild Grass** (see page 144) but you may try to reserve on T03775-273392; ask to call Dulal Saikia (the head priest) to the phone, then ring back after 10 mins.

Sibsagar *p141*
E Siddhartha, BG Rd, T0376-222 3276. 29 rooms, restaurant, bar, modern.
E-F Brahmaputra, BG Rd, T0376-222 2000. 48 rooms, restaurant, helpful, clean.
G Tourist Lodge, near Siva Dol, T0376-222 2394. Helpful tourist office, 6 rooms often full.

Dibrugarh, Tinsukia and Borajan Reserve Forest *p141*
B Chang Bungalow, near Dibrugarh. A Heritage Planter's bungalow, sparkling clean, fabulous food, excellent staff, car and guide included. Contact **Purvi Discovery**, T0373-230 1166, csn@purvidiscovery.com.
C-E Mona Lisa, Mancotta Rd, Chowkidinghee, Dibrugarh, T0373-232 0416. Good restaurant, bar,19 rooms, some a/c, best in new wing.
D-E Goswami, near **Mona Lisa**, Dibrugarh, T0373-232 1250. Some a/c in 12 rooms, dining hall, **Green Valley Tours**, bus pick-up.

D-E **Highway**, AT Rd, Tinsukia, T0374-233 5383, 500 m from New Tinsukia station. Modern, 20 rooms, some a/c, vegetarian restaurant.

D-E **Jyoti**, Rangagora Rd, Tinsukia, T0374-233 9573. Restaurant, 20 rather grubby rooms, some a/c, hot water.

G **President**, Station Rd, Tinsukia, T0374-232 0789. Basic, noisy, 32 rooms, vegetarian restaurant, TV.

G **Retiring Rooms**, Tinsukia. Very basic vegetarian refreshments.

There is G paying guest accommodation in Dibrugarh in an Assamese home, about Rs 200 including breakfast, contact Binoy Dowerah, T0373-232 2289.

⦿ Eating

Guwahati *p135, map p136*

Assamese *thalis* including rice, fish and vegetable curry, often cooked with mustard. You might try vegetarian *Kharoli*, Omita *Khar* (papaya cooked with burnt 'bark' of the banana plant). Larger hotels, including Bellevue and Rajmahal, serve continental food and have bars.

††† **Dynasty**, for Chinese. Recommended.

†† **Ming Room**, Rajgarh Rd, near Chandmari Flyover. Very good Chinese.

† **Apple Pie**, MC Rd. Pastries, ice creams.

† **Hits Cafeteria**, near Central School, Khanapara, T0361-230 0090. Out in the suburbs, offers great lunch and dinner.

† **Lantosh**. Assamese. Takeaway and ice cream, clean.

† **Magic Mushroom**, MC Rd. International. Clean, good quality, varied menu, psyche-delic decor, very friendly and helpful owner.

† **Magnolia**, Orchid Hotel, B Barua Rd.

† **Paradise**, GNB Rd, Chandmari, T0361-254 6904. Assamese. Great *thalis* (Rs 55), very clean and friendly, closes 1530-1800 (cycle rickshaw from station, Rs 10).

† **Station restaurant**, good omelettes.

† **Woodlands**, AT Rd (older branch on GS Rd). Indian vegetarian. Clean, a/c, specializes in lunch and dinner thalis (Rs 40).

Northeast Assam *p140*

On Majuli Island, food is available at simple eateries. Carry drinking water. Those listed below are situated in Jorhat.

Belle Amies Food & Fun Junction, Gar-Ali. Indian/Chinese. Colour-coded menu to indicate hotness!

Canteen at State Bus Stand. Cheap, does good *roti breakfasts (toilets)*.

Rajhans, AT Rd. Indian snacks.

Woodlands, BG Rd (between MG Rd and Gar Ali). Indian. Good thalis.

⊛ Festivals and events

Guwahati *p135, map p136*

Jan Magh Bihu, wee-long festivities celebrated with singing and dancing.

Mid-Apr Rongali Bihu similar to Magh Bihu.

Jun Ambubachi marks the end of Mother Earth's menstrual cycle with a fair at Kamakhya Temple.

Sep The Manasa Festival honours the Snake goddess. You can watch devotees dancing and entering into trances from galleries on the hillside.

26-28 Dec Assam Tea Festival is celebrated with events in various places.

⦿ Shopping

Guwahati *p135, map p136*

Silk and handicrafts

Muga, pat and *endi* silks, hats, bamboo and cane baskets, flutes, drums and pipes are typical of the area. Guide prices: silk per metre: *muga* Rs 400+ (saris Rs 4000+), *pat* Rs 250 (saris Rs 2000+), *endi* Rs 150-300. *Pat mikhala* and *shador*, Rs 1500, *endi* shawls Rs 300+. Bargain in Pan Bazar and Fancy Bazar.

Assam at Ambari, sells silks, bamboo, wood, brass and ceramics.

Assam Co-op Silk House, HB Rd, Pan Bazar, for pure silk items.

Khadi Gramudyog, near Guwahati Emporium.

Manipur, Paltan Bazar.

Purbashree, GNB Rd, has traditional crafts.

Tantuja, Ulubari, has Bengal handloom.

▲ Activities and tours

Guwahati *p135, map p136*

Assam Bengal Navigation, 10 Barley Mow Passage, London, W4 4PH, T020-8995 3642, assambengal@aol.com. Runs long-distance cruises along the Brahmaputra aboard *RV Charaidew* and *RV Sukapha*, with 12 en suite

cabins. It also runs Bansbari Lodge in Manas National Park and Diphlu River Lodge, a new luxurious resort, in Kaziranga National Park.
Assam Tourism, Tourist Lodge, Station Rd, T0361-254 7102. City: Basistha Ashram, Zoo, Museum, Kamakhya Temple, Govt Sales Emporium. 0900-1500. Rs 90. Tue, Sun (minimum 10). River cruises: from near Janardhan Temple, winter 1500, 1600; summer 1600, 1700, 1 hr, Rs 50. Kaziranga: Nov-Apr, departs 0900, arrives 1600, return 1600 on following day, Rs 600, foreigners Rs 1250 (inclusive) allows only from 1500 to 1000 (on next day) in the park. Separate morning buses, departs 0700, 5½ hrs. Shillong: departs 0700, Rs 255 (tiring, as the windy hill roads take 3½ hrs each way). Private companies (see below) may be more reliable.
Hemanta Doley, Sankardeva Udyan, Machkhowa, T0361-251 2121, for river trips.
Network Travels, GS Rd, T0361-251 2700. Imaginative tours including river cruises, Indian Airlines agent, efficient and reliable.
Purvi Discovery, T0373-230 1166, csn@purvidiscovery.com. Varied tours, excellent service.
Rhino, M Nehru Rd, T0361-254 0061. For visiting game reserves and Shillong.
Traveland, 1st floor, Brahmaputra Ashok, MG Rd, T0361-254 1064, rchaliha@hotmail.com. Knowledgeable and helpful.
Wild Grass, Barua Bhavan, 107 MC Rd, Uzan Bazar, T0361-254 6827, wildgrass@sancharnet.in. Very helpful, knowledgeable, efficient. Highly recommended for good value wildlife, tribal tours and Arunachal (can get a permit in 5 days), free travel advice on phone (Nov-Apr).

Kaziranga National Park p138, map p138
Assam Tourism offers a 2-day tour, also see **Wild Grass**; both under Guwahati above.

Tezpur and around p139
Assam Anglers' Association, T03712-220004, assamangling@yahoo.com, operates a strict 'catch-record-release' system to conserve the golden mahseer.
Eco camp, Potasali, T03714-244246, organizes whitewater rafting and mahseer fishing on the Bhoreli. Rafting, for fishing or nature watching, for two people on rubber rafts, Rs 650 per day, Rs 300 transport to/from raft.

Guwahati p135, map p136
Air
Information T0361-245 2859. Transport to town: Indian Airlines and Rhino Travels coaches connect with Kolkata flights, Rs 40, 1 hr. Taxi, Rs 300, share taxi, Rs 100, 45 mins. Auto-rickshaw, Rs 150. **Indian Airlines**, Ganeshguri, near Dispur, T0361-226 4425, airport, T0361-284 0279, www.indian-airlines.nic.in; 0900-1600. 2 daily to **Kolkata** and one to **Delhi**; several a week to **Agartala**, **Bagdogra**, **Imphal**, **Lilabari**. Jet Airways, Panchvati, GNB Rd, T0361-266 2202, airport T0361-284 0130, www.jetairways.com: to **Bagdogra**, **Delhi**, **Imphal**, **Kolkata**. Also flights with Air Deccan, T3300-8888, www.airdeccan.net, and Spicejet, T1800-180 3333, www.spicejet.com. **Helicopter**: Meghalaya Transport Corp, T0361-284 0300, to **Shillong**, Mon-Sat, Rs 1000, on to **Tura**; tickets at airport.
Airlines Air India, GS Rd, T0361-260 4165; BA, Pelican Travels, Hotel Brahmaputra Ashok, T0361-263 0123, or try agents at Rajmahal Hotel.

Bus
Between midnight and 0500 buses are not allowed to enter the city, but taxis are.
Local Red minibus 'canters' or 'Omni taxis' cover main roads. Prone to accidents.
Long distance Private coaches (and taxis) operate from Paltan Bazar, with waiting rooms, left-luggage, snack bars. Operators: **Assam Valley**, T0361-254 6133, **Blue Hill**, T0361-252 0604, **Green Valley**, T0361-254 2852, and others have buses to all the Hill States. **Assam STC Stand**, Paltan Bazar, T0361-254 4709. Left luggage, Rs 3 per day. Reservations 0630-1230, 1330-1700. Meghalaya STC, T0361-254 7668, 222 3129. Buses to: **Aizawl** (11 hrs); **Imphal** (579 km); **Itanagar** (11 hrs); **Jorhat via Kohora (for Kaziranga)** (6 hrs); **Kaziranga and Upper Assam**: bus for Tinsukia and Digboi (0700 a/c; 0730), halt at Wild Grass Resorts after 4 hrs. **Kohima** 2000, 2015, 2030 (13 hrs); **Shillong** (103 km) hourly, 0600-1700, Rs 40 (3½ hrs); **Silchar** 1730; **Siliguri**; **Tezpur** every 30 mins (3½ hrs). **City Bus Stand**, Station Rd (north end): to **Hajo**, (1½ hr). **Adabari Bus Stand**,

AT Rd (4 km west of centre) reached by 'canters' from MG Rd, has buses to Hajo, Orang and Nalbari.

Ferry
To **North Guwahati** from MG Rd Ferry Ghat. To **Peacock Island**: Rs 6 each way. 0700-1700.

Rickshaw
From Paltan Bazar to Fancy Bazar Rs 25, Fancy Bazar to Navagraha Temple Rs 30.

Taxi
Local Sightseeing Rs 100 per hr (excluding petrol); **Guwahati Taxis**, Paltan Bazar, near Police Station; **Green Valley**, Silpukhuri, T0361-254 2852, cars/jeeps Rs 1100 per day plus overnight Rs 150. **Traveland**, 1st floor, Brahmaputra Ashok, MG Rd, T0361-254 1064, F252 0762. Reliable and efficient. **Chandana**, Goswami Villa, Zoo Narengi Rd, T0361-255 7870, has Tata Sumo (a/c), Rs 1500 per day.
Long distance From Paltan Bazar: **Shillong**, Rs 1100, shared taxis fill up quickly when trains arrive).

Train
Station has snack bars, chemists, tourist information, left luggage (trunks and suitcases only), on showing ticket. Enquiries: T0361-254 0330. Reservations: 100 m north of the station on Station Rd, T0361-254 1799, 0800-1330, 1400-2000; Foreign Tourists, Counter 3, where great patience is needed. To **Kolkata (H)**: *Kanchenjunga Exp 5658*, 2230, 21½ hrs (via **New Jalpaiguri**, 9 hrs); *Kamrup Exp 5960* (AC/II), 0715, 23½; *Saraighat Exp 3026*, except Wed and Sun, 1900, 17 hrs (via **New Jalpaiguri**, 7 hrs). To **Delhi (ND)**: *Rajdhani Exp 2423*, via Patna and Kanpur, Mon, Thu-Fri, 0700, 28 hrs; *Rajdhani Exp 2435*, via Lucknow, Mon-Tue, Fri-Sat, 32½ hrs. To **Dibrugarh** Via Dimapur: *Brahmaputra Mail 4056*, 1445, 14 hrs; *Kamrup Exp 5959*, 1645, 14½ hrs.

Manas National Park *p137*
Buses travel on a good fair weather road between Guwahati and Barpeta Rd but no buses beyond; taxis charge, Rs 450-600 per journey. The nearest train station is at Barpeta Rd (40 km) with trains to **Guwahati** and **Kolkata**.

Kaziranga National Park *p138, map p138*
Air
Nearest airport is at Jorhat (88 km). See below. Foreign tourists must use Guwahati's Borjhar airport, see page 135.

Road
Best to ask **Wild Grass** if they have a vehicle going from Guwahati, or confirm timings of private buses. ASTC buses between Guwahati and Jorhat via **Kohora** stopping at **Nagaon** (30 mins, where you can stop overnight); departs 0900, 1000, 1100, 1230, Rs 85, 5-6 hrs. **Private**: Green Valley (office behind bus station) coaches depart Guwahati for Tinsukia and Digboi, 0700 (non a/c, Rs 95), 0730 (a/c, Rs 135); lunch stop at Wild Grass Resorts, after 4 hrs. **Guwahati**: a/c bus from Dibrugarh stops at resort for lunch; leaves at 1330. Kaziranga Forest Lodge has 10 seats reserved on the Express coach between Golaghat and Guwahati. Assam Tourism bus, depart 0930 from **Bonashree Lodge**, arrive Guwahati 1600, Rs 85 (lunch Rs 40). It is a very bumpy ride. From **Shillong** get a Jorhat bus and switch at **Jorabat** for Kaziranga.

Train
Furkating (75 km) has the nearest station with trains from Guwahati and Dibrugarh; buses via Golaghat.

Tezpur and around *p139*
Air Saloni airport is to the north of Tezpur: Indian Airlines, T03712-231657, www.indian-airlines.nic.in. Flies to/from **Kolkata** via **Imphal** twice weekly, and also to **Dimapur** twice weekly. Frequent **buses** to/from **Guwahati**; **Kaziranga** until 1400. Daily to **Itanagar** (4 hrs); **Tawang** (12 hrs). **Taxi** To **Orang/Nameri**, Rs 550 plus petrol.

Jorhat *p140*
Air Jorhat has the main airport 7 km from town with airlines coach or autos for transfer. Private taxis Rs 100 to town or Rs 600 to Kaziranga. **Indian Airlines**, T0376-232 1521, airport, T0376-234 0294, www.indian-airlines .nic.in, to **Kolkata** via **Dimapur**; Jet Airways, Hotel Paradise, T0376-232 5652, airport, T0376-234 0881, ww.jetairways.com; **Kolkata**, Wed-Thu, Fri, Sun. **Imphal**, Wed-Fri, Sun. **Bus** ASTC Stand on AT Rd has a good canteen. Private buses leave from outside

ASTC: to **Guwahati**, 0600-0730 and 2000-2130, 7 hrs; **Sibsagar** (55 km); **Dibrugarh** (131 km). Ticket booths are nearby.

Train Station (3 km southeast of bus stand) has no toilets. To **Guwahati**: *Jan Shatabdi Exp 2068*, Mon-Sat 1345, 7 hrs, via Lumding, narrow gauge to **Haflong**: 0715, 4½ hrs – beautiful route but tourists are discouraged; Haflong Tourist Lodge is occupied by the army.

Majuli Island *p140*

Bus from Jorhat (at junction of MG and AT Roads) to **Neemati** (13 km north); allow 1 hr.

Government **ferry** from **Neemati**, 1000, 1600, return 1330 (confirm timings); crossing time varies seasonally as boats have to circumnavigate sand bars. Buses run from the ghat to **Kamalabari** (about 5 km) and **Garmur** (8½ km). You can also arrange private boats at the jetty for transporting a car.

Sibsagar *p141*

Nearest airport: Jorhat (60 km). Nearest railway station: Simaluguri (20 km). Regular buses to Guwahati, Kaziranga, Simaluguri.

Dibrugarh *p141*

Air The airport is 16 km from town. Indian Airlines, T0373-230 0114, www.indian-airlines.nic.in, to **Kolkata**, Tue-Thu, Sun.

Private **bus** stand on AT Rd. Green Valley bus to Guwahati (Rs 190), Kaziranga (Rs 150) pick up from Goswami Guest House at 0715.

Train To **Guwahati**: *Brahamaputra Mail 4055*, 2245, 13½ hrs; *Rajdhani Exp 2423A*, Thu, 2015, 10 hrs (continues to **New Delhi** in further 28 hrs); *Kamrup Exp 5660* (AC/II), 1800, 13½ hrs (continues to **NJP** and **Kolkata (H)** in further 24 hrs). Local *BG Pass* to Ledo (via Tinsukia), 0700, 1600 (not Sat).

Tinsukia *p141*

ASTC bus stand on AT Rd; private buses from top end of Rangagora Rd. To **Jorhat**, Rs 80. The 2 train stations are 3 km apart. New Tinsukia has most of the long-distance trains.

🟢 Directory

Guwahati *p135, map p136*

Banks United Bank of India, HB Rd, Pan Bazar. ATM and TCs, minimum Rs 50 commission. **Grindlays/SC Bank**, Dighali

Pukhari, GNB/Earl roads, Mon-Fri 1000-1500, Sat 1000-1230. ATM plus TCs, commission 1% or Rs 100 but quick and efficient. **Hospitals** Christian Hospital, Chatribari, T0361-254 0193. **Good Health**, GS Rd, T0361-256 6911. **Medical College**, Bhangagarh, T0361-256 1477. With 24-hr chemists outside. **MM Choudhury Hospital**, Pan Bazar, T0361-254 3998. **Internet** Sangita Communications, Anuradha Cinema Complex, GNB Rd, 0830-2000. **Post** GPO (entrance on Shillong Rd) with Speed Post (7 days). Counter 1 for evaluation and 14 for stamps, then basement for franking. CTO: in Pan Bazar. **Tourist offices** Assam, Directorate, Station Rd, T0361-254 7102, www.assamtourism.org. **Tourism**, B Barua Rd, T0361-245 4421, astdcorpn@ sancharnet.in. Counters at airport and railway station. **Arunachal Pradesh**, RG Barua Rd, Bhaskar Nagar, T0361-241 2859. **India**, GS Road, T0361-245 6158, 254 7407. Mon-Fri 0930-1730, Sat 1000-1300, airport counter, helpful for planning trips to other parts of India. **Manipur**, Rajgarh Rd, T0361-254 0707. **Meghalaya**, Ulubari, GS Rd, T0361-252 7276. 1000-1700 except Sun; Rehabari, AK Azad Rd, T0361-254 4343. **Nagaland**, 6th Mile, T0361-233 8426.**Tripura**, Ajanta Path, T0361-222 3034. **Useful numbers** Ambulance: T0361-266 5114. Fire: T0361-254 0222. **Police**: T100.

Kaziranga National Park *p138, map p138*

Post Near the Tourist Lodge and at the park. **Useful addresses** The Wildlife Society has a library of books and magazines and may show wildlife films to groups. Range Officer, T03776-226 2423. Director, Tourist Complex, Bokakhat, T03776-268095. **Kaziranga Safari**, T03776-325468, F325782, can book accommodation.

Jorhat *p140*

Banks State Bank of India, AT Rd. Exchanges TCs (show proof of purchase). **Internet** Sigma, AT Rd (near Gar-Ali). **Tourist office** Station Rd.

Tinsukia *p141*

Internet Sygma Systems, near Railway Overbridge, AT Rd. **Travel agent** Classic Travels AT Rd, T0374-278 6125.

Meghalaya → *Entry permits, see page 134. Population: 2.3 mn. Area: 22,500 sq km.*

Meghalaya, the 'abode of the clouds', with its pine-clad hills, beautiful lakes, high waterfalls and huge caverns, has been called the Scotland of the East because of the similarity of climate, terrain and scenery. The wettest region in the world, between May and September the rain comes down like waterfalls as the warm monsoon air is forced up over the hills. Home to the Garo, Khasi and Jaintia tribes, the hill state retains an untouched feel. There are traditional Khasi villages near Shillong with views into Bangladesh.▶▶ *For Sleeping, Eating and other listings, see pages 151-153.*

The land
Much of the plateau is made up of the same ancient granites as are found in peninsular India; its south facing slope, overlooking Bangladesh, is very steep. The hills rise to heights just under 2000 m which makes it pleasantly cool but it is also one of the wettest places on the earth (Mawsynram has received more than 20 m of rainfall in one year). Much is still densely forested. Shillong is the only important town; 80% of the people live in villages. Compact and isolated, Meghalaya's rolling plateau lies in a severe earthquake belt. In 1897, Shillong was entirely destroyed in an earthquake.

History
The Khasi, Jaintia and Garo tribes each had their own small kingdoms until the 19th century when the British annexed them. The Garos, originally from Tibet, were animists. The Khasis are believed to be Austro-Asiatic. Jaintias are Mongolian and similar to the Shans of Burma. They believed in the universal presence of god and so built no temples. The dead were commemorated by erecting **monoliths** and groups of these can be seen in Khasi villages in central Meghalaya between Shillong and Cherrapunji. In the 19th century many Jaintias were converted to Christianity by missionaries, although they continued many of their old traditions.

People
Meghalaya is divided into three distinct areas, the Garo, Khasi and Jaintia Hills, each with its own language, culture and particular customs. All three tribes are matrilineal, passing down wealth and property through the female line, with the youngest daughter taking the responsibility of caring for the parents.

Government
The hill state was created on 21 January 1972. Since 1980 the Congress Party has dominated Lok Sabha elections, but it has never won more than 25 of the 60 State Assembly seats. The Hill Peoples Union, despite being a minority, has claimed the largest number of seats, but the Congress won both Lok Sabha seats in the 2004 elections.

Shillong ⬤🎷🎸⭕🔺🚍☕ ▶▶ *pp151-153. Colour map 2, grid B4.*

→ *Phone code: 0364. Population: 132,900. Altitude: 1496 m.*

Shillong, situated among pine-clad hills and lakes, retains a measure of its colonial past particularly around the Ward Lake. Elsewhere in the town, unattractive newer buildings have encroached and you can see that an air of decay is beginning to set in.

The horseshoe-shaped **Ward Lake** set in a landscaped botanical garden and popular for boating is near Raj Bhavan, a two-minute walk from Police Bazar. The **Botanical Garden**ⓘ *0900-1700*, is behind it. The **Butterfly Museum**ⓘ *1000-1600*, is in a private house between Police Bazar and Wahingdoh, where butterflies are bred for conservation and sale. The golf course, amidst pines, is ideal for an early morning walk. **Tee & Putt** provides excellent freshly brewed coffee. **Bara Bazar** is well worth a visit to see authentic local colour. It attracts tribal people, mainly women, who come to buy and sell produce – vegetables, spices, pots, baskets, chickens and even bows and arrows. Small stalls sell real Khasi food.

Just over 1 km away is **Lady Hydari Park**ⓘ *0830-1630, Rs 2, cameras Rs 10*, which is designed like a Japanese garden, where you will see the pine native to the area – *Pinus khasiana*. It is well laid out with its **Forest Museum** and **Mini Zoo**.

The nearby **Crinoline Waterfalls** has a swimming pool surrounded by orchids, potted bonsais and a rock pool with reeds and water lilies. At Lumparing, Laban, the Buddhist **Lamasery** near the Assam Club is interesting but a steep climb.

Shillong Peak (10 km, 1960 m) is 3 km from the Cherrapunji Road, commanding spectacular views. **Laitkor Peak** is on the same ridge, 3 km from the Shillong-Jowai Road, and is under Air Force control; visitors have to report at the barrier. Buses drop you at the appropriate junction.

> Due to simmering ethnic tension it's unsafe to walk in unfamiliar parts of town after dark, although it's OK to travel by car.

Elephant Falls (12 km), off the Cherrapunji Road, is a picturesque spot with two high waterfalls. You can walk down to the lowest pool and get a good view, though the falls themselves are less impressive between November and May. The attractive **Umiam Lake** (Barapani), 16 km, offers fishing and boating.

Rhino Memorial Museum, Hospital Road, in a striking building, has a good tribal collection with a bizarre mix of military paraphernalia.

⚡ The Archery Stakes

The Archery Stakes, unique to Shillong, take place Monday to Saturday. Members of different clubs shoot 1500 arrows at a cylindrical bamboo target for four minutes. The punters count the number that stick and anyone who has guessed the last two digits of the number of arrows that stick is rewarded with an 80:1 win. A second shoot takes place an hour later when the odds are 6:1 but if you correctly forecast both results the odds are as high as 4500:1. Naturally, the bookies are the best-dressed men in town.

Start times of the event vary so ask locally in the morning, and to find the exact field, go to the Polo Ground and ask. There are bookies' shops all over town and elsewhere in the state; bets are even placed as far off as Kolkata and Mumbai. The Stakes were legalized only in 1983 when the state government realized that it could raise a hefty 40% tax on the daily money spinner.

Around Shillong ⊜🟋⊜ ⇥ pp151-153.

Mawsynram → 55 km from Shillong.

Mawjymbuin Cave has water dripping from a breast-shaped stone on to what looks like a Siva lingam. The rainfall record in Mawsynram has beaten that of Cherrapunji with over 20 m in one year. Take a bus from Bara Bazar in Shillong at 1400. It takes three hours (Rs 20). **Jakrem**, 64km away, has hot springs. Buses leave Shillong at 1400, taking three hours.

Cherrapunji → Colour map 2, grid B4. Altitude: 1,300 m.

The old administrative headquarters of the Khasis, picturesque Cherrapunji is a pleasant, quiet town spread out along a ridge with gravestones dotting the surrounding hillocks. The best time to visit for spectacular views is during the drier months of October to January. The heat and humidity can be oppressive much of the year. By March it is hazy most days and the odd torrential shower is not unusual. It once held the record as the wettest place on earth, but nearby **Mawsynram** has surpassed this. On average it still gets 11,500 mm annually.

The colourful **Ka Iewbah Sohrarim market** is held every eight days. The local orange flower honey is sold from a house (clearly signposted) just below Cherra Bazar (about 100 m on the road; avoid plastic bottles). Surprisingly, a variety of banana here actually contains seeds.

Nohkalikai Falls, reputedly the world's fourth highest, is 5 km away, near Sohrarim. A vendor sells good orange flower honey. Montana Tourism, Cherra Bazar, arranges group tours (US$10). Limestone caves nearby include Krem Mawmluh (4503 m) with a five river passage and Krem Phyllut (1003 m) at **Mawsmai**, with a large fossil passage and two stream ways. Mawsmai also has high waterfalls in the wet season.

Jowai

Jowai, 64 km southeast of Shillong on NH44, is the headquarters of the **Jaintia Hills**, circled by the Myntdu River. The market, full of tribal women, is particularly colourful. From Shillong cars take 2½ hours, buses a little longer. **Syndai**, 40 km south, has many caves used by ancient warriors as hide-outs, like Krem Sweep with a vast chamber. India's longest (6381 m) and deepest (106.8 m) Eocene Age cave with cataracts and falls is **Krem Um-Lawan**, 60 km southeast of Jowai near **Lumshnong**.

Tura

The centre of the West Garo Hills District, Tura, 220 km southwest of Guwahati, sits at the foot of the jungle-clad 1457 m Nokrek Peak. It is a spread-out town with a slow pace of life. Tura Bazar is dominated by the new supermarket, a red-and-white mini shopping mall, with an underground car park. The small fruit and vegetable market in the basement is well organized. A Museum-cum-Cultural Complex is planned 200 m west of **Orchid Lodge**. Weekly tribal markets are held in surrounding villages.

Nokrek Peak can be reached by a 5 km trek, but involves rock climbing, so is best not attempted alone. **Nokrek National Park** is 55 km away. Jeeps from Tura Bazar cost Rs 1150-1500 for the round trip (daily rate). Ask the tourist office for a guide. **Naphak Lake**, 112 km, near the Simsang River is good for fishing and birdwatching.

Siju → *Colour map 2, grid B3.*

Southeast of Tura just below the town, with others nearby, is one of India's longest caves (4.8 km) with a fine river passage. Groups of at least four are needed for caving so look out on noticeboards. It is more enjoyable and cheaper to travel this way. Bus to Baghmara, 45 km, 1½ hours; from there to Tura, leaves at 0900.

● Sleeping

Shillong *p148, maps p149 and p151*

A-C Tripura Castle, Cleve Colony, T0364-250 1111. The first heritage hotel in the northeast, with 10 art deco-style rooms with brass fireplaces, tea lounge, holistic therapy.
B Polo Towers, Polo Grounds, Oakland Rd, T0364-222 2341, www.hotelpolotowers.com. 50 well-appointed rooms, exchange (cash), modern and efficient, popular bar on Sat.
B-C Centre Point, GS Rd, Police Bazar, T0364-222 5210, centrepoint91@rediffmail .com. 24 comfortable modern rooms with views,

good restaurant (Indian, Chinese).
C-D Alpine Continental, Thana-Quinton Rd, T0364-222 0991, alpine@sancharnet.in. 41 comfortable rooms and suites, hot water (0730-1030), reasonable restaurant, small cosy bar, exchange (cash, TCs), terrace garden, prompt room service.
D Pinewood, Rita Rd, near Raj Bhavan, T0364-222 3146. Well located, otherwise disappointing, 40 old-fashioned rooms (in need of painting), **B** suites, a Raj relic, spacious grounds, restaurants, bar, exchange, golf.
D Summit, Sikandra, 23 Lachaumiere (south of NH between Dhankheti and Malki), T0364-222 6216, fmh_sikandra@hotmail.com. Well-furnished, comfortable rooms, good food, family atmosphere. Recommended.
E Shillong Club, MG Rd (near Ward Lake), T0364-222 5533, resi@hotmail.com. 18 rooms in 'colonial' club, Indian restaurant, bar, tennis, billiards.
E-F Baba Tourist Lodge, GS Rd, T0364-221 1285. Basic, friendly, clean, restaurant, 27 rooms.
E-F Pine Borough, Police Bazar Rd, T0364-222 0698. Restaurant, bar, 20 rooms with bath.
F Yalana, Main Rd, Laitumkrah (near Don Bosco), T0364-221 1240. Comfortable hotel, 17 rooms, good restaurant, very friendly.

Tura *p151*

E Orchid Lodge (MTDC), New Tura (4 km from Tura Bazar), city bus to Dakopgre stops outside, or auto-rickshaw (Rs 50; Rs 70 at night), T03651-222568. Dorm (Rs 70),

Shillong centre

Sleeping ⬤
Alpine Continental 1
Baba Tourist Lodge 2
Centre Point 3
Pine Borough 5

Eating ⬤
Abba 1
Bakery 2
Eecee 3
Jadoh Stall 4

N

0 metres 50
0 yards 50

7 rooms, TV (variable reception despite a giant satellite dish), dining hall meals at set times, Tourist Office (tours of Siju, Balpakram).
E Rikman Continental, Tura Bazar, T03651-220744. Clean, 16 rooms, attached bath, restaurant.

Siju *p151*
F Tourist Lodge (MTDC). Take your own provisions, a chowkidar will cook for you. Another at Baghmara.

● Eating

Shillong *p148, maps p149 and p151*
Try a local pork dish, *dokhkleh* (minced brains with onion and spices) with *jadoh* (rice flavoured with turmeric or pig's blood!) and *saag* (greens) with spicy *tung tap* (hot chutney made with dried fish) at places in Bara Bazar and a stall behind Centre Point.
♈ Abba, Malki Point and GS Rd. Delicious Chinese, closed Sun.
♈ Bakery, serves pizzas and fast food. Recommended.
♈ Eecee, near Bus Stand, Police Bazar. Western. Good restaurant and great cakes.
♈ Elektra Cafè Hits, Nazareth Hospital, Laitumkhra. International. Excellent breakfast and lunch. Also has delicious chocolate cake.
♈ New World, GS Rd. Good Chinese.

Around Shillong *p150*
Orchid Restaurant, Cherrapunji, opposite the falls, serves good food. **Cherra Bazar** has a few eateries.

● Bars and clubs

Shillong *p148, maps p149 and p151*
Better bars at **Pinewood**, **Polo Towers** and **Shillong Club** for more atmosphere. *Kiad*, the local rice wine, is popular in roadside bars.

○ Shopping

Shillong *p148, maps p149 and p151*
You can get handwoven shawls, canework, Khasi jewellery, handicrafts, orange flower honey. Govt Emporia are on Jail Rd and GS Rd. In Bara Bazar, tribal women sell attractive Khasi silver, gold and amber jewellery.

▲ Activities and tours

Shillong *p148, maps p149 and p151*
Golf
Golf Club, T0364-222 3071. 19-holes, clubs for hire; the wettest, and also one of the most beautiful, 'natural' courses in the world.

Swimming and watersporsts
Club near **Crinoline Waterfalls**, 0600-1630 (women 1100-1200, 1400-1500). **Umiam Lake** (16 km), waterskiing, boating and fishing.

Tour operators
Blue Hill Travels, Police Bazar. Very helpful.
Cultural Pursuits, Mawlai, Nongpdeng, T0364-222 3337. Organizes eco-adventure tours of Assam, Meghalaya.
Meghalaya Adventurers, Hotel Centre Point, T0364-222 5210. Offers cave tours. Visitors may contact Patricia Mukkim, a local teacher-cum-journalist, T0364-223 0593, patria@technologist.com. She is well informed about local culture and history.
Meghalaya Tourism, T0364-222 6220, departs from MTDC, Jail Rd, local tours stopping a few mins at most sights, (2½ hrs at Umiam Lake). 0830-1530, Rs 85. Cherrapunji, Nohkalikai Falls, Mawsmai cave (torch essential) and Falls: 0800-1600 (15-20 mins at each place). Rs 100. Recommended.

⊖ Transport

Shillong *p148, maps p149 and p151*
Air
Alliance Air flies 3 times a week to **Kolkata** and **Dimapur**. Bookings through **Sheba Travels**, Police Bazar, T0364-222 7222, who also runs an airport coach. **Meghalaya Helicopter** at Meghalaya Transport Corporation (MTC), T0364-222 3200, flies from Guwahati (Mon-Sat) and Tura, maximum 10 kg baggage, but poor safety record. Tickets from MTC Bus Stand, Jail Rd. Transport to **Guwahati airport** (127 km): taxi, Rs 850 (3 hrs), nearly double for departures after 1100, or hourly bus, Rs 50.

Bus
Meghalaya TC, Jail Rd, T0364-222 3200. To **Guwahati**, frequent, 0600-1700, 3½ hrs; **Silchar**, 2100, 11½ hrs. Also from stands near Anjali Cinema, Bara Bazar to towns in

Meghalaya. Private bus companies have offices/booths around Police Bazar for long-distance connections in the Northeast.

Taxi

Local Metered, yellow-top taxis pick up passengers to share rides. Flag one down and hop in if he is going your way; short hops, eg Police Bazar to Laitumkhrah, Rs 10. MTDC taxis at Pinewood Ashok or the Tourist Office. Sightseeing, Rs 1400 (8 hrs, 100 km).

Long distance Tourist Taxi Association, Police Bazar, T094361-16824, share taxi to Guwahati, Rs 170 each, 3 hrs.

Train

Guwahati (103 km) the nearest railhead. Tickets from MTC Bus Stand, T0364-222 3200. 0600-1100, 1300-1600.

Cherrapunji *p150*

Bus from Shillong (Bara Bazar), to Cherrapunji, 1½ hrs; Mawmluh, 2 hrs.
Taxi from Cherra Bazar for Nohkalikai Falls, Krem Mawmluh and views over the plains of Bangladesh, Rs 300; also share taxis. Meghalaya Tourism, Shillong, runs tours.

Tura *p151*

Helicopter services to/from **Shillong** and **Guwahati**.

Bus to **Baghmara** 106 km (for Siju, none direct), 1300, 4-5 hrs, along the Bangladesh border. Buy tickets the day before from booth near MTC Bus Stand, Tura Bazar; ask your hotel to buy your ticket for a small fee. Private buses to **Guwahati** (8 hrs), **Shillong** (12 hrs, night bus arrives at 0400), **Siliguri** from Tura Bazar. Booking offices are easy to find.

● Directory

Shillong *p148, maps p149 and p151*
Banks State Bank of India, MG Rd, 1st floor. Mon-Fri 1130-1400. **Indian Overseas Bank**, GS Rd (Police Bazar end). Both currency and TCs. **Hospitals** Civil Hospital, GS Rd, T0364-222 6381. Nazareth Hospital, Laitumukhrah, T0364-222 4052. **Ambulance**, T0364-222 4100. **Chemists** in Police Bazar. **Internet** On GS Rd and Police Bazar Rd. **Post** GPO GS Rd, Police Bazar. **Tourist offices** India, GS Rd, Police Bazar, T0364-222 5632. 1000-1700, free Shillong map. Meghalaya, opposite Meghalaya Bus Stand, Jail Rd, T0364-222 6220. **Directorate of Tourism**, Nokrek Building, 3rd Meghalaya Secretariat, Lower Lachaumiere, T0364-222 6054, www.meghalaya tourism.com, 0700-1800. Very helpful. MTDC, **Orchid Hotel**, T0364-222 4933, mtdc@meghalaya.ren.nic.in. 1030-1630. **Useful addresses** Foreigners' Registration Office, Lachumiere near Museum.

Arunachal Pradesh

→ *Population: 1.1 mn. Area: 84,000 sq km.*

This is Northeast India's largest and most remote state. The Tawang Monastery, birthplace of the sixth Dalai Lama and home to countless Buddhist treasures, is a major attraction, along with the state's rich tribal heritage and its wonderful variety of orchids. ➹ *For Sleeping, Eating and other listings, see pages 156-157.*

The land

On the Northeast frontier of India, Arunachal Pradesh is India's least densely populated state with just 13 people per sq km. It stretches from the foothills of the eastern Himalaya to their permanently snow-capped peaks to the north. The Brahmaputra, known here as the Siang River, enters the state from China and flows through a deeply cut valley. Stretching from the Himalaya to the steamy plains of the Brahmaputra valley, Arunachal Pradesh has an extraordinary range of forests from the Alpine to the subtropical – from rhododendrons to orchids, reeds and bamboo. It is an orchid lover's paradise with over 550 species identified. The wildlife includes elephants, clouded leopard, snow leopard, tiger, sloth bear, Himalayan black bear, red panda and musk deer. The Namdapha National Park is near Miao.

⁝ Entering Arunachal

Permits may be given by the Resident Commissioner, Government of Arunachal Pradesh, Nyaya Marg, Delhi, T011-301 3956 or Liaison Officer, Roxi Cinema, JL Nehru Road, Kolkata, or Arunachal State Government (ask Wild Grass, page 144). Foreigners must book a group tour through an approved Indian travel agent. Independent travel is not encouraged. Itanagar, Ziro, Along, Pasighat, Miao, Namdapha, Tipi and Bhalukpong are open to tourists. The daily tariff requirement is US$150 (US$50 to the state government and US$100 to cover the costs of the travel agent). See page 134.

History

The entire region had remained isolated since 1873 when the British stopped free movement. After 1947 Arunachal became part of the North East Frontier Agency (NEFA). Its strategic significance was demonstrated by the Chinese invasion in 1962, and the Indian government subsequently broke up the Agency giving statehood to all the territories surrounding Assam. Arunachal became the 24th state in 1987, though China continues to argue that until the international border between it and India are agreed some of the territory remains disputed. At the same time the state is disputing its southern border with Assam, and in April 2001 the state government lodged a petition with India's Supreme Court against the government of Assam for "large scale encroachment" on its territory. Having long borders with China and Myanmar, it is a truly frontier State. The state was opened to tourists in 1995 with the first foreigners being given permission to trek only as recently as 1998.

Culture

The Arunachali people are the state's greatest attraction. In the capital Itanagar you may even see Nishi warriors wearing hornbill feathers in their caps, carrying bearskin bags and their knives in monkey-skin scabbards.

A great diversity of the tribal people speak over 60 different dialects. Most have an oral tradition of recording their historic and cultural past by memorizing verses handed down through generations. Some Buddhist tribes have, however, maintained written records, largely recording their religious history. Some tribes worship Donyi and Polo, the Sun and Moon gods.

Itanagar-Naharlagun 🖾🖸▲🖾🖸 » *pp156-157.*

Colour map 2, grid A5.

→ *Phone code: 0360. Population: 61,900.*

Itanagar, the new capital, and Naharlagun, the old town 10 km away, together provide the capital's administrative offices. Itanagar, sited between two hills, has the Governor's Residence on one and a new Buddhist temple on the other, with shops, bazar, traditional huts and more recent earthquake-proof wooden-framed buildings in between. The capital has been identified as Mayapur, the 11th-century capital of the Jitari Dynasty.

Ins and outs

Getting there Visitors arriving at Lilabari or North Lakhimpur in Assam take two hours by bus (or a little less by taxi) to Itanagar, calling at Naharlagun Bus Station before climbing up along a scenic road to the new capital. Regular buses from Guwahati and Shillong. » *See Transport, page 157, for further details.*

Getting around Frequent buses run between Itanagar and Naharalagun from 0600 until 2000. Cycle-rickshaws only available in Naharalagun.

Sights

The yellow-roofed **Buddhist Temple** stands in well-kept gardens on a hilltop with good views. The **Gyaker Sinyi** (Ganga Sekhi Lake), 6 km, is reached by a rough road through forests of bamboo and tree ferns. On reaching the foot of the hill, walk across a bamboo bridge, up steps cut on the hillside to reach a ridge overlooking the forest lake. The brick fort (14th-15th century) is believed to have been built by King Ramachandra. In Naharalagun, the **Polo Park** is on top of a ridge with interesting botanical specimens including the cane thicket, which looks like palm, as well as a small **zoo**.

Jawaharlal Nehru Museum ⓘ *Tue-Sun*, has good coverage of tribal people: collection of art, wood carvings, musical instruments and religious objects. The first floor has archaeological finds from Malinthan, Itafort, Noksaparbat and others.

Bomdila and Tawang Monastery 🖦🛆 ⤑ *pp156-157.*
Colour map 2, grid A4.

The whole journey, to reach Tawang from Tezpur in Assam – the nearest airport – is spectacular, passing waterfalls, terraced paddy fields, alpine forests and mountain streams. The road north crosses the border at **Bhalukpong**, see page 140, and continues towards Bomdila passing through low wooded slopes for about 60 km. On the bank of the Bhoreli River in the upper plains is **Tipi**, with the Orchid Research Centre and a glasshouse with 500 species of orchids. From there the road rises sharply to reach Bomdila.

Bomdila → *Altitude: 2530 m.*

Bomdila has marvellous views of the snow-capped mountains. It has a craft centre, apple and cherry orchards and Buddhist *gompas*. Buses from the main bus stand. Lower Town Tezpur and Tawang take eight hours. Private buses from Himalayan Holidays to Tezpur take seven hours.

To Tawang

For the next 180 km the route passes through the pretty Dirang Valley shrouded in pine woods, then climbs to the **Sela Pass** at 4215 m which presents a far starker view. The successor to Lama Guru Rimpoche has been found in a village nearby. Stop a while here, along one of the highest motorable roads in the world. **Jaswantpur**, 4 km from the pass, has the *samadhi* to the brave Jawan (soldier) Jaswant Singh which commemorates how he, his fiancé and her friend valiantly held up the advancing Chinese army in 1962 for three days before laying down their lives. Drivers along this road, many of them ex-army personnel, stop to pay their respects at the poignant memorial. You see a high-altitude lake and the trout hatchery at Nuranang just below the pass before reaching Tawang.

Tawang Monastery → *Phone code: 03794. Population: 4600.*

Set in breathtakingly beautiful scenery at over 3000 m, the monastery, one of the largest in India, is the birthplace of the sixth Dalai Lama. Dating originally from 1642, it is the second oldest Buddhist monastery in the world (after Lhasa), and houses over 500 *lamas* belonging to the Gelugpa (Reformed) Sect of Mahayana Buddhist monks. Buddhism arrived in the area with Padmasambhava in the eighth century but the local Monpas were converted to the Tantric Buddhist cult only after the establishment of the monastery here in the 17th century. During renovations, the main building was completely rebuilt. Treasures include a 5½ m high Buddha, numerous sculptures, *thangkas* and priceless manuscripts. Tawang also has the 350-year-old Tawang Gompa among dense forest which is the only Lady Lamasery (Buddhist Monastery for nuns) in Asia. The three-day annual **Losar festival** is usually in early January. Prayers are held every morning and afternoon. A craft centre produces woollen carpets.

To reach the monastery take one of the regular buses or Tata Sumo services from Bomdila and Tezpur. Cars take nearly two days from Guwahati (400 km) through rough terrain. Foreigners should travel in a small group in a hired vehicle from Tezpur (12 hrs). Check feasibility locally and don't travel after dark – visibility on the narrow mountain roads can be very poor at night.

Lake District

Just above Tawang beyond the monastery is the **Lake District**, an exceptionally beautiful area with about 30 high-altitude lakes. After a fork and an army outpost, the road continues towards **Klemta**, just a few kilometres from the Indian border. There are a few scattered monasteries and a shrine to all faiths at the spot where Guru Nanak rested as he trekked into Tibet, 500 years ago. **Ptso**, 25 km from Tawang, has a small cabin by a lake. To explore this area hire a jeep and guide, carry snacks and drinks, and be prepared for steep, treacherous mountain roads. It is all worth it for the breathtaking mountain scenery.

Ziro → *150 km north of Itanagar. Altitude: 1,475 m.*

Ziro lies in a picturesque level valley of the Apatani plateau, surrounded by pine-covered mountains. The **Apatani tribals** who live in small, densely populated villages have evolved a sophisticated system of irrigated paddy cultivation. You can also visit Nisi tribal settlements. There are daily buses from Itanagar (200 km away) and Lilabari (100 km).

Parasuram Kund

This lake in Eastern Arunachal attracts thousands of pilgrims at **Makar Sankranti** (mid-January) who come to the fair and to take a holy bath. Spartan Government **Tourist Lodge**; contact Dy Commissioner, Tezu, well in advance. From Tinsukia, launch along the Brahmaputra (1½ hrs) to Sadiya Ghat, there are buses to Parasuram Kund.

Namdapha National Park

This park, at an altitude of 200-4500 m, is close to the Myanmar border and can be approached from Deban. It is unique as it is home to four members of the cat family: tiger, leopard, snow leopard and clouded leopard. There are also elephants, sambhar, deer, gaur, goral and wild hogs and a rich birdlife. The best season to visit is from October to April. The variety of vegetation is fascinating.

You can obtain an entry permit from the Field Director, Miao; accommodation is in Deban, 25 km away. Dibrugarh (140 km) has the nearest airport. State buses from there go to Miao, the entry point, via Margherita (64 km), the nearest railhead where you can also hire taxis.

⬤ Sleeping

Itanagar-Naharlagun *p154*
Make sure that you reserve hotels at least a month in advance.
C Donyi-Polo Ashok, Sector C, Itanagar, T0360-221 2626. Arunachal's most upmarket hotel, in a decaying concrete building with 20 rooms, 2 a/c suites and average restaurant.

E Arun Subansiri, Zero Point, Itanagar, T0360-221 2806. Comfortable and modestly stylish rooms, hot shower, decent value.
F Hornbill, Naharlagun, T0360-224 4419. 14 rooms, some de luxe.
G Youth Hostel, Naharlagun. Basic, with 60 beds.

Bomdila *p155*
C-F Siphiyang Phong, Tourist Lodge and La,
are a few of the options in town.

Tawang Monastery *p155*
D-E **Paradise**, Old Bazar, T03794-
222063, F222307. A private lodge with
pleasant, clean, spacious rooms with
bath, some de luxe, small dining room serving
simple, freshly cooked meals. The manager
also arranges jeep hire and takes guided tours.
D-E **Tourist Lodge**, T03794-222359. A
lodge with 20 well-furnished but poorly
maintained rooms, contact the Deputy
Commissioner to make reservations.

Ziro *p156*
D **Model Village**, bookings through
Arunachal Tourism, T0360-221 4745.
Interestingly decorated huts in tribal
style, modern amenities and a restaurant
serving local specialities.
F **Blue Pine** and other guest houses.
G **Inspection Bungalow** and
Circuit House, 8 rooms. Reservations:
Dy Comm, Lower Subansiri District.

Namdapha National Park *p156*
E **Camp Namdapha**, offers bamboo huts and
log cabins as well as tented accommodation.
G **Deban Forest Bungalow**, overlooking the
Noa Dihing River, make bookings through
Arunachal Tourism, T0360-221 4745.

O Shopping

Itanagar-Naharlagun *p154*
The cotton textiles available here are colourful
and are beautifully patterned. You can also
get wooden masks and figures, cane belts
and caps. **Handicrafts centres** have shawls,
thangkas, handloom, wood carvings, cane
and bamboo work and carpets; you can
watch tribal craftsmen trimming, cutting
and weaving cane. **Bomdila** is good for
handwoven Monpa carpets.

▲ Activities and tours

Itanagar-Naharlagun *p154*
Arunachal Travels, Itanagar, agents for
Indian Airlines.
Himalayan Holidays, Naharlagun, T0360-
224 6232, www.himalayan-holidays.com.

Nature Expeditions India, Gurgaon,
T0124-236 8601, www.himalaya-india.com.

Bomdila *p155*
Himalayan Holidays, ABC Buildings,
Main Market, T03782-222017,
www.himalayan-holidays.com.

Tawang Monastery *p155*
Himalayan Holidays, T03794-223151,
www.himalayan-holidays.com.
Organizes tours and jeep hire.

⊖ Transport

Itanagar-Naharlagun *p154*
Air The nearest airport is **Lilabari** in
Assam, 57 km from Naharlagun, 67 km from
Itanagar, which has twice weekly flights from
Guwahati. Transfer by bus. **Indian Airlines**,
T03752-223725, www.indian-airlines.nic.in,
from Kolkata via **Dibrugarh** (1½ hrs), Mon,
Wed, Fri, Sun. **Air Deccan**, T3900-8888,
www.airdeccan.net, 3 times weekly to
Kolkata and Guwahati.

Bus APST from Naharlagun Bus Station.
Guwahati, 381 km, 8 hrs, Rs 135; **Shillong**,
481 km, Rs 170. Ziro, 6 hrs, **North Lakhimpur**;
Bomdila, Mon, Thu, 12 hrs. Blue Hills
overnight coach to Guwahati, 11½ hrs.
Enquiries: T0360-2244221.

Taxi Naharlagun/Itanagar, Rs 170
plus fuel; Rs 25 (shared taxi).

Train The nearest railhead is North
Lakhimpur in Assam, 50 km from Naharlagun
and 60 km from Itanagar; Harmoti station is
23 km from Naharlagun. **Railway Out Agency**,
Naharlagun bus station, T0360-224 4209.
Nearest railheads for the bigger towns:
Along: Silapathar; **Tezu**: Tinsukia;
Namdapha: Margherita.

⊙ Directory

Itanagar-Naharlagun *p154*
There are banks and post offices.
Hospitals Itanagar, Naharlagun.
Tourist offices India, Sector 'C', Itanagar,
T0360-221 2949. Arunachal Pradesh,
Naharlagun, T0360-224 1752, 221 4745,
www.arunachaltourism.com.

Nagaland

→ *Entry permits, see page 134. Population: 2 mn. Area: 16,579 sq km.*

Nagaland, the narrow strip of mountain territory, has a long border with Myanmar (Burma) to the east. There are green valleys with meandering streams, high mountains with deep gorges and a rich variety of wildlife and flora. ►► *For Sleeping, Eating and other listings, see pages 159-160.*

History

The British reached peace with the Nagas at the end of the 19th century and found them useful allies in the war against the Japanese, who advanced as far as Kohima before finally retreating from the region. After Indian Independence, Nagaland became a separate state on 1 December 1963. A separatist movement for full Independence continues, as the 1975 Shillong Accord was rejected. A series of month-to-month ceasefires in effect during the 1990s came to a drastic end in 2004, when insurgents attacked the railway station in Dimapur. As elsewhere in the northeast, check with your consulate before travelling to Nagaland, and avoid road travel at night.

Culture

Tribal groups Nagaland is almost entirely inhabited by 15 groups of the Tibeto-Burmese tribes – among them are the Angamis, Aos, Konyaks, Kukis, Lothas, Semas and Wanchus, collectively known as the **Nagas**. There are many tribal languages spoken: Angami, Ao, Chang are a few. The Nagas were once head hunters and have been known for their fierceness and the regular raids they made on Assam and Burma. The warring tribes believed that since the enemy's animated soul (*yaha* in Wanchu dialect) was to be found at the nape of the neck, it could only be set free once beheaded. However, since the spiritual soul, *mio*, resided in the head and brought good fortune, enemy heads (and those of dead comrades) were prized as they could add to a community's own store of dead ancestors. The hilltop villages are protected by stone walls. The *morung*, a meeting house, acts as a boys' dormitory, and is used for storing weapons and once displayed the prizes of war (enemy heads). The huge sacred drum stands by each *morung* is a hollowed-out tree trunk resembling a buffalo head. Some believe that the Nagas' ancestors came from the seafaring nation of Sumatra and retain this link in legends, village drums and ceremonial jewellery, which uses shells.

Religion Today 90% of the Nagas are Christians. Originally, although they revered natural spirits, the Nagas believed in a single overseeing but unknown superforce, and hence incorporated the Christian Gospel into their cosmology quite readily. The Bible was translated into many of the Naga dialects (nearly every village has a church), yet many old customs have been retained. There are also remains of the Hindu Kingdom of the Kacharis at Dimapur near the present capital Kohima, which was destroyed by the Assamese Ahoms in the 16th century.

Crafts The ancient craft of weaving on portable looms is still practised by the women. The strips of colourful cloth are stitched together to produce shawls in different patterns which distinguish each tribe. Ao warriors wear the red and black striped shawl with a central white band embroidered with symbols.

Kohima → *Phone code: 0370. Colour map 2, grid B5. Population: 78,600. Altitude: 1,500 m.*

The British-built town of Kohima lies in the valley between higher hills, alongside the immaculately kept war cemetery. Kohima attracted world attention during the Second World War because it was here that the Japanese advance was halted by the British and Indian forces. The original Angami Kohima Village is set on a hill above overlooking the Main Bazar. There may be a strong military presence in town.

The **Second World War Cemetery** is in a beautiful setting, with well-maintained lawns where rose bushes bloom in season. Two tall crosses stand out at the lowest and highest points. The stone markers each have a polished bronze plaque with epitaphs commemorating the men who fell here, to halt "the invasion of India by the forces of Japan in April 1944" by the British 14th Army under General William Slim. The flowering cherry tree which was used by Japanese soldiers as a snipers' post was destroyed; what grew from the old stump marks the limit of the enemy advance. At the base of the 2nd Division lower cross, near the main entrance, are the lines: "When you go home/Tell them of us and say/For your tomorrow/We gave our today."

Three kilometres away by road, the striking red-roofed **Cathedral of Reconciliation** (1995) overlooks the cemetery from a hill. Part funded by the Japanese government, representatives from both sides of the conflict attended the inauguration.

The **Main Bazar** attracts colourful tribal women who come to buy and sell their produce. The vast **Kohima Village** (Bara Basti) has a traditional Naga ceremonial gateway carved with motifs of guns, warriors and symbols of prosperity, though the 20th century has had its impact. The traditional Naga house here has crossed horns on the gables, carved heads to signify the status of the family, huge baskets to hold the grain in front of the house and a trough where rice beer is made for the community.

Nagaland State Museum ⓘ *Bayavu Hill Colony, 1½ km from centre, Mon-Sat 0930-1430, closed 2nd Sat,* has a collection of anthropological exhibits of the different Naga tribes. The basement has birds and animals of the Northeastern Hill states.

Around Kohima

Khonoma is an authentic tribal village, 20 km southwest, with a proud past, and is surrounded by extensive terraces for rice cultivation. Another 20 km along the same road takes you to **Dzulekie**, at 2134 m, with attractive waterfalls and trout streams in a deep rocky gorge. There is a Tourist Rest House and Cottages.

Trek to **Jopfu Peak**, at 3043 m, which is 15 km south, between November and March for clear mountain views. **Dzukou Valley**, at 2438 m, 15 km further south, is best from June to September for its colourful rhododendrons, lilies and meadow flowers. A new campsite should be ready on the Jakhama route.

Dimapur

Dimapur, on the edge of the plains northwest of Kohima, is the railhead and has Nagaland's only airport. It is the state's main commercial and trading centre.

This was the old capital of the Kacharis (13th-16th century) and the **Kachari relics**, including a huge brick-built arch, are 1 km from the NST Bus Station. Nearby are 30 huge mushroom-shaped carved megaliths believed to represent the fertility cult. Visit **Chumukedima** old village on a hill above town, or trek to the **Triple Falls** at Seithekima.

● Sleeping

Kohima *p158*
C Japfu Ashok, (ITDC), PR Hill, T0370-224 0211, hoteljapfu@yahoo.co.in. 27 large heated rooms in motel arrangement, restaurants.
F Pine, Phool Bazar, T0370-222 2234. 7 rooms with bath.
G Bonanza Lodge, opposite main Bus Stand. Friendly and helpful, some rooms with bath.

Dimapur *p159*
C-E Tragopan, Circular Rd near Overbridge, T03862-230351. Some

of the 22 rooms have a/c, restaurant, library, internet.
D Tourist Lodge, near Nagaland bus station, T03862-226335. Doubles, tourist office.

❼ Eating

Kohima *p158*
Nagaland can be tough for vegetarians outside the cities. Local dishes are simple but may include such exotica as water snails, eels, silkworm curry, hornet larvae

or fermented fish. Most places offer Indian and Chinese dishes.

♨ **Dimori Cove**, 13 km along NH39 towards Manipur. The eatery has a small swimming pool, good views.

♨ **Naga**, Secretariat, also offers Japanese. Pleasant, lively.

✪ Festivals and events

Kohima *p158*
The different tribes celebrate their special festivals when priests perform ceremonies followed by dancing, singing and drinking.
Feb Sekrenyi is celebrated by Angamis for 10 days when all work in the fields ceases.
Apr Konyak Aoling, a 6-day 'New Year' festival marking the beginning of spring.
May Ao Moatsu, 6-day festival marking the beginning of the growing season.
Dec Hornbill Festival, when all tribes gather in Kisama to display traditional, sports, dance and food.

✪ Shopping

Kohima *p158*
Warm, colourful Naga shawls are excellent. You can also get beads, shoulder bags, decorative spears, table mats, wood carvings and bamboo baskets. **Gürttel** is recommended.

▲ Activities and tours

Kohima *p158*
Nagaland Tourism, offers 4-5-day group cultural, adventure (trekking, tribal) tours.

✪ Transport

Kohima *p158*
Air and train Dimapur has the nearest airport and railhead; buses (Rs 50) and taxis take 3 hrs to Kohima centre. See below for details.

Bus Blue Hills luxury coaches go to other capitals in the Northeast; Green Hills, Taxi Stand, for coaches and flight bookings.

Taxi From Dimapur, Rs 500, shared Rs 100. Nagaland State Transport, T0370-222 2265.

Dimapur *p159*
Air The airport is 5 km from town. Indian Airlines, T03862-229366. Airport, T038622-242441. www.indian-airlines.nic.in.
To **Kolkata** daily.

Bus From Golaghat Rd to **Guwahati** 292 km (10-11 hrs), **Imphal** 142 km (5-6 hrs); from Nagaland Bus Stand to **Kohima** hourly, 3 hrs.

Train Enquiries: T03862-131. To **Delhi (OD)**: *Brahmaputra Mail 4055*, 0540, 48 hrs.
Dibrugarh: *Kamrup Exp 5959*, 2155, 8½ hrs. *Brahmaputra Mail 4056*, 2000, 8½ hrs.
Guwahati: *Rajdhani 2423A*, Thu 0120, 5½ hrs; *Jan Shatabdi Exp 2068*, except Sun 1610, 4½ hrs.

✪ Directory

Kohima *p158*
There are banks, a post office and hospital, T0360-222 2916. Tourist office, T0360-227 0107.

Manipur

→ *Population: 2.4 mn. Area: 22,327 sq km.*
The former princely state of Manipur, the 'land of jewels', bordering Myanmar, has a low-lying basin in its centre surrounded by hills that rise to over 2000 m. The reedy Lake Loktak, the largest freshwater lake in the Northeast, and the flat-bottomed basin and river valleys that drain into it, add to the beauty of the land. It is the land of graceful Rasa dances, of the famous Women's market in Imphal, of rare orchids and the endangered thamin, the brow-antlered deer. ▸▸ *For Sleeping, Eating and other listings, see page 163.*

History

Manipur has always been quite independent of its neighbouring tribal areas. It was often invaded from Burma but also enjoyed long periods of relatively stable government. At the end of the Indo-Burmese War in 1826 it was brought into India by the Treaty of Yandabo, British sovereignty being recognized in 1891. In 1939 a remarkable women's social revolt ('Nupilan' from 'nupi', meaning women, and 'lan', war) led to government action against monopolistic traders. The contemporary party Nisha Bandh consists of an all-women patrol that seeks to keep the streets safe at night. The role of women traders can be seen most colourfully in the women's market. During the Second World War Imphal was occupied by the Japanese. After Indian Independence Manipur became a Union Territory and achieved statehood in 1972.

People
The majority of the population are Vaishnavite Hindus. They belong to the *Meithe* tribe and are related to the *Shans* of Burma, who live in the valleys. The 20 or so hill tribes who constitute about a third of the population are Christian. Like the Nagas, the Manipuris have a reputation for being great warriors, still practising their skills of wrestling, sword fighting and martial arts. Most of wars were fought across the border in Burma. They are also keen on sport, and polo, which is said to have originated in Manipur, is the principal sport.

Dance, drama and music
The ancient musical forms of the valley dwellers are closely connected to the worship of Vishnu, expressed in Manipuri dancing. The *Rasa* dances performed at every ceremony are characterized by graceful and restrained movements and delicate hand gestures. The ornate costumes worn by the veiled women are glittering and colourful; the stiff, heavy skirts barely move. The *Sankirtana* dance often precedes the *Rasa*. It is usually performed by men and is vigorous, rhythmic and athletic, and they play on the *pung* (drums) and cymbals while they dance. The tribal ritual dances, some of which are performed by priests and priestesses before deities, may end in a trance. Others can last several days, observing a strict form and accompanied by the drone of a bowed instrument, *pana*. *Thang-ta* is a skilful martial art performed to beating drums, and is practised by both sexes dressed in black.

Political developments
Troubled by a variety of internal conflicts since the late 1980s and with separatist movements voicing open dissent with rule from New Delhi, Manipur's State Assembly has had an unsettled recent history. One recent bone of contention is the Tipaimukh Dam, a 1500 mw hydro and flood protection project that has stirred up strong opposition from some quarters in Manipur and across the border in Bangladesh. The foundation stone for the project was laid in December 2006. Democracy is very popular, with over 90% of the electorate turning out to vote in recent elections, but it has not produced stability. In the February 2007 elections the Indian National Congress under Chief Minister Okram Ibobi Singh won half the 60 seats, but it is too early to judge whether the long-running disturbances in the state will be resolved. Be sure to find out about the current situation before travelling to Manipur.

Imphal ⊖🏨🚾❄️🔺⊖👶 » p163. Colour map 2, grid B5.

→ *Phone code: 0385. Population: 217,300.*

The capital Imphal (from *yumpham*, homestead) lies in the heart of an oval-shaped valley cut through by narrow rivers and surrounded by forested hills. The city has the large open space of the Polo Ground but is otherwise not particularly attractive. Due to its location it has become a principal export route for Myanmar's illegal drugs.

Getting there and around The airport is 8 km south of the city with taxis and autos available for transfers. Bus travel is tiring due to long distances involved. The dusty centre and the Ima Market are easy to cover on foot. Auto- and cycle-rickshaws can take you to places beyond the centre. ▸▸ *See Transport, page 163, for further details.*

Sights

The **Shri Govindaji Temple** to Krishna with two golden domes adjoins the royal palace. This Vaishnavite centre with shrines to Vishnu, Balaram, Krishna and Jagannath has regular performances of ceremonial dancing; Manipuri dancing originated here in Imphal. Overlooking the University, the historic palace of **Langthaband**, with its ceremonial houses and temples, stands on the hills among formally planted pine and jackfruit trees, 8 km along the Indo-Burma road.

Khwairamband Bazar (Ima Market) ① *0700-1900*, in the town centre is the largest women's bazar anywhere in the country. It is an excellent place for handicrafts, handloom goods, jewellery and cosmetics as well as fish vegetables, pickles, orange honey and other foodstuffs. Up to 3000 women gather here every day. It represents a form of family work-sharing, for while younger mothers stay at home to look after children, the older women come to market. The women do not bargain and will be offended if you try to pick through fruit or vegetables, as they take great pride in serving only the best quality at a fair price. Their own union helps to maintain the bazar and is a potent political force.

The **War Cemeteries** are managed by the Commonwealth War Graves Commission, one on the Imphal-Dimapur NH39 and the other on the Imphal-Ukhrul Road. They are beautifully maintained and serenely peaceful sites.

The **Konghampat Orchidarium** ① *best season is Apr-May*, 12 km along NH39, set up by the Forest Department, has over 120 species of orchids including some rare ones.

The **Manipur State Museum** ① *near the Polo Ground, T0385-222 0709, Tue-Sun 1000-1630*, has a collection of art (including portraits), archaeology, natural history, geology, old arms, costumes and textiles. **Matua Museum** is a private collection of art, textiles and manuscripts to preserve the identity of Manipuri culture.

Around Imphal

Moirang, 45 km from Imphal, on Loktak Lake, is noted for its early Manipuri folk culture and the traditional folk dance form. The temple to the forest god, known as *Thankgjing*, has robes of the 12th-century Moirang kings and holds a ritual dance festival each summer. During the Second World War Moirang was the HQ of the Indian National Army (INA) for a short time, and their flag was raised in the palace grounds as a symbol of national independence for the first time on 12 April 1944. There is an INA memorial and a war museum. You can stay on **Sendra Island** in Loktak Lake, see page 163.

Keibul Lamjao National Park ● ▸▸ *p163.*

The park, covering 25 sq km, is the only floating sanctuary of its kind. It has a small population of thamin (Sangai), the endangered brow-antlered deer. The sanctuary was set up in 1977 on Loktak Lake when the swamps, the natural habitat of the thamin, were reclaimed for cultivation resulting in the near extinction of this 'dancing deer'. The thamin feed on mats of floating humus covered with grass and *phumdi* reeds until the rainy season when they move to the hills. You can travel through the creeks on small boats. There is also a viewing tower on Babet Ching hillock. Other wildlife include hog deer, wild boar, panther, fishing cat and water birds.

Travel restrictions for foreigners as elsewhere in the Northeast. The nearest airport and railway are at Dimapur, 32 km from Imphal. The best time to visit is December to May. Temperatures range from 41°C to 0°C and annual rainfall is 1280 mm.

⊕ Sleeping

Imphal *p161, map below*
D **Anand Continental**, Khoyathong Rd,
T0385-222 3422. Good rooms with bath, TV.
D **Imphal**, Dimapur Rd, T0385-222 0459,
manipur@x400.nicgw.nic.in. 60 large rooms,
some a/c, modern facilities, restaurant.
E-F Excellency, Airport Rd, T0385-222 5401.
Varied rooms, some a/c, restaurant.
G **Sendra Tourist Home**, on Sendra
Island, contact the Department of Tourism, in
Imphal, T0385-222 0802. A very peaceful spot
with lovely views of the lake where fishermen,
who live on islands of floating weeds, use nets
to farm fish and water chestnut (*singhara*).
Cheap beds, small restaurant.
G **Youth Hostel**, Khuman Lampak, T0385-
222 3423. Dorm (Rs 30).

Keibul Lamjao National Park *p162*
Forest Lodges at Phubala and Sendra.

⊕ Eating

Imphal *p161, map below*
Manipur is a 'dry' state. In hotel restaurants,
try *iromba*, the Manipuri savoury dish of
fish, vegetables and bamboo shoots and
the sweet *Kabok* made with molasses
and rice. Govindaji Temple prepares local
dishes with advance notice. **Sangam** and
Welcome are inexpensive.

Imphal

To Dimapur & Konghampat Orchidarium

War Cemetery · Stadium
Thangal Bazar · Indian Airlines
Khwairamband Bazar
Kangchup Rd · Laxmi Bazar
Manipur State Museum
Handloom House · Palace Rd
War Cemetery
KANGLA · CHECKON
To & Airport
Old Palace
Jail Rd
Shri Govindaji Temple

N · Not to scale

Sleeping ⊕
Excellency 4
Imphal 2

Eating ⊕
Sangam 1
Welcome 2

⊕ Entertainment

Imphal *p161, map below*
Cultural shows with Manipuri dancing
at **Rupmahal**, BT Rd, and at **Kala Academy**.

⊛ Festivals and events

Imphal *p161, map below*
Feb-Mar Yaosang on full moon night,
boys and girls dance the Thabal Chongba
and sing in a circle in the moonlight.
May-Jun A festival is held in honour
of forest gods.
Sep Heikru Hitongba is mainly non
religious, when there are boat races along
a 16-m wide moat in narrow boats with
large numbers of rowers.

⛰ Activities and tours

Imphal *p161, map below*
Manipur Tourism tours to Sri Govindaji
Temple, Bishnupur, INA Memorial, Moirang,
KL National Park and the Loktak Lake,
depart **Hotel Imphal**, Sun 0800.
Seven Sisters, North AOC, T0385-222
8778. For touring the region.

⊖ Transport

Imphal *p161, map opposite*
Air Taxi to town, Rs 150. **Indian Airlines**,
MG Av, T0385-222 0999, airport T222 0888,
www.indian-airlines.nic.in: **Kolkata**, daily
(some via **Aizwal**); **Delhi**, **Guwahati**,
Jorhat, **Silchar**, 2-3 times weekly, **Jet
Airways**, Hotel Nirmala, MG Av, T0385-244
1546, airport T2455054: **Guwahati**, Tue,
Wed; **Kolkata** (via Guwahati), Tue, Wed
(via Jorhat), Thu, Sun.

Bus Buses connect Dimapur (215 km)
the nearest railhead, with **Imphal** (8 hrs),
Rs 60; share taxi Rs 250. Daily private buses
(some a/c) for **Guwahati** (579 km), 24 hrs,
via Silchar (198 km) to Shillong, through:
Blue Hills, MG Av, T0385-222 6443. **Manipur
Golden Travels**, MG Av, T0385-222 1332.
Kangleipak, T0385-222 2131.

Taxi Tourist taxis are available from
the visitor information centre.

❶ Directory

Imphal *p161, map below*
Banks Banks in Bazar, Thangal Bazar and MG Av. **Hospital** Hospitals at Porompat and Lamphalpat. **Post** There is a GPO. **Tourist**

offices **India**, Old Lambulane, Jail Rd, T0385-222 1131. Closed Sat-Sun, airport desk opens for flights. **Manipur**, Hotel Imphal, T0385-222 0802, manipur@x400.nicgw .nic.in. Mon-Sat 0900-1630, closed 2nd Sat. **Meghalaya**, Hotel Imphal, T0385-222 0459.

Mizoram

→ *Population: 891,100. Area 21,000 sq km.*

The southernmost of the Northeastern Hill States, Mizoram lies between Myanmar (Burma) and Bangladesh. Until 1972 it was known as the Lushai Hills, a district of Assam. The six or so parallel north-south ranges of hills, which rise to an altitude of over 2000 m, are covered in dense forests of bamboo and wild banana. At the bottom of the deep gorges the rivers run in narrow ribbons. ►► *For Sleeping, Eating and other listings, see page 165.*

Culture

Tribal groups **Mizo** is derived from *mi* (man) and *zo* (highland), a collective name given by their neighbours to a number of tribes that settled in the area. The different groups of tribal people are thought to have originally come from Northwest China in the seventh century, gradually travelled southwards and reached this area less than

‼ *Entry permits, see page 134. The state government can also issue permits.*

300 years ago. The Mizos were animists, believing in good and evil spirits of the woodland. Mizo villages perch on top of the ridges with the chief's house and the *zawlbuk* (bachelors' dormitory) in the centre. Built on steep slopes, houses often have front doors at street level while the backs stand precariously on stilts. Every home proudly displays orchids and pots of geranium, begonia and balsam. Over 1000 varieties of medicinal plants grow wild.

Religion The raiding of British tea plantations up until the end of the 19th century led to the introduction of Inner Line permits which restricted movement of people but gave free access to missionaries, who carried out their religious duties and introduced literacy, which is exceptionally high in this state, the language having adopted the Roman script. Most Mizos are Christian converts and have a strong tradition of Western choral singing. The mainly nomadic Chakmas along the western border practise a religion which combines Hinduism, Buddhism and animism. Some even claim descent from one of the lost tribes of Israel. A few **Kukis** who were once headhunters, and **Chins**, have converted to Judaism.

Economy

Rice and maize, supplemented by shifting cultivation, supports 75% of the population. There are no mineral resources exploited yet and no large-scale industries though the government has sponsored some light industrial development in Aizawl. Handicrafts and handwoven textiles predominate.

Aizawl → *Phone code: 0389. Colour map 2, grid B5/C5. Population: 229,700. Altitude: 1132 m.*

The road from Silchar comes upon the isolated capital Aizawl (pronounced Eye-jull), built along a central ridge and several surrounding spurs. White-painted churches stand out above the residential buildings that cling precariously to the hillsides.

Bara Bazar, the main shopping centre, is on the other side of the central ridge. The steep Zion Street is lined with stalls selling garments and Mizo music cassettes. In the main market people gather in their traditional costumes to sell produce from farms and homesteads including river crab in little wicker baskets.

At the **Weaving Centre** you can watch women at their looms weaving traditional shawls which are for sale. **Luangmual Handicrafts Centre**, 7 km away, has a *khumbeu* ceremonial bamboo hat made using waterproof wild *hnahthial* leaves.

Mizoram State Museum ① *McDonald's Hill, Mon 1200-1600, Tue-Fri 0930-1600*, is small but has an interesting collection of historical relics, ancient costumes and traditional implements.

Champhai
Champhai, on the Indo-Myanmar border and known as the fruit bowl of the Northeast, is worth a visit for its stunning location and sense of history.

🛌 Sleeping

Mizoram *p164*
D **Ahimsa**, Zarkawt, T0389-234 1133. Comfortable rooms, restaurant.
F-G **Ritz**, Bara Bazar, Chaltlang, T0389-232 3358. Comfortable rooms, some with bath, good restaurant.
F-G **Tourist Lodge**, Chaltlang, T0389-234 1083. Has 14 large but tired rooms, good restaurant, good views.

🍴 Eating

Mizoram *p164*
Labyrinth, Chandmari, serves cheap Chinese and Indian food. You can also find cheap local Mizo food around Bara Bazar.

🎉 Festivals and events

Mizoram *p164*
Early Mar **Chapchar Kut**, a traditional spring festival marking the end of *Jhumming* is celebrated with singing dancing and feasting. **Cheraw** is performed by nimble-footed girls who dance in and out of bamboo poles, clapped together by teams of young men. Similar dances are performed in Myanmar, Thailand and the Philippines.

🚌 Transport

Mizoram *p164*
Air Flights connect Aizawl with Kolkata, Guwahati and Imphal. Travellers from the rest of the Northeast usually arrive by bus via Silchar to the north.
   New **Langpui Airport** (37 km north); for tickets and bus transfer contact **Quality Travels**, Chandmari, T0389-234 1265.
   Indian Airlines, T0389-234 1265, airport T0389-234 4733, www.indian-airlines.nic.in, flies to **Kolkata** and **Guwahati**, Mon, Wed, Fri, with some flights via Imphal.

Bus The major operator in the state is Mizoram State Transport. It runs buses to **Silchar**, 180 km (9 hrs), Rs 150, which is the nearest railhead; the 4WD Sumos, however, are quicker and not too pricey. Private buses to **Guwahati** via Silchar and Shillong, Rs 280.

Taxi Rs 200 for 2 hrs' sightseeing in town.

🏛 Directory

Mizoram *p164*
Bank State Bank of India. **Post** GPO, Treasury Sq. **Hospital** Civil Hospital, T0389-232 2318, **Presbyterian Hospital**, Durtland (7 km), T0389-236 1222. **Tourist office** Mizoram, Treasury Sq, T0389-231 2473; for permits apply to Mizoram House.

⬤ *For an explanation of the sleeping and eating price codes used in this guide, see the inside*
● *front cover. Other relevant information is found on pages 35-39.*

Northeastern Hill States Mizoram Listings

Tripura

→ *Population: 3.19 mn. Area: 10,492 sq km.*

Still extensively forested, the tiny former Hindu Princely State of Tripura managed to retain a large degree of independence through much of the last millennium. Extensively forested, its predominantly tribal people retain centuries-old practices, though Agartala begins to show signs of modern development. ⤷ *For Sleeping, Eating and other listings, see page 168.*

The land

Covering just under 10,500 sq km, Tripura is almost surrounded on the north, west and south by Bangladesh. The north falls into four valleys, separated by hills rising to just under 1000 m. The more open land of the south is still forested. Indian hardwoods include sal. Parts of the state get over 4000 mm of annual rainfall.

History

Tripura is believed to have existed in the times of the epic *Mahabharata*. Historically, it was ruled by the **Manikyas** of Indo-Mongolian origin from the 14th century. Since Tripura was constantly feuding with her neighbours, particularly the Nawabs of Bengal, the British offered help to the Maharaja and established a protectorate, separating the princely state from tribal lands outside the control of the Hindu rajas. The Manikyas ruled continuously right up to 15 October 1949 when Tripura acceded to India. It became a full state in 1972. In the 1930s, Maharaja Bir Bikram made his kingdom more accessible by opening an airport. **Rabindranath Tagore** based his play *Visarjan* and novel *Rajasri* on the legends of the Manikyas.

Culture

Tripura remains predominantly tribal, with distinctive customs. A typical tribal welcome involves building a bamboo arch, garlanding the honoured guest while wafting incense. An egg, believed to absorb evil spirits, is rubbed in paddy, dipped in water and then symbolically thrown away. You may notice brightly coloured parasols in the village pond which are put there in honour of dead ancestors.

Modern Tripura

Rice is the main crop while rubber has gained importance (now second only to Kerala in production). Jute, cotton, tea and fruit are important cash crops. Suga rcane, mustard and potatoes are also grown. In the last 10 years the Indian government has encouraged small industries. Weaving, carpentry, pottery and basket making are common. Tripura suffers from the continuing failure of Bangladesh and India to agree a trade and travel treaty, which would allow goods to be taken in transit across Bangladesh. This adds hugely to the time and cost of transport to Kolkata, still a major market for Tripura goods, and lorries can take two weeks to make a journey that could take two days by the direct route.

The **democratic process** in the state operates under severe constraints. Politically motivated killings and kidnaps are common. The Disturbed Areas Act operates in the majority of the 45 police station areas. Reang refugees continue to flood in from Mizoram and the temporary camps in the north are full. The 60 member state assembly is controlled by the Left Front.

There is a high degree of **literacy** in the state, and despite its small size it has no less than 17 daily newspapers (two in English and 15 in Bengali).

Agartala 🚌🚹🚐🏦 ›› p168. Colour map 2, grid C4.

→ Phone code: 0381. Population: 189,300. Altitude: 1280 m.

Once a pleasant city, Agartala has mushroomed unchecked and the growth in population has far outstripped essential services. The city's red brick official buildings contrast with the British preference for white paint, still obvious on some important structures, notably the Maharaja's palace. While there are some pleasant suburbs, the centre's open drains with wooden covers are prone to flooding in the monsoons.

Ins and outs

Getting there The most convenient way to get to Agartala is by air but tickets are in short supply. Travellers must register their arrival and departure. Transfer from the airport is by taxi or bus which arrive at the Motor stand to the southeast of the palace.

Getting around The centre can be covered on foot; otherwise you can get a rickshaw. There may be a strong military presence in town. ›› See Transport, page 168, for further details.

Climate Summer maximum 35°C, minimum 24°C. Winter maximum 27°C, minimum 13°C. Annual rainfall: 2240 mm, June-August. Best season: September-March.

Sights

The airport road from the north of town leads to the **Ujjayanta Palace**. Built by Maharaja Radha Kishore Manikya in 1901, it stands amidst large well-kept Mughal gardens with pools and floodlit musical fountains. The vast palace has magnificent tiled floors, a carved wooden ceiling in the Chinese room and beautifully crafted front doors. Now the State Legislature, it is normally closed to visitors, but you may ask to look around when the Assembly is not in session. The late 19th-century **Jagannath temple** across an artificial lake in front of the palace, rises to a striking orange four-storeyed *sikhara*.

The **Temple of Chaturdasa Devata**, 8 km east, near Old Agartala, is dedicated to 14 gods and goddesses, represented by their heads only. It combines the Bengali Bankura style with a Buddhist *stupa*-type structure. In July, *Kharchi Puja,* which has evolved from a tribal festival, attracts worshippers from all over Tripura.

Tripura Government Museum ⓘ *HG Basak Rd, Mon-Fri 1000-1700*, has a small but well-displayed collection of rare stone images, old coins, Bengal *kantha* embroidery and archaeological finds from the region including eighth- to 10th-century Buddhist sculptures from Pilak.

Around Agartala

Travelling outside Agartala is hazardous because of tribal insurgents who have taken to kidnapping for ransom. Some sections of the Agartala-Assam Highway are closed except to vehicles travelling in convoy; there are usually three or four daily. Seek advice before travelling around the state.

Sepahijala The **botanical garden** ⓘ *0700-1600*, 33 km away, with a small zoo and a boating lake, is well worth a visit. The zoo is beautifully kept and new enclosures provide a more natural habitat. There are tigers, lions, cheetahs, bears and a rhino; the spectacle monkeys live in the trees above while the lake attracts migrating birds. Elephant rides are offered too. It may be possible to visit a rubber plantation and watch the processing on a trip. There are hourly buses from Agartala.

Neermahal Some 53 km south, this water-palace, in the middle of **Rudrasagar Lake**, was built in 1930 by the late Maharaja. The striking white and red fairytale castle with towers, kiosks, pavilions and bridges is fun to explore. Now being restored, it is particularly beautiful illuminated at night. The lake itself attracts migratory birds. Tourist coaches leave from Agartala, and once there, singing boatmen row you across the lake!

Tripura Sundari Temple This temple, 57 km away, in the ancient capital Udaipur, was built on Dhanisagar hill in the mid-16th century. The Matabari is believed to be one of the 51 holy *pithasthans* mentioned in the *Tantras*, where the Mother Goddess is served by red-robed priests. The pond behind has huge turtles which are delighted to be fed. A large fair is held during **Diwali** in October/November. There is a good lodge. Buses and jeeps from Agartala.

● Sleeping

Agartala *p167*
Most **D-E** have some a/c rooms.
D-F Welcome Palace, HG Basak Rd, T0381-231 3887, welcome_palace@usa.net. The newest and most comfortable hotel with some very clean a/c rooms, good restaurant.
D-F Rajdhani, BK Rd, near Indian Airlines (northeast of Palace), T0381-222 3387. 27 clean rooms with bath plus **A** suites, car hire, "first lift in Tripura!"
D-F Royal Guest House, Palace Compound, West Gate, T0381-222 5652. Rooms with bath, restaurant.
D-E Brideway, Palace Ground, T0381-220 7298. Some of the 12 rooms have a/c and bath, room service (Indian, Chinese).
F-G Meenakshi, Hawkers Corner, Khushbagan (near Museum), T0381-238 5810. Indian food.
F-G New Sonali, GB Hospital Rd, Kunjaban, T0381-222 5322. Has 12 rooms, Indian and Chinese food.
G Ambar, Sakuntala Rd (south of Palace), T0381-222 8439. Rooms with bath (some a/c), restaurant.

Around Agartala *p167*
Sepahijala
G Forest Bungalow, in well-kept gardens above the lake, meals provided. Contact Chief Conservator of Forests, Agartala, T0381-222 3779.

Neermahal
F-G Sagarmahal Tourist Lodge, on the lake, with 44 comfortable rooms and dorm, restaurant.

● Eating

Agartala *p167*
Kurry Klub, at Welcome Palace, offers comfortable a/c, and serves good Indian and Chinese.
Shankar, NSCB Rd, for interesting Bengali and Tripuri dishes.

Around Agartala *p167*
Neermahal
Superb Bengali snacks and sweets are sold along the road and simple clean restaurants serve good meals (Rs 25-40).

● Transport

Agartala *p167*
Air Airport transfer, 13 km: taxi, Rs 135; auto-rickshaw, Rs 70. Flights to **Kolkata** and **Guwahati** with **Indian Airlines**, Palace Compound, T0381-232 5470, airport, T0381-234 2020; **Jet Airways**, T0381-234 1400; **Air Deccan**, T3900-8888; **Kingfisher**, T1800-1800101.

Bus Travelling around Agartala is difficult. Tripura STC Bus Stand is on LN Bari Rd. To/from **Dharmanagar**, 8 hrs. There are private buses to **Silchar** (317 km). Bangladesh border crossing, just 2 km from the centre, is convenient for anyone with a visa to get to Dhaka which is 4 hrs by road and 3 hrs by train. The Bangladesh Visa Office is by **Brideway Hotel**; the fee for UK nationals is about US$46 for 6 months; US$23 for nationals of USA and Australia.

Taxi Tourist taxi from Directorate of Information, Rs 700 per day, T0381-222 2419.

Train Kumarghat, 140 km, is the nearest railhead. Bookings at State Bus Stand, T0381-232 5533.

● Directory

Agartala *p167*
Bank State Bank of India, HG Basak Rd.
Hospital GB Hospital, Kunjaban. **Post** GPO: Chowmohani. **Tourist office** Ujjayant Palace, East Wing, T0381-222 5930, tripura.nic.in.

Orissa

Footprint features

Introduction

The Sun Temple at Konark acted as a beacon for sailors
for nearly a millennium, while the great and architecturally
astonishing temples of Bhubaneswar and Puri have drawn
pilgrims in their millions from across India. Meanwhile,
holidaymakers from Kolkata have enjoyed Puri's broad
and sandy beaches for years.

Over 2000 years ago, the fertile delta on which the modern
capital Bhubaneswar stands witnessed one of the most
significant battles of India's history, when the Emperor Asoka,
having massacred his Kalingan opponents, converted to
Buddhism and laid the foundations for one of the great
empires of world history.

Inland, Orissa's beautiful hills, home to the tribal peoples, are
among the least densely populated and most densely forested
regions of India. Beneath them lie rich resources of iron ore,
coal, bauxite and other minerals, but despite some mining
activity much of the interior retains its remote charm.

★ Don't miss ...

1 **Bhubaneswar** Visit a few of the 500 or so temples surrounding Bindusagar Tank, then see a performance of the classical Odissi dance, page 177.

2 **Rani Gumpha** Visit the Jain Caves at Udayagiri; this one is particularly fine, page 183.

3 **Puri** Watch the Kolkata crowd enjoying themselves here, especially at the end of June during the car festival (Rath Yatra) when 500,000 celebrate in a riot of colour and noise, page 185.

4 **Konark** Check out the temple porch at this World Heritage Site, which has some of the best sculptures in India, page 187.

5 **Paradeep** If you can cope with the pollution and lack of accommodation, Paradeep, at the mouth of the Mahanadi River, is the place to watch the giant Olive Ridley turtles lay their eggs, page 197.

6 **Nandapur and Ramgiri** Visit the interesting and picturesque markets, page 206.

Background → *Population: 36.7 mn. Area: 156,000 sq km.*

The land
Geography   Near the coast it is easy to get the impression that Orissa is nothing but a flat alluvial plain composed of mile after mile of paddy fields. The coastline has shifted significantly in the last 2000 years as the land has risen relative to sea level, leaving the shallow Chilika Lake, which with an area of 1100 sq km is Asia's largest brackish lake, cut off from the sea; the lake now maintains its salinity levels by means of a man-made channel.

Inland, the alluvial soils give way to the ancient rocks of peninsular India, some of which bear huge iron ore resources. Until recently the densely forested hills were made inhospitable both by the difficulty of clearing the forest and by the devastating prevalence of malaria. Dense deciduous *sal* forest, peopled only by tribal groups living in isolation, dominated the landscape, and shifting cultivation was widely practised. Much of the forest has now been severely thinned and cultivation has spread up many of the valleys, but there remain remote and sparsely populated areas and roads that rarely see traffic, and the scenic rewards for the slowness of parts of the journey are great. The lakes to the south of Koraput in the 3000-million-year-old hills are particularly striking.

Climate   Lying just south of the Tropic of Cancer, Orissa is very warm throughout the year, though the hills are sufficiently high to bring a welcome coolness. January and February are dry, but showers increase through the spring and the monsoon from June to September is one of the wettest in India; travelling in this period is best avoided. Coastal districts are particularly at risk from cyclones in October and November. The most recent of these was the catastrophic cyclone of October 1999 which caused the death of over 8000 people, and an estimated three million cattle, as well as inflicting massive damage to villages, forests and agricultural land.

History
Coastal Orissa formed a part of the ancient kingdom of Kalinga, which grew wealthy through trading, extending its colonial influence as far afield as modern Indonesia from the port of Kalinganagar as early as the fourth century BC. The Mauryan Emperor Asoka crushed the Kalingan Kingdom at Dhauligiri in 262 BC, but after experiencing the horrors of war and the accompanying bloodshed he converted to Buddhism. He preached the philosophy of peace, and while Buddhism flowered, his tolerance allowed Jainism and Hinduism to continue. After Asoka, the first century BC King Kharavela, a fervent Jain, built up a vast empire, recorded in the remarkable Udayagiri caves near Bhubaneswar. After Kharavela, separate political territories emerged in the north and centre of the region. Maritime trade flourished and Buddhism became popular again.

The greatest period of temple building in Bhubaneswar coincided with the **Kesaris** (sixth-11th century), to be followed by the Ganga Dynasty (11th-15th century), who were responsible for the Jagannath Temple in Puri (circa 1100) and the Sun Temple at Konark (circa 1250).

Orissa resisted the annexation of her territory by **Muslims**. After a short period of Afghan rule, the powerful Mughals arrived as conquerors in 1592 and during their reign destroyed many of the Bhubaneswar temples. It was their violent disruption of temple life in Puri and Bhubaneswar that later led the Brahmin community to ban all non-Hindus from the precincts of the Lingaraj and Jagannath temples. The Mughals were followed by the Marathas in 1751.

In 1765 after Clive's win at Plassey, parts of Orissa, Bihar and Bengal were acquired by the **East India Company** with further gains in Cuttack and Puri at the beginning of the following century. Thus, by 1803, British rule extended over the whole region.

Culture

Tribal groups Orissa has the third highest concentration of tribals in India. The tribal population, nearly 25% of the total, live mainly in the Koraput, Kandhamal, Sundargarh and Mayurbhanj districts. Some 62 *Adivasi* ('ancient inhabitants') or tribal groups live in remote hill regions of the state, some virtually untouched by modern civilization, and so have kept their tribal traditions alive. Each has a distinct language and pattern of social and religious customs. They are not economically advanced and literacy is low.

> **:** *Suggested reading: Norman Lewis* A Goddess in the Stones.

However, the tribal groups have highly developed artistic ability, as seen in their body paintings, ornaments, weaving and wall paintings. Music and dance also form an integral part of life-cycle ceremonies and seasonal festivals. They are remarkable in having maintained their distinct identities in a hostile and exploitative environment. There has been a new interest in their rich heritage and the Tourism Department is keen to promote visits to tribal areas, see page 205.

The **Khonds**, the most numerous (about 100,000), live mainly in the west and speak Kuvi, a Dravidian language, and Kui. They used to practise human Meriah sacrifice (now replaced by animal sacrifice), offering the blood to their supreme goddess represented by a piece of wood or stone, to ensure fertility of the soil. They use bows and arrows to protect themselves against wild animals.

The **Santals**, the second most numerous group, come from the northern districts of Mayurbhanj and Balasore. In the northwestern industrial belt, they have abandoned their aboriginal lifestyle to work in the steel mills. They belong to 12 patrilineal clans (*paris* or *sibs*) and speak Santali, one of the oldest languages in India. Santals believe that evil spirits in trees, forests and rivers have to be appeased by magic. The women practice witchcraft while the *ojhas* are the medicine men. Music and dance are an integral part of their daily life, especially in festivals in October-November and March-April.

In the southern districts, especially in Koraput, there are about 6000 of the **Bondos** ('naked people') of Tibeto-Burmese origin. They live isolated on high hills, growing rice by shifting cultivation and keeping domesticated cows and goats, and can only be seen when they come to trade in local markets. Bondo women are noticeable for their striking bead, brass and silver necklaces, and their shaved heads, decorated with plaits of palmyra leaves.

The **Saoras**, another major tribe, mostly live in hilly areas of Parlakhemundi (Gajapati district) and Gunupur (Rayagada district). Saoras live in extended families (*birindas*), descended from a common ancestor, under a headman who is helped by a religious leader. The *shamans* are able to communicate with watchful deified ancestors. Village houses of mud and stone walls are raised on plinths with high wooden platforms inside to store grain. The walls are decorated with remarkable paintings; traditional designs now incorporate hunters on aeroplanes and bicycles.

The **Koya** who live in villages in clearings in the middle of dense forest are distinguished by their headgear made of bison horn.

Dance, drama and music The region's magnificent temple sculpture gave rise to a classical dance form, **Odissi**, which shadows the postures, expressions and lyrical qualities of the carved figures. The dance was a ritual offering performed in the *nata mandirs* by the *maharis* (temple dancers) resplendent in their costume and jewellery. The subject is often Jayadev's *Gita Govinda* (12th century), which explores the depths of Krishna's love for Radha, the dancer expressing the sensual and the devotional.

Orissan temples

Orissan temples are graced by a tall, curvilinear tower, the deul (pronounced day-ool) or rekha deul, and a much lower, more open structure or porch in front of the entrance to the tower, the jagamohana. The dark interior of the sanctuary is designed to allow only a glimpse of the presiding deity and to enable priests to conduct ritual worship. A dancing hall (nata mandir) and a hall of offering (bhoga mandir) were often added in later temples.

The square plan of the sanctuary tower and the porch are broken vertically by the inward curving form of the main tower. Each exterior face of the sanctuary tower is divided by vertical, flat-faced projections (rathas).

Some Orissan architects likened the structure of the temple to that of the human body, and the names given to the vertical sections correspond to main parts of the body.

1 The platform (pishta) Early temples had no platform. In contrast, in highly developed temples (eg Surya temple at Konark), the platform may be more than 3 m high.

2 The lower storey (bada) relates to the lower limbs. In early temples this was divided into three parts, the base (the foot), above which was a perpendicular section corresponding to the shin. This was topped by a set of mouldings. In some mature temples the scale of this section was greatly elongated and was itself then divided into five layers.

3 The upper storey (gandi, or human trunk) is a curvilinear spire in the case of the sanctuary, or a pyramidal roof in the case of the porch.

4 The head (mastaka) with crowning features. Divided into a series of elements, the 'head' or mastaka of the sanctuary developed over time. The 'neck' (beki) – a recessed cylindrical portion, is surmounted by the skull, amla. This is represented by a symbolic fruit, the amalaka. On the amla rests a 'water pot', an auspicious symbol, then on top of all comes the sacred weapon of the deity.

Orissan temple

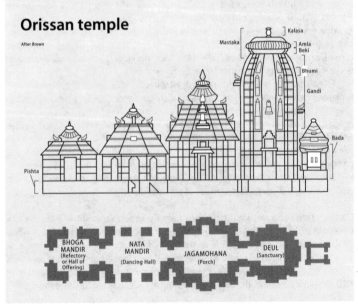

After Brown

Kalasa
Mastaka — Amla / Beki
Bhumi
Gandi
Bada
Pishta

BHOGA MANDIR (Refectory or Hall of Offering) — NATA MANDIR (Dancing Hall) — JAGAMOHANA (Porch) — DEUL (Sanctuary)

The **folk dances** usually performed during festivals take various forms – day-long
Danda Nata, the traditional fishermen's dance, *Chaitighoda* which requires a horse
dummy, the battle dance called *Paika Nritya*, and *Chhau*, the dance-drama
reminiscent of Orissa's martial past. There are also tribal dances performed in
colourful costumes with distinctive headgear made of animal horns and shells, to the
accompaniment of string instruments, flutes and drums.

Food and drink Rice forms the staple food, wheat taking second place. Meals
include lightly spiced side dishes of vegetables and pulses, chutneys and pickles.
Fresh seafood, especially prawns and the flat *pomfret* fish, are common in coastal
areas. Try *mahura* or *saga bhaja* (fried mustard or spinach leaves), *dahi baigono*
(aubergines cooked with yoghurt) or the festive *besara* (vegetables cooked with
mustard seed paste).

Orissa is particularly noted for its milk sweets – *rasamalai, khiramohan, rajbhoga,
rabidi, chhenapodapitha* and *kalakanda. Khiri* is prepared with milk and rice, semolina
or vermicelli while special *pithas* are often filled with sweetened coconut.

Art and architecture
The temples of Bhubaneswar, along with those of Puri and Konark, represent a
remarkably full record of the development of Orissan architecture from the seventh to
the 13th century AD. Although some of the temples have suffered structural damage
many are virtually intact and some are still in everyday use; centres of active
pilgrimage, worship and faith.

Crafts
Stone carving has been highly developed in Orissa for over 2000 years. The artistry
that produced the early sculptures and the superb carvings on Orissan temples in
Bhubaneswar, Puri and Konark is still kept alive by modern craftsmen. They produce
beautiful figures, bowls or plates carved out of soft soapstone, hard *kochila* or
multicoloured serpentine from Khiching. Orissa also has a tradition of **hornwork** in
Parlakhemundi and Cuttack, buffalo horn being carved into the typical small flat
figures of animals and birds.

Silver filigree is perhaps one of the most distinctive and exquisite works of the
Cuttack jewellers who turn fine silver wire into beautiful, fragile objects with floral
patterns. The metal used is close to sterling silver and is drawn through finer and finer
holes to make the wire.

Metalwork is popular. Craftsmen use brass (alloy of copper and zinc) and
bell-metal (alloy of copper and tin) to produce small figurines, vases and plates. The
tribal metal casting in the *dhokra* style by the lost-wax (*cire perdue*) process is found
in Dhenkanal and Mayurbhanj districts. A clay core of the basic shape is covered by
fine wax 'threads' before the whole is enclosed in a shell of straw and clay and then
baked in a tiny charcoal fire. At the firing, molten metal is poured in, to displace the
melting wax. Similar casting is done by tribal peoples in Bihar, Madhya Pradesh,
Manipur and West Bengal.

Brightly coloured **wood carvings** of the deities in the Jagannath temple, and
figures of animals and birds make attractive gifts. **Ivory** inlay (now replaced by plastic)
was traditionally carried out for rich patrons of the Puri temple, and also for making
illustrated wooden covers for palm leaf manuscripts. The tradition of using **papier-
mâché** masks of deities and animal characters to tell stories from the epics also
comes from Orissa.

The *chitrakars* (picture makers), particularly from the village of Raghurajpur,
12 km from Puri, **paint** the *pattachitras* on specially prepared cloth, coated with earth
to stiffen it and finally finished with lacquer after painting, producing pictures and
attractive playing cards. Old sets of *ganjapa* cards consisted of 96 discs. The vibrant

colours traditionally came from earth, stone, leaves and flowers. The best *chitrakars* are those allowed the honour to paint the Puri temple deities and their 'cars' each year. They are also commissioned by the rich to produce fine temple murals and manuscripts on paper and palmleaf. However, what are usually available in the bazars are cruder examples for pilgrims to take home.

Finds of the 16th century reveal how illustrated manuscripts were produced by holding an iron stylus stationary while moving a **palm leaf** underneath. It was a technique that helped to give the Oriya script its rounded form. The leaves were first prepared by drying, boiling, drying again, and then flattening them before coating with powdered shell. After inscribing, the grooves were rubbed with soot or powdered charcoal, while colour was added with a brush. The leaves were then stacked and strung together and placed between decorative wooden covers. The *pattachitra* artists in Raghurajpur have also revived this art form.

Pipli, a small town about 20 km southwest of Bhubaneswar, is well known for its **appliqué** work using brightly coloured embroidered cloth, probably originally designed for use in the Jagannath temple. The roadside stalls sell items for the house and garden – parasols, cushion covers, wall hangings – using striking animal, bird and flower patterns on a backcloth. Unfortunately, mass production has resulted in the loss of attention to detail of the original fine Pipli work which picked out the motifs by cleverly stuffing sections of the pattern. Today, the best pieces of work are usually sent away to be sold in the government emporia in Bhubaneswar, Delhi and Kolkata.

Textile weaving has been a traditional craft throughout Orissa for generations and thousands are still employed in this cottage industry. It is one of the few regions in India producing **ikat** – the technique of resist-dyeing the warp or weft thread, or both, before weaving, so that the fabric that emerges from the loom has a delicate enmeshed pattern. The favourite designs include rows of flowers, birds and animals, using either tussar or cotton yarn. **Berhampur, Sambalpur, Mayurbhanj** and **Nuapatna** all produce silk and cotton ikat saris. Some also produce tapestry, bedspreads and embroidered fabric.

Crafts villages While some (for example, Raghurajpur and Pipli) are used to passing tourists, others are rarely visited by foreigners. It is worth visiting to see craftsmen at work and perhaps buy their goods. In **Raghurajpur** (reached via Chandapur, 10 km from Puri on the Bhubaneswar road), you can watch artists painting *pattachitras* in bright folk-art style or etching palm leaves (see *chitrakars* above). Sadly, the village has now been reduced to a sales exercise. **Pipli**, on the Bhubaneswar-Puri Road, specializes in appliqué work, **Balakati**, 10 km from Bhubaneswar, in bell-metal, while there is a community of Tibetan carpet weavers at **Chandragiri** near the Taptapani Hot Springs in tribal country. Adjacent to the Buddhist site of **Lalitgiri** is a stone-carvers' village. Master-weavers work at their looms in **Nuapatna** and **Maniabandha**, 100 km from Bhubaneswar, and in the narrow streets next to the temple at **Berhampur**. **Cuttack** remains famous for silver filigree work.

Modern Orissa

Political power in Orissa has alternated between the Congress and Opposition parties, most recently the BJD (the Biju Janata Dal, named after its former leader Biju Patnaik), which in alliance with the BJP won an overwhelming majority in the Assembly elections of February 2000. Chief Minister Naveen Patnaik, the son of Biju Patnaik, has held a range of ministerial posts in both state and central governments and has a strong reputation for integrity. In the 2004 State Assembly elections the BJD won 61 of the 147 seats and the BJP, its coalition partners, 32, leaving the Congress trailing on 38.

Mahanadi Delta

Bhubaneswar 🔲🚗🎵❄️✳️🏛️⛰️📷🌙 ►► *pp190-194. Colour map 3, grid A6.*

→ *Phone code: 0674. Population: 647,300.*

Set on the edge of the lush green rice fields of the Mahanadi Delta, the pleasantly broad but increasingly crowded streets of the planned town of Bhubaneswar offer a striking contrast to the architectural legacy of its period of greatness over one thousand years ago. Named after 'The Lord of the Universe', Bhubaneswar still has some 500 of the original '7000' temples that once surrounded Bindusagar Tank. The graceful towers of those early temples, complemented by the extraordinary fineness of the stone carving, make Bhubaneswar one of the most rewarding destinations in East India.

Ins and outs

Getting there The airport, served by direct flights from Delhi, Mumbai and Kolkata, is 4 km from the centre. Trains on the main Kolkata-Chennai line stop at Bhubaneswar station, from where many hotels are within walking distance. The new bus stand is 6 km out of town, but many long-distance buses stop at the Old Bus Stand in the centre first. Buses for Konark and Puri can be boarded by the State Museum.

Getting around The temples are a long way from the modern centre and most hotels so it is best to hire a rickshaw to reach them. Once you're there it's easy enough to explore the old city on foot. ►► *See Transport, page 193, for further details.*

Tourist Information **Orissa Tourism** ① *Panthanivas Hotel, Lewis Rd, T0674-243 2382, www.orissatourism,gov.in.* **India Tourism** ① *B-21, BJB Nagar, T0674-243 2203, itobbs@ori.nic.in.* Obscure location, but very helpful.

History

Several sites testify to the importance of the Bhubaneswar region far earlier than the seventh to 11th centuries, when the Kalinga kings ruled over the area. Both Jain and Buddhist shrines give clear evidence of important settlements around Bhubaneswar in the first two centuries BC. The remains of a ruined moated city, Sisupalgarh (opposite the Dhauligiri battlefield and Asokan edicts), show that it was occupied from the beginning of the third century BC to the middle of the fourth century AD and the pottery shows Roman influence. Bhubaneswar is the capital of Orissa, chosen in 1948 in place of Cuttack partly because it was the ancient capital of the Kalinga Empire.

Sights

Parsuramesvara Temple The seventh-century temple, though small, is highly decorated, and is the best preserved of the early Bhubaneswar temples. The rectangular porch and the stepped roof indicate an early date. Even so, the porch was probably built after the sanctuary itself, as suggested by the rather crude junction between the two. In the early period the masonry was kept in place by weight and balance alone. Other features include the carving of a goddess and two sea-monsters on the lintel over the sanctuary door.

> ● *Temple priests will approach you for donations; these are not compulsory, but if you do decide to give, a token Rs 10 is sufficient.*

The temple marks an important stage in the development of Hindu power at the expense of Buddhism in seventh-century Orissa, illustrated by the frequent representation of **Lakulisa**, the seventh-century priest responsible for Hindu proselytism. He is sculpted in Buddha-like form, and often surrounded by disciples. Note also, the distinctive *chaitya* windows developed earlier in Buddhist *chaitya* halls, as at Ajanta. There are two on the front of the sanctuary tower.

The sanctuary is divided horizontally and vertically into three sections. The carvings show motifs and styles that were to reach their full flowering in later temples. The base, for example, has a top moulding (close to the ground) decorated with scrolls, birds, humans and floral motifs. At about eye level, the mouldings are distinctive. The recessed frieze (discarded in later designs) is embossed with early examples of the amorous couples which were to become such a prominent feature of

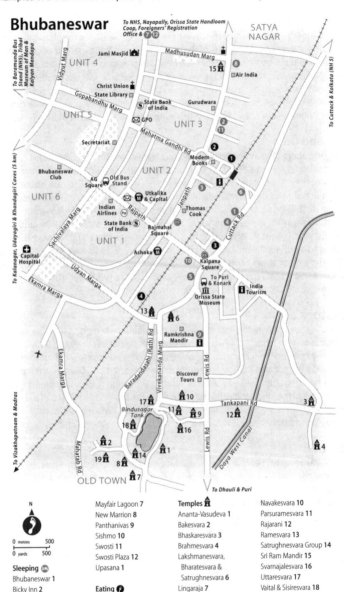

Bhubaneswar

the Konark temple, interspersed with *vyalas* (rampant lions) astride crouching elephants. In addition to the main entrance to the porch there is a door on the south side and four latticed windows. The vigorous and graceful sculptures of musicians and dancers he carvings on each side of the western doorway are outstanding.

The main accessory deities are placed in niches on each side of the sanctuary housing the principal deity. The Parsurameswara Temple was dedicated to Siva; only two of the three original deities survive. On the south of the sanctuary, at eye level in the middle of the tower, is the four-armed elephant-headed Ganesh, his trunk curled towards a bowl of *laddus,* his favourite sweet. In the southern niche is Karttikeya (Subrahmanya) with a peacock, carrying a fruit in his right hand and a spear in his left. The lintel above Karttikeya illustrates the marriage of Siva and Parvati; to their right are Agni (Fire), the kneeling Brahma, and Surya (Sun).

Muktesvara Temple Beautifully decorated with outstanding carvings, this late 10th-century temple belongs to the end of the first phase of temple building. Although it still has the three-fold horizontal division of the lower storey, a feature of the early period, the plan of the sanctuary is now divided into the five-sectioned form. Also, the platform here consists of five mouldings, as in later temples.

New designs include graceful female figures and pilasters carved with *nagas* and *naginis* (snakes). Strikingly, the porch has a new and more dramatic layered form. Ketu, too, is introduced as the ninth planet and Ganesh is joined by his mount, the mouse.

The Muktesvara displays the unique gateway arch (*torana*) dated at about AD 900; although the upper portion is restored, the original skill can still be seen in the graceful female figures. The rectangular tank at its east end, used by priests and devotees, and the well to the south, into which women still toss coins in the hope of curing infertility, symbolize the continued holiness of the site. On the door frame of the well is the figure of Lakulisa (see Parsuramesvara above).

The *chaitya* windows carved on the sanctuary tower show the finest examples of the *bho* motif – the grinning face of a lion with beaded tassels emerging from its mouth, flanked by two dwarves. Notice the monkey scenes on the outer frame of the diamond-shaped lattice windows on the north and south walls.

Siddhesvara Temple Immediately to the northwest of the Muktesvara is the later Siddhesvara Temple. It shows the mature Orissan temple form almost complete. The vertical lower section is divided into five parts and the *amla* on top of the sanctuary is supported by four squatting figures. However, the overall effect is comparatively plain, as sculptures marked out on the rock were never executed.

Gauri Temple The Gauri Temple to the south is probably of the late 10th century but it is built in the *khakhara* form (see Vaital Deul below), and has been substantially repaired. The porch was rebuilt in the early 20th century but still has a few original sculptures of real merit. Note the girl shown leaning against a post with a bird perched on it, on the south face of the eastern projection of the sanctuary. On the western projection is an equally beautiful sculpture of a girl removing her anklets.

Rajarani Temple ⓘ *0600-1800, foreigners Rs100, video camera Rs 25.* The entrance to the early 11th-century temple is 300 m east of the main road, set back from the road. It no longer has an image of the deity in the sanctuary and is out of use. The main tower is surrounded by four miniature copies, giving the sanctuary a near-circular appearance.

The porch (*jagmohana*) is plain although it has the mature style of a pyramidal roof. Many carvings are unfinished but give an insight into the method of cutting the stone into sections ('blocking out') followed by rough shaping ('boasted'), to be finished by the master sculptor. The finished work in the main sanctuary is impressive.

Perhaps the best-preserved features of the temple are the *Dikpalas* (Guardians of the eight cardinal directions) who protect the central shrine from every quarter. They are placed in pairs about 3 m above ground level, in the lower section of the main tower.

Dikpalas: the Directional Guardians

Starting from the left (south) of the porch they appear in the following order:

1 Facing east, **Indra**, the guardian of the east, holds a thunderbolt and an elephant goad, and his vehicle is the elephant.

2 At right angles to Indra, facing south, is the pot-bellied and bearded **Agni**, god of fire, riding a ram, guarding the southeast.

3 Moving a few metres along the wall, on the far side of the projection, is the south-facing **Yama**, holding a staff and a noose, with his vehicle the buffalo. The skull on his staff is a Tantric symbol.

4 Again at right angles to Yama is the west-facing **Nirritti**, guardian of the southwest. Nirritti, the god of misery, holds a severed head and a sword over the lying figure of a man.

5 Again facing west, but on the north side of the sanctuary's central projection, is the guardian of the west, **Varuna**. He holds the noose symbolizing fate in his left hand. His vehicle is the sea creature *makara*.

6 At right angles to Varuna, facing north, is **Vayu** (meaning 'wind'), guardian of the northwest. He holds a fluttering banner, and his vehicle is the deer.

7 The last pair of guardians are on the further side of the central projection, on the north and east facing sides respectively. First is **Kubera**, guardian of the north (pot-bellied to symbolize prosperity), placed above seven jars of precious stones. He has a horse.

8 **Ishana**, guardian of the northeast, symbolizing fecundity, is shown as was customary, with an erect phallus and accompanied by an emaciated figure.

Brahmesvara Temple The temple (built in 1060) is still in use today. Entering from the north you pass through the two enclosure walls, the inner forming a compact surround for the temple complex, raised on a platform. Facing you is a well-oiled image of Lakshmi, covered in cloth, with incense sticks burning in front. The sanctuary itself houses a Siva *linga*. There are minor shrines in each corner of the compound.

The sanctuary tower has a five-fold vertical division, typical of the later temples. The base (*pabhaga*) and the top of the wall (*varanda*) have rich carvings. The lower section of the wall is decorated alternately by miniature *khakhara* style 'temples', sculptures of rampant lions, while the central niches of the miniature temple carvings at the corners of the lower section have *Dikpalas*. In the corresponding spaces of the upper section are miniatures of the normal temple sanctuary towers, and graceful secular figures, including erotic couples.

Satrughnesvara Group The **Lakshmanesvara**, **Bharatesvara** and **Satrughnesvara** temples are almost certainly the oldest in Bhubaneswar, dating from the late sixth century. The southernmost temple in the group has been rebuilt by the Archaeological Department of Orissa. Only the cores of these three temple are now visible.

Vaital Temple A major feature of this small, late eighth-century temple is its form. Seen from the road the semi-cylindrical shape in section of the *deul* is immediately seen. Its *khakhara* style derives, as Percy Brown says, from the shape of the *gopurams* of Dravida temples in South India, taken originally from the Buddhist *chaitya* halls. Another striking feature is the temple's tantric associations, marked by its presiding deity, Chamunda (a terrible form of Durga). Durga herself appears on the north face of the *bada* as the eight-armed *Mahishasuramardini* (slayer of the buffalo demon) holding a snake, bow, shield, sword, trident, thunderbolt and an arrow, piercing the neck of the demon.

Outside, on the east face of the *deul*, the lower of the two *chaitya* windows has a beautifully carved figure of the sun god Surya, with Usha (Dawn) and Pratyusha shooting arrows on either side of him while Aruna (also Dawn) drives a chariot in front. It has a certain incongruity in view of the image within the sanctum itself. The upper *chaitya*window has a 10-armed Nataraja, or dancing Siva.

Further evidence of the tantric basis of the temple comes from the stone post to which sacrifices were tethered, just in front of the *jagamohana*. The figure of Chamunda in the central niche is extremely difficult to see without artificial light, though very early morning sun penetrates the gloom of the interior. The most chilling of the other figures is that of a male on the north wall "rising from the ground after filling his skull-cup with the blood of a person whose severed head lies on the right; on the pedestal is an offering of two more heads".

Lingaraja Temple Along with the Jagannatha Temple at Puri the Lingaraja Temple (AD 1000), built 100 years earlier, represents the peak of achievement of the Orissan middle period. Non-Hindus are not allowed inside but you may get a view from a special platform outside the north perimeter wall (donations sought); early morning and late afternoon are best for photography.

Even from a distance the sanctuary's 54-m high tower (the *Sri Mandir*) dominates the landscape. It is one of the four main buildings in the temple compound, with several subsidiary shrines. To the left of the tower is the *Jagamohana* (pillared porch), then the *Nata Mandir* (dancing hall) and finally the *Bhoga Mandir* (Hall of Offering). The latter two were added a century after the sanctuary and the porch.

The monumental tower which rises in a distinctive curve, is 17 m sq in plan with projecting faces. The *amla* head with a pot-shaped pinnacle carrying the trident of Siva is supported by four mythical gryphons. The middle section has vertical lines of miniature towers sculpted in sharp relief on a background of horizontal mouldings. The massive protruding sculpture of a lion crushing an elephant on each side is a common symbol in Orissan architecture.

Ekamra Kanan ① *Mar-Oct 0800-2000, Nov-Feb 0900-1900, Rs 5.* The Government Regional Plant Resource Centre in Nayapally (north of town) has a large rose garden (Flower Show, December/January), woods, flowerbeds and a large lake which attracts migratory birds. It also boasts a Cactus Garden with over 550 species of cacti and succulents, one of the largest collections in India.

Orissa State Museum ① *Gautam Nagar, Tue-Sun 1400-1700 (last entry 1600), closed government holidays, Rs 5, foreigners Rs 60.* The collection includes archaeological exhibits, copper plates, coins, sculptures, musical instruments and rare palm leaf manuscripts; good anthropological section. Allow an hour or two.

Tribal Museum of Man ① *CRP Square, Mon-Sat 1000-1700, northwest of town, off NH5 on bus route.* The Tribal Research Institute's museum has a collection of tribal dress, weapons and jewellery.

Kalanagar ① *Khandagiri Rd, Mon-Sat 1000-1700.* This place offers displays of traditional art and crafts, stone sculptures, *pattachitras*, brass casting, horn ware, terracotta and silver filigree.

Nandan Kanan ⓘ *Tue-Sun 0800-1700, summer 0730-1730, Rs 10, foreigners Rs 100, camera Rs 5, video Rs 500. Cable car across the lake, Rs 22, last return 1600. Safari Rs 15.* The subsidiary road from Bhubaneswar to Cuttack, the medieval regional capital, passes Nandan Kanan after 20 km where the zoo and botanical garden are surrounded by dense forest. There are tigers, including rare white ones, lion and white tiger safaris, rhinos, panthers, leopards, wildfowl and reptiles in their natural surroundings. It has also succeeded in breeding black panthers and *gharials* in captivity. The botanical gardens with its cactus house and rosarium are across the lake; much of it is derelict. **Shradhanjali Restaurant** near the entrance serves good *thalis and snacks.*

Udayagiri and Khandagiri caves ⬤ ⟫ *p190. Colour map 3, grid A5.*

The caves, 6 km from Bhubaneswar, on the two low hills of Udayagiri and Khandagiri, date from the time of Jain occupation of the region, at least the second century BC. A narrow valley winds between the hills, the route of an early Buddhist pilgrim track leading to a stupa which probably stood on the present site of Bhubaneswar. The coarse-grained sandstone which forms Khandagiri ('broken hill') and Udayagiri ('hill of the sunrise') rises nearly 40 m above the surrounding lateritic and infertile plain. The crumbling nature of the sandstone into which the caves were dug has exposed them to severe damage, moderately repaired by the Archaeological Survey of India.

Ins and outs
ⓘ *Foreigners US$2, video Rs 25 for Udayagiri. Khandagiri is free. 0800-1800.*
The caves are very easy to visit by car, bus, rickshaw (Rs 120 return, includes waiting) or bicycle from Bhubaneswar, but the area can get very crowded. You can take the path up towards Udayagiri to the right of the hills as you face them, and follow the route indicated to visit the caves in order. Some with sculptures are protected by wire-meshed gates. Allow two to three hours.

Around Bhubaneswar & Cuttack

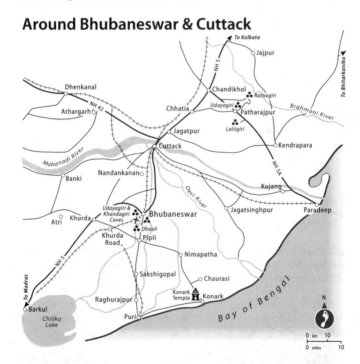

The **Jain caves** are among the earliest in India. Furthermore, some of the rock inscriptions found above the *Hati Gumpha* (Elephant Cave, No 14) and elsewhere, speak of the Chedi Dynasty who ruled over Kalinga from their capital, probably at Sisupalgarh, 9 km southeast of Khandagiri.

Kharavela, according to his own record, extended his rule across a large part of North, Central and South India. At home he made great efforts to improve canals, rebuild his capital city of Kalinganagara, and also to excavate some of the caves at Udayagiri-Khandagiri. Probably all the caves now visible were constructed during the 150 years before Christ. Designed for the ascetic life of Jain monks, they simply provided dry shelter, with no concessions to any form of comfort. Too low to stand in, the cells are no more than cramped sleeping compartments.

Although the Jains did not enjoy royal patronage after the fall of Kharavela's Dynasty, Jain occupation was continuous throughout successive Buddhist and Hindu periods in the region. The Parsvanatha temple on top of Khandagiri was built in the early 19th century, while the Hindu temple dates from the 1970s.

Udayagiri

Cave 1 The **Rani Gumpha**, on the path to the right, is the largest and most impressive of the caves. It is a double-storeyed monastery cut on three sides of a quadrangle with fine wall friezes and some pillars that have been restored. The right wing of the lower storey is

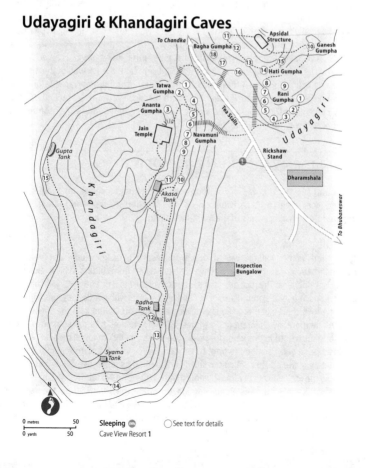

Udayagiri & Khandagiri Caves

To Chandka

Apsidal Structure ⑪

Bagha Gumpha ⑫

⑱

⑰ ⑬ ⑩ Ganesh Gumpha

⑯ ⑮

⑭ Hati Gumpha

Tatwa Gumpha ② ①

④ ⑧ ⑨

Ananta Gumpha ③ ⑤ ⑦ Rani Gumpha ①

⑥ ⑥

Jain Temple ⑦ Navamuni Gumpha ⑤

⑧ ④ ③

⑨ ②

Gupta Tank Tea Stalls

⑮ ⑪ ⑩ Rickshaw Stand

Akasa Tank *Udayagiri*

Khandagiri Dharamshala

To Bhubaneswar

Inspection Bungalow

Radha Tank ⑫

⑬

Syama Tank

⑭

N

0 metres 50
0 yards 50

Sleeping 😴
Cave View Resort **1**

○ See text for details

guarded by two sentries. The pilasters at the entrance to the cell and the arches are beautifully carved with religious and royal scenes while the main central wing celebrates the king's victory march. There are two small guard rooms with decorative outer walls. In the upper storey, the doorway arches to the cells are ornately carved; auspicious Jain symbols (snake and lotus) appear among vivid secular friezes of a woman's abduction, an elopement, and a duel between a man and a woman.

Cave 10 Ganesh Gumpha About 50 m from the top of the steps. Friezes illustrate the Sanskrit love story of Udayan and Bassavadatta. From Cave 10 head up the path to the right, where an **apsidal structure** was unearthed in 1958. It is similar to a Buddhist *chaitya* hall in plan and it was almost certainly a place of worship used by Jain monks.

Cave 12 Bagha Gumpha is carved bizarrely into the shape of a tiger's open mouth, an inscription showing it to have been the cave of the town judge.

Cave 14 The last important cave on Udayagiri, the **Hati Gumpha** (Elephant Cave), has the most important inscription, that of King Kharavela. Protected by a masonry shelter since 1902, it is in the Magadhi script.

Khandagiri

Caves 1 and 2 Known as **Tatwa Gumpha** from the parrots carved on their door arches. Two sentries in *dhotis* guard Cave 1 which bears the name **Kusuma**. Modern steps lead up to the more elaborately carved Cave 2 on the left. On the back of the cell are Brahmi inscriptions in red pigment (first century BC to first century AD).

Cave 3 Ananta Gumpha, at the top of the flight of steps, named after the two serpents on the door arches, has some very interesting reliefs using unique motifs; note especially the sculpted façade. On the back wall of the cell, among the various symbols is the *svastika*, auspicious to the Jains.

Cave 7 Navamuni Gumpha, named after the nine Tirthankaras (*munis*) carved on the back and right walls, was originally a residential cell. On the back wall of the original right hand cell are seven Tirthankaras in high relief including Parsvanatha under a seven-hooded canopy, and Risabanatha with a halo, seated on a bull. There are lovely carvings of Digambara Jains on the back wall of the shrine with a corrugated iron roof half way up to the Jain temple.

Bhubaneswar to Puri and Konark

The round trip to Puri, one of the four holiest pilgrimage centres for Hindus, and Konark, according to Mark Twain one of the wonders of the world, crosses the irrigated rice growing plains of the Mahanadi delta.

Dhauli

The horrors of the Kalinga war at Dhauli led Asoka to acknowledge the value of Buddhist teachings. The two 'Kalinga Edicts' differ from others which expound Buddhist principles. The rock edicts at the bottom of the hill (circa 260 BC) give detailed instructions to Asoka's administrators to rule his subjects with gentleness and fairness. "… You are in charge of many thousand living beings. You should gain the affection of men. All men are my children, and as I desire for my children that they obtain welfare and happiness both in this world and next, the same do I desire for all men …". Above the inscription you can see the front of an elephant carved out of an enormous rock. Unfortunately, the edict is difficult to see clearly behind its protective cage.

Now the rock edicts are almost ignored by the bus loads of tourists who are taken on up the hill to the Buddhist **Peace Pagoda**. Known as the **Shanti Stupa**, the Pagoda was built in the early 1970s by the Japan Buddha Sangha and Kalinga Nippon Buddha Sangha. The old Hindu temple of Lord Dhavaleswar which was reconstructed in 1972 is also on the hilltop here.

Puri ⬤⬤⬤⬤⬤⬤▲⬤⬤ → pp190-194. Colour map 3, grid A5.

→ *Phone code: 06752. Population: 157,600.*

Puri's tourist guest houses cater to the flocks of Kolkata holidaymakers who take advantage of the highly revered Jagannath Temple and the good sandy beach to combine pilgrimage with relaxation. The massive curvilinear temple tower dominates the skyline, and the otherwise sleepy town seethes with life during the car festival (*Rath Yatra*). Yet for most of the year Puri feels like an out of season backwater with quiet shady lanes and prettily painted houses.

Ins and outs

Getting there and around The station is about 1 km from the main hotels and the bus stand, 500 m north of it, on Grand Road. Cycle-rickshaws tout for business all across town. It is well worth hiring a bike to visit the temple, bazar and explore the coast if you don't wish to hire a rickshaw. → *See Transport, page 193, for further details.*

History

The Sabaras, an *adivasi* tribal group who predated the Dravidians and Aryans, were believed to have inhabited the thickly wooded area around Puri. Some believe that this was **Dantapura**, which once held the holy Buddhist Tooth relic. According to

Puri

N

0 metres 500
0 yards 500

Sleeping
Arya Palace 1
Asian Inn Beach Resort 2
BNR 3

Derby 4
Gandhara, Sun Row
  Cottage & Internet 5
Hans Coco Palms 6
Holiday House, Kasi's Castle
  & Loknath Books 7
Lotus 8
Love & Life 9
Mayfair Beach Resort 10

Nilachal Ashok 11
Panthanivas & OTDC
  Tourist Office 12
Pearl Beach Club 13
Pink House 14
Puri 15
Santana 16
Shankar International 17
Toshali Sands 18

Vijoya International 19
Youth Hostel 20
Z 21

Eating
Chung Wah 1
Harry's Café 3
Peace 4
Wild Grass 2

Orissa Mahanadi Delta

⁑ Rath Yatra

Traditionally the only occasion on which non-Hindus and Hindus of low caste can set eyes on one of India's most beloved deities, Lord Jagannath's 'car festival' brings Puri's streets to life in an extraordinary riot of colour and noise. Shaped like a temple sanctuary and brightly decorated, Lord Jagannath's 13-m tall 'car', the largest, has 16 wheels each 2 m in diameter. Loud gongs announce the boarding of the deities onto the chariots with the arrival of the Raja of Puri accompanied by bedecked elephants. With a golden broom and sprinkling holy water, the Raja fulfils his role as the 'sweeper of the gods', symbolizing that all castes are equal before God. The procession is led by Balabhadra's car, followed by Subhadra's with Lord **Jagannath**'s bringing up the rear, about 4000 people being needed to draw each chariot. The 3 km journey may take as much as 24 hours.

During the week away, the deities are daily dressed in new garments and treated to special rice cakes (podapitha) before they return with a similar procession. The ceremonies and the fairs attract more than 500,000 devotees to Puri each year. In the past some were said to have thrown themselves under the massive wheels to die a blessed death. After the festival, the raths are broken up and bits are sold to pilgrims as relics.

Murray, in Japan and Sri Lanka, the **Tooth Festival** of Buddha was celebrated with three chariots and the similarity with the **Rath Yatra** at Puri further strengthens the theory that the deities here evolved from Buddhist symbols.

Sights

Jagannath Temple This temple is the major attraction of Puri and, for Hindus, to remain here for three days and three nights is considered particularly rewarding. The temple attracts thousands on feast days and particularly during **Rath Yatra**. Non-Hindus are not allowed inside this temple. The fact that in the eyes of Jagannath (Lord of the Universe), there are no caste distinctions, has made Puri a very popular destination with the devout. The wooden figures of the three deities, **Jagannath**, **Balabhadra** and **Subhadra** stand in the sanctuary garlanded and decorated by the priests. The extraordinary form that Jagannath takes is believed to be the unfinished work of the craftsman god Viswakarma, who in anger left this portrayal of Lord Vishnu incomplete. Small wooden replicas of the three images are available around the temple. There are vantage points for viewing the temple; for example, the roof of Raghunandan Library opposite the main entrance to the east or from the **Jaga Balia Lodge** nearby. A small donation is expected in return.

The temple is referred to by some as the white pagoda (the Konark Temple being the black pagoda) and was completed in the late 12th century. The original temple built in the Kalinga style consisted of the **deul** (sanctuary) and the **jagamohan** (audience hall) in front of it. It was only in the 14th or 15th century that the *nata mandir* (dance hall) and the *bhoga mandir* (hall of offerings) were added in alignment in the style of other Orissan temples. The **nata mandir** is unusual in that it has 16 pillars in four rows to support the large ceiling. The site is a virtual 200 m sq enclosed within an outer wall 6 m high. Within is another concentric wall which may have acted as fortification, inside which stands the tallest temple in Orissa, 65 m high, crowned by the wheel of Vishnu and a flag. On the higher ground in the enclosure are 30 small shrines, much in the Buddhist stupa tradition. Pilgrims are expected to visit at least three of these smaller temples before proceeding to the main temple. The outer wall has the main **Lion entrance**. On this east side there is an intricately carved 10-m high free-standing stone pillar with a small figure of *Aruna*, the charioteer of the Sun. This once stood in front of the *nata mandira* at Konark, see page 188. To the left of the main entrance is the temple kitchen which daily prepares 56 varieties of food making up the *Bhogas* which are offered to the deities five times a day; the *mahaprasada* is then distributed from the Ananda Bazar to thousands. At festival times as many as 250,000 are served daily. The temple is supposed to be a self-sufficient community, served by 6000 priests and over 10,000 others who depend on it for their livelihood. The four sacred *tanks* in Puri provide thousands of pilgrims with the opportunity to take a holy dip. The **Narendra Tank** is particularly famous since the deities are taken there during the Snana Yatra.

Gundicha Ghar The terminus of the **Rath Yatra**, where the deities from the Jagannath Temple spend a week, is open to Hindus only. It shows the unique and ingenious way wrought-iron framework supported the laterite lintels of the massive temples.

The beach The long stretch of Puri's golden beach is shallow enough to walk out a long distance. Sunrise is particularly striking. The currents can be treacherous at times. Take great care and avoid swimming out too far. The best hotels have a stretch of fairly clean sand. The customary *nolia*, fisherman-turned-lifeguard in a distinctive conical hat, may be hired for either half or a full day, at a small price. The fishing villages along the coast are worth visiting, but be prepared to pick your way carefully!

Konark ⬛🏃❄🛏🌙 ▸ *pp190-194. Colour map 3, grid A6.*

Konark (Konarak) is one of the most vivid architectural treasures of Hindu India and is a World Heritage Site. It no longer stands as a landmark on the seashore since the land has risen and the sea is now 2 km away. Though much of it now lies in ruins, the porch is still magnificent.

Ins and outs
Getting there and around The 35 km drive from Puri (small toll charged) through attractive scenery passes a Turtle Research Centre off the Marine Drive after 10 km and through coastal villages with beautifully decorated houses including Chaitan, a stone carvers' hamlet. The energetic can cycle to Konark and bring the bike back on the bus. The site is very compact and can only be seen on foot. ▸ *See Transport, page 194, for details.*

History
The Sun Temple was built by King Langula Narasimha Deva in the 13th century, although there may have been an older ninth-century temple on the same site. Built of *khondalite*, it is said to have taken 1200 masons 16 years to complete. It was only in 1901 that the first tentative steps were taken to reclaim the ruins of the temple from the encroaching sand. By that stage not only had the sanctuary or *deul* collapsed but a number of the statues had been removed, many in the 1830s by the Hindu Raja of Khurda, who wanted them to decorate temples he was building in his own fort, 100 km away, and at Puri. There has been substantial renovation, some of it protective and some replacing fallen stonework and sculptures.

The site
ⓘ *0600-1800, foreigners, US$5/Rs 250, video Rs 25. Official guides, Rs 100 per hr.*
The **Surya Temple** is set back 180 m from the road and is reached by a wide laterite path. The sanctuary (closed for safety reasons at the time of writing) has no deity for worship, so shoes may be worn. The exception is the small structure in the northeast corner of the site which houses the old *Navagraha* (nine planets) doorway arch,

removed from the temple. The path to the temple is lined with beggars, as in major centres of Hindu pilgrimage.

Archaeological Survey and Government approved **guides** conduct tours of less than an hour. Unofficial guides will press their services, but can be unreliable.

The temple compound

The temple presents its most imposing aspect from the steps of the *bhoga mandira* (refectory) at the eastern end of the complex, an isolated hall with pillars raised on a richly decorated platform guarded by a pair of stone lions; some believe this may have been a *nata mandira* (dancing hall). To its west is an open space leading to the porch (*jagamohana*) which rises magnificently to its original height of 39 m. The massive lower section of the original sanctuary (*deul*) was once over 60 m tall.

From the south wall you can see that the temple was built in the form of a war chariot. Twelve pairs of great wheels were sculpted on either side of the temple platform. In front of the eastern entrance a team of seven horses were shown straining to pull the chariot towards the dawn. In Hindu mythology the Sun god traverses the sky in a chariot drawn by seven horses, each representing a day of the week. The 12 pairs of wheels may have symbolized the 12 months of the year, and the eight spokes in each wheel, the divisions of the day into eight *prahars*. Each wheel also functions as a sundial.

The sculptures

The walls of the *bhoga mandir* are covered by carvings, but as Debala Mitra writes, they are of "mediocre quality". The platform gives an excellent view of the whole east front of the main temple with its porch doorway, and the large, remarkably vivid carvings on the terraces of its pyramidal roof, unique in Orissan architecture, see page 175.

The sculptures draw for their subject from every aspect of life – dancers, musicians, figures from mythology, scenes of love and war, of court life, hunting, elephant fights. Since the temple was conceived to reflect a rounded picture of life and since *mithuna* or union in love is a part of that, a significant section of the sculpture is erotic art. Konark is unusual in that the carvings are found both on the outer and inner surfaces.

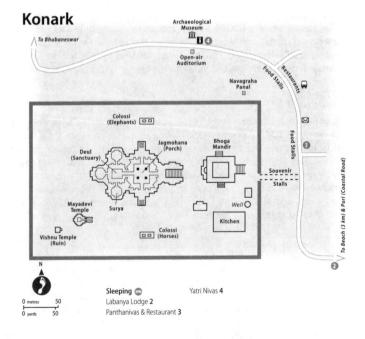

Konark

Sleeping 🛏️
Labanya Lodge **2**
Panthanivas & Restaurant **3**
Yatri Nivas **4**

The porch roof is divided into three tiers, separated by terraces. Above the bottom and middle tiers is a series of musicians vividly captured in a variety of rhythmic poses playing drums, cymbals and *vinas*. On the bottom tier at either end of the central segments are dramatic sculptures of Siva as the awe-inspiring Bhairava. The top of the porch is crowned with the flattened spheres typical of Orissan temples.

The plinth (*upana*), a few centimetres high, runs right round the base of the temple, and is decorated with a variety of friezes – elephants (estimated at over 1700, and each different), including wild elephants being trapped, military marches, hunting, journeys, and a variety of other animals including crocodiles and a giraffe.

The platform is divided into the same five horizontal layers that characterize the temple itself. These are richly decorated with creepers and scrolls, and end with tiny motifs of *chaitya* windows. Along the lower mouldings are spaced miniature temple-like façades – *khakhara-mundis* – which contain niches. Set into these are figures, often of young women – caressing a bird, washing hair, playing the *vina*. The slabs between have a variety of carvings – some are erotic, some are *nagas* or *naginis*, each with a human head but with the tail of a snake.

The middle of the platform has three horizontal mouldings at about eye level. Above this, the *upper jangha* is richly sculpted, sometimes with religious scenes such as *Mahishasuramardini* (Durga as the Goddess of destruction) and *Jagannatha*, enshrined in a temple. Other sculptures show royal courts or simple family scenes. Along the top of the platform is the veranda, consisting of two mouldings separated by a narrow recess. Though severely damaged, these are decorated with friezes.

From the platform you will see the intricately carved eight-spoked wheels, each shown with its axle, a decorated hub and an axle pin. Floral motifs, creepers and the widely shown *chaitya* windows cover the stonework. Medallions with gods such as Surya and Vishnu, erotic figures, nobles and animals all add life to the structure.

The sanctum sanctorum

Although the *jagmohana* is now the dominant building of the complex, the scale of the sanctuary is still evident. The climb up the outer walls allows you to see at close quarters the remarkable chlorite statues of Surya, on the outer north, west and south walls. The large grey-green statues stand in sharp contrast with the surrounding yellowish-orange *khondalite* stone. Surya stands on a chariot drawn by his seven horses, lashed by Aruna, the charioteer, surrounded by two four-armed gods, a pot-bellied Brahma on the right and possibly Vishnu on the left. Below them are possibly four wives of Surya.

The sanctuary itself is currently inaccessible, awaiting a new stairway which has been in the pipeline since at least 2003. The main feature inside is the chlorite platform at the western end of the 10 m sq room intended for the presiding deity. This image from the pedestal was moved to the Jagannath Temple complex in Puri. The platform that remains is nonetheless outstanding; some carvings almost certainly show the King, the donor of the temple, accompanied by priests. The hollows on top of the platform's eastern edge resulted from the placing of pots over a long period.

The Colossi

Originally each of the three staircases to the porch was guarded by a pair of colossi – rampant lions on top of a crouching elephant to the east, decorated elephants to the north, and war horses to the south. The last two pairs have been remounted a short distance from their original sites. The lions have been put in front of the eastern steps up to the *Bhoga mandira* near the entrance.

Archaeological Museum

ⓘ *Sat-Thu 1000-1700, Rs 5, near Travellers' Lodge.* This museum has a small collection including many important pieces from the Sun Temple complex. Occasional lectures and film shows. Archaeological Survey publications for sale.

Orissa Mahanadi Delta

● Sleeping

Bhubaneswar *p177, map p178*

L-A Mayfair Lagoon, 8B Jaydev Vihar, Nayapalli, 5 km from centre, T0674-236 0101, mayfairlagoon@hotmail.com. Modern, low-level palace-style hotel with 63 attractive cottages set around lagoon, all facilities, very stylish, friendly efficient staff. Best of the 5-star hotels. Recommended.

AL-A The New Marrion, 6 Janpath, opposite Sri Ram Mandir, T0674-238 0850, www.the marrion.com. Spacious rooms and suites boasting a fresh, contemporary look, the latter with huge balconies overlooking large pool, Irish-themed sports bar, good food nearby (see Eating, page 192).

A Kalinga Ashok, Gautam Nagar, T0674-243 1055, www.theashokgroup.com. 32 clean rooms (4 **A** suites), all a/c, TV, hot bath, restaurant, coffee shop, bar, exchange.

A Sishmo, 86/A1 Gautam Nagar, T0674-243 3600, www.hotelsishmo.com. Well-run place but in need of freshening up, with 72 comfortable a/c rooms, some getting musty and threadbare, good facilities including health club and renovated pool, restaurant.

A Swosti, 103 Janpath, T0674-253 5771, www.swosti.com. 60 a/c rooms, restaurant, bar, overpriced compared to those out of town, good discounts when quiet.

A Swosti Plaza, P-1 Jaydev Vihar, 5 km from centre, T0674-230 0008, www.swosti.com. 147 a/c rooms in distinctive hotel based on Orissan temple design, fair-sized rooms though some suffer from road noise, 3 restaurants, Scottish theme bar, pool.

C-D Bicky Inn, 61 Janpath, T0674-253 6435. 26 small, but well-kept rooms, mostly a/c, Indian-style hotel, rooftop restaurant.

D-E Upasana, Cuttack Rd, behind Bhubaneswar, T0674-231 4144. 20 good clean rooms, some a/c, with all-important mosquito mesh on windows, away from main road so quieter, decent room service, friendly, 24-hr checkout. Recommended.

D-E Bhubaneswar, Cuttack Rd, T0674-231 3245. Generally cleanish and good value but staff could be more helpful. 42 rooms with bath, some a/c, some decrepit.

D-E Chandrakala, 74 Ashok Nagar, T0674-231 0944. Handy for station, 31 small, clean rooms with bath, TV, vegetarian room service.

E-F Panthanivas, Lewis Rd, T0674-243 2314, www.panthanivas.com. Clean, spacious rooms, hot bath, some a/c, restaurant, punitive 0800 check out, tourist office.

E Ekamra, Kalpana Square, T0674-231 1732. Simple, grubby rooms, though clean linen, cheap singles, restaurant, internet café below. Mainly used by Indian workers.

E-F Lingaraj, Old Station Bazar, T0674-231 3565. Basic clean rooms, dorm.

Udayagiri and Khandagiri caves
p182, map 183

D-E Cave View Resort, T0674-247 2288. 5 rooms.

Puri *p185, map p185*

Avoid arriving at your hotel by rickshaw as commission will be added to the room rate. Instead, get down nearby and walk. Most backpackers stay in hotels on CT Rd towards the fishing village at the eastern end. Domestic visitors prefer the seaside resorts along Marine Drive. Most check out at 0800 and several have a 2200 curfew. Check before staying out late. Top hotels will arrange pick-up from the station.

A Hans Coco Palms, Swargdwar, off New Marine Drive, T06752-230038, www.hans hotels.com. 40 good sea-facing a/c rooms with balconies/terraces, palm-filled restaurant, pleasant garden, good pool, friendly staff, knowledgeable manager, book ahead in season. Recommended.

A Mayfair Beach Resort, CT Rd, T06752-227800, mayfair1@sancharnet.in. Very well run, 34 well-furnished a/c cottages and rooms, some with sea view, rampant tropical garden, good pool (residents only), clean section of beach, decent restaurants, friendly staff. Recommended.

A Toshali Sands, Konark Marine Drive (8 km), T06752-250571, www.toshalisands. Com. 104 rooms (mostly suites) in cottages and villas set in attractive and extensive gardens (butterflies' paradise), all very comfortable, 2 km to very quiet beach, sports facilities though pool could be cleaner, pricey restaurant with no choice nearby.

B Pearl Beach Club, Sipasurabali, 5 km west of Marine Parade by rough sandy track, T06752-230109. Large modern resort, first of several destined to appear in this area.

224 comfortable a/c rooms with all facilities, boat service to cross river to beach.

B-C Asian Inn Beach Resort, New Marine Drive, T06752-231307. New hotel, 31 rooms, some a/c and suites, smallish but clean and comfortable, TV, good restaurant, well run.

C-D Nilachal Ashok (ITDC), next to Raj Bhavan, VIP Rd, T06752-223639, www.the ashokgroup.com. 34 clean, good-sized a/c rooms, TV, some with sea view, beach access via scrubby back garden.

C-E Arya Palace, CT Rd, T06752-232688, neeraj21jain@indiatimes.com. 32 rooms (some a/c) in new hotel, clean and airy, hot bath, TV, generous discounts when quiet.

C-E Samudra, CT Rd, T06752-222705, hsamudra@yahoo.co.in. 52 decent clean rooms, all with breezy sea-facing balconies, better at front on higher floors with sea view, TV, restaurant, friendly staff.

C-E Vijoya International, CT Rd, T06752-222702, hotelvijoya@rediffmail.com. 44 clean but dark rooms, half a/c, large garden, quiet, friendly staff, pool and health club.

D-E Shankar International, CT Rd, T06752-222696. Indian-style hotel set around lawn, 30 rooms with beach views, plus 6 cottages, small but clean, restaurant.

D-F Panthanivas (OTDC), CT Rd, T06752-222740, www.panthanivas.com. 48 rooms including 3 **C** suites, a few a/c, rooms in old block run down, better in newer block, tour booking, pleasant garden with beach access.

E BNR, CT Rd, T06752-222063, bnrhotel@ hotmail.com. Revamped, 34 large, clean rooms, some a/c, first floor better with wide verandas overlooking sea, siestas encouraged (quiet hours 1400-1600), an old-world curiosity, claim to serve the best continental food, billiards, croquet.

E Gandhara, CT Rd, T06752-224117, www.hotelgandhara.com. Clean, comfortable rooms, some a/c, friendly, good value, cheap dorms, restaurant, popular.

E-F Kasi's Castle, CT Rd, T06752-224522. 9 spotless rooms with attached bath in friendly family house, good choice but avoid arriving by rickshaw (commission demanded).

E-F Puri, Marine Parade, T06752-222114, www.purihotelindia.com. Huge hotel on seafront with 127 rooms, including 9- and 10-bed rooms. Popular Indian family hotel so quieter during the week, wide choice, clean, some a/c, vegetarian restaurant.

E-G Holiday House, CT Rd, T06752-223782, F224363. 45 reasonable, good-sized clean rooms, better sea facing (prices rise with altitude!), restaurant.

E-G Lotus, CT Rd, T06752-223852. Quite clean, 9 simple rooms (mostly **G**), good restaurant (**Harry's Café**, see page 192).

E-G Love & Life, CT Rd, T06752-224433, loveandlife@hotmail.com. Good value rooms in 3 storey, airy building with cottages at rear, theoretical hot water, nets, dorm, very clean, good choice.

E-G Sun Row Cottage, CT Rd, T06752-223259. Set around small, colourful garden, 10 simple rooms in double cottages restaurant, long-stay discounts.

E-G Z, CT Rd, T06752-222554, www.zhotel india.com. 12 spacious rooms plus dorm in old mansion, best sea facing, terrace, some wirh clean shared bath, good food, friendly, solar powered, pleasant garden, TV/games room, popular. Recommended, book ahead.

F-G Derby, CT Rd, T06752-223961. Popular, 10 sea-facing rooms with bath, garden.

G Pink House, CT Rd, T06752-222253. 15 rooms, some 3-5 bedded, directly on beach, friendly, popular with backpackers, beach shack restaurant (suspect hygiene).

G Santana, CT Rd, at the end of the fishing village, T06752-223491. Simple rooms in friendly, secure hotel, popular with Japanese visitors.

G Youth Hostel, CT Rd, T06752-222424. Separate, though somewhat dishevelled male and female dorms, some 2-3 bedded, camping, good Indian meals.

Konark *p187, map p188*

E-F Yatri Nivas, T06758-236820. 38 good value, clean rooms with nets, some 4-bedded, 8 a/c with geyser and TV, pleasant gardens, restaurant, dorm beds in open-air auditorium except during festival, free cultural programme on weekend evenings during season.

F-G Panthanivas (OTDC), opposite temple, T06758-236831. Smaller rooms a bit dark, 11 clean rooms with nets, 2 a/c with hot bath, separate **Geetanjali** restaurant.

G Labanya Lodge, away from temple, T06758-236824, labanyalodge1@rediffmail .com. Most popular of the budget lodges. 13 musty rooms, mostly with attached bath, cycle hire, travel.

Orissa Mahanadi Delta Listings

🍴 Eating

Bhubaneswar *p177, map p178*

🍴🍴🍴 **Mayfair Lagoon**, pleasant restaurants include outdoor truck stop-style. Great Western fast food and sweets.

🍴🍴🍴 **Swosti**. Varied menu. Dimly lit, generous portions, local specialities to advance order.

🍴🍴 **Banjara**, Station Square. Good Indian for lunch and dinner.

🍴🍴 **Hare Krishna**, Lalchand Complex, Janpath, T0674-2503188. Strict vegetarian. Upstairs, a/c, smart, tasty food.

🍴🍴 **Panthanivas**, local specialities, ask ahead.

🍴 **Deep Down South**, in New Marrion Hotel complex (see page 190). An excellent, almost trendy choice for unusual South Indian: try tomato and chilly sponge dosa, or mint and dhania gunpowder dosa. Good lassis too.

🍴 **New Ganguram Sweets**, various locations. Delicious Indian sweets and snacks.

🍴 **Tulsi**, Hotel Pushpak Complex, Kalpana Square. Clean and simple café serving excellent Orissan vegetarian food and sweets, and good fresh juices.

🍴 **Venus Inn**, 217 Bapuji Nagar (2nd floor). Good South Indian vegetarian.

Puri *p185, map p185*

Puri's signature dish is the *mahaprasad* of rice, dahl, vegetables and sweet prepared by 400 cooks at the Jagannath Temple. It can be bought at the Anand Bazaar in the temple complex. There is an abundance of fresh fish; ensure all is fresh and thoroughly cooked. Hotels expect advance notice for non-residents.

🍴🍴 **Chung Wah**, Hotel Lee Garden, VIP Rd. Good Chinese.

🍴🍴 **Wild Grass**, VIP Rd. Pleasant open-air restaurant with rustic theme. Good North Indian vegetarian and non-vegetarian, some Orissan specialities, friendly. Recommended.

🍴 **Harry's Café**, CT Rd. Pure vegetarian (no onion or garlic) South Indian. Good *thalis and snacks*.

🍴 **Peace**, CT Rd. Friendly garden café.

Konark *p187, map p188*

Plenty of choice, with *thalis and snacks*.

🍴 **Sun Temple Hotel**. Good choice among the many basic eating places lining the road opposite the temple entrance. Friendly service, everything cooked fresh, and the breakfast parathas are fantastic.

🎭 Entertainment

Bhubaneswar *p177, map p178*

Programmes of Odissi and folk dances and folk drama are staged regularly and are worth seeking out. **Rabindra Mandap**, near GPO and **Suchana Bhavan** near Bus Stand.

Puri *p185, map p185*

Top hotels and resorts have bars. Classical *Odissi* dance, folk dances and drama which are always performed for festivals are also staged from time to time and are worth seeking out.

🎉 Festivals and events

Bhubaneswar *p177, map p178*

End-Jan: Tribal Fair attended by groups from different regions – excellent performances and crafts exhibitions.

Mar/Apr: Asokashtami, the Lingaraja Car Festival. The image of Siva is drawn on a chariot from the Lingaraja Temple to visit the Ramesvara Temple for 4 days.

Puri *p185, map p185*

Mid-Apr: 21-day Chandan Yatra coincides with the Hindu New Year when images of Jagannath, his brother and sister are taken out in boats on the Narendra Tank. *Chandan* is the sandal paste used to anoint the deities. **Snana Yatra**, which follows, marks the ritual bathing of the deities on a special barge. For 15 days the gods are kept out of sight, when worshippers may only pray before *pattachitras* (paintings). Every few years new images of the deities are carved from specially selected trees and the old ones are secretly buried by the temple priests.

Jun/Jul: Rath Yatra, see box on page 186.

Nov: Beach Festival, 1 week of cultural shows, crafts and food stalls.

Konark *p187, map p188*

Feb: Honouring the Sun god; pilgrims flock here from evening to sunrise.

1-5 Dec: Classical dance festival at the open-air auditorium opposite *Yatri Nivas*.

🛍 Shopping

Bhubaneswar *p177, map p178*

Many shops close on Thu and close for lunch. Market Building shops have fixed prices.

Khadi Gramodoyag Bhavan, Kalpana Sq. Hand-spun cotton garments.
Orissa State Handloom (West Market) is recommended for saris and handloom fabrics.
Utkalika (East Tower) sells Orissa handloom and handicrafts.

Puri *p185, map p185*
Visit the vast **bazar** around the Jagannath Temple, along Bada Danda and Swargadwara, but you have to bargain. Pathuria Sahi is the stone carvers' quarter and Raghurajpur (12 km) produces *pattachitras* and etchings on palm leaf, see page 175. See also page 176.

Books
Loknath, CT Rd. Second-hand, sale/ exchange, library (Rs 7 per day), postcards.

Handicrafts
Stone carvings, papier-mâché masks, painted wood figures, paintings, appliqué, hornwork all make good buys.
Akbar, CT Rd. Cheap painted cards.
Odissi, Dolamandap Sahi. Handlooms.
Sudarshan, Station Rd. Stone carving, where you can also watch masons at work carving out images of deities.
Sun Crafts, Tinikonia Bagicha.
Utkalika and **Crafts Complex**, Mochi Sahi Sq.
Weavers' Co-op Society, Grand Rd. Handlooms.

▲ Activities and tours

Bhubaneswar *p177, map p178*
OTDC: by 'luxury' coach from Transport Unit, behind *Panthanivas*, T0674-243 1515. Ask about special tours to Chilika Lake. They will also pick up/drop off at hotels. Daily tours to Nandankanan, Khandagiri, Udaigiri, Dhauli and **museum** with guide. Tue-Sun 0900-1730, Rs 130 (Rs 180 a/c). **Pipli, Konark** and **Puri**. 0900-1800, Rs 150/180. **Puri** and **Satapada**. 0830-1800, Rs 175. **Barkul** and **Narayani**. 0830-1800, Rs 175. **OTDC** and private operators have a/c and non a/c cars for full and half day sightseeing. A round trip by car visiting Konark and Puri from Bhubaneswar takes 6-8 hrs. Allow at least 1 hr for Konark.
Discover Tours, 463 Lewis Rd, T0674-2430477, www.orissadiscover.com. For special interest tours (cultural, treks, wildlife parks, tribal and textile villages), from US$25

per day per person sharing a twin room. Sarat Acharya and Bijaya Pattnaik are excellent guides and have won awards from the Regional Tourist Board. Tours organized even at short notice, though ask ahead for full service. Highly recommended.
Swosti Travels, 103 Janpath, T0674-253 5773, www.swosti.com. Good – but expensive – specialist tours (tribal, architectural, wildlife), though not the most welcoming.

Puri *p185, map p185*
Tourist Office has a list of government-approved tour companies. Almost every hotel on CT Rd has a travel office.
Heritage Tours, Mayfair Beach Resort, T06752-223656, is reliable and offers a good benchmark for comparing prices.
OTDC, T06752-223526, to Konark, Dhauli, Bhubaneswar, Khandagiri, Udayagiri and Nandankanan Zoo. It is a long day. 0630-1900, Rs 130 non a/c, Rs 160 a/c. Chilika Lake (Satapada), 0630-1930, Rs 110. Private operators offer similar tours at cheaper rates, including more leisurely Konark-only tours and specialized cultural trips.

◉ Transport

Bhubaneswar *p177, map p178*
Air
Airport 4 km. Taxi transfer, Rs 100 through OTDC. From airport Rs 100-150. **Indian Airlines**, Rajpath, T0674-253 0533, airport, T253 4472, www.indian-airlines.nic.in. Daily to **Delhi, Kolkata, Chennai**, Mumbai and **Bengaluru (Bangalore)**. Air Sahara, T0674-253 5007, airport T0674-253 5729, www.air sahara.net. Daily to **Kolkata** and **Hyderabad**, 3 flights weekly to **Mumbai**. Air Deccan, daily to **Kolkata**, 4 times a week to **Raipur**.

Bus
Local City buses are cheap and cover major routes but avoid evening rush hour.
Long distance New Bus Stand is at Baramunda on the NH5 (6 km from centre) where there are auto-rickshaws for transfer. Enquiries T0674-235 4695. Some long-distance buses go through the city first, stopping at the Old Bus Stand, off Rajpath. Regular buses to **Puri** and **Konark** (both 1½-3 hrs) pick up passengers from outside the museum on Lewis Rd. Most are quite

full though local people will often offer their seats to foreigners. Buses usually thin out at Pipli. Buses to **Cuttack** (1 hr) stop on the opposite side of the road.

Taxi
Tourist taxis, unmetered. OTDC (Transport), T0674-243 1515, cars Rs 600, a/c, Rs 800, for 8 hrs or 80 km. Out-of-town rates are higher.

Train
Reservations, T0674-253 2350; enquiries, T0674-253 2233. Computerized booking hall is in separate building opposite the station. Auto- and cycle-rickshaws for transfer. **Chennai**: *Coromandal Exp 2841*, 2140, 21 hrs; *Howrah Chennai Mail 2603*, 0643, 25½ hrs. **Kolkata (H)**: *Dhauli Exp 2822*, 1315, 7 hrs; *Coromandal Exp 2842*, 0500, 7½ hrs; *Falaknuma Exp 2704*, 1100, 8½ hrs; *Chennai Howrah Mail 2604*, 2045, 9 hrs; *Jagannath Exp 8410*, 0015, 8 hrs; *East Coast Exp 8646*, 0735, 10½ hrs. **Mumbai (CST)**: *Konark Exp 1020*, 1515, 38½ hrs. **Secunderabad**: *Falaknuma Exp 2703*, 1410, 20½ hrs; *Konark Exp 1020*, 1515, 21 hrs; *East Coast Exp 8645*, 1940, 24 hrs; *Visakha Exp 7015*, 0825, 25 hrs. **New Delhi**: *Purushottam Exp 2801*, 2330, 30 hrs, via **Mughal Sarai (Varanasi)**.

Puri *p185, map p185*
Air
Bhubaneswar, 60 km, is the nearest airport. Prepaid taxi to Puri Rs 600, 1-1½ hrs.

Bicycle and motorcycle
Hiring a bike or a motorbike is a good option for exploring the coast. There are several outlets on CT Rd. Cycles costs Rs 20-30 per day. Motorbikes Rs 250-300 per day.

Bus
The huge, open bus stand on Grand Road runs regular buses to **Bhubaneswar** and **Konark**. Minibuses are faster. There are also services to **Cuttack, Visakhapatnam** and **Kolkata**. Enquiries, T06752-224461.

Rickshaw
Cycle-rickshaws available all over town. Bus Stand to CT Rd, Rs 20; railway station Rs 10. To prevent commission being added to room price, ask to be dropped off at BNR and walk along CT Rd to your hotel.

Taxi
Tourist taxis from large hotels, CT Rd agencies, and taxi stand, T06752-222161; Rs 700 per 8 hrs or 80 km. To Bhubaneswar around Rs 550.

Train
Enquiry, T131. **Kolkata (H)**: *Jagannath Exp 8410*, 2230, 11½ hrs. **New Delhi**: *Purushottam Exp 2801*, 2145, 32½ hrs. **Guwahati (H)**: *Guwahati Exp 5639*, 1400 (Sat only), 32 hrs via **New Jalpaiguri**, 24 hrs.

Konark *p187, map p188*
OTDC 'luxury' coach or ordinary, very crowded bus from Puri (1½ hrs) and Bhubaneswar (up to 3 hrs). Prepaid taxi from Bhubaneswar airport costs Rs 600.

❶ Directory

Bhubaneswar *p177, map p178*
Banks State Bank of India, Rajpath, by Police Station. Exchange on 1st floor, cash and TCs (closed Sun). ICICI, near Shree Raj Talkies, Janpath, and Thomas Cook, 130 Ashok Nagar, Janpath, for exchange. Many ATMs on Janpath and around Kalpana Sq. **Hospital** Capital Hospital, Unit 6, T0674-240 1983. **Internet** At Ekamra Hotel and on Kalpana Sq. **Post** GPO, Sachivalaya Marg. **Tourist offices** Orissa, Jayadev Marg, behind Panthanivas, T0674-243 1299. Mon-Sat 1030-1700. Airport counter, T0674-253 4006. Rly station counter, T0674-253 0715. **Govt of India**, B-21, BJB Nagar, T0674-243 2203. **Useful addresses** Foreigners' Registration Office, Sahid Nagar, T0674-254 0555.

Puri *p185, map p185*
Banks Allahabad Bank, Temple Rd is best for changing cash. Other exchanges on CT Rd. Several ATMs on Grand Rd and CT Rd. **Hospital** District HQ Hospital, T06752-222062. TB Hospital, Red Cross Rd, T06752-222094. **Internet** Nanako, near Sun Row Cottage on CT Rd. **Post** GPO on Kutchery Rd. PCOs and internet on CT Rd. **Tourist office** Orissa, Station Rd, T06752-222664, Mon-Sat 1000-1700, with a museum above. Tourist counter, railway station, T06752-223536.

Konark *p187, map p188*
Post Sub Post Office, near Panthanivas. **Tourist office** Yatri Nivas, T/F06758-236821.

The Northeast

It is possible to visit several places of historic and religious interest in the north of Orissa in three to seven days, as well as to see outstandingly beautiful scenery and the Similipal National Park. Some of the accommodation is excellent value (particularly at Chandipur), though it is very basic. ▸▸ *For Sleeping, Eating and other listings, see pages 199-201.*

Cuttack 🛏️🍴🛍️🏛️⛰️🚌🎭 ▸▸ *pp199-201. Colour map 3, grid A6.*

→ *Phone code: 0671. Population: 535,100.*

Cuttack occupies an important strategic position in relation to the network of canals in the region. Situated at the head of the Mahanadi delta and surrounded by the great river and its tributary the Kathjuri, the town is almost an island, its crowded streets and bazars clustered up towards its western end.

Cuttack is one of Orissa's oldest cities and its medieval capital. It was founded by Nrupat Kesari (ruled 920-935). It remained the administrative centre until the end of the British Raj and was the state capital until 1956. The ancient **stone embankment** to the south was built in the 11th century by the Kesari ruler to protect the town from flooding by the Kathjuri River. It still stands as a reminder of the engineering skills practised 900 years ago. The **Qadam-i-Rasul** (Kadam Rasul) in the centre of the old city, visited as a

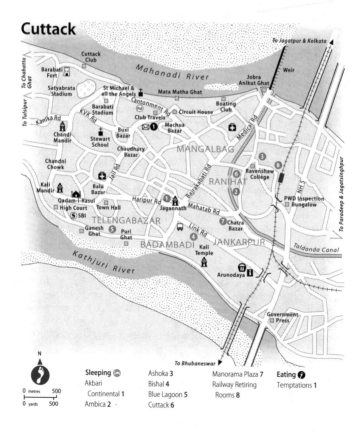

Cuttack

Sleeping 🛏️
Akbari
Continental **1**
Ambica **2**
Ashoka **3**
Bishal **4**
Blue Lagoon **5**
Cuttack **6**
Manorama Plaza **7**
Railway Retiring
Rooms **8**

Eating 🍴
Temptations **1**

0 metres 500
0 yards 500

To Bhubaneswar

Orissa The Northeast

shrine by Muslims and Hindus, has three 18th-century mosques with beautiful domes and a music gallery. The shrines contain relics of the Prophet Mohammad; the Prophet's footprint is carved on a circular stone. The famous silver filigree shops are in Balu Bazar.

To the northwest the blue granite 13th-century **Barabati Fort** is being excavated by the Archaeological Survey. Its wide moat and gateway remain but the nine-storeyed palace has disappeared. Probably built by a Ganga ruler, it was in Marhatta hands when it was taken by the British in 1803. Close to the fort is the vast **Barabati Stadium** where major sporting and cultural events are held. The **Church of St Michael and all the Angels** (CNI) by the river, typical of Raj-style church buildings, is worth a visit.

Ratnagiri, Udayagiri and Lalitgiri ⬤⬤ » *pp199-201.*
Colour map 3, grid A6.

The beautiful hills and rice growing lands are home to remarkable Buddhist remains of the Vajrayana sect, set in an idyllic situation surrounded by green fields. The excavations at the three sites have revealed Buddhist structures, both stupas and monasteries, as well as sculptures and Buddha images.

Ins and outs
Getting there and around The sites can all be visited in a day from Cuttack or Bhubaneswar by car. If you go by bus you will need to stay overnight. Rickshaws can be hired at Patharajpur. » *See Transport, page 200, for further details.*

Ratnagiri → *70 km from Cuttack, 115 km from Bhubaneswar .*
ⓘ *Museums, Sat-Thu 1000-1700, foreigners US$2.*
Ratnagiri, the site of the 'Jewel Hill', on the bank of River Keluo, has produced the best finds. The extensive remains show excellent sculptural skill combining different coloured stones, from blue-green chlorite to the purple-red garnets encrusted in brownish silver khondalite. The finds include three monasteries (two quadrangular), eight temples and several stupas believed to date from the seventh-century. The largest monastery (No 1) is 55 m sq with a surrounding veranda with 60 pillars built around a courtyard entered through a carved gateway. At one end a shrine has a khondalite Buddha image and remnants of about 24 cells for monks which were built of brick but had stone door frames. Look for the intricate carving on the doorway of the back porch wall: a dancer stamping her feet; a royal lady with her arm around a maid; a woman meditating. The seventh-century University of *Pushpagiri* may have flourished here; Hiuen Tsang, the Chinese traveller, after his visit in AD 639 described it as one of Orissa's two Buddhist centres of learning. Four galleries display fine sculptural figures dating from the ninth to the 10th centuries, terracotta and ivory objects, inscribed copper plates and miniature bronzes produced by the lost-wax process.

Udayagiri
ⓘ *10 km south of Ratnagiri, foreigners US$2.*
Excavations by the Archaeological Department (in progress in mid 2001) have unearthed better preserved carvings including the door jambs to the sanctum. The monastery, within a large compound, has 18 cells with a veranda arranged around a courtyard. The 3 m Lokesvar Buddha image here has an eighth-century inscription on it. Further up the hill, fragments of sculpture have been excavated among the ruins.

Lalitgiri
ⓘ *Foreigners US$2.*
The site about 3 km south of Bandareswar village was first excavated by the ASI in 1985. Large architectural remains including a 20 m high apsidal temple have been found

together with sculptures and decorated door jambs. A stone platform with inscriptions dates this site closer to the second century although Kushana Brahmi inscriptions on an underlying brick stupa suggest Buddhist occupation around the first century BC. Three caskets were also found, two of which contained stone, silver and gold caskets with preserved relics inside. The caretaker will open the small museum. There is a stone-carvers' village at the base of Lalitgiri which traces its connections back to ancient times and produces excellent pieces of sculpture.

The coastal towns 🚇🚌🛈 ⇥ *pp199-201.*

Paradeep → *94 km from Cuttack on the NH5A.*
Paradeep is a port at the mouth of the Mahanadi River. Some 2500 years ago Orissan sailors regularly set sail for Indonesia and mainland Southeast Asia from this point. Thousands of giant Pacific Ridley turtles migrate from as far afield as South America yearly to lay their eggs but now many face their death as they approach the shore, see box page 198. Visitors today find they can't escape industrial pollution even here – "a layer of black dust settles on every surface in no time". There are a few overnight options. Regular buses arrive from Cuttack and Bhubaneswar.

Baleshwar
Northeast from Bhubaneswar, this medieval maritime trading port was first established by the British in 1642 with subsequent competition from the French who called it *Farasidinga* and the Dutch *Dinamardinga*. Ruins of **Dutch tombs** can still be seen and traces of **canals**, up which ocean-going ships were hauled inland. The Khirachora Gopinath Temple is at Remuna (9 km) and Panchalingesvar Temple, 30 km away.

Chandipur
On the coast 16 km from Balashwar, Chandipur has one of Orissa's finest beaches. The tide recedes 5 km daily and the dunes and casuarina groves make it particularly attractive and a pleasant, quiet stopping place. When the tide is in scores of fisherfolk trawl for small fish along the coast. About 3 km north of *Panthanivas* is the fishing harbour at Balarama Gadi where fresh fish can be bought daily. The occasional explosions that can be heard come from the missile testing site nearby, which is on the road to Baleshwar.

Mayurbhanj District 🚇🚌🛈 ⇥ *pp199-201.*

The district is thickly forested with hills, waterfalls and streams and is home to abundant wildlife, which can best be seen at Similipal National Park. There are prehistoric sites at Kuchai and Kuliana. The historic sites are Khiching, Baripada and Haripur, where the Bhanja rulers have left their mark.

The area produces excellent tussar silk, carvings in multi-coloured translucent serpentine stone (from Khiching) and tribal metal casting of toys and cult images. The tribal people have enriched the culture of the district particularly with their traditional dances. Accommodation throughout the district is very basic.

Haripur → *16 km southeast of Baripada.*
Haripur was founded by Maharaja Harihar in 1400 as the capital of the Bhanja Dynasty. A later king built the magnificent **Rasikaraya Temple** which, though now in ruins, is a unique example of a brick-built Orissan temple. The area is still fascinating as it has several more historic buildings nearby. The ruins of Ranihamsapur, the inner apartment of the queen, is to the north of the courtyard while the remains of the Durbar Hall with its

Turtles in peril

Virtually every species of mangrove is found in the the Bhitarkanika Wildlife Sanctuary, north of Paradeep, but their swamps are better known for their estuarine crocodiles, water monitors, cobras and above all Olive Ridley turtles (*Lepidochelys olivacea*), which have mysteriously arrived each year in vast numbers to lay eggs on a 10 km stretch of Gahirmatha beach.

Sea turtles are believed to return to nest where they hatched so the cycle continues. They arrive at night, for a fortnight around the full moon from October to May, with a spectacular arribadas (from the Portuguese,

meaning 'the coming') in February, when record numbers find their way from the Indian Ocean or from Australia, via the Pacific. They lay their eggs in nests excavated in the sand, a safe distance above the waterline and shed a salty 'tear' afterwards. The eggs hatch about two months later, the incubation temperature deciding the sex; clutches are male around 24-26°C and female around 30-32°C, mixed when temperatures are in between.

The turtles compete for food with the fishermen and thousands have met their death when trapped by their nets.

beautiful sculptured stone columns and arches is to the east. The brick **Radhamohan Temple** and 14th-century **Jagannath Temple** are interesting architecturally although the deities were moved and are now worshipped nearby in **Pratapapur**.

Baripada

The district headquarters has a **museum** ⓘ *Tue-Sun 0700-1200 summer, 1000-1700 winter, closed holidays*, to the east of town with a small collection of stone sculpture, coins, seals, terracottas and inscriptions. **Chhau dance festival**, known as **Chaitra Parba**, is held in mid-April; the **Rath Yatra** in July is unique because the chariot carrying *Subhadra* is drawn by women.

Similipal National Park → *Colour map 3, grid A6.*

ⓘ *Foreigners Rs 100 per day, Indians Rs 10; vehicle charge, Rs 100; trekking/nature trail, Rs 100 (Indians Rs 20); camera fee, amateur Rs 100 for 3 days, professional Rs 400 per camera per day. Video cameras, Rs 1000 per day, professional Rs 10,000. Malaria prophylaxis is strongly recommended. Entry is from Pithabata, near Baripada (NH5), or Jashipur (NH6). Entry permits from the Range Officer, Pithabata Check Gate or the Assistant Conservator of Forests, Khairi, Jashipur, T06797-232474. Some tour operators in Bhubaneswar can make all the arrangements (eg Discover Tours) but need 4 weeks' notice – otherwise try for a permit on the day with a local agent (try Ambika in Baripada, see Sleeping). Entry for day visitors is 0600-1200, those with reservations 0600-1400. All must leave before sunset. Best time to visit: Nov to Feb (park open 1 Nov-15 Jun); May to Jun can be very hot. Temperature, 45-5°C. Rainfall, 2000 mm.*

Similipal is Orissa's principal wildlife sanctuary covering 2,750 sq km at the heart of which is one of the country's earliest tiger reserves. The area has majestic sal forests interspersed with rosewood and flowering trees, as well as broad expanses of grass-land, waterfalls, gorges and valleys. Spend two to three days to make a visit worthwhile.

The 42 species of animals include tiger (99), elephant (449), leopard (119), wolf, chital, sambar, deer, gaur and flying squirrel. There are over 230 species of birds including mynahs, parakeet and peacocks. To view the park's inhabitants, open jeeps or Tata Sumos (more comfortable, though enclosed) are the usual choice of vehicle inside the park (Rs 1200-1500 for up to five passengers). Jeep hire can be arranged through the Forest Office, Jashipur, Baripada Tourist Office or **Ambika** in

Baripada (see Sleeping, page 200) which can also help to arrange accommodation. However, logging disturbance and dense vegetation make viewing difficult and is further hindered by visitors who ignore the signs asking for silence, and there is an increasing problem of litter in the park. Visitors are allowed to go to the waterfalls, the **Chahala woodland** and **Nawana valley,** in the core area, on the dedicated forest road. The **Barehipani waterfall,** with a drop of 400 m, and the **Joranda Falls,** 150 m, are both very impressive as are the **Bachhurichara grassland** where you might see a herd of elephants and the 1158 m peak of Meghasani. However, most of the larger wildlife prefer to remain further inside the core area which does not allow visitors.

Khiching → 20 km west of Joshipur along the NH6.

The capital of the **Bhanja** rulers in the 10th to the 11th century, a visit to Khiching can be combined with an excursion to Similipal from Chandipur (see above). The local deity **Kichakesvari**, once the family goddess of the Mayurbhanj royal family, has a unique temple built entirely of chlorite slabs. The reconstructed 20th-century temple, which has fine carvings, is believed to have used the traditional temple building skills which date back to the eighth century. Nearby there are a number of other temples built in the Kalinga style, some of which are still in use.

● Sleeping

Cuttack p195, map p195
C-E Akbari Continental, Haripur Rd, Dolmundai, T0671-242 3251. A bit tatty, 60 rooms, central a/c, hot bath with tubs, balconies view of garden obscured by ugly extension, inefficient reception.
D-E Blue Lagoon, Ring Rd, near Puri Ghat, T0671-263 1884. Central a/c, cramped singles, river views, overpowering blue decor, decent restaurant and fast food corner, overly helpful staff, newish but showing signs of wear, plush in design though not in execution.
D-G Ashoka, Ice Factory Rd, College Square, T0671-264 7509. Handy for trains, 50 clean rooms, half a/c with bath, chaotic reception but rooms OK. Restaurant, taxi service.
E-G Ambica, Pilgrim Rd, College Sq, T0671-261 0137, hotelambica@yahoo.com. Range of rooms from a/c to cheap singles with shared bath, clean and simple, friendly manager, vegetarian restaurant, close to railway.
F-G Bishal, Link Rd, Badambadi, T0671-231 0993. Handy for bus station but suffers from road noise, 15 rooms (4 a/c), quite comfortable and clean, hot bath, TV.
F-G Manorama Plaza, Mahatab Rd, T0671-233 1681. Most of the 54 clean, reasonable though small rooms have a/c. Restaurant, travel desk, bizarre birdsong doorbells.
G Railway Retiring Rooms. 4 rooms (1 a/c), cheap dorm.
G Cuttack, College Rd, T0671-261 0766. Basic, but serviceable, some with bath.

Ratnagiri, Udayagiri and Lalitgiri p196
G Panthasala, Patharajpur, Cuttack, T0671-231 2225. Simple rooms, caretaker may provide a meal with advance notice.

Baleshwar p197
C-E Torrento, Januganj, 4 km from centre near NH5, T06782-263481. Some a/c in the 28 comfortable rooms, good restaurant, exchange, pool and health club.
E-G Swarnachuda, Sahadev Khunta (close to bus stand), T06782-262657. Wide range of rooms with bath, some a/c, restaurant/bar.
G Railway Retiring Rooms. A/c and non a/c rooms, dorm (Rs 30).

Chandipur p197
Other hotels on the main road are reluctant to accept foreigners.
E-F Panthanivas (OTDC), on beach, T06782-270051, www.pathanivas.com. 34 rooms, a few a/c, dorm (Rs 70), nets, ISD/internet, decent food, helpful staff, newer block better, ample mosquitoes and cockroaches in old block nearer beach. Tours including Similipal (minimum 10 people). 0800 checkout.
E-F Shubnam, T06782-270025. With 29 rooms (6 a/c), clean, friendly, nets, better maintained than Panthanivas.
F Chandipur, T06782 270030. Small, simple rooms with attached bath, clean linen, nets.

E-G **Sibapriya**, Traffic Square, T06792-255138. 20 rooms, "best in town" but non a/c rooms grubby, a/c better, restaurant.

F-G **Ambika**, Roxy Rd, T06792-252557. 10 reasonably clean rooms, some a/c, friendly and helpful staff, decent restaurant, tour of Similipal arranged, good value.

F-G **Mahapatra**, opposite Bus Stand, T06792-255226. Bit grubby, 8 simple rooms, some a/c, balconies overlook the bus stand.

G **Ganesh Bhavan**, Main Market, T06792-252784. Some of the 32 basic rooms have bath.

Similipal National Park *p198*

D **Camp Polpola Retreat**, inside the park, can be booked through Pugmarks, 10 Meher Ali Rd, Kolkata, T033-287 3307, who organizes tours to Simlipal.

E **Forest Rest Houses**, the booking process is complicated. All food provisions should be taken with you, but the caretaker at each will help you to cook a meal. Most rooms have several beds and cost around Rs 200-400 per head for foreigners if full, otherwise it can work out quite expensive. Maximum stay is 3 nights. Those at **Chahala** (an old hunting lodge, 35 km from Jashipur), **Nomana** (60 km), **Joranda** (72 km) and **Barehpani** (with view of waterfall, 52 km) must be booked through Field Director, Similipal Tiger Reserve Office, PO Bhanjpur, Baripada, 757002 Orissa, T06792-252593, F256705. Write enclosing an SAE self-addressed envelope (minimum 30 days, maximum 60 days before proposed date of stay) and include names of group members, sex, age, nationality, visa/ passport details. Rest Houses at **Badampahar** (16 km from Jashipur), **Gudgudia** (25 km), and **Jamuani** (25 km), though not in the core area, are easier to reserve, in person, up to 10 days in advance from DFO, Karanjia, Jashipur, T06796-220226, T251613. Reservation counter open 1000-1330 every day.

E-F **Aranyanivas** (OTDC), at Lulung (3 km from Pithabata Gate), reserve at Baripada Tourist Office, T06792-252710, or visit www.panthanivas.com. 8 double rooms, 2 dorms with 12 beds each, only restaurant inside park, completely run on solar power.

Panthasala, outside the park area, 35 km from Baripada towards Jashipur, has 4 doubles. Reservations as for Aranyanivas.

Khiching *p199*

Inspection Bungalow, contact Executive Engineer, PO Baripada.

Revenue Rest Shed, PO Khiching, contact District Magistrate, PO Baripada.

🍴 Eating

Cuttack *p195, map p195*

Outside the better hotels there are few decent eateries. In the evenings street stalls set up around Buxi Bazar for cheap bites.

Temptations, near Buxi Bazar, has the best ice creams in town, reasonable pizzas and snacks.

🎭 Entertainment

Cuttack *p195, map p195*

You can try a makeshift pedalo on the Mahanadi River. **Mahanadi Boating Club** (2 men, a few chairs and an umbrella), on the Ring Rd, charges Rs 15 per person per 30 minutes. Also power boat at Rs 550 per hr.

🛍 Shopping

Cuttack *p195, map p195*

Utkalika, Jail Rd, has a very good selection of textiles and handicrafts including horn and brass objects and jewellery. The famous silver filigree shops are in Nayasarak and Balu Bazar.

⛰ Activities and tours

Cuttack *p195, map p195*

Club Travels, Mani Sahu Chowk, Buxi Bazar, T0671-230 4999.

🚌 Transport

Cuttack *p195, map p195*

Bus Long-distance buses stop at the bus stand in Link Rd. Services to all points in Orissa from the main bus stand in Badambari. Regular services to **Bhubaneswar**. Also state transport to major towns in **Andhra Pradesh**, **Chhattisgarh**, **Madhya Pradesh** and **West Bengal** (including Kolkata).

Taxi At the railway station and some hotels. Full day trip to **Lalitgiri**, **Ratnagiri** and **Udayagiri** (excluding entrance fees), Rs 600-800, depending on bargaining skills.

Train

East of town, Enquiries T131. **Bhubaneswar** and **Puri**: Several express and passenger trains, but timings are unreliable, so quicker to take bus. **Chennai**: *Coromandal Exp 2841*, 2043, 21½ hrs; *Howrah Chennai Mail 2603*, 0607, 26½ hrs. **Kolkata (H)**: *Dhauli Exp 2822*, 1345, 7½ hrs; *Coromandal Exp 2842*, 0540, 6½ hrs; *Falaknuma Exp 2704*, 1143, 8 hrs; *Jagannath Exp 8410*, 0105, 9 hrs; *East Coast Exp 8646*, 0811, 8 hrs. **New Delhi**: *Purushottam Exp 2801*, 0015, 30½ hrs. **Secunderabad**: *Falaknuma Exp 2703*, 1318, 21½ hrs; *East Coast Exp 8645*, 1840, 24 hrs.

Ratnagiri, Udayagiri and Lalitgiri *p196*

A day excursion from Cuttack or Bhubaneswar is possible by car (Rs 800). Get to Chandikhol on NH5 (43 km), with some roadside eating places, and turn right on NH5A (towards Paradeep) and then take the first turn left (at '12 km', before Patharajpur). Udayagiri is 1½ km west of the road (8 km from NH5A) and Ratnagiri, 10 km further north. Return to the NH5A and continue towards Paradeep passing the Patharajpur **Panthasala** (Rest House) on the right. Turn right (south) at 20 km for Lalitgiri, 5 km away. Alternatively, buses from Cuttack stop at Chandikhol where you can hire a car for a 85 km return journey. Or take another bus to Patharajpur, hire a rickshaw and visit the first 2 sites.

Baleshwar *p197*

Bus stand, Sahadevkhunta Rd, has services to all major towns, but few to **Chandipur**. **Train** Spelt **Balasore** in timetables, the railway station is 500 m from Bus Stand, on the main Chennai-Kolkata line. **Bhubaneswar**: best is *Dhauli Exp 2821*, 0946, 3½ hrs. **Chennai**: *Coromandel Exp 2841*, 1807, 24½ hrs; *Howrah Chennai Mail 2603*, 0248, 29½ hrs. **Kolkata (H)**: *Coromandel Exp 2842*, 0805, 4½ hrs; *Falaknuma Exp 2704*, 1357, 4½ hrs; *East Coast Exp 8646*, 1135, 5½ hrs. **New Delhi**: *Rajdhani Exp 2421*, 1232 (Wed, Sun), 21½ hrs; *Purushottam Exp 2801*, 0235, 27 hrs. **Puri**: *Jagannath Exp 8409*, 2240, 6½ hrs. **Secunderabad**: *Falaknuma Exp 2703*, 1031, 24½ hrs.

Chandipur *p197*

There are only 4-5 **buses** per day to/from **Baleshwar**. Ask at Panthanivas for timings. Ask for Rs 170 for a **taxi** to/from **Baleshwar**.

Baripada *p198*

Private and government **buses** serve the region's main towns. You can hire a **jeep** to visit Similipal. Ask at **Ambika** (see page 200) or tourist office. The nearest train stations are at Baleshwar (Balasore) and Tata Nagar.

Similipal National Park *p198*

The road from Baripada is via Lulung, 30 km west, which has a regular **bus** service. The nearest **train** stations on the Southeastern Railways are at Tatanagar and Balasore.

Khiching *p199*

Bus Regular buses from Baripada, 150 km. Nearest **train** station is 96 km away, but it is better to get down at Balasore, 210 km, which has a fast service on the Southeast Railway.

---

❶ Directory

Cuttack *p195, map p195*

Banks State Bank of India, near High Court, sterling and US$ TCs and cash exchange. Forex on first floor. **Hospital** Christian Mission Hospital, recommended. Private clinics on Medical Rd. **Internet** 3 on Jail Rd next to Rajtarangiri Cinema. Decent connections, Rs 25 per hr. **Tourist offices** Orissa, Arunodaya Market Building, Link Rd, T0671-231 2225. Railway Station Counter, T0671-261 0507. Both have helpful staff.

Baleshwar *p197*

Banks State Bank of India, Branch, near ITT, 3 km from railway station; the only bank authorized to deal in foreign exchange between Cuttack and Kolkata, so come prepared. **Tourist office** Orissa, Panthanivas hotel, Police Line, T06782-262048.

Baripada *p198*

Banks Nearest foreign exchange is at Baleshwar. The Central Co-op Bank paints a list of its top ten defaulters on the wall outside! **Tourist office** Baghra Rd, near the Bus Stand, T06792-252710. **Tiger Reserve Office**, Bhanjpur (2 km), T06792-252593, simitig@dte.vsnl.net.in. **Useful services** There is a district hospital, post office and shops selling local handicrafts and handloom.

Western Orissa

Settled in ancient times, Ptolemy's text of the second century refers to this area as a diamond trading centre. In the eighth century King Indrabhuti became a Buddhist and a preacher of the Vajrayana sect. ➤➤ *For Sleeping, Eating and other listings, see pages 203-204.*

Sambalpur and around → *Phone code: 0663. Colour map 3, grid A5.*

Sambalpur is a pleasant, small town with a number of decent hotels and a few restaurants grouped in the centre. The presiding deity Samalesvari to whom a temple was built here by the Chauhans in the mid-16th century probably accounts for the town's name. The district is famous for its textiles, particularly its tie-and-dye ikat work.

The villages and the countryside are pleasant in themselves and you might consider visiting **Baragarh**, 1½ hours, and **Barpali**, three hours' drive, with a guide, if you are interested in weaving. **Sonepur**, a lively small town with a colourful market square and temple, is particularly rewarding. A scenic road from Sambalpur along the Mahanadi River ends in a footpath down across the wide sandbank over half the river in the dry season. Small boats ferry passengers across the remainder.

Debjharan Sanctuary has been recently created and developed as a picnic spot in forest situated 35 km south of Sambalpur, 5 km east of the NH6. There is a small waterfall and a dam with waterhole at Chaura Asi Mal and a Forest Rest House. Taxis from Sambalpur cost Rs 300-400 for a return day trip.

Ushakothi → *48 km east of Sambalpur on the NH6.*

Ushakothi Wildlife Sanctuary is densely forested and covers 130 sq km. The sanctuary has wild elephant, leopard, tiger, bison, wild boar and *chital (barking deer). The best time to visit is from November to June, at night. Take a guide with search lights and see* the wildlife from the watchtowers sited near watering points to which the animals come. Open hooded jeeps are recommended. Permits to visit, and guides, from the Forest Range Officer, PO Badrama. *Forest Rest House, Badrama, 3 km away, is very basic with no electricity; when on site ask for Choudhary Babu, Dealing Clerk, from 1000 to 1600.*

Hirakud Dam

The Mahanadi created enormous problems every year through devastating floods of the delta region and in order to combat these the Hirakud Dam was built about 20 km northwest of Sambalpur. The key section is a 1100 m long masonry dam, with a further earth dam of over 3500 m. One of the longest mainstream dams in the world, it is over 60 m high and drains an area twice the size of Sri Lanka. Since its completion in 1957 there have been no serious floods in the Mahanadi delta and it allows the irrigation of vast areas of high-quality land. You get an excellent view from the revolving tower, Gandhi Minar at one end of the dam. Contact the Deputy Superintendent of Police, Security Force, Hirakud before visiting. There are regular buses from Sambalpur.

Debrigarh Wildlife Sanctuary

This sanctuary adjoins Hirakud Lake, around 50 km from Sambalpur. With an area of 347 sq km, the dry deciduous forest is home to tiger, leopard, sloth bear, chital, sambar, nilgai and a number of resident and migratory birds. Muggar crocodiles and freshwater turtles are amongst the reptiles present. Entry to the sanctuary is at Dhodrokusum, with a watchtower at Pathedurga. There are basic **Forest Rest Houses** at Dhodrokusum and Dechua, or a **Tourist Cottage** at Chaurasimal. The best season to visit is from October to May. For permission and guides, contact DFO (Wildlife), Motijharan, T0663-240 2741. For information contact Chief Wildlife Warden (Orissa), Bhubaneswar, cwlwob@hotmail.com.

Huma has a famous **Leaning Temple**, on the bank of the Mahanadi, dedicated to Lord Siva. The temple leans southwards but the pinnacle is vertical. The colourful Kudo fish, which are easily seen from January to June, are believed to belong to Siva so are never caught by fishermen; visitors may feed them grain. Country boats are available for hire. There are regular buses from Sambalpur to Huma Chowk, then walk 2 km to the temple.

Sundargarh District

To the north of Sambalpur is Sundargarh District. In the tribal heartland, it is an area of undulating hills with the richest deposits of mineral wealth in the state. Cave paintings are evidence of the existence of early man. Once relatively untouched by modern civilization, the district was chosen for the siting of the first public sector steel plant at Rourkela. The route from Sambalpur to Rourkela runs north, 192 km, passing through some glorious scenery. The Brahmani flows along a wide rocky and sandy bed, a torrent in the monsoon, with forested hills on either side. A large industrial town girdled by a range of hills and encircled by rivers, **Rourkela** has a major steel plant and fertilizer complex, both of which may be visited with permission from the PRO. There are banks, post offices, shops and hospitals.

● Sleeping

Sambalpur *p202*

D-F Saket, T0663-240 2345. Some a/c in 30 decent, clean rooms, hot bath, TV, restaurant.
D-F Sheela Towers, VSS Marg, T0663-240 3111. The 41 smallish rooms are clean and comfortable, TV, 2 restaurants.
E-F Panthanivas (OTDC), Brook's Hill, end of VSS Marg, T0663-241 1282, www.pantha nivas.com. Despite all having balconies, few of the 34 rooms (clean linen, 13 a/c with TV) have decent views. Restaurant, bar.
E-G Uphar, T0663-240 3078. Slightly cheaper sister concern of **Uphar Palace**.
E-G Uphar Palace, T0663-240 0519. 29 good clean rooms with bath, some a/c, TV, 2 restaurants (good South Indian).
G Rani Lodge, next to **Uphar Palace**, T0663-252 2173. Clean, simple rooms with bath, nets, early morning mosque noise.

Hirakud Dam *p202*
E Ashok Nivas, good guesthouse at end of dam.

Sundagarh District *p203*
B Mayfair Garden, Panposh Rd, 3 km from Rourkela, T0661-252 0001, rkl_mayfair@ sancharnet.in. Touted as a 'farm resort', 18 comfortable rooms, decent restaurant, pool.
E Radhika, Bisra Rd, opposite railway station, Rourkela, T0661-251 0300. Reasonably clean, 60 large rooms, helpful staff.
E-G Panthanivas (OTDC), Sector 5, 2 km from Rourkela, T0661-264 3280,

www.panthanivas.com. With 31 rooms, some a/c, restaurant/bar.

▲ Activities and tours

Sambalpur *p202*
Providing jeeps and taxis for sightseeing: **Nalini Travels**, Buddharaja, near flyover, and **Swati Travels**, near Ashoka Talkies.

● Transport

Sambalpur *p202*
Bus
Sambalpur has 2 bus stands, one for private buses, near Laxmi Talkies, and the other for government buses. Both are a short cycle-rickshaw ride from VSS Marg. The former has more regular services to major towns.

Jeep/taxi
Jeep/taxi hire is the easiest way to visit wildlife sanctuaries. See Directory for travel agents or contact the tourist office. Return jeeps to **Debjharan**, Rs 300-400; to **Ushakothi** (1600-0400), Rs 500.

Train
There are 2 stations: Sambalpur and Sambalpur Rd, both 2-3 km from hotels on VSS Marg. **Kolkata (H)**: *Koraput Howrah Exp 8006*, 1925, 13 hrs. **Puri** (via **Bhubaneswar**): *Tapaswini Exp 8451*, 2250, 9½ hrs (7½ hrs).

Bus Rourkela's New Bus Stand is in walking distance of Bisra Rd hotels; turn right and right again. Buses to all major destinations.

Rourkela's **train** station is a 1-min walk from Bisra Rd and hotels. **Kolkata (H)**: *Ispat Exp 2872*, 1135, 8 hrs. **Mumbai (CST)** : *Gitanjali Exp 2860*, 2005, 26 hrs. **Patna**: *South Bihar Link Exp 3287*, 1510, 18 hrs. **Puri** via **Bhubaneswar** (all stop at Balasore and Cuttack): *Tapaswini Exp 8451*, 1930, 12½ hrs (10 hrs); *Utkal Exp 8478*, 1710, 16 hrs (12½ hrs).

● Directory

Sambalpur *p202*

Bank State Bank of India, near Collectorate, for foreign exchange. **Post** Main post office, near Collectorate. Several internet cafés on VSS Marg, Rs 20-25 per hour. **Tourist offices** Orissa, at Panthanivas, T0663-241 1118. Very helpful staff, worth a visit to plan excursions. Railway counter at Khetrajpur, T2521661. Tours are often cancelled due to lack of passengers.

Southern Orissa

Chilika Lake ●●● ⇢ *pp206-208. Colour map 3, grid A5 and B5.*

ⓘ *Boats from Barkul, Book Rambha and Satapada, 1½ hrs, Rs 20. Nalabana bird-watching trip, Rs 120, 4 hrs. Pay 0730 on the day and wait until the boat is full.*

Chilika is the largest brackish water lake in Asia (1100 sq km) stretching across the Khurdha, Puri and Ganjam districts, and forms an enormous lagoon as it is joined to the Bay of Bengal with a narrow mouth, a sandy ridge separating it from the sea.

The lake is the winter home of migratory birds, some flying great distances from Iran, Central Asia and Siberia. During the winter months, from November to February, you can watch white bellied sea eagles, ospreys, golden plovers, sandpipers, flamingoes, shovellers, pelicans and gulls. The lake attracts fishermen who come in search of prawn, mackerel and crab. Some ornithologists blame the growth in prawn farming, as well as the increasing discharge from rivers, silting and salinity for reduced bird numbers. The large Nalabana Island (Reed Island) sanctuary is often below water.

The **Kalijai Temple** stands on one of the tiny rock islands. Weekends get very crowded. **Satapada**, on the other side of the lake, has a Tourism Complex.

Ganjam District ●●● ⇢ *pp206-208. Colour map 3, grid A5 and B5.*

Ganjam District, south of Chilika Lake, takes its name from the Persian '*Ganj – Am*', meaning granary of the world, a testimony to its agricultural fertility. Still largely covered in dense forest, it was settled in prehistoric times and came under the influence of Emperor Asoka's rule. The handicrafts of the region include brass and bell-metal ware, hornwork, wood carvings, silks and carpets.

Ganjam

Ganjam was the District Headquarters, but the administration was moved to Chatrapur because of its unhealthy location. Its chief interest is the small East India Company fort and a Christian cemetery at the north end of town, near a large factory between the main road and the sea. An interesting excursion inland takes you to Aska (52 km) and Bhanjanagar (85 km).

Berhampur

A trading centre for silk fabric, Berhampur is the major commercial town of the District. The **Thakurani, Jagannath** and **Nilakanthesvar Siva temples** ⓘ *near DIG Residence,* all worth visiting. Berhampur is also a good place to shop for silks. The museum has a sculpture, anthropological and natural history specimens; no photos are permitted.

Gopalpur → *Phone code: 0680.*

Gopalpur was an ancient sea port from which early settlers from Kalinga sailed as far as Java, Bali and Sumatra. Then it was a port for the export of Aska sugar and 'coolie' labour to the Assam tea gardens. Later still it became a popular seaside resort for the British offering a beautiful sandy beach. Today, however, it has a rather faded feeling and appearance. Sand dunes, groves of coconut and casuarinas separate the small town from the beach, while the backwaters, creeks and lagoons give some variety. A red and white lighthouse opens to visitors briefly each afternoon; there are good views but photography is not allowed.

Taptapani

Water from the very hot sulphur springs discovered at Taptapani in a forest setting, 50 km from Berhampur, is channelled to a pool for bathing. There is a shrine to goddess Kandhi inside the original *kund* (pool) as it is believed to cure infertility – tribal women come to the hot water pool near the **Panthanivas hotel** (D-E) to try to pick up a seed pod from the mud at the bottom. Direct buses leave from Berhampur, 50 km away, and Bhubaneswar, 240 km away.

Chandragiri

In the tribal hills, 32 km south of Taptapani, Tibetan carpet weavers have settled in a refugee colony at Chandragiri. The temple and Buddhist prayer flags lend a distinctive atmosphere. You can watch weavers and craftsmen at work; good prices.

Jaugada → *35 km north of Berhampur.*

Jaugada in the Malati Hills is famous for one of **Asoka's 'Kalinga Edicts'** (see Dhauli, page 184), which was discovered at the beginning of the 19th century, but the shelter was built only in 1975. Emperor Asoka's doctrine of conquest through love instead of the sword and his declaration "All men are my children" appear here. Sadly, some parts of the inscriptions have now disappeared. The old fort (circa sixth century) contains stone images of the five *Pandavas* which are worshipped in the Guptesvar Temple. Jaugada is reached by a jeep road from Purusottampur which has buses from Berhampur.

Buguda, a few kilometres away, has the Viranchinarayan Temple with its beautifully carved wooden *Jagamohan* and murals depicting stories from the epic Ramayana. Also, close by, **Buddhakhol** has Buddhist sculptures as well as shrines to Siva.

Tribal areas ▣⦿▲▣◖ ⇢ *pp206-208. Colour map 3, grid A5 and B5.*

Orissa's rich tribal heritage has survived among the hills and forests across the districts of Koraput, Kandhamal, Kalahandi, Ganjam, Keonjhar, Dhenkanal and Mayurbhanj. The state government is actively promoting tourism in some of these areas, see page 173. It is best to book a tour at least a month ahead to allow time to get permits to visit tribal territories. Without permits, tours are restricted to roadside villages where development programmes are already changing traditional values and in some cases the influx of tourism has created a disappointing 'circus' effect, with demands of money for photos, dances and sweets for the children. With permits and a guide, it is possible to visit the more isolated villages. Individual visitors face difficulties from the local police, so it is best to take a guide in any instance. Always seek out the village chief for permission to enter a village. Photography is prohibited in Bondo and Dongariya territories. Permission should always be asked before taking photographs of tribal people. Respect their privacy should they decline. Walking around settlements with a video camera glued to the eye is not appreciated. Away from the main towns accommodation is very basic and some camping is necessary when trekking. Transport is usually by non-air conditioned car, jeep or minibus. Foreign exchange is only available in Sunubeda so it's best to change money in advance.

Tribal markets

Typical 'Social Interest' tours offered by travel agents include a number of tribal villages with a chance to attend interesting festivals and markets. Some of the tribes seen in these areas may include Dongariya Kondhs, Dhurubas, Parajas, Koyas, Bondos and Gadabas. In Koraput District, **Ramgiri**, 70 km southwest of Jeypore, has a picturesque Tuesday market where Kondh people come to sell fresh vegetables and baskets and to buy salt. **Nandapur**, 44 km south of Koraput, brings tribal women to the colourful Wednesday market where they sell beedi leaves and large almond-flavoured seeds. **Ankadeli**, 90 km southwest of Koraput, has a Thursday market where Bondo women, clad entirely in bead, come to sell handloom fabric, beads and exquisite woven grass headbands. **Rayagada** has some good accommodation. Sleeping and eating are also available at **Laxmipur** and **Baliguda** (see page 207).

Jeypore → *Phone code: 06854.*

Jeypore itself is unspoilt by tourism and is surrounded by beautiful scenery. There are several monuments including a fort and palace. It is quite possible to organize your own tour from Jeypore and reportedly easier to get permits to visit tribal areas in Koraput rather than in Bhubaneswar.

Koraput

Koraput is a useful base for visiting the tribal areas. There is a small tribal **museum** ① *closed Wed, 1500-1700, Sun 1000-1600*, although you may need a guide to understand the exhibits. The Orissa Coffee Planters' Association, located around 20 km from Koraput, are happy to show visitors around the plantation which has fruits and spices as well as coffee.

Kotapad → *46 km northwest of Jeypore on N43.*

The clean area of weavers' houses in Kotapad has large pots of cotton and tussore silk soaking in natural dyes, while skeins hang drying. Weavers are happy to show you work in progress. The Co-op ensures even pricing – Rs 350-600 buys a 3-m shawl. It is worth seeking out award winner Jagabandhu Samarth. As the word gets around, weavers will find you to show their pieces but there is no pressure to buy.

◉ Sleeping

Chilika Lake *p204*
E-F Panthanivas (OTDC), 1 km from road end, Barkul, T06756-220488, www.panthanivas.com. 35 small rooms, some a/c, bar, restaurant, tourist office, boating complex, 0800 checkout, busy at weekends and holidays.
E-F Panthanivas (OTDC), Rambha, T06810-278346, www.panthanivas.com. 11 rooms, some a/c, half rate for day visitors 0900-1700.
F-G Yatri Nivas, Satapada, on the north side of the lake, closest to Puri, T06752-262077. Attractive location, decent

rooms. First floor rooms have balconies and the best views.
G Shree Khrishna Lodge, Barkul (500 m from **Panthanivas**), T06756-221195. Simple, clean rooms, some with bath.

Berhampur *p204*
Few visitors stay overnight, preferring to head to Gopalpur. If arriving late, there are options:
D-F Kameswari, close to railway station on Station Rd, T0680-1283, radhahotel bam@rediffmail.com. 28 rooms, 7 a/c.

E-GHotel Radha, near the Old Bus Stand, T0680-222 2341. Some a/c in the 45 rooms.
F-GGitanjali, close to the railway station, T0680-220 4822.
F-GUdipi, near the Old Bus Stand, T0680-222 2196.
GPuspa, Gatekeeper's Square, 1½ km from the New Bus Stand, T0680-222 1117. Basic.

Gopalpur *p205*
ALOberoi Palm Beach, T0680-222021, pbeach@sancharnet.in. Renovated with 18 rooms around gardens, good restaurants, bar, private beach, sports facilities, relaxing.
C-DSea Pearl, T0680-224 2556. Decent, albeit pricey rooms with bath, TV and balcony, although some face the building next door.
DSong of the Sea, next to lighthouse, T0680-224 2347. Clean, light and airy rooms in family run hotel, peaceful location, simple restaurant. The best rooms are at the front on the first floor with sea view, pleasant though pricey.
D-EGreen Park, T0680-224 2016, greenpark016@yahoo.com. 17 clean rooms (some a/c), simple Indian-style hotel, best with sea view.
D-EHoliday Home, T0680-224 2049. Simple rooms, some with TV, clean bath and linen, small singles, restaurant, terrace with sea views.
D-ESea Side Breeze, T0680-224 2075. Only hotel right on the beach, 14 clean rooms, food on order, ideal for backpackers.
EMermaid, T0680-224 2050. Good, clean breezy rooms, better on first floor with sea-facing balconies, one of the best place to stay, although the food is not so good.
FHeaven Spot, Rewu St, T0680-224 3274. 5 small, basic but clean rooms with attached bath, away from beach, serves as a base.
FNataraj, T0680-224 2340. Away from the beach, 10 simple rooms, food available.
FRosalin, T0680-224 2071. Friendly but prepare for mosquitoes, 9 basic rooms with attached bath. Small garden, food on order.
FSai Tourist Lodge, T0680-224 2041. 6 basic rooms in family house with attached or shared bath.

Tribal areas *p205*
Rayagada
D-GSai International, JK Rd, T06856-222 5555. Staff not used to foreigners but excellent value, 40 good, comfortable rooms, several a/c, TV, hot bath, restaurant and bar.

F-GJyoti Mahal, Convent Rd, T06856-222 3015. Bit grubby but friendly, 25 reasonably sized rooms with bath, good restaurant.
F-GSwagath, New Colony, T06856-222 2208. 44 clean rooms, good local-style restaurant.

Laxmipur
Hotel Konark, green building by Ambedkar Chowk. Good *thalis, friendly young English-speaking owner. Decent lunch stop.*

Baliguda
Baliguda is basically a one-street town, a quiet, friendly place with a slow pace of life.
GSantosh, off Main Road, with 16 rooms, best on the first floor with attached bath.

Jeypore *p206*
CHello Jeypore, East Octroi Check Post, NH43, 2 km centre, T06854-223 1127, hellojeypore@yours.com. Best in town though noisy area, 30 comfortable, well-furnished a/c rooms overlooking lovely garden, hot shower in mornings, TV, efficient service, excellent restaurant (try *alu raita*). Recommended.
F-GMadhumati, NKT Rd, T06854-224 0307. 30 large rooms, some a/c, TV, mosquitos, restaurant, bar, very helpful manager.
F-GPrincess, near Bus Stand, NH43 (corner of Main Rd), T06854-223 0027, princessco@vsnl.com. 40 reasonable rooms, some a/c, hot bath, TV, cheaper singles, good restaurant, accommodating staff, well run.
GRoseland Lodge, T06854-223 0639. Very cheap rooms (all under Rs 100), common bath, basic but friendly.

Koraput *p206*
FAmbica Heavens, T06852-251136. Decent rooms with bath, TV, quiet at back.
FAthithi Bhavan, T06852-250610. Managed by the Jagannath Temple Trust, simple rooms with bath, TV, temple food, can be noisy.

❷ Eating

Jeypore *p206*
Girija, Main Rd. Good Chinese. **Hello Jeypore**, see Sleeping, excellent food. **Kasturi**, *thalis. Princess, see Sleeping, reasonable but dark.*

Koraput *p206*
Dolphin's Plaza, below Ambica Heavens, is worth a try for meals.

▲ Activities and tours

Jeypore *p206*
Discover Tours, see Bhubaneswar, page 193. Highly recommended.
Perfect Travels, Rajmahal Chowk, T06854-242 1856. Car and driver, Rs 850 per day.
Travel Care, Sardar Patel Marg, T06854-2422291, F2423286. For tours write to Mr Pujari 4-6 weeks in advance with a photocopy of the relevant passport pages.

◉ Transport

Chilika Lake *p204*
Chilika Lake is easiest to reach by road (NH5) from Barkul, 6 km south of Balugaon or Rambha at the south end of the lake.

Bus Buses from **Bhubaneswar** and **Berhampur**. Satapada at the northern end can only be reached via **Puri** from where there are day trips offering 'dolphin safaris'.

Ferry OTDC motor launches are available from Barkul, Rambha and Satapada although during the week it may not be cost effective. Dolphin watching is the main focus of boats from Satapada. Private country boats are also available at Barkul and Rambha.

Train Slow passenger trains on the Chennai-Kolkata line stop at **Balugaon**, **Chilika**, **Khallikote** and **Rambha**.

Berhampur *p204*
Bus The Old and New Bus Stands are about 3 km from the railway station, 2 km from each other. Government buses use the Old Bus Stand, private buses (which are more regular and reliable) the New Bus Stand and cover major towns in Orissa and neighbouring states. Several buses to Bhubaneswar a day, Rs80, 4 hrs on a good road.

Train Berhampur, sometimes referred to as **Brahmapur** in timetables, is on the main Chennai-Kolkata line, enquiries T131. **Chennai**: *Coromandel Exp 2841*, 0010, 18 hrs; *Howrah Chennai Mail 2603*, 0915, 22½ hrs. **Kolkata (H)** via **Bhubaneswar**:

Coromandel Exp 2842, 0230, 11½ hrs; *Falaknuma Exp 2704*, 0805, 11½ hrs; *East Coast Exp 8646*, 0430, 14½ hrs. **Secunderabad**: *Falaknuma Exp 2703*, 1655, 17½ hrs; *Konark Exp 1020*, 1800, 18 hrs; *East Coast Exp 8645*, 2240, 20 hrs; *Visakha Exp 7015*, 1105, 21½ hrs.

Gopalpur *p205*
There are regular private buses from the New Bus Stand, Berhampur (Rs 6, 30 min).

Jeypore *p206*
Frequent **bus** service to Koraput. Also to Sambalpur and Bhubaneswar (16 hrs). Night buses from Berhampur.
   If travelling by **car** from the coast, make sure the car can manage the hill roads and the driver isn't worried about entering tribal areas.
   The **train** station is 7 km away. A daily train connects with Vishakhapatnam. From Vizag, *Kirandol Exp*, 0745, 8 hrs. Superb views for first 3 hrs uphill then down to Araku Valley; 2nd class is full of firewood and farm produce and best avoided. From the north, travel to Vizianagaram station, and then by bus or taxi.

Koraput *p206*
Trains to **Bhubaneswar**: *Hirakhand Exp 8448*, 1825, 14 hrs. From Bhubaneswar, *Hirakhand Exp 8447*, 2000, 14½ hrs. **Kolkata (H)**: *Koraput Howrah Exp 8006*, 0745, 25 hrs.

❶ Directory

Chilika Lake *p204*
There is a post office, government dispensary and a tourist office at **Barkul**, T06756-220855.

Berhampur *p204*
Bank State Bank of India, Main Branch, State Bank Rd, changes foreign cash and TCs. **Tourist office** New Bus Stand, 1st floor, T0680-228 0226. Railway station counter, T0680-220 3870. **Useful services** Christian Mission Hospital, post offices and shops.

Koraput *p206*
Bank Sunabeda, 18 km away. State Bank of India, the only one in the area. **Tourist office** Orissa, Koraput Club, T06852-250318.

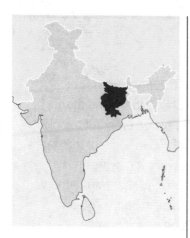

Bihar and Jharkhand

❖ Footprint features

Introduction

Bihar, which takes its name from the word 'vihara', or monastery, was the early home of Buddhism and the birthplace of one of India's most revered emperors, Asoka. His Buddhist legacy has left its imprint in some of the state's most visited pilgrimage sites, for while it may be on the outskirts of modern Patna, Kumrahar still has fragmentary remains of the early Mauryan capital; in Bodh Gaya and Nalanda, Buddhism's tradition is powerfully visible.

After the creation of the new state of Jharkhand modern Bihar is confined to the densely populated, and desperately poor, Ganges plains. The state has a chequered recent political history. Separated from Bengal in 1912, in 1936 another partition led to the creation of Orissa. After Independence the reorganization of Indian states saw the transfer of territory from Bihar to West Bengal, while the tribal groups had already begun to campaign for a separate state for the tribal areas of the Chota Nagpur plateau in South Bihar. On 15 November 2000 this dream was finally achieved with the division of Bihar into two, the mineral-rich Chota Nagpur plateau becoming the new state of Jharkhand.

In recent years Bihar in particular has acquired an unfortunate, now almost proverbial, reputation for crime and banditry. Travellers intending to visit or travel through should be aware that this is one of India's poorest regions, and should strictly avoid travelling by night on rural roads. Nevertheless, most travellers who adopt the necessary precautions emerge unscathed.

★ Don't miss ...

1 **Kolhua Asoka Pillar** Take the pleasant 5-km walk at Vaishali to one of the only two Asoka pillars that remain in situ, page 217.

2 **Sonepur Fair** One of Asia's most remarkable cattle fairs takes place in November, page 217.

3 **Nalanda** Visit the impressive ruins here, possibly the site of the world's oldest university, page 220.

4 **Bodh Gaya** This place can resemble a medieval encampment as pilgrims from all over the world visit one of the holiest Buddhist pilgrimage centres, page 224.

5 **Sher Shah's mausoleum** The tomb, at Sasaram, appears to float in an artificial tank; the area around is a great place for relaxing, page 226.

6 **Parasnath Hill** Join pilgrims at 0400 and climb the hill to catch superb views of the sunrise and surrounding countryside, page 231.

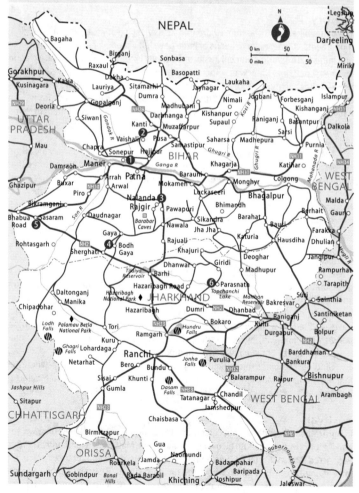

Bihar & Jharkhand

Background → *Population: Bihar 82.88 mn, Jharkhand 26.9 mn. Area: Bihar 174,000 sq km, Jharkhand 80,000 sq km.*

The land

Bihar and Jharkhand form a region of transition. The wet lowlands to the east give way to the much drier and now more prosperous alluvial plains to the west. From north to south, the two states stretch 600 km from the foothills of the Himalaya across the flat plains to the forested and mineral-rich hills of Chota Nagpur (now in Jharkhand). The River Ganga runs through the heart of the plains, joined by its tributaries from the Nepal Himalaya to the north and from the Vindhyan Hills of the Peninsula to the south. To the north of the Ganga are the scars of old river beds which often form chains of lakes during the monsoon and provide a vital source of fish. North Bihar is India's biggest producer of freshwater fish, over half of which is sold to Kolkata. Torrential rain in the Himalayan foothills and the flatness of the Ganga valley floor cause some of the rivers, like the Kosi, to flood catastrophically. Over a period of 130 years the Kosi has moved over 110 km westwards.

History

The name Bihar is derived from *vihara* (monastery), suggesting its wealth of religious monuments. All the major religions of India have left a mark, most notably Buddhism and Jainism. The world's first university of Buddhist learning was founded at Nalanda, southeast of Patna. Bihar was settled from the west as Aryan tribes moved down the Ganga valley, clearing the forest and developing cultivation. Agriculture provided the base for the Magadhan kings who ruled from the sixth to the fourth centuries BC. The early Magadhan kings had their capital at **Rajgir,** 100 km southeast of modern Patna. It was surrounded by 40 km of stone walls which can still be seen. Later they moved their capital to **Pataliputra,** the site of modern Patna.

The Guptas, who played a central role in the flowering of Hindu culture of the classical period, rescued Magadha in the fourth to fifth centuries AD from more than 600 years of obscurity. They were followed by the Palas of Bengal who ruled until defeated by the Muslims in 1197. The Delhi sultans and a succession of independent Muslim rulers controlled the region until the arrival of the Mughals who retained it until the British won the Battle of Buxar in 1764. Subsequently Bihar was separated from Bengal and became a province under British rule until India's Independence in 1947.

Culture

There is a sharp division between the agricultural plains of north Bihar, with three-quarters of the combined population total, and the Chota Nagpur plateau to the south, where a high proportion of India's mineral resources are concentrated. The plains are peopled largely by Hindus but five centuries of Muslim political dominance have resulted in a significant Muslim population (14% today). Aboriginal **tribal peoples** in Jharkhand, include Santal, Oraon, Munda Kharia and Ho tribes. Some have converted to Christianity in large numbers.

Hindi is dominant throughout the plains, with related dialects elsewhere (eg Maithili, Bhojpuri, Magahi). Urdu is spoken by many Muslims, and tribal languages by nearly 10% of the population (eg Austro-Asiatic Santali and Dravidian Oraon).

Festivals

In **April/May** is **Buddha Jayanti,** celebrating the Buddha's birth, when Bodh Gaya and Rajgir attract Buddhists from all over the world, while **Mahavira Jayanti** brings Jains to the sacred Parasnath Hill. In **June** a unique 14-day **marriage market** takes place in a large mango grove in Saurath where the nation's Mithila Brahmins gather. Parents come with horoscopes to arrange marriages of their sons and daughters.

⦂ Bihar's plains: gift of the Himalaya?

Severe flooding of Bihar's rivers has prompted some environmentalists to blame deforestation in Nepal. A rising population, commercial logging and bad agricultural practices have been held responsible for widespread damage on Bihar's plains. But recent research sheds doubt on this simple cause and effect. The River Kosi has been shifting its course for decades, and floods have for centuries washed down Himalayan silt, without which the plains would not exist. A protective embankment along the southern flank of the Himalaya was built in 1960 to limit the flooding and westward movement of the river, and to protect agricultural land. Attempts to control the Kosi by building dams in Nepal are still under consideration, but the huge amounts of silt, plus the fact that the Himalayan foothills are a zone of major earthquakes, makes projects extremely difficult to implement effectively. To add to the problem, when the Ganga is in full flow it rises higher than the tributaries which join it from the south, so it is also subject to severe floods between July and October. Those in August 2007 were declared the "worst in living memory" by the UN, leaving hundreds of thousands of people homeless.

October/November has **Pataliputra Festival** starting with **Dasara** in October and ends with the Sonepur Fair. **Durga puja, Dasara** and **Diwali** are celebrated. **Chhath** or **Surya Puja** takes place six days after **Diwali**. To mark the harvest, fresh paddy, sweets and fruit are offered by devotees in procession; women, waist deep in the Ganga, offer homage at sunrise and sunset. **Sonepur Fair** is one of Asia's most remarkable cattle fairs in November.

Food and drink

The typical Bihari meal consists of rice, unleavened bread, lentils and vegetables cooked with hot spices. *Sattoo*, a grain mix, is made into a dough and eaten as a savoury, or sweetened with sugar or jaggery. The mixture can also be taken as a drink with milk or water and flavoured with cardamoms and cloves. *Puri-aloo*, deep fried Indian bread with potatoes cooked with onions and garlic, and *kachoris*, made with wheat and lentil flour and then served with *kala chana* (black gram), are delicious snacks.

Modern Bihar

From its pre-eminent position in the culture and politics of early and classical India, Bihar has declined today to one of India's poorest and most badly administered states. There are periodic outbreaks of caste-based violence in the countryside. Bihar is one of the most troubled political administrations of modern India. Successive governments have been charged with corruption and maladministration and it is widely regarded across India as the most lawless state in the country.

Through the mid-1990s and the first half of this decade the state government was run by current railways minister Laloo Prasad Yadav and his wife Rabri Devi, presently at the head of the Rabri Janata Dal (RJD). While they have been accused by some of effectively stripping the state of its wealth, they retain a strong core of support. Nonetheless, their Rabri Janata Dal Party won only 65 of the 243 state assembly seats in the re-run November 2005 election, being ousted by the Janata Dal (United)-BJP coalition. Nitish Kumar was sworn in as chief minister. Having been railways minister in the previous Indian government, there is an irony in the fact that that post should now be held by the former Bihar chief minister, Laloo Prasad Yadav.

Patna

→ *Phone code: 0612. Colour map 1, grid B5. Population: 1.4 mn.*

Bihar's straggling capital, Patna, has the air more of a semi-rural provincial town in its more attractive areas, despite its size. However, it is one of India's poorest cities, stretching along the south bank of the Ganga for about 15 km. Divided in two by the large open Maidan, the central city is crowded, dusty and has little of architectural interest. Scant evidence remains of its earlier wealth and political supremacy. Many thousands sleep on the streets and there are few street lights at night. However, around the station food stalls are neatly set out and illuminated, and it can be interesting to take a cycle-rickshaw round by day or night. Many tribal people come into the town, often working on roads or building sites. ▸▸ *For Sleeping, Eating and other listings, see pages 217-219.*

Ins and outs

Getting there and around Patna airport, 7 km from town, has coaches and taxis for transfer. Long-distance State buses arrive at the Gandhi Square Bus Stand, which is between 15-25 minutes' walk from most budget hotels. These are strung out down Fraser Road towards Patna Junction railway station and Vir Kunwar Singh (Hardinge) Bus Stand (serving Gaya, Varanasi and Nepal). The centre is compact enough to walk around, though rickshaws are easily available. Hire an unmetered taxi from major hotels for longer trips. ▸▸ *See Transport, page 218, for further details.*

History

At the confluence of the rivers Son, Punpun, Gandak and Ganga, Patna's history can be traced back 2500 years. Ajatasatru, the second Magadha king who ruled from

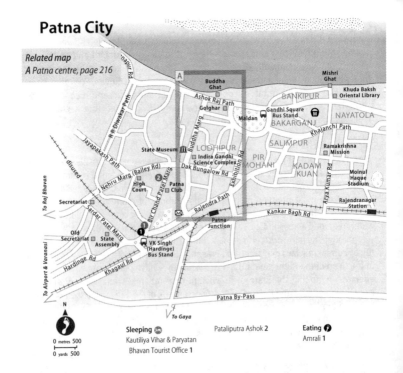

Patna City

Related map
A Patna centre, page 216

Sleeping
Kautiliya Vihar & Paryatan
Bhavan Tourist Office 1

Pataliputra Ashok 2

Eating
Amrali 1

Rajgir, built a small fort at Pataligrama. Later Chandragupta Maurya founded the
Mauryan Empire with Pataliputra as its capital. Buddhist histories suggest that it was
here that Asoka usurped the throne of his father, Bindusara, murdering all his rivals
and starting a reign of terror, before a conversion eight years later. It marked the
beginning of perhaps the greatest reforming kingship the world has known. The
Greek ambassador Megasthenes was deeply impressed by the efficiency of the
Chandragupta administration and the splendour of the city. Ruins can be seen at
Kumrahar, Bhiknapahari and Bulandhi Bagh with its 75 m wooden passage.
Excavations date the site back to the pre-Mauryan times of 600 BC. In the 16th
century the Pathan Sher Shah Suri established the foundations of a new Patna,
building a majestic mosque in 1540 which dominates the skyline.

Sights

Patna's buildings reflect its administrative and educational functions. The Collectorate,
Court and educational institutions are all close to the river bank in the western part of
the city, along with the Raj Bhavan, the High Court and the better residential areas. To
the east is Old Patna with its bazars, old mosques, Har Mandir and St Mary's Church.

The central area
State Museum ⓘ *Tue-Sun 1030-1630, Buddha Marg*, has a collection of coins,
paintings, terracotta, bronze and stone sculptures including the famous Mauryan
Didarganji Yakshi (circa 200 BC), Jain sculptures (second, third centuries) and finds
from Bodh Gaya, Nalanda, etc. The presentation is uneven, with scarcely any labels and
some moth-eaten exhibits. However, the first floor gallery is well lit with a collection of
terracotta heads from the third century BC; the mezzanine floor has an interesting

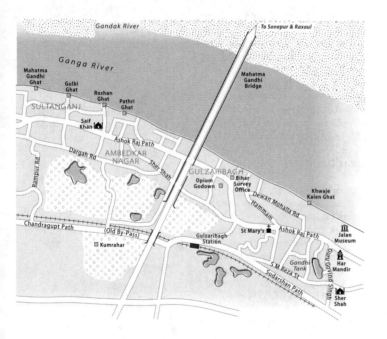

collection of Tibetan *thangkas*. **Indira Gandhi Science Complex**, corner of Buddha Marg and Bailey Road, includes a planetarium. Just to the east of the centre is **Khuda Baksh Oriental Public Library** (1900), with one of the largest private collections of books and rare Persian and Arabic manuscripts, Rajput paintings and the only books rescued from the Moorish University of Cordoba, Spain. It is now a national library.

Golghar

The *Gola* (round house), an extraordinary ovoid dome between the Maidan and the Ganga, was built of stone slabs in 1786 by Captain John Garstin of the Bengal Engineers, who planned this grain store for the army in case of a repeat of the 1770 famine. It has a base 125 m wide, where the wall is 3.6 m thick, with two brick staircases that spiral up the outside; the workforce were to carry the grain up one and descend by the other. It was never completed so the last line of the inscription "First filled and publicly closed by ..." remains unfinished. Sometimes, it is possible to go inside and listen to the remarkable echo. It is well climbing the steps for an excellent view of the city and the Ganga. From July to September the river can be over 5 km wide at this point.

Kumrahar

Excavations at the site of the ancient capital of Pataliputra have revealed ruins enclosed within a high brick wall. These date back to 600 BC, the first of four distinct periods of settlement over the following 1200 years. The buildings, mainly of wood, were devastated by a fire and lay hidden in the silt. The more recent fifth phase dates from the early 17th century.

The most important finds are rare wooden ramparts and a large Mauryan three-storeyed assembly hall, that was 77 m square, with 15 rows of five highly polished sandstone pillars dating back to 400-300 BC. The garden site has little to show today other than the single 6-m intact pillar. The tiny museum has its small collection of valuable finds almost invisibly shut away in a dark room.

Gulzaribagh

About 8 km east of the Golghar near Kumrahar, at Gulzaribagh, are the former East India Company's principal opium *godowns* (warehouses), which are now home to a government printing press. The three long buildings with porticoes on each side were strategically placed by the river for boats to carry the opium down to Kolkata. The old *godowns*, ballroom and hall are open to visitors.

Har Mandir and around

Har Mandir is in the Chowk area of old Patna. The *gurudwara* built by Maharaja

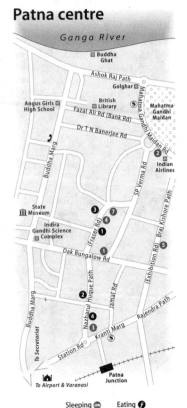

Patna centre

Sleeping
AAEI 1
Maurya Patna 2
Mayur 3
Rajasthan 4
Republic 5
Sheodar 7

Eating
Ashok 1
Marwari Awas
Griha 3
Mayfair 4
Nalanda at Satkar
International Hotel 2

0 metres 300
0 yards 300

Ranjit Singh is the second of the four great *takhts* (thrones) of the Sikhs and consecrates the birthplace of the 10th Guru, Gobind Singh, in 1660. The shrine of white marble with kiosks on the terrace above has a museum on the third floor.

Jalan Museum ① *get prior permission from the owner, Mr BM Jalan, Hira Pl, Dak Bungalow Rd, Patna 1, T0612-222 5070, quilahouse@hotmail.com*, in Quila House , is across the road from Har Mandir. The private house was built over the ruins of Sher Shah's fort and is a museum containing Chinese paintings and a valuable collection of jade and silver filigree work of the Mughal period.

Saif Khan's Mosque (Pathar-ki-Masjid), on the river bank, was built in 1621 by Parwez Shah, the son of the Mughal Emperor Jahangir.

Around Patna

Sonepur → *Colour map 3, grid A4.*

Near its confluence with the Gandak, 22 km across the Ganga, Sonepur has a station on the Northeast Railway. Sonepur has Asia's biggest cattle market, beginning on the full moon of the Hindu month of **Kartik Purnima** (October/ November). The two-week fair draws thousands to the magic shows, folk dances, contests and stalls selling handicrafts and handlooms. Mark Shand's *Travels on my Elephant* gives a colourful account of the fair. Elephants, camels, horses and birds are bought and sold but numbers are dwindling. Bihar Tourism sets up a Tourist Village a week before and Swiss Cottage Tents are furnished, with attached baths.

❖ *Sonepur and Vaishali can both be visited comfortably in a day. You can hire a taxi or take a tour.*

Vaishali → *Colour map 1, grid B5.*

Vaishali – derived from King Visala, from the *Ramayana* – dates back to the sixth century BC when it was a flourishing city of the Lichchavis, reputedly one of the first cities in the world to adopt a republican form of government. This is where the Buddha preached his last sermon and announced his approaching Nirvana. In 383 BC, 100 years later, it was the venue of the second Buddhist Council, when two stupas were erected. Jains of the Svetambara sect believe that Mahavir was born in Vaishali in 599 BC. Today, the district is part of the Mithila region, famous for Madhubani paintings on village houses.

The **Asoka Pillar** at **Kolhua**, also known as Bhimsen-ki-Lathi (stick), is a single 18 m piece of highly polished red sandstone with a bell-shaped inverted lotus capital and a life-sized lion carved on top. Asoka pillars (*stambhas*) were unornamented, with a circular section tapered like a palm tree trunk. They may have been forerunners of temples developed from the ancient form of worshipping in the forest. This is one of two Asoka pillars that remain in situ. The Wheel of Law on top of many pillars, and appears on the Indian flag, is the mark of the social and political order laid down by the Emperor.

Ramkund is also known as Monkey Tank since it was thought to have been dug by monkeys who offered the Buddha a bowl of honey. The two Buddhist **stupas** are said to hold urns containing the Buddha's ashes; the second was only excavated in 1958. The ancient **Coronation Tank** (*Kharauna Pokhar*) contains holy water which was used for anointing the ruler of Vaisali at his coronation. The **Lotus Tank** nearby is thought to be a picnic spot of the sixth century BC.

A pleasant, easy 5-km walk from the **Tourist Bungalow** to the Asoka Pillar goes through pretty villages, passing the Japanese stupa, museum and an old small stupa.

◉ **Sleeping**

Patna *p214, maps p214 and p216*
Some streets have been renamed: Bir Chand Patel Path (or Marg) has replaced Gardiner Rd.

Some old names continue to be used, eg Bailey Rd (J Nehru Marg), Fraser Rd (Nazharul Huque Path), Exhibition Rd (Braj Kishore Path).

AL-A Maurya Patna, Fraser Rd, S Gandhi
Maidan, T0612-220 3040, www.maurya.com.
80 centrally a/c rooms and suites, modern,
best in town. Pool (Rs 150 per day for
non residents).
B Pataliputra Ashok (ITDC), Bir Chand Patel
Path, T0612-222 6270, patashok@bih.nic.in.
45 rooms (half-day rates), good restaurant,
travel, tourist office.
C Rajasthan, Fraser Rd, T0612-222 5102.
20 rooms some a/c, good vegetarian meals,
very welcoming.
C Republic, Lauriya Bagh, Exhibition Rd,
T0612-232 0021, lawlysen@sancharnet.in.
35 a/c rooms, dining hall (very good
vegetarian meals), exchange, roof garden.
D-E Kautiliya Vihar (Bihar Tourism),
Bir Chand Patel Path, T0612-222 5411.
44 rooms, some a/c, dorm beds (Rs 50),
restaurant, exchange, travel.
E Mayur, Fraser Rd, T0612-222 4149.
Basic and clean rooms, some with bath,
good restaurant.
E Sheodar, Fraser Rd, T0612-222 7210.
15 fairly clean rooms, some a/c.
F AAEI, Dak Bungalow Rd. 1 room with bath,
good value, worth trying even if you are not
a member.
Avoid **Railway Retiring Rooms**.

🍴 Eating

Patna *p214, maps p214 and p216*
Hotels on Fraser Rd and Ashok Rajpath
usually have a restaurant.
▥▥▥ Pataliputra Ashok. International. Good
food, excellent kebabs, poolside barbecue,
but slow service.
▥▥ Amrali, Bir Chand Patel Path (Kautilya
Vihar building). Indian vegetarian.
Excellent dishes, quick service. Dimly lit
but recommended.
▥▥ Ashok (1st floor). Rather dark but good
Indian. Good Chinese.
▥▥ Nalanda, at Satkar International. Indian.
Pleasant atmosphere, good food.
▥ Marwari Awas Griha. Small, busy
dining hall that serves some excellent
vegetarian thalis.
▥ Mayfair, inexpensive snacks and
ice creams.

🛍 Shopping

Patna *p214, maps p214 and p216*
Patna and its surrounding villages are known
for wooden toys, inlay work, silver jewellery
in beaten rustic style, *tussar* silk, lacquerware,
leather shoes and *Madhubani* paintings.
Government emporia at **Bihar** on E Gandhi
Maidan, **Khadi Gramudyog** and shops at
Patna Market, New Market, Maurya Lok
Complex and Boring Canal Rd. Government
Lacquerware, Maghalpura for lacquer
on wood.

🏔 Activities and tours

Patna *p214, maps p214 and p216*
Ashok, Hotel Pataliputra Ashok, T0612-
222 3238.
TCI, Maurya Hotel, T0612-222 1699.
Bihar Tourism (BSTDC), **Ashok Travels &
Tours** and **Patna Tours**. All run city sight-
seeing Oct-Mar, Rajgir, Nalanda and Pawa-
puri, usually 0800-2200, Rs 80-100. Also
to Vaishali, Bodh Gaya, Buxar and Sasaram.
Buses can be slow and uncomfortable.

🚍 Transport

Patna *p214, maps p214 and p216*
Air
Transport to town, taxis, or **Indian Airlines**.
Coach to City Office via some hotels, Rs 30;
Tourist taxi transfers, about Rs 120 (Rs 350
deluxe). Airport enquiry, T0612-222 3199.
Indian Airlines, Gandhi Maidan, T0612-222
2554, www.indianairlines.nic.in. Daily to
Delhi, **Lucknow**, **Mumbai** and **Ranchi**. Jet
Airways, www.jetairways.com, and **Air
Deccan**, www.airdeccan.net, also fly to Delhi.

Bus
Luxury and Express bus services between
Patna and regional centres including
Kolkata, **Siliguri**, **Bhagalpur**, **Ranchi**,
Hazaribagh, **Monghyr** and **Gumra**.
Bihar SRTC, Gandhi Maidan, opposite
GPO, T0612-267 1682; Reservations:
1030-1800; at Junction Railway Station,
T0612-222 1093. Private bus stand opposite
Vir Kunwar Singh (Harding) Park.

● *For an explanation of the sleeping and eating price codes used in this guide, see the inside*
● *front cover. Other relevant information is found on pages 35-39.*

To Nepal STRCs and private buses run daily from Harding Park Bus Stand to Raxaul (5-7 hrs, Rs 60). However, timings are difficult and the buses packed and uncomfortable. Night buses reach the border early in the morning. Morning buses from Patna connect with the night bus to Kathmandu. Either way you have an overnight bus journey, unless you stay at Birganj – an unenviable option, though there are two modest hotels. Raxaul has little to offer; Ajanta, Ashram Rd, has rooms with bath. In **Raxaul** the tempo stand is south of the railway line and the Immigration and Customs office. You can cross the border to **Birganj** by rickshaw/ tempo (15-20 mins). In Birganj the tempo stand and Bus Park are in Adarsh Nagar, to the south of town. In the morning, buses depart from the Bus Stand east of the Clock Tower. To **Tandi Bazar** (4 hrs, for Chitwan, Rs 60), **Pokhara** (11-12 hrs, Rs 90) and **Kathmandu** (11-12 hrs, Rs 95). Even Express buses are slow and packed. Tourist minibuses are the only moderately comfortable option. You need an exit stamp in **Raxaul** from the Indian Immigration office (round the corner, and across the road from the Customs office), which is a great hassle. You may need customs clearance first. After crossing the border you need to get an entry stamp from the Nepalese Immigration counter (usually open early morning to late evening). Occasionally an unjustified additional fee is demanded for 'extras', eg registration card, or a 'visa' fee in US$.

From Nepal When travelling to India via Patna it is best to stay overnight in **Hetauda** and catch the 0530 bus to Birganj (3 hrs); go to the Bus Stand at 0500 to get a seat. At **Birganj**, walk or get a (pricey) horse-drawn rickshaw to the auto-tempo stand at the second crossroads. From there travel to Raxaul. Remember to get an exit stamp from Nepalese Immigration before crossing the border and an entry stamp from Indian Immigration in Raxaul.

Car
Tourist taxis, TCI, competitive rates, including longer tours; also **Ashok Travels and Tours**, about Rs 500 per 4 hrs to Rs 1000 per 8 hrs for a/c. Out-of-town touring (600 km), eg Vaishali, Rs 1200-1700; Bodh Gaya, Rajgir, Nalanda, Rs 4500 (a/c).

Taxi
Private unmetered taxis available from the airport, railway station, some hotels and important tourist sites. Fix rates beforehand. The same applies to rickshaws and tongas.

Train
Reservations on Northeast Railways, ie to Gorakhpur, Raxaul, must be made at Sonepur station, not Patna.

Patna Junction railway Station, enquiries, T131/0612-242 7812, reservations, T0612-222 2197. **Delhi (ND):** *Vikramshila Exp 2367,* 1705, 16½ hrs; *Rajdhani Exp 2423,* 2150, not Mon or Fri, 13 hrs. **Delhi (OD):** *Brahmaputra Mail 4055,* 1310, 15½ hrs. **Dhanbad:** *Damodar Exp 3330,* 2325, 6½ hrs. **Gaya:** *Patna Hatia Exp 8625,* 1130, 2½ hrs; *Palamau Exp 3348,* 2157, 2½ hrs. **Guwahati:** *NE Exp 2506,* 2200, 20½ hrs; *Rajdhani Exp 2424,* 0200, not Thu or Sun, 16 hrs. **Kolkata:** *Toofan Exp 3008,* 0630, 12½ hrs; *Rajdhani Exp 2306,* 0555, Mon, Fri, 7½ hrs; *Poorva Exp 2304,* 0755, Wed, Thu, Sat, Sun, 9 hrs. **Mumbai (Lokmanya Tilak):** *Rajendranagar Lokmanya Tilak Exp 2142,* 1105, 28 hrs. **Varanasi:** *Farraka Exp 3413/3483,* 0525, 6 hrs; *Shramjeevi Exp 2391,* 1050, 4 hrs.

Directory

Patna p214, maps p214 and p216
Banks State Bank of India, Gandhi Maidan, may refuse to cash Amex TCs. **Trade Wings,** Hotel Maurya complex. Efficient, good rate.
Hospitals Patna Medical College Hospital, Ashok Rajpath E, T0612-267 0132. **Nalanda Medical College Hospital,** T0612-263 1159, By-Pass Rd. **Library** British Library, Bank Rd, near Gandhi Maidan. 1030-1830 Tue-Sat. Very good collection and helpful staff.
Post GPO: Station Rd. **Central Telegraph Office,** Buddha Marg. **Tourist offices** India, Sudama Bhawan near Overbridge, Kankarbagh, T0612-234 5776. 1000-1700, excellent service, arranges local tours and excursions. Bihar, Paryatan Bhawan, Beer Chand Patel Marg, T0612-222 5411, F223 6218. Counters at Pataliputra Ashok, T223 2238, Airport and Patna Junction Railway Station T0612-222 1093. ITDC, Pataliputra Ashok, T0612-222 6270. **Tourism Department,** Government of Bihar, 9D Hutment, Secretariat, T/F0612-222 4531.

Patna to Bodh Gaya

→ *Colour map 1, grid B5/6.*

The area to the south of Patna has many major Buddhist sites, and also some Muslim and Hindu places of pilgrimage. This circular route to the southwest of Patna visits the ruins of Nalanda, one of the world's oldest universities, Rajgir, royal capital of the Magadh Empire, the Barabar Caves and Bodh Gaya. On the return journey to Patna, you can take a longer route via the immense tombs of Sher Shah at Sasaram. It is preferable to take at least two days even for the shorter trip. Once out of Patna the countryside is often very attractive, the early morning being particularly crisp and inviting. From March through to the monsoon it gets extremely hot during the day.

▸▸ *For Sleeping, Eating and other listings, see pages 226-228.*

Biharsharif and Pawapuri

On the NH31, these two towns can be visited prior to arriving at Nalanda. **Biharsharif**, 13 km from Nalanda, remained an Islamic cultural centre up to the 16th century. The *dargahs* (tombs) of Mukhdoom Shah, a 13th-century saint and Malik Ibrahim Baya, draw large numbers of Muslims, particularly during the annual **Urs fair**.

Pawapuri, also Apapuri which means 'sinless town', is particularly sacred to the Jains since Mahavir, the founder of Jainism, gained enlightenment here. The lotus pond where he bathed and on whose bank he was cremated has a white marble temple, the *Jalamandir*, in its centre and Samosharan Temple.

Nalanda 🖥️🚆 ▸▸ *pp226-228. Colour map 1, grid B6.*

Nalanda ① *0900-1750*, has the ruins of one of the world's oldest universities, founded in the fifth century AD on an ancient site of pilgrimage and teaching which had been visited by the Buddha and Mahavir (who spent '14 rainy seasons' in the area). According to Ghosh, Hiuen Tsang ascribed its name, which means 'charity without intermission', to the Buddha's liberality in an earlier birth.

History
Nalanda was hidden under a vast mound for centuries. Its archaeological importance was only established in the 1860s with most of the excavation taking place over about 20 years from 1916. The monasteries went through varying periods of occupation, and in one case nine different levels of building have been discovered. The Buddhist monastic movement resulted in large communities withdrawing into retreats. Even in the seventh century, according to Hiuen-Tsang, Buddhism was declining except in Bihar and Bengal where it enjoyed royal patronage and the support of the laity. The sanctuaries were often vast, as is the one here (500 m by 250 m).

The site
The remains of 11 monasteries and several *chaityas* (temples) built mainly in red brick, have been found as well as a large stairway, a library, lecture halls, dormitories, cells, ovens and wells. The buildings are in several storeys and tiers on massive terraces of solid brick, with stucco decorations of the Buddha as well as Hindu deities, and secular figures. Several of the monasteries have a guarded entrance on the western wall; the monks' cells are around a central courtyard with a wide

veranda (or a high wall in some cases). Opposite the entrance, the centre of the eastern wall has a shrine which must have contained an impressive image. Remains of drains which carried sewage to the east, and staircases giving access to the different storeys can be seen.

The monasteries are numbered one to 11, from south to north. The path from the gate enters the complex between one and four and goes across an open space to **Temple No 3**, the largest here. Almost certainly this was originally built by Asoka. The earliest temples were small structures, completely incorporated into the successively larger mounds. The north facing shrine chamber on top may have once contained an enormous Buddha image. The highest point gives a commanding view over the site as a whole, which is particularly impressive in the evening light.

> ♟ Nalanda by A Ghosh, 6th ed, 1986, gives excellent detailed descriptions of the site and the museum

Returning east, **Monasteries 1**, **1A** and **1B** are the most important of the monastery group. Ghosh suggests that the lower monastery was built by a Sumatran king in the reign of the third Pala king, Devapala, between AD 810-850. There was an earlier monastery underneath, which had been substantially damaged. It is possible to walk around all three of these southern monasteries.

There are several interesting features in the other monasteries: double rows of cells in **Monastery 5**, brick courtyards and two sets of double ovens in the upper courtyard of **6**, and evidence of three successive monasteries built on the same site at **7**.

Nalanda

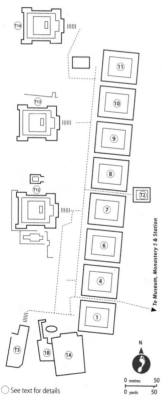

○ See text for details

0 metres 50
0 yards 50

▲ To Museum, Monastery 5 & Station

There is an imposing shrine and unique doorway in **8**, striking drains in **9** and arched doorways in **10**. The fragments of 25 stone pillars were recovered from the ruins of **11**, which stood 1 m apart and 2 m high. Ghosh suggests that fire was a recurrent hazard, and that every monastery was deserted and reoccupied.

In addition to the monasteries and the main temple, four other temples have been excavated. **Temples 12, 13** and **14** are in a line stretching north from the main temple. They all have a square outline and originally had large Buddha images, now destroyed. On the north of Temple **13** a brick smelting furnace was discovered, while the niches of the image's pedestal in Temple **14** contain the only example of mural painting in Nalanda. Little remains.

Temple site 2, east of monasteries seven and eight and reached by a path between them, has a sculpted dado with over 200 panels showing a wide variety of scenes depicting Hindu deities. Apart from the monasteries and temples there are several images, including the Buddha and Marachi (the Buddhist goddess of dawn).

Excavations to the northeast in **Sarai Mound** show evidence of a brick temple with frescoes of elephants and horses. **Bargaon** and **Begampur** to the north and **Jagadishpur** to the southwest contain impressive Buddhist and Hindu images.

⁝ Monastic University for the Buddhist world

It is assumed that the Gupta emperors were responsible for Nalanda's first monasteries. In the seventh century Hiuen-Tsang spent 12 years, both as a student and a teacher, at Nalanda which once had over 3000 teachers and philosophers. The monks were supported by 200 villages, and a library of nine million manuscripts attracted men from countries as far flung as Java, Sumatra, Korea, Japan and China. Great honour was attached to a Nalanda student and admission was restricted with seven or eight out of 10 applicants failing to gain a place.

I-Tsing, another Chinese scholar, arrived here in AD 673 and also kept detailed records, describing the severe lifestyle of the monks. The divisions of the day were measured by a water clock, and the syllabus involved the study of Buddhist and Brahmanical scriptures, logic, metaphysics, medicine and Sanskrit grammar.

The University flourished until 1199 when the Afghan Bhaktiar Khalji sacked it, burning, pillaging and driving the surviving residents into hiding. It was the end of living Buddhism in India until the modern revival.

Nava Nalanda Mahavihar

About 2 km from the principal site is a postgraduate Institute for Research into Buddhism and Pali literature set up by the Bihar government, which has many rare manuscripts; it is now the site of the Indira Gandhi Open University. There is a colourful **Thai Temple** built in the 1980s. **Kundalpur**, 1½ km north of Nalanda, is believed by the Digambara sect of Jains to be the birthplace of Mahavir.

Rajgir 🏨🚻🚌 ➤ *pp226-228. Colour map 1, grid B6.*

➔ *Phone code: 6119. Population: 33,700.*

Encircled by rugged forested hills, Rajgir is held sacred by both Buddhists and Jains for its association with Mahavir, who taught here for many years, and the Buddha. You can still see parts of the 40-km cyclopean dry stone wall that once enclosed the ancient city and fort. Today, the *kund* (hot springs) with large open-air baths are a special attraction. Non-Hindus are not allowed into the Surya Temple. The Kund Market nearby, where buses stop, has shops, stalls and local eating places with basic rooms.

The site

Gridhrakuta, the 'Hill of Vultures', was one of the Buddha's favourite places where he delivered many important sermons, and was where he is believed to have converted the Magadhan King **Bimbisara**, who had built the old stone road leading up the hill. It was used by Hiuen-Tsang in the seventh century and still provides the best access. Rock cut steps lead to the two natural caves; plaques and Buddhist shrines were found in the area (now in Nalanda Museum). The first Buddhist Council was held in the **Saptaparni Cave** on Vaibhara Hill, six months after the Buddha's death, and his teachings were written down for the first time. On the way to the cave is the large, 7-m high **Pippala stone house**, an extraordinary 'watchtower' built of blocks of stone. On all sides there are small cells for guards which were later used by monks.

Little survives of the fifth-century BC **Ajatasatru Fort**. The outer wall was built with blocks of stone up to 1½ m long, with smaller boulders in its core. In places it was 4 m

⁝ Rajgir *by Md Hamid Kuraishi, 5th ed, 1987, describes the site with maps.*

high and over 5 m wide. Of the 32 large gates (and 64 small ones) mentioned in ancient texts, only one to the north has survived. Of the inner city wall, which was about 5 km long and roughly pentagonal, only a section to the south remains, with three gaps through which the old roads ran. In the valley, a 6-m high circular brick structure, decorated with stucco figures, had an old Jain shrine called **Maniyar Math**.

Nearby **Venuvana**, the bamboo grove where the Buddha spent some time, where excavations revealed a room, some stupas and the Karanda Tank, is now a deer park with a small zoo. To the south of Venuvana there are Jain and Hindu temples. The ruins of Buddha's favourite retreat within the valley, called the **Jivakamarvana Monastery** (fourth to third century BC), have been found with four halls and several rooms.

The **Visva Santi Stupa** ① *cable car (600 m) for access, usually 0900-1300, 1500-1700, (good for the views)*, built by the Japanese on top of Ratnagiri, is dedicated to world peace. The large white Nipponzan Myohoji stupa has four golden statues of the Buddha representing his birth, enlightenment, preaching and death.

Mahavir spent "14 rainy seasons" in Rajgir and the 20th Tirthankara was born here so it is a major Jain pilgrimage centre, with temples on most of the hilltops.

Gaya ●●● ⟩⟩ *pp228-228. Colour map 1, grid B5.*

→ *Phone code: 0631. Population: 383,200.*

Gaya, on slightly raised ground in the valley between two hills, was blessed by Vishnu with the power to absolve all temporal sins. Its many sacred shrines attract Hindus at Pitrapaksh Tarpan (September-October), when prayers are offered for the dead before pilgrims take a dip in the seasonal holy River Phalgu. Cremations take place on funeral pyres in the burning ghats along the river.

Gaya

Sights

There are several old Buddhist temples and monastery remains around Gaya. In the centre of the town is the **Vishnupad Temple**, which is supposed to have been built over Vishnu's footprint, imprinted on a rock set in a silver basin. The 30-m high temple has eight rows of beautifully carved pillars supporting the *mandapa* (pavilion), which were refurbished in 1787. Only Hindus are permitted into the sanctum and temple grounds which has the *Akshayabat* (the immortal banyan tree under which the Buddha is believed to have meditated for six years), where the final puja for the dead takes place. Brahmayoni Hill, 1 km southwest, with its 1000 stone steps, which lead to a vantage point for viewing both Gaya and Bodh Gaya.

The **Surya Temple** at **Deo**, 20 km away, dedicated to the Sun God, attracts large crowds in November when **Chhatt Puja** is celebrated.

Sleeping ●	
Ajatshatru 1	Royal Surya 4
Akash 2	Siddhartha
Railway Retiring	International 5
Rooms 3	Vishu
	International 6

0 metres 500
0 yards 500

N

Bihar & Jharkhand Patna to Bodh Gaya

Barabar Caves is 35 km north. The 22-km rough track leading to the caves in the impressive granite hill turns east off the main road to Patna at **Belagunj** (30 minutes from Gaya, two hours from Patna) where buses stop. From here allow four hours to walk up ("a real challenge" by four-wheel drive). It is only safe to go in daylight and not alone; a solitary sadhu is inclined to jump out at you from nowhere! Enquire about safety at Belagunj Police Station.

The whale-backed quartzite gneiss hill stands in wild and rugged country. Inscriptions reveal that, on instructions from Asoka, four chambers were excavated, cut and chiselled to a high polish by the stonemasons, as retreats for ascetics who belonged to a sect related to Jainism. Percy Brown pointed out that the extraordinary caves, particularly the *Lomas Rishi* and the *Sudama*, are exact copies of ordinary beehive shaped huts built with bamboo, wood and thatch. The barrel-vaulted chamber inside the *Sudama* is 10 m long, 6 m wide and 3½ m high which through a doorway leads to a circular cell of 6 m diameter. The most impressive craftsmanship is seen on the façade of the *Lomas Rishi* which replicates the horseshoe shaped gable end of a wooden structure with two lunettes which have very fine carvings of lattice-work and rows of elephants paying homage to Buddhist stupas. Excavation is incomplete as there was a possibility of the cave collapsing. There is also a Siva temple on the Siddheshwar peak.

> ❈ *The caves inspired the setting of EM Forster's A Passage to India. They date from the third century BC and are the earliest examples of rock-cut sanctuaries.*

At **Nagarjuna Hill** there are three further rock-cut sanctuaries, 1 km northeast from Barabar. The *Gopi* (Milkmaid's) cave having the largest chamber. Inscriptions date these to about 50 years after the excavations at Barabar.

Bodh Gaya ⬤🔵🔴⬤ ➤ *pp228-228. Colour map 1, grid B5.*

→ *Phone code: 0631. Population: 30,900.*

Bodh Gaya, a quiet village near the river Niranjana (Phalgu), is one of the holiest Buddhist pilgrimage centres. It was under the Bo tree here that Gautama, the prince, attained enlightenment to become the Buddha.

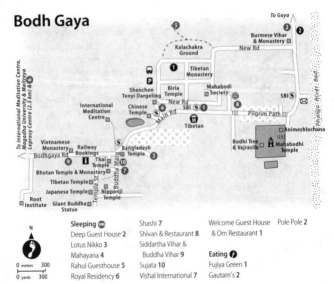

Bodh Gaya

Sleeping		Shashi 7	Welcome Guest House	Pole Pole 2
Deep Guest House 2		Shivan & Restaurant 8	& Om Restaurant 1	
Lotus Nikko 3		Siddartha Vihar &		
Mahayana 4		Buddha Vihar 9	**Eating**	
Rahul Guesthouse 5		Sujata 10	Fujiya Green 1	
Royal Residency 6		Vishal International 7	Gautam's 2	

N
0 metres 300
0 yards 300

Ins and outs

Getting there and around Travel in daylight only, for your own safety. Buses run from Gaya, Patna, Nalanda and Rajgir. The hotels, temple and monasteries are a few minutes' walk from the bus stand. ▶▶ *See Transport, page 228, for further details.*

The site

Bodh Gaya was 'lost' for centuries until rediscovered by Burmese Buddhists in 1877 which led to restoration work by the British. UNESCO has recently given its preliminary approval to declare Bodh Gaya as a World Heritage Site, with the event to be marked by the arrival of a 152 m high bronze statue (made in the UK).

Lamas, Rimpoches and Buddhists from all over the world assemble here during the *monlam* when the area north of the bus station resembles a medieval encampment with tents serving as informal restaurants and accommodation. The food is smoky and there are long waits, but it is atmospheric and full of colour. The 'tourist season' draws to a close at the end of February when many restaurants close and meditation courses stop running. Unfortunately the air can get heavily polluted, partly due to badly serviced buses, making a walk along the road rather unpleasant.

Mahabodhi Temple

ⓘ *0500-2100, cameras Rs 20.*

Asoka's original shrine near the Bodhi tree was replaced by this temple in the second century, which in turn went through several alterations. The temple on a high and broad plinth, with a soaring 54-m high pyramidal spire with a square cross-section and four smaller spires, houses a gilded image of the Enlightened Buddha. The smaller spires may have been added when Burmese Buddhists attempted extensive rebuilding in the 14th century. An ornately carved stone railing in bas relief surrounds the temple on three sides and several carved Buddhist stupas depict tales from the Buddha's early life. Unlike earlier circular railings this had to conform to the quadrangle of the temple structure. Its height of 2 m, its lighter proportions and the quality of the carving dates it to the Sunga period (early first century BC). The lotus pond where the Buddha may have bathed is to the south. To the north is the *Chankramana*, a raised platform (first century) with lotus flowers carved on it, which marks the consecrated promenade used by the Buddha while meditating. Numerous attempts to restore the temple have obscured the original. The candle-lit evening ceremony is worth attending.

The original Bodhi tree (pipal or *Ficus religiosa*) was supposedly destroyed by Asoka before he was converted, and others which replaced it also died. The present tree behind the temple is believed to come from the original stock – Prince Mahinda carried a sapling from the sacred Bo tree to Sri Lanka when he went to spread Buddhism there. This in turn produced a sapling which was brought back to Bodh Gaya. The red sandstone slab, the **Vajrasila**, under the tree marks the place where Gautama sat in meditation. Today, pilgrims tie pieces of coloured cloth on its branches when they come to pray.

Animeshlochana is another sacred spot where the Buddha stood to gaze in gratitude at the Bodhi tree for a week, after his Enlightenment. The temple also attracts Hindu pilgrims since the Buddha is considered to be one of the *avatars* or incarnations of Vishnu.

Other temples

Pilgrims from many lands have built their own temples. You can start at the giant 20-m stone **Buddha statue** which was installed at the end of the road in 1989. The modern two-storey, spotless **Japanese Temple** ⓘ *0700-1200, 1400-1800*, next door with beautiful polished marble floors has gold images of the Buddha. The **Tibetan Temple** and **Monastery** next to this (1938) is ornately painted and has a *Dharma*

Chakra (Wheel of Law) which must be turned three times when praying for forgiveness of sins. A large 2-m metal ceremonial drum in red and gold is also on display. Opposite is the **Nipponji Temple** complex with a free clinic, monastery and a Peace Bell (rung from 0600-1200 and at 1700). Returning to the Mahabodhi Temple you will pass the colourful **Bhutan Temple** protected by carved Himalayan deities, a glittering pagoda-style **Thai Temple** and a **Bangladesh Temple**. The **Chinese Temple** houses an enormous, revolving ceremonial prayer drum.

Teaching centres

Magadha University, an international centre for studies in history, culture and philosophy, is about 3 km from the Mahabodhi Temple. The **Tibetan Medical and Astro Institute** carries out research and gives advice. **Meditation courses** varying from a week to a month during the winter, follow both the Mahayana and Hinanyana traditions; enquire at the Burmese, Tibetan and Thai monasteries. Insight Meditation, www.insightmeditation.org, runs retreats during January and February in the Thai monastery. The **International Meditation Centre** ① *contact via Woodland Rd, Denbury, Devon, UK, TQ12 6DY*, opposite the Thai monastery, T0631-220 0707, also holds courses. The **Root Institute**, off the Magadha University Road, is involved in community self-help schemes and gives popular short introductory courses.

Sasaram → *Colour map 1, grid B5.*

Sher Shah Suri, who was responsible for the tombs, asked the master-builder Aliwal Khan to build a tomb for his father **Hasan Khan** around 1535. This later inspired the building of the impressive second tomb for Sher Shah himself. The first imitated the octagonal structure and walled enclosure of the earlier Lodi tombs but was rather plain. What followed, however, was extraordinary not only in scale, but also in its conception. **Sher Shah's mausoleum** ① *Mar-Jul 0700-1800, Aug-Feb 0800-1700, Rs 100*, 500 m away, was set in a large artificial lake so it appears to float. A modern redbrick gateway opposite the Dak Bungalow leads down to the tombs. You enter it by a causeway after going through a guard room on the north bank (originally visitors approached by barge from the ghat on the east side). The grounds and lake provide a relaxing break, though travellers report a certain amount of hassle from local youth.

This Muslim site, between Gaya and Varanasi, is well worth a visit. The tombs are a short rickshaw ride from the railway station, which has left luggage (Rs 10)

⬤ Sleeping

Nalanda *p220*
E Tathaghat Vihar. Modest rooms.
F Ajatashatru Vihar. Very basic, dorm only.
F Burmese Rest House, beyond museum.
F Inspection Bungalow, meals to order, contact Superintendent, Archaeological Survey of India, Patna.
F Youth Hostel.

Rajgir *p222*
There are several Jain Dharamshalas near the station.
AL Indo Hokke, 2 km from Kund Market, T06112-255245, www.theroyalresidency.net. 44 comfortable rooms (few Western style), primarily for Japanese pilgrims, excellent Japanese restaurant (with fresh ingredients daily), open Nov-Mar, reserve well ahead (guarantees 'beds' not 'rooms' in high season).
AL The Rajgir Residency, T06112-255404, www.rajgir-residency.com. 28 a/c rooms plus authentic Korean, Japanese and Thai food.
D Gautam Vihar, T06112-225273, 15 rooms (some a/c) with bath and veranda.
D-E Siddharth, near Kund Market, T06112-255616. Good rooms with bath, and decent food.
D-E Tathagat Vihar, T06112-225176. 32 simple rooms (some a/c), dorm, Indian restaurant, open Nov-Mar.

Gaya *p223, map p223*

Mostly very basic with non a/c rooms.

B-C Siddhartha International, off Station Rd, T0631-243 6243, www.rajgir-residency .com. Some a/c rooms, modern, great food, but noisy and overpriced.

D-E Ajatshatru, opposite railway station, T0631-243 4584. Range of rooms with bath (hot water), some gloomy and noisy, but popular ground floor restaurant has large menu, cheap but good basic food.

D-E Royal Surya, Dak Bungalow Rd, T0631-242 3730. Spacious, bright rooms, 24-hr checkout, affable staff.

D-E Vishu International, Swarajpuri Rd, T0631-243 1146. Clean and new, large public balcony and an all-important generator.

G Akash, in the alley opposite the station, T0631-222 2205. Rooms with air cooler around an Islamic-style courtyard, bucket hot water, the best bottom-rung option in town.

G Railway Retiring Rooms, at Gaya Junction. 6 rooms, 2 a/c, dorm Rs 50 (not for women).

Bodh Gaya *p224, map p224*

Simple budget hotels often quote higher rates so bargain. Good off-season discounts are available.

AL-A The Royal Residency, Dumahan Rd, T0631-220 0124, www.theroyal residency.net. 67 rooms, central a/c, most luxurious in town.

A-B Lotus Nikko Hotel, next to Mahabodhi Temple, T0631-220 0700, www.nikko hotels.com. Clean and spacious renovated rooms, most a/c, those on first floor preferable. Good location.

B Sujata, Buddha Marg, past the Bangladesh Temple, T0631-220 0481. Large and lovely rooms, Japanese baths, soulless restaurant.

D-E Mahayana, Main Rd, T0631-220 0756, mahayanagt@yahoo.com. Huge bright rooms in an airy building with courtyards, peaceful vibe and charming staff, a good choice.

E Root Institute, Magadha University Rd, T0631-220 0714. Rooms in traditional local huts in a peaceful rural setting, shared bath, excellent food.

E Shashi, Buddha Marg, T0631-220 0459. Small, clean rooms, restaurant.

E Vishal International, Buddha Marg, T0631-220 0633, htlvishal@gmail.com. Brand new place with fussy but clean rooms, best ones at the front.

E-G Siddartha Vihar, Bodhgaya Rd, T0631-220 0445. Decent a/c rooms with balconies in a quirky circular building; next door **Buddha Vihar** (Bihar Tourism) has very cheap dorm beds.

G Deep Guest House, next to Burmese Monastery, near Sujata Bridge, T0631-220 0463. Clean rooms, friendly staff, roof terrace, peaceful atmosphere.

G Rahul Guest House, behind Kalachakra Ground, T0631-220 0709. Clean and cheery rooms, plus a good terrace, in a super-peaceful location.

G Shivan, opposite temple, T0631-220 0425. Clean rooms, some with bath, hot water, friendly, restaurant downstairs.

G Welcome Guest House, above Om restaurant on Main Rd, T0631-220 0377. Caters to backpackers, and is in a good central location.

Monasteries

Some monasteries provide spartan accommodation primarily for pilgrims; contact the monk in charge. They expect guests to conform to certain rules of conduct.

G Bhutan Monastery, Buddha Rd. 18 rooms in guest houses, shared facilities.

G Burmese Vihar, Gaya Rd. Simple rooms (some newer) with nets, dorm, no fan, garden (eat at **Pole Pole** opposite).

Sasaram *p226*

It is advisable to avoid staying overnight here if possible.

F Shilpa Deluxe, GT Rd, T06184-222 3305. 15 rooms, dirty, staff have TV on loud non stop.

F Youth Hostel.

Station Refreshment Room for breakfast and simple thalis, fairly clean, "nice waiters at least try to chase the rats"!

● *For an explanation of the sleeping and eating price codes used in this guide, see the inside*
● *front cover. Other relevant information is found on pages 35-39.*

🍴 Eating

Rajgir p222

Green, Kund market near Bus Stop. Basic, cheap, simple Indian – tables on veranda.

Bodh Gaya p224, map p224

Most of the tent restaurants operate in winter only.

🍴 **Café Om**, decent Western fare draws in every backpacker in town.

🍴 **Fujiya Green**, near Kalachakra Ground. Extensive vegetarian/non-vegetarian menu, specializes in Tibetan but it has every continent covered. Attractive interior lives up to the name, friendly service.

🍴 **Gautam's**, opposite Burmese Vihar, for apple strudel and cinnamon rolls.

🍴 **Lotus Nikko**, good a/c restaurant serving tasty food.

🍴 **Pole Pole**, tent opposite Burmese Vihar. Clean, excellent management, good though not exceptional food.

🍴 **Shiva**, diagonally opposite entrance to temple. Japanese food and simple Western.

🚌 Transport

Nalanda p220

Regular buses from **Patna** (90 km north), **Rajgir** (15 km) with the nearest railway station. Cycle-rickshaw and tonga: outside the Tourist Information Centre.

Rajgir p222

Bus to **Patna** (105 km), 4 hrs; and **Gaya** 3 hrs. Auto-rickshaw or share-taxi to visit the sites, and Nalanda.

Gaya p223, map p223
Bus
Long distance From Stand across the river: to **Rajgir**; from Gandhi Maidan Bus Stand: Patna, Ranchi and Hazaribagh. To **Bodh Gaya**: buses from the station, but very crowded. Shared 6-seater auto-rickshaws leave from station (Rs 10) and from main auto stand opposite the market (Rs 8). After 1800 only private auto-rickshaws are available: bargain hard, Rs 50-100. A cycle-rickshaw from the station to main auto stand is Rs 8-10.

Rickshaw
Auto- and cycle-rickshaws are easily available.

Train
Gaya is on the Grand Chord line of the Delhi-Kolkata section of Eastern Railway. Gaya Junction railway Station, enquiries and reservations: T0631-243 2031, 0900-1600. **Delhi (ND)**: *Rajdhani Exp 2301/2421*, 2211, 12 hrs; *Purushottam Exp 2801*, 1415, 15 hrs;. **Kolkata (H)**: *Howrah Exp 2308*, 2043, 8 hrs; *Kalka-Howrah Mail 2312*, 2242, 7½ hrs; *Rajdhani Exp 2302/2422*, 0433, 6½ hrs; plus others. **Patna**: *Palamau Exp 3347*, 0345, 2½ hrs; *Hatia Patna Exp 8624/8626*, 0410, 2½ hrs. **Varanasi**: *Doon Exp 3009*, 0515, 5½ hrs; *Poorva Exp 2381*, 1657, Wed, Thu, Sun, 3½ hrs; plus lots that arrive/depart in middle of night, and others that go to Mughal Sarai, with transfer by auto-rickshaw to Varanasi.

Bodh Gaya p224, map p224

Patna has the nearest airport, while Gaya (16 km) has the nearest train station. Computerized train bookings next to the Tourist Office, Mon-Sat 0800-1400. Auto-rickshaws take 30 mins to Gaya; the last shared one leaves 1800, then private hire (Rs 50-100) until 2100.

Sasaram p226

Train to **Gaya**, *Doon Exp 3009*, 1908, 2 hrs. From **Gaya**, 0607, 1½ hrs; to **Varanasi**, 0755, 3½ hrs; from **Varanasi**: 1620, 2½ hrs.

ℹ️ Directory

Gaya p223, map p223
Banks State Bank of India ATMs, at station and next to market. **Post** Station Rd and GB Rd. Warning from travellers whose mail/parcels were pilfered here. **Tourist office** Bihar, Gaya Junction Railway Station Main Hall, T0631-242 0155, 0600-2100.

Bodh Gaya p224, map p224
Banks State Bank of India has an ATM on Main Rd, and changes cash, TCs, Mon-Fri 1030-1430, Sat 1030-1230. **Post** T0631-240 0742. Mon-Fri 1000-1530, Sat 1000-1230. **Internet** Several options in the town centre. **Tourist office** Bihar, corner of Bodhgaya Rd and Temple St, T0631-220 0672.

Jharkhand

Background

The land Jharkhand lies on the once densely forested northern edge of the Indian Peninsula. The rolling plateau, between 300-400 m, with occasional outcrops rising to nearly 1000 m, is mostly granite and gneiss of ancient Gondwanaland. On the north it drops quite sharply to the plains of the Ganges, while a great fault has created the valley of the mineral rich Damodar. The plateau still has an open feel, forest being interspersed by agricultural land, except where coal and iron ore mining have created a scarred industrial landscape of mines and soil tips. To the south of the Damodar valley are the Ranchi plateaus, broken up by remarkable looking flat-topped hillocks or *mesas*. Up to 20% is still forested, though exploitation of this continues. The soils are often poor, sometimes lateritic, and easily eroded if conservation measures are not adopted.

Politics The inauguration of the state in the early hours of 15 November 2000 was set symbolically on the birth anniversary of Birsa Munda, leader of the Santhal rebellion in 1831-1832. The origins of the present state can be traced to the formation of the Chota Nagpur Unnati Samaj in 1921, which proposed the creation of a separate Jharkhand state in 1928. Jharkhand's future is heavily dependent upon the exploitation of its mineral wealth. Many of the tribal peoples have been under pressure from agricultural settlers from the plains, and increasingly from both state and national governments keen to exploit the mineral wealth that lies beneath their lands. By way of resistance, some tribal people have joined Maoist militias, the so-called Naxalites, while many others have been conscripted into a government-backed opposing force, the ironically named Salva Judum (Peace March). In 2006 battles between the rival groups resulted in a number of deaths. Often in desperation the poor have moved to cities like Kolkata and Mumbai, or to work on tea estates.

Ranchi ⬛🅾🅘 ▸ *pp231-232. Colour map 1, grid C6.*

→ *Phone code: 0651. Population: 846,500.*

Once the summer capital of Bihar state, Ranchi still attracts holidaymakers for its location on higher ground in the heart of the Chota Nagpur tribal country. An industrial town and a major educational centre, Ranchi is also known for its mental asylum at Kanke, 9 km north. The town is surrounded by rolling forests with waterfalls and lakes in the heart of one of India's great tribal belts. The Ranchi district has been the recent scene of violently suppressed demonstrations, opposed to Koel-Karo dam project.

Ranchi Lake is popular for local people to relax, while the adjacent **Ranchi Hill** offers good views of the town and surrounding countryside. **Tagore Hill**, 3 km away, is named after Rabindranath Tagore who wrote several books and poems here. **Ranchi University** ① *1100-1700*, has ethnographic collections of central Indian states and Andaman and Nicobar Islands. **Ranchi Museum** ① *Tribal Research Institute Building, Morabadi Rd, Mon-Sat 1030-1700, free*, 4 km away, has a collection of stone sculpture, terracottas and arms as well as ethnological objects at the Institute itself.

The 17th-century **Jagannath Temple** on a hillock at Jagannathpur, 10 km southwest, is in the style of the great temple in Puri (annual **Ratha Yatra** in June/July).

Around Ranchi

The Subhanarekha River, which rises southeast of the town, is interrupted by several impressive waterfalls, within easy range of Ranchi. **Hundru Falls**, 45 km east, are formed by the 100 m drop of the river, particularly impressive just after the monsoons.

You can picnic and bathe in the pools at the bottom. Others in the area include **Johna**, 40 km east on the Purulia Road, and **Dassamghagh Falls** (34 km) which has a tea house. It is dangerous to bathe at Dassamghagh; several people have drowned. Mundas believe that the god of the Falls demands sacrifices.

Chota Nagpur plateau 💻 ➡ *p231. Colour map 1, grid B5 and C5.*

There are game reserves set in often stunningly beautiful and remote scenery on the Chota Nagpur plateau, which can be easily reached from Ranchi. This is one of the poorest areas of India, with extensive missionary activity, though efforts are in place to conserve traditional tribal culture, which the government sees as a strong tourist draw.

Palamau (Betla) National Park was once the home of the extinct Indian cheetah and the world's first tiger census was taken in this Project Tiger Reserve in 1932. Recent developments in the park have not been encouraging: a survey taken by forest rangers reported that in 2006 visitors sighted a grand total of two tigers. The wildlife also includes leopard, gaur, sambar, muntjac and nilgai, Indian wolf and many species of birds. The North Koel River and its tributary run through the park but in the summer animals become dependent on waterholes. The wooden towers at **Hathibajwa** and **Kamaladah**, and the hide at **Madhuchuhan**, are good vantage points. Elephants can be seen from the end of the monsoon until the waterholes begin to dry up in March. The Flame of the Forest (*Butea monosperma*) and *mahua* flowers attract birdlife: over 200 species of water and woodland birds have been recorded, while hot springs and the remains of two 16th-century **forts** of Chero kings who once ruled from here add to the interest. Palamau's vegetation is mainly *sal* and bamboo, though it is now considerably degraded. Jeeps for viewing the animals can be hired from the Forest Department. The park is open throughout the year, though the best time to visit is from October to April.

Hazaribagh Wildlife Sanctuary ① *Evening park tour from Divisional Forest Office, Hazaribagh, 1700-2200, Rs 150,* is a Project Tiger Reserve, part of the Chota Nagpur plateau in forested tribal territory, interspersed with grass meadows and some deep waterways. Hazaribagh ('thousand gardens') town is close to the wildlife sanctuary, waterfalls, Tilaiya Dam (55 km) and Konar Dam (51 km). The sanctuary is set in hilly terrain but is slightly lower than the town at 550 m. The park supports sambar, nilgai, deer, chital, leopard, tiger, wild boar and wild cat, though here too animal numbers are dwindling. There are 10 watchtowers and hides for viewing. Roads allow easy access; the NH33 takes you to the Pokharia gate, 16 km from Hazaribagh. The best time to visit is from February to April.

The Hazaribagh area also has some Mesolithic shelters where rock art can be seen and several Neolithic monuments including dolmens similar to those found in Celtic Europe. For more details contact Bulu Imam at Sanskriti crafts store, Hazaribagh ① *T06546-264820, www.sanskritihazaribagh.com*, who sells authentic tribal artworks and has founded a Tribal Women's Artists' Cooperative for traditional arts.

Eastern Jharkhand 💻🗨🅘 ➡ *pp232-232.*

Jamshedpur → *Phone code: 0657. Population: 570,300.*

This flourishing steel town lies 130 km southeast of Ranchi, established as a planned township by the Parsi industrialist Jamshedji Tata in 1908. Located close to rich iron and coal deposits, there are also limestone quarries and some magnesite. The town has retained much of its natural attraction, with its lakes and rivers enclosed by the Dolma hills, in spite of the pollution from its heavy plants. The town is split in two by the steel plant and rail sidings. **Keenan Stadium** in Bistupur, north of town, is the venue for international cricket matches. **Dalma Wildlife Sanctuary**, a few kilometres out of Jamshedpur, on the Ranchi Road is noted for its elephant population.

Other centres have emerged along the **Damodar Valley**, which cuts through a rocky, thickly wooded section of the Chota Nagpur plateau, the home of the many aboriginal tribal people of Jharkhand. The Santals, Bedia, Khond, Munda and Oraon were the original inhabitants of this land, and though a few still live in isolated villages, most have joined the workforce in the industrial townships. The river valley has a number of hydroelectric power stations and large dams. Industrial activities in the valley include coal in Dhanbad, and locomotives in Chittaranjan and Bokaro.

Parasnath Hill → *Colour map 1, grid B6. Altitude: 1366 m.*

The holy hill of Parasnath is about 150 km along the Kolkata Road from Bodh Gaya, near Dumri and Madhuban; note that Madhuban's dharamshalas and lodges may be full during holidays and festivals. Particularly sacred to the Jains, a track winds up through Parasnath's forested slopes to the 24 shrines which crown the hilly northern outcrops of the Indian Peninsula. The shrines are rarely visited by foreigners but are a regular pilgrimage site for thousands of devout Jains and Hindus. The highest shrine is dedicated to the last forerunner of Mahavir himself, Lord Parsvanatha, see page 314, who is believed to have achieved enlightenment while meditating in the cave, now enshrined in the temple.

Most pilgrims start climbing at 0400, the best time to catch superb views of sunrise and the countryside. It is a three-hour climb but *dhoolis* are available; allow eight hours in all. The super-fit can manage a climb in just over two hours and run down much faster. A visit is highly recommended. Leather items are not allowed on the hill.

● Sleeping

Ranchi *p229*
Most hotels in Ranchi are generally full. Book in advance if possible.
AL-A Capitol Hill, Main Rd, T0651-233 1330, www.hotelcapitolhill.com. Smart rooms with minibar and internet, good central location, multi-cuisine restaurant, 24-hr room service.
A Yuvraj Palace, Doranda, T0651-248 0326, www.hotelyuvrajpalace.com. Best in town, 25 central a/c rooms and elegant suites, multi-cuisine restaurant, bar, 24-hr café.
B-D BNR, Station Rd, T0651-220 8044.
22 rooms in cottages in station building, some a/c, restaurant, lawns, tennis, old-world feel.
C Hindustan, Main Rd, T0651-220 6039.
32 reasonable rooms with TV, some a/c, decent restaurant, overpriced but likely to have vacancies.
C Kwality Inns, Station Rd, T0651-246 0128.
36 rooms, mostly a/c, reasonable, clean, restaurant, though lacklustre staff.
C-D Yuvraj, Doranda, T0651-248 2423.
35 rooms, some a/c, restaurant/bar.
E-F Birsa Vihar (JTDC), Main Rd, T0651-233 1828. Dorm, 30 simple rooms, tourist office.

Chota Nagpur plateau *p230*
D Tree House, Betla, Palamau National Park, book through Conservator of Forests,
T06562-222650, fdptrpalamau@yahoo.co.in.
Rickety little shack perched in a tree amid forest, lots of deer and other wildlife, the most atmospheric choice by far.
D Tree House, Maromar, bookings as above.
Another Robinson Crusoe affair, built entirely of wood but it has modern facilities.
D-F Van Vihar, inside reserve, Betla, T06567-226513. Reports of no electricity or food, 25 rooms, fairly comfortable a/c, good deer viewing, tourist information.
E Debjani, food available.
E Forest Rest Houses, Kehr and Kechki. Reservations: Field Director, Project Tiger, Palamau, Daltonganj, T06562-222650.
E Rest Houses at Mundu, Garu, Chhipadohar and Baresand, contact Div Forest Officer, S Forest Div, Daltonganj, T06562-222427.
E Tourist Lodge, near reserve. 10 rooms.

Hazaribagh *p230*
D-E Tourist Lodge, T06546-224337.
9 rooms, some a/c, tourist information.
F Govt Guest House, 12 rooms, near bus stand.
G Canary Hill Rest House, on hill overlooking lake, get permission from Forest Officer, T06546-222339. Very simple and basic but great views, wake up to birdsong.

Budget hotels in Jamshedpur are close to Tata
Nagar railway station. Mid-range hotels are
2-3 km from bus and train stations in Bistupur.
A Fortune Hotel Centrepoint, 2, Inner
Circle Road, Bistupur, T0657-222 4200, www
.fortuneparkhotels.com. 42 rooms, central
a/c, health club, good business facilities.
B-C Darshan, opposite Ram Mandir,
Main Rd, T0657-242 4317, F2430973.
26 decent, clean a/c rooms, restaurant.
C-E South Park, Q Rd, Bistupur, T0657-243
5001. Inviting rooms, some a/c, clean hot bath,
good restaurant, helpful. Recommended.
D-E Boulevard, Main Rd, Bistupur, T0657-242
5321, www.theboulevardhotel.org. Stately old
place, large, sparse rooms, TV, hot bath, clean,
friendly, well located. Recommended.

Transport

Ranchi *p229*
Air
The airport is 13 km away. **Indian Airlines**,
Main Rd, T0651-220 6160, airport, T141, T250
1554, www.indian-airlines.nic.in. Daily to
Delhi, **Mumbai** and **Patna**. Four flights a
week to **Kolkata** and **Lucknow**.

Bus
Private bus stand at Kantatoli, 2 km from Main
Rd, T0651-230 8907; serves major towns in
Jharkhand and surrounding states.
Government bus stand, Station Rd, T0651-
230 4328. Also Ratu Rd bus stand (4 km) for
buses to Madhya Pradesh (eg Daltonganj).

Train
Enquiries, T131. Reservations, T135.
Computerized Reservation Centre, G-41 Sainak
Market, Main Rd, T0651-230 1097. **Dhanbad**:
Maurya Exp 5027, 1750, 4 hrs. **Gaya**: *Hatia Patna
Exp 8626*, 0620, 6½ hrs; *Rajendranagar Exp 8624*,
1930, 8½ hrs. Both continue to **Patna**, 10 hrs
and 11½ hrs. **Kolkata (H)**: *Hatia Howrah Exp
8616*, 2150, 9 hrs. **New Delhi**: *Rajdhani Exp
2439*, 1730 (Wed and Sun), 18 hrs; *Jammu
Tawi Exp 8101/ 86011*, 1530, 27 hrs.

Chota Nagpur plateau *p230*
The nearest airport to Palamau is at Ranchi,
140 km away. If in a car, take the road west-
north west out of Ranchi for **Kuru** (57 km),
in Kuru fork right to Tori, then towards

Daltonganj. The closest stations are
Daltonganj (25 km) and **Barwadih** (15 km).

Hazaribagh Wildlife Sanctuary
If in a car, go north from Ranchi on the
NH33 through Ramgarh to Hazaribagh
(91 km) and to the main gate at Pokharia.
The nearest train station is Koderma (60 km).

Jamshedpur *p230*
Bus
Jamshedpur Bus Stand is at Mango, 4 km
from Bistupur; services to the main centres.

Rickshaw
Shared auto-rickshaws (unmetered) run along
main routes, or you have to take a 'reserved
rickshaw'; expect to bargain. Don't pay more
than Rs 30 for Tata Nagar to Bistupur.

Train
Tata Nagar station is on the SE railway on
Kolkata (Howrah)-Mumbai line. Enquiries, T131.
To **New Delhi**: *Purushottam Exp 2801*, 0650,
22½ hrs. **Kolkata (H)**: *Jan Shatabdi Exp, 2022*,
1710 (not Sun), 4½ hrs; *Steel Exp 2814*, 0615,
4½ hrs; *Gitanjali Exp 2859*, 0830, 4 hrs. **Puri**
via **Bhubaneswar**: *Purushottam 2802*, 2015,
10½ hrs (8 hrs); *Utkal Exp 8478*, 2030, 10 hrs.
Ranchi: *Howrah Hatia Exp 8615*, 0147, 6 hrs.

Parasnath Hill *p231*
From Dhanbad, the nearest large town with
hotels (see Damodar Valley): Train *Asansol-
Varanasi Pass 129*, 0805, then minibus from
Parasnath station to Madhuban, Rs 15,
40 mins, or taxi, Rs 200. Buses also from
Dhanbad, 0545, to Isri; then taxi (for return
that day) or another bus to Madhuban at
1000, and stay overnight in a dharamshala.
Return bus from Madhuban at 1530.

Directory

Ranchi *p229*
Tourist office Birsa Vihar Tourist Complex,
5 Main Rd, T0651-233 08522, jharkhandtourism
@yahoo.co.in, train station, T0651-2208815.

Jamshedpur *p230*
Banks Bank of Baroda, Main Rd, Bistupur,
cash on credit cards. ICICI, K Rd, Bistupur; ATM
Visa withdrawals. **Tourist office** Jharkhand,
near Air India office, Bistupur, T0657-2432892.

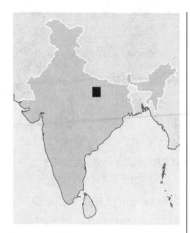

⦂ Footprint features

Introduction

Varanasi is both life and death. It encapsulates India: all that is wonderful and sacred combine with all that is dark and mysterious. The sacred river *Ganga Ma* – regarded by Hindus as the physical and spiritual life-source of the country – draws millions of pilgrims to the bathing ghats at Varanasi every year, making them buzz with activity each dawn and dusk. The burning funeral pyres cast ashes on the Brahmin priests and tribespeople who come to perform purifying rites, just as they have for time immemorial: Varanasi is thought to be the oldest living city in the world.

Otherwise known as Benares or Kashi (City of Light), there are 1500 temples, shrines and palaces towering over the ghats or hiding in the teeming, confusing alleyways. To the west, the broader streets are dusty, chaotic and noisy to an extreme degree. Arrival at the station, finding the hotel of your choice, or trying to negotiate boat hire is almost always fraught, but nothing can detract from the intensely spiritual atmosphere that pervades the old city and the waterfront at all times.

The Jains also deem Varanasi to be holy, while nearby Sarnath is an centre of Buddhism and ancient Jaunpur contains the remains of Islamic masterpieces. Although these timeless seats of religion are now surrounded by a land transformed by great irrigation schemes, their majesty remains undiminished.

★ Don't miss ...

1 **A boat ride on the Ganga** Whether at dawn with the bathers shrouded in mist or at dusk among the leaf-boat lamps, a boat trip is worth the haggling, page 240.

2 **Walk the ghats** Mingling with the pilgrims and saffron-draped holy men on the steps by Mother Ganges is a stimulating occupation in the City of Light, pages 240-242.

3 **Ramnagar Fort** Cross the Ganges and visit the Maharajah's former home, enjoy a *Ramlila* performance (October/November) or just to view the holy city from another perspective, page 243.

4 **Sarnath** Pay homage to one of Buddhism's holiest sites, or watch the monk's playing cricket in the deer park, page 243.

5 **Jaunpur** Admire the fine regional Islamic architecture and unique arches of the Akbari bridge, with a guarantee that there'll be no other tourists in sight, page 245.

6 **Shopping** Browse for aarti bowls, wrap yourself in the finest silk saris, choose between inlaid sitars or ornate tablas – shopping in Varanasi can be a fantastic experience, page 250.

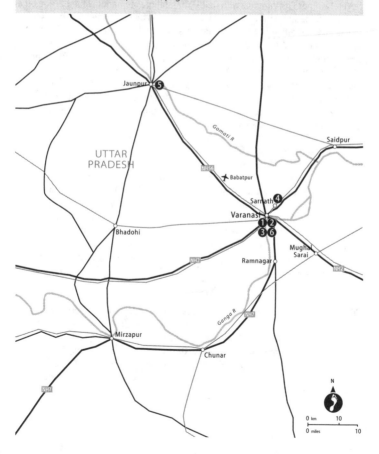

Varanasi

Varanasi and around

→ *Phone code: 0542. Colour map 1, B4. Population: over 1.3 mn.*

Perhaps the holiest of India's cities, Varanasi defies easy description. A highly congested maze of narrow alleys winding behind its waterfront ghats, at once highly sacred yet physically often far from clean. As an image, an idea and a symbol of Hinduism's central realities, the city draws pilgrims from around the world, to worship, to meditate, and above all to bathe. It is a place to be born and a place to die. In the cold mists of a winter's dawn, you can see life and death laid bare. For an outside observer it can be an uncomfortable, albeit unmissable experience, juxtaposing the inner philosophical mysteries of Hinduism with the practical complications of living literally and metaphorically on the edge. More holy places surround Varanasi: Sarnath, one of Buddhism's major centres; and Jaunpur, a city with a strong Islamic history.

▶▶ *For Sleeping, Eating and other listings, see pages 247-252.*

Ins and outs

Getting there

Several airlines link Varanasi with Delhi, Khajuraho, Kathmandu, Mumbai and other cities. From Babatpur airport, 22 km away, there is an unreliable airport bus to the Indian Airlines office in the Cantonment area. It's better to take a taxi from the prepaid booth. Most long-distance buses arrive at the bus stand near the crossroads 500 m northeast of the Junction Station. Most trains stop at the Junction Station near the Cantonment, about 6 km northwest of the Old City and the budget hotels. Some trains (eg Delhi–Kolkata *Rajdhani* and *Expresses* to New Jalpaiguri and Guwahati) do not pass through Varanasi itself but stop at Mughal Sarai, 27 km away, which is easily accessible by rail or road from Varanasi. A rickshaw to Assi Ghat should cost around Rs 140.

Getting around

The only way to really see the heart of the Old City is on foot, though no visit is complete without an early morning boat trip along the Ghats. Yet Varanasi is quite spread out: the university to the south is nearly 7 km from the spacious Cantonment area and the Junction Station to the north. Around town, cycle-rickshaws are common, while autos are usually shared. Buses are hopelessly crowded so you might consider hiring a bike if you are staying a few days. Unmetered taxis are best for longer sightseeing trips. The city has some of the disadvantages of pilgrimage centres, notably rickshaw drivers who seem determined to extort as much as possible from unsuspecting visitors. ▶▶ *See Transport, page 250, for further details.*

Tourist information

UP Tourist Bungalow ⓘ *Parade Kothi, T0542-220 6638, Mon-Sat 1000-1700*, is very helpful, Japanese spoken. **Tourist Information Counter** ⓘ *Junction Railway Station, near 'Enquiry', T0542-250 6670, 0600-2000*, provides very helpful maps and information. **Government of India Tourist Office** ⓘ *15B The Mall, Cantt, T/F0542-250 1784, Mon-Sat 0900-1730*, is well run, with very helpful manager and staff; guides available, about Rs 450 (half day), Rs 600 (full day) depending on group size. They also have a counter at Babatpur Airport.

⁞ Polluted Ganga purifies itself

All along the Ganga, the major problem of waste disposal (of human effluent and industrial toxins) has defied the best efforts of the Ganga Action Plan set up in 1986 to solve it. The diversion and treatment of raw sewage in seven main cities was planned. In Varanasi however, the 17th-century sewers, the inadequate capacity of the sewage works, the increased waterflow during the monsoons and the erratic electricity supply (essential for pumping) have all remained problems. In addition, although most Hindus are cremated, an estimated 45,000 uncremated or partially cremated bodies are put in the Ganga each year. A breed of scavenger turtles which dispose of rotting flesh was introduced down river but the turtles disappeared.

The Uttar Pradesh Water Board (Jal Nigam) has put forward a Ganga Action Plan II, but critics of the first failed scheme are proposing an alternative under the guidance of a Banaras Hindu University engineering professor Veer Bhadra Mishra. It remains to be seen whether his proposal of a massive educational programme backed by advanced engineering will help Varanasi purify the tide of filth that enters it every day.

Although the Ganga may be one of the world's most polluted rivers, like many tropical rivers it can cleanse itself quickly. Scientists had discovered the river's exceptional property in the last century. The cholera microbe did not survive three hours in Ganga water whereas in distilled water it survived 24 hours!

Background

Varanasi derives its name from two streams, the Varuna to the north and the Assi, a small trickle, on the south. **Banaras** is a corruption of Varanasi but it is also called **Kashi** (The City of Light) by Hindus. As one of the seven sacred cities of Hinduism, see page 299, it attracts well over one million pilgrims while about 50,000 Brahmins are permanent residents. The Jains too consider it holy because three *tirthankars* (seventh Suarsvanath, 11th Shyeyanshnath, 23rd Parsvanath) were born here.

Varanasi is said to combine the virtues of all other places of pilgrimage, and anyone dying within the area marked by the **Panch Kosi Road** is transported straight to heaven. Some devout Hindus move to Varanasi to end their days and have their ashes scattered in the holy Ganga. Every pilgrim, in addition to visiting the holy sites, must make a circuit of the Panch Kosi Road which runs outside and round the sacred territory of Varanasi. This starts at Manikarnika Ghat, runs along the waterfront to Assi Ghat, then round the outskirts in a large semi-circle to Barna Ghat. The 58-km route is lined with trees and shrines and the pilgrimage is supposed to take six days, each day's walk finishing in a small village, equipped with temples and *dharamshalas*.

Varanasi was probably already an important town by the seventh century BC when Babylon and Nineveh were at the peak of their power. The Buddha visited it in 500 BC and it was mentioned in both the *Mahabharata* and the *Ramayana*. It became a centre of culture, education, commerce and craftsmanship but was raided by **Mahmud of Ghazni's** army in 1033 and by Qutb-ud-din Ghuri in 1194. **Ala-ud-din Khalji**, the King of Delhi (1294-1316), destroyed temples and built mosques on their sites. The Muslim influence was strong so even in the 18th century the city, for a brief period, was known as Mohammadabad. Despite its early foundation hardly any building dates before the 17th century, and few are more than 200 years old.

The city stands as the chief centre of **Sanskrit learning** in North India. Sanskrit, the oldest of the Indo-European languages, used for Hindu ritual has been sustained here long after it ceased to be a living language elsewhere. The Banaras Hindu **University** has over 150,000 rare manuscripts. Hindu devotional movements flourished here, especially in the 15th century under Ramananda, and **Kabir**, one of India's greatest poets, lived in the city. It was here that **Tulsi Das** translated the Ramayana from Sanskrit into Hindi.

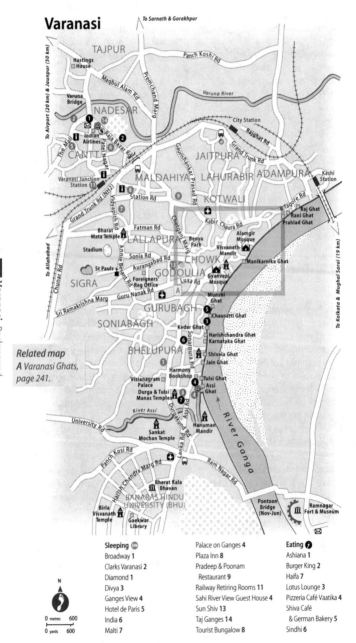

Varanasi

Related map
A Varanasi Ghats,
page 241.

Sleeping	Palace on Ganges 4	Eating
Broadway 1	Plaza Inn 8	Ashiana 1
Clarks Varanasi 2	Pradeep & Poonam	Burger King 2
Diamond 1	Restaurant 9	Haifa 7
Divya 3	Railway Retiring Rooms 11	Lotus Lounge 3
Ganges View 4	Sahi River View Guest House 4	Pizzeria Café Vaatika 4
Hotel de Paris 5	Sun Shiv 13	Shiva Café
India 6	Taj Ganges 14	& German Bakery 5
Malti 7	Tourist Bungalow 8	Sindhi 6

N

0 metres 600
0 yards 600

Sights

The city's focus extends from Raj Ghat in the north, to Assi Ghat in the south. At dawn the riverbank's stone steps begin to hum with activity. Early risers immerse themselves in the water as they face the rising sun, boatmen wait expectantly on the waterside, pilgrims flock to the temples, flower sellers do brisk business, astrologers prepare to read palms and horoscopes while families carry the dead to their last rites by the holy river. A few steps away from the ghats, motor bikers speed through the lanes narrowly missing a motley band of wandering sadhus, hopeful beggars, curious visitors and wandering cows, while packs of stray dogs scavenge among the piles of rubbish.

Old Centre

Visvanath Temple has been the main Siva temple in Varanasi for over 1000 years. The original temple, destroyed in the 12th century, was replaced by a mosque. It was rebuilt in the 16th, and again destroyed within a century. The present **'Golden' temple** was built in 1777 by Ahilya Bai of Indore. The gold plating on the roof was provided by Maharaja Ranjit Singh in 1835. Its pointed spires are typically North Indian in style and the exterior is finely carved. Bags are not allowed inside, and you may be searched on entering; only Hindus are allowed into the inner sanctum; the 18th-century **Annapurna Temple** (*anna* food; *purna* filled) nearby, built by Baji Rao I, has shrines dedicated to Siva, Ganesh, Hanuman and Surya. Ask for directions as you make your way through the maze of alleys around the temples.

The **Gyan Kup** (Well of Knowledge) next door is said to contain the Siva lingam from the original temple – the well is protected by a stone screen and canopy. The **Gyanvapi Mosque** (Great Mosque of Aurangzeb) with 71-m-high minarets shows evidence of the original Hindu temple, in the foundations, the columns and at the rear.

The 17th-century **Alamgir Mosque** (Beni Madhav ka Darera), impressively situated on Panchganga Ghat, was Aurangzeb's smaller mosque. It was built on the original Vishnu temple of the Marathas, parts of which were used in its construction. Two minarets are missing – one fell and killed some people and the other was taken down by the government as a precaution. You can climb to the top of the mosque for fantastic views (donation expected); again, bags are prohibited and you may be searched.

Back lanes

The maze of narrow lanes, or *galis*, along the ghats through the old quarters exude the smells and sounds of this holy city. They are fascinating to stroll through though easy to get lost in! Some find it all too over-powering. Near the Town Hall (1845) built by the Maharaja of Vizianagram, is the **Kotwali** (Police Station) with the Temple of **Bhaironath**, built by Baji Rao II in 1825. The image inside is believed to be of the Kotwal (Superintendent) who rides on a ghostly dog. Stalls sell sugar dogs to be offered to the image. In the temple garden of **Gopal Mandir** near the Kotwali is a small hut in which Tulsi Das is said to have composed the *Binaya Patrika* poem.

The **Bhelupura Temple** with a museum marks the birthplace of the 23rd Jain Tirthankar **Parsvanath** who preached non-violence. The **Durga Temple** (18th-century) to the south along Durga Kund Road, was built in the Nagara style. It is painted red with ochre and has the typical five spires (symbolizing the elements) merging into one (Brahma). Non-Hindus may view from the rooftop nearby. Next door in a peaceful garden, the **Tulsi Manas Temple** (1964) in white marble commemorates the medieval poet Tulsi Das. It has walls engraved with verses and scenes from the *Ramcharitmanas*, composed in a Hindi dialect, instead of the conventional Sanskrit, and is open to all (closed 1130-1530). Good views from the second floor of 'Disneyland-style' animated show. **Bharat Mata Temple**, south of Varanasi Junction Station, has a relief map of 'Mother India' in marble.

The hundred and more **ghats** on the river are the main attraction for visitors to Varanasi. Visit them at first light before sunrise, 0430 in summer, 0600 in winter when Hindu pilgrims come to bathe in the sacred Ganga, facing the rising sun, or at dusk when synchronized *pujas* are performed, culminating in leaf-boat lamps being floated down the river, usually from 1800 (try Mir or Assi Ghat). Start the river trip at Dasasvamedha Ghat where you can hire a boat quite cheaply especially if you can share, bargain to about Rs 60-120 per hour for two to eight at dawn. You may go either upstream (south) towards Harishchandra Ghat or downstream to Manikarnika Ghat. You may prefer to have a boat on the river at sunset and watch the lamps floated on the river, or go in the afternoon at a fraction of the price quoted at dawn. For photographs, visit the riverside between 0700-0900. The foggy sunshine early in the morning often clears to produce a beautiful light.

Kite flying is a popular pastime, as elsewhere in India, especially all along the riverbank. The serious competitors endeavour to bring down other flyers' kites and so fortify their twine by coating it with a mix of crushed light bulbs and flour paste to make it razor sharp! The quieter ghats, eg Panchganga, are good for watching the fun – boys in their boats on the river scramble to retrieve downed kites as trophies that can be re-used even though the kites themselves are very cheap.

Dasasvamedha Ghat Commonly called 'Main Ghat', Dasasvamedha means the 'Place of Ten Horse Sacrifices' performed here by **Brahma**, God of Creation. Some believe that in the age of the gods when the world was in chaos, **Divodasa** was appointed King of Kashi by Brahma. He accepted, on condition that all the gods would leave Varanasi. Even **Siva** was forced to leave but Brahma set the test for Divodasa, confident that he would get the complex ceremony wrong, allowing the gods back into the city. However, the ritual was performed flawlessly, and the ghat has thus become one of the holiest, especially at eclipses. Bathing here is regarded as being almost as meritorious as making the sacrifice.

Moving south You will pass **Munshi Ghat**, where some of the city's sizeable Muslim population (25%) come to bathe. The river has no religious significance for them. Close by is **Darbhanga Ghat** where the mansion had a hand-operated cable lift. Professional washermen work at the **Dhobi Ghat**; there is religious merit in having your clothes washed in the Ganga. Brahmins have their own washermen to avoid caste pollution. The municipality has built separate washing facilities away from the ghat.

Narad and **Chauki Ghats** are held sacred since the **Buddha** received enlightenment here under a *peepul* tree. Those who bathe together at Narad, supposedly go home and quarrel! The pink water tower here is for storing Ganga water. High water levels are recorded at **Raj Ghat**. The flood levels are difficult to imagine when the river is at its lowest in January and February. **Mansarovar Ghat** leads to ruins of several temples around a lake. **Kedar Ghat** is named after Kedarnath, a pilgrimage site in the Uttarakhand, with a Bengali temple nearby.

Photography is not permitted at the burning ghats. Travellers may be told that it is allowed and then a large fine is demanded. Also beware of conmen collecting 'donations' for wood for burning the poor.

The **Harishchandra Ghat** is particularly holy and is dedicated to King Harishchandra. It is now the most sacred *smashan* or cremation ghat although Manikarnika is more popular. Behind the ghat is a *gopuram* of a Dravidian-style temple. The **Karnataka Ghat** is one of many regional ghats which are attended by priests who know the local languages, castes, customs and festivals.

The **Hanuman Ghat** is where Vallabha, the leader of a revivalist Krishna bhakti cult was born in the late 15th century. **Shivala Ghat** (Kali Ghat) is privately owned by the ex-ruler of Varanasi. **Chet Singh's Fort**, Shivala, stands behind the ghat. The fort, the old palace of the Maharajas, is where the British imprisoned him but he escaped by

climbing down to the river and swimming away. **Anandamayi Ghat** is named after the 241
Bengali saint Anandamayi Ma (died 1982) who received 'enlightenment' at 17 and
spent her life teaching and in charitable work. **Jain Ghat** is near the birthplace of
Tirthankar Shyeyanshnath. **Tulsi Ghat** commemorates the great saint-poet **Tulsi Das**
who lived here (see Tulsi Manas Temple, page 239). Furthest upstream is the **Assi Ghat**,
where the River Assi meets the Ganga, one of the five that pilgrims should bathe from in a
day. The order is Assi, Dasasvamedha, Barnasangam, Panchganga and Manikarnika.
Upstream on the east bank is the Ramnagar Fort, the Maharaja of Varanasi's residence
(see page 243). Here the boat will turn to take you back to Dasasvamedha Ghat.

Moving north Leaving from Dasasvamedha Ghat, you will pass the following: **Man
Mandir Ghat** ① *normally 0930-1730 but if you enquire locally you may be able to get
in at dawn or dusk*, built by Maharajah Man Singh of Amber in 1600 and one of the
oldest in Varanasi. The palace was restored in the last century with brick and plaster.
The beautiful stone balcony on the northeast corner gives an indication of how the
original looked. Maharaja Jai Singh of Jaipur converted the palace into an **observatory**
in 1710. Like its counterparts in Delhi, Jaipur and Ujjain, the observatory contains a
fascinating collection of instruments built of brick, cement and stone. The most
striking of these, at the entrance, is the Bhittiyantra, or wall quadrant, over 3 m high
and just under 3 m broad and in the same plane as the line of longitude. Similarly
placed is the Samratyantra which is designed to slope upwards pointing at the Pole
Star. From the top of the Chakra Yantra there is a superb view of the ghats and the
town. Near the entrance to the observatory is a small **Siva Temple** whose shrine is a
lingam immersed in water. During droughts, water is added to the cistern to make it
overflow for good luck.

Varanasi Ghats

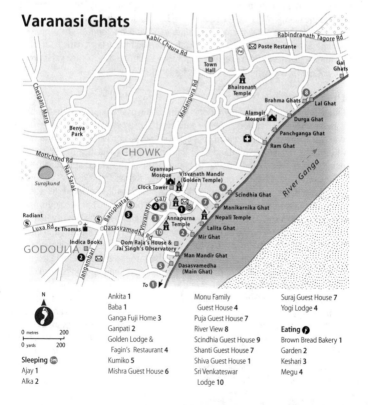

Sleeping 🛏
Ajay **1**
Alka **2**
Ankita **1**
Baba **1**
Ganga Fuji Home **3**
Ganpati **2**
Golden Lodge &
  Fagin's Restaurant **4**
Kumiko **5**
Mishra Guest House **6**
Monu Family
  Guest House **4**
Puja Guest House **7**
River View **8**
Scindhia Guest House **9**
Shanti Guest House **7**
Shiva Guest House **1**
Sri Venkateswar
  Lodge **10**
Suraj Guest House **7**
Yogi Lodge **4**

Eating 🍴
Brown Bread Bakery **1**
Garden **2**
Keshari **3**
Megu **4**

The **Dom Raja's House** is next door, flanked by painted tigers. The **doms** are the 'Untouchables' of Varanasi and are integral to the cremation ceremony. As Untouchables they can handle the corpse, a ritually polluting act for Hindus. They also supply the flame from the temple for the funeral pyre. Their presence is essential and also lucrative since there are fees for the various services they provide. The Dom Raja is the hereditary title of the leader of these Untouchables. You can climb up through the astronomical observatory (which is overrun by monkeys) to the Raja Dom's Palace – a guide will take you round the court room, and on to the roof which has the best view of the river.

Mir Ghat leads to a sacred well; widows who dedicate themselves to prayer, are fed and clothed here. Next is **Lalita Ghat** with the distinctive Nepalese-style temple with a golden roof above and a Ganga mandir at water level. Above **Manikarnika Ghat** is a well into which Siva's dead wife Sati's earring is supposed to have fallen after she committed suicide. The Brahmins managed to find the jewel from the earring (*manikarnika*) and returned it to Siva who blessed the place. Offerings of *bilva* flowers, milk, sandalwood and sweetmeats are thrown into the tank where pilgrims come to bathe. Between the well and the ghat is *Charanpaduka*, a stone slab with Vishnu's footprint. Boatmen may ask you to leave a 'private' offering to perform a *puja* (a ploy to increase their earnings)!

The adjoining **Jalasayin Ghat** is the principal burning ghat of the city. The expensive scented sandalwood which the rich alone can afford is used sparingly; usually not more than two kilos. You may see floating bundles covered in white cloth; children, and those dying of 'high fever', or smallpox in the past, are not cremated but put into the river. This avoids injuring *Sitala* the goddess of smallpox.

Scindia Ghat, originally built in 1830, was so large that it collapsed. **Ram Ghat** was built by the Maharaja of Jaipur. Five rivers are supposed to meet at the magnificent **Panchganga Ghat** – the Ganga, Sarasvati, Gyana, Kirana and Dhutpapa. The stone column can hold around 1000 lamps at festivals. The impressive flights of stone steps run up to the Alamgir Mosque (see above). At **Gai Ghat** there is a statue of a sacred cow whilst at **Trilochana Ghat** there is a temple to Siva in his form as the 'Three-eyed' (*Trilochana*); two turrets stand out of the water. **Raj Ghat** is the last on the boat journey. Excavations have revealed a site of a city from the eighth century BC on a grassy mound nearby. Raj Ghat was where the river was forded until bridges were built.

Other sights

Varanasi is famous for ornamental brasswork, silk weaving and for its glass beads, exported worldwide. *Zari* work, whether embroidered or woven, once used silver or gold thread but is now done with gilded copper or brass. You can watch weavers at work in Piti Kothi, the Muslim area inland from Raj Ghat. The significance of **silk** in India's traditional life is deep-rooted. Silk was considered a pure fabric, most appropriate for use on ceremonial and religious occasions. Its lustre, softness and richness of natural colour gave it precedence over all other fabrics. White or natural coloured silk was worn by the Brahmins and others who were 'twice born'. Women wore bright colours and the darker hues were reserved for the lowest caste in the formal hierarchy, few of whom could afford it. Silk garments were worn for ceremonials like births and marriages, and offerings of finely woven silks were made to deities in temples. This concept of purity may have given impetus to the growth of silk-weaving centres around ancient temple towns like Kanchipuram, Varanasi, Bhubaneswar and Ujjain, a tradition that is kept alive today.

Banaras Hindu University (BHU) is one of the largest campus universities in India to the south of the city and enjoys a pleasant, relaxed atmosphere. Founded at the turn of the 19th century, it was originally intended for the study of Sanskrit, Indian art, music and culture and has the Bharat Kala Bhavan Museum (see below). The **New Visvanath Temple** (1966), one of the tallest in India, is in the university semicircle and was financed by the Birla family. It was planned by Madan Mohan Malaviya (1862-1942), chancellor of the university, who believed in Hinduism without caste distinctions. The marble Shiva temple modelled on the old Visvanath Temple, is open to all.

Bharat Kala Bhavan ① *BHU, T0542-230 7621, Mon-Sat 1100-1630, closed*
holidays, Rs 40 foreigners, Rs 10 Indians, Rs 20 camera, exhibits include sculptures from Mathura and Sarnath, excellent Mughal miniature paintings and Benarasi brocades.

Across the river in a beautiful setting among narrow crowded streets is the run-down 17th-century **Ramnagar Fort**, the former home of the Maharaja of Varanasi. The ferry costs Rs 10 return, or there are rickshaws from centre which cross a crumbling double-decker bridge, Rs 75, ask the driver to wait or take a boat back or else walk over the pontoon bridge. The Durbar Hall houses a **museum** ① *T0542-233 9322, summer 0900-1200, 1400-1700, winter 1000-1700, Rs 7*, with palanquins, elephant *howdahs*, costumes, arms and furniture gathering dust. See the amazing locally made astrological clock and single cylinder steam driven fan. Nearby Ramnagar village has *Ramlila* performances during Dasara (October to November).

Chunar → *Colour map 1, B4.*

Chunar, 35 km southwest of Varanasi, is famous for Chunar sandstone, the material of the Asoka pillars, highly polished in a technique said to be Persian. The town is also noted for its **fort** built on a spur of the Kaimur Hills, 53 m above the surrounding plain. It was of obvious strategic importance and changed hands a number of times. The army occupies the fort today, but you can look around. There is an impressive well with steps leading down to a water gate; watch out for snakes. The British Cemetery below the fort overlooks the Ganga. Islamic tombs of Shah Kasim Suleiman and his son here, feature in paintings by Daniells and others. Buses from City Station, Varanasi take 1½ hours, Rs 75 return.

Sarnath 🚌⊗🚌 ➤➤ *pp247-252. Colour map 1, B4.*

Sarnath, 10 km northeast of Varanasi, is one of Buddhism's major centres in India. Given its great historic importance visitors may be disappointed to find the stupas neglected and the very limited collection in the museum, although it houses some superb pieces. Nevertheless, many find the deer park a place of peace and reflection despite distractions of loud transistor radios and young monks running around or playing cricket!

History

When he had gained enlightenment at Bodh Gaya, the **Buddha** came to the deer park at Sarnath and delivered his first sermon (circa 528 BC), usually referred to as *Dharmachakra* (The Wheel of Law). Since then, the site has been revered. The Chinese traveller Hiuen Tsang described the *sangharama* (monastery) in AD 640 as having 1500 monks, a 65-m-high *vihara*, a figure of the Buddha represented by a wheel, a 22-m-high stone stupa built by Asoka, a larger 90-m-high stupa and three lakes. The remains here and the sculptures now at the Indian Museum, Kolkata and the National Museum, Delhi, reveal that Sarnath was a centre of religious activity, learning and art, continuously from the fourth century BC until its abandonment in the ninth century AD and ultimate destruction by Muslim armies in 1197.

Enclosure

A separate entrance leads to the enclosure on the far right. The statue on the right is of **Anagarika Dharmapala**, the founder of the Mahabodhi Society which has assumed responsibility for the upkeep of Sarnath and Bodh Gaya. The modern **Mulagandhakuti Vihara** (1929-1931) contains frescoes by the Japanese artist Kosetsu Nosu depicting scenes from the Buddha's life. An urn in the ground is supposed to hold a Buddha relic obtained from Taxila (Pakistan). The **Bodhi tree** (*pipal, Ficus religiosa*), planted in 1931, is a sapling of the one in Sri Lanka which was grown from a cutting taken there circa 236 BC by Mahinda's sister Princess Sanghamitta.

Here is the **Dhamekh Stupa** (fifth to sixth century AD) ⓘ *US$2/Rs 100 foreigners, Rs 5 Indians, video camera Rs 25*, or Dharma Chakra, the most imposing monument at Sarnath, built where the Buddha delivered his first sermon to his five disciples. Along with his birth, enlightenment and death, this incident is one of the four most significant. The stupa consists of a 28-m-diameter stone plinth which rises to a height of 13 m. Each of the eight faces has an arched recess for an image. Above this base rises a 31-m-high cylindrical tower. The upper part was probably unfinished. The central section has elaborate Gupta designs, eg geometric patterns, birds and flowers. The Brahmi script dates from the sixth to ninth centuries. The stupa was enlarged six times and the well-known figures of a standing Boddhisattva and the Buddha teaching were found nearby.

Other sights

The **deer park** is holy to Jains because **Shyeyanshnath**, the 11th Tirthankar, was born near the Dhamekh stupa. The temple to your left as you move between the stupas commemorates him; 'Sarnath' may be derived from his name. The monastery (fifth century onwards) in the southwest corner is one of four in the deer park. The others are along the north edge. All are of brick with cells off a central courtyard which are in ruins.

Dharmarajika Stupa was built by the Emperor Asoka to contain relics of the Buddha. It was enlarged on several occasions but was destroyed by Jagat Singh, Dewan of the Maharaja of Benares, in 1794, when a green marble casket containing human bones and pearls was found. The British Resident at the Maharaja's court published an account of the discovery thereby drawing the attention of scholars to the site.

Sarnath

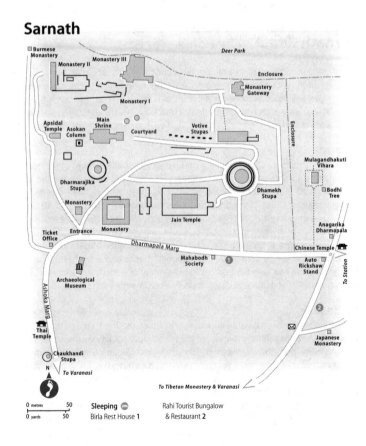

```
0 metres    50
0 yards     50
```

Sleeping 🛏
Birla Rest House **1**

Rahi Tourist Bungalow
& Restaurant **2**

The **Main shrine** is a rectangular building, 29 m by 27 m, with doubly recessed corners and is 5½ m high. The building, marking the place of the Buddha's meditation, is attributed to Asoka and the later Guptas. The concrete path and interior brick walls were added later to reinforce the building. To the rear is the 5-m-lower portion of a polished sandstone **Asokan Column** (third century BC). The original was about 15 m high with a lion capital which is now in the Archaeological Museum. The four lions sitting back to back with the wheel of law below them is now the symbol of the Indian Union. The column was one of many erected by Asoka to promulgate the faith and this contained a message to the monks and nuns not to create any schisms and to spread the word.

The modern **Burmese monastery** is worth the short detour from the road. It is very colourful and peaceful with no hawkers and hardly any tourists. Tibetan, Thai and Chinese monasteries have also been built around the old complex. The Central Institute of Higher Tibetan Studies, near the ruins, runs courses and carries out research. The library has a good collection of texts and manuscripts.

The **museum** ⓘ *Sat-Thu 1030-1630*, has a well-displayed collection of pieces from the site, including the famous lion capital (Asokan Column), a Sunga Period (first century BC) stone railing, Kushana Period (second century AD) Boddhisattvas, Gupta Period (fifth century AD) figures, including the magnificent seated Buddha. Allow about one hour. Tickets are Rs 2 from across the road where Archaeological Survey booklets are for sale. Cameras and bags are not normally allowed.

Chaukhandi, 500 m south, has a fifth-century stupa. On top of this is an octagonal brick tower built by Akbar in 1588 to commemorate the visit his father Humayun made to the site. The inscription above the doorway reads "As Humayun, king of the Seven Climes, now residing in paradise, deigned to come and sit here one day, thereby increasing the splendour of the sun, so Akbar, his son and humble servant, resolved to build on this spot a lofty tower reaching to the blue sky".

Jaunpur 🏛🍴🚌 → *pp247-252. Colour map 1, B4.*

→ *Phone code: 05452. Population: 321,000.*

Jaunpur, 58 km from Varanasi, is a uniquely important centre of 14th- and 15th-century regional Islamic architecture. Once the short-lived capital of the Sharqi Dynasty, today only the ruins of some magnificent mosques and its famous Akbari Bridge distinguish it from hundreds of other dusty and congested Uttar Pradesh towns. The buildings that remain remind us of its brief period as one of India's main centres of political, architectural and artistic development and so is well worth a visit if you can spare the time.

History

Located at a strategic crossing point of the Gomti River, Jaunpur was established by Feroz Shah Tughluq in 1360 as part of his drive to the East. Earlier Hindu and Jain structures were destroyed to provide material for the mosques with which the Sharqi Dynasty rapidly embellished their capital. The Sharqi kings – named 'Kings of the East' by Feroz Shah – established effective independence from the Tughluqs who had been crushed in Timur's sack of Delhi in 1398. They maintained it until 1479, when Husain Shah, the last Sharqi king, was violently deposed by Ibrahim Lodi. Although all the secular buildings, including palaces and courts, were razed to the ground, Ibrahim Lodi spared at least some of the mosques. Some of the city's destruction visible today can be put down to much later events – floods in 1773 and 1871 and an earthquake in 1934. According to Rushbrook Williams this last catastrophe destroyed seven of the 15 arches in the great 200-m-long Akbari Bridge, designed by the Afghan architect Afzal Ali and built between 1564-1568. The stone lion above an elephant at the end of the bridge marks the point from which distances from the city were measured.

The **bridge** emphasized Jaunpur's role as the centre of a pre-Mughal trading network. In the 17th century the Gomti allowed ships up to 18 tons to navigate over 200 km upstream. Under the great king Shams-ud-din-Ibrahim (1402-1436) Jaunpur became a centre of the arts and university education. Today, however, it is the remains of the fort and the mosques which are most worth visiting.

The **Old Shahi Fort** ① *Rs 100*, just north of the Akbari Bridge, is an irregular grassy quadrangle enclosed by ruined stone walls. It shelters the oldest **mosque** in Jaunpur (1377), a narrow arcade (40 m by 7 m) supported by carved pillars, named after its builder, Ibrahim Naib Barbak, Feroz Shah Tughluq's brother. In the mid-19th century Fergusson described some distinctive yellow and blue enamelled bricks on the fine 15-m-high stone gateway, and an inscribed monolith (1766) at the entrance, still visible today. Of particular interest is the almost perfect model of a **hammam** (Turkish bath) which you can wander around.

Perhaps the most striking of the surviving mosques, the **Atala**, stands less than 400 m to the north of the fort. Built in 1408 on the site of the Hindu Atala Devi temple, it marks the triumphant beginning of Shams-ud-din-Ibrahim's reign and introduces unique features of Jaunpuri style. An arched gateway or 'pylon' fronts the sanctuary on the west side of the 50-m-square court; the remaining three sides are spacious cloisters, two-storeyed and five aisles deep. The pylon has sloping sides, as in other Tughluq building, and its central arch is over 22 m high – along with the arch of the great Jami Masjid nearby, the highest in India. Other features borrowed from the Tughluq style are a recessed arch with its ornamented fringe, and tapering turrets on the west wall. Although artisans were brought in from Delhi, Jaunpur builders soon articulated their Tughluq traditions in a highly distinctive way. Note the beautiful sanctuary interior with its decorated nave and transepts, and the perforated stone screens. At the far end, the transepts are two-storeyed, with the upper section screened off for the zenana.

The same weakness applies to the 'most ambitious' of Jaunpur's mosques, the **Jami Masjid**, about 1 km north of the fort. Begun by Shah Ibrahim in 1438 it was completed by Husain Shah, the last Sharqi king, in 1470. Raised about 6 m on an artificial platform, the worshipper is forced to climb a steep flight of steps to enter the

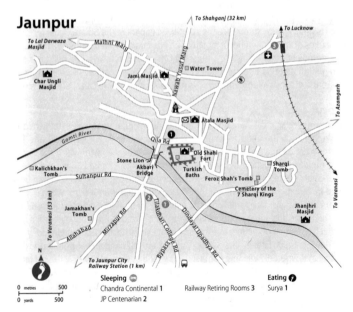

Jaunpur

To Shahganj (32 km)

To Lucknow

To Lal Darwaza Masjid

Malhni Marg

Nawab Yusuf Marg

Water Tower

Char Ungli Masjid

Jami Masjid

Atala Masjid

Gomti River

Qila Rd

Stone Lion

Kalichkhan's Tomb

Sultanpur Rd

Akbari Bridge

Old Shahi Fort

Turkish Baths

Feroz Shah's Tomb

Sharqi Tomb

Cemetery of the 7 Sharqi Kings

To Azamgarh

To Varanasi

To Varanasi (53 km)

Jamakhan's Tomb

Allahabad

Mirzapur Rd

Tilakdhari College Rd

Dindayal Upadhya Rd

Bypass Rd

Jhanjhri Masjid

N

To Jaunpur City Railway Station (1 km)

0 metres 500
0 yards 500

Sleeping
Chandra Continental 1
JP Centenarian 2

Railway Retiring Rooms 3

Eating
Surya 1

60-m-sq courtyard. Built on an even grander scale than the Atala Mosque, the 25-m-high central pylon dominates the sanctuary. Note the unsupported transept halls which create a remarkable clear covered open space. Despite the lack of pillars they have survived earthquakes as well as normal ageing. Allow three hours on foot for the main sights.

● Sleeping

Varanasi *p239, maps p238 and p241*
Off-season discounts in Jun and Jul. Be prepared for power cuts and carry a torch at night. Some rickshaw drivers insist on taking you to hotels where they get a commission. Hotels on the riverfront can be difficult to locate, particularly at night. Local people will often show you the way but may expect a commission from the hotel, thus increasing the rate you pay. Most **E** hotels have rooms with TV and attached baths. Rooms with river view are worth the extra.

LL-L Taj Ganges, Nadesar Palace Ground, T0542-250 3001, www.tajhotels.com. 130 rooms, good restaurants (spotless kitchen), pool, top-class facilities, busy, but efficient service, taxis from here overcharge.

L-AL Clarks Varanasi, The Mall, T0542-250 1011. In a quiet location with good facilities, pool (non-residents, Rs 200), buffet-biased restaurant with expensive drinks, beginning to feel a little outdated.

A Palace on Ganges, B-1/158 Assi Ghat, T0542-231 5050, www.palaceonganges.com. 24 rooms, each decorated in the style of a different Indian state, in a converted old palace, restaurant with live Indian classical music plus a small rooftop restaurant. The most luxurious hotel on the banks of the Ganga.

B-D Ganges View, Assi Ghat, T0542-231 3218, hotelgangesview@yahoo.com. Old patrician home converted into welcoming guesthouse with a tastefully decorated range of small rooms, very pleasant atmosphere, interesting clientele (artists and academics), lovely riverside verandas, vegetarian food (restaurant for guests only).

C Hotel de Paris, 15 The Mall, T0542-250 5131, hoteldeparis@indiananetwork.com. Fairly basic but spacious rooms in 100-year-old palace, very well-kept lawns, not bad value.

C Pradeep, Jagatganj, T0542-220 4963. Clean rooms, most a/c, near noisy junction, excellent **Poonam** restaurant (see Eating, below), very attractive roof top bar/

restaurant with real lawn, friendly staff, not bad value, recommended.

C-E Plaza Inn, S.21/116H, Parade Kothi, Cantt, T0542-220 5504, www.hotelplaza inn.com. Spacious, modern rooms, very professional staff, interesting Nawab restaurant and bar, reasonable value, handy for railway station.

D Diamond, Bhelupura, T0542-227 6696, www.hotel-diamond.com. 40 rooms, most a/c though regular rooms are just as good, restaurant, money exchange, gardens, reasonable value.

D India, 59 Patel Nagar, Cantt, T0542-250 7593, www.hotelindiavns.com. 73 bright, modern a/c rooms, better in renovated building, restaurant (popular so service can be slow), bar, good rooftop garden, very clean, good value.

D-E Divya, behind Assi Ghat, T0542-231 1305, www.hoteldivya.com. New and clean rooms meeting all standards, conveniently close to ghats, good mid-range choice. Attached **Yafah** restaurant has kitchens on view.

E Broadway, near Vijaya Cinema Crossing, Bhelupur, T0542-227 7097, info@newhotel broadway.com. 25 clean, modern rooms, can be noisy lower down, but very good service and **Mughlai** restaurant.

E Rahi Tourist Bungalow (UP Tourism), off Parade Kothi, opposite railway station, T0542-220 8413. A/c and air-cooled rooms and dorm (Rs 100) in barrack-style 2-storey building, restaurant, bar, shady veranda, pleasant garden, simple, clean and efficient, very helpful tourist office.

E-F Malti, 31/3 Vidyapith Rd, T0542-222 3878, www.hotelmalti.com. Simple rooms, some a/c with balcony, restaurant. Avoids early morning heat and includes transport to/from ghat north of Alamgir mosque, not bad value.

E-G Alka, Mirghat, T0542-240 1681, www.hotelalkavns.com. Good variety of spotless rooms, prime riverside location, often full, book ahead.

E-G Ganga Fuji Home, D7/21 Shakarkand Gali, near Golden Temple, T0542-239 7333.

Clean rooms, some deluxe a/c, some with common bath, very friendly family, a/c **Nirmala** restaurant on rooftop restaurant with exceptional city views, entertainment 1930 every night, serves beer.

E-G Ganpati, next to Alka on Mir ghat, T0542-239 0059, www.ganpatiguest house.com. Great views from rooftop, very good restaurant, pleasant staff.

E-G Puja Guest House, D1/45 Lalita Ghat (near Nepali Temple), T0542-240 5027. 42 cleanish rooms, some a/c, very gloomy so check a few, less touristy than most. Cheap restaurant on highest rooftop in town, help with air, bus, train tickets, not recommended for single women.

E-G Sahi River View Guest House, Assi Ghat, T0542-236 6730, sahi_rvgh@sify.com. 12 rooms (more coming) of all standards, great views from balcony and rooftop, food from spotless kitchen, free local and received calls, owner eager to please, no commission. Recommended.

E-G Shanti Guest House, 8/129 Garwasi Tola, near Manikarnika Ghat, T0542-239 2568. Rooms vary, some **D** a/c, open-air dorm, 24-hr rooftop restaurant serving tasty food, free boat trips twice a day, motorbike hire.

F Sun Shiv, D 54/16-D Ravi Niketan, Jaddumandi Rd (off Aurangabad Rd), T0542-241 0468, hotelsunshiv@rediffmail.com. 16 modest but charming rooms with balconies in unusual, art deco-inspired 1960s family house, room service, quiet, no commission to rickshaws. Highly engaging, multi-lingual owner. Recommended.

F-G Ajay, near Munshi Ghat, T0542-245 0970, ajayguesthousebns@yahoo.co.in. Rooms on several levels, all with bath, clean, rooftop restaurant with great views, good service, tasty food. **Elena Hotel** run by brother next door.

F-G River View,Brahma Ghat, T094156-97507, hotel_riverview@hotmail.com. 9 rooms (6 more underway) in peaceful, clean and friendly hotel away from tourist scene, some with bath, TV, air cooler, great views (watch dawn from front rooms), cute breezy restaurant, discounts on longer stay. Ask to be picked up from GPO.

F-G Scindhia Guest House, Scindhia Ghat, T0542-242 0319. Excellent ghat-side location, many rooms have dream views from balcony.

F-G Sri Venkateswar Lodge, D5/64 Dasaswamedh, T0542-239 2357. Very clean rooms in calm, well-run hotel, all water solar heated, strictly no alcohol or drugs.

F-G Yogi Lodge, D8/29 Kalika Gali, near Golden Temple, T0542-240 4224, yogilodge @yahoo.com. Simple rooms, shared bath, dorm (Rs 55), meals on roof terrace or in pleasant courtyard, open kitchen, internet, friendly staff, recommended.

G Baba Guest House, D20/15 Munshi Ghat, T0542-245 5452, babaguesthouse@ yahoo.com. Basic, freshly painted rooms, some with bath, dorm, huge Korean menu, food served in downstairs café when it's too hot to use rooftop restaurant.

G Golden Lodge, D8/35 Kalika Lane, near Golden Temple, T0542-239 8788. Cell-like clean rooms, 3 on roof, 24-hr hot water, enthusiastic proprietor, a/c restaurant (**Fagin's**), has character, free washing machine.

G Kumiko, riverside near Dasasvamedha Ghat, T0542-309 1356, kumiko_house@hotmail.com. Rooms and dorm, breakfast and dinner, Japanese spoken, friendly and eccentric owners. Very welcoming, recommended.

G Mishra Guest House, near Manikarnika Ghat, T0542-240 1143, vsn1@sify.com. Large *haveli*-style hotel, most rooms have balcony, some with extra long beds, best with river view.

G Monu Family Guest House, D8/4 Kalika Ghat near Golden Temple, T093356-68877. Sweet, atmospheric and a bargain, music lessons and language courses available.

G Railway Retiring Rooms, Varanasi Junction. Some a/c rooms and dorm.

G Suraj Guest House, Lalita Ghat near Nepali Temple, T0542-239 8560. Tucked away behind a tiny temple, quaint simple rooms owned by eccentric family, extremely cheap.

G Shiva Guest House, D20/14 Munshi Ghat, T0542-245 2108, shiva_guest_house@hot mail.com. 17 simple, clean rooms, some with hot bath, rooftop restaurant (good food, great views), family-run, friendly, recommended.

Sarnath *p243, map p244*

E Rahi Tourist Bungalow (UP Tourism), T0542-259 5965, www.up-tourism.com. Rooms and dorm (Rs 70), Indian restaurant, tourist office, tours.

F-G Golden Buddha Hotel, T0542-258 7933. Clean rooms, friendly owner, recommended.

G Birla Rest House, near Mulagandhakuti Vihara. Dorm (Rs 50).

Jaunpur *p245, map p246*
E-G Hotel JP Centenarian, Olandganj,
T05452-268056. Cleanish rooms in central
location, helpful staff.
F Chandra Continental, Tilakdhari
College Rd, Olandganj, T05452-264388.
12 clean rooms, restaurant in basement.
G Railway Retiring Rooms, 2 rooms (Rs 75).

❷ Eating

Varanasi *p239, maps p238 and p241*
Restaurants outside hotels tend to be vegetarian and are not allowed to serve alcohol.
Dry days on the 1st and 7th of each month,
and some public holidays. Many cheap eateries
on Bengali Tola (large alley running from
Main Ghat to Assi Ghat) some excellent and
cheap South Indian places at southern end.
Ashiana, Clark Rd, Varuna Bridge.
Reliable Indian and Chinese.
Brown Bread Bakery, Tripura Bhairavi
(near Golden Temple, T0542-645 0232.
Excellent salads and Thai meals in attractive
haveli setting with cushions for lounging,
live sitar music in evening, food delicious
and plentiful but service negligible.
Burger King, Nai Bazar, Cantt (next to
Taj Ganges) Vegetarian only! Not a branch of
the international chain. Good cheese burger,
ice creams, also chow miens, soups, no seats
but recommended if waiting for the train.
Ganga Fuji, see Sleeping. International.
Reasonable, safe food, tempered down for
Western palate, live classical music in the
evenings, helpful and friendly owner, popular.
Recommended for ambiance and hospitality.
Haifa, in pleasant garden, good Middle
East dishes, great atmosphere.
Keshari, off Dasasvamedha Ghat. Excellent
vegetarian thalis, "the longest menu in town",
quick efficient service. Highly recommended.
Lotus Lounge, Mansarovar Ghat, T98385-
67717. Top spot for Ganga views from
chilled-out terrace, prices a step up but the
inventive Asian and Western dishes are too.
Poonam, in Pradeep Hotel. Indian. Good
variety, clean, professional staff, order banana
lassi, *masala*, and finish with *Shahi tukra*.
Alka, Mir Ghat. Very good vegetarian,
clean kitchen, great location.
Fagin's, Golden Lodge (see Sleeping).
International. A/c, in a rather dark basement,
but tasty food and friendly staff.

Ganpati, see Sleeping. Rooftop restaurant
with sublime views, and courtyard with
Mediterranean feel, both serving quality food.
Garden, opposite Sushil Cinema, Godoulia.
Indian, Chinese and continental. Excellent
food (if a bit slow), pleasant rooftop, friendly.
Megu, Kalika Lane near Golden Temple.
Specializes in Japanese food, popular.
Monalisa, Bengali Tola. Western
favourites, always busy.
Pizzeria Café Vaatika, Assi Ghat,
wonderful shady terrace on the Ganga,
friendly staff, Italian and Indian food,
excellent coffee.
Shanti, off Bengali Tola. Japanese restaurant
with a loyal following. Closed May-Jun.
Shiva Café and German Bakery, Bengali
Tola near Naraol Ghat. Very popular, especially
for breakfasts, spartan decor but lovely staff.
Sindhi, Bhelupura, next to Lalita Cinema.
Excellent Indian vegetarian, difficult for
foreigners to get fully-sugared Indian *chai*.
Spicy Bites, Bengali Tola. Western snacks
are good. Nachos are a treat, friendly service,
travellers' notice board but little effort
with decor.

Jaunpur *p245, map p246*
Surya, Qila Rd, for snacks, clean.

❸ Entertainment

Varanasi *p239, maps p238 and p241*
Clarks Cultural Centre, Peshwa Palace,
Raj Ghat, in an old Brahmin refectory,
enquire at **Clarks Varanasi**, The Mall,
T0542-250 1011. Evening entertainment
organized on request for groups, begins at
sunset with *Ganga aarti* with floating of
lamps, performance of music and dance;
US$80-100 including pick-up from hotel
1730, return 2030. At dawn, witness prayers
with chanting and singing; provides
a vantage point for photographs.

❈ Festivals and events

Varanasi *p239, maps p238 and p241*
Feb Ganga Water Rally, organized by UP
Tourism, is an international and national
kayak get-together from Allahabad to
Chunar Fort. A 40-km race from Chunar
to Varanasi happens on the final day.
Also International Yoga Week.

Late Feb/early Mar 3 days at Sivaratri, festival of Dhrupad music attracts performers from near and far, beginners and stars, in a very congenial atmosphere, a wonderful experience, many *naga babas* (naked sadhus) set up camp on ghats.

Mar/Apr Holi is celebrated with fervour.

Apr Pilgrims walk around 'Kashi', as laid down in the scriptures. Jain Mahavir Jayanti.

Apr/May Sankat Mochan Music Festival, Sankat Mochan Mandir. Non-stop temple music, open to all.

May Ganga Dasara celebrates the day the waters of the Ganga reached Haridwar.

Jul/Aug Month-long **carnival** with funfair opposite Monkey Temple, monsoon fever makes it particularly crazy.

Oct/Nov Dasara Ramlila at Ramnagar. **Ganga Festival** is organized by UP Tourism alongside a 10 day craft fair. **Nagnathaiya** draws up to 50,000 worshippers to Tulsi Ghat, re-enacting the story of Krishna jumping into the Yamuna to overcome *Kalija*, the King of the Serpents. **Nakkataiya** A fair at Chetganj recalling Rama's brother, Lakshmana, cutting off Ravana's sister's nose when she attempted to force him into a marriage! At Nati Imli, **Bharat Milap**, the meeting of Rama and Bharat after 14 years' separation is celebrated – the Maharaja of Varanasi attends in full regalia on elephant back.

Dec-Feb Music festivals.

Sarnath *p243, map p244*
May On first full-moon, **Buddha Jayanti** marks the Buddha's birthday. A fair is held and relics which are not on public display at any other time are taken out in procession.

O Shopping

Varanasi *p239, maps p238 and p241*
Varanasi is famous for silks including brocades (Temple Bazar, Visvanath Gali), brassware, gold jewellery, sitar making and hand-block printed goods. The main shopping areas are Chowk, Godoulia, Visvanath Gali, Gyanvapi and Thatheri Bazar.

Handloom and handicrafts
Benares Art Culture, 2/114 Badhaini Assi. Aims to promote local artists, interesting selection of sculpture, paintings and silks at fixed prices.

Bhagwan Stores, in Visvanath Gali and K37/32 Golghar. Recommended.

Brijraman Das, in Visvanath Gali and K37/32 Golghar. Recommended.

Ganga Handlooms, D10/18 Kohli Katra, off Viswanath Gali, near Golden Temple (ask locally). 1100-2000. Large selection of beautiful cotton fabrics, ikats, vegetable dyes, good tailors, great patterns (Western).

Mohan Silks, in Visvanath Gali and K37/32 Golghar. Recommended.

Muslim Silk Weaving Centre is next door.

▲ Activities and tours

Varanasi *p239, maps p238 and p241*
Body and soul
International Yoga Clinic and Meditation Centre, Man Mandir Ghat, T0542-239 7139. Hour-long classes, maximum 3 students.

Panch Mandir, Assi Ghat. Drop-in classes each morning 0600-0930, open to all, reasonably priced.

Satya Foundation, B-37/54B Rukma Bhawan, Birdopur, T093368-77455, www.satya foundation.com. Music, meditation and yoga, highly authentic teachings. Recommended.

Yoga Institute, BHU, T0542-230 7208. One-month courses.

Tour operators
Many small travel agents in laneways of Old City, usually charge Rs 50-70 for train tickets.

TCI, Sri Das Foundation, S20/51-5 and S20/52-4, The Mall, T0542-250 5928, tcivaranasi@tci.co.in. Highly recommended.

Tiwari Tours and Travel, Assi Ghat, T0542-236 6727, www.tiwaritravel.com. Excellent service, bus tickets to high-end tours.

Travel Bureau, 52 Patel Nagar, Mint House Rd, T0542-250 7632. Highly recommended.

UP Roadways Tour I: River trip, temples, Benaras Hindu University. Tour II: Sarnath and Ramnagar Fort. Daily, summer 1430-1825, winter 1400-1755. Starts from **Tourist Bungalow**, picking up from Govt of India Tourist Office, The Mall. Tickets on bus.

☉ Transport

Varanasi *p239, maps p238 and p241*
Air
Transfer by taxi, a/c Rs 300, non-a/c Rs 200. Some taxis offer free transfer and claim a

commission from hotel on arrival. A minibus to the aiport runs from Assi Ghat for Rs 175 per person, contact **Tiwari Tours**. Complimentary bus for **Indian Airlines'** passengers leaves from office at 52 Yadunath Marg, Cantonment, at 0900, returns from airport at 1700, T0542-250 2529, airport T0542-262 2494.

Indian Airlines flies daily to **Delhi** and **Mumbai**; to **Khajuraho** Wed, Fri, Sun; **Kathmandu**, Mon, Tue, Thu, Sat. **Jet Airways**, S20/56D Kennedy Rd, The Mall, T0542-250 6444, www.jetairways.com, flies to Delhi and Khajuraho daily. **Kingfisher**, T1800-1800101, and **Spicejet**, T1800-1803333, both fly to Delhi and Mumbai. **Thai Airways** 3 flights per week to **Bangkok**, Oct-Mar only.

Bicycle

Cycle and motorcycle hire: near **Hotel Hindustan International**, Maldahiya.

Boat

This is the best way to enjoy Varanasi. It is necessary to bargain especially for an early-morning ghats visit; shared boat, Rs 40 per person per hr is the official rate for a boat carrying up to 10 people, but bargaining is possible. Ask around for others to share boat; river crossing about Rs 30 return. A boat ride at dusk is also recommended.

Bus

UP Roadways Bus Stand, Sher Shah Suri Marg, is oppposite Junction Station, open 24 hrs, T0542-2203476. Private buses stop opposite the railway station. Buses to **Sarnath**, 9 km, Rs 5 (see below). Frequent services to **Allahabad**, 0330-2300, 122 km, 3 hrs, better than train, many private operators run deluxe buses; **Gorakhpur**, hourly, 7 hrs, Rs 121; **Jaunpur**, 1 hr, Rs 30. For **Delhi** go via **Kanpur**, depart in evening until 2300, 8 hrs, Rs 172; **Lucknow**, hourly, 286 km, 8 hrs, Rs 160. **Khajuraho**: 1 direct per day, 0430, 565 km, 12 hrs, Rs 248. **Agra**, 1 per day, 1700, 14 hrs, Rs 318. **Gaya**: better by rail.

Rickshaw

Most tempos and auto-rickshaws run on fixed routes; those near hotel gates overcharge (fix the fare before hiring). They are not allowed in the narrow streets of the old city but will go to Godoulia in the centre near Dasasvamedha Ghat, Rs 40-60 from station, or Rs 50-60 to Assi

Ghat. There is a prepaid taxi and rickshaw booth near the station Reservations office.

Taxi

Private taxis from agents and hotels. Full day (80 km; 8 hrs), a/c Rs 900-1200, non a/c Rs 700.

Train

Note The large 'Tourist Information Counter' at Junction station is run by travel agents and adds large commissions to tickets. The official Reservations office is outside the station on the left as you exit. Be careful on trains bound for Varanasi as theft is common.

Most trains stop at the **Junction** (or Cantonment) **Station**, T0542-234 8031 or 131, with 24-hr left luggage; to reach a Cantonment hotel on foot, use the back exit. Can be very crowded; use a retiring room if you have a long wait. **Mughal Sarai** station, T0542-225 5703, has the **Delhi/Kolkata** *Rajdhani Exp* (though some go via Patna); see below. Get your tickets (preferably a day in advance) from the **Foreign Tourist Assistance** inside the main hall which is very helpful and efficient, passport required (0800-2200, Sun 0800-1400). When it is closed use the computerized railway reservations (0800-1400, 1430-2000). **Agra Fort**: *Marudhar Exp 4853/4863*, 1720/1830, 12½ /11¼ hrs (book ahead); or go to Tundla from Mughal Sarai (see below). **Allahabad**: *Mahanagari Exp 1094*, 1130, 3½ hrs; *Sarnath Exp 4260*, 1230, 2¾ hrs; *Kamayani Exp 1072*, 1550, 3¾ hrs. **Chennai**: *Ganga-Kaveri Exp 2670*, 2025, Mon, Wed, 48 hrs, reserve early. **Dehra Dun**: *Doon Exp 3009*, 1040, 24 hrs, book in advance (no Tourist Quota); *Janta Exp 4265*, 0830, 24 hrs; *Varanasi Dehra Dun Exp 4265*, 0830, 24¼ hrs, no a/c class. **Gaya**: *Dehra Dun Exp 3010*, 1615, 5¼ hrs; *Chauri Chaura Exp 5004*, 0025, 6 hrs. **Gorakhpur** (for Nepal): *Krishak Exp 5002*, 1630, 5½ hrs; *Manduadih Gorakhpur Exp 5104A*, 0550, 5¼ hrs; **Jaunpur**: *Sutlej Doon Exp 3307*, 0640 1¼ hr; *Farakka Exp 3483*, 1230, 50 mins. **Kanpur**: *Neelachal Exp 8475*, 0742, Mon, Wed, Sat, 7¼ hrs; **Kolkata** (**H**): *Amritsar-Howrah Mail 3006*, 1650, 14¾ hrs; *Doon Exp 3010*, 1615, 14¾ hrs. **Lucknow**: *Varuna Exp 4227*, 0455, 5 hrs; *Kashi-Visvanath Exp 4257*, 1345, 6½ hrs. **Mahoba** (for **Khajuraho**): *Bundelkhand Exp 1108*, 1330, 12¼ hrs (onward bus, 0600). **Satna** (for **Khajuraho**): *Satna Mahanagari*

Exp 1094, 1145, 6½ hrs (from Satna, bumpy bus next day, 5 hrs). **Mumbai** (CST): *Varanasi Lokmanya Tilak Exp 1066*, 2025, Tue, Thu, Sun, 25¾ hrs. **New Delhi**: *Lichchavi Exp 5205*, 1500, 13½ hrs; *Shramjeevi Exp 2401*, 1520, 14¼ hrs.

Mughal Sarai station (with retiring rooms and left luggage). Take a connecting train from Varanasi (45 mins), or allow plenty of time as you need to cross the Ganga and there are huge jams. Best to take a taxi from Varanasi as buses are not dependable and a rickshaw would feel very vulnerable next to the speeding juggernauts. Mughal Sarai has several trains to **Gaya**; a good one is *Purushottam Exp 2802*, 1030, 3 hrs. Also to: **Kolkata (H)**: *Rajdhani Exp 2302/2422*, 0235, 8-10 hrs; *Kalka Howrah Mail 2312*, 2030, 10½ hrs. **New Delhi**: *Poorva Exp 2381/2303*, 1910/2045, Wed, Thu, Sun, 13/11½ hrs; *Neelanchal Exp 8475*, 0655, Mon, Wed, Sat, 14½ hrs; *Rajdhani Exp 2301/5*, 0050, 9¼ hrs. **New Jalpaiguri** (for Darjeeling): *Mahananda Exp 4084*, 2120, 18½ hrs; *NE Exp 2506*, 1835, 16 hrs and to **Guwahati**, 24¼ hrs.

Transport to Nepal

Payment for Nepalese visa at border in cash only. Try to carry exactly US$30 (other currencies not accepted), as money changers at the border give terrible exchange rates. It is illegal to carry Rs 500 and Rs 1000 notes into Nepal.

To **Kathmandu**, the journey requires an overnight stay near the border plus about 20 hrs on the road so can be tiring. **UP Roadways** buses go via **Gorakhpur** to **Sonauli**, depart 4 or 5 times per day, check at bus stand for timings, 9-10 hrs, Rs 130; from Sonauli, 0600. Private buses (agents near UP Tourist Bungalow, around Bengali Tola/Assi Ghat and opposite railway station), often demand inclusive fares for hotel stay; you may prefer to opt for their deluxe buses to the border. Well organized bus service by **Paul Travels**, T0542-220 8137, near **Tourist Bungalow**, Rs 600; departs 0830, reaches Sonauli 1830, overnight in "horrific" dorms on Nepali side, next morning depart 0830 for Kathmandu (10-11 hrs). Also possible to buy tickets direct to Chitwan National Park and Pokhara (both Rs 600).

Sarnath *p243, map p244*
Infrequent bus service; also included in coach tours. From Varanasi, autos from opposite railway station (Rs 50), tempo seat (Rs 10). The road is bumpy; cycling is not recommended as trucks travel along it at great speed. Taxis take 30 mins (Rs 600 including wait).

Jaunpur *p245, map p246*
Bus Frequent service along NH56 to/from **Varanasi** and **Lucknow** including *Express* (under 2 hrs). Ask to be dropped at the Akbari Bridge (crossroads north of the bus stand) where you can pick up a cycle rickshaw.
Taxi From Varanasi, Rs 850 return.
Train To **Varanasi** *Sutlej Exp 3308*, 1820, 2 hrs; *Varuna Exp 4228*, 2200.

⊙ Directory

Varanasi *p239, maps p238 and p241*
Banks Most banks refuse to change money. Travellers are often stopped and asked for 'change'. State Bank of India at Hotel Kashika (Mon-Fri 1000-1400), and Godoulia (near Indica Books), takes 1 hr, changes Visa, TCs. Also at Clarks Varanasi and at airport. Radiant Services, D48/139A Misir Pokhra (by Mazda Cinema), Luxa Rd, Godoulia, T0542-235 8852. Daily 0700-2200, changes TCs, has a 24-hr counter at Shanti Guest House, T0542-239 2017, and Cantt Office, above Union Bank of India, on the Mall, T0542-251 1052. Shops changing money offer a poor rate. **Hospitals** Heritage Hospital, Lanka (near BHU main entrance), T0542-236 8888. Private hospital. Many hotels have a doctor on call. **Internet** Many along Bengali Tola and around Assi Ghat, about Rs 30 per hr. **Post** Head Post Office: Bisheshwarganj (parcel packing outside). Post office in Cantt, Mon-Sat 1000-1800. A man offers to 'help' get a parcel posted for a fee (Rs 100), but you can do this yourself. Couriers: City Airlinkers, Cantt, T0542 234 4214. **Useful addresses** Ambulance: T0542-233 3723. Fire: T101, T0542 232 2888. Police: T100. Foreigners' Registration Office: Sidh Giri Bagh (not easy to find), T0542-241 1968.

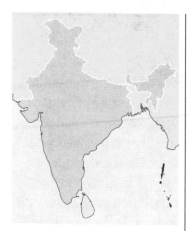

Andaman and Nicobar Islands

Introduction

The Andaman and Nicobar Islands were, until the tsunami in December 2004, a little-known chain of tropical islands in the Bay of Bengal. Thickly forested with rainforest and tropical trees, edged by mangrove swamps and pristine palm-fringed, white-sand beaches and coral reefs, these remote islands easily rival the likes of the Maldives or the Caribbean in terms of natural beauty. The only thing they lack is five-star all-inclusive resorts. However, joining the hammocks and wood cabins are some small resorts with all the creature comforts.

The sparkling clear water and pristine corals make it one of the best places in the world to explore the seabed with rare species – dugong, grey teal, Estuarine crocodile and marine turtles – as well as tropical fish and coral. Birdwatchers are also in paradise with 242 species recorded. The canopied rainforests harbour 3000 species of plants including mangroves, ferns, orchids, palms, climbers and tropical fruits. Of the 58 species of mammals and 83 reptiles, many are endemic, as the islands are isolated.

The islands' aboriginal tribal people are of special interest to anthropologists. Some, like the Jarawas and Sentinalese in the Andamans, have remained isolated and hostile to outsiders even up to the late 20th century. Others, the Great Andamanese for example, have interacted with non-tribal settlers for decades and now there are very few left. The Indian government keeps the Primitive Tribal Reserve Areas out of bounds.

The tsunami devasted parts of this paradise; the southern chain of islands, the Nicobars, was badly hit resulting in many deaths. Only the southernmost island in the Andamans – Little Andaman – was substantially affected. Parts of the Andaman are accessible to foreigners, the Nicobars are off-limits.

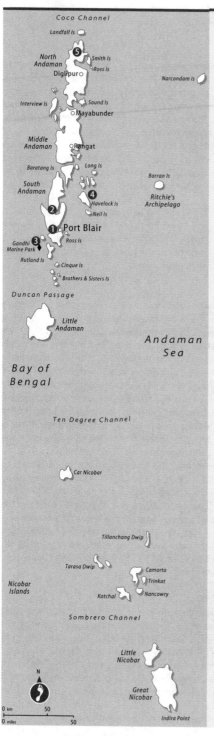

★ Don't miss ...

1 **Port Blair** Learn about the area's penal past with a visit to the eerie, abandoned Viper Island and then take a trip to Cellular Jail, page 259.

2 **South Andaman** Hire a scooter and explore the island along its quiet roads, page 265.

3 **Mahatma Gandhi Marine National Park** When access is allowed, here you can experience some of the world's finest coral reefs, page 267.

4 **Havelock Island** The most developed of all the islands, this is home to an award-winning beach and some great places to stay, page 268.

5 **Saddle Peak National Park** Get active and explore this beautiful area, page 272.

Andaman & Nicobar Islands

Background → *Population: 356,300. Area: 8,249 sq km.*

The land

Geography The Andaman and Nicobar group comprises about 300 islands formed by a submarine mountain range which divides the Bay of Bengal from the Andaman Sea. The islands lie between latitudes 6° to 14° north (about level with Chennai and longitudes 92-94° east, a span of 725 km). The land rises to 730 m (Saddle Peak), formed mainly of limestones, sandstones and clays. The Andamans are separated from the Nicobars by a 90-m deep 150 km strait. The Andamans group has 204 islands (26 inhabited) with its three main islands of North, Middle and South, which are separated by mangrove-fringed islets and are together called Great Andaman. The Nicobar Islands comprise 12 inhabited and seven uninhabited islands including the three groups, Car Nicobar in the north, Camorta and Nancowry in the middle and the largest, Great Nicobar in the south.

Climate Tropical. Temperature: 20°C to 32°C. Annual rainfall: 2,540 mm. Monsoons – usually May to mid-September, and November to mid-December (though the first may arrive as early as mid-April, bringing heavy rain on most days). Best season is end-November to mid-April. The climate has no extremes, the main contrasts coming with the arrival of the monsoons and tropical storms.

History

Lying on the trade route between Burma and India the islands appeared on Ptolemy's second century map and were also recorded by the Chinese traveller I-Tsing in the seventh century. At the end of the 17th century the Marathas established a base there to attack the trading British, Dutch and Portuguese ships. Dutch pirates and French Jesuits had made contact with the islands before the Danish East India Company made attempts to evangelize the islands in the mid-18th century. The reputation of ferocity attributed to the Nicobarese may have been partly due to Malay pirates who attacked and killed sailors of any trading vessel that came ashore (some anthropologists believe that in spite of common belief, the aboriginals themselves were not cannibals). The first British attempt to occupy the islands was made in 1788 when the Governor General of India sent Lt Blair (whose name was given to the first port) and, although the first convicts were sent there in 1794, it was abandoned within a couple of years.

After the 'First War of Independence' (the 'Mutiny') in 1857 the British gained control of most of the islands and used them as a penal colony for its prisoners (who until then had been sent to Sumatra) right up to Indian Independence, with a short break from 1942-1945 when the Japanese occupied Port Blair, Ross Island and the Nicobar Islands. However, political prisoners were sent in large numbers only after the completion of the Cellular Jail in 1906. Each revolt on the mainland resulted in the transportation of people from various parts of India, hence the presence of Bengalis, Malayans and Burmese among others. Subhas Chandra Bose, the Indian Nationalist, first raised the Indian tricolour here in 1943.

Culture

Sir Arthur Conan Doyle in 1890 described the islanders as "perhaps ... the smallest race upon this earth ... fierce, morose and intractable". In the mid-19th century, the British guessed the tribal population was around 5000 but the number has been steadily dwindling. Today most of the inhabitants are Indians, Burmese and Malays – some, descendants of the criminals who were transported there. Since the 1950s, refugees from East Pakistan (now Bangladesh), Burma and Indian emigrants from Guyana have settled on the main islands to be followed more recently by Tamils from Sri Lanka. The largest concentration is around the capital, Port Blair, with the majority of the tribal people (about 15% of the population) living in the Nicobars.

Tribals of Andaman and Nicobar

One story goes that the monkey god Hanuman stopped in the Andamans on his way to Lanka in search of Sita (see page 293), giving the islands his name. They have been inhabited by Aboriginal tribes (some Negrito) for thousands of years but remained unexplored because anyone attempting to land would be attacked. Today there are only a few **Andamanese**, who once inhabited the Great Andamans, some **Onges** in Little Andaman who traditionally painted their naked bodies, the fierce **Jarawas** on South Andaman and the **Sentinelese** on North Sentinel. Car Nicobar (Carnic) is inhabited by the mongoloid **Nicobarese**, the most numerous groups, and **Shompens** who may have been of pre-Dravidian stock, live in Great Nicobar.

Hunting wild pigs, fishing with nets and catching turtles with harpoons from dug-out canoes, the islanders used iron for arrowheads and metal from wrecks for harpoons. Some tribes made pottery but the **Andamanese** particularly were exceptional since they had not discovered fire-making.

The Anthropological Survey of India and the Andaman Administration have been jointly trying to establish friendly contact with the Jarawas and Sentinelese since the 1960s. They consistently repelled groups of explorers with poisoned arrows. More recently, some **Sentinelese** have picked up coconuts (which do not grow on their island) that were left on the beach as a gesture of friendship by anthropologists. In January 1991, Indian anthropologists succeeded in landing on North Sentinel and in February, a few Sentinelese boarded a lifeboat to accept gifts of coconuts. Study groups have made regular visits, removing most of their clothes in order to be accepted. The 400 or so Sentinelese do not appear to have a hierarchical social structure; they are naked, painting their bodies with chalk and ochre and wearing bead and bone ornaments.

The **Jarawas** remain in the Tribal Reserve set aside to the west of the Andaman Trunk Road, all along the South and Middle Andamans.

Hindi, Bengali, Tamil, Malayalam and English are spoken. The Andamanese language, which bears no resemblance to any other language, uses prefixes and suffixes to indicate the function of a word and is extraordinary in using simply two concepts of number, 'one' and 'greater than one'.

Modern Andaman and Nicobar

Economy Tourism before the tsunami was rapidly becoming the Andamans' most important industry and the runway at the airport was extended in 2003. Forests represent an important resource. The government has divided 40% of the forests into Primitive Tribal Reserve areas which are only open to Indian visitors with permits, and the remaining 60% as Protected Areas set aside for timber for export as plywoods, hardwoods and matchwoods (a Swedish multinational owns extensive logging rights). Rubber and mahogany have been planted in addition to teak and rosewood which are commercially in demand. Fishing – lobsters, prawns and sea fish – and agriculture are also important, with rice a staple food crop.

Government As a Union Territory the Andamans and Nicobar Islands have a Lieutenant Governor, Shri Nagendra Nath Jha, a retired member of the Indian Foreign Service and member of the BJP's National Executive since 1994.

⚉ Tsunami

In December 2004, following the powerful earthquake off the coast of Indonesia, devastating tidal waves hit many countries. In this region, the aboriginal tribals living on the Nicobar Islands bore the brunt of the casualties. The official human fatalities are daunting: 8000 died in the Nicobars alone, and 80 died on Little Andaman. But this published death toll is contested by aid agencies, who say it is likely that more than half the archipelago's population of 35,000 were lost to the waves. As with all the countries affected, tourism is being encouraged as a direct way of spurring the economic revival that is needed to fund the relief effort and visitor permits are being issued to the Andamans, but the Nicobars, long closed to tourism to protect their tribal cultures, remain so. Of the 572 islands, Car Nicobar was the worst affected. Elsewhere, Little Andaman's two resorts were razed, and many of the other businesses on the islands have let go of staff, but hotels are open and operating. Port Blair, the Andaman's capital, was unscathed. Havelock Island, the government's prime focus for tourism, was not badly damaged, and the corals around Ritchie's Archipelago are all mostly intact and marine life abundant – so there's still good reason, besides those humanitarian, to visit.

Ins and outs

Getting there

Foreigners with tourist visas for India are allowed a maximum stay of 30 days on arrival at Port Blair, the capital, by air or sea, but may not visit tribal areas or restricted islands including Nicobar. It is no longer necessary to get a permit in advance. CID will extend your permit up to a maximum stay of 15 days without difficulty, but only when your initial period of approval is about to expire. Any extension is only valid for staying in Port Blair. Foreign tourists may now apply and get a Restricted Area Permit after Registration at Immigration at a cost of US$30 (payable in dollars or rupees, but must be cash). Officially, permits allow foreigners to visit and stay overnight in Port Blair, Havelock, Long Island, Neil Island, entire islands of South and Middle Andaman (excluding tribal reserve), Baratang, Rangat, Mayabunder, Diglipur, North Passage Island, Little Andaman Island (excluding tribal reserve), and all islands in Mahatma Gandhi Marine National Park except Boat, Hobay, Twin Island, Tarmugli, Malay and Pluto Island. You can also visit Jolly Buoy, Red Skin, South Cinque, Mount Harriet and Madhuban, Ross Island, Narcondam, Interview, Brother, Sister and Barren Island during the daytime. In practice, requests to visit remote islands such as Barren, North Passage and Narcondam, which have recently been opened to tourists, are often refused even though ships sail to them. Some dive companies arrange overnight stays on courses. Foreigners working in the Andamans can get a four-month visa but to extend the stay, the person must leave India and re-enter with a new visa and permit. Indians may visit the Andamans and Nicobars without a permit but must obtain a permit for restricted areas. See also http://tourism.andaman.nic.in ▸ *For Transport details, see page 263.*

Getting around

Hiring a scooter can be handy for visiting place around Port Blair. Recommended particularly for trips to Wandoor, Chiriya Tapu, Mt Harriet and Corbyn's Cove. Buses cover sights and towns on the limited road network. Inter-island ferries sail to coastal towns and islands which are far more relaxing than the capital.

Port Blair

→ Phone code: 03192. Colour map 3. Population: 100,200.

Port Blair, the capital, about 1200 km from Kolkata and Chennai, has only a handful of sights. The small town has changed in the last 30 years from one which saw a ship from the mainland once a month if the weather permitted to a place connected by flights from Chennai and Kolkata several times a week. It now has a hospital, shops, schools and colleges and a few museums, in addition to resort hotels and watersports facilities. ➤➤ *For Sleeping, Eating and other listings, see pages 261-265.*

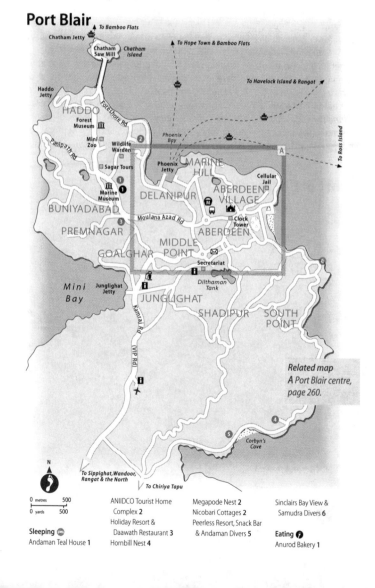

Related map
A Port Blair centre, page 260.

0 metres 500
0 yards 500

Sleeping 🛌
Andaman Teal House 1

ANIIDCO Tourist Home
  Complex 2
Holiday Resort &
  Daawath Restaurant 3
Hornbill Nest 4

Megapode Nest 2
Nicobari Cottages 2
Peerless Resort, Snack Bar
  & Andaman Divers 5

Sinclairs Bay View &
  Samudra Divers 6

Eating 🍴
Anurod Bakery 1

Getting there and around Lamba Line airport, 3 km south of Port Blair, has flights from Kolkata and Chennai. You can get a bus or taxi to town. Ships from the mainland dock at Haddo jetty where you can get taxis but they invariably overcharge. As Port Blair is very small, you can easily see the sights in a couple of days. Aberdeen Village with the bazar in the town centre has most of the budget hotels, the bus station, shops and offices. ▸▸ *For further information, see Transport, page 263.*

Sights

North of Aberdeen Jetty, the **Cellular Jail** ① *Tue-Sun 0900-1200, 1400-1700, Rs 5, camera, Rs 10, video camera, Rs 50, allow 1 hr,* dating from 1886-1906, was originally built by the British to house dangerous criminals. Subsequently it was used to place Indian freedom fighters until 1938; it could hold 698 solitary prisoners in small narrow cells. The Japanese used it for their prisoners of war during their occupation from 1942-1945. Three of the original seven wings which extended from the central guard tower survive; the jail was renovated in 1998. There is a site **museum**, photographs and lists of 'convicts' held, a 'death house' and the gallows, where you can get an impression of the conditions within the prison in the early 1900s and the implements used in torture. There is a well-presented 45-minute **Sound and Light show** ① *daily at 1915, Rs 100, in English,* on prison life. Highly recommended.

Chatham Saw Mill ① *Mon-Sat 0630-1430 (0830 is a good time to arrive to avoid the lunch break), allow about 1½ hrs, photography is not allowed,* is one of the oldest in Asia, employing 1000 workers. Tours take you through the different processes of turning logs into 'seasoned' planks. For tours, report to the Security Office just outside

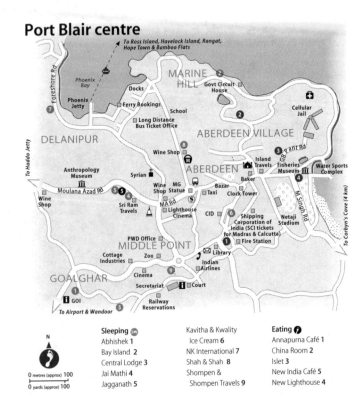

Port Blair centre

To Ross Island, Havelock Island, Rangat, Hope Town & Bamboo Flats

MARINE HILL

Phoenix Bay

Docks

Govt Circuit House

Phoenix Jetty

Ferry Bookings

School

Cellular Jail

Long Distance Bus Ticket Office

ABERDEEN VILLAGE

DELANIPUR

Wine Shop

To Haddo Jetty

Anthropology Museum

Syrian

ABERDEEN

Island Travels

Fisheries Museum

Water Sports Complex

Pant Rd

Moulana Azad Rd

Wine Shop

MG Road

Bazar

Baker

To Corbyn's Cove (4 km)

Wine Shop

Sri Ram Travels

Taxi

Clock Tower

CID

Lighthouse Cinema

Shipping Corporation of India (SCI tickets for Madras & Calcutta)

Netaji Stadium

M Singh Rd

PWD Office

MIDDLE POINT

Library

Fire Station

Cottage Industries

Zoo

Indian Airlines

GOALGHAR

Cinema

Secretariat

Court

GOI

Railway Reservations

To Airport & Wandoor

N

0 metres (approx) 100
0 yards (approx) 100

Sleeping 😴
Abhishek 1
Bay Island 2
Central Lodge 3
Jai Mathi 4
Jagganath 5

Kavitha & Kwality
  Ice Cream 6
NK International 7
Shah & Shah 8
Shompen &
  Shompen Travels 9

Eating 🍴
Annapurna Café 1
China Room 2
Islet 3
New India Café 5
New Lighthouse 4

the main gate. The **Forest Museum** ⓘ *0800-1200, 1430-1700*, here has unusual local woods including red paduk, satin and marble woods and shows the use of different woods in the timber industry and methods of lumbering and finishing.

The **Mini Zoo** ⓘ *Tue-Sun 0800-1700*, has a small, uninspiring collection in some very old wooden cages with a few specimens of unusual island fauna including a sea crocodile farm. **Marine Museum** ⓘ *opposite Andaman Teal House, Tue-Sun 0830-1200, 1400-1700, Rs 10, camera, Rs 20, video camera, Rs 40, allow 30 mins*, has a collection of corals and shells and a display of 350 species of marine life. The **Anthropological Museum** ⓘ *Tue-Sun 1000-1230, 1400-1600*, it worth a visit; it has a small but interesting collection of photographs and artefacts and records of exploratory expeditions.

At **Sippighat Farm** ⓘ *Tue-Sun 0600-1100, 1200-1600*, 14 km away, you can see cash crops such as spices and other plants being propagated. The Andaman Water Sports Complex has been developed nearby (see page 263).

Viper Island, near Haddo Wharf, is at the mouth of Port Blair harbour where convicts were interned before the Cellular Jail was built.

Although the only beach close to Port Blair, **Corbyn's Cove**, 5 km from Port Blair, is only busy at weekends. The water is warm with gentle surf and the white sand beach is clean and palm fringed. A government eco-friendly tourist village is under way 1½ km north of the Cove.

● Sleeping

Port Blair *p259, maps p259 and p260*
Many hotels offer discounts Apr-Sep.
A Bay Island, Marine Hill, 2 km, T03192-234101, www.fortunehotels.in. 48 a/c rooms, some small, replica local huts (not all have sea view), cool open lounge and restaurant, good gardens but poor tennis court, sea water pool, keen on conservation , far from beach but excellent view across harbour entrance.
A-B Peerless Resort, Corbyn's Cove (4 km), set back from beach, T03192-233461, ppbeachin@sancharnet.in. 48 rooms, 4 cottages, good Snack Bar (see page 262), pleasant and airy, well-kept gardens, tennis, beach nearby (take snorkelling equipment), dive centre, excellent service, warm ambience, free airport transfer but need taxis to town.
B Megapode Nest, Haddo Hill, www.niva link.com/megapodenest. 25 good a/c rooms off central lounge area, short walk from restaurant, large terrace, very peaceful, very good but no food or drink outside mealtimes.
B Sinclairs Bay View, South Pt, T03192-233236, www.nivalink.com/bayview. Refurbished resort hotel in elevated location overlooking Ross Island, no beach, 24 rooms, some a/c, restaurant, excellent and popular bar, pool, dive centre.
B-D Shompen, 2 Middle Point, T03192-233236, hotelshompen@hotmail.com. 40 rooms (noisy in front, windowless and very hot in centre), 15 a/c overpriced,

rooftop restaurant, free airport transfer, tours, popular with backpackers, friendly, helpful staff, off-season/long stay discounts.
B-E Hornbill Nest, 10 mins' walk from Corbyn's Cove, T03192-246042, hornbillresort @rediffmail.com. Clean rooms, some on hillside overlooking sea, central open-air lounge and restaurant, transport difficult (stop a returning empty taxi), best for those wanting cheapish shared room near beach.
C Nicobari Cottages, Haddo Hill, T03192-232207. Mainly for officials, 2 a/c rondavels.
C-E Holiday Resort, Prem Nagar, T03192-230516, holidayresort88@hotmail.com. Large clean rooms with bath, bucket hot water, good restaurant, TV in lounge, helpful manager, stores luggage, internet.
D NK International, Fore Shore Rd, T03192-233066. Functional grey concrete block, 31 very simple rooms, some a/c with bath, few with good view across Phoenix Jetty.
D Tourist Home, Haddo Hill, reservations: New Marine Dry Docks, T03192-32376. 18 refurbished rooms attached to the reception area, restaurant, very good value.
D-E Abhishek, Goalghar, T03192-233565, hotelabhishek@hotmail.com. Inconvenient location. Friendly, helpful management, good restaurant and bar, snorkel equipment for hire, free transfer (usually meets flights).
E Andaman Teal House, Delanipur, T03192-232642. Good views, 27 cleanish rooms with

bath, some a/c, comfortable wicker furniture, spacious lounge-restaurant.

E Jagannath, Moulana Azad Rd, 7 mins from bazar, T03192-232148. Some of the 15 clean rooms have bath and balcony in newer block but no hot water, filtered water, helpful staff.

F ANIIDCO Tourist Home Complex, Haddo Hill, T03192-32380. Central restaurant, bar and gardens with superb views.

F Central Lodge Middle Point, Goalghar, T03192-33634. Some rooms with bath but often full, camping. Set back off road.

F Jai Mathi, 78 Moulana Azad Rd, T03192-33457. Large rooms, clean but variable, bucket hot water, very good cheap food (try ginger fish, prawn *biriyani*), bar, helpful staff.

F Kavitha, Aberdeen Bazar, opposite CID, T03192-233762. Often has room when all others full (at time of ship arrive/depart), 24 rooms, 1 night only.

F Shah and Shah, near Aberdeen Bazar, T03192-233696, shahnshahrediff@mail.com. 23 excellent large clean rooms, huge first floor balcony. Recommended.

⊘ Eating

Port Blair *p259, maps p259 and p260*
Good seafood is widely available and even the cheapest hotels offer prawn and crab curries. Larger hotels have a wider selection, but meals (most ingredients imported from the mainland) and drinks can be expensive. There are several juice bars between the bus stand and clock tower. Government Guest Houses are open to non-residents. All Indian restaurants have excellent fish fry for under Rs 15. Highly recommended, especially for trips out of Port Blair.

♥♥♥ Bay Island, Marine Hill. International. Luxurious surroundings, seafood recommended, lunch buffet Rs 350.

♥♥♥ China Room, Aberdeen Village. Chinese. Owned by Burmese/Punjabi couple. Eat in pleasant shady outdoor yard, dinner by candlelight (but mosquito problem), freshly prepared with home-grown vegetables, not drenched in oil, soya or tomato sauce, order seafood 'specials' the day before, beer.

♥♥♥ Islet, 1st floor, GB Pant Rd (takeaway downstairs). Indian, Chinese. Relax with a cool beer on the narrow balcony with views across stadium, generous portions but quality overrated.

♥♥ New India Café, next to Hotel Jaimathi. Good Indian, some Western dishes. Great food and prices, continental breakfast, lobster and other specials on request, but very slow service (wait an hour for dinner).

♥♥ New Lighthouse, opposite Municipal Guest House. Wide choice of Indian and Chinese in small open-air café, evening BBQ.

♥♥ Shompen Rooftop. Indian, Continental. Limited menu (try *aloo jeera* and dhal), fish dishes a bit hit-and-miss.

♥ Annapurna Café, Aberdeen Bazar. Wide selection. Try their different dosas and Indian sweets, good for European-style breakfast, a/c rooms, very popular. Recommended.

♥ Anurod Bakery, towards Teal House. Sells good cakes, snacks and cornflakes.

♥ Daawath, below Holiday Resort. Good breakfasts and curries, avoid Western food.

♥ Kwality ice cream next door to Kavita.

♥ Snack Bar at Peerless Beach Resort serves reasonable food (fish and chips), open all day, friendly staff, quick service, good toilets at resort with lockers and changing rooms.

♥ Teal Bakery behind bus stand. Good cakes.

♥ Tourist Home Complex, Haddo. Indian. Excellent *thali lunches*, try the chicken dishes.

⊙ Bars and clubs

Port Blair *p259, maps p259 and p260*
Peerless Beach Resort, Sinclairs Bay View, Tourist Home Complex, Abishek and Shompen have bars. Beers and spirits from bar below **Shalimar Hotel**, Delanipur.

⊛ Festivals and events

Port Blair *p259, maps p259 and p260*
End-Feb Island Tourism Festival for 10 days, with music and dancing from all over India and focusing on local crafts, culture and food.

○ Shopping

Port Blair *p259, maps p259 and p260*
Local curio shops are by the clocktower and opposite the post office. Tailors sell hammocks. **Andaman Teal House**, hires out tents, good condition (deposit, Rs 2,500, Rs 50-70 per day). **Sagarika Cottage Emporium**, next to tourist office, open 0900-1800, closed Sun. Selection of souvenirs in wood and shell (the government limits for collection of shells).

፧ Into the deep

There are many excellent locations for snorkelling. The most popular site was MG National Marine Park though this is currently off-limits to the vast majority of visitors. Another site, Chiriya Tapu, is very easy to reach from Port Blair. It is best to bring your own mask and snorkel. You may need to pay up to Rs 5000 as deposit when hiring equipment. Most close from early May during the monsoons.

Scuba diving is a boom business in the Andamans and the number of

diving schools is growing. It is difficult to find a cheaper and more beautiful location to learn to dive in the world. For fanatics, longer dive trips can be organized to unexplored sites around the Andamans providing enough people are interested. The best dive sites for a day trip are in the vicinity of Cinque Island though the government tax of Rs 1000 for dives makes it pricey.

Do not remove dead coral even if you find pieces on the beach.

▲ Activities and tours

Port Blair *p259, maps p259 and p260*
Diving
Havelock also has dive centres.
Andaman Divers, Peerless Resort, see Sleeping. Runs PADI courses and trips.
Samudra, Sinclair Bay View Hotel, see Sleeping. PADI courses and trips.

Swimming
Swimming is excellent. The best spot is the crescent-shaped Corbyn's Cove or one of the uninhabited islands which tourists may visit.

Tour operators
A&N Islands Tours and Travels, 20/4 Air Rd, Delanipur, T01392-245068, anislands@rediff mail.com. Efficient and professional.
Island Travel, Aberdeen Bazar, T03192-233358. Indian Airlines/Alliance Air, Jet Airways agents, good for excursions, car hire.
Sagar Tours, 7 Krishna Building, Haddo, T03192-233703.
Shompen Travels, 2 Middle Pt, T03192-232644. Local tours, Wandoor to Jolly Buoy/Red Skin ferry.

Watersports
Andaman Adventure, near Holiday Inn, has good snorkelling equipment for hire, Rs 60/day, US$100 deposit.
Andaman Water Sports Complex, next to Fisheries Museum, Sippighat, T03192-230769. 0700-1100, 1500-2000. Sailing, paddle boats, wind surfing, paragliding.

⊝ Transport

Port Blair *p259, maps p259 and p260*
Make sure you confirm reservations. Problems can occur Apr-May and for the Tourism Festival.

Air
Alliance Air flights from Kolkata and Chennai, 5 times a week and **Jet Airways** daily from Chennai. The new extended runway may permit flights to/from Delhi. Transport to town: most buses pass the airport entrance. Taxis should charge Rs 30 per person; fix fare first. Some hotels send taxis. Flights are always fully booked at least a month ahead (earlier for Apr-May). However, because of the strict enforcement of the 30-day stay regulations, officials may find you a seat to fly out even at the last moment. If stuck, try for tickets from **Island Travels** or from **Jet Airways**, or **Indian Airlines/Alliance Air**, and ask the office manager to be placed on the priority waiting list. Book well ahead. You may request your international carrier to get Andaman's tickets, preferably 6 months ahead. Reconfirm on arrival in India, and after you get to Port Blair. Avoid mid-Apr when the summer holiday rush starts. **Indian Airlines**, G55 Middle Pt, behind PO, T03192-234744. Airport T03192-32983. **Jet Airways**, 189 Main Rd, Junglighat, T03192-236922, airport T03192-235911.

Bicycle
Hire from shop between Aberdeen Bazar and the bus stop (about Rs 5 per hr) but you need to be very fit to manage the hilly island.

Central Bus Station near Aberdeen Bazar serves state and private buses, T03192-232278. Regular service to villages and districts. Bus stops at **Shompen Hotel** and near the airport. A few private buses run between Chatham jetty and the Cellular Jail. To **Rangat**, 2 private buses daily (6-7 hrs), 1 via Mayabunder at 0420. **Mayabunder** daily departs 0530-0630, Rs 70 (de luxe, Rs 120); often noisy video bus. Buy tickets a day ahead from agents around the bus stand. For state buses go to the transport office opposite entrance to Phoenix jetty; numbered tickets go on sale at 1400. Long queues, plenty of touts. *Diglipur Express* is the quickest to the far north, and the only way of reaching Diglipur (which involves crossing 3 creeks) the same night. Depart 0530, arrive 1930 (Rs 90). Others to Mayabunder miss the last ferry to Kalighat (1630) which connects to Diglipur.

Ferry

There are a bewildering range of **inter-island and harbour ferries** operating from Port Blair. Most operate from Phoenix Bay Jetty. Details from Directorate of Shipping Services, Port Blair, T03192-232426. Passengers may feel seasick! Regular sailings to **Havelock, Neil** and **Long Islands, Rangat Bay, Mayabunder** and **Aerial Bay** appear in the *Daily Telegrams* newspaper (or ring Shipping Corp of India for times, T03192-233347). There are 2 decks and hawkers sell snacks on board. **Diglipur** via Aerial Bay Jetty, Tue evening and Fri morning, Rs 90, 14 hrs. **Havelock,** Rs 25, 4 hrs, direct. **Neil,** Wed and Fri, 4 hrs. **Rangat,** 4 a week, 7 hrs. There are also less frequent services to the 2 volcanic islands of Narcondam and Barren. **Little Andaman** (Hut Bay), once a week, Rs 25-70, 8 hrs. Fares are often doubled if tickets are not bought in advance. A Harbour ferry operates from Phoenix Jetty (vehicular only) to Hope Town, Bamboo Flats, Ross Island daily except Wed, 0830, 1000, 1230, Rs 20; Cholunga Wharf, Phoenix Bay: Harbour Cruise, Rs 25, 1500-1700, including Viper Island. From Chatham Jetty to Bamboo Flats and Dundas Pt, about hourly, 0600-2025 (2 hrs).

Mainland ferries sail between **Haddo Jetty**, Port Blair and Kolkata (66 hrs) and Chennai (60 hrs) run to a schedule of sorts 3 to 4 times a month. Also **Vishakapatnam** (56 hrs) once a month. For immigration formalities, see page 258. Tentative schedules for the month are usually available at the end of the previous month; times of departure and arrival appear about a week before in the local papers. Last minute changes are made depending on weather conditions and tides. Tickets are issued 7 days ahead but are not sold on the day of sailing. They can be difficult to get. Apply with 3 photos to **Shipping Corporation of India**, 2 Supply Rd, near Mosque, T03192-233347, for tickets. Sailing schedules are also available opposite **Lakshmi Narayan Hotel**, Aberdeen Bazar. The Directorate of Tourism has a tourist quota of 12 bunk class berths for each sailing from Port Blair to Kolkata and Chennai. Put your name down well in advance. A few days before sailing, collect a form which entitles you to claim a berth from the Shipping Corporation of India before tickets go on public sale. Ships vary but prices are approximately: Deluxe Cabin (2 beds, shower), Rs 3900 each; 1st/A Class (4 bunks, shower), Rs 2400; B Class (4/8 berth), Rs 2800; 2nd Class (for 6), Rs 2700; a/c dormitory, Rs 1800 (on MV *Akbar* only); Bunk Class, Rs 1150. The ships are 25 to 65 years old! Meals cost Rs 120 (cabin), Rs 60 (bunk) per day but some may not find them suitable. Carry some snacks. A kiosk sells snacks, cigarettes, mineral water, soft drinks. Disembarkation can be chaotic and a free-for-all. Taxis demand Rs 50 to go anywhere.

Motorbike

Prashant Travels, Phoenix Bay, next to **Jagannath Hotel**, Has a newish fleet of motorbikes for hire, Rs 150 per day (Rs 1000 deposit) return by 1900; scooters, Rs 120. Also try **TSG** (TS Guruswamy), Moulana Azad Rd, near Anthropology Museum, T03192-232894. **GDM**, further up the road, has good Kinetic Hondas, Rs 200 per day (very good condition, start first time!). Check insurance papers.

Rickshaw and taxi

Please use pre-paid **Traffic Complaint Cards** to report taxi and rickshaw drivers who refuse to use a meter to take you to your destination etc. In time, this may lead to positive action. Available from the Inspector, Traffic Branch, Police Station, Aberdeen (opposite Bus Stand), T03192-234472, ext 309. **Central Taxi Stand**, opposite bus station and by clocktower,

Aberdeen Bazar, charge Rs 20 about town, Rs 50 for Corbyn's Bay and Haddo Jetty. They often refuse to use meters and are overpriced.

Train
Railway Reservations Office, near Secretariat, T03192-233042, 0800-1230, 1300-1400. Supposedly separate queues for Kolkata and Chennai, but a chaotic free-for-all. Buy tickets in advance on the mainland if possible.

⊙ Directory

Port Blair *p259, maps p259 and p260*
Banks Credit cards not accepted anywhere in the Andamans. TCs are only changed at **Island Travels**, Aberdeen Bazar, Port Blair. **Shompen** and **Bay Island** hotels will change TCs if you spend foreign currency there. **State Bank of India** opposite bus station, 0900-1300, Sat 0900-1100. **Laundry** Near Bazar Taxi stand. **Libraries** State Library, near Annapoorna Café, has a small collection of reference books on the Andamans, useful for identification of corals and fish. Open 1230-1945. **Post** GPO, near centre, by Indian Airlines office. Mon-Fri 0700-2200, Sat-Sun 0800-1800. **CTO**, for international calls and fax service. Also several private STD and ISD booths. Make your important international calls in Port Blair since links elsewhere are unreliable. **Tourist offices** Govt of India, 2nd floor (above Super Shoppe), 189 Junglighat Main Rd (VIP Rd), T03192-233006. Enthusiastic officer (printout of local information). **Director of Tourism**, opposite Indian Airlines, T03192-232694. Register on the Tourist Quota for boats to Kolkata and Chennai. Unhelpful reception desk. Airport counter open at flight times, T03192-232414. **ANIIDCO** (Andaman and Nicobar Islands Integrated Development Corporation), New Marine Dry Docks (first gate after entrance to Phoenix jetty), T03192-32098/33695. Airport counter T03192-232414. Runs Tourist Home Complex, Haddo. Screens occasional films about the islands. **Useful addresses** Fire, T03192-232101. **Hospital**, T03192-232102. **Police**, T03192-233077. **Chief Conservator of Forests**, T03192-233321; Deputy, T03192-232816. **PWD Office**, between Shompen and Lighthouse Cinema, T03192-233050.

South Andaman and the Marine National Park

Chiriya Tapu
Chiriya Tapu, 28 km from Port Blair, at the southern tip of South Andaman, is only an hour by road. Popular for birdwatching, it has excellent beaches with good snorkelling. From the bus stop, which has some tea shops, a track past the **Forest Guest House** (not possible to stay here), leads to the first beach. Continue along the trail through the forest for 20 minutes (several smaller trails are ideal for birdwatching), until you reach a second beach with very good corals 50 m out; at low tide you can walk a long way. The corals are not so spectacular along the coastline, but there is a large range of fish.
▶▶ *For Sleeping, Eating and other listings, see page 267.*

Mount Harriet
The hill is good for either a morning or a whole day trip but make an early start to avoid the heat. A path through the forest starts by the derelict water viaduct in Hope Town, which joins the surfaced road near the top (excellent vines for would-be-Tarzans here!). Allow 1½ hours to the top. Alternatively, the bus from the jetty stops in Hope Town near the viaduct, or will drop you at the start of the road up the hill with a 4-km walk from here. Near the top of the road lie the ruins of the Chief Commissioner's bungalow, abandoned in 1942. Signs show where the rooms were.

It is also possible to ride a scooter to the top but you will pass the **Forest Check Post** ⊙ *Rs 10, scooter Rs 10, camera Rs 25, video camera Rs 1,500,* where national park fees are charged. Taking the forest path on foot avoids the check post and fees.

Black Rocks

Black Rocks (Kalapathar) is 2 km from Mount Harriet and **Madhuban** via Mount Carpenter, 16 km. A signpost marks the start of the nature trail from Mount Harriet which is easy to follow as far as the Black Rocks, the spot where prisoners were pushed to their death. After Black Rocks, the trail is unclear so take a guide if you plan to walk the whole route. The walk back along the rocky coast is uninteresting; you can get a bus 5 km after the lighthouse. **Madhuban Beach** is on the east side where young elephants are trained for forestry; at **Burma Nalla**, 3 km away, they are used for lumbering.

Ross Island

Ross Island was originally developed under the British as the Residence of the Chief Commissioner, and the administrative headquarters. During the Second World War, it was occupied by the Japanese whose legacy is an ugly complex of concrete bunkers which are still intact. The rest of the buildings on the island are ruins with spotted deer living peacefully among them. In many cases the walls are only still standing because of the climbing trees. The church in the centre and the Subalterns' club are impressive. The small **museum** ⓘ *dawn to dusk, except Wed, Rs 10; foreigners must sign a registration book, allow 2 hrs, boat charter Rs 1000 (no tourist boat)*, by the cafeteria has interesting old photos. The island is still under the jurisdiction of the Indian Navy and swimming is not allowed despite the clear enticing waters by the jetty.

South Andaman & Marine National Park

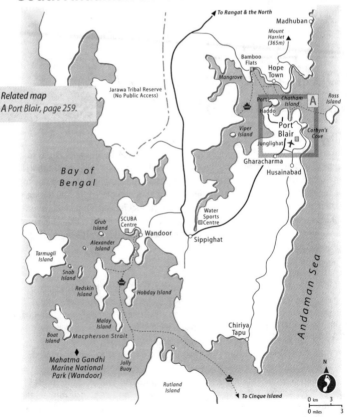

Mahatma Gandhi Marine National Park

About 30 km southwest of Port Blair, the Mahatma Gandhi Marine National Park protects some exceptional coral beds and underwater life off some of these uninhabited islands. Covering an area of 280 sq km, the park is a group of 15 islands with blue waters separating them. It includes Grub, Redskin, Jolly Buoy, Pluto, Boat Island, with Tarmugli to the west, Kalapahar or Rutland to the east and the Twins to the south. It is very rich, not only in marine life, but also in the variety of tropical flowers and birds. The dense forests come down to the beach where the mangrove thrives on the water's edge. There are angelfish, green parrot, yellow butterfly, black surgeon, blue damsel fish, silver jacks, squirrel, clown fish and sweetlips as well as sea cucumbers, sea anemones, starfish and a variety of shells – cowries, turbots, conches and the rarer giant clam, up to a metre wide (coral and shell collecting is strictly forbidden). There are turtles, sharks and barracudas on the outer reefs and many beautiful corals including brain, finger, mushroom and antler, the colours derived from the algae that thrive in the living coral.

● Sleeping

Chiriya Tapu *p265*
There are excellent camping spots here, with fresh water, in the village set back from the Munda Pahar Beach. The trail continues through the forest to some smaller beaches.

Mount Harriet *p265*
Forest Guest House (with permission). You can get water and tea from the caretaker. There is an octagonal viewing platform at the top with good views of Ross Island, and a small garden for picnics.

● Eating

Ross Island *p266*
A small café sells drinks and snacks. Take a picnic if you plan to spend the day. If the café is shut, try cracking open a fallen coconut.

● Transport

Chiriya Tapu *p265*
Buses leave from Port Blair stand at 0500, 0730, 1030, 1200 (1 hr) but often late; returns 10 mins after arrivals; last at 1900. It is an easy journey by hired scooter but beware of oncoming traffic; the single-track road has many blind bends. Taxi Rs 120 one way.

Mount Harriet *p265*
Tours are operated by the Directorate of Shipping from Phoenix Bay Jetty, T03192-232725. Vehicles must take a ferry from Phoenix Bay to Bamboo Flats. Chatham to Hope Town or Bamboo Flats carry foot passengers only; from Bamboo Flats it is a

20-min walk along the coast to Hope Town. A bus (0600, 0800) runs along this road. For return from Hope Town jetty: 1315, 1415 to Bamboo Flats and 1500 to Phoenix Bay; Bamboo Flats to Chatham Jetty: 1520, 1615, 1735, 1830. Taxis charge Rs 350 return to the top from Bamboo Flats jetty. By road alone it is 45 km instead of 15 km.

Ross Island *p266*
Boats (daily except Wed) from Phoenix Jetty, 0830, 1030, 1230, 1400, 1500. Go early as later boats get crowded, especially at weekends. Return boat at 0840, 1040, 1240, 1410, 1640.

▲ Activities and tours

Mahatma Gandhi National Park *p267*
Tours depend on demand, minimum 10 people; ask your hotel to enquire. The cost, around Rs 1000, covers transport to/from any hotel in Port Blair, park entry fee, packed lunch, soft drinks and bottled water. You will be picked up around 0530 and taken to Wandoor Village by boat (3½-4 hrs, depending on tide) allowing a maximum of 4 hrs on the island since boats must return before dark.

● Transport

Mahatma Gandhi National Park *p267*
From Port Blair there are frequent public buses to Wandoor, where from the wooden jetty by the Park Reception Centre, tour boats leave daily at 1000 and return about 1430. Bus, Rs 8 (tour operators charge Rs 100 return); 0830 bus connects with the 1000 tour.

Ritchie's Archipelago

The archipelago lies between 20 and 40 km off the east coast of south Andaman and Baratang Islands. Most are inhabited, but only three are open to foreign visitors: Havelock, Neil and Long Island. They are the focus of the government's tourist effort and can be reached by the regular ferry service between Port Blair (Phoenix Jetty) and Rangat Bay (Nimbutala Jetty). ▶▶ *For Sleeping, Eating and other listings, see pages 269-270.*

Havelock Island

This beautiful island with pristine white beaches is the government's principal centre for tourist development outside Port Blair. It is the island chosen by most visitors as an escape from Port Blair. Despite its popularity, you can – as anywhere in the Andamans – escape from other visitors and find your private bit of beach for the day. You can cycle

South Andaman & Ritchie's Archipelago

along the road to Radhnagar beach (No 7), 11 km to the southwest of the Jetty (No 1), and one of the best in the Andamans. Beach No 3 is 3 km from the jetty; No 5 is further south. A week-long **Mela** marking the birth of Subhas Chandra Bose is held in January with special Bengali cultural programmes. On arrival passports and permits are checked at the jetty where touts pester new arrivals. There is a confusing system of referring to beaches and settlements on the island by numbers. Sand flies can be a nuisance.

Neil Island

Neil is the smallest island in the Andamans you can stay on. Lushly forested with good snorkelling, it is very relaxed and attracts fewer visitors than Havelock. The best beach is close to the jetty and you will find shops sell provisions and basic camping gear but not tents or hammocks. Camping is allowed. Beach No 1 is unspoilt and peaceful though visitors often leave litter behind. Ask to get water from a farm well.

Long Island

A beautiful island, its main beach – Lalaji beach – is pristine. It is a two-hour walk through woods or by boat (Rs 200). There is camping by a small coconut plantation. The beach is lined with coconut trees and cattle steal any food left lying about! The drinking water quality from the well near the beach is suspect though, so come prepared. The baker is helpful and sells good coconut croissants. There is also a plywood factory on the island.

◉ Sleeping

Havelock Island *p268*
Beach camping is not allowed on the island.
AL-A Barefoot (formerly **Jungle Resort**), Beach No 7, T03192-237656, www.barefoot india.com. Remote and shaded, 9 small, bamboo, Nicobari cottages on stilts with nets, 8 a/c Andaman villas, excellent, 1 duplex and 4-bed cottage. Restaurant, promotes 'eco-friendly tourism', well-equipped dive centre.
B Wild Orchid, Beach No 3, T03192-282472, islandtravel@yahoo.com. Thai-style cottages a/c, bath, veranda, gardens, good restaurant.
B-D Dolphin Yatri Niwas, Beach No 5, bus stops 100 m from entrance, then walk down sandy track to campsite, T01392-282411. Popular with Indian tourists, book ahead, 18 huts on stilts, thin walls, pleasant gardens, restaurant, no decent beach nearby.
E Café del Mar, Beach No 3. 6 simple but comfortable bungalows, good restaurant, spacious, diving run by 2 experienced Swiss.
E MS, Jetty (No 1), T01392-282439. Rooms with bath and open-sided thatched huts with floor mattress, net, good food.
E Maya Sea View, Jetty (No 1), T03192-282367. Some of the 8 rooms have a bath and sea view, shabby but good meeting place.
E Pristine Beach, Beach No 3, next to Café del Mar, T03192-82344. 6 simple huts, bar.
F Tented Camp, Beach No 5. A bit run-down, tents, lunch and dinner thalis (order ahead),

popular and cheap, very peaceful. Reservation Secretariat, Director of Tourism, Port Blair, T03192-32694. Naval base near the beach.

Neil Island *p269*
D-E Hawabill Nest, T03192-82630. Simple, clean rooms (Rs 400-800 if a/c works) with hot shower, dorm (Rs 75), cook (buy provisions in the market and ask him to prepare meal), snorkel hire. Reservations, Secretariat, Director of Tourism, Port Blair, T03192-82694.

Long Island *p269*
G Forest Dept Guest House, on path uphill to the left from jetty, simple but only Rs 20. Must book ahead in Port Blair or Rangat.

⊘ Eating

Havelock Island *p268*
Near Jetty No 1 there are several basic places serving reasonable fish, vegetable and rice dishes: **Das** is the friendliest and best; **MS**, wonderful garlic fish (pick your own).
Women's Co-op Café does good *thalis*.
At Beach No 7, aside from the resorts:
Harmony, near the beach. Excellent lunch/ dinner, Rs 60, but order early, great atmosphere, packed in the evening, may have to wait 2 hrs in season, but chess, backgammon and *carom* to pass the time.

Chand, in the village, has chickpea *dhal*, egg rolls and *vadais*.
Shanti, next door, is also good.

O Shopping

Havelock Island *p268*
Village No 3 has a good market.
General Stores, varied camping equipment.

▲▲ Activities and tours

Havelock Island *p268*
Andaman Scuba Club, Beach No 3 at Café del Mar. Better areas and prices than from Port Blair, Swiss run, professional and friendly, digital equipment, PADI course, 2-dive trip.
Barefoot Scuba, Beach No 7 at Barefoot. Good equipment and trips.

⊖ Transport

Havelock Island *p268*
Two taxis and a jeep drive from the jetty to Beach No 3, 5 and 7, Rs 10-30.

Bikes For hire at Jetty (ask at hotel) or at the *paan* shop under **Susmita Electronics**, or outside **Dolphin Yatris Niwas**. Bikes, Rs 35.
Bus Regular service from Jetty (No 1) all the way to Radhnagar Beach (No 7), via Village No 3 and **Dolphin Resort** (No 5); 2 hourly, 0700-1100, 1500-1900; from No 7, 0600-1000, 1400-1800. Lots of school children at 0800 and 1500.
Ferry Inter-island, from Phoenix Jetty to Havelock, daily, 0600, 4-6 hrs; new faster service on Rangat 0600, 1200 (not daily, usually weekends), 2 hrs (buy ticket at Phoenix Jetty the day before 0900-1100).

Neil Island *p269*
Neil Island to Port Blair takes 4 hrs, Rs 9; Neil Island to Havelock, 2½ hrs, Rs 6.

Long Island *p269*
There are usually 3 boats a week from Port Blair, Phoenix Bay Jetty, via Havelock.

❶ Directory

Havelock Island *p268*
Bank for exchange. **Internet** at No 7.
Medical centre at No 3.

Middle and North Andamans

The Andaman Trunk Road is the only road to the north from Port Blair. Since it passes through the restricted Jarawa tribal reserve, it is not possible to drive along this yourself. There are daily buses to Rangat and Mayabunder. Occasionally the more adventurous Jarawas hitch a lift on the bus to the edge of the reserve. The route runs through some spectacular forest but sadly, despite controls, there has already been a lot of selective clearance of hardwoods. Accommodation options are limited.
▸▸ *For Sleeping, Eating and other listings, see pages 272-274.*

Middle Andaman ⬛🟡⊖❶ ▸▸ *pp272-274.*

Rangat
It is the only place with private accommodation for at least 20 visitors. **Amkunj Beach**, 8 km away, has little shade but there is good snorkelling off the rocks at the top end of the beach. From Rangat, take any bus heading for Nimbutala or Mayabunder up to the fork for Rangat Bay, then walk 1 km along track to right just after the helipad.

There is a good sandy beach across the road from **Hawksbill Nest**. Ideal for swimming but it is a wildlife sanctuary where turtles nest between November to April. In order to step onto the beach permission is needed from the Forest Department at Rangat, Mayabunder or the Beat Officer at Betapur, 4 km north of Hawksbill Nest; entrance fee is Rs 10 per day. Those caught on the beach without permission are promised "an unpleasant experience".

Mayabunder

Mayabunder is the administrative centre for Middle and North Andaman. All amenities are situated along a single road which runs along the brow of a ridge sticking out into the bay; the port is at the north end.

You can visit **Karmateng Beach**, 25 minutes away by bus. A shallow sandy slope over 1 km long, with a few rocks at the north end, it is not so good for snorkelling or swimming, as it is exposed and the sea is choppy. A short distance from Karmateng is another idyllic beach popular with foreign tourists at **Gujinala**. You need permission from DFO in Mayabunder or from Beat Officer at Karmateng.

There are several islands in the bay opposite the jetty which can be reached by *dunghy*; ask fishermen and expect to pay Rs 120 for a boat charter for several hours. All offer safe beaches for swimming but there is no good coral.

Avis Island and around

This tiny island is just east of Mayabunder but its ownership is disputed between the Forestry Department and The Coconut Society of Mayabunder. To visit, get permission from DCF, Mayabunder, and charter a *dunghy*. Foreign tourists are also permitted to visit (with permission from DCF, Mayabunder) **Curlew Island**, **Rayhill Island**, **Sound Island**, **Interview Island** and **Mohanpur** on the eastern coast of North Andaman. Tourists are encouraged to destroy illegal deer traps they find.

Interview Island

The island which has wild elephants now has a protected forest. Day visits can in theory be organized from Mayabunder, 20 km away. You may be able to stay overnight at the **Forest Department Guest House** with three rooms; contact DCF, Mayabunder. It can only be visited in a private boat.

Barren Islands

Across to the east from Middle Andaman, Barren has India's only active volcano which erupted in 1991 causing widespread destruction. Smoky fire belches from the side of the crater. It is only possible to visit on a day trip with no landings permitted. Sailings are infrequent and it is essential to get a permit from the tourist office in Port Blair.

North Andaman 🚌🚶🚐 → pp272-274.

Kalighat

It is a small settlement at the point where the creek becomes too shallow for the ferry to go any further. Of no particular interest, it still makes a very pleasant and peaceful stopover between Port Blair and the north. You can cross the river by the mangrove footbridge and follow the path up into the forest which is good for birdwatching. Sadly you also get a good impression of how many hardwoods are being logged.

You can (with some effort; little English spoken) take a bus to the beach at Ramnagar (11 km). Better still, hire a cycle for Rs 5 per hour and enjoy a very pleasant push, ride, free-wheel, with a refreshing swim at the end as a reward.

Diglipur

Previously known as Port Cornwallis, Diglipur is the most northerly commercial centre that foreigners can visit. There is a good market and shops; a special **Mela** is held during January/February that attracts many traders.

Aerial Bay

The small fishing village is the last peaceful location before returning to Port Blair. Most of the fish is taken to the market in Diglipur.

From Aerial Bay, you can visit the islands just north where it is possible to camp on pleasant forested beaches (though there are plans to build bungalows here, in which case free camping may be banned). You need permission from the Range Officer, opposite Jetty entrance. The ferry leaves at 0600 and 1400 (Rs 5), or hire a dunghy.

Saddle Peak National Park

Theoretically 'Lamia Bay Permits' for Saddle Peak and Lamia Bay are available from the Beat Officer in Lamia Bay. However, the path from Lamia Bay to Saddle Peak is very overgrown. **Kalipur** is a small group of farm houses on both sides of the road with a shop and a **Yatri Niwas** a few kilometres south of Aerial Bay. There is a very interesting beach at Kalipur with Saddle Peak as an impressive backdrop, accessible via a small path almost opposite the **Turtle Resort**.

Lamia Bay has a pebble beach south of Kalipur which you can walk to. From the bus stop the road leads straight ahead onto a path which is easy to follow (30 minutes). It is possible to camp under a small, round palm-leaf shelter. To the north, there are small bays strewn with large eroded boulders, whilst the beaches to the south lead towards Saddle Peak (730 m), 4½ km away.

Despite the relatively short distance to **Saddle Peak**, the rocky beach, the steep climb, the thick forest and the heat, mean that you need a whole day for the trek, starting early in the morning after camping in Lamia Bay. Don't attempt the whole trip in a day from Aerial Bay.

Narcondam Island

East of North Andaman, this is the most remote island in the group. An extinct craterless volcano, it is covered in luxuriant forest that is the home of the unique Narcondam hornbill was declared a sanctuary in 1977. It is a birdwatchers' paradise though permission to visit is hard to get and only 24-hour stops are allowed. Occasional sailings from Aerial Bay.

● Sleeping

Rangat *p270*
E **Hawksbill Nest**, Cuthbert Bay, 18 km from Rangat (take bus to Mayabunder, ask for Yatri Niwas). 8 clean sea-facing rooms (Rs 250), 2 a/c (Rs 400) 4-bed dorms (Rs 75). Book at Secretariat, Director of Tourism, Port Blair, T03192-282630.
F **Chandra Mohan Lodge**, blue wooden building on edge of town, run down, friendly.

Mayabunder *p271*
E **Swiftlet Nest**, 10 km from Mayabunder, away from the beach, contact Directorate of Tourism, T03192-273495, overlooking paddy fields (forest not cleared at beach). 10 good rooms (Rs 250), 4 a/c (Rs 400), dorm (Rs 75), good food, helpful staff.

North Andaman

Cape Price
Cape Henning
Elizabeth Bay
Reef Island
Cape Kyd
Gibb Creek
Paget Island
Point Island
Cold Stream Bay
Smith Island
Ross Island
Aerial Bay
Hudson Bay
Milangram
Casuarina Bay
Kalipur
Diglipur
Saddle Peak National Park
Lamia Bay
Kalara
Saddle Peak (737m)
Kalighat
Taralait Bay
Cliff Bay
under construction
Stewart Island
Sound Island
Bacon Bay
Austin Strait
Mayabunder
Avis Island
Seaward Bay
Karmatang Beach
0 km   5
0 miles   5
N
▼ To Rangat

F Dhanalakshmi and **Lakshmi Narayan** have small, dirty rooms.
As a last resort, **Jetty Waiting Rooms** provide some shelter and canteen food.

Kalighat *p271*

There are a few hotels near the jetty.
F PWD Rest House, on a hill, 2 mins' walk from jetty (book ahed in Port Blair). 3 rooms (1 for VIPs only), friendly housekeeper, excellent vegetable thalis, generous portions.

Diglipur *p271*

G Drua, 15 rooms (Rs 200), unhelpful manager.
G Laxmi, 4 clean rooms with common bath (Rs 120), friendly, helpful. Recommended.
G Sports Stadium, with clean, spacious, guarded area for travellers with immaculate toilets and showers. Recommended.

Aerial Bay *p271*

F PWD Rest House high up on a hill (book ahead in Port Blair). 2 rooms, often full.
Also an unmarked wooden hotel on the left, coming into town from Diglipur.

Saddle Peak National Park *p272*

E-F Turtle Resort Yatri Niwas, 8 rooms, Rs 250 (4 a/c, Rs 400), dorm (Rs 75), poor food, dirty public areas, unhelpful staff. Tranquil, on a hill overlooking paddy fields with thick forests leading up to the Saddle Peak National Park. The rooms are named after birds like Ostrich and Penguin. Contact T03192 2747.

☻ Eating

Rangat *p270*

Annapurna, on corner of vegetable market (from bus stand, turn left opposite **Krishna Lodge**, then right and left again). Good food.
Darbar Bakery, near bus stand (at start of road to PWD Rest House). Good selection.

Kalighat *p271*

Viji has okay food, with a **bakery**, next door.

Diglipur *p271*

Plenty of snack bars, tea houses and fresh fruit in the market.

Aerial Bay *p271*

Excellent fish is sold near harbour gates; larger fish (tuna and barracuda) in the afternoon

(Rs20-30 per kg). Shops sell basic provisions and there is a small market by the bus stand.
Mohan, owner speaks some English and is helpful, will prepare excellent fish dishes for you, good thalis, selection of drinks.

☻ Transport

Rangat *p270*

Bus To **Mayabunder** 0600, connects with ferry to Kalighat at 0930, later bus at 1145; to **Port Blair** *Exp* (B), daily, 0800, 0900 (Rs 33). From **Port Blair** by bus to Rangat there are 2 ferry crossings (Nilambur and Gandhi Ghat). Takes up to 8 hrs to Rangat town, depending on bus connections, ie whether your bus goes on this ferry and/or if bus is waiting on other side at Nilambur.
Ferry The jetty is at Rangat Bay (Nimbutala), 7 km from town. To **Port Blair** 0600, 7 hrs, buy tickets (Rs 30) on board. There is an 'Inner' (Creek) and an 'Outer' route, the latter via Strait, Havelock (30-min stop) and Neil Islands (see Transport under Port Blair). Lumber boats from Mangrove Jetty go to **Long Island**; **Mayabunder**, 3 per week, 3 hrs.

Mayabunder *p271*

Bus Port Blair *Exp* (A) and (C), depart 0600, tickets sold from 1500 the day before, at bus station (2 km from jetty). **Rangat** local bus, 0830-1700. Also some private buses.
Karmateng many for beach, 0715-1700 (return bus approx 35 mins after these times).
Diglipur the road is still under construction.
Ferry For **Diglipur** take local ferry to Kalighat, or wait for the inter-island ferry from Port Blair which calls here en route to Aerial Bay every 11-12 days. **Kalighat** small sea ferry daily, 0930, 1445, 2½ hrs (Rs 3), is very crowded, with little shade. Private *dunghies* leave at dawn; they can carry 20 people (Rs 25 each) and the occasional scooter; a charter costs Rs 400. **Port Blair** Check outside Asst Commissioner's office near police station for schedules.

Kalighat *p271*

Bus To **Diglipur** Regular local service (45 mins), 0630, 0800, 1030, 1130, 1400, connect with ferry from Mayabunder.
Ferry To **Mayabunder** daily, 0500, 1230, 2 hrs (Rs 3), can get very crowded and virtually no shade; also *Dunghy*, 0600, 2 hrs

(Rs 15); or charter a *dunghy* at any time for about Rs 300 (the rate for a full boat).

Diglipur *p271*
Buses to all the surrounding villages and beaches. Regular service to Kalighat, 45 mins (last at 1900) and Aerial Bay (30 mins) which has the occasional boat to Port Blair.

Aerial Bay *p271*
Bus It is not possible to reach Port Blair by bus in 1 day, the furthest you can hope to get is Rangat. Private and public buses to **Diglipur** and **Kalipur**, approximately every hour.
Ferry To **Mayabunder** and **Port Blair** (2 sailings a month). The jetty ticket office is not always sure when the next boat is due; better to contact the coastguard tower who have radio contact with Port Blair (no telephone connection with South Andaman).

Fare: bunk Rs 47, deck Rs 27 (cabins for Govt officials only); Indian canteen meals. Tickets go on sale the day before departure at the Tehsildar's office, next to Diglipur *Rest House*; to avoid a long wait there, buy on the boat, though you may sometimes have to pay more, and only get a deck ticket.

Saddle Peak National Park *p272*
Bus Buses Diglipur–Kalipur, via Aerial Bay. From Kalipur: departs 1230, 1330, 1530, 1740, 2015; to Aerial Bay, 25 mins, Rs 2.

◑ Directory

Rangat *p270*
Banks State Bank of India, by the bus stand.
Post Opposite the Police Station.

Little Andaman Island

This large island lies 120 km south of Port Blair across the Duncan Passage. It takes about eight hours to get here. The main village, **Hut Bay** to the southeast, is 2 km away from the jetty. Heavily deforested during the 1960s and 1970s, much of the island has become virtually treeless. Betel, red palm and banana plantations dominate the scenery. There were two resorts, both were razed during the tsunami. Prior to the arrival of the resorts, it was possible to camp on the large beach in the north of the island, around 22 km from the jetty. If you do make the trip take food and water. Be aware that the area is notorious for malaria.

Nicobar Islands

The names given by travellers and sailors from the east and the west all referred to these islands as the Land of the Naked – Nicobar is derived from the Tamil word *nakkavaram*. The islands which lay on the trade route to the Far East were visited in the 11th century by the seafaring Cholas during the rule of King Rajendra I who attempted to extend his rule here. Before the British used the Nicobars as a penal territory in the late 19th century, European missionaries (particularly the Danish) made converts during the 17th and 18th centuries but few survived the difficulties of the climate and most died of fever within a year.

The islands, including **Katchal** with a large rubber plantation, **Nancowry** harbour, **Indira Point**, India's southernmost tip and **Campbell Bay** (Great Nicobar), are closed to foreign visitors; Car Nicobar to the north can be visited by Indians with a permit. The significant tribal population live in distinctive huts, which look like large thatched domes that are raised on stilts about 2 m high and are entered through the floor. The Nicobarese enjoy wrestling, fishing, swimming and canoeing but are best known for their love of music. Villages still participate in competitions of traditional unaccompanied singing and dancing which mark every festivity.

History

The first village communities in South Asia grew up on the arid western fringes of the Indus Plains 10,000 years ago. Over the following generations successive waves of settlers – sometimes bringing goods for trade, sometimes armies to conquer territory and sometimes nothing more than domesticated animals and families in search of land and peace – moved across the Indus and into India. They left an indelible mark on the landscape and culture of all the countries of modern South Asia.

The first settlers

A site at Mehrgarh, where the Indus Plains meet the dry Baluchistan Hills in modern Pakistan, has revealed evidence of agricultural settlement as early as 8500 BC. By 3500 BC agriculture had spread throughout the Indus Plains and in the thousand years following there were independent settled villages well to the east of the Indus. Between 3000 BC and 2500 BC many new settlements sprang up in the heartland of what became the Indus Valley civilization.

Most cultural, religious and political developments during that period owed more to local development than to external influence, although India had extensive contacts with other regions, notably with Mesopotamia. At its height the Indus Valley civilization covered as great an area as Egypt or Mesopotamia. However, the culture that developed was distinctively South Asian. Speculation continues to surround the nature of the language, which is still untranslated.

India from 2000 BC to the Mauryas

In about 2000 BC Moenjo Daro, widely presumed to be the capital of the Indus Valley Civilization, became deserted and within the next 250 years the entire Indus Valley civilization disintegrated. The causes remain uncertain: the violent arrival of new waves of Aryan immigrants (a theory no one now accepts), increasing desertification of the already semi-arid landscape, a shift in the course of the Indus and internal political decay have each been suggested as instrumental in its downfall. Whatever the causes, some features of Indus Valley culture were carried on by succeeding generations.

Probably from about 1500 BC northern India entered the Vedic period. Aryan settlers moved southeast towards the Ganga valley. Classes of rulers *(rajas)* and priests *(brahmins)* began to emerge. Grouped into tribes, conflict was common. In one battle of this period a confederacy of tribes known as the Bharatas defeated another grouping of 10 tribes. They gave their name to the region to the east of the Indus which is the official name for India today – Bharat.

The centre of population and of culture shifted east from the banks of the Indus to the land between the rivers Yamuna and Ganga, the doab (pronounced *doe-ahb*, literally 'two waters'). This region became the heart of emerging Aryan culture, which, from 1500 BC onwards, laid the literary and religious foundations of what ultimately became Hinduism, spreading to embrace the whole of India.

The Vedas The first fruit of this development was the Rig Veda, the first of four Vedas, composed, collected and passed on orally by Brahmin priests. While some scholars date the oral originsas early as the beginning of the second millennium BC, the date of 1300 BC to about 1000 BC still seems more probable. In the later Vedic period, from about 1000 BC to 600 BC, the Sama, Yajur and Artha Vedas show that the Indo-Aryans developed a clear sense of the Ganga-Yamuna *doab* as 'their' territory.

From the sixth to the third centuries BC the region from the foothills of the Himalaya across the Ganga plains to the edge of the Peninsula was governed under a variety of kingdoms or Mahajanapadhas – 'great states'. Trade gave rise to the birth of towns in

the Ganga plains themselves, many of which have remained occupied to the present.
Varanasi (Benaras) is perhaps the most famous example, but a trade route was established that ran from Taxila (20 km from modern Islamabad in Pakistan) to Rajgir 1500 km away in what is now Bihar. It was into these kingdoms of the Himalayan foothills and north plains that Mahavir, founder of Jainism, and the Buddha, were born.

The Mauryas

Within a year of the retreat of Alexander the Great from the Indus in 326 BC, **Chandragupta Maurya** established the first indigenous empire to exercise control over much of the subcontinent. Under his successors, that control was extended to all but the extreme south of peninsular India.

The centre of political power had shifted east into wetter, more densely forested but also more fertile regions. The Mauryans had their base in the region known as Magadh (now Bihar) and their capital at Pataliputra, near modern Patna. Their power was based on massive military force and a highly efficient, centralized administration.

The greatest of the Mauryan emperors, **Asoka** took power in 272 BC. He inherited a full-blown empire, but extended it further by defeating the Kalingans in modern Orissa, before turning his back on war and preaching the virtues of pacifism, see page 184. Asoka's empire stretched from Afghanistan to Assam and from the Himalaya to Mysore.

The state maintained itself by raising revenue from taxation – on everything, from agriculture, to gambling and prostitution. He decreed that 'no waste land should be occupied and not a tree cut down' without permission because all were potential sources of revenue for the state. The *sudras* (lowest of Hindu castes) were used as free labour for clearing forest and cultivating new land.

Asoka (described on the edicts as 'the Beloved of the Gods, of Gracious Countenance') left a series of inscriptions on pillars and rocks across the subcontinent. Over most of India these inscriptions were written in *Prakrit*, using the *Brahmi* script, although in the northwest they were in Greek using the *Kharoshti* script. They were unintelligible for over 2000 years after the decline of the empire until James Prinsep deciphered the Brahmi script in 1837. Through the edicts Asoka urged all people to follow the code of **dhamma** or dharma – translated by the Indian historian Romila Thapar as 'morality, piety, virtue and social order'. He established a special force of *dhamma* officers to try to enforce the code, which encouraged toleration, non-violence, respect for priests and those in authority and for human dignity.

However, Romila Thapar suggests that the failure to develop any sense of national consciousness, coupled with the massive demands of a highly paid bureaucracy and army, proved beyond the abilities of Asoka's successors to sustain. Within 50 years of Asoka's death in 232 BC the Mauryan Empire had disintegrated and with it the whole structure and spirit of its government.

A period of fragmentation: 185 BC to AD 300

Beyond the Mauryan Empire other kingdoms had survived in South India. The Satavahanas dominated the central Deccan for over 300 years from about 50 BC. Further south in what is now Tamil Nadu, the early kingdoms of the Cholas and the Pandiyas gave a glimpse of both power and cultural development that was to flower over 1000 years later. In the centuries following the break up of the Mauryan Empire these kingdoms were in the forefront of developing overseas trade, especially with Greece and Rome. Internal trade also flourished and Indian carried goods to China and Southeast Asia.

The classical period – the Gupta Empire: AD 319-467

Although the political power of Chandra Gupta and his successors never approached that of his unrelated namesake nearly 650 years before him, the Gupta Empire which was established with his coronation in AD 319 produced developments in every field of Indian culture. Their influence has been felt profoundly across South Asia to the present.

Geographically the Guptas originated in the same Magadhan region that had given rise to the Mauryan Empire. Extending their power by strategic marriage alliances, Chandra Gupta's empire of Magadh was extended by his son, Samudra Gupta, who took power in AD 335, across North India. He also marched as far south as Kanchipuram in modern Tamil Nadu, but the heartland of the Gupta Empire remained the plains of the Ganga.

Chandra Gupta II reigned for 39 years from AD 376 and was a great patron of the arts. Political power was much less centralized than under the Mauryans and as Thapar points out, collection of land revenue was deputed to officers who were entitled to keep a share of the revenue, rather than to highly paid bureaucrats. Trade with Southeast Asia, Arabia and China all added to royal wealth.

That wealth was distributed to the arts on an unprecedented scale. Some went to religious foundations, such as the Buddhist monastery at Ajanta, which produced some of its finest murals during the Gupta period. But Hindu institutions also benefited and some of the most important features of modern Hinduism date from this time. The sacrifices of Vedic worship were given up in favour of personal devotional worship, known as bhakti. Tantrism, both in its Buddhist and Hindu forms, with its emphasis on the female life force and worship of the Mother Goddess, developed. The focus of worship was towards a personalized and monotheistic deity, represented in the form of either Siva or Vishnu. The myths of Vishnu's incarnations arose in this period.

The Brahmins, the priestly caste who were in the key position to mediate change, refocused earlier literature to give shape to the emerging religious philosophy. In their hands the *Mahabharata* and the *Ramayana* were transformed from secular epics to religious stories. The excellence of contemporary sculpture both reflected and contributed to an increase in image worship and the growing role of temples as centres of devotion.

The spread of Islamic power – the Delhi Sultanate

From about AD 1000 the external attacks which inflicted most damage on Rajput wealth and power came increasingly from the Arabs and Turks. Mahmud of Ghazni raided the Punjab virtually every year between 1000 and 1026, attracted both by the agricultural surpluses and the enormous wealth in cash, golden images and jewellery of North India's temples which drew him back every year. He sacked the wealthy centres of Mathura (UP) in 1017, Thanesar (Haryana) in 1011, Somnath (Gujarat) in 1024 and Kannauj (UP). He died in 1030, to the Hindus just another *mlechchha* ('impure' or sullied one), as had been the Huns and the Sakas before him, soon to be forgotten. Such raids were never taken seriously as a long-term threat by kings further east and as the Rajputs often feuded among themselves the northwest plains became an attractive prey.

Muslim political power was heralded by the raids of Mu'izzu'd Din and his defeat of massive Rajput forces at the Second Battle of Tarain in 1192. Mu'izzu'd Din left his deputy, Qutb u'd Din Aibak, to hold the territorial gains from his base at Indraprastha. Mu'izzu'd Din made further successful raids in the 1190s, inflicting crushing defeats on Hindu opponents from Gwalior to Benaras. The foundations were then laid for the first extended period of such power, which came under the Delhi sultans.

Qutb u'd Din Aibak took Lahore in 1206, although it was his lieutenant **Iltutmish** who really established control from Delhi in 1211. Qutb u'd Din Aibak consolidated Muslim dominion by an even-handed policy of conciliation and patronage. In Delhi he converted the old Hindu stronghold of Qila Rai Pithora into his Muslim capital and began several magnificent building projects, including the Quwwat-ul-Islam mosque and the Qutb Minar, a victory tower. Iltutmish was a Turkish slave – a *Mamluk* – and the Sultanate continued to look west for its leadership and inspiration. However, the possibility of continuing control from outside India was destroyed by the crushing raids of **Genghis Khan** through Central Asia and from 1222 Iltutmish ruled from Delhi completely independently of outside authority. He annexed Sind in 1228 and all the territory east to Bengal by 1230.

A succession of dynasties followed, drawing on refugees from Genghis Khan's raids and from still further to the west to strengthen the leadership. In 1290 the first dynasty was succeeded by the Khaljis, which in turn gave way to the Tughluqs in 1320. **Mohammad bin Tughluq** (ruled 1324-1351) was described by the Moorish traveller Ibn Batuta as 'a man who above all others is fond of making presents and shedding blood'. Despite its periodic brutality, this period marked a turning point in Muslim government in India, as Turkish Mamluks gave way to government by Indian Muslims and their Hindu allies. The Delhi sultans were open to local influences and employed Hindus in their administration. In the mid-14th century their capital, Delhi, was one of the leading cities of the contemporary world but in 1398 their control came to an abrupt end with the arrival of the Mongol Timur.

Timur's limp caused him to be called Timur-i-leng (Timur the Lame, known to the west as Tamburlaine). This self-styled 'Scourge of God' was illiterate, a devout Muslim, an outstanding chess player and a patron of the arts. Five years before his arrival in India he had taken Baghdad and three years before that he had ravaged Russia, devastating land and pillaging villages. India had not been in such danger from Mongols since Genghis Khan had arrived on the same stretch of the Indus 200 years before.

After Timur, it took nearly 50 years for the Delhi Kingdom to become more than a local headquarters. The revival was slow and fitful. The last Tughluqs were succeeded by an undistinguished line of Sayyids, who began as Timur's deputies who were essentially Afghan soldier/administrators. They later called themselves sultans and Lodi kings (1451-1526) and moved their capital to Agra. Nominally they controlled an area from Punjab to Bihar but they were, in fact, in the hands of a group of factious nobles.

The Mughal Empire

In North India it is the impact of the Mughal rule that is most strikingly evident today. The descendants of conquerors, with the blood of both Tamburlaine (Timur) and Genghis Khan in their veins, they came to dominate Indian politics from Babur's victory near Delhi in 1526 to Aurangzeb's death in 1707. Their legacy was not only some of the most magnificent architecture in the world, but a profound impact on the culture, society and future politics of South Asia.

Babur (the tiger) Founder of the Mughal Dynasty, Babur was born in Russian Turkestan on 15 February 1483, the fifth direct descendant on the male side of Timur and 13th on the female side from Genghis Khan. He established the Mughal Empire by leading his cavalry and artillery forces to a stupendous victory over the combined armies of Ibrahim Lodi, last ruler of the Delhi Sultanate and the Hindu Raja of Gwalior, at **Panipat**, 80 km north of Delhi, in 1526. When he died four years later, the Empire was still far from secured, but he had not only laid the foundations of political and military power but had also begun to establish courtly traditions of poetry, literature and art which became the hallmark of subsequent Mughal rulers.

Babur, used to Persian gardens and cool Afghan hills, was unimpressed by what he saw of India. In his autobiography he wrote: "Hindustan is a country that has few pleasures to recommend it. The people are not handsome. They have no idea of the charms of friendly society, of frankly mixing together, or of familiar intercourse. They have no genius, no comprehension of mind, no politeness of manner, no kindness or fellow-feeling, no ingenuity or mechanical invention in planning or executing their handicraft works, no skill or knowledge in design or architecture; they have no horses, no good flesh, no grapes or musk melons, no good fruits, no ice or cold water, no good food or bread in their bazars, no baths or colleges, no candles, no torches, not a candlestick".

Babur's depressing catalogue was the view of a disenchanted outsider. Within two generations the Mughals had become fully at home in their Indian environment and brought some radical changes. Babur was charismatic. He ruled by keeping the loyalty of his military chiefs, giving them control of large areas of territory.

Humayun However, their strength posed a problem for Humayun, his successor. Almost immediately after Babur's death Humayun was forced to retreat from Delhi through Sind with his pregnant wife. His son Akbar, who was to become the greatest of the Mughal emperors, was born at Umarkot in Sindh, modern Pakistan, during this period of exile, on 23 November 1542.

Akbar Akbar was only 13 when he took the throne in 1556. The next 44 years were one of the most remarkable periods of South Asian history, paralleled by the Elizabethan period in England, where Queen Elizabeth I ruled from 1558 to 1603. Although Akbar inherited the throne, it was he who really created the empire. He also gave it many of its distinguishing features.

Through his marriage to a Hindu princess he ensured that Hindus were given honoured positions in government, as well as respect for their religious beliefs and practices. He sustained a passionate interest in art and literature, matched by a determination to create monuments to his empire's political power and he laid the foundations for an artistic and architectural tradition which developed a totally distinctive Indian style. This emerged from the separate elements of Iranian and Indian traditions by a constant process of blending and originality of which he was the chief patron.

But these achievements were only possible because of his political and military gifts. From 1556 until his 18th birthday in 1560, Akbar was served by a prince regent, Bairam Khan. However, already at the age of 15 he had conquered Ajmer and large areas of Central India. Chittor and Ranthambore fell to him in 1567-1568, bringing most of what is now Rajasthan under his control. This opened the door south to Gujarat.

Afghans continued to cause his empire difficulties, including Daud Karrani, who declared independence in East India in 1574. That threat to Mughal power was finally crushed with Karrani's death in 1576. Bengal was far from the last of his conquests. He brought Kabul back under Mughal control in the 1580s and established a presence from Kashmir, Sind and Baluchistan in the north and west, to the Godavari River on the border of modern Andhra Pradesh in the south.

Akbar deliberately widened his power base by incorporating Rajput princes into the administrative structure and giving them extensive rights in the revenue from land. He abolished the hated tax on non-Muslims *(jizya)* – ultimately reinstated by his strictly orthodox great grandson Aurangzeb – and ceased levying taxes on Hindus who went on pilgrimage. He also ended the practice of forcible conversion to Islam.

Artistic treasures abound from Akbar's court – paintings, jewellery, weapons – often bringing together material and skills from across the known world. Akbar's eclecticism had a political purpose, for he was trying to build a focus of loyalty beyond that of caste, social group, region or religion. Like Roman emperors before him, he deliberately cultivated a new religion in which the emperor himself attained divinity, hoping thereby to give the empire a legitimacy which would last. While his religion disappeared with his death, the legitimacy of the Mughals survived another 200 years, long after their real power had almost disappeared.

Jahangir Akbar died of a stomach illness in 1605. He was succeeded by his son, Prince Salim, who inherited the throne as Emperor Jahangir ('*world seizer*'). He added little to the territory of the empire, consolidating the Mughals' hold on the Himalayan foothills and parts of central India but restricting his innovative energies to pushing back frontiers of art rather than of land. He commissioned works of art and literature, many of which directly recorded life in the Mughal court. Hunting scenes were not just romanticized accounts of rural life, but conveyed the real dangers of hunting lions or tigers; implements, furniture, tools and weapons were made with lavish care and often exquisite design.

From early youth Jahangir had shown an artistic temperament, but he also became addicted to alcohol and then to opium. In his autobiography, he wrote: "I had not drunk until I was 18, except in the time of my infancy two or three times my mother and wet nurses gave it by way of infantile remedy, mixed with water and rose water to take away a cough ... years later a gunner said that if I would take a glass of wine it would drive away the feeling of being tired and heavy ... After that I took to drinking wine... until wine made from grapes ceased to intoxicate me and I took to drinking arrack (local spirits). By degrees my potions rose to 20 cups of doubly distilled spirits, 14 during the daytime and the remainder at night".

Nur Jahan Jahangir's favourite wife, Nur Jahan, brought her own artistic gifts. Born the daughter of an Iranian nobleman, she had been brought to the Mughal court along with her family as a child and moved to Bengal as the wife of Sher Afgan. She made rapid progress after her first husband's accidental death in 1607, which caused her to move from Bengal to be a lady in waiting for one of Akbar's widows.

At the Mughal court in 1611, she met Jahangir. Mutually enraptured, they were married in May. Jahangir gave her the title Nur Mahal (Light of the Palace), soon increased to Nur Jahan (Light of the World). Aged 34, she was strikingly beautiful and had an astonishing reputation for physical skill and intellectual wit. She was a crack shot with a gun, highly artistic, determined yet philanthropic. Throughout her life Jahangir was so captivated by her that he flouted Muslim convention by minting coins bearing her image.

By 1622 Nur Jahan effectively controlled the empire. She commissioned and supervised the building in Agra of one of the Mughal world's most beautiful buildings, the **I'timad ud-Daula** ('Pillar of government'), as a tomb for her father and mother. Her father, **Ghiyas Beg**, had risen to become one of Jahangir's most trusted advisers and Nur Jahan was determined to ensure that their memory was honoured. She was less successful in her wish to deny the succession after Jahangir's death at the age of 58 to Prince Khurram. Acceding to the throne in 1628, he took the title Shah Jahan (*Ruler of the World*) and in the next 30 years his reign represented the height of Mughal power.

Shah Jahan The Mughal Empire was under attack in the Deccan and the northwest when Shah Jahan became Emperor. He tried to re-establish and extend Mughal authority in both regions by a combination of military campaigns and skilled diplomacy. Akbar's craftsmen had already carved outstandingly beautiful *jalis* for the tomb of Salim Chishti in Fatehpur Sikri, but Shah Jahan developed the form further. Undoubtedly the finest tribute to these skills is found in the Taj Mahal, the tribute to his beloved wife Mumtaz Mahal, who died giving birth to her fourteenth child in 1631.

Aurangzeb The need to expand the area under Mughal control was felt even more strongly by Aurangzeb ('*The jewel in the throne*'), than by his predecessors. He had shown his intellectual gifts in his grandfather Jahangir's court when held hostage to guarantee Shah Jahan's good behaviour, learning Arabic, Persian, Turkish and Hindi. When he seized power at the age of 40, he needed all his political and military skills to hold on to an unwieldy empire that was in permanent danger of collapse from its own size.

Aurangzeb realized that the resources of the territory he inherited from Shah Jahan were not enough. One response was to push south, while maintaining his hold on the east and north. Initially he maintained his alliances with the Rajputs in the west, which had been a crucial element in Mughal strategy. In 1678 he claimed absolute rights over Jodhpur and went to war with the Rajput clans at the same time embarking on a policy of outright Islamisation. However, for the remaining 39 years of his reign he was forced to struggle continuously to sustain his power.

The East India Company and the rise of British power

The British were unique among the foreign rulers of India in coming by sea rather than through the northwest and in coming first for trade rather than for military conquest. The ports that they established – Madras, Bombay and Calcutta – became completely new centres of political, economic and social activity. Before them Indian empires had controlled their territories from the land. The British dictated the emerging shape of the economy by controlling sea-borne trade. From the middle of the 19th century railways transformed the economic and political structure of South Asia and it was those three centres of British political control, along with the late addition of Delhi, which became the foci of economic development and political change.

The East India Company in Madras and Bengal

In its first 90 years of contact with South Asia after the Company set up its first trading post at **Masulipatnam**, on the east coast of India, it had depended almost entirely on trade for its profits. However, in 1701, only 11 years after a British settlement was first established at Calcutta, the Company was given rights to land revenue in Bengal.

The Company was accepted and sometimes welcomed, partly because it offered to bolster the inadequate revenues of the Mughals by exchanging silver bullion for the cloth it bought. However, in the south the Company moved further towards consolidating its political base. Wars between South India's regional factions gave the Company the chance to extend their influence by making alliances and offering support to some of these factions in their struggles, which were complicated by the extension to Indian soil of the European contest for power between the French and the British.

Robert Clive The British established control over both Bengal and Southeast India in the middle of the 17th century. Robert Clive, in alliance with a collection of disaffected Hindu landowners and Muslim soldiers, defeated the new Nawab of Bengal, the 20-year-old Siraj-ud-Daula, in June 1757. At **Plassey** (Palashi), about 100 km north of Calcutta.

Hastings and Cornwallis The essential features of British control were mapped out in the next quarter of a century through the work of **Warren Hastings**, Governor-General from 1774 until 1785 and **Lord Cornwallis** who succeeded and remained in charge until 1793. Cornwallis was responsible for putting Europeans in charge of all the higher levels of revenue collection and administration and for introducing government by the rule of law, making even government officers subject to the courts.

The decline of Muslim power

The extension of East India Company power in the Mughal periphery of India's south and east took place against a background of the rising power of Sivaji and his Marathas.

Sivaji and the Marathas Sivaji was the son of a Hindu who had served as a small-scale chief in the Muslim-ruled state of Bijapur. The weakness of Bijapur encouraged Sivaji to extend his father's area of control and he led a rebellion. The Bijapur general Afzal Khan, sent to put it down, agreed to meet Sivaji in private to reach a settlement. In an act which is still remembered by both Muslims and Marathas, Sivaji embraced him with steel claws attached to his fingers and tore him apart. It was the start of a campaign which took Maratha power as far south as Madurai and to the doors of Delhi and Calcutta.

Although Sivaji himself died in 1680, Aurangzeb never fully came to terms with the rising power of the Marathas, though he did end their ambitions to form an empire of their own. While the Maratha confederacy was able to threaten Delhi within 50 years of Aurangzeb's death, by the early 19th century it had dissolved into five independent states, with whom the British ultimately dealt separately.

Nor was Aurangzeb able to create any wide sense of identity with the Mughals as a legitimate popular power. Instead, under the influence of Sunni Muslim theologians, he retreated into insistence on Islamic purity. He imposed Islamic law, the *sharia*, promoted only Muslims to positions of power and authority, tried to replace Hindu administrators and revenue collectors with Muslims and reimposed the *jizya* tax on all non-Muslims. By the time of his death in 1707 the empire no longer had either the broadness of spirit or the physical means to survive.

Bahadur Shah The decline was postponed briefly by the five year reign of Aurangzeb's son. Sixty-three when he acceded to the throne, Bahadur Shah restored some of its faded fortunes. He made agreements with the Marathas and the Rajputs and defeated the Sikhs in Punjab before taking the last Sikh guru into his service. Nine emperors succeeded Aurangzeb between his death and the exile of the last Mughal ruler in 1858. It was no accident that it was in that year that the British ended the rule of its East India Company and decreed India to be its Indian empire.

Mohammad Shah remained in his capital of Delhi, resigning himself to enjoying what Carey Welch has called "the conventional triad of joys: the wine was excellent, as were the women and for him the song was especially rewarding". The idyll was rudely shattered by the invasion of **Nadir Shah** in 1739, an Iranian marauder who slaughtered thousands in Delhi and stole priceless Mughal treasures, including the Peacock Throne.

The East India Company's push for power

Alliances In the century and a half that followed the death of Aurangzeb, the British East India Company extended its economic and political influence into the heart of India. As the Mughal Empire lost its power India fell into many smaller states. The Company undertook to protect the rulers of several of these states from external attack by stationing British troops in their territory. In exchange for this service the rulers paid subsidies to the Company. The British extended their territory through the 18th century as successive regional powers were annexed and brought under direct Company rule.

Progress to direct British control was uneven and often opposed. The Sikhs in Punjab, the Marathas in the west and the Mysore sultans in the south, fiercely contested British advances. **Haidar Ali** and **Tipu Sultan**, who had built a wealthy kingdom in the Mysore region, resisted attempts to incorporate them. Tipu was finally killed in 1799 at the battle of Srirangapatnam, an island fort in the Kaveri River just north of Mysore, where Arthur Wellesley, later the Duke of Wellington, began to make his military reputation.

The Marathas were not defeated until the 1816-18 war. Even then the defeat owed as much to internal fighting as to the power of the British-led army. Only the northwest of the subcontinent remained beyond British control until well into the 19th century. Thus in 1799 **Ranjit Singh** was able to set up a Sikh state in Punjab, surviving until the late 1830s despite the extension of British control over much of the rest of India.

In 1818 India's economy was in ruins and its political structures destroyed. Irrigation and road systems had fallen into decay and gangs terrorized the countryside. Thugs and dacoits controlled much of rural areas in Central India and often robbed and murdered even on town outskirts. The stability of the Mughal period had long since passed. From 1818 to 1857 there was a succession of local and uncoordinated revolts in different parts of India. Some were bought off, some put down by military force.

A period of reforms

While existing political systems were collapsing, the first half of the 1800s was also a time of radical social change in territories governed by the East India Company. **Lord William Bentinck** became governor-general at a time when England was undergoing major reform. In 1828 he banned the burning of widows on the funeral pyres of their husbands (**sati**) and then moved to suppress **thuggee** (the ritual murder and robbery carried out in the name of the goddess Kali). But his most far reaching change was to introduce education in English.

From the late 1830s massive new engineering projects began to be taken up; first canals, then railways. The innovations stimulated change and change contributed to the growing unease with the British presence. The development of the telegraph, railways and new roads, three universities and the extension of massive new canal irrigation projects in North India seemed to threaten traditional society, a risk increased by the annexation of Indian states to bring them under direct British rule. The most important of these was Oudh.

The Rebellion

Out of the growing discontent and widespread economic difficulties came the Rebellion or 'Mutiny' of 1857. On 10 May 1857 troops in Meerut, 70 km northeast of Delhi, mutinied.

They reached Delhi the next day, where **Bahadur Shah**, the last Mughal Emperor, took sides with the mutineers. Troops in Lucknow joined the rebellion and for three months Lucknow and other cities in the north were under siege. Appalling scenes of butchery and reprisals marked the struggle, only put down by troops from outside.

The Period of Empire

The 1857 rebellion marked the end not only of the Mughal Empire but also of the East India Company, for the British government in London took overall control in 1858. Yet within 30 years a movement for self government had begun and there were the first signs of a demand among the new Western-educated elite that political rights be awarded to match the sense of Indian national identity.

Indian National Congress Established in 1885, this was the first all-India political institution and was to become the key vehicle of demands for independence. However, the educated Muslim elite of what is now Uttar Pradesh saw a threat to Muslim rights, power and identity in the emergence of democratic institutions which gave Hindus, with their built-in natural majority, significant advantages. Sir Sayyid Ahmad Khan, who had founded a Muslim University at Aligarh in 1877, advised Muslims against joining the Congress, seeing it as a vehicle for Hindu and especially Bengali, nationalism.

The Muslim League The educated Muslim community of North India remained deeply suspicious of the Congress, making up less than 8% of those attending its conferences between 1900-20. Muslims from UP created the All-India Muslim League in 1906. However, the demands of the Muslim League were not always opposed to those of the Congress. In 1916 it concluded the Lucknow Pact with the Congress, in which the Congress won Muslim support for self-government, in exchange for the recognition that there would be separate constituencies for Muslims. The nature of the future independent India was still far from clear, however. The British conceded the principle of self-government in 1918, but however radical the reforms would have seemed five years earlier, they already fell far short of heightened Indian expectations.

Mahatma Gandhi Into a tense atmosphere Mohandas Karamchand Gandhi returned to India in 1915 after 20 years practising as a lawyer in South Africa. He arrived as the government of India was being given new powers by the British parliament to try political cases without a jury and to give provincial governments the right to imprison politicians without trial. In opposition to this legislation Gandhi proposed to call a *hartal*, when all activity would cease for a day, a form of protest still in widespread use. Such protests took place across India, often accompanied by riots.

On 13 April 1919 a huge gathering took place in the enclosed space of Jallianwala Bagh in Amritsar. It had been prohibited by the government and General Dyer ordered troops to fire on the people without warning, killing 379 and injuring at least a further 1,200. It marked the turning point in relations with Britain and the rise of Gandhi to the key position of leadership in the struggle for complete independence.

The thrust for Independence Through the 1920s Gandhi developed concepts and political programmes that were to become the hallmark of India's Independence struggle. Ultimately political Independence was to be achieved not by violent rebellion but by *satyagraha* – a "truth force" which implied a willingness to suffer through non-violent resistance to injustice.

Mahatma Gandhi

Mohandas Karamchand Ghandi, a westernized, English educated lawyer, had lived outside India from his youth to middle age. He preached the general acceptance of some of the doctrines he had grown to respect in his childhood, which stemmed from deep Indian traditions – notably ahimsa, or non-violence. On his return the Bengali Nobel Laureate poet, Rabindranath Tagore, had dubbed him 'Mahatma' – Great Soul. From 1921 he gave up his Western style of dress and adopted the hand spun dhoti worn by poor Indian villagers.

Yet, he was also fiercely critical of many aspects of traditional Hindu society. He preached against the discrimination of the caste system which still dominated life for the overwhelming majority of Hindus. Often despised by the British in India, his death at the hands of an extreme Hindu chauvinist in January 1948 was a final testimony to the ambiguity of his achievements: successful in contributing so much to achieving India's Independence, yet failing to resolve some of the bitter communal legacies which he gave his life to overcome.

In 1930 the Congress declared that 26 January would be Independence Day – still celebrated as Republic Day in India today. Mohammad Iqbal, the Leader of the Muslim League, took the opportunity of his address to the League in the same year to suggest the formation of a Muslim state within an Indian Federation. Also in 1930 a Muslim student in Cambridge, **Chaudhuri Rahmat Ali**, coined a name for the new Muslim state **PAKISTAN**. The letters were to stand 'P' for Punjab, 'A' for Afghania, 'K' for Kashmir, 'S' for Sind with the suffix '*stan*', Persian for country. The idea still had little real shape however and waited on developments of the late 1930s and 1940s to bear fruit.

By the end of the Second World War the positions of the Muslim League, now under the leadership of **Mohammad Ali Jinnah** and the Congress led by **Jawaharlal Nehru**, were irreconcilable. While major questions of the definition of separate territories for a Muslim and non-Muslim state remained to be answered, it was clear to General Wavell, the British Viceroy through the last years of the war, that there was no alternative but to accept that independence would have to be given on the basis of separate states.

Independence and Partition

One of the main difficulties for the Muslims was that they made up only a fifth of the total population were scattered throughout India. It was therefore impossible to define a simple territorial division which would provide a state to match Jinnah's claim of a '*two-nation theory*'. On 20 February 1947, the British Labour Government announced its decision to replace Lord Wavell as Viceroy with Lord Mountbatten, who was to oversee the transfer of power to new independent governments. It set a deadline of June 1948 for British withdrawal. The announcement of a firm date made the Indian politicians even less willing to compromise and the resulting division satisfied no one.

Independence arrived on 15 August for India and the 14 August for Pakistan because Indian astrologers deemed the 15th to be the most auspicious moment. Several key Princely States had still not decided firmly to which country they would accede. Kashmir was the most important of these, with results that have lasted to the present day.

Modern India

India, with an estimated 1.13 billion people in 2007, is the second most populated country in the world after China. That population size reflects the long history of human occupation and the fact that an astonishingly high proportion of India's land is relatively fertile. Sixty percent of India's surface area is cultivated today, compared with about 10% in China and 20% in the United States.

Although the birth rate has fallen steadily over the last 40 years, initially death rates fell faster and the rate of population increase has continued to be nearly 2% – or 18 million – a year. Today over 320 million people live in towns and cities.

Politics and institutions

When India became independent on 15 August 1947 it faced three immediate crises. Partition left it with a bitter struggle between Muslims on one side and Hindus and Sikhs on the other which threatened to tear the new country into pieces at birth. An estimated 13 million people migrated between the two new countries of India and Pakistan.

In the years since Independence, striking political achievements have been made. With the two year exception of 1975-1977, when Mrs Gandhi imposed a state of emergency in which all political activity was banned, India has sustained a democratic system in the face of tremendous pressures. The general elections of May 2004 saw the Congress Party return as the largest single party, with 220 of the 540 Lok Sabha seats. They managed to forge alliances with some of the smaller parties and thus formed the new United Progressive Alliance government under the prime ministership not of the Congress Party's leader, Sonia Gandhi, but of ex-finance minister, Manmohan Singh.

The constitution

Establishing itself as a sovereign democratic republic, the Indian parliament accepted Nehru's advocacy of a secular constitution. The president is formally vested with all executive powers exercised under the authority of the prime minister.

Parliament has a lower house (the *Lok Sabha* – House of the people) and an upper house (the *Rajya Sabha* – Council of States). The former is made up of directly elected representatives from the 543 parliamentary constituencies (plus two nominated members from the Anglo-Indian community), the latter of a mixture of members elected by an electoral college and of nominated members.

India's federal constitution devolves certain powers to elected state assemblies. Each state has a governor who acts as its official head. Many states also have two chambers, the upper generally called the Rajya Sabha and the lower (often called the Vidhan Sabha) being of directly elected representatives. In practice many of the state assemblies have had a totally different political complexion from that of the Lok Sabha. Regional parties have played a far more prominent role, though in many states central government has effectively dictated both the leadership and policy of state assemblies.

States and Union Territories Union territories are administered by the president "acting to such an extent as he thinks fit". In practice Union territories have varying forms of self-government. Pondicherry has a legislative Assembly and Council of Ministers. The 69th Amendment to the Constitution in 1991 provided for a legislative assembly and council of ministers for Delhi, elections for which were held in December 1993. The Assemblies of Union Territories have more restricted powers of legislation than full states. Some Union Territories – Dadra and Nagar Haveli, Daman and Diu, all of

which separated from Goa in 1987 when Goa achieved full statehood – Andaman and
Nicobar Islands and Lakshadweep, have elected bodies known as Pradesh Councils.

Secularism One of the key features of India's constitution is its secular principle. Some see the commitment to a secular constitution as having been under increasing challenge from the Hindu nationalism of the Bharatiya Janata Party, the BJP.

The judiciary India's Supreme Court has similar but somewhat weaker powers to those of the United States. The judiciary has remained effectively independent of the government except under the Emergency between 1975-1977.

The civil service India continued to use the small but highly professional administrative service inherited from the British period. Renamed the Indian Administrative Service (IAS), it continues to exercise remarkable influence across the country. The administration of many aspects of central and regional government is in the hands of this elite body, who act largely by the constitutional rules which bind them as servants of the state. Many Indians accept the continuing efficiency and high calibre of the top ranking officers in the administration while believing that the bureaucratic system as a whole has been overtaken by widespread corruption.

The police India's police service is divided into a series of groups, numbering nearly one million. While the top ranks of the Indian Police Service are comparable to the IAS, lower levels are extremely poorly trained and very low paid. In addition to the domestic police force there are special groups: the Border Security Force, Central Reserve Police and others. They may be armed with modern weapons and are called in for special duties.

The armed forces Unlike its immediate neighbours Pakistan and Bangladesh, India has never had military rule. It has around one million men in the army, one of the largest armed forces in the world. Although they have remained out of politics the army has been used increasingly frequently to put down civil unrest especially in Kashmir.

The Congress Party The Congress won overall majorities in seven of the 10 general elections held before the 1996 election, although in no election did the Congress obtain more than 50% of the popular vote. In 1998 its popular support completely disappeared in some regions and fell below 30% nationally and in the elections of September-October 1999 Sonia Gandhi, Rajiv Gandhi's Italian-born widow, failed to achieve the much vaunted revival in the Party's fortunes. Through 2001 into 2002 a sea change began with the BJP losing power in state assemblies in the north and becoming increasingly unpopular nationally, and the Congress picking up a wide measure of support, culminating in their victory in the May 2004 general election.

The Non-Congress Parties Political activity outside the Congress can seem bewilderingly complex. There are no genuinely national parties. The only alternative governments to the Congress have been formed by coalitions of regional and ideologically based parties. Parties of the left – Communist and Socialist – have never broken out of their narrow regional bases. The **Communist Party of India** split into two factions in 1964, with the Communist Party of India Marxist (**CPM**) ultimately taking power in West Bengal and Kerala. In the 1960s the **Swatantra Party** (a liberal party) made some ground nationally, opposing the economic centralization and state control supported by the Congress.

At the right of the political spectrum, the **Jan Sangh** was seen as a party of right wing Hindu nationalism with a concentrated but significant base in parts of the north, especially among higher castes and merchant communities. The most organized political force outside the Congress, the Jan Sangh merged with the **Janata Party** for the elections of 1977. After the collapse of that government it re-formed itself as the **Bharatiya Janata Party (BJP)**. In 1990-1991 it developed a powerful campaign focusing on reviving Hindu identity against the minorities. The elections of 1991 showed it to be the most powerful single challenger to the Congress in North India. In the decade that followed it became the most powerful single party across northern India and established a series of footholds and alliances in the South. Elsewhere a succession of regional parties dominated politics in several key states, including Tamil Nadu and Andhra Pradesh in the south and West Bengal and Bihar in the east.

Recent developments By mid-2001 the gloss had worn off the popularity of the BJP and it had suffered a series of scandals, but the prime minister had kept the core of the government together. In July 2001 Pakistan's military ruler General Pervez Musharraf visited New Delhi and Agra for talks at the Indian Government's invitation, but they ended in a shambles.

The attacks on New York and Washington on 11 September and the US-led 'War on Terror' has had major repercussions in India and Pakistan. While the Taliban's rapid defeat brought a new government to power in Afghanistan, strongly supported by India, the Kashmir dispute between India and Pakistan deepened. Both India and Pakistan sought political advantage from the war on terror, and when a terrorist attack was launched on the Indian parliament on 13 December 2001 the Indian government pushed massive reinforcements to the Pakistan border from Gujarat and Rajasthan to Kashmir. India demanded that President Musharraf close down all camps and organizations which India claimed were the source of the attacks in Delhi and Kashmir. Although President Musharraf closed down *Lashkar e Taiba* and *Jaish e Mohammad*, two of the most feared groups operating openly in Pakistan, cross-border firing intensified along the Line of Control in Kashmir and attacks in Kashmir continued. On 16 May 2002 terrorists launched a devastating attack on an army camp in Jammu, killing at least 20 people, and Sonia Gandhi demanded that the Government translate rhetoric into action. Since the change of government in May 2004, however, things have improved dramatically, with the new Indian prime minister seeming to enjoy a genuinely warm rapport with Pakistan's Pervez Musharraf. Progress over the following three years has been slow and is complicated by the continuing unrest in Pakistan itself and the challenge of apparently renewed support for the Taliban in some of its border regions. Work continues, however, on resolving the Kashmir problem.

Economy

Agriculture

Although agriculture now accounts for less than 30% of India's GDP, it remains the most important single economic activity. Over half of India's people depend directly on agriculture and its success has a crucial effect on the remainder of the economy.

Indian agriculture is enormously varied due to different climate, soil and relief. Cereal farming dominates, but wheat, grown as a winter crop, is most important in western Uttar Pradesh through Haryana to Punjab. Rice, the most important single foodgrain, is concentrated in the wetter regions of the east and south. Production of both crops has more than doubled in the last 20 years.

Other cereal crops – sorghum and the millets – predominate in central India and unirrigated parts of the north. In addition to its cereals and a range of pulses, India produces important crops of tea, cotton and sugar cane. All have seen significant growth, tea and cotton manufacturers making major contributions to export earnings.

Between Independence and the late 1960s most of the increase in India's agricultural output came from extending the cultivated area. In the last 20 years increasingly intensive use of land through greater irrigation and use of fertilizer, pesticides and high-yielding varieties of seeds (HYVs) has allowed growth to continue. The area under irrigation has risen to over 35% in 2002, while fertilizer use has increased 25 times since 1961. Indian agriculture is dominated by small holdings. Only 20% of the land is farmed in units of more than 10 ha (compared with 31% 20 years ago), while nearly 60% of farms are less than 1 ha. While the Green Revolution – the package of practices designed to increase farm output – has had its opponents, it has now transformed the agricultural productivity of many regions of India, allowing a population twice the size of that thirty years ago to be fed without recourse to imports or aid. Much of this has been achieved as the result of seed breeding and agricultural research in India's own agricultural research institutions.

Resources and industry

India has extensive resources of iron ore, coal, bauxite and some other minerals. Reserves of coal at likely rates of use are estimated at well over 100 years (at least 30 billion tonnes, plus six billion tonnes of coking coal). Medium and high grade iron ore reserves (five billion tonnes) will last over 200 years at present extraction rates. Although iron ore is found widely across peninsular India, coal is largely restricted to West Bengal, Bihar and Orissa. India's coal output reached over 250 million tonnes in 2002 and iron ore 60 million tonnes, much of which was exported to Japan.

The search for oil intensified after the oil price rises of the 1970s and late 1980s. Development of the Bombay High, off the coast of Gujarat, has contributed to the total output of over 26 million tonnes. Oil, coal and gas provide the energy for just over half of India's 100 million kw electric generation capacity, 20 million kw being hydro and two million mw nuclear.

By 2002 India's power production had grown to over 470 billion kwh, but demand has risen so fast that many states continue to have power blackouts or 'loadshedding'. Firewood is estimated to provide nearly 30% of the total energy requirement, agricultural waste 9% and cow dung, a universal fuel in some poorer areas, 7%. A recent report highlights the health risk of the continuing dependence on traditional fuels for cooking, suggesting that noxious fumes released in kitchens are responsible for up to 500,000 deaths a year from cancers and related illnesses.

India's Five Year Plans

In the early 1950s India embarked on a programme of planned industrial development. Borrowing planning concepts from the Soviet Union, the government tried to stimulate development through massive investment in the public sector, imposing a system of tight controls on foreign ownership of capital in India and playing a highly interventionist role in all aspects of economic policy. The private sector was allowed to continue to operate in agriculture and in a wide range of 'non-essential' industrial sectors.

Although significant achievements were made in the first two Five Year Plans (1951-1956, 1956-1961), the Third Five Year Plan failed catastrophically. Agriculture was particularly hard hit by three poor monsoons. After a period of dependence on foreign aid at the end of the 1960s, the economy started moving forward again. The Green Revolution enabled Indian agriculture to increase production faster than demand and through the 1980s it was producing surplus foodgrains, enabling it to build up reserves.

Achievements and problems

India today has a far more diversified industrial base than seemed imaginable at Independence. It produces goods, from aeroplanes and rockets to watches and computers, from industrial and transport machinery to textiles and consumer goods. The influence of India's manufacturing industry reaches every village. The most striking modern development is in the IT sector. According to the London *Financial Times* since the early 1990s India has become one of the world's leading centres for software development and India is rapidly transforming itself into a computer-based society. Yet despite economic successes, many in India claim that the weaknesses remain profound. Perhaps half of the population continues to live in absolute poverty and despite surplus grain production many still lack an adequate diet.

Culture

Language

The graffiti written on the walls of any Indian city bear witness to the number of major languages spoken across the country, many with their own distinct scripts. In all the states of North and West India an Indo-Aryan language – the easternmost group of the Indo-European family – is predominant. Sir William Jones, the great 19th-century scholar, discovered the close links between Sanskrit (the basis of nearly all North Indian languages) German and Greek. He showed that they all must have originated in the common heartland of Central Asia, being carried west, south and east by the nomadic tribes who shaped so much of the following history of both Europe and Asia.

Sanskrit As the pastoralists from Central Asia moved into South Asia from 2000 BC onwards, the Indo-Aryan languages they spoke were gradually modified. Sanskrit developed from this process, emerging as the dominant classical language of India by the sixth century BC, when it was classified in the grammar of **Panini**. It remained the language of the educated until about AD 1000, though it had ceased to be in common use several centuries earlier.

Hindi and Urdu The Muslims brought Persian into South Asia as the language of the rulers, where it became the language of the numerically tiny but politically powerful elite. The most striking example of Muslim influence on the earlier Indo-European languages is that of the two most important languages of India and Pakistan, Hindi and Urdu respectively. Most of the other modern North Indian languages were not written until the 16th century or after. Hindi developed into the language of the heartland of Hindu culture, stretching from Punjab to Bihar and from the foothills of the Himalaya to the marchlands of central India.

Bengali At the east end of the Ganga plains Hindi gives way to Bengali (Bangla), the language today of over 50 million people in India, as well as more than 115 million in Bangladesh. Linguistically it is close to both Assamese and Oriya.

Gujarati and Marathi South of the main Hindi and Urdu belt of India and Pakistan is a series of quite different Indo-Aryan languages. Panjabi in both Pakistan and India (on the Indian side of the border written in the Gurumukhi script) and Gujarati and Marathi, all have common features with Urdu or Hindi, but are major languages in their own right.

The Dravidian languages The other major language family of South Asia today, Dravidian, has been in India since before the arrival of the Indo-Aryans. Four of South Asia's major living languages belong to this family group – Tamil, Telugu, Kannada and Malayalam, spoken in Tamil Nadu (and northern Sri Lanka), Andhra Pradesh, Karnataka and Kerala respectively.

Each has its own script. All the Dravidian languages were influenced by the prevalence of Sanskrit as the language of the ruling and educated elite. There have been recent attempts to rid Tamil of its Sanskrit elements and to recapture the supposed purity of a literature that stretches back to the early centuries BC. Kannada and Telugu were clearly established by AD 1000, while Malayalam, which started as a dialect of Tamil, did not develop its fully distinct form until the 13th century. Today the four main Dravidian languages are spoken by over 180 million people.

It is impossible to spend even a short time in India or the other countries of South Asia without coming across several of the different scripts that are used. The earliest ancestor of scripts in use today was **Brahmi**, in which Asoka's famous inscriptions were written in the third century BC. Written from left to right, a separate symbol represented each different sound.

Devanagari For around 1000 years the major script of northern India has been the Nagari or Devanagari, which means literally the script of the 'city of the gods'. Hindi, Nepali and Marathi join Sanskrit in their use of Devanagari. The Muslim rulers developed a right to left script based on Persian and Arabic.

Dravidian scripts The Dravidian languages were written originally on leaves of the palmyra palm. Cutting the letters on the hard palm leaf made particular demands which had their impact on the forms of the letters adopted. The letters became rounded because they were carved with a stylus. This was held stationary while the leaf was turned. The southern scripts were carried overseas, contributing to the form of the non-Dravidian languages of Thai, Burmese and Cambodian.

Numerals Many of the Indian alphabets have their own notation for numerals. This is not without irony, for what in the western world are called 'Arabic' numerals are in fact of Indian origin. In some parts of South Asia local numerical symbols are still in use, but by and large you will find that the Arabic number symbols familiar in Europe and the West are common.

Literature

Sanskrit was the first all-India language. Its literature has had a fundamental influence on the religious, social and political life of the entire region. Its early literature was memorized and recited. The hymns of the Rig Veda probably did not reach their final form until about the sixth century BC.

The Vedas

The Rig Veda is a collection of 1028 hymns, not all religious. Its main function was to provide orders of worship for priests responsible for the sacrifices that were central to the religion of Indo-Aryans. Two later texts, the Yajurveda and the Samaveda, served the same purpose. A fourth, the Atharvaveda, is largely a collection of magic spells.

The Brahmanas Central to the Vedic literature was a belief in the importance of sacrifice. At some time after 1000 BC a second category of Vedic literature, the Brahmanas, began to take shape. Story telling developed as a means to interpret the significance of sacrifice. The most famous and the most important of these were the Upanishads, probably written at some time between the seventh and fifth centuries BC.

The Mahabharata The Brahmanas gave their name to the religion emerging between the eighth and sixth centuries BC, Brahmanism, the ancestor of Hinduism. Two of its texts remain the best known and most widely revered epic compositions in South Asia, the *Mahabharata* and the *Ramayana*.

Dating the Mahabharata

Tradition puts the date of the great battle described in the *Mahabharata* at precisely 3102 BC, the start of the present era, and names the author of the poem as a sage, Vyasa. Evidence suggests however that the battle was fought around 800 BC, at

Kurukshetra. It was another 400 years before priests began to write the stories down, a process which was not complete until 400 AD. The *Mahabharata* was probably an attempt by the warrior class, the Kshatriyas, to merge their brand of popular religion with Brahmanism ideas. The original version was 3000 stanzas long, but it now has over 100,000; eight times as long as Homer's Iliad and the Odyssey put together.

Good and evil The battle was seen as a war of good and evil, the **Pandavas** being interpreted as gods and the **Kauravas** as devils. The arguments were elaborated and expanded until the fourth century AD by which time, as Shackle says, "Brahmanism had absorbed and set its own mark on the religious ideas of the epic and Hinduism had come into being". A comparatively late addition to the *Mahabharata*, the *Bhagavad-Gita* is the most widely read and revered text among Hindus in South Asia today.

The Ramayana

Valmiki is thought of in India as the author of the second great Indian epic, the *Ramayana*, though no more is known of his identity than is known of Homer's. Like the *Mahabharata*, it underwent several stages of development before it reached its final version of 48,000 lines.

Sanskrit literature

Sanskrit was always the language of the court and the elite. Other languages replaced it in common speech by the third century BC, but it remained in restricted use for over 1000 years after that period. The remarkable Sanskrit grammar of Panini (see page 197) helped to establish grammar as one of the six disciplines essential to understanding the Vedas properly and to conducting Vedic rituals. The other five were phonetics, etymology, meter, ritual practice and astronomy. Sanskrit literature continued to be written in the courts until the Muslims replaced it with Persian, long after it had ceased to be a language of spoken communication. One of India's greatest poets, **Kalidasa**, contributed to the development of Sanskrit as the language of learning and the arts.

Literally 'stories of ancient times', the Puranas are about Brahma, Vishnu and Siva. They were not compiled until the fifth century AD. The stories are often the only source of information about the period immediately after the early Vedas. Each Purana dealt with five themes: "the creation of the world (sarga); its destruction and recreation (pratisarga); the genealogy of gods and patriarchs (vamsa); the reigns and periods of the Manus (manvantaras); and the history of the solar and lunar dynasties".

The Muslim influence

Persian In the first three decades of the 10th century AD Mahmud of Ghazni carried Muslim power into India. For considerable periods until the 18th century, Persian became the language of the courts. Classical Persian was the dominant influence, with Iran as its country of origin and Shiraz its main cultural centre, but India developed its own Persian-based style. Two poets stood out at the end of the 13th century AD, when Muslim rulers had established a sultanate in Delhi, Amir Khusrau, who lived from 1253 to 1325 and the mystic Amir Hasan, who died about AD 1328.

Turki The most notable of the Mughal sponsors of literature, Akbar (1556-1605) was himself illiterate. Babur left one of the most remarkable political autobiographies of any generation, the Babur-nama (History of Babur), written in Turki and translated into Persian. His grandson Akbar commissioned a biography, the Akbar-nama, which reflected his interest in all the world's religions. His son Jahangir left his memoirs, the Tuzuk-i Jahangiri, in Persian. They have been described as intimate and spontaneous and showing an insatiable interest in things, events and people.

⁞ The story of Rama

Under Brahmin influence, Rama was transformed from the human prince of the early versions into the divine figure of the final story. Rama, the 'jewel of the solar kings', became deified as an incarnation of Vishnu. The story tells how Rama was banished from his father's kingdom. In a journey that took him as far as Sri Lanka, accompanied by his wife Sita and helper and friend Hanuman (the monkey-faced God depicted in many Indian temples, shrines and posters), Rama finally fought the king **Ravana**, again changed in late versions into a demon. Rama's rescue of Sita was interpreted as the Aryan triumph over the barbarians. The epic is widely seen as South Asia's first literary poem and is known and recited in all Hindu communities.

The Colonial Period

Persian was already in decline during the reign of the last great Muslim Emperor, **Aurangzeb** and as the British extended their political power so the role of English grew. There is now a very wide Indian literature accessible in English, which has thus become the latest of the languages to be used across the whole of South Asia.

In the 19th century English became a vehicle for developing nationalist ideals. However, notably in the work of **Rabindranath Tagore**, it became a medium for religious and philosophical prose and for a developing poetry. Tagore himself won the Nobel Prize for Literature in 1913 for his translation into English of his own work, Gitanjali. Leading South Asian philosophers and thinkers of the 20th century have written major works in English, including not only MK Gandhi and Jawaharlal Nehru, the two leading figures in India's Independence movement, but S Radhakrishnan, Aurobindo Ghose and Sarojini Naidu, who all added to the depth of Indian literature in English.

Several South Asian regional languages have their own long traditions of both religious and secular literature which are discussed in the relevant sections of this book.

Science

Views of the universe   Early Indian views of the universe were based on the square and the cube. The earth was seen as a square, one corner pointing south, rising like a pyramid in a series of square terraces with its peak, the mythical Mount Meru. The sun moved round the top of Mount Meru in a square orbit and the square orbits of the planets were at successive planes above the orbit of the sun. These were seen therefore as forming a second pyramid of planetary movement. Mount Meru was central to all early Indian schools of thought, Hindu, Buddhist and Jain.

However, about 200 BC the Jains transformed the view of the universe based on squares by replacing the idea of square orbits with that of the circle. The earth was shown as a circular disc, with Mount Meru rising from its centre and the Pole Star above it.

The science of early India   By about 500 BC Indian texts illustrated the calculation of the **calendar**, although the system itself almost certainly goes back to the eighth or ninth century BC. The year was divided into 27 *nakshatras*, or fortnights, years being calculated on a mixture of lunar and solar counting.

Technology The only copy of Kautiliya's treatise on government (which was only discovered in 1909) dates from about 100 BC. It describes the **weapons** technology of catapults, incendiary missiles and the use of elephants, but it is also evident that gunpowder was unknown. Large-scale **irrigation** works were developed, though the earliest examples of large tanks may be those of the Sri Lankan King Panduwasa at Anuradhapura, built in 504 BC. During the Gupta period dramatic progress was made in **metallurgy**, shown in the pure iron pillar which can be seen in the Qutb Minar in Delhi.

Mathematics Conceptions of the universe and the mathematical and geometrical ideas that accompanied them were comparatively advanced in South Asia by the time of the Mauryan Empire and were put to use in the rules developed for building temple altars. Indians were using the concept of zero and decimal points in the Gupta period. Furthermore in AD 499, just after the demise of the Gupta Empire, the astronomer Aryabhatta calculated Pi as 3.1416 and the length of the solar year as 365.358 days. He also postulated that the earth was a sphere rotating on its own axis and revolving around the sun and that the shadow of the earth falling on the moon caused lunar eclipses. The development of science in India was not restricted to the Gupta court. In South India, Tamil kings developed extensive contact with Roman and Greek thinkers during the first four centuries of the Christian era. Babylonian methods used for astronomy in Greece remained current in Tamil Nadu until very recent times. The basic texts of astronomy (the Surya Siddhanta) were completed by AD 400.

Architecture

Over the 4000 years since the Indus Valley civilization flourished, art and architecture have developed with a remarkable continuity through successive regional and religious influences and styles. The Buddhist art and architecture of the third century BC left few remains, but the stylistic influence on early Hindu architecture was profound. From the sixth century AD the first Hindu religious buildings to have survived into the modern period were constructed in South and East India.

Hindu temple buildings

The principles of religious building were laid down by priests in the *Sastras*. Every aspect of Hindu, Jain and Buddhist religious building is identified with conceptions of the structure of the universe. This applies as much to the process of building – the timing of which must be undertaken at astrologically propitious times – as to the formal layout of the buildings. The cardinal directions of north, south, east and west are the basic fix on which buildings are planned. George Michell suggests that in addition to the cardinal directions, number is also critical to the design of the religious building. The key to the ultimate scale of the building is derived from the measurements of the sanctuary at its heart. Indian temples were nearly always built according to philosophical understandings of the universe. This cosmology, of an infinite number of universes, isolated from each other in space, proceeds by imagining various possibilities as to its nature. Its centre is seen as dominated by **Mount Meru** which keeps earth and heaven apart. The concept of *separation* is crucial to Hindu thought and social practice. Continents, rivers and oceans occupy concentric rings around the mountain, while the stars encircle the mountain in another plane. Humans live on the continent of **Jambudvipa**, characterized by the rose apple tree (*jambu*). For more information on temple architecture specific to the South, see Footprint's *South India*.

Mandalas The Sastras show plans of this continent, organized in concentric rings and entered at the cardinal points. This type of diagram was known as a **mandala**. Such a geometric scheme could be subdivided into almost limitless small compartments, each of which could be designated as having special properties or be devoted to a particular deity. The centre of the mandala would be the seat of the major god; they provided the ground rules for the building of stupas and temples across India and gave the key to the symbolic meaning attached to every aspect of religious buildings.

Temple design The focal point of the temple, its sanctuary, was the home of the presiding deity, the 'womb-chamber' (*garbhagriha*). A series of doorways, in large temples leading through a succession of buildings, allowed the worshipper to move towards the final encounter with the deity to obtain *darshan* – a sight of the god. Both Buddhist and Hindu worship encourage the worshipper to walk clockwise around the shrine, performing *pradakshina*.

The elevations are symbolic representations of the home of the gods. Mountain peaks such as Kailasa are common names for the most prominent of the towers. In North and East Indian temples the tallest of these towers rises above the *garbagriha* itself, symbolizing the meeting of earth and heaven in the person of the enshrined deity. In later South Indian temples the gateways to the temple come to overpower the central tower. In both, the basic structure is usually richly embellished with sculpture. When first built this would usually have been plastered and painted and often covered in gems. In contrast to the extraordinary profusion of colour and life on the outside, the interior is dark and cramped but here it is believed, lies the true centre of divine power.

Muslim religious architecture

Although the Muslims adapted many Hindu features, they also brought totally new forms. Their most outstanding contribution, dominating the architecture of many North Indian cities, are the mosques and tomb complexes (*dargah*). The use of brickwork was widespread and they brought with them from Persia the principle of constructing the true arch. Muslim architects succeeded in producing a variety of domed structures, often incorporating distinctively Hindu features such as the surmounting finial. By the end of the great period of Muslim building in 1707, the Muslims had added magnificent forts and palaces to their religious structures, a statement of power as well as of aesthetic taste.

European buildings

Nearly two centuries of architectural stagnation and decline followed the demise of Mughal power. The Portuguese built a series of remarkable churches in Goa that owed nothing to local traditions and everything to Baroque developments in Europe. Not until the end of the Victorian period, when British imperial ambitions were at their height, did the British colonial impact on public rather than domestic architecture begin to be felt. Fierce arguments divided British architects as to the merits of indigenous design. The ultimate plan for New Delhi was carried out by men who had little time for Hindu architecture and believed themselves to be on a civilizing mission. Others at the end of the 19th century wanted to recapture and enhance a tradition for which they had great respect. They have left a series of buildings, both in formerly British ruled territory and in the Princely States, which illustrate this concern through the development of what became known as the Indo-Saracenic style.

In the immediate aftermath of the colonial period, Independent India set about trying to establish a break from the immediately imperial past, but was uncertain how to achieve it. In the event foreign architects were commissioned for major developments, such as Le Corbusier's design for Chandigarh and Louis Kahn's buildings in Dhaka and Ahmadabad. The latter, a centre for training and experiment, contains a number of new buildings such as those of the Indian architect Charles Correa.

Background Culture

Music and dance

Music Indian music can trace its origins to the metrical hymns and chants of the Vedas, in which the production of sound according to strict rules was thought to be vital to the continuing order of the Universe. Through more than 3000 years of development, India's musical tradition has been handed on almost entirely by ear. The chants of the **Rig Veda** developed into songs in the **Sama Veda** and music found expression in every sphere of life, reflecting the cycle of seasons and the rhythm of work.

Over the centuries the original three notes, which were sung strictly in descending order, were extended to five and then seven and developed to allow freedom to move up and down the scale. The scale increased to 12 with the addition of flats and sharps and finally to 22 with the further subdivision of semitones. Books of musical rules go back at least as far as the third century AD. Classical music was totally intertwined with dance and drama, an interweaving reflected in the term *sangita*.

At some point after the Muslim influence made itself felt in the north, North and South Indian styles diverged, to become Carnatic (Karnatak) music in the south and Hindustani music in the north. However, they still share important common features: *svara* (pitch), *raga* (the melodic structure) and *tala* or *talam* (metre).

Hindustani music probably originated in the Delhi Sultanate during the 13th century, when the most widely known of North Indian musical instruments, the *sitar*, was believed to have been invented. **Amir Khusrau** is also believed to have invented the small drums, the *tabla*. Hindustani music is held to have reached its peak under *Tansen*, a court musician of Akbar. The other important northern instruments are the stringed *sarod*, the reed instrument *shahnai* and the wooden flute. Most Hindustani compositions have devotional texts, though they encompass a great emotional and thematic range. A common classical form of vocal performance is the *dhrupad*, a four-part composition.

The essential structure of a melody is known as a **raga** which usually has five to seven notes and can have as many as nine (or even 12 in mixed ragas). The music is improvised by the performer within certain rules and although theoretically thousands of ragas are possible, only around a 100 are commonly performed. Ragas have become associated with particular moods and specific times of the day. Music festivals often include all night sessions to allow performers a wider choice of repertoire.

Dance The rules for classical dance were laid down in the Natya shastra in the second century BC, which is still one of the bases for modern dance forms. The most common sources for Indian dance are the epics, but there are three essential aspects of the dance itself, Nritta (pure dance), Nrittya (emotional expression) and Natya (drama). The religious influence in dance was exemplified by the tradition of temple dancers, *devadasis*, girls and women who were dedicated to the deity in major temples. In South and East India there were thousands of *devadasis* associated with temple worship, though the practice fell into widespread disrepute and was banned in independent India. Various dance forms (for example Odissi, Manipuri, Bharat Natyam, Kathakali, Mohinyattam) developed in different parts of the country. India is also rich in folk dance traditions which are widely performed during festivals.

The cinema Film goers around the world are taking greater note of Indian cinema, both home-grown and that produced and directed by Indians abroad. Not all fall into the category of a Bollywood '*masala* movie' or 'curry western' churned out by the Mumbai (Bombay) film industry but many offer an insight into what draws millions to watch diverse versions of Indian life on the silver screen. A few titles, both all time favourites as well as new releases include: Viewing: *Pather Panchali, Mother India; Titash Ekti Nadir Naam; Sholay; Bombay; Kuch Kuch Hota Hai; Lagaan; Kabhie Khushi Kabhie Cham; Monsoon Wedding; The Guru; The Warrior.*

Religion

It is impossible to write briefly about religion in India without greatly oversimplifying. Over 80% of Indians are Hindu, but there are significant minorities. Muslims number about 125 million and there are over 23 million Christians, 19 million Sikhs, six million Buddhists and a number of other religious groups. One of the most persistent features of Indian religious and social life is the caste system. This has undergone substantial changes since Independence, especially in towns and cities, but most people in India are still clearly identified as a member of a particular caste group. The government has introduced measures to help the backward, or 'scheduled' castes, though in recent years this has produced a major political backlash.

Hinduism

It has always been easier to define Hinduism by what it is not than by what it is. Indeed, the name 'Hindu' was given by foreigners to the peoples of the subcontinent who did not profess the other major faiths, such as Muslims or Christians. While some aspects of modern Hinduism can be traced back more than 4000 years before that, other features are recent.

Key ideas

According to the great Indian philosopher and former president of India, S Radhakrishnan, religion for the Hindu "is not an idea but a power, not an intellectual proposition but a life conviction. Religion is consciousness of ultimate reality, not a theory about God". There is no Hindu organization, like a church, with the authority to define belief or establish official practice. Not all Hindu groups believe in a single supreme God. In view of these characteristics, many authorities argue that it is misleading to think of Hinduism as a religion at all. Be that as it may, the evidence of the living importance of Hinduism is visible across India. Hindu philosophy and practice has also touched many of those who belong to other religious traditions, particularly in terms of social institutions such as caste, and in post-Independence India religious identity has become an increasingly politicized feature of national life.

Darshan One of Hinduism's recurring themes is 'vision', 'sight' or 'view' – **darshan**. Applied to the different philosophical systems themselves, such as *yoga* or *vedanta*, 'darshan' is also used to describe the sight of the deity that worshippers hope to gain when they visit a temple or shrine hoping for the sight of a 'guru' (teacher). Equally it may apply to the religious insight gained through meditation or prayer.

The four human goals Many Hindus also accept that there are four major human goals; material prosperity (*artha*), the satisfaction of desires (*kama*) and performing the duties laid down according to your position in life (*dharma*). Beyond those is the goal of achieving liberation from the endless cycle of rebirths into which everyone is locked (*moksha*). It is to the search for liberation that the major schools of Indian philosophy have devoted most attention. Together with dharma, it is basic to Hindu thought.

The *Mahabharata* lists 10 embodiments of **dharma**: good name, truth, self-control, cleanness of mind and body, simplicity, endurance, resoluteness of character, giving and sharing, austerities and continence. In *dharmic* thinking these are inseparable from five patterns of behaviour: non-violence, an attitude of equality, peace and tranquillity, lack of aggression and cruelty and absence of envy. Dharma, an essentially secular concept, represents the order inherent in human life.

⁝ The four stages of life

Popular Hindu belief holds that an ideal life has four stages: that of the student, the householder, the forest dweller and the wandering dependent or beggar (*sannyasi*). These stages represent the phases through which an individual learns of life's goals and of the means of achieving them.

One of the most striking sights today is that of the saffron-clad *sannyasi* (sadhu) seeking gifts of food and money to support himself in the final stage of his life. There may have been sadhus even before the Aryans arrived. Today, most of these have given up material possessions, carrying only a strip of cloth, a *danda* (staff), a crutch to support the chin during *achal* (meditation), prayer beads, a fan to ward off evil spirits, a water pot, a drinking vessel, which may be a human skull and a begging bowl. You may well see one, almost naked, covered only in ashes, on a city street.

Karma The idea of *karma*, 'the effect of former actions', is central to achieving liberation. As C Rajagopalachari put it: "Every act has its appointed effect, whether the act be thought, word or deed. The cause holds the effect, so to say, in its womb. If we reflect deeply and objectively, the entire world will be found to obey unalterable laws. That is the doctrine of karma". See also box opposite.

Rebirth The belief in the transmigration of souls (*samsara*) in a neverending cycle of rebirth has been Hinduism's most distinctive and important contribution to Indian culture. The earliest reference is in one of the *Upanishads*, around the seventh century BC, at about the same time as the doctrine of *karma* made its first appearance.

Ahimsa AL Basham pointed out that belief in transmigration must have encouraged a further distinctive doctrine, that of non-violence or non-injury – *ahimsa*. The belief in rebirth meant that all living things and creatures of the spirit – people, devils, gods, animals, even worms – possessed the same essential soul. One inscription threatens that anyone who interferes with the rights of Brahmins to land given to them by the king will 'suffer rebirth for 80,000 years as a worm in dung'. Belief in the cycle of rebirth was essential to give such a threat any weight!

Schools of philosophy

It is common now to talk of six major schools of Hindu philosophy. *Nyaya, Vaisheshika, Sankhya, Yoga, Purvamimansa* and *Vedanta*.

Yoga Yoga, can be traced back to at least the third century AD. It seeks a synthesis of the spirit, the soul and the flesh and is concerned with systems of meditation and self denial that lead to the realization of the Divine within oneself and can ultimately release one from the cycle of rebirth.

Vedanta These are literally the final parts of the Vedic literature, the *Upanishads*. The basic texts also include the Brahmasutra of Badrayana, written about the first century AD and the most important of all, the *Bhagavad-Gita*, which is a part of the epic the *Mahabharata*. There are many interpretations of these basic texts. Three are given here.

Advaita Vedanta holds that there is no division between the cosmic force or principle, *Brahman* and the individual Self, *atman* (also referred to as 'soul'). The fact that we appear to see different and separate individuals is simply a result of ignorance. This is termed *maya* (illusion), but Vedanta philosophy does not suggest

Karma – an eye to the future

According to the doctrine of karma, every person, animal or god has a being or 'self' which has existed without beginning. Every action, except those that are done without any consideration of the results, leaves an indelible mark on that 'self', carried forward into the next life.

The overall character of the imprint on each person's 'self' determines three features of the next life: the nature of his next birth (animal, human or god),

the kind of family he will be born into if human and the length of the next life. Finally, it controls the good or bad experiences that the self will experience. However, it does not imply a fatalistic belief that the nature of action in this life is unimportant. Rather, it suggests that the path followed by the individual in the present life is vital to the nature of its next life and ultimately to the chance of gaining release from this world.

that the world in which we live is an illusion. *Jnana* (knowledge) is held as the key to understanding the full and real unity of Self and Brahman. **Shankaracharya**, born at Kalady in modern Kerala, in the seventh century AD, is the best known Advaitin Hindu philosopher. He argued that there was no individual Self or soul separate from the creative force of the universe, or Brahman and that it was impossible to achieve liberation (*moksha*), through meditation and devotional worship, which he saw as signs of remaining on a lower level and of being unprepared for true liberation.

The 11-12th-century philosopher, **Ramanuja**, repudiated ideas of **Vishishtad-vaita**. He transformed the idea of God from an impersonal force to a personal God and viewed both the Self and the World as real but only as part of the whole. In contrast to Shankaracharya's view, Ramanuja saw *bhakti* (devotion) as of central importance to achieving liberation and service to the Lord as the highest goal of life.

Dvaita Vedanta was developed by the 14th-century philosopher, Madhva. He believed that Brahman, the Self and the World are completely distinct. Worship of God is a key means of achieving liberation.

Worship

Puja For most Hindus today, worship ('performing puja') is an integral part of their faith. The great majority of Hindu homes will have a shrine to one of the gods of the Hindu pantheon. Individuals and families will often visit shrines or temples and on special occasions will travel long distances to particularly holy places such as Benaras or Puri. Such sites may have temples dedicated to a major deity but may also have numerous other shrines in the vicinity dedicated to other favourite gods.

Acts of devotion are often aimed at the granting of favours and the meeting of urgent needs for this life – good health, finding a suitable wife or husband, the birth of a son, prosperity and good fortune. Puja involves making an offering to God and *darshan* (having a view of the deity). Hindu worship is generally, though not always, an act performed by individuals. Thus Hindu temples may be little more than a shrine on a river bank or in the middle of the street, tended by a priest and visited at special times when a darshan of the resident God can be obtained. When it has been consecrated, the image, if exactly made, becomes the channel for the godhead to work.

Holy places Certain rivers and towns are particularly sacred to Hindus. Thus there are seven holy rivers – the Ganga, Yamuna, Indus and mythical Sarasvati in the north and the Narmada, Godavari and Kaveri in the Peninsula. There are also seven holy places – Haridwar, Mathura, Ayodhya and Varanasi, again in the north, Ujjain, Dwarka and Kanchipuram to the south. In addition to these seven holy places there are four holy abodes: Badrinath, Puri and Ramesvaram, with Dwarka in modern Gujarat having the unique distinction of being both a holy abode and a holy place.

Rituals and festivals The temple rituals often follow through the cycle of day and night, as well as yearly lifecycles. The priests may wake the deity from sleep, bathe, clothe and feed it. Worshippers will be invited to share in this process by bringing offerings of clothes and food. Gifts of money will usually be made and in some temples there is a charge levied for taking up positions in front of the deity in order to obtain a darshan at the appropriate times.

Every temple has its special festivals. At festival times you can see villagers walking in small groups, brightly dressed and often high spirited, sometimes as far as 80-100 km.

Hindu deities

Today three Gods are widely seen as all-powerful: Brahma, Vishnu and Siva. While Brahma is regarded as the ultimate source of creation, Siva also has a creative role alongside his function as destroyer. Vishnu in contrast is seen as the preserver or protector of the universe. Vishnu and Siva are widely represented have come to be seen as the most powerful and important. Their followers are referred to as Vaishnavite and Shaivites respectively and numerically they form the two largest sects in India.

Brahma Popularly Brahma is interpreted as the Creator in a trinity, alongside Vishnu as Preserver and Siva as Destroyer. In the literal sense the name Brahma is the masculine and personalized form of the neuter word Brahman.

In the early Vedic writing, *Brahman* represented the universal and impersonal principle which governed the Universe. Gradually, as Vedic philosophy moved towards a monotheistic interpretation of the universe and its origins, this impersonal power was increasingly personalized. In the *Upanishads*, Brahman was seen as a universal and elemental creative spirit. Brahma, described in early myths as having been born from a golden egg and then to have created the Earth, assumed the identity of the earlier Vedic deity Prajapati and became identified as the creator.

By the fourth and fifth centuries AD, the height of the classical period of Hinduism, Brahma was seen as one of the trinity of Gods – *Trimurti* – in which Vishnu, Siva and Brahma represented three forms of the unmanifested supreme being. It is from Brahma that Hindu cosmology takes its structure. The basic cycle through which the whole cosmos passes is described as one day in the life of Brahma – the *kalpa*. It equals 4,320 million years, with an equally long night. One year of Brahma's life – a cosmic year – lasts 360 days and nights. The universe is expected to last for 100 years of Brahma's life, who is currently believed to be 51 years old.

By the sixth century AD Brahma worship had effectively ceased (before the great period of temple building), which accounts for the fact that there are remarkably few temples dedicated to Brahma. Nonetheless images of Brahma are found in most temples. Characteristically he is shown with four faces, a fifth having been destroyed by the fire from Siva's third eye. In his four arms he usually holds a copy of the Vedas, a sceptre and a water jug or a bow. He is accompanied by the goose, symbolizing knowledge.

Sarasvati Seen by some Hindus as the 'active power' of Brahma, popularly thought of as his consort, Sarasvati has survived into the modern Hindu world as a far more important figure than Brahma himself. In popular worship Sarasvati represents the goddess of education and learning, worshipped in schools and colleges with gifts of fruit, flowers and incense. She represents 'the word' itself, which began to be deified as part of the process of the writing of the Vedas, which ascribed magical power to words. The development of her identity represented the rebirth of the concept of a mother

⁝ Auspicious signs

Some of Hinduism's sacred symbols are thought to have originated in the Aryan religion of the Vedic period.

Om The Primordial sound of the universe, 'Om' (or more correctly the three-in-one 'Aum') is the Supreme syllable. It is the opening and sometimes closing, chant for Hindu prayers. Some attribute the three constituents to the Hindu triad of Brahma, Vishnu and Siva. It is believed to be the cosmic sound of Creation which encompasses all states from wakefulness to deep sleep and though it is the essence of all sound, it is outside our hearing.

Svastika Representing the Sun and it's energy, the svastika usually appears on doors or walls of temples, in red, the colour associated with good fortune and luck. The term, derived from the Sanskrit 'svasti', is repeated in Hindu chants. The arms of the symbol point in the cardinal directions which may reflect the ancient practice of lighting fire sticks in the four directions. When the svastika appears to rotate clockwise it symbolizes the positive creative energy of the sun; the anti-clockwise svastika, symbolizing the autumn/winter sun, is considered unlucky.

Six-pointed star The intersecting triangles in the 'Star of David' symbol represents Spirit and Matter held in balance. A central dot signifies a particle of Divinity. The star is incorporated as a decorative element in some Muslim buildings such as Humayun's Tomb in Delhi.

Lotus The 'padma' or 'kamal' flower with it's many petals appears not only in art and architecture but also in association with gods and godesses. Some deities are seen holding one, others are portrayed seated or standing on the flower, or as with Padmanabha it appears from Vishnu's navel. The lotus represents purity, peace and beauty, a symbol also shared by Buddhists and Jains and as in nature stands away and above the impure, murky water from which it emerges. In architecture, the lotus motif occurs frequently.

Om

Svastika

Six-pointed star

Lotus

goddess, which had been strong in the Indus Valley Civilization over 1000 years before and may have been continued in popular ideas through the worship of female spirits.

In addition to her role as Brahma's wife, Sarasvati is also variously seen as the wife of Vishnu and Manu or as Daksha's daughter, among other interpretations. Normally white coloured, riding on a swan and carrying a book, she is often shown playing a vina. She may have many arms and heads, representing her role as patron of all the sciences and arts.

Vishnu Vishnu is seen as the God with the human face. From the second century a new and passionate devotional worship of Vishnu's incarnation as Krishna developed in the South. By AD 1000 Vaishnavism had spread across South India and it became closely associated with the devotional form of Hinduism preached by **Ramanuja**, whose followers spread the worship of Vishnu and his 10 successive incarnations in animal and human form. For Vaishnavites, God took these different forms in order to save the world from impending disaster. AL Basham has summarized the 10 incarnations.

Rama and Krishna By far the most influential incarnations of Vishnu are those in which he was believed to take recognizable human form, especially as Rama (twice) and Krishna. As the Prince of Ayodhya, history and myth blend, for Rama was probably a chief who lived in the eighth or seventh century BC. Although Rama is now seen as an earlier incarnation of Vishnu than Krishna, he came to be regarded as divine very late, probably after the Muslim invasions of the 12th century AD. Rama (or Ram, pronounced to rhyme with *calm*) is a powerful figure in contemporary India. His supposed birthplace at Ayodhya became the focus of fierce disputes between Hindus and Muslims in the early 1990s which continue today. Krishna is worshipped extremely widely as perhaps the most human of the gods. His advice on the battlefield of the *Mahabharata* is one of the major sources of guidance for the rules of daily living for many Hindus today.

Lakshmi Commonly represented as Vishnu's wife, Lakshmi is widely worshipped as the goddess of wealth. Earlier representations of Vishnu's consorts portrayed her as Sridevi, often shown in statues on Vishnu's right, while Bhudevi, also known as Prithvi, who represented the earth, was on his left. Lakshmi is popularly shown in her own right as standing on a lotus flower, although eight forms of Lakshmi are recognized.

Hanuman The *Ramayana* tells how Hanuman, Rama's faithful servant, went across India and finally into the demon Ravana's forest home of Lanka at the head of his monkey army in search of the abducted Sita. He used his powers to jump the sea channel separating India from Sri Lanka and managed after a series of heroic and magical feats to find and rescue his master's wife. Whatever form he is shown in, he remains almost instantly recognizable.

Siva Professor Wendy Doniger O'Flaherty argues that the key to the myths through which Siva's character is understood, lies in the explicit ambiguity of Siva as the great ascetic and at the same time as the erotic force of the universe.

Siva is interpreted as both creator and destroyer, the power through whom the universe evolves. He lives on Mount Kailasa with his wife **Parvati** (also known as **Uma, Sati, Kali** and **Durga**) and two sons, the elephant-headed Ganesh and the six-headed Karttikeya, known in South India as Subrahmanya. In sculptural representations Siva is normally accompanied by his 'vehicle', the bull (*Nandi* or *Nandin*).

Siva is also represented in Shaivite temples throughout India by the *linga*, literally meaning 'sign' or 'mark', but referring in this context to the sign of gender or phallus and *yoni*. On the one hand a symbol of energy, fertility and potency, as Siva's symbol it also represents the yogic power of sexual abstinence and penance. The *linga* is now the most important symbol of the cult of Siva. O'Flaherty suggests that the worship of the *linga* of Siva can be traced back to the pre-Vedic societies of the Indus Valley civilization (circa 2000 BC), but that it first appears in Hindu iconography in the second century BC. From that time a wide variety of myths appeared to explain the origin of *linga* worship. The myths surrounding the 12 **jyotirlinga** (*linga* of light) found at centres like Ujjain go back to the second century BC and were developed to explain and justify *linga* worship.

Siva's alternative names Although Siva is not seen as having a series of rebirths, like Vishnu, he none the less appears in very many forms representing different aspects of his varied powers. Some of the more common are:

Chandrasekhara – the moon (*chandra*) symboilizes the powers of creation and destruction.

Mahadeva – the representation of Siva as the god of supreme power, which came relatively late into Hindu thought, shown as the *linga* in combination with the *yoni*, or female genitalia.

Nataraja – the Lord of the Cosmic Dance. The story is based on a legend in which Siva and Vishnu went to the forest to overcome 10,000 heretics. In their anger the heretics attacked Siva first by sending a tiger, then a snake and thirdly a fierce black dwarf with a club. Siva killed the tiger, tamed the snake and wore it like a garland and then put his foot on the dwarf and performed a dance of such power that the dwarf and the heretics acknowledged Siva as the Lord.

Rudra – Siva's early prototype, who may date back to the Indus Valley Civilization.

Virabhadra – Siva created Virabhadra to avenge himself on his wife Sati's father, Daksha, who had insulted Siva by not inviting him to a special sacrifice. Sati attended the ceremony against Siva's wishes and when she heard her father grossly abusing Siva she committed suicide by jumping into the sacrificial fire. This act gave rise to the term *sati* (*suttee*, a word which simply means a good or virtuous woman). Recorded in the *Vedas*, the self immolation of a woman on her husband's funeral pyre probably did not become accepted practice until the early centuries BC. Even then it was mainly restricted to those of the Kshatriya caste.

Nandi – Siva's vehicle, the bull, is one of the most widespread of sacred symbols of the ancient world and may represent a link with Rudra, who was sometimes represented as a bull in pre-Hindu India. Strength and virility are key attributes and pilgrims to Siva temples will often touch the Nandi's testicles on their way into the shrine.

Ganesh One of Hinduism's most popular gods, Ganesh is seen as the great clearer of obstacles. Shown at gateways and on door lintels with his elephant head and pot belly, his image is revered across India. Meetings, functions and special family gatherings will often start with prayers to Ganesh and any new venture, from the opening of a building to inaugurating a company, will not be deemed complete without a Ganesh puja.

Shakti, The Mother Goddess Shakti is a female divinity often worshipped in the form of Siva's wife Durga or Kali. As Durga she agreed to do battle with Mahish, an *asura* (demon) who threatened to dethrone the gods. Many sculptures and paintings illustrate the story in which, during the terrifying struggle which ensued, the demon changed into a buffalo, an elephant and a giant with 1000 arms. Durga, clutching weapons in each of her 10 hands, eventually emerges victorious. As Kali ('black') the mother goddess takes on her most fearsome form and character. Fighting with the chief of the demons, she was forced to use every weapon in her armoury, but every drop of blood that she drew became 1000 new giants just as strong as he. The only way she could win was by drinking the blood of all her enemies. Having succeeded she was so elated that her dance of triumph threatened the earth. Ignoring the pleas of the gods to stop, she even threw her husband Siva to the ground and trampled over him, until she realized to her shame what she had done. She is always shown with a sword in one hand, the severed head of the giant in another, two corpses for earrings and a necklace of human skulls. She is often shown standing with one foot on the body and the other on the leg of Siva.

The worship of female goddesses developed into the widely practised form of devotional worship called Tantrism. Goddesses such as Kali became the focus of worship which often involved practices that flew in the face of wider Hindu moral and legal codes. Animal and even human sacrifices and ritual sexual intercourse were part of Tantric belief and practice, the evidence for which may still be seen in the art and sculpture of some major temples. Tantric practice affected both Hinduism and Buddhism from the eighth century AD; its influence is shown vividly in the sculptures of Khajuraho and Konark and in the distinctive Hindu and Buddhist practices of the Kathmandu Valley in Nepal.

Skanda The God of War, Skanda (known as Murugan in Tamil Nadu and by other regional names) became known as the son of Siva and Parvati. One legend suggests that he was conceived by the Goddess Ganga from Siva's seed.

Hindu deities

Deity	Association	Relationship
Brahma	Creator	One of Trinity
Sarasvati	Education and culture, "the word"	Wife of Brahma
Siva	Creator/destroyer	One of Trinity
Bhairava	Fierce aspect of Siva	
Parvati (Uma)	Benevolent aspect of female divine power	Consort of Siva, mother of Ganesh
Kali	The energy that destroys evil	Consort of Siva
Durga	In fighting attitude	Consort of Siva
Ganesh/ Ganapati	God of good beginnings, clearer of obstacles	Son of Siva
Skanda (Karttikkeya, Murugan, Subrahmanya)	God of War/bringer of disease	Son of Siva and Ganga
Vishnu	Preserver	One of Trinity
Prithvi/ Bhudevi	Goddess of Earth	Wife of Vishnu
Lakshmi	Goddess of Wealth	Wife of Vishnu
Agni	God of Fire	
Indra	Rain, lightning and thunder	
Ravana	King of the demons	

Ardhanarisvara, the male/female form of Siva

Vishnu, Preserver of the Universe

Krishna, eighth incarnation of Vishnu

Durga, Mother-goddess, destroyer of demons

Attributes	Vehicle
4 heads, 4 arms, upper left holds water pot and rosary or sacrificial spoon, sacred thread across left shoulder	Hamsa (goose/swan)
Two or more arms, vina, lotus, plam leaves, rosary	Hamsa
Linga; Rudra, matted hair, 3 eyes, drum, fire, deer, trident; Nataraja, Lord of the Dance	Bull – Nandi
Trident, sword, noose, naked, snakes, garland of skulls, dishevelled hair, carrying destructive weapons	Dog
2 arms when shown with Siva, 4 when on her own, blue lily in right hand, left hand hangs down	Lion
Trident, noose, human skulls, sword, shield, black colour	Lion
4 arms, conch, disc, bow, arrow, bell, sword, shield	Lion or tiger
Goad, noose, broken tusk, fruits	Rat/ mouse/ shrew
6 heads, 12 arms, spear, arrow, sword, discus, noose cock, bow, shield, conch and plough	Peacock
4 arms, high crown, discus and conch in upper arms, club and sword (or lotus) in lower	Garuda - mythical eagle
Right hand in abhaya gesture, left holds pomegranate, left leg on treasure pot	
Seated/standing on red lotus, 4 hands, lotuses, vessel, fruit	Lotus
Sacred thread, axe, wood, bellows, torch, sacrificial spoon	2-headed ram
Bow, thunderbolt, lances	
10 heads, 20 arms, bow and arrow	

Background Religion

Siva as Nataraj

Ganesh, bringer of prosperity

Parvati, wife of Siva

Kali, the "black" Mother-goddess

Gods of the warrior caste Modern Hinduism has brought into its pantheon over many generations gods who were worshipped by the earlier pre-Hindu Aryan civilizations. The most important is **Indra**, often shown as the god of rain, thunder and lightning. To the early Aryans, Indra destroyed demons in battle, the most important being his victory over Vritra, 'the Obstructor'. By this victory Indra released waters from the clouds, allowing the earth to become fertile. To the early Vedic writers the clouds of the southwest monsoon were seen as hostile, determined to keep their precious treasure of water to themselves and only releasing it when forced to by a greater power. Indra, carrying a bow in one hand, a thunderbolt in another and lances in the others and riding on his vehicle Airavata, the elephant, is thus the Lord of Heaven. His wife is the relatively insignificant **Indrani**.

Mitra and **Varuna** have the power both of gods and demons. Their role is to sustain order, Mitra taking responsibility for friendship and Varuna for oaths and as they have to keep watch for 24 hours a day Mitra has become the god of the day or the sun, Varuna the god of the moon.

Agni, the god of fire, is a god whose origins lie with the priestly caste rather than with the Kshatriyas, or warriors. He was seen in the Vedas as being born from the rubbing together of two pieces of dead wood and as Masson-Oursel writes "the poets marvel at the sight of a being so alive leaping from dry dead wood. His very growth is miraculous". Riding on a ram, wearing a sacred thread, he is often shown with flames leaping from his mouth and he carries an axe, wood, bellows or a fan, a torch and a sacrificial spoon, for he is the god of ritual fire.

The juice of the soma plant, the nectar of the gods guaranteeing eternal life, **Soma** is also a deity taking many forms. Born from the churning of the ocean of milk in later stories Soma was identified with the moon. The golden haired and golden skinned god **Savitri** is an intermediary with the great power to forgive sin and as king of heaven he gives the gods their immortality. **Surya**, the god of the sun, fittingly of overpowering splendour is often described as being dark red, sitting on a red lotus or riding a chariot pulled by the seven horses of the dawn (representing the days of the week). **Usha**, sometimes referred to as Surya's wife, is the goddess of the dawn, daughter of Heaven and sister of the night. She rides in a chariot drawn by cows or horses.

Devas and Asuras In Hindu popular mythology the world is also populated by innumerable gods and demons, with a somewhat uncertain dividing line between them. Both have great power and moral character and there are frequent conflicts and battles between them.

The **Rakshasas** form another category of semi-divine beings devoted to performing magic. Although they are not themselves evil, they are destined to cause havoc and evil in the real world.

The multiple-hooded cobra head often seen in sculptures represents the fabulous snake gods the **Nagas**, though they may often be shown in other forms, even human. In South India it is particularly common to find statues of divine Nagas being worshipped. They are usually placed on uncultivated ground under trees in the hope and belief, as Masson-Oursel puts it, that "if the snakes have their own domain left to them they are more likely to spare human beings". The Nagas and their wives, the **Naginis**, are often the agents of death in mythical stories.

Hindu society
Dharma Dharma is seen as the most important of the objectives of individual and social life. But what were the obligations imposed by dharma? Hindu law givers, such as those who compiled the code of Manu (AD 100-300), laid down rules of family conduct and social obligations related to the institutions of caste and jati which were beginning to take shape at the same time.

Caste Although the word caste was given by the Portuguese in the 15th century AD, the main feature of the system emerged at the end of the Vedic period. Two terms – varna and jati – are used in India itself and have come to be used interchangeably and confusingly with the word caste.

Varna, which literally means colour, had a fourfold division. By 600 BC this had become a standard means of classifying the population. The fair-skinned Aryans distinguished themselves from the darker skinned earlier inhabitants. The priestly varna, the Brahmins, were seen as coming from the mouth of Brahma; the Kshatriyas were warriors, coming from Brahma's arms; the Vaishyas, a trading community, came from Brahma's thighs and the Sudras, classified as agriculturalists, from his feet. Relegated beyond the pale of civilized Hindu society were the untouchables or outcastes, who were left with the jobs which were regarded as impure, usually associated with dealing with the dead (human or animal) or with excrement.

Many Brahmins and Rajputs are conscious of their varna status, but the great majority of Indians do not put themselves into one of the four varna categories, but into a **jati** group. There are thousands of different jatis across the country. None of the groups regard themselves as equal in status to any other, but all are part of local or regional hierarchies. These are not organized in any institutional sense and traditionally there was no formal record of caste status. While individuals found it impossible to change caste or to move up the social scale, groups would sometimes try to gain recognition as higher caste by adopting practices of the Brahmins such as becoming vegetarians. Many used to be identified with particular activities and occupations used to be hereditary. Caste membership is decided by birth. Although you can be evicted from your caste by your fellow members, usually for disobedience to caste rules such as over marriage, you cannot join another caste and technically you become an outcaste.

Right up until Independence in 1947 such punishment was a drastic penalty for disobeying one's dharmic duty. In many areas all avenues into normal life could be blocked, families would disregard outcaste members and it could even be impossible for the outcaste to continue to work within the locality.

Gandhi spearheaded his campaign for independence from British colonial rule with a powerful campaign to abolish the disabilities imposed by the caste system. Coining the term *Harijan* (meaning 'person of God'), which he gave to all former outcastes, Gandhi demanded that discrimination on the grounds of caste be outlawed. Lists – or 'schedules' – of backward castes were drawn up during the early part of this century in order to provide positive help to such groups. The term itself has now been widely rejected by many former outcastes as paternalistic and as implying an adherence to Hindu beliefs (Hari being a Hindu deity) which some explicitly reject and today the use of the secular term '**dalits**' – the 'oppressed' has been adopted in its place. There are several websites devoted to dalit issues, including www.dalits.org.

Marriage, which is still generally arranged by members of all religious communities, continues to be dictated almost entirely by caste and clan rules. Even in cities, where traditional means of arranging marriages have often broken down and where many people resort to advertising for marriage partners in the columns of the Sunday newspapers, caste is frequently stated as a requirement. Marriage is mainly seen as an alliance between two families. Great efforts are made to match caste, social status and economic position, although rules governing eligibility vary from region to region. In some groups marriage between first cousins is common, while among others marriage between any branch of the same clan is strictly prohibited.

Hindu reform movements

In the 19th-century English education and European literature and modern scientific thought, alongside the religious ideas of Christian missionaries, all became powerful influences on the newly emerging western educated Hindu opinion. That opinion was challenged to re-examine inherited Hindu beliefs and practice.

Some reform movements have had regional importance. Two of these originated, like the **Brahmo Samaj**, in Bengal, see box above. The **Ramakrishna Mission** was named after a temple priest in the Kali temple in Calcutta, Ramakrishna (1834-1886), who was a great mystic, preaching the basic doctrine that 'all religions are true'. He believed that the best religion for any individual was that into which he or she was born. One of his followers, **Vivekananda**, became the founder of the Ramakrishna Mission, which has been an important vehicle of social and religious reform, notably in Bengal, see page 66.

Aurobindo Ghose (1872-1950) links the great reformers from the 19th century with the post-Independence period. Educated in English – and for 14 years in England itself – he developed the idea of India as 'the Mother', a concept linked with the pre-Hindu idea of Shakti, or the Mother Goddess. For him 'nationalism was religion'. After imprisonment in 1908 he retired to Pondicherry, where his ashram became a focus of an Indian and international movement.

The Hindu calendar While for its secular life India follows the Gregorian calendar, for Hindus, much of religious and personal life follows the Hindu calendar. This is based on the lunar cycle of 29 days, but the clever bit comes in the way it is synchronized with the 365 day Gregorian solar calendar of the west by the addition of an 'extra month' (*adhik maas*), every 2½-3 years.

Hindus follow two distinct eras. The *Vikrama Samvat* which began in 57 BC (and is followed in Goa), and the *Salivahan Saka* which dates from AD 78 and has been the official Indian calendar since 1957. The *Saka* new year starts on 22 March and has the same length as the Gregorian calendar. In most of South India (except Tamil Nadu) the New Year is celebrated in the first month, *Chaitra* (corresponding to March-April). In North India (and Tamil Nadu) it is celebrated in the second month of *Vaisakh*.

The year itself is divided into two, the first six solar months being when the sun 'moves' north, known as the *Makar Sankranti* (which is marked by special festivals), and the second half when it moves south, the *Karka Sankranti*. The first begins in January and the second in June. The 29 day lunar month with its 'dark' (*Krishna*) and 'bright' (*Shukla*) halves based on the new (*Amavasya*) and full moons (*Purnima*), are named after the 12 constellations, and total a 354 day year. The day itself is divided into eight *praharas* of three hours each and the year into six seasons: *Vasant* (spring), *Grishha* (summer), *Varsha* (rains), *Sharat* (early autumn), *Hemanta* (late autumn), *Shishir* (winter).

Islam

Even after partition in 1947 over 40 million Muslims remained in India and today there are around 120 million. Islamic contact with India was first made around AD 636 and then by the navies of the Arab Mohammad al Qasim in AD 710-712. These conquerors of Sindh made very few converts, although they did have to develop a legal recognition for the status of non-Muslims in a Muslim-ruled state. From the creation of the Delhi Sultanate in 1206, by Turkish rather than Arab power, Islam became a permanent living religion in India.

The victory of the Turkish ruler of Ghazni over the Rajputs in AD 1192 established a 500-year period of Muslim power in India. By AD 1200 the Turkish sultans had annexed Bihar in the east, in the process wiping out the last traces of Buddhism with the massacre of a Buddhist monastic order, sacked Varanasi and captured Gwalior. Within 30 years Bengal had been added to the Turkish empire and by AD 1311 a new Turkish dynasty, the Khaljis, had extended the power of the Delhi Sultanate to the doors of Madurai.

⁝ The five pillars of Islam

In addition to the belief that there is one God and that Mohammed is his prophet, there are four obligatory requirements imposed on Muslims. Daily prayers are prescribed at daybreak, noon, afternoon, sunset and nightfall. Muslims must give alms to the poor. They must observe a strict fast during the month of Ramadan. They must not eat or drink between sunrise and sunset. Lastly, they should attempt the pilgrimage to the Ka'aba in Mecca, known as the Hajj. Those who have done so are entitled to the prefix Hajji before their name.

Islamic rules differ from Hindu practice in several other aspects of daily life. Muslims are strictly forbidden to drink alcohol (though some suggest that this prohibition is restricted to the use of fermented grape juice, that is wine, it is commonly accepted to apply to all alcohol). Eating pork, or any meat from an animal not killed by draining its blood while alive, is also prohibited. Meat prepared in the appropriate way is called Halal. Finally, usury (charging interest on loans) and games of chance are forbidden.

Background Religion

The early Muslim rulers looked to the Turkish ruling class and to the Arab caliphs for their legitimacy and to the Turkish elite for their cultural authority. From the middle of the 13th century, when the Mongols crushed the Arab caliphate, the Delhi sultans were left on their own to exercise Islamic authority in India. From then onwards the main external influences were from Persia. Small numbers of migrants, mainly the skilled and the educated, continued to flow into the Indian courts. Periodically their numbers were augmented by refugees from Mongol repression in the regions to India's northwest as the Delhi Sultanate provided a refuge for craftsmen and artists from the territories the Mongols had conquered from Lahore westwards.

Muslim populations Muslims only became a majority of the South Asian population in the plains of the Indus and west Punjab and in parts of Bengal. Elsewhere they formed important minorities, notably in the towns of the central heartland such as Lucknow. The concentration at the east and west ends of the Ganga valley reflected the policies pursued by successive Muslim rulers of colonizing forested and previously uncultivated land. In the central plains there was already a densely populated, Hindu region, where little attempt was made to achieve converts.

The Mughals wanted to expand their territory and their economic base. To pursue this they made enormous grants of land to those who had served the empire and particularly in Bengal, new land was brought into cultivation. At the same time, shrines were established to Sufi saints who attracted peasant farmers. The mosques built in East Bengal were the centres of devotional worship where saints were venerated. By the 18th century many Muslims had joined the **Sunni** sect of Islam. The characteristics of Islamic practice in both these regions continues to reflect this background.

In some areas Muslim society shared many of the characteristic features of the Hindu society from which the majority of them came. Many of the Muslim migrants from Iran or Turkey, the elite **Ashraf** communities, continued to identify with the Islamic elites from which they traced their descent. They held high military and civil posts in imperial service. In sharp contrast, many of the non-Ashraf Muslim communities in the towns and cities were organized in social groups very much like the *jatis* of their neighbouring Hindu communities. While the elites followed Islamic practices close to those based on the Qur'an as interpreted by scholars, the poorer, less literate communities followed devotional and pietistic forms of Islam.

Muslim beliefs The beliefs of Islam (which means 'submission to God') could apparently scarcely be more different from those of Hinduism. Islam, often described as having "five pillars" of faith (see box above) has a fundamental creed; 'There is no God but God; and Mohammad is the Prophet of God' (*La Illaha illa 'Ilah Mohammad Rasulu 'Ilah*). One book, the Qur'an, is the supreme authority on Islamic teaching and faith. Islam preaches the belief in bodily resurrection after death and in the reality of heaven and hell.

The idea of heaven as paradise is pre-Islamic. Alexander the Great is believed to have brought the word into Greek from Persia, where he used it to describe the walled Persian gardens that were found even three centuries before the birth of Christ. For Muslims, Paradise is believed to be filled with sensuous delights and pleasures, while hell is a place of eternal terror and torture, which is the certain fate of all who deny the unity of God.

Islam has no priesthood. The authority of Imams derives from social custom and from their authority to interpret the scriptures, rather than from a defined status within the Islamic community. Islam also prohibits any distinction on the basis of race or colour and most Muslims believe it is wrong to represent the human figure. It is often thought, inaccurately, that this ban stems from the Qur'an itself. In fact it probably has its origins in the belief of Mohammad that images were likely to be turned into idols.

Muslim sects During the first century after Mohammad's death Islam split in to two sects which were divided on political and religious grounds, the Shi'is and Sunni's. The religious basis for the division lay in the interpretation of verses in the Qur'an and of traditional sayings of Mohammad, the Hadis. Both sects venerate the Qur'an but have different *Hadis*. They also have different views as to Mohammad's successor.

The **Sunnis** – always the majority in South Asia – believe that Mohammad did not appoint a successor and that Abu Bak'r, Omar and Othman were the first three caliphs (or vice-regents) after Mohammad's death. Ali, whom the Sunni's count as the fourth caliph, is regarded as the first legitimate caliph by the Shi'is, who consider Abu Bak'r and Omar to be usurpers. While the Sunni's believe in the principle of election of caliphs, Shi'is believe that although Mohammad is the last prophet there is a continuing need for intermediaries between God and man. Such intermediaries are termed Imams and they base both their law and religious practice on the teaching of the Imams.

Akbar, the most eclectic of Mughal emperors, went as far as banning activities like cow slaughter which were offensive to Hindus and celebrated Hindu festivals in court. In contrast, the later Mughal Emperor, Aurangzeb, pursued a far more hostile approach to Hindus and Hinduism, trying to point up the distinctiveness of Islam and denying the validity of Hindu religious beliefs. That attitude generally became stronger in the 20th century, related to the growing sense of the Muslim's minority position within South Asia and the fear of being subjected to Hindu rule.

The Islamic calendar The calendar begins on 16 July 622 AD, the date of the Prophet's migration from Mecca to Medina, the Hijra, hence AH (Anno Hejirae). *Murray's Handbook for travellers in India* gave a wonderfully precise method of calculating the current date in the Christian year from the AH date: "To correlate the Hijra year with the Christian year, express the former in years and decimals of a year, multiply by .970225, add 621.54 and the total will correspond exactly with the Christian year".

The Muslim year is divided into 12 lunar months, totalling 354 or 355 days, hence Islamic festivals usually move 11 days earlier each year according to the solar (Gregorian) calendar. The first month of the year is *Moharram*, followed by *Safar, Rabi-ul-Awwal, Rabi-ul-Sani, Jumada-ul-Awwal, Jumada-ul-Sani, Rajab, Shaban, Ramadan, Shawwal, Ziquad* and *Zilhaj*.

Buddhism

India was the home of Buddhism, which had its roots in the early Hinduism, or Brahmanism, of its time. Today it is practised only on the margins of the subcontinent, from Ladakh, Nepal and Bhutan in the north to Sri Lanka in the south, where it is the religion of the majority Sinhalese community. Most are very recent converts, the last adherents of the early schools of Buddhism having been killed or converted by the Muslim invaders of the 13th century. However, India's Buddhist significance is now mainly as the home for the extraordinarily beautiful artistic and architectural remnants of what was for several centuries the region's dominant religion.

India has sites of great significance for Buddhists around the world. Some say that the Buddha himself spoke of the four places his followers should visit. **Lumbini**, the Buddha's birthplace, is in the Nepali foothills, near the present border with India. **Bodh Gaya**, where he attained what Buddhists term his 'supreme enlightenment', is about 80 km south of the modern Indian city of Patna; the deer park at **Sarnath**, where he preached his first sermon and set in motion the Wheel of the Law, is just outside Varanasi; and **Kushinagara**, where he died at the age of 80, is 50 km east of Gorakhpur. There were four other sacred places of pilgrimage – **Rajgir**, where he tamed a wild elephant; **Vaishali**, where a monkey offered him honey; **Sravasti**, associated with his great miracle; and **Sankasya**, where he descended from heaven. The eight significant events associated with the holy places are repeatedly represented in Buddhist art.

In addition there are remarkable monuments, sculptures and works of art, from Gandhara in modern Pakistan to Sanchi and Ajanta in central India, where it is still possible to see the vivid evidence of the flowering of Buddhist culture in South Asia. In Sri Lanka, Bhutan and Nepal the traditions remain alive.

The Buddha's Life Siddharta Gautama, who came to be given the title of the Buddha – the Enlightened One – was born a prince into the warrior caste in about 563 BC. He was married at the age of 16 and his wife had a son. When he reached the age of 29 he left home and wandered as a beggar and ascetic. After about six years he spent some time in Bodh Gaya. Sitting under the Bo tree, meditating, he was tempted by the demon Mara, with all the desires of the world. Resisting these temptations, he received enlightenment. These scenes are common motifs of Buddhist art.

The next landmark was the preaching of his first sermon on 'The Foundation of Righteousness' in the deer park near Benaras. By the time he died the Buddha had established a small band of monks and nuns known as the *Sangha* and had followers across North India. His body was cremated and the ashes, regarded as precious relics, were divided among the peoples to whom he had preached. Some have been discovered as far west as Peshawar, in Pakistan and at Piprawa, close to his birthplace.

After the Buddha's death From the Buddha's death, or *parinirvana*, to the destruction of Nalanda (the last Buddhist stronghold in India) in AD 1197, Buddhism in India went through three phases. These are often referred to as Hinayana, Mahayana and Vajrayana, though they were not mutually exclusive, being followed simultaneously in different regions.

Hinayana The Hinayana or Lesser Way insists on a monastic way of life as the only path to the personal goal of *nirvana*, see box page 312, achieved through an austere life. Divided into many schools, the only surviving Hinayana tradition is the **Theravada Buddhism**, which was taken to Sri Lanka by the Emperor Asoka's son Mahinda, where it became the state religion, and spread to southeast Asia as practised in Thailand, Myanmar, Cambodia and Laos today. Suffering, sorrow and dissatisfaction are the

⁝ The Buddha's Four Noble Truths

The Buddha preached Four Noble Truths: that life is painful; that suffering is caused by ignorance and desire; that beyond the suffering of life there is a state which cannot be described but which he termed nirvana; and that nirvana can be reached by following an eightfold path.

The concept of nirvana is often understood in the west in an entirely negative sense – that of 'non-being'. The word has the rough meaning of 'blow out' or 'extinguish', meaning to blow out the fires of greed, lust and desire. In a more positive sense it has been described by one Buddhist scholar as "the state of absolute illumination, supreme bliss, infinite love and compassion, unshakeable serenity and unrestricted spiritual freedom". The essential elements of the eightfold path are the perfection of wisdom, morality and meditation.

nature of ordinary life and can only be eliminated by giving up desire. In turn, desire is a result of the misplaced belief in the reality of individual existence. Theravada Buddhism taught that there is no soul and ultimately no God. *Nirvana* is a state of rest beyond the universe, once found never lost.

Mahayana In contrast to the Hinayana schools, the followers of the Mahayana school (the Great Way) believed in the possibility of salvation for all. They practised a far more devotional form of meditation and new figures came to play a prominent part in their beliefs and their worship – the **Bodhisattvas,** saints who were predestined to reach the state of enlightenment through thousands of rebirths. They aspired to Buddhahood, however, not for their own sake but for the sake of all living things. The Buddha is believed to have passed through numerous existences in preparation for his final mission. Mahayana Buddhism became dominant over most of South Asia and its influence is evidenced in Buddhist art from Gandhara in north Pakistan to Ajanta in Central India and Sigiriya in Sri Lanka.

Vajrayana A new branch of Buddhism, Vajrayana, or the Vehicle of the Thunderbold, appeared which began to lay stress on secret magical rituals and cults of female divinities. This new 'Diamond Way' adopted the practice of magic, yoga and meditation. It became associated with secret ceremonies, chanting of mystical 'mantras' and taking part in orgiastic rituals in the cause of spiritual gain in order to help others. The ideal of Vajrayana Buddhists is to be 'so fully in harmony with the cosmos as to be able to manipulate the cosmic forces within and outside himself'. It had developed in the north of India by the seventh century AD, matching the parallel growth of Hindu Tantrism. The magical power associated with Vajrayana requires instruction from a teacher or Lama, hence the Tibetan form is sometimes referred to as 'Lamaistic'.

Buddhist beliefs Buddhism is based on the Buddha's own preaching. However, when he died none of those teachings had been written down. He developed his beliefs in reaction to the Brahmanism of his time, rejecting several of the doctrines of Vedic religion which were widely held in his lifetime: the Vedic gods, scriptures and priesthood and all social distinctions based on caste. However, he did accept the belief in the cyclical nature of life and that the nature of an individual's existence is determined by a natural process of reward and punishment for deeds in previous lives – the Hindu doctrine of karma, see page 298. In the Buddha's view, though, there is no eternal soul. He denied the identification of the Self with the everchanging Mind-Body (here, some see parallels in the Advaita Vedanta philosophy of

Self-*Brahman* in Hinduism). In Buddhism, *Anatta* (no-Self), overcame the egoistical Self, given to attachment and selfishness.

Following the Buddha's death a succession of councils was called to try and reach agreement on doctrine. The first three were held within 140 years of the Buddha's death, the fourth being held at Pataliputra (modern Patna) during the reign of the Emperor Asoka (272-232 BC), who had recently been converted to Buddhism. Under his reign Buddhism spread throughout South Asia and opened the routes through Northwest India for Buddhism to travel into China, where it had become a force by the first century AD.

Buddhism's decline The decline of Buddhism in India probably stemmed as much from the growing similarity in the practice of Hinduism and Buddhism as from direct attacks. Mahayana Buddhism, with its reverence for Bodhisattvas and its devotional character, was increasingly difficult to distinguish from the revivalist Hinduism characteristic of several parts of North India from the seventh to the 12th centuries AD. The Muslim conquest dealt the final death blow, as it was also accompanied by the large scale slaughter of monks as well as the destruction of monasteries. Without their institutional support Buddhism faded away.

Jainism

Like Buddhism, Jainism started as a reform movement of the Brahmanic religious beliefs of the sixth century BC. Its founder was a widely revered saint and ascetic, Vardhamma, who became known as **Mahavir** – 'great hero'. Mahavir was born in the same border region of India and Nepal as the Buddha, just 50 km north of modern Patna, probably in 599 BC. His family, also royal, were followers of an ascetic saint, Parsvanatha, who according to Jain tradition had lived 200 years previously.

Mahavir's life story is embellished with legends, but there is no doubt that he left his royal home for a life of the strict ascetic. He is believed to have received enlightenment after 12 years of rigorous hardship, penance and meditation. Afterwards he travelled and preached for 30 years, stopping only in the rainy season. He died aged 72 in 527 BC. His death was commemorated by a special lamp festival in the region of Bihar, which Jains claim is the basis of the now-common Hindu festival of lights, Diwali.

Unlike Buddhism, Jainism never spread beyond India, but it has survived continuously into modern India, with four million adherents. In part this may be because Jain beliefs have much in common with puritanical forms of Hinduism and are greatly respected and admired. Some Jain ideas, such as vegetarianism and reverence for all life, are widely recognized by Hindus as highly commendable. The value Jains place on non-violence has contributed to their importance in business, as they regard nearly all occupations except banking and commerce as violent.

Jain beliefs Jains (from the word Jina, literally meaning 'descendants of conquerors') believe that there are two fundamental principles, the living (*jiva*) and the non-living (*ajiva*). The essence of Jain belief is that all life is sacred and that every living entity, even the smallest insect, has within it an indestructible and immortal soul. Jains developed the view of ahimsa – often translated as 'non-violence', but better perhaps as 'non-harming'. Ahimsa was the basis for the entire scheme of Jain values and ethics and alternative codes of practice were defined for householders and for ascetics.

The five vows may be taken both by monks and by lay people: not to harm any living beings (Jains must practise strict vegetarianism-and even some vegetables, such as potatoes and onions, are believed to have microscopic souls); to speak the truth; not to steal; to give up sexual relations and practice complete chastity; to give up all possessions-for the *Digambara* sect that includes clothes.

Celibacy is necessary to combat physical desire. Jains also regard the manner of dying as extremely important. Although suicide is deeply opposed, vows of fasting to death voluntarily may be regarded as earning merit in the proper context. Mahavir himself is believed to have died of self-starvation. The essence of all the rules is to avoid intentional injury, which is the worst of all sins. Like Hindus, the Jains believe in *karma*.

Jains have two main **sects**, whose origins can be traced back to the fourth century BC. The more numerous **Svetambaras** – the 'white clad' – concentrated more in eastern and western India, separated from the **Digambaras** – or 'sky-clad'– who often go naked. The Digambaras may well have been forced to move south by drought and famine in the northern region of the Deccan and they are now concentrated in the south of India.

Unlike Buddhists, Jains accept the idea of God, but not as a creator of the universe. They see him in the lives of the 24 **Tirthankaras** (prophets, or literally 'makers of fords' – a reference to their role in building crossing points for the spiritual journey over the river of life), or leaders of Jainism, whose lives are recounted in the Kalpsutra – the third century BC book of ritual for the Svetambaras. Mahavir is regarded as the last of these great spiritual leaders. Much Jain art details stories from these accounts and the Tirthankaras play a similar role for Jains as the Bodhisattvas do for Mahayana Buddhists. The first and most revered of the Tirthankaras, Adinatha, also known as Rishabnath, is widely represented in Jain temples.

Sikhism

Guru Nanak, the founder of the religion was born just west of Lahore and grew up in what is now the Pakistani town of Sultanpur. His followers, the Sikhs, (derived from the Sanskrit word for 'disciples') form perhaps one of India's most recognizable groups. Beards and turbans give them a very distinctive presence and although they represent less than 2% of the population they are both politically and economically significant.

Sikh beliefs The first Guru, accepted the ideas of *samsara* – the cycle of rebirths – and *karma*, see page 298, from Hinduism. However, Sikhism is unequivocal in its belief in the oneness of God, rejecting idolatry and any worship of objects or images. Guru Nanak believed that God is One, formless, eternal and beyond description.

Guru Nanak also fiercely opposed discrimination on the grounds of caste. He saw God as present everywhere, visible to anyone who cared to look and as essentially full of grace and compassion. Some of Guru Nanak's teachings are close to the ideas of the Benaras mystic **Kabir**, who, in common with the Muslim mystic sufis, believed in mystical union with God. Kabir's belief in the nature of God was matched by his view that man was deliberately blind and unwilling to recognize God's nature. He transformed the Hindu concept of *maya* into the belief that the values commonly held by the world were an illusion.

Guru Nanak preached that salvation depended on accepting the nature of God. If people recognized the true harmony of the divine order (*hookam*) they would be saved. Rejecting the prevailing Hindu belief that such harmony could be achieved by ascetic practices, he emphasized three actions: meditating on and repeating God's name (*naam*), 'giving', or charity (*daan*) and bathing (*isnaan*).

Many of the features now associated with Sikhism can be attributed to **Guru Gobind Singh**, who on 15 April 1699, started the new brotherhood called the *Khalsa* (meaning 'the pure', from the Persian word *khales*), an inner core of the faithful, accepted by baptism (*amrit*). The 'five ks' date from this period: *kesh* (uncut hair), the most important, followed by *kangha* (comb, usually of wood), *kirpan* (dagger or short sword), *kara* (steel bangle) and *kachh* (similar to 'boxer' shorts). The dagger and the shorts reflect military influence.

In addition to the compulsory 'five ks', the new code prohibited smoking, eating *halal* meat and sexual intercourse with Muslim women. These date from the 18th century, when the Sikhs were often in conflict with the Muslims. Other strict prohibitions include: idolatry, caste discrimination, hypocrisy and pilgrimage to Hindu sacred places. The Khalsa also explicitly forbade the seclusion of women, one of the common practices of Islam. It was only under the warrior king Ranjit Singh (1799-1838) that the idea of the Guru's presence in meetings of the Sikh community (the *Panth*) gave way to the now universally held belief in the total authority of the **Guru Granth**, the recorded words of the Guru in the scripture.

Sikh worship The meditative worship Guru Nanak commended is a part of the life of every devout Sikh today, who starts each day with private meditation and a recitation of the verses of Guru Nanak himself, the *Japji*. However, from the time of the third Guru, Sikhs have also worshipped as congregations in Gurudwaras ('gateways to the Guru'). The Golden Temple in Amritsar, built at the end of the 16th century, is the holiest site of Sikhism.

The present institutions of Sikhism owe their origins to 19th-century reform movements. Under the Sikh Gurudwaras Act of 1925 all temples were restored to the management of a Central Gurudwara Management Committee, thereby removing them from the administrative control of the Hindus under which many had come. This body has acted as the religion's controlling body ever since.

Christianity

There are about 23 million Christians in India. Christianity ranks third in terms of religious affiliation after Hinduism and Islam and there are Christian congregations in all the major towns of India.

The great majority of the Protestant Christians in India are now members of the Church of South India, formed from the major Protestant denominations in 1947, or the Church of North India, which followed suit in 1970. Together they account for approximately half the total number of Christians. Roman Catholics make up the majority of the rest. Many of the church congregations, both in towns and villages, are active centres of Christian worship.

Origins Some of the churches owe their origin either to the modern missionary movement of the late 18th century onwards, or to the colonial presence of the European powers. However, Christians probably arrived in India during the first century after the birth of Christ. There is evidence that one of Christ's Apostles, **Thomas,** reached India in 52 AD, only 20 years after Christ was crucified. He settled in Malabar and then expanded his missionary work to China. It is widely believed that he was martyred in Tamil Nadu on his return to India in AD 72 and is buried in Mylapore, in the suburbs of modern Chennai. St Thomas' Mount, a small rocky hill just north of Chennai airport, takes its name from him. Today there is still a church of Thomas Christians in Kerala.

Northern missions Protestant missions in Bengal from the end of the 18th century had a profound influence on cultural and religious development. In November 1793 the Baptist missionary **William Carey** reached the Hugli River. Although he went to India to preach, he was also interested in languages and education and the work of 19th-century missions rapidly widened to cover educational and medical work as well. See page 69.

Converts were made most readily among the backward castes and in the tribal areas. The Christian populations of the tribal hill areas of Nagaland and Assam stem from such late 19th-century and 20th-century movements. But the influence of Christian missions in education and medical work was greater than as a proselytizing force.

Education in Christian schools stimulated reformist movements in Hinduism itself and mission hospitals supplemented government-run hospitals, particularly in remote areas. Some of these Christian-run hospitals, such as that at Vellore, continue to provide high class medical care.

Christian beliefs Christian theology had its roots in Judaism, with its belief in one God, the eternal Creator of the universe. Judaism saw the Jewish people as the vehicle for God's salvation, the 'chosen people of God' and pointed to a time when God would send his Saviour, or Messiah. Jesus, whom Christians believe was 'the Christ' or Messiah, was born in the village of Bethlehem, some 20 km south of Jerusalem. Very little is known of his early life except that he was brought up in a devout Jewish family. At the age of 29 or 30 he gathered a small group of followers and began to preach in the region between the Dead Sea and the Sea of Galilee. Two years later he was crucified in Jerusalem by the authorities on the charge of blasphemy – that he claimed to be the son of God.

Christians believe that all people live in a state of sin, in the sense that they are separated from God and fail to do his will. They believe that God is personal, 'like a father'. As God's son, Jesus accepted the cost of that separation and sinfulness himself through his death on the cross. Christians believe that Jesus was raised from the dead on the third day after he was crucified and that he appeared to his closest followers. They believe that his spirit continues to live today and that he makes it possible for people to come back to God.

The New Testament of the Bible, which, alongside the Old Testament, is the text to which Christians refer as the ultimate scriptural authority, consists of four 'Gospels' (meaning 'good news') and a series of letters by several early Christians referring to the nature of the Christian life.

Christian worship Although Christians are encouraged to worship individually as well as together, most forms of Christian worship centre on the gathering of the church congregation for praise, prayer and the preaching of God's word, which usually takes verses from the Bible as its starting point. Different denominations place varying emphases on the main elements of worship, but in most church services today the congregation will take part in singing hymns (songs of praise), prayers will be led by the minister, priest or a member of the congregation, readings from the Bible will be given and a sermon preached. For many Christians the most important service is the act of Holy Communion (Protestant) or Mass (Catholic) which celebrates the death and resurrection of Jesus in sharing bread and wine, which are held to represent Christ's body and blood given to save people from their sin.

Zoroastrianism

The first Zoroastrians arrived on the west coast of India in the mid-eighth century AD, forced out from their native Iran by persecution of the invading Islamic Arabs. Until 1477 they lost all contact with Iran and then for nearly 300 years maintained contact with Persian Zoroastrians through a continuous exchange of letters. They became known by their now much more familiar name, the **Parsis** (or Persians).

Although they are a tiny minority (approximately 100,000), even in the cities where they are concentrated, they have been a prominent economic and social influence, especially in West India. Parsis adopted westernized customs and dress and took to the new economic opportunities that came with colonial industrialization. Families in West India such as the Tatas continue to be among India's leading industrialists, just part of a community that in recent generations has spread to Europe and north America.

⁝ Hill tribes

The hill tribes of the 635 "scheduled" tribes listed in the Indian Constitution, 213 have their traditional homelands in the remote hill states of Northeast India. Bordered by Bhutan and China to the north, Myanmar to the east and Bangladesh to the west, the people are of Mongoloid origin, speaking a variety of Sino-Tibetan languages. Tribal culture and religion is firmly rooted in the flora and fauna of the forests that once covered this humid tropical region; traditional dress comprises woven shawls, often in black, red and yellow, sometimes accompanied by extravagant headgear decorated with the beaks and feathers of the indigenous hornbill. Early anthropologists declared the various tribal religions to be animistic, but many scholars argue that the core tribal belief is in a single "High God" – a fact that may have expedited the widespread conversion to Christianity, now the dominant religion in the region.

Until the arrival of the British in the 1820s, the hill tribes had remained beyond the reach of colonising Indian empires, but since the creation of Assam, a strategic move in the 19th century "Great Game" designed to forestall Chinese expansion in India, and especially since the creation of Bangladesh after Partition in 1947, the hill regions have been flooded with immigrants from the Ganges delta. Despite the government granting ethnically based territories to some of the major tribal groups – the States of Nagland, Mizoram and Manipur – displacement by Bengali migrants has rendered tribes a minority elsewhere in the northeast. Rapid economic development in the region has caused much of the region's cultural heritage to disappear, while separatist groups in Nagaland, Manipur and Assam have begun to adopt political violence as a means to win independence from India.

Origins Zoroastrians trace their beliefs to the prophet Zarathustra, who lived in Northeast Iran around the seventh or sixth century BC. His place and even date of birth are uncertain, but he almost certainly enjoyed the patronage of the father of Darius the Great. The passage of Alexander the Great through Iran severely weakened support for Zoroastrianism, but between the sixth century BC and the seventh century AD it was the major religion of peoples living from North India to central Turkey. The spread of Islam reduced the number of Zoroastrians dramatically and forced those who did not retreat to the desert to emigrate.

Parsi beliefs The early development of Zoroastrianism marked a movement towards belief in a single God. **Ahura Mazda**, the Good Religion of God, was shown in rejecting evil and in purifying thought, word and action. Fire plays a central and symbolic part in Zoroastrian worship, representing the presence of God. There are eight Atash Bahram – major fire temples – in India; four are in Mumbai, two in Surat and one each in Navsari and Udwada. There are many more minor temples, where the rituals are far less complex – perhaps 40 in Mumbai alone.

Earth, fire and air are all regarded as sacred, while death is the result of evil. Dead matter pollutes all it touches. Where there is a suitable space therefore, dead bodies are simply placed in the open to be consumed by vultures, as at the Towers of Silence in Mumbai. However, burial and cremation are also common.

Land and environment

Geography

The origins of India's landscapes

Only 100 million years ago the Indian Peninsula was still attached to the great land mass called 'Pangaea' alongside South Africa, Australia and Antarctica. Then as the great plates on which the earth's southern continents stood broke up, the Indian Plate started its dramatic shift northwards, eventually colliding with the Asian plate. As the Indian Plate continues to get pushed under the Tibetan Plateau so the Himalaya continue to rise. Northeast India falls into two major geological regions. The north is enclosed by the great arc of the Himalaya, while along their southern flank lie the alluvial plains of the Ganga.

The Himalaya The Himilaya dominate the northern borders of India, stretching 2500 km from northwest to southeast. Of the 94 mountains in Asia above 7300 m, all but two are in the Himalaya. Nowhere else in the world are there mountains as high. The Himalaya proper, stretching from the Pamirs in Pakistan to the easternmost bend of the Brahmaputra in Assam, can be divided into three broad zones. On the southern flank are the Shiwaliks, or Outer Ranges. To their immediate north run the parallel Middle Ranges of Pir Panjal and Dhauladhar and to the north again is the third zone, the Inner Himalaya, which has the highest peaks, many of them in Nepal. The central core of the Himalayan ranges did not begin to rise until about 35 million years ago. The latest mountain building period, responsible for the Shiwaliks, began less than five million years ago and is still continuing, raising some of the high peaks by as much as 5 mm a year. Such movement comes at a price and the boundary between the plains and the Himalayan ranges is a zone of continuing violent earthquakes and massive erosion.

The Gangetic Plains As the Himalaya began their dramatic uplift, the trough which formed to the south of the newly emerging mountains was steadily filled with the debris washed down from the hills, creating the Indo-Gangetic plains. Today the alluvium reaches depths of over 3000 m in places (and over 22 km at the mouth of the Ganga in Bangladesh), and contains some of the largest reserves of underground water in the world. These have made possible extensive well irrigation, especially in Northwest India, contributing to the rapid agricultural changes which have taken place.

The Indo-Gangetic plains are still being extended and modified. The southern part of Bengal only emerged from the sea during the last 5000 years. The Ganga and the Indus have each been estimated to carry over one million tonnes of silt every year – considerably more than the Mississippi. The silts washed down from the Himalaya have made it possible for intensive rice cultivation to be practised continuously for hundreds of years, though they cause problems for modern irrigation development. Dams in the Himalayan region are being rapidly filled by silt, over 33 million tonnes being deposited behind the Bhakra Dam on the Sutlej River alone.

Climate

The monsoon The term monsoon refers to the wind reversal which replaces the dry northeasterlies, characteristic of winter and spring, with the very warm and wet southwesterlies of the summer. The arrival of the monsoon is as variable as is the amount of rain which it brings. What makes the Indian monsoon quite exceptional is not its regularity but the depth of moist air which passes over the subcontinent. Over India, the highly unstable moist airflow is over 6000 m thick compared with 2000 m over Japan, giving rise to the bursts of torrential rain which mark out the wet season.

Winter In winter, high pressure builds up over Central Asia. Most of India is protected from the cold northeast monsoon winds that result by the massive bulk of the Himalaya and daytime temperatures rise sharply in the sun. Right across the Ganga plains night temperatures fall to below 5°C in January and February. To the south the winter temperatures increase having a minimum temperature of around 20°C. Although much of North India often has beautiful weather from November through to March, there are periods when it is cool and overcast.

Summer From April onwards much of India becomes almost unbearably hot. Temperatures of over 50°C are not unknown. It is a time of year to get up to the hills. At the end of May very moist southwesterlies sweep across South India and the Bay of Bengal. They then double back northwestwards, bringing tremendously heavy rain first to the eastern Himalaya then gradually spreading northwestwards.

The wet season The monsoon season, which lasts from between three and five months depending on the region, brings an enveloping dampness which makes it very difficult to keep things dry. If you are travelling in the wetter parts of India during the monsoon you need to be prepared for extended periods of torrential rain and major disruption to travel. However, many parts of India receive a total of under 1000 mm a year, mainly in the form of heavy isolated showers.

Storms Some regions of India suffer major storms. Cyclones may hit the east coast causing enormous damage and loss of life, the risk being greatest between the end of October and early December. In Northwest India, 'the Loo', between April and June, brings dust storms and very hot winds. In Bengal Nor'westers can cause enormous damage in April-May

Humidity The coastal regions have humidity levels above 70% for most of the year which can be very uncomfortable. However, sea breezes often bring some relief on the coast itself. Moving north and inland, between December-May humidity drops sharply, often falling as low as 20% during the daytime.

Vegetation

India's tropical location and its position astride the wet monsoonal winds ensured that 16 different forest types were represented in India. The most widespread was tropical dry deciduous forest. Areas with more than 1700 mm of rainfall had tropical moist deciduous, semi-evergreen or wet evergreen forest, while much of the remainder had types ranging from tropical dry deciduous woodland to dry alpine scrub, found at high altitudes. However, today forest cover has been reduced to about 13% of the surface area, mainly the result of the great demand for wood as a fuel.

Deciduous forest Two types of deciduous tree remain particularly important, **Sal** (*Shorea robusta*), now found mainly in eastern India and **Teak** (*Tectona grandis*). Most teak today has been planted. Both are resistant to burning, which helped to protect them where people used fire as a means of clearing the forest.

Mountain forests and grassland At between 1000-2000 m in the eastern hill ranges of India and in Bhutan, for example, wet hill forest includes evergreen oaks and chestnuts. Further west in the foothills of the Himalaya are belts of subtropical pine at roughly the same altitudes. Deodars (*Cedrus deodarus*) form large stands and moist temperate forest, with pines, cedars, firs and spruce, is dominant, giving many of the valleys a beautifully fresh, alpine feel. Between 3000-4000 m alpine forest predominates. Rhododendron are often mixed with other forest types. Birch, juniper, poplars and pine are widespread.

There are several varieties of coarse grassland found along the southern edge of the Terai and alpine grasses are important for grazing above altitudes of 2000 m. A totally distinctive grassland is the bamboo (*Dendo calamus*) region, which is found in the eastern Himalaya.

Flowering trees Many Indian trees are planted along roadsides to provide shade and they often also produce beautiful flowers. The **Silk Cotton Tree** (*Bombax ceiba*), up to 25 m in height, is one of the most dramatic. The pale greyish bark of this buttressed tree usually bears conical spines. It has wide spreading branches and keeps its leaves for most of the year. The flowers, which appear when the tree is leafless, are cup-shaped, with curling, rather fleshy red petals up to 12 cm long while the fruit produce the fine, silky cotton which gives it its name.

Other common trees with red or orange flowers include the Dhak (also called 'Flame of the forest' or *Palas*), the Gulmohur, the Indian coral tree and the Tulip tree. The smallish (6 m) deciduous **Dhak** (*Butea monosperma*), has light grey bark and a gnarled, twisted trunk and thick, leathery leaves. The large, bright orange and sweet pea-shaped flowers appear on leafless branches. The 8-9 m high umbrella-shaped **Gulmohur** (*Delonix regia*), a native of Madagascar, is grown as a shade tree in towns. The fiery coloured flowers make a magnificent display after the tree has shed its feathery leaves. The scarlet flowers of the **Indian Coral Tree** (*Erythrina indica*) appear when its branches with thorny bark are leafless. The tall **Tulip Tree** (*Spathodea campanulata*) (not to be confused with the North American one) has a straight, darkish brown, slender trunk. It is usually evergreen except in the drier parts of India. The scarlet bell-shaped, tulip-like, flowers grow in profusion at the ends of the branches from November to March.

Often seen along roadsides the **Jacaranda** (*Jacaranda mimosaefolia*), has attractive feathery foliage and purple-blue thimble-shaped flowers up to 40 mm long. When not in flower it resembles a Gulmohur, but differs in its general shape. The valuable **Tamarind** (*Tamarindus indica*), with a short straight trunk and a spreading crown, often grows along the roadside. An evergreen with feathery leaves, it bears small clusters of yellow and red flowers. The noticeable fruit pods are long, curved and swollen at intervals. In parts of India, the rights to the fruit are auctioned off annually for up to Rs 4000 (US$100) per tree.

Of these trees the Silk cotton, the Dhak and the Indian coral are native to India. Others were introduced mostly during the last century: the Tulip tree from East Africa, the Jacaranda from Brazil and the Tamarind, possibly from Africa.

Fruit trees The familiar apple, plum, apricot and cherry grow in the cool upland areas of India. In the warmer plains tropical fruits flourish. The large, spreading **Mango** (*Mangifera indica*) bears the delicious, distinctively shaped fruit that comes in hundreds of varieties. The evergreen **Jackfruit** (*Artocarpus heterophyllus*) has dark green leathery leaves. The huge fruit (up to 90 cm long and 40 cm thick), growing from a short stem directly off the trunk and branches, has a rough, almost prickly skin and is almost sickly sweet. The **Banana** plant (*Musa*), actually a gigantic herb (up to 5 m high) arising from an underground stem, has very large leaves which grow directly off the trunk. Each large purplish flower produces bunches of up to 100 bananas. The **Papaya** (*Carica papaya*) grows to about 4 m with the large hand-shaped leaves clustered near the top. Only the female tree bears the fruit, which hang down close to the trunk just below the leaves.

Palm trees **Coconut Palms** (*Cocos nucifera*) are extremely common all round the coast of India. It has tall (15-25 m), slender, unbranched trunks, feathery leaves and large green or golden fruit with soft white flesh filled with milky water, so different from the brown fibre-covered inner nut which makes its way to Europe. The 10-15 m high **Palmyra palms** (*Borassus flabellifer*), indigenous to South and East India, have very distinctive fan-like leaves, as much as 150 cm across. The fruit, which is smaller than a coconut, is round, almost black and very shiny. The **Betel Nut Palm** (*Areca catechu*) resembles the coconut palm, its slender trunk bearing ring marks left by fallen leaf stems. The smooth, round nuts, only about 3 cm across, grow in large hanging bunches. **Wild Date Palms** (*Phoenix sylvestris*), originally came from North

Africa. About 20-25 m tall, the trunks are also marked with the ring bases of the leaves which drop off. The distinctive leaflets which stick out from the central vein give the leaf a spiky appearance. Bunches of dates are only borne by the female tree.

All these palm trees are of considerable **commercial importance**. From the fruit alone the coconut palm produces coir from the outer husk, copra from the fleshy kernel from which coconut oil or coconut butter is extracted, in addition to the desiccated coconut and coconut milk. The sap is fermented to a drink called toddy. A similar drink is produced from the sap of the wild date and the palmyra palms which are also important for sugar production. The fruit of the betel nut palm is wrapped in a special leaf and chewed. The trunks and leaves of all the palms are widely used in building and thatching.

Other trees Of all Indian trees the **Banyan** (*Ficus benghalensis*) is probably the best known. It is planted by temples, in villages and along roads. The seeds often germinate in the cracks of old walls, the growing roots splitting the wall apart. If it grows in the bark of another tree, it sends down roots towards the ground. As it grows, more roots appear from the branches, until the original host tree is surrounded by a 'cage' which eventually strangles it. The famous one in Kolkata's Botanical Gardens is more than 400 m in circumference.

Related to the banyan, the **Pipal** or Peepul (*Ficus religiosa*), also cracks open walls and strangles other trees with its roots. With a smooth grey bark, it too is commonly found near temples and shrines. You can distinguish it from the banyan by the absence of aerial roots and its large, heart-shaped leaf with a point tapering into a pronounced 'tail'. It bears abundant 'figs' of a purplish tinge which are about 1 cm across.

The **Ashok** or **Mast** (*Polyalthia longifolia*) is a tall evergreen which can reach 15 m or more in height. One variety, often seen in avenues, is trimmed and tapers towards the top. The leaves are long, slender and shiny and narrow to a long point.

Acacia trees with their feathery leaves are fairly common in the drier parts of India. The best known is the **Babul** (*Acacia arabica*) with a rough, dark bark. The leaves have long silvery white thorns at the base and consist of many leaflets while the flowers grow in golden balls about 1 cm across.

The **Eucalyptus** or **Gum Tree** (*Eucalyptus grandis*), introduced from Australia in the 19th century, is now widespread and is planted near villages to provide both shade and firewood. There are various forms but all may be readily recognized by their height, their characteristic long, thin leaves which have a pleasant fresh smell and the colourful peeling bark.

The wispy **Casuarina** (*Casuarina*) grows in poor sandy soil, especially on the coast and on village waste land. It has the typical leaves of a pine tree and the cones are small and prickly to walk on. It is said to attract lightning during a thunder storm.

Bamboo (*Bambusa*) strictly speaking is a grass which can vary in size from small ornamental clumps to the enormous wild plant whose stems are so strong and thick that they are used for construction and for scaffolding and as pipes in rural irrigation schemes.

Flowering plants

Common in the Himalaya is the beautiful flowering shrub or tree, which can be as tall as 12 m, the **Rhododendron** which is indigenous to this region. In the wild the commonest colour of the flowers is crimson, but other colours, such as pale purple occur too. From March to May the flowers are very noticeable on the hill sides. Another common wild flowering shrub is **Lantana**. This is a fairly small untidy looking bush with rough, toothed oval leaves, which grow in pairs on the square and prickly stem. The flowers grow together in a flattened head, the ones near the middle being usually yellowish, while those at the rim are pink, pale purple or orange. The fruit is a shiny black berry.

Many other flowering plants are cultivated in parks, gardens and roadside verges. The attractive **Frangipani** (*Plumeria acutifolia*) has a rather crooked trunk and stubby branches, which if broken give out a white milky juice which can be irritating to the skin. The big, leathery leaves taper to a point at each end and have noticeable parallel veins. The sweetly scented waxy flowers are white, pale yellow or pink. The **Bougainvillea** grows as a dense bush or climber with small oval leaves and rather long thorns. The brightly coloured part (which can be pinkish-purple, crimson, orange, yellow, etc) which appears like a flower is not formed of petals, which are quite small and undistinguished, but by large papery bracts.

The unusual shape of the **Hibiscus**. The trumpet shaped flower, as much as 7 or 8 cm across, has a very long 'tongue' growing out from the centre and varies in colour from scarlet to yellow or white. The leaves are somewhat oval or heart-shaped with jagged edges. In municipal flowerbeds the commonest planted flower is probably the **Canna Lily**. It has large leaves which are either green or bronzed and lots of large bright red or yellow flowers. The plant can be more than 1 m high.

On many ponds and tanks the floating plants of the **Lotus** (*Nelumbo nucifera*) and the **Water Hyacinth** (*Eichornia crassipes*) are seen. Lotus flowers which rise on stalks above the water can be white, pink or a deep red and up to 25 cm across. The very large leaves either float on the surface or rise above the water. Many dwarf varieties are cultivated. The rather fleshy leaves and lilac flowers of the water hyacinth float to form a dense carpet, often clogging the waterways.

Crops

Of India's enormous variety, the single most widespread crop is **rice** (commonly *Orysa indica*). This forms the most important staple in South and East India, though other cereals and some root crops are also important elsewhere. The rice plant grows in flooded fields called *paddies* and virtually all planting or harvesting is done by hand. Millets are favoured in drier areas inland, while wheat is the most important crop in the northwest.

There are many different sorts of millet, but the ones most often seen are finger millet, pearl millet (bajra) and sorghum (jowar). **Finger millet**, commonly known as ragi (*Eleusine corocana*), is so-called because the ear has several spikes which radiate out, a bit like the fingers of a hand. Usually less than 1 m high, it is grown extensively in the south. Both **pearl millet** (*Pennisetum typhoideum*, known as *bajra* in the north and *cumbu* in Tamil Nadu) and **sorghum** (*Sorghum vulgare*, known as *jowar* in the north and *cholam* in the south) look superficially similar to the more familiar maize though each can be easily distinguished when the seed heads appear. Pearl millet, mainly grown in the north, has a tall single spike which gives it its other name of bulrush millet. Sorghum bears an open ear at the top of the plant.

Tea (*Camellia sinensis*) is grown on a commercial scale in tea gardens in areas of high rainfall, often in highland regions. Over 90% comes from Assam and West Bengal in the Northeast and Tamil Nadu and Kerala in the South. Left to itself tea grows into a tree 10 m tall. In the tea gardens it is pruned to waist height for the convenience of the tea pluckers and forms flat topped bushes, with shiny bright green oval leaves.

Coffee (*Coffea*) is not as widely grown as tea, but high quality arabica is an important crop in parts of South India. Coffee is also a bush, with fairly long, shiny dark green leaves. The white, sweet smelling flowers, which yield the coffee berry, grow in groups along the stems. The coffee berries start off green and turn red when ripe.

Sugar cane (*Saccharum*) is another important crop. It looks like a large grass, standing up to 3 m tall. The crude brown sugar is sold as jaggery and tastes like molasses.

Of the many spices grown in India, the two climbers pepper and vanilla and the grass-like cardamom are the ones most often seen. The **pepper** vine (*Piper Nigrum*) is indigenous to India where it grows in the warm moist regions. As it is a vine it needs support such as a trellis or a tree. It is frequently planted up against the betel nut palm and appears as a leafy vine with almost heart-shaped leaves. The peppercorns cluster along hanging spikes and are red when ripe. Both black and white pepper is produced from the same plant, the difference being in the processing.

Vanilla (*Vanilla planifolium*), which belongs to the orchid family, also grows up trees for support and attaches itself to the bark by small roots. It is native to South America, but grows well in India in areas of high rainfall. It is a rather fleshy looking plant, with white flowers and long slender pods.

Cardamom (*Elettaria cardomomum*) is native to India and is planted under shade. It grows well in highland areas such as Sikkim and the Western Ghats. It is a herbaceous plant looking like a big clump of grass, with long leafy shoots springing out of the ground up to 2-3 m. The white flowers grow on shoots which can be upright, but usually sprawl on the ground. It is from these flowers that the seed bearing capsules grow.

The **cashew nut** tree (*Anacardium occidentale*) was introduced into India, but now grows wild as well as being cultivated. It is a medium sized tree with bright green, shiny, rounded leaves. The nut grows on a fleshy fruit called a cashew apple and hangs down below this. **Cotton** (*Gossypium*) is important in parts of the west and south. The cotton bush is a small knee-high bush and the cotton boll appears after the flower has withered. This splits when ripe to show the white cotton lint inside.

The **castor oil** plant (*Ricinus Communis*) is cultivated as a cash crop and is planted in small holdings among other crops and along roads and paths. It is a handsome plant up to about 2 m in height, with very large leaves which are divided into some 12 'fingers'. The young stems are reddish and shiny. The well known castor oil is extracted from the bean which is a mottled brown in colour.

Wildlife

India has an extremely rich and varied wildlife, though many species only survive in very restricted environments. Alarmed by the rapid loss of wildlife habitat the Indian government established the first conservation measures in 1972, followed by the setting up of national parks and reserves. Some 25,000 sq km were set aside in 1973 for Project Tiger. Tigers are reported to be increasing steadily in several game reserves but threats to their survival continue, mainly due to poaching. The same is true of other less well-known species. Their natural habitat has been destroyed both by people and by domesticated animals. There are now nearly 70 national parks and 330 sanctuaries, as well as programmes of afforestation and coastline preservation. Most sanctuaries and parks are open October-March; in the northeast they are closed April-September.

The animals

The big cats Of the three Indian big cats the Asiatic lion is virtually confined to a single reserve. The other two, the tiger and leopard, occasionally occur outside. The **tiger** (*Panthera tigris*), which prefers to live in fairly dense cover, is most likely to be glimpsed as it lies in long grass or in dappled shadow or in the mangroves of the Sunderbans. The **asiatic lion** (*Panthera leo*) is now found only in the Gir National Park. Less sleek than the African lion, it has a more shaggy coat and a smaller, often black mane. The **leopard** or **panther** as it is often called in India (*Panthera pardus*), is far more numerous than the tiger, but is even more elusive. The all-black form is not uncommon in areas of higher rainfall in Northeast India, though the typical form is seen more often.

Elephant and rhino The **Indian elephant** (*Elephas maximus*) has been domesticated for centuries and today it is still used as a beast of burden. In the wild it inhabits hilly country with forest and bamboo, where it lives in herds which can number as many as 50 or more individuals. They are adaptable animals and can live in all sorts of forest, except in dry areas. Wild elephants are mainly confined to reserves, but occasionally move out into cultivation, where they cause great damage. The **great Indian one-horned rhinoceros** (*Rhinoceros unicornis*) has folds of skin which look like rivet covered armour plating. It stands at up to 170 cm at the shoulder.

⦂ Tiger, tiger

At one time the tiger roamed freely throughout the subcontinent and at the beginning of this century the estimated population was 40,000 animals. Gradually, due mainly to increased pressure on its habitat by human encroachment, the numbers of this beautiful animal dwindled to fewer than 2000 in 1972. This was the low point and alarmed at the approaching extinction of the tiger, concerned individuals with the backing of the Government and the World Wildlife Fund, set up Project Tiger in 1973. Initially nine parks were set up to protect the tiger and this was expanded over the years. However, despite encouraging signs in the first decade the latest tiger census suggests that there are still fewer than 2500.

Deer, antelope, oxen and their relatives Once widespread, these animals are now largely confined to the reserves. The male deer (stags) carry antlers which are branched, each 'spike' on the antler being called a tine. Antelopes and oxen, on the other hand, have horns which are not branched. There are several deer species in India, mainly confined to very restricted ranges. Three species are quite common. The largest and one of the most widespread, is the magnificent **sambar** (*Cervus unicolor*) which can be up to 150 cm. It has a noticeably shaggy coat, which varies in colour from brown with a yellow or grey tinge through to dark, almost black, in the older stags. The sambar is often found on wooded hillsides and lives in groups of up to 10, though solitary individuals are also seen. The **barasingha** or **swamp deer** (*Cervus duvauceli*), standing about 130 cm at the shoulder, is also quite common. The females are usually lighter and some are spotted, as are the young. The antlers are much more complex than those of the sambar, having as many as 20 tines, but 12 is more usual. Barasingha prefer swampy habitat, but are also seen in grassy areas, often in large herds. The small **chital** or **spotted deer** (*Axis axis*), only about 90 cm tall, are seen in herds of 20 or so, in grassy areas. The bright rufous coat spotted with white is unmistakable; the stags carry antlers with three tines.

These animals live in open grasslands, never too far from water. The beautiful **blackbuck** or **Indian antelope** (*Antilope cervicapra*), up to 80 cm at the shoulder, occurs in large herds. The distinctive colouring and the long spiral horns make the stag easy to identify. The coat is chocolate brown above, sharply demarcated from the white of the underparts. The females do not usually bear horns and like the young, have yellowish brown coats. The larger, heavier **nilgai** or **blue bull** (*Boselaphus tragocamelus*) is about 140 cm at the shoulder and has a horse-like sloping back. The male has a dark grey coat; the female is sandy coloured. Both sexes have two white marks on the cheek, white throats and a white ring above each hoof. The male carries short, forward-curving horns and has a tuft of long black hairs on the front of the neck.

The very graceful **chinkara** or **Indian gazelle** (*Gazella gazella*) is only 65 cm at the shoulder. The light russet colour of the body has a distinct line along the side where the paler underparts start. Both sexes carry slightly S-shaped horns. Chinkara live in small groups in rather broken hilly countryside.

The commonest member of the oxen group is the **Asiatic wild buffalo** or water buffalo (*Bubalus bubalis*). About 170 cm at the shoulder, the wild buffalo, which can be aggressive, occurs in herds on grassy plains and swamps near rivers and lakes. The black coat and wide-spreading curved horns, carried by both sexes, are distinctive.

In the high Himalaya, the **yak** (*Bos grunniens*) is domesticated. The wild yak, found on bleak Himalayan hillsides has a shaggy, blackish brown coat and large horns; the domesticated animals are often piebald and the horns much smaller.

The **Indian bison** or **gaur** (*Bos gaurus*) can be up to 200 cm at the shoulder with a heavy muscular ridge across it. Both sexes carry curved horns. The young gaur is a

⦂ Elephants – a future in the wild?

The Indian elephant (*Elephas maximas*), smaller than the African, is the world's second largest land mammal. Unlike the African elephant, the male rarely reaches a height of over 3 m; it also has smaller ears. Other distinguishing features include the high domed forehead, the rounded shape of the back and the smooth trunk with a single 'finger' at the end. Also the female is often tuskless or bears small ones called tushes and even the male is sometimes tuskless (makhnas). The Indian elephant has five nails on its front feet and four on the back (compared to the African's four and three respectively). There are approximately 6500 elephants living in the wild in northern West Bengal, Assam and Bhutan.

The loss of habitat has made wild elephants an increasing danger to humans and about 300 people are killed every year by wild elephants, mainly in the northeast. The tribal people have developed skilled techniques for capturing and training wild elephants, which have been domesticated in India for about 5000 years. They need a lot of feeding – about 18 hours a day. Working elephants are fed on a special diet, by hand straight at the mouth and they eat between 100 and 300 kg per day.

light sandy colour, which darkens with age, the old bulls being nearly black with pale sandy coloured 'socks' and a pale forehead. Basically hill animals, they live in forests and bamboo clumps and emerge from the trees to graze.

The rare **asiatic wild ass** (*Equus hemionus*) is confined to the deserts of the Little Rann of Kachchh. The fawn body has a distinctive dark stripe along the back. The dark mane is short and erect. The **wild boar** (*Sus scrofa*) has a mainly black body and a pig-like head; the hairs thicken down the spine to form a sort of mane. A mature male stands 90 cm at the shoulder and, unlike the female, bears tusks. The young are striped. Quite widespread, they can often cause great destruction among crops.

One of the most important scavengers of the open countryside, the **striped hyena** (*Hyena hyena*) usually comes out at night. It is about 90 cm at the shoulder with a large head with a noticeable crest of hairs along its sloping back.

The **common giant flying squirrel** are common in the larger forests of India, except in the northeast (*Petaurista petaurista*). The body can be 45 cm long and the tail another 50 cm. They glide from tree to tree using a membrane stretching from front leg to back leg which acts like a parachute.

In towns and villages The **common langur** (*Presbytis entellus*), 75 cm, is a long-tailed monkey with a distinctive black face, hands and feet. Usually a forest dweller, it is found almost throughout India. The **rhesus macaque** (*Macaca mulatta*), 60 cm, is more solid looking with shorter limbs and a shorter tail. It can be distinguished by the orange-red fur on its rump and flanks.

Palm squirrels are very common. The **five-striped** (*Funambulus pennanti*) and the **three-striped palm squirrel** (*Funambulus palmarum*), are both about the same size (30 cm long, about half of which is tail). The five-striped is usually seen in towns.

The two bats most commonly seen in towns differ enormously in size. The larger so-called **flying fox** (*Pteropus giganteus*) has a wing span of 120 cm. These fruit eating bats, found throughout, except in the driest areas, roost in large noisy colonies where they look like folded umbrellas hanging from the trees. In the evening they can be seen leaving the roost with slow measured wing beats. The much smaller **Indian pipistrelle** (*Pipistrellus coromandra*), with a wing span of about 15 cm, is an insect eater. It comes into houses at dusk, roosting under eaves and has a fast, erratic flight.

The **jackal** (*Canis aureus*), a lone scavenger in towns and villages, looks like a cross between a dog and a fox and varies from brown to black. The bushy tail has a dark tip.

The **common mongoose** (*Herpestes edwardsi*) lives in scrub and open jungle. It kills snakes, but will also take rats, mice and chicken. Tawny coloured with a grey grizzled tinge, it is about 90 cm in length, of which half is pale-tipped tail.

The **sloth bear** (*Melursus ursinus*), about 75 cm at the shoulder, lives in broken forest, but may be seen on a lead accompanying a street entertainer who makes it 'dance' to music as a part of an act. They have a long snout, a pendulous lower lip and a shaggy black coat with a yellowish V-shaped mark on the chest.

If you take a boat trip on the Ganga or the Brahmaputra rivers, look out for the fresh water **gangetic dolphin** (*Platanista gangetica*) as it comes to the surface to breathe.

Birds

Town and village birds Some birds perform a useful function scavenging and clearing refuse. One of the most widespread is the brown **pariah kite** (*Milvus migrans*, 65 cm). The more handsome chestnut and white **brahminy kite** (*Haliastur indus*, 48 cm) is largely confined to the waterside. The common brown **white-backed vulture** (*Gyps bengalensis*, 90 cm) looks ungainly and has a bare and scrawny head and neck. The smaller **scavenger vulture** (*Neophron percnopterus*, 65 cm) is mainly white, but often has dirty looking plumage and the bare head and neck of all vultures. In flight its wedge-shaped tail and black and white colouring are characteristic.

The **house crow** (*Corvus splendens*, 45 cm) on the other hand is a very smart looking bird with a grey body and black tail, wings, face and throat. It occurs in almost every town and village in India. The **jungle crow** (*Corvus macrorhynchos*, 50 cm) originally a bird of the countryside has started to move into populated areas and in the hill stations tends to replace the house crow. Unlike the house crow it is a glossy black all over and has a much deeper, hoarser caw.

The **feral pigeon**, or **blue rock dove** (*Columba livia*, 32 cm), found throughout the world, is generally a slaty grey in colour. It invariably has two dark bars on the wing and a white rump. The **little brown dove** (*Streptopelia senegalensis*, 25 cm) is bluey grey and brown above, with a pink head and underparts and a speckled pattern on the neck. The **collared dove** (*Streptopelia decaocto*, 30 cm) with a distinct half collar on the back of its neck, is common, especially in the drier parts of India.

Bulbuls are common in gardens and parks. The **red-vented bulbul** (*Pycnonotus cafer*, 20 cm), a mainly brown bird, can be identified by the slight crest and a bright red patch under the tail. The **house sparrow** (*Passer domesticus*, 15 cm) can be seen in towns. The ubiquitous **common myna** (*Acridotheres tristis*, 22 cm), feeds on lawns, especially after rain or watering. Look for the white under the tail and the bare yellow skin around the eye, yellow bill and legs and in flight the large white wing patch.

A less common, but more striking bird also seen feeding in open spaces, is the **hoopoe** (*Upupa epops*, 30 cm), easily identified by its sandy plumage with black and white stripes and long thin curved bill. The marvellous fan-shaped crest is sometimes raised. Finally there is a member of the cuckoo family which is heard more often than seen. The **koel** (*Eudynamys scolopacea*, 42 cm), is commonly heard during the hot weather: kuoo-kuoo-kuoo, the double note starts off low and flute-like, rises in pitch and intensity, then suddenly stops, only to start all over again. The male is all black with a greenish bill and a red eye; the female streaked and barred.

Water and waterside birds The *jheels* (marshes or swamps) of India form one of the richest bird habitats in the world. Cormorants abound; the commonest, the **little cormorant** (*Phalacrocorax niger*, 50 cm) is found on most inland waters. An almost entirely black bird with just a little white on the throat, it has a long tail and a hooked bill. The **coot** (*Fulica atra*, 40 cm), another common black bird, seen especially in winter has a noticeable white shield on the forehead.

The magnificent **sarus crane** (*Grus antigone*, 150 cm) is one of India's tallest birds. It is widespread year round across northern India, usually in pairs. The bare red head and long red legs combined with its height and grey plumage make it easy to identify. The commonest migrant crane is the **common crane** (*Grus grus*, 120 cm), present only in winter, often in flocks. It has grey plumage with a black head and neck. There is a white streak running down the side of the neck and above the eye is a tuft of red feathers.

The **openbill stork** (*Anastomus oscitans*, 80 cm) and the **painted stork** (*Ibis leucocephalus*, 100 cm) are common too and breed in large colonies. The former is white with black wing feathers and a curiously shaped bill. The latter, mainly white, has a pinkish tinge on the back and dark marks on the wings and a broken black band on the lower chest. The bare yellow face and yellow down-curved bill are conspicuous.

By almost every swamp, ditch or rice paddy up to about 1200 m you will see the **paddy bird** (*Ardeola grayii*, 45 cm). An inconspicuous, buff-coloured bird, it is easily overlooked as it stands hunched up by the waterside. As soon as it takes off, its white wings and rump make it very noticeable. The **bronze-winged jacana** (*Metopidius indicus*, 27 cm) has very long toes which enable it to walk on the floating leaves of water-lilies and there is a noticeable white streak over and above the eye. Village ponds often have their resident bird.

The commonest and most widespread of the Indian kingfishers is the jewel-like **common kingfisher** (*Alcedo atthis*, 18 cm). With its brilliant blue upperparts and orange breast it is usually seen perched on a twig or a reed beside the water.

Open grassland, light woodland and cultivated land The **cattle egret** (*Bubulcus ibis*, 50 cm), a small white heron, is usually seen near herds of cattle, frequently perched on the backs of the animals. Equal in height to the sarus crane is the impressive, but ugly **adjutant stork** (*Leptopilos dubius*, 150 cm). This often dishevelled bird is a scavenger and is thus seen near rubbish dumps and carcasses. It has a naked red head and neck, a huge bill and a large fleshy pouch which hangs down the front of the neck.

The **rose-ringed parakeet** (*Psittacula krameri*, 40 cm) is found throughout India up to about 1500 m while the **pied myna** (*Sturnus contra*, 23 cm) is restricted to northern and central India. The rose-ringed parakeet often forms huge flocks, an impressive sight coming in to roost. The long tail is noticeable both in flight and when the bird is perched. They can be very destructive to crops, but are attractive birds which are frequently kept as pets. The pied myna, with its smart black and white plumage is conspicuous, usually in small flocks in grazing land or cultivation. It feeds on the ground and on village rubbish dumps. The all black **drongo** (*Dicrurus adsimilis*, 30 cm) is invariably seen perched on telegraph wires or bare branches. Its distinctively forked tail makes it easy to identify.

Weaver birds are a family of mainly yellow birds, all remarkable for the intricate nests they build. The most widespread is the **baya weaver** (*Ploceus philippinus*, 15cm) which nest in large colonies, often near villages. The male in the breeding season combines a black face and throat with a contrasting yellow top of the head and the yellow breast band. In the non-breeding season both sexes are brownish sparrow-like birds.

Hill birds Land above 1500 m supports different species, although some, such as the ubiquitous **common myna**, are found in the highlands as well as in lower lying terrain.

The highland equivalent of the red-vented bulbul is the **white-cheeked bulbul** (*Pycnonotus leucogenys*, 20 cm) which is found in gardens and woodland in the Himalaya up to about 2500 m. It has white underparts with a yellow patch under the tail. The black head and white cheek patches are distinctive. The crest varies in length and is most prominent in birds found in Kashmir, where it is very common in gardens. The **red-whiskered bulbul** (*Pycnonotus jocosus*, 20 cm) is widespread in the Himalaya and the hills of South India up to about 2500 m. Its pronounced pointed crest, which is sometimes so long that it flops forward towards the bill, white underparts and red and white 'whiskers' serve to distinguish it. It has a red patch under the tail.

In the summer the delightful **verditer flycatcher** (*Muscicapa thalassina*, 15 cm) is a common breeding bird in the Himalaya up to about 3000 m. It is tame and confiding, often builds its nest on verandas and is seen perching on telegraph wires. In winter it is more widely distributed throughout the country. It is an active little bird which flicks its tail up and down in a characteristic manner. The male is all bright blue green with darker wings and a black patch in front of the eyes. The female is similar, but duller.

Another species associated with man is the **white wagtail** (*Motacilla alba*, 21 cm), very common in the Himalayan summer up to about 3000 m. It is found near water, by streams and lakes, on floating vegetation and among the house boats in Kashmir. Its black and white plumage and constantly wagging tail make it easy to identify.

Yet another species common in Kashmir and in other Himalayan hill stations is the **red-billed blue magpie** (*Urocissa erythrorhyncha*, 65 cm). With a long tail and pale blue plumage, contrasting with its black head, it is usually seen in small flocks as it flies from tree to tree. Its habitats of choice are tea gardens, open woodland and cultivation.

The highlands of India, especially the Himalaya, are the home of the ancestors of **domestic hens** and also of numerous beautiful **pheasants**. These are mainly forest dwellers and are not easy to see as they tend to be shy and wary of man.

Last but not least is India's national bird, the magnificent **Peafowl** (*Pavo cristatus*, male 210 cm, female 100 cm), which is more commonly known as the peacock. Semi-domesticated birds are commonly seen and heard around towns and villages, especially in the northwest of India. In the wild it favours hilly jungles and dense scrub.

Reptiles and amphibians

India is famous for its reptiles, especially its snakes which feature in many stories and legends. One of the most common is the **Indian rock python** (*Python molurus*) a 'constrictor' which kills it's prey by suffocation. Usually about 4 m in length, they can be much longer. Their docile nature make them favourites of snake handlers.

The other large snakes favoured by street entertainers are cobras. The various species all have a hood which is spread when the snake draws itself up to strike. They are all highly venomous and the snake charmers prudently de-fang them to render them harmless. The best known is probably the **spectacled cobra** (*Naja naja*), which has a mark like a pair of spectacles on the back of its hood. The largest venomous snake in the world is the **king cobra** (*Ophiophagus hannah*) which is 5 m in length. It is usually brown, but can vary from cream to black and lacks the spectacle marks of the other. In their natural state cobras are generally inhabitants of forest regions.

Equally venomous, but much smaller, the **common krait** (*Bungarus caeruleus*) is just over 1 m long. The slender, shiny, blue-black snake has thin white bands. They are found all over the country except in the northeast where the cannibalistic **banded krait** with bold yellowish and black bands have virtually eradicated them.

In houses everywhere you cannot fail to see the **gecko** (*Hemidactylus*). This small harmless, lizard is active after dark. It lives in houses behind pictures and curtain rails and at night emerges to run across the walls and ceilings to hunt insects. It is not usually more than about 14 cm long, with a transparent, pale yellowish brown body.

At the other end of the scale is the **monitor lizard** (*Varanus*), which can grow to 2 m in length. They can vary from a colourful black and yellow, to plain or speckled brown. They live in different habitats from cultivation and scrub to waterside places and desert.

The most widespread crocodile is the freshwater **mugger** or Marsh crocodile (*Crocodilus palustrus*) which grows to 3-4 m in length. The only similar fresh water species is the **gharial** (*Gavialis gangeticus*) which lives in large, fast flowing rivers. Twice the length of the mugger, it is a fish-eating crocodile with a long thin snout and, in the case of the male, an extraordinary bulbous growth on the end of the snout.

The huge, aggressive **estuarine** or **saltwater crocodile** (*Crocodilus porosus*) is restricted to the brackish waters of the Sundarbans, on the east coast and in the Andaman and Nicobar Islands. It grows to 7 m in length and is sleeker than the mugger.

Books

Art and architecture

T Richard Burton *Hindu Art*, British Museum P. Well illustrated; a broad view of art and religion.

Ilay Cooper and Barry Dawson *Traditional Buildings of India*, Thames & Hudson.

George Michell *The Hindu Temple*, Univ of Chicago Press, 1988. An authoritative account of Hindu architectural development.

Henri Sterlin *Hindu India*. Köln, Taschen, 1998. Traces the development from early rock-cut shrines, detailing famous examples.

Giles Tillotson *The tradition of Indian architecture*, Yale 1989. Superbly clear writing on development of Indian architecture under Rajputs, Mughals and the British.

Current affairs and politics

Patrick French *Liberty or Death*, Harper Collins, 1997. Well researched and serious but readable.

Granta 57 *India: the Golden Jubilee* Superb edition devoted to India's 50th anniversary of Independence, 22 international writers give brilliant snapshot accounts of India today.

Sunil Khilnani *The idea of India*, Penguin, 1997. Excellent introduction to contemporary India.

Robert B Silver and Barbara Epstein *India: a mosaic*. New York, NYRB, 2000. Distinguished essays on history, politics and literature including Amartya Sen on Tagore, Pankaj Mishra on nuclear India.

Shashi Tharur *India: from midnight to the millennium*. Viking, 1997.

Mark Tully *No full stops in India*, Viking, 1991. An often superbly observed but controversially interpreted view of contemporary India.

History

Bridget and Raymond Allchin *Origins of a civilisation*, Viking, Penguin Books, 1997. The most authoritative up-to-date survey of the origins of Indian civilizations.

AL Basham *The Wonder that was India*, London, Sidgwick & Jackson, 1985. Still one of the most comprehensive and readable accounts of the development of India's culture.

John Beames *Memoirs of a Bengal Civilian*. A readable insight into the British Raj in the post-Mutiny period, London, Eland, 1991.

Michael Edwardes *The Myth of the Mahatma*. Presents Gandhi in a whole new light.

Rajmohan Gandhi *The Good Boatman* Viking/Penguin 1995. An excellent biography by one of Gandhi's noted grandson's.

Bamber Gascoigne *The Great Moghuls*, London, Cape, 1987.

John Keay *India: a History*, Harper Collins, 2000. A popular history of the subcontinent.

Jawaharlal Nehru *The discovery of India*, New Delhi, ICCR, 1976.

Francis Robinson (ed) *Cambridge Encyclopaedia of India*, Cambridge, 1989. An introduction to South Asian society.

Percival Spear & Romila Thapar *A history of India*, 2 vols, Penguin, 1978.

Stanley Wolpert *A new history of India*, OUP, 1990.

Language

Rupert Snell and Simon Weightman *Teach Yourself Hindi*. An excellent, accessible teaching guides with cassette tapes.

H Yule and AC Burnell (eds), *Hobson-Jobson*, 1886. New paperback edition, 1986. A delightful insight into Anglo-Indian words and phrases.

Literature

Upamanyu Chatterjee *English August*. London, Faber, 1988. A wry modern account of an Indian civil servant's year in a rural posting.

Nirad Chaudhuri Four books give vivid, witty and often sharply critical accounts of India across the 20th century. *The autobiography of an unknown Indian*, Macmillan, London; *Thy Hand, Great Anarch!*, London, Chatto & Windus, 1987.

Firdaus Kanga *Trying to grow*, Bloomsbury, 1989; Mumbai life seen through the experiences of a Parsi family.

Rohinton Mistry *A fine balance*. Faber, 1995. A tale of the struggle to survive in the modern Indian city.

VS Naipaul *A million mutinies now*, Penguin, 1992. Naipaul's 'revisionist' account of India turns away from the despondency of his earlier 2 India books (*An Area of darkness* and *India: a wounded civilisation*).

RK Narayan has written many gentle and humorous novels and short stories of South India. *The Man-eater of Malgudi* and *Under the*

Banyan tree and other stories, *Grandmother's stories*, London, Penguin, 1985.
AK Ramanuja: *The collected essays*. Ed by V Dhawadker. New Delhi, OUP, 1999. Brilliant essays on Indian culture and literature.
Arundhati Roy *The God of Small Things*. Indian Ink/Harper Collins, 1997. Excellent first novel about family turmoil in a Syrian Christian household in Kerala.
Salman Rushdie *Midnight's children*, London, Picador, 1981. A novel of India since Independence, offering funny and bitterly sharp critiques of South Asian life in the 1980s.
Paul Scott *The Raj Quartet*, London, Panther, 1973; *Staying on*, Longmans, 1985. Outstandingly perceptive novels of the end of the Raj.
Vikram Seth *A Suitable Boy*, Phoenix House London, 1993. Prize-winning novel of modern Indian life.
Simon Weightman (ed) *Travellers Literary Companion: the Indian Sub-continent*. An invaluable introduction to the diversity of Indian writing.

People
Elisabeth Bumiller *May you be the mother of one hundred sons*, Penguin, 1991. An American woman journalists' account of coming to understand the issues that face India's women.
Lakshmi Holmstrom *The Inner Courtyard*, a series of short stories by Indian women, translated into English, Rupa, 1992.
Norman Lewis *A goddess in the stones*. An insight into tribal life in Orissa and Bihar.
Sarah Lloyd *An Indian Attachment*, London, Eland, 1992. A very personal and engaging account of time spent in an Indian village.

Religion
Wendy Doniger O'Flaherty *Hindu Myths*, London, Penguin, 1974. A sourcebook translated from the Sanskrit.
JP Jain *Religion and Culture of the Jains*. 3rd ed. New Delhi, Bharatiya Jnanapith, 1981.
IH Qureshi *The Muslim Community of the Indo-Pakistan Sub-Continent 610-1947*, OUP, Karachi, 1977.
Walpola Rahula *What the Buddha Taught*.
H Singh *The heritage of the Sikhs*, 2nd ed. New Delhi, 1983.
R Waterstone *India, the cultural companion*, Duncan Baird, Winchester, 2002. India's spiritual traditions brought up to date, well illustrated.
RC Zaehner *Hinduism*, OUP.

Travel
Trevor Fishlock *Cobra Road*. London, John Murray, 1991. Impressions of a news journalist.
Alexander Frater *Chasing the monsoon*, London, Viking, 1990. A prize winning account of the human impact of the monsoon's sweep across India.
John Hatt *The tropical traveller: the essential guide to travel in hot countries*, Penguin, 3rd ed 1992. Wide ranging and clearly written common sense, based on extensive experience and research.
John Keay *Into India*. London, John Murray, 1999. Seasoned traveller's introduction to understanding and enjoying India.

Trekking
Chris Bonnington *Annapurna South Face*, London, Cassell, 1971; *Everest the hard way*, London, Hodder & Stoughton, 1979.
Justine Hardy *The Ochre Border* 1995, Constable, London. An account of crossing the Puri Parvati Pass from Kullu to Spiti.
Edmund Hillary *High Adventure*, New York, Dutton, 1955. Both classic accounts of Himalayan climbs.
Harish Kapadia *Spiti: Adventures in the Trans-Himalaya*, 1996, Indus.
GD Khosla *Himalayan Circuit*. 1989 OUP. An early account of travel into this then virtually unknown region of Kinnaur and Spiti.
Audrey Salkeld *The History of Great Climbs*, 1995 The Royal Geographical Society. A magnificently illustrated and written account of historic climbs.
More practical publications include:
T Iozawa *Trekking in the Himalayas*, Delhi, Allied Publishers, 1980. *Nest & Wings*, Post Box 4531, New Delhi 110016, T6442245: 'Trekking', 'Holiday & Trekking' and 'Trekking Map' titles (Rs 40-140) cover most trekking destinations in the Indian Himalaya; trekking itineraries are listed in brief but some booklets give additional insight into the history and culture of the area.
Hugh Swift *Trekking in Pakistan and India*, London, Hodder & Stoughton, 1990. Practical guide, based on extensive experience.
Also useful are:
Himalayan Club's *Himalayan Journal* (annual) from PO Box 1905, Mumbai 400001.
Indian Mountaineering Foundation's *Indian Mountaineer* (six-monthly) from Benito Juarez Rd, New Delhi 110021.

Footnotes

Food and drink glossary

Meat and fish

gosht, mas	meat, usually mutton (sheep)
jhinga	prawns
macchli	fish
murgh	chicken

Vegetables (sabzi)

aloo	potato	khumbhi	mushroom
baingan	aubergine	matar	peas
band gobi	cabbage	piaz	onion
bhindi	okra, ladies' fingers	phool gobi	cauliflower
gajar	carrots	sag	spinach

Styles of cooking

Many items on restaurant menus are named according to methods of preparation, roughly equivalent to terms such as 'Provençal' or 'sauté'.

bhoona in a thick, fairly spicy sauce

chops minced meat, fish or vegetables, covered with mashed potato, crumbed and fried

cutlet minced meat, fish, vegetables formed into flat rounds or ovals, crumbed and fried (eg prawn cutlet, flattened king prawn)

do piaza with onions (added twice during cooking)

dum pukht steam baked

jhal frazi spicy, hot sauce with tomatoes and chillies

jhol thin gravy (Bengali)

Kashmiri cooked with mild spices, ground almonds and yoghurt, often with fruit

kebab skewered (or minced and shaped) meat or fish; a dry spicy dish cooked on a fire

kima minced meat (usually 'mutton')

kofta minced meat or vegetable balls

korma in fairly mild rich sauce using cream /yoghurt

masala marinated in spices (fairly hot)

Madras hot

makhani in butter rich sauce

moli South Indian dishes cooked in coconut milk and green chilli sauce

Mughlai rich North Indian style

Nargisi dish using boiled eggs

navratan curry ('9 jewels') colourful mixed vegetables and fruit in mild sauce

Peshwari rich with dried fruit and nuts (Northwest Indian)

tandoori baked in a tandoor (special clay oven) or one imitating it

tikka marinated meat pieces, baked quite dry

vindaloo hot and sour Goan meat dish using vinegar

Typical dishes

aloo gosht potato and mutton stew

aloo gobi dry potato and cauliflower with cumin

aloo, matar, kumbhi potato, peas, mushrooms in a dryish mildly spicy sauce

bhindi bhaji lady's fingers fried with onions and mild spices

boti kebab marinated pieces of meat, skewered and cooked over a fire

dhal makhani lentils cooked with butter

dum aloo potato curry with a spicy yoghurt, tomato and onion sauce

matar panir curd cheese cubes with peas and spices (and often tomatoes)

murgh massallam chicken in creamy marinade of yoghurt, spices and herbs with nuts
nargisi kofta boiled eggs covered in minced lamb, cooked in a thick sauce
rogan josh rich, mutton/beef pieces in creamy, red sauce
sag panir drained curd (panir) sautéd with chopped spinach in mild spices
sarson-ke-sag and **makkai-ki-roti** mustard leaf cooked dry with spices served with maize four roti from Punjab
shabdeg a special Mughlai mutton dish with vegetables
yakhni lamb stew

Rice
bhat/sada chawal plain boiled rice
biriyani partially cooked rice layered over meat and baked with saffron
khichari rice and lentils cooked with turmeric and other spices
pulao/pilau fried rice cooked with spices (cloves, cardamom, cinnamon) with dried fruit, nuts or vegetables. Sometimes cooked with meat, like a biriyani

Roti – breads
chapati (roti) thin, plain, wholemeal unleavened bread cooked on a tawa (griddle), usually made from ata (wheat flour). Makkaikiroti is with maize flour.
nan oven baked (traditionally in a tandoor) white flour leavened bread often large and triangular; sometimes stuffed with almonds and dried fruit
paratha fried bread layered with ghi (sometimes cooked with egg or with potatoes)
poori thin deepfried, puffed rounds of flour

Sweets
These are often made with reduced/thickened milk, drained curd cheese or powdered lentils and nuts. They are sometimes covered with a decorative, edible silver leaf.
barfi fudgelike rectangles/diamonds
gulab jamun dark fried spongy balls, soaked in syrup
halwa rich sweet made from cereal, fruit, vegetable, nuts and sugar
khir, payasam, paesh thickened milk rice/vermicelli pudding
kulfi cone-shaped Indian ice cream with pistachios/almonds, uneven in texture
jalebi spirals of fried batter soaked in syrup
laddoo lentil based batter 'grains' shaped into rounds
rasgulla (roshgulla) balls of curd in clear syrup
sandesh dry sweet made of curd cheese

Snacks
bhaji, pakora vegetable fritters (onions, potatoes, cauliflower etc) deep-fried in batter
chat sweet and sour fruit and vegetables flavoured with tama rind paste and chillis
chana choor, chioora ('Bombay mix') lentil and flattened rice snacks mixed with nuts and dried fruit
dosai South Indian pancake made with rice and lentil flour; served with a mild potato and onion filling (masala dosai) or without (ravai or plain dosai)
iddli steamed South Indian rice cakes, a bland breakfast given flavour by spiced accompaniments
kachori fried pastry rounds stuffed with spiced lentil/ peas/potato filling
samosa cooked vegetable or meat wrapped in pastry triangles and deep fried
utthappam thick South Indian rice and lentil flour pancake cooked with spices/onions/tomatoes
vadai deep fried, small savoury lentil 'doughnut' rings. **Dahi vada** are similar rounds in yoghurt

Glossary

Words in *italics* are common elements of words, often making up part of a place name

A

aarti (arati) Hindu worship with lamps

abad peopled

acharya religious teacher

Adi Granth Guru Granth Sahib, holy book of the Sikhs

Adinatha first of the 24 Tirthankaras, distinguished by his bull mount

agarbathi incense

Agni Vedic fire divinity, intermediary between gods and men; guardian of the Southeast

ahimsa non-harming, non-violence

amrita ambrosia; drink of immortality

ananda joy

Ananda the Buddha's chief disciple

Ananta a huge snake on whose coils Vishnu rests

anna (ana) 1/16 of a rupee

Annapurna Goddess of abundance; one aspect of Devi

apsara celestial nymph

Ardhanarisvara Siva represented as half-male and half-female

Arjuna hero of the Mahabharata, to whom Krishna delivered the Bhagavad Gita

arrack alcoholic spirit fermented from potatoes or grain

asana a seat or throne (Buddha's) pose

ashram hermitage or retreat

Ashta Matrikas The eight mother goddesses who attended on Siva or Skanda

astanah threshold

atman philosophical concept of universal soul or spirit

aus summer rice crop (Apr-Aug) Bengal

Avalokiteshwara Lord who looks down; Bodhisattva, the Compassionate

avatara 'descent'; incarnation of a divinity

ayah nursemaid

B

babu clerk

bagh garden

bahadur title, meaning 'the brave'

baksheesh tip 'bribe'

Balabhadra Balarama, elder brother of Krishna

bandh a strike

Bangla (Bangaldar) curved roof, based on thatched roofs in Bengal

bania merchant caste

basti Jain temple

bazar market

begum Muslim princess/woman's courtesy title

Bhagavad-Gita Song of the Lord; section of the Mahabharata

Bhagiratha the king who prayed to Ganga to descend to earth

bhai brother

Bhairava Siva, the Fearful

bhakti adoration of a deity

bhang Indian hemp

Bharata half-brother of Rama

bhavan building or house

bhikku Buddhist monk

Bhima Pandava hero of the Mahabharata, famous for his strength

Bhimsen Deity worshipped for his strength and courage

bidi (beedi) Indian cigarette, tobacco wrapped in tendu leaves

bo-tree (or Bodhi) *Ficus religiosa*, pipal tree associated with the Buddha

Bodhisattva Enlightened One, destined to become Buddha

bodi tuft of hair on back of the shaven head (also *tikki*)

Brahma Universal self-existing power; Creator in the Hindu Triad.

Brahmachari religious student, accepting rigorous discipline (eg chastity)

Brahman (Brahmin) highest Hindu (and Jain) caste of priests

Brahmanism ancient Indian religion, precursor of modern Hinduism

bundh (literally closed) a strike

burqa (burkha) over-dress worn by Muslim women observing purdah

bustee slum

C

cantonment planned military or civil area in town

chaam Himalayan Buddhist masked dance

chadar sheet worn as clothing

chai tea

chakra sacred Buddhist wheel of the law; also Vishnu's discus

chala Bengali curved roof

Chamunda terrifying form of the goddess Durga

Chandra Moon; a planetary deity

char bagh formal Mughal garden, divided into quarters

char bangla (char-chala) 'four temples' in Bengal, built like huts

charpai 'four legs' – wooden frame string bed

chatt(r)a ceremonial umbrella on stupa (Buddhist)

chaukidar (chowkidar) night-watchman; guard

chhang strong mountain beer of fermented barley maize rye or millet or rice

chhatri umbrella shaped dome or pavilion

chhetri (kshatriya) Hindu warrior caste

chikan shadow embroidery on fine cotton

chogyal heavenly king (Sikkim)

choli blouse

chorten Himalayan Buddhist relic shrine or a memorial stupa

chowk (chauk) a block; open place in a city where the market is held

coir fibre from coconut husk

crore 10 million

D

dacoit bandit

dada (dadu) grandfather; elder brother

dahi yoghurt

dak post

dakini sorceress

Dakshineshvara Lord of the South; name of Siva

dan gift

dandi wooden 'seat' carried by bearers

darbar (durbar) a royal gathering

darshan (darshana) viewing of a deity or spiritual leader

darwaza gateway, door

deodar Himalayan cedar; from *deva-daru*, the 'wood of the gods'

dervish member of Muslim brotherhood, committed to poverty

deul in Bengal and Orissa, generic name for temple; the sanctuary

devala temple or shrine (Buddhist or Hindu)

Devi Goddess; later, the Supreme Goddess

dhaba roadside restaurant

dharamshala (dharamsala) pilgrims' rest house

dharma moral and religious duty

dharmachakra wheel of 'moral' law (Buddhist)

dhobi washerman

dhol drums

dhooli (dhooli) swinging chair on a pole, carried by bearers

dhoti loose loincloth worn by Indian men

dhyana meditation

digambara literally 'sky-clad' Jain sect in which the monks go naked

dighi village pond (Bengal)

dikshitar person who makes oblations or offerings

divan (diwan) smoking-room; also a chief minister

Diwali festival of lights (Oct-Nov)

diwan chief financial minister

diwan-i-am hall of public audience

diwan-i-khas hall of private audience

Draupadi wife-in-common of the five Pandava brothers in the Mahabharata

duar (dwar) door, gateway

dun valley

dupatta long scarf worn by Punjabi women

Durga principal goddess of the Shakti cult

durrie (dhurrie) thick handloom rug

E

ek the number 1, a symbol of unity

ekka one horse carriage

F

firman edict or grant issued by a sovereign

G

gaddi throne

gadi/gari car, cart, train

gali (galli) lane; an alley

gana child figures in art

Ganesh (Ganapati) elephant-headed son of Siva and Parvati

Ganga goddess personifying the Ganges

ganj market

ganja Indian hemp

gaon village

garbhagriha literally 'womb-chamber'; a temple sanctuary

---

garh fort

Garuda Mythical eagle, half-human Vishnu's vehicle

Gauri 'Fair One'; Parvati, consort of Shiva.

Gaurishankara Siva with Parvati

ghagra (ghongra) long flared skirt

ghanta bell

ghat hill range, hill road; landing place; steps on the river bank

ghazal Urdu lyric poetry/love songs, often erotic

ghee clarified butter for cooking

gherao industrial action, surrounding home or office of politician or industrial manager

giri hill

godown warehouse

gola conical-shaped storehouse

gompa Tibetan Buddhist monastery

Gopala (Govinda) cowherd; a name of Krishna

Gopis cowherd girls; milk maids who played with Krishna

Gorakhnath historically, an 11th-century yogi who founded a Saivite cult; an incarnation of Siva

gosain monk or devotee (Hindi)

gram chick pea, pulse

gram village; gramadan, gift of village

gumbaz (gumbad) dome

gur gur salted butter tea (Ladakh)

gurudwara (literally 'entrance to the house of God'); Sikh religious complex

---

H

Haj (Hajj) annual Muslim pilgrimage to Mecca

hakim judge; a physician (usually Muslim)

halwa a special sweetmeat

Hanuman Monkey devotee of Rama; bringer of success to armies

Hara (Hara Siddhi) Siva

Hari Vishnu Harihara, Vishnu-Siva as a single divinity

hartal general strike

hat (haat) market

hathi (hati) elephant

hathi pol elephant gate

hauz tank or reservoir

haveli a merchant's house usually in Rajasthan

havildar army sergeant

hindola swing

hiti a water channel; a bath or tank with water spouts

Holi spring festival (Feb-Mar)

hookah 'hubble bubble' or smoking vase

---

howdah seat on elephant's back, sometimes canopied

hundi temple offering

huzra a Muslim tomb chamber

I

lat pillar, column

Id principal Muslim festivals

Idgah open space for Id prayers

ikat 'resist-dyed' woven fabric

imam Muslim religious leader

imambara tomb of a Shiite Muslim holy man; focus of Muharram procession

Indra King of the gods; God of rain; guardian of the East

Ishana Guardian of the North East

Ishvara Lord; Siva

iwan main arch in mosque

J

jadu magic

jaga mohan audience hall or ante-chamber of an Orissan temple

Jagadambi literally Mother of the World; Parvati

Jagannath literally Lord of the World; particularly, Krishna worshipped at Puri

jagati railed parapet

jaggery brown sugar, made from palm sap

jahaz ship: building in form of ship

Jambudvipa Continent of the Rose-Apple Tree; the earth

Jami masjid (Jama, Jumma) Friday mosque, for congregational worship

Jamuna Hindu goddess who rides a tortoise; river

Janaka Father of Sita

jangha broad band of sculpture on the outside of the temple wall

jarokha balcony

jataka stories accounts of the previous lives of the Buddha

jatra Bengali folk theatre

jawab literally 'answer,' a building which duplicates another to provide symmetry

jawan army recruit, soldier

jheel (jhil) lake; a marsh; a swamp

jhilmil projecting canopy over a window or door opening

-ji (jee) honorific suffix added to names out of reverence and/or politeness; also abbreviated 'yes' (Hindi/Urdu)

Jina literally 'victor'; spiritual conqueror or Tirthankara, after whom Jainism is named

Jogini mystical goddess

jorbangla double hut-like temple in Bengal

Jyotirlinga luminous energy of Siva manifested at 12 holy places, miraculously formed lingams

K

kabigan folk debate in verse

kacheri (kutchery) a court; an office for public business

Kailasa mountain home of Siva

Kali literally 'black'; terrifying form of the goddess Durga, wearing a necklace of skulls/heads

Kalki future incarnation of Vishnu on horseback

kalyanamandapa marriage hall

kameez women's shirt

kanga comb (one of five Sikh symbols)

kantha Bengali quilting

kapok the silk cotton tree

karma impurity resulting from past misdeeds

Kartikkeya (Kartik) Son of Siva, God of war

kati-roll Muslim snack of meat rolled in a 'paratha' bread

khadi cotton cloth made from home-spun cotton (or silk) yarn

khal creek; a canal

khana food or meal, also suffix for room/office/place

khanqah Muslim (Sufi) hospice

khet field

khola river or stream in Nepal

khondalite crudely grained basalt

khukri traditional curved Gurkha weapon

kirti-stambha 'pillar of fame,' free standing pillar in front of temple

kos minars Mughal 'mile' stones

kot (kota/kottai/kotte) fort

kothi house

kotla citadel

Kubera chief yaksha; keeper of the treasures of the earth, Guardian of the North

kumar a young man

Kumari virgin; Durga

Kumbhayog auspicious time for bathing to wash away sins

kumhar (kumar) potter

kund lake, well or pool

kurta Punjabi shirt

kurti-kanchali small blouse

kutcha (cutcha/kacha) raw; crude; unpaved; built with sun-dried bricks

kwabgah bedroom; literally 'palace of dreams'

L

la Himalayan mountain pass

lakh 100,000

Lakshmana younger brother of Rama

Lakshmi Goddess of wealth and good fortune, consort of Vishnu

lama Buddhist priest in Tibet

lassi iced yoghurt drink

lathi bamboo stick with metal bindings, used by police

lena cave, usually a rock-cut sanctuary

lingam (linga) Siva as the phallic emblem

Lingaraja Siva worshipped at Bhubaneswar

Lokeshwar 'Lord of the World', Avalokiteshwara to Buddhists and form of Siva to Hindus

lungi wrapped-around loin cloth, normally checked

M

madrassa Islamic theological school or college

maha great

Mahabharata Sanskrit epic about the battle between the Pandavas and Kauravas

Mahabodhi Great Enlightenment of Buddha

Mahadeva 'Great Lord'; Siva

mahal palace, grand building

mahalla (mohulla) division of a town; a quarter; a ward

mahant head of a monastery

maharaja great king

maharani great queen

maharishi (Maharshi) literally 'great teacher'

Mahavira literally 'Great Hero'; last of the 24 Tirthankaras, founder of Jainism

Mahayana The Greater Vehicle; form of Buddhism practised in East Asia, Tibet and Nepal

Mahesha (Maheshvara) Great Lord; Siva

mahout elephant driver/keeper

mahseer large freshwater fish found especially in Himalayan rivers

maidan large open grassy area in a town

Maitreya the future Buddha

makara crocodile-shaped mythical creature symbolizing the river Ganga

makhan butter

mali gardener

Manasa Snake goddess; Sakti

mandala geometric diagram symbolizing the structure of the Universe

mandi market

mandir temple

mani stones with sacred inscriptions at Buddhist sites

Mara Tempter, who sent his daughters (and soldiers) to disturb the Buddha's meditation

marg wide roadway

masjid literally 'place of prostration'; mosque

mata mother

math Hindu or Jain monastery

maulana scholar (Muslim)

maulvi religious teacher (Muslim)

maund measure of weight about 20 kg

maya illusion

meena enamel work

mela festival or fair, usually Hindu

memsahib married European woman, term used mainly before Independence

Meru mountain supporting the heavens

mihrab niche in the western wall of a mosque

mimbar pulpit in mosque

Minakshi literally 'fish-eyed'; Parvati

minar (minaret) slender tower of a mosque

mitthai Indian sweets

mithuna couple in sexual embrace

mofussil the country as distinct from the town

moksha salvation, enlightenment; literally 'release'

momos Tibetan stuffed pastas

mudra symbolic hand gesture

muezzin mosque official who calls the faithful to prayer

Muharram period of mourning in remembrance of Hasan and Hussain, murdered sons of Ali

mullah religious teacher (Muslim)

musalla prayer mat

muthi measure equal to 'a handful'

N

nadi river

Naga (nagi/nagini) Snake deity; associated with fertility and protection

nagara city, sometimes capital

nallah (nullah) ditch, channel

namaaz Muslim prayers, worship

namaste Hindu greeting (with joined palms) translated as: 'I salute all divine qualities in you'

namda rug

Nandi a bull, Siva's vehicle and a symbol of fertility

Narayana Vishnu as the creator of life

Nataraja Siva, Lord of the cosmic dance

nath literally 'place' eg Amarnath

natya the art of dance

nautch display by dancing girls

navagraha nine planets, represented usually on the lintel or architrave of the front door of a temple

navaranga central hall of temple

navaratri literally '9 nights'; name of the Dasara festival

nawab prince, wealthy Muslim, sometimes used as a title

niwas small palace

nritya pure dance

P

pada foot or base

padam dance which tells a story

padma lotus flower, Padmasana, lotus seat; posture of meditating figures

paga projecting pilaster-like surface of an Orissan temple

pahar hill

paisa (poisa) one hundredth of a rupee

palanquin covered litter for one, carried on poles

pali language of Buddhist scriptures

palli village

pan leaf of the betel vine; sliced areca nut, lime and other ingredients wrapped in leaf for chewing

panchayat a 'council of five'; a government system of elected councils

pandal marquee made of bamboo and cloth

pandas temple priests

pandit teacher or wise man; a Sanskrit scholar

pankah (punkha) fan, formerly pulled by a cord

Parinirvana the Buddha's state prior to nirvana, shown usually as a reclining figure

parishads political division of group of villages

Parsi (Parsee) Zoroastrians who fled from Iran to West India in the 8th century to avoid persecution

Parvati daughter of the Mountain; Siva's consort

Pashupati literally Lord of the Beasts; Siva

pata painted hanging scroll

patan town or city (Sanskrit)

patel village headman

pattachitra specially painted cloth (especially Orissan)

pau measure for vegetables and fruit equal to 250 g

peon servant, messenger (from Portuguese *peao*)

pida (pitha) basement

pida deul hall with a pyramidal roof in an Orissan temple

pinjrapol animal hospital (Jain)

pipal Ficus religiosa, the Bodhi tree

pir Muslim holy man

pithasthana place of pilgrimage

pralaya the end of the world

prasadam consecrated temple food

prayag confluence considered sacred by Hindus

puja ritual offerings to the gods; worship (Hindu)

pujari worshipper; one who performs puja (Hindu)

pukka literally 'ripe' or 'finished'; reliable; solidly built

punya merit earned through actions and religious devotion (Buddhist)

Puranas literally 'the old' Sanskrit sacred poems

purdah seclusion of Muslim women from public view (literally curtains)

pushkarani sacred pool or tank

Q

qabr Muslim grave

qibla direction for Muslim prayer

qila fort

qutb axis or pivot

R

rabi winter/spring season crop

Radha Krishna's favourite consort

raj rule or government

raja king, ruler (variations include rao, rawal)

rajbari palaces of a small kingdom

Rajput dynasties of western and central India

Rakshakas Earth spirits

Rama Seventh incarnation of Vishnu

Ramayana Sanskrit epic – the story of Rama

Ramazan (Ramadan) Muslim month of fasting

rana warrior (Nepal)

rani queen

rath chariot or temple car

Ravana Demon king of Lanka; kidnapper of Sita

rawal head priest

Rig (Rg) Veda oldest and most sacred of the Vedas

Rimpoche blessed incarnation; abbot of a Tibetan Buddhist monastery (gompa)

rishi 'seer'; inspired poet, philosopher

ryot (rayat/raiyat) a subject; a cultivator; a farmer

S

sabha columned hall (sabha mandapa, assembly hall)

sabzi vegetables, vegetable curry

sadar (sadr/saddar) chief, main especially Sikh

sadhu ascetic; religious mendicant, holy man

sagar lake; reservoir

sahib title of address, like 'sir'

Saiva (Shaiva) the cult of Siva

sal a hall

sal hardwood tree of the lower slopes of the Himalayan foothills

salaam literally 'peace'; greeting (Muslim)

salwar (shalwar) loose trousers (Punjab)

samadh(i) literally concentrated thought, meditation; a funerary memorial

samsara transmigration of the soul

samudra large tank or inland sea

sangam junction of rivers

sangarama monastery

sangha ascetic order founded by Buddha

sankha (shankha) the conch shell (symbolically held by Vishnu); the shell bangle worn by Bengali women

sanyasi wandering ascetic; final stage in the ideal life of a man

sarai caravansarai, halting place

saranghi small four-stringed viola shaped from a single piece of wood

Saraswati wife of Brahma and goddess of knowledge

sarkar the government; the state; a writer; an accountant

sarod Indian stringed musical instrument

sarvodaya uplift, improvement of all

sati (suttee) a virtuous woman; act of self-immolation on a husband's funeral pyre

Sati wife of Siva who destroyed herself by fire

satyagraha 'truth force'; passive resistance

seer (ser) weight (about 1 kg)

sepoy (sepai) Indian soldier, private

serow a wild Himalayan antelope

seth merchant, businessman

seva voluntary service

shahtush very fine wool from the Tibetan antelope

Shakti Energy; female divinity often associated with Siva

Shankara Siva

sharia corpus of Muslim theological law

shastras ancient texts defining temple architecture

shastri religious title (Hindu)

sheesh mahal palace apartment with mirror work

sherwani knee-length coat for men

Shesha (Sesha) serpent who supports Vishnu

shikar hunting

shloka (sloka) Sanskrit sacred verse

sindur vermilion powder used in temple ritual; married women mark their hair parting with it (East India)

singh (sinha) lion; Rajput caste name adopted by Sikhs

Sita Rama's wife, heroine of the Ramayana epic

sitar classical stringed musical instrument with a gourd for soundbox

Siva (Shiva) The Destroyer in the Hindu triad of Gods

Sivaratri literally 'Siva's night'; a festival (Feb-Mar)

soma sacred drink mentioned in the Vedas

sri (shri) honorific title, often used for 'Mr'; a sign of great respect

stupa hemispheric Buddhist funerary mound

subahdar (subedar) the governor of a province; viceroy under the Mughals

sudra lowest of the Hindu castes

sufi Muslim mystic; sufism, Muslim mystic worship

Surya Sun; Sun God

svami (swami) holy man; a suffix for temple deities

svastika (swastika) auspicious Hindu/ Buddhist cross-like sign

swadeshi home-made goods

swaraj home rule

swatantra freedom

T

tabla a pair of drums

tahr wild goat

takht throne

talao (tal, talar) water tank

taluk administrative subdivision of a district

tamasha spectacle; festive celebration

tandava (dance) of Siva

tapas (tapasya) ascetic meditative self-denial

Tara literally 'star'; a goddess

tarkashi Orissan silver filigree

Teej Hindu festival

tehsil subdivision of a district (North India)

tempo three-wheeler vehicle

terai narrow strip of land along Himalayan foothills

thakur high Hindu caste; deity (Bengal)

thakur bari temple sanctuary (Bengal)

thana a police jurisdiction; police station

thangka (thankha) cloth (often silk) painted with a Tibetan Mahayana deity

tiffin snack, light meal

tika (tilak) vermilion powder, auspicious mark on the forehead; often decorative

tirtha ford, bathing place, holy spot (Sanskrit)

Tirthankara literally 'ford-maker'; title given to 24 religious 'teachers', worshipped by Jains

Tollywood the Bengali film industry

tonga two-wheeled horse carriage

Trimurti the Hindu Triad, Brahma, Vishnu and Siva

trisul the trident chief symbol of the god Siva

triveni triple-braided

tsampa ground, roasted barley, eaten dry or mixed with milk, tea or water (Himalayan)

tulsi sacred basil plant

U

Uma Siva's consort in one of her many forms

untouchable 'outcastes', with whom contact of any kind was believed by high caste Hindus to be defiling

Upanishads ancient Sanskrit philosophical texts, part of the Vedas

ustad master

uttarayana northwards

V

vahana 'vehicle' of the deity

vaisya the 'middle-class' caste of merchants and farmers

Valmiki sage, author of the Ramayana epic

Vamana dwarf incarnation of Vishnu

vana grove, forest

Varaha boar incarnation of Vishnu

varna 'colour'; social division of Hindus into Brahmin, Kshatriya, Vaishya and Sudra

Varuna Guardian of the West, accompanied by Makara

Veda (Vedic) oldest known Hindu religious texts

vedi (bedi) altar, also a wall or screen

vihara Buddhist or Jain monastery with cells around a courtyard

Vishnu a principal Hindu deity; the Preserver (and Creator)

W

-wallah suffix often used with an occupational name, eg rickshaw-wallah

wazir chief minister of a raja (from Turkish 'vizier')

Y

yagya (yajna) major ceremonial sacrifice

Yaksha (Yakshi) a demi-god, associated with nature

Yama God of death, judge of the living

yantra magical diagram used in meditation; instrument

yatra pilgrimage

Yellow Hat Gelugpa Sect of Tibetan Buddhism – monks wear yellow headdress

yoni a hole symbolising female sexuality; vagina

Z

zamindar a landlord granted income under the Mughals

zari silver and gold thread for weaving or embroidery

zarih cenotaph in a Muslim tomb

zenana segregated women's apartments

ziarat holy Muslim tomb

zilla (zillah) district

Acknowledgements

Vanessa Betts

For support and help along the way, my thanks go to Jane Betts, Nicola Gibbs, Alex Melamed, Niamh Moran, Rod Pereira, Sandip Sammadar, David Stott and the staff at the West Bengal tourist office.

David Stott

To everyone who helped out along the road, including but not limited to: Renzino, Kinzong and Chaweng in Sikkim; Gobind Bhuyan in Bhubaneswar; Janneke Hindrikson and Darna Weinstein, somewhere in the Himalayas on their red and yellow bicycles; Rebecca and Peter, without whom this book would have been a mere shadow of itself. Also to the readers who wrote in with their experiences, especially Julie Desormiers and Douglas Inglis, Ben Hall, Alison Cleary, and Stuart Heard. At Footprint, thanks go to Nicola Gibbs, and to Robert and Roma Bradnock, whose work provided the foundation of this book. Most of all to Helen, for logistical assistance, porter services and the occasional kick in the backside.

Credits

Footprint credits

Editor: Nicola Gibbs
Map editor: Sarah Sorensen
Picture editor: Robert Lunn

Publisher: Patrick Dawson
Editorial: Sophie Blacksell, Felicity Laughton, Alan Murphy, Jo Williams
Cartography: Robert Lunn, Kevin Feeney
Design: Mytton Williams
Sales and marketing: Andy Riddle, Zoë Jackson, Hannah Bonnell
Finance and administration: Elizabeth Taylor

Photography credits

Front cover: Alamy (Buddhist protector in Namchi Nyingma, Sikkim)
Back cover: Vanessa Betts (South Kolkata market)
Inside colour section: Vanessa Betts, SuperStock.inc, Heather Lewis/shutterstock, agefotostock/SuperStock, Alamy, Eitan Simanor/Robert Harding, Richard Durnan/SuperStock

Print

Manufactured in Italy by LegoPrint
Pulp from sustainable forests

Footprint feedback

We try as hard as we can to make each Footprint guide as up to date as possible but, of course, things always change. If you want to let us know about your experiences – good, bad or ugly – then don't delay, go to **www.footprintbooks.com** and send in your comments.

Publishing information

Footprint Northeast India
1st edition
© Footprint Handbooks Ltd
October 2007

ISBN: 978 1 906098 17 9
CIP DATA: A catalogue record for this book is available from the British Library

® Footprint Handbooks and the Footprint mark are a registered trademark of Footprint Handbooks Ltd

Published by Footprint

6 Riverside Court
Lower Bristol Road
Bath BA2 3DZ, UK
T +44 (0)1225 469141
F +44 (0)1225 469461
discover@footprintbooks.com
www.footprintbooks.com

Northeast India

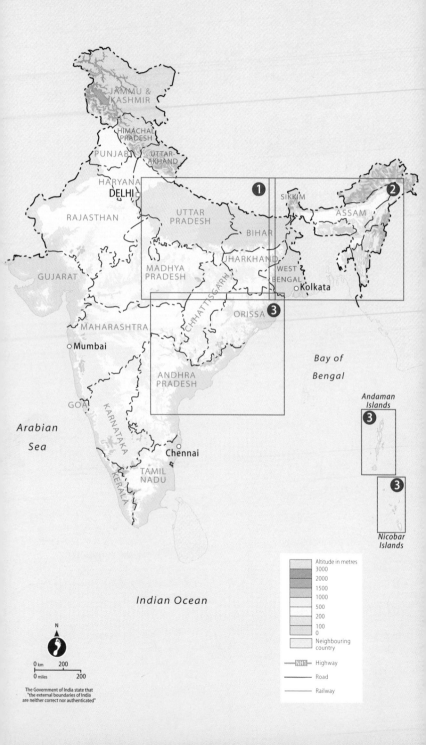

The Government of India state that "the external boundaries of India are neither correct nor authenticated"

Altitude in metres
3000
2000
1500
1000
500
200
100
0
Neighbouring country

NH1 Highway
Road
Railway